Open Systems
Interconnection

Other McGraw-Hill Communications Books of Interest

BALL • *Cost-Efficient Network Management*

BERSON • *APPC: A Guide to LU6.2*

BERSON • *Client/Server Architecture*

BLACK • *Network Management Standards*

BLACK • *TCP/IP and Related Protocols*

BLACK • *The V Series Recommendations*

BLACK • *The X Series Recommendations*

BROWN/SIMPSON • *OSI Dictionary of Acronyms and Related Abbreviations*

CHORAFAS • *The Complete LAN Reference*

COOPER • *Computer and Communications Security*

DAYTON (RANADE, ED.) • *Integrating Digital Services*

DAYTON • *Multi-Vendor Networks*

DAYTON • *Telecommunications*

FEIT • *TCP/IP*

FOLTS • *McGraw-Hill's Compilation of Open Systems Standards*

FORTIER • *Handbook of LAN Technology*

GRAY • *Open Systems: A Business Strategy for the 1990s*

HELDMAN • *Future Telecommunications*

HELDMAN • *Global Telecommunications*

HUGHES • *Data Communications*

INGLIS • *Electronic Communications Handbook*

KESSLER • *ISDN*

KESSLER/TRAIN • *Metropolitan Area Networks*

KIMBERLEY • *Electronic Data Interchange*

KNIGHTSON • *Standards for Open Systems Interconnection*

MCCLAIN • *The Open Systems Interconnection Handbook*

MCCLIMANS • *Communications Wiring and Interconnection*

NAUGLE • *Local Area Networking*

NEMZOW • *The Ethernet Management Guide*

PELTON • *Voice Processing*

RADICATI • *Electronic Mail*

RANADE • *Advanced SNA Networking*

RANADE • *Introduction to SNA Networking*

RHEE • *Error Correction Coding Theory*

RORABAUGH • *Communications Formulas and Algorithms*

ROSE • *Programmer's Guide to Netware*

SCHLAR • *Inside X.25*

TERPLAN • *Effective Management of Local Area Networks*

WHITE • *Interworking and Addressing*

To order, or to receive additional information on these or any other McGraw-Hill titles, please call 1-800-822-8158 in the United States. In other countries, please contact your local McGraw-Hill office.   MH93

Open Systems Interconnection

Its Architecture
and Protocols

Bijendra N. Jain
Indian Institute of Technology, Delhi

Ashok K. Agrawala
University of Maryland at College Park

Revised Edition

McGraw-Hill, Inc.

New York   San Francisco   Washington, D.C.   Auckland   Bogotá
Caracas   Lisbon   London   Madrid   Mexico City   Milan
Montreal   New Delhi   San Juan   Singapore
Sydney   Tokyo   Toronto

Library of Congress Cataloging-in-Publication Data

Jain, Bijendra N.
  Open systems interconnection : its architecture and protocols /
Bijendra N. Jain and Ashok K. Agrawala.—Rev. ed.
      p.   cm. — (McGraw-Hill series on computer communications)
  Includes bibliographical references and index.
  ISBN 0-07-032385-2
  1. Computer networks. 2. Computer network architectures.
  3. Computer network protocols. I. Agrawala, Ashok K. II. Title.
  III. Series.
  TK5105.5.J35   1993
  004.6'2—dc20   92-38964
                                                            CIP

Portions of this book were first published by Elsevier in 1990.

  2 3 4 5 6 7 8 9 0   DOC/DOC   9 9 8 7 6 5 4 3

ISBN 0-07-032385-2

*The sponsoring editor for this book was Neil Levine, the editing supervisor
was David E. Fogarty, and the production supervisor was Suzanne W.
Babeuf. This book was set in Century Schoolbook by McGraw-Hill's
Professional Book Group composition unit.*

Printed and bound by R. R. Donnelley & Sons Company.

To
Madhu, Tarun and Tushit
and
Radhika, Maneesh and Geetika

Contents

Preface

Computer networks, today, play a vital role in providing fast, reliable, secure and cost-effective means of communication and information sharing. They have also changed the way computing resources are acquired and used to satisfy data processing needs of an organization. It is, therefore, not surprising that the industry has witnessed tremendous growth of computer networks technology. Evolving network standards have played a significant role in sustaining this growth. Whether these standards are proprietary or industry-wide, they have encouraged the development of standardized products and services, and thereby, made this technology available to a larger user community.

Open Systems Interconnection (OSI), which is the new international standard, is now mature enough to be adopted by users, manufacturers, and organizations that provide network services. It not only specifies the seven-layer architecture, and the services and protocols of each layer, but it also defines a general framework using those other services and protocols that can be developed. Further, in terms of services available to application programs, the OSI environment provides a far richer set of services than is available under TCP/IP, SNA or DECNET. It is, therefore, to be expected that OSI-based products and services would soon be available.

In the book we have attempted to provide a comprehensive coverage of OSI architecture and the basic principles used in defining OSI services and protocols of each of its seven layers. Throughout, the emphasis has been on fundamentals, be it architectural concepts or functions incorporated in each layer. We discuss the motivation behind incorporating a certain functionality in a layer, and the use to which it can be put by a higher layer entity. In many instances, we also present the rationale behind choosing its particular realization and adopting it as part of the protocol standards.

It was never our intention to describe OSI standards in all their variety and detail. We have, therefore, avoided a detailed discussion on syntax of messages and service parameters. In view of the fact that OSI standards run into several thousand pages, we have limited the discussion to those issues that we believe are significant and of sufficient interest. In particular, optional facilities, or protocols that are widely understood, have been covered only briefly. Further, we have tried to emphasize higher layer services and protocols.

This book is intended for professionals in the area of computer networks who wish to gain an in-depth understanding of OSI architecture, its services and protocols. It may also be used as a text for a graduate or senior undergraduate course on Computer Networks where the emphasis is on layered architectures and network protocols. Further, the book could form the basis for short-term training programs for industry professionals. In either case, we assume that the reader has some background in computer architecture and programming, and familiarity with computer networks and data communication.

The first four chapters are devoted to a discussion of the OSI architecture, whereas the last six (but one) chapters cover various applications. Chapters 5 through 8 contain a discussion of the bottom six layers. Fundamental concepts of layered architecture are discussed in Chapter 2. Chapter 4, on the other hand, provides an overview of the seven layers, but with an emphasis on functions implemented in each layer. Chapter 3 is devoted to a discussion on how to define the service provided by a given layer, or to specify a protocol that realizes a given service.

Subsequent chapters of the book cover services and protocols for each layer. The emphasis is on basic principles, rather than on details of primitives and their parameters, or on syntax. Protocols for Physical layer through Network layer have been around for some time, and are discussed in Chapter 5. A discussion of local area networks and internetworking is also contained in the chapter.

The protocols used at the Transport layer (Layer 4) can be very complex. They depend upon the characteristics of the underlying network. Several Transport protocols are, therefore, available. These are discussed in Chapter 6. The Session layer provides services using which application processes may structure their interaction. Related concepts of synchronization points and activities are covered in Chapter 7. Application programs are generally free to represent information using a local syntax. The problem of information representation and its solution are discussed in Chapter 8.

The purpose of interconnecting open systems is to permit user-defined application programs to exchange information. These programs are modelled as users of application services, provided as part of the OSI environment. Therefore, a number of application layer services and protocols have been defined. Related concepts, services and protocols are presented in Chapters 9 through 14. Commonly used application services are discussed in Chapter 9, whereas specific applications, including Directory services, Message Handling System, File Transfer, Access and Management, and Virtual Terminal are covered in Chapters 10 through 14. The book concludes with a discussion of major issues concerning implementation of OSI-based networks. An appendix on OSI Standards Documents has been added to help the reader identify other ISO documents.

Many individuals have directly or indirectly helped us in the preparation of the book. In particular, we would like to thank S. Y. Han, John Waclawski and Sandra Murphy for having reviewed the book on several occasions. Their suggestions have, we believe, contributed greatly to improving both its structure and content. In the preparation of the manuscript, several of our research students and associates have contributed their time and energy. They include Sandeep Gupta, Rajiv Jain, and Ravi Mittal, Lisa, Lata, Sangeeta, Maneesh and Geetika prepared most of the figures. To all of them we are extremely grateful.

Throughout this project, we have received encouragement from numerous colleagues, including Pramod Bhatt, Jayant Deshpande, Ali Khujoory, S. Ramakrishnan, S. V. Raghavan, Sam Lomonaco, and Satish Tripathi. We gratefully acknowledge their support.

Part of the work was supported by research and development grants from Government of India, UNDP, and several industrial organizations. Without such support, the book would never have been completed. Portions of the book were written when the first author was on short-term appointment with University of Maryland and AT&T Bell Laboratories. To these and our respective institutions, we owe our deepest gratitude.

Finally, we wish to thank our respective families for their constant encouragement, support and, above all, patience.

BIJENDRA N. JAIN
New Delhi

ASHOK K. AGRAWALA
College Park, Md.

Introduction

1.1 Introduction

Information has always played a pivotal role in our society. The ability to gather, process, store and distribute information has been a key factor in the growth of most civilizations in the history of mankind. During the second half of the twentieth century we have seen major technological developments which have transformed all our traditional notions of handling information. Information gathering and distribution has been supported by communication technology, and information processing and storage by computer technology.

Communication technology, as well as computer technology, have sustained an exponential growth during the last few decades. Highly reliable, wide bandwidth communication links have come into existence, providing easy communication over long distances. Computers have steadily become smaller, cheaper and more powerful, to the extent that a single user workstation on a desk today has more computational capabilities than what was available to large organizations only a few years ago. The most remarkable development, however, has been the ability to implement systems in which both computer and communication technologies are integrated. Today most large organizations, with many offices in geographically diverse areas, have the capability of routinely obtaining current information stored in any of their computers. As our ability to gather, process, store and distribute information improves, our desire to implement more sophisticated information processing functions and applications involving multiple organizations grows even more rapidly.

In order to implement large communication systems it is essential that the systems make use of some information processing capabilities. On the other hand, the computer systems of today with multiple processing units have to be able to transfer information from one place to another within a system. The merger of communication technology and computer technology is proceeding systematically and rapidly.

1.2   Integration of Networks

In order to meet information processing needs of organizations it is essential that the computer systems being used within an organization be allowed to communicate with each other, as well as with computers of other organizations. As we start examining the inter-computer communication needs, we note that several factors have to be considered in designing such a system. The most important factors in these regards are communication bandwidth and the distance between the two end points of a communication system. In Table 1.1 we present a simple classification of the organization of processors and the kind of networks.

When the distance between processors is small and they are located on the same board, they require connections with very high bandwidth. Such connections are found within a computer system and are not considered as computer networks. The communication technique used is tightly integrated into the design of processors and other components on the board. Even when we consider processors which are up to a few meters apart, the communication is among processing elements within a single system. As distances grow from 100 meters to a few kilometers the communication bandwidth requirements are usually from 10 K to 10 M bytes per second. These types of networks are referred to as *Local Area Networks (LANs)*. The term *Metropolitan Area Network (MAN)* is used to refer to networks which interconnect processors within a metropolitan area. In order to connect processors which are farther away *Wide Area Networks (WANs)* are used. When connecting a group of processors on a local area network, for example, to another similar group, an interconnection between the two LANs is required. Such connections fall within the domain of *internetworking*. Internetworking has been used to interconnect a large number of networks throughout the world.

TABLE 1.1   Classification of Networks

Inter-processor distance	Processor Location	Bandwidth Range	Example Network
0.1 m	Circuit board	1-10 G Bytes/sec	Dataflow machines
1 m	System	10M -1 G Bytes/sec	System
10 m	Room	100K - 10 M Bytes/sec	LAN
100 m	Building	10 K - 10 M Bytes/sec	LAN
1 km	Campus	10 K - 10 M Bytes/sec	LAN
10 km	City	10 K - 10 M Bytes/sec	MAN
100 km	Country	1 K - 1 M Bytes/sec	WAN
1000 km	Continent	1 K - 100 K Bytes/sec	Internetwork
10000 km	Planet	1 K - 100 K Bytes/sec	Internetwork

The above classification is based on the technical factors, inter-processor dis:ance and bandwidth. Alternatively, one may classify networks based on the common applications or on the common hardware/software. For example, the UNIX[1] operating system has supported networking at the kernel level for a long time. Today a large number of UNIX machines form a rather loosely coupled *uucp* network which is used primarily for message passing (see [OReilly 89]). UNIX machines exchange messages possibly using either dedicated or dial-up telephone connections. In order to communicate over the network, a machine has to know which other machine on the network is willing to act as a store-and-forward node for this machine. Several thousand UNIX machines are part of the uucp network throughout the world today.

Another type of networking, developed over the last few years, is in the form of PC networks. As use of PCs in the work place increases, the need for interconnecting them for information exchange, as well as resource sharing, requires that they be interconnected in the form of LANs. Several companies now provide dedicated PC networks which use some variant of standard LAN technologies, but adapted to the PC environment.

1.3   Network Applications

When we replace a single mainframe computer by a collection of smaller workstations connected via a LAN, the major impact is on reliability and productivity of its users. This transition does not promote any new application which could not be developed for a single mainframe environment. But, when we consider the availability of MANs and WANs, and an internetwork connecting them, a variety of new applications become feasible. Let us consider some of them.

One of the major uses of wide area networks has been to provide researchers with common interests an easy means of communicating with each other. It is well recognized that in the fast development of high temperature superconductors, electronic bulletin boards played a significant role in speeding up exchange of scientific information, resulting in a faster pace of development. This means of communication replaced the traditional means of refereed journal publications, or even technical reports. While the use of computer networks for electronic mail and file transfer has primarily been by the academic community, the potential of its use by the public at large is enormous, with a corresponding impact on the society in a variety of ways.

---

[1]UNIX is a trademark of AT&T Bell Labs.

Access to large databases through networks is another major application area. Today one can access the complete airline schedule from a home computer and make reservation for an airline seat as well as for hotel and car rental. Many stock brokers provide customers with direct access to their accounts over a computer network. The latter enables automated acceptance and processing of transaction orders.

Supercomputers are being used for a variety of applications today. They, however, continue to be an expensive resource such that only a few supercomputer centers exist. High speed access to supercomputer resources can be provided to a number of users at locations far away from the center through a network, thereby making this highly valued and unique resource easily accessible by a large user community.

These are just a few examples where computer networks play a significant role. Many more examples of such applications exist and newer ones are being formulated every day. The ability of multiple computers to communicate with each other at high speeds opens up a whole new horizon for development of new and innovative applications. In summary, we note that computer networks provide easy access to expensive information processing or communication resources. At the very least, networks make resource sharing possible and cost-effective.

1.4   Standards

Interconnection of computers for exchange of information has gone on for a long time. In the early days each computer manufacturer had its own equipment and software for networking. Some computer manufacturers even had several. As a consequence, users had to obtain all their computing and communication equipment from a single vendor. They had to rely on that vendor for all new developments in applications, software and hardware, or had a very difficult time making computers from different manufacturers communicate with each other. Through the use of standards for networking, it becomes possible for any computer following the standard to communicate with any other computer following the same standard.

A major impact of the standards is not only to permit computers from different vendors to communicate with each other, but also to open up new markets for their products that follow the standards. A vendor has a much bigger market and can, therefore, exploit techniques of mass production and VLSI implementation thereby benefitting from economies of scale.

Standards are formed in two ways. When a product starts dominating the market, its practices are followed by other vendors as well. A good example of this is the IBM PC which has become a *de facto* standard for personal computers. On the other hand there are *de jure* standards which are established through a formal, legal procedure and adopted by some standards body. Both, voluntary and through treaty, organizations for international standardization have contributed to the standardization efforts in the area of communications.

We may also distinguish between public standards and proprietary standards. Public standards specify the details without referring to any specific implementation. On the other hand, proprietary standards are applicable to a specified hardware/software. For example, *Systems Network Architecture (SNA)* is a standard for networking of a range of IBM computers (see [IBM 75]). It was designed to allow IBM customers to implement their own private networks. Digital Equipment Corporation offers DECNET for the same purpose. Some of the largest networks in the world today use these proprietary standards. Networks based on proprietary standards are usually owned by a single company or organization.

The main advantage of proprietary standards is that they are controlled by a single manufacturer or vendor. They can, therefore, be controlled, modified and adapted more easily than public standards, which have a very formal procedure for their adoption. The major disadvantage of proprietary standards is that they do not address the problems of interconnecting computers of different vendors. Therefore, they address only a subset of the problems of providing a general purpose communications environment to a variety of users.

Yet another variety of standards are industry standards. These are standards which the whole industry accepts. Their applicability is limited to the portions of the industry accepting them and using them. In this regard, industry standards fall in the category of *de facto* standards. *uucp* protocol is a good example of this type of standard. Another *de facto* national standard in USA is the TCP/IP standard which is used extensively in Internet, and many other networks (see [Comer 88]).

Every country has some organizations which develop standards. In USA, for example, some of the organizations involved in standardization activity are IEEE, NIST, ANSI and EIA. ECMA is one of Europe's main standardization bodies in the field of computers. These organizations have defined standards which are in use today. For example, IEEE has defined the IEEE 802.x^2 series of standards for local area networks. These standards are considered national standards as they were formulated by a national group.

International standards are formulated and adopted by international organizations. The main organization for international stan-

---

^{2}See [IEEE 802.2] through [IEEE 802.5].

dardization is *International Standards Organization* (*ISO*), which is a voluntary, non-treaty organization founded in 1946. It has 89 national standards organizations as its members. It has over 200 technical committees (TC), each identified by a number and dealing with a specific technical area. TC97 (now known as JTC1) deals with computers and information processing. Each TC has subcommittees which are further organized into working groups (WG).

Comité Consultatif International de Télégraphique et Téléphonique (CCITT) is one of the groups under International Telecommunications Union (ITU), an agency of the United Nations. CCITT has five classes of members. A class members are national Post, Telegraph, and Telephone departments. B class members are private administrations such as AT&T. C class members are scientific and industrial organizations. D class members are international organizations, and E class members are those with primary interest in another field but have some interest in CCITT's activities. Only A class members have voting rights. The main task of CCITT is to make *Recommendations,* for example, V.24 (also known as EIA RS-232 in the USA) and X.25.

There is wide ranging cooperation among standards organizations. For example, ISO and CCITT adopt each other's standards whenever found necessary or desirable. ISO adopts standards through a consensus. The starting point for establishing any standard is to form a **working group** (WG). The WG comes up with a *Draft Proposal* (DP). The DP is circulated to all member bodies for comments for a period of six months. If a substantial majority approves, a revised document, called DIS (*Draft International Standard*), is produced and circulated for comments and voting. The final text of the IS (*International Standard*) is prepared, approved and published subsequently. When a disagreement exists a DP or DIS may have to go through several rounds of revision.

For most of the standards the WGs start with some other standard, either international, national, or an industry standard. New developments in technology and in the application area are then reflected in the DP prepared by the WG.

1.5   OSI Reference Model

In the area of computer networks ISO activities started with the formulation of *Open Systems Interconnection* (*OSI*) *Reference Model.* This model provides the basic framework for development of standards for interconnection of two or more systems [ISO 7498].

It is now well recognized, from experience derived from implementing a number of proprietary networks, that interconnection of several systems into a computer network requires a large number of functions to be carried out by each communicating system. The major contributions of the OSI Reference Model have been:

1. to identify the collection of functions that are fundamental to providing reliable, cost-effective, secure and transparent communication between systems,
2. to give a precise definition of each function without necessarily providing details of how the functionality is to be achieved,
3. to define the concept of layered architecture in terms of *services*, functions and *protocols*,[3] and
4. to specify the seven-layer OSI architecture in terms of the functionality of each layer (see Figure 1.1).

The concept of services is central to the description of the OSI architecture. It is an abstract specification of the interface between subsystems in two adjacent layers. Each layer in OSI provides a set of services to subsystems in the layer above. Further, in providing these services, a layer uses the services made available by the layer(s) below. In order to bridge the gap between the services available to a layer and those that it provides, several functions have to be implemented. This collection of functions, and a mechanism to realize each of them, is specified by a protocol.

---

[3]These and other concepts will be discussed in Chapter 2.

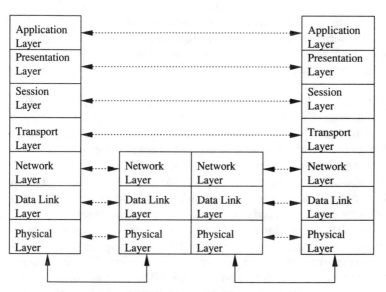

Figure 1.1 Seven layers of OSI Reference Model.

The framework laid down by the OSI Reference Model opens the way for developing standards, for both services and protocols, for each layer in the OSI architecture. Such development can, at least in theory, take place independently for each layer, once the services offered by the lower layer are defined. Specifying the OSI architecture in terms of services has yet another advantage. The realization of a service in terms of functions to be implemented and the supporting layer protocol, can be made totally independent of how this service is to be used or how the supporting lower layer service is provided.

Within the OSI framework, ISO and CCITT, together with IEEE, have developed, or adopted, standards for each of the seven layers. For each layer, related documents specify the service to be provided and the protocol to be implemented by each system that claims conformance to OSI standards. These standards do not give details of how a service will be accessed by a local subsystem within the system. Instead, the service is specified in abstract terms. Similarly, the OSI standards documents specify only the procedural aspects of protocols, without giving details on how a given procedure is implemented or invoked. Note that it is the protocol which specifies what information needs to be exchanged between systems and when. Therefore, a protocol must go one step beyond to also specify the structure and format of all information exchanged across system boundaries.

In summary, the OSI architecture is concerned more with the external and visible behavior of communicating systems rather than with issues that are local or are implementation related. The resulting advantage is that manufacturers are free to implement interfaces between subsystems and protocol procedures the way they like. Therefore, systems from various manufacturers, based upon different machine architectures or supporting different operating environments, are *open* to communication with each other as long as they all conform to the same OSI standards.

The standard protocols of OSI are the only set of accepted international standards. These standards provide for connectivity between systems so that application programs running on different machines can exchange information in a reliable, cost-effective, secure and transparent manner. The development, within the OSI framework, of a notation to specify the syntax of information exchanged between application programs is considered significant. It introduces a certain amount of formalism in specifying the structure of information objects.

The OSI architecture places equal or greater emphasis on standardization of protocols for commonly used distributed applications. These include file transfer, electronic mail and remote login. These network applications are well known to users of TCP/IP-based networks, for example. Several new application protocols have been developed, or are being developed, within the framework of OSI. These include *Directory Services, Network Resource Management, Job Transfer and Manipulation, Transaction Processing, Office Documentation Architecture,* and *Remote Databases.* To support the above applications, the OSI architecture provides for inter-process communication services, including *Association Control, Reliable Transfer* and *Remote Operations.*[4] With completion of standardization of these applications, OSI is likely to provide a rich environment for development of end-user applications that are truly distributed.

1.6 Outline of the Book

This book attempts to provide a comprehensive coverage of the OSI architecture and the basic principles used in defining the services and protocols of each of the seven layers. The first four chapters are devoted to a discussion of the OSI architecture, whereas the last six chapters cover various applications. Chapters 5 through 8 contain a discussion of the bottom six layers.

The OSI Reference Model is covered in Chapters 2 and 4. The fundamental concepts of layered architecture, *connections, connection-oriented vs. connection-less data transfer, addressing,* etc., are discussed in Chapter 2. Chapter 4, on the other hand, provides an overview of each of the seven layers, but with an emphasis on the functions implemented in each layer. These seven layers, together, provide OSI-based application services to user-written application programs.

Chapter 3 is devoted to a discussion on how to define the service provided by a given layer, and to specify a protocol that realizes the service. Each layer, together with the layers below, is modelled as a *service-provider,* while sub-systems in the next higher layer are viewed as its *users.* This model uses the concept of *service primitives* to define the interaction between a service provider and its user, and as a consequence, between the two users themselves. Chapter 3 also covers techniques for protocol specification. State tables are a convenient way to specify protocol procedures that a layer implements. A state table corresponding to the Transport layer is also studied in the chapter, but with a view to illustrate the specification of a protocol, and its correspondence with the service that it realizes.

Subsequent chapters of the book cover services and protocols for each layer in some detail. The emphasis is, however, on basic principles, rather than on details concerning service primitives and their parameters, or on formats of information exchanged between peer entities.

---

[4]These and other Application layer services are discussed in Chapters 9 through 14.

Protocols for layers 1, 2, and 3 have been around for some time (see Figure 1.1). Together, these layers provide for end-to-end relaying and routing of information through one or more sub-networks. Services and protocols concerning the three bottom layers are discussed in Chapter 5. A brief discussion of local area networks is also contained in the chapter.

The protocols used at the Transport layer (Layer 4) can be very complex, depending upon the error characteristics of the Network service. A variety of Transport protocols are available. These are discussed in Chapter 6. The Session layer provides services using which application processes may structure their interaction. Related concepts of *synchronization points* and *activities* are covered in Chapter 7.

In the OSI architecture, user information is transferred transparently. This facility is also available to application programs, which are free to represent information using a locally defined syntax. It is the responsibility of the Presentation layer to suitably encode the information using a common representation before transferring it. The *abstract syntax notation* for describing the structure of user information and the corresponding encoding rules are discussed in Chapter 8 along with the Presentation layer services and protocols.

The main purpose of interconnection of open systems is to permit exchange of information among user-defined application programs. These application programs are modelled as users of a number of application services provided as part of the OSI environment. Therefore, a number of application layer services and protocols have been defined for the Application layer. Related concepts, services and protocols are presented in Chapters 9 through 14.

Common application services, including Association control, Reliable Transfer and Remote Operations, are discussed in Chapter 9. A detailed discussion of the specific applications, Directory services, Message Handling System, File Transfer, Access and Management, and Virtual Terminal are, respectively, contained in Chapters 10 through 13. Other applications are briefly covered in Chapter 14.

In Chapter 15, the book concludes with a discussion of major issues concerning implementation of OSI-based networks. Specifically, we discuss *protocol profiles* and strategies for transition to OSI protocols and applications.

A Reference Model

This chapter is an introduction to Open Systems Interconnection and to its description at the highest level of abstraction. It includes a detailed discussion of its layered architecture. In particular we discuss the notions of services offered by different layers and protocols that govern communication within each layer. Discussion of services offered by each layer and the supporting protocols required to be implemented, however, are contained in subsequent chapters. A notation for identifying different objects, including data units, within the Open Systems Interconnection environment, is given. Also, we bring out the distinction between connection-oriented and connection-less data transfer schemes in the last two sections of this chapter.

2.1 Introduction

In this section we present the distinction between *open systems* and *real systems,* and emphasize the point that the primary concern of Open Systems Interconnection is with the externally visible behavior of systems. It is pointed out that the Reference Model is simply an abstract model that permits a detailed specification of interactions between open systems (see [ISO 7498] and [CCITT X.200]).

2.1.1 Open Systems

Open Systems Interconnection (OSI) is concerned with exchange of information between systems, in fact, between *open* systems. Within OSI, a distinction is made between *real* systems and open systems. A *real system* is a computer system together with the associated software, peripherals, terminals, human operators, physical processes, and even sub-systems that are responsible for information transfer. It is assumed that the components of a computer system listed above form an autonomous whole and are in themselves capable of processing and transferring information. On the other hand, *an open system* is only a representation of a real system that is known to comply with the architecture and protocols as defined by OSI. In fact, the representation takes into account only those aspects of a real system that pertain to information exchange between such open systems and are consistent with OSI. Put differently, an open system is that portion of a real system which is visible to other open systems in their attempts to transfer and process information jointly.

2.1.2   Systems Interconnection

Information transfer is not the only concern of OSI. The term *systems interconnection* suggests much more. It also includes aspects that are necessary for systems to work together cooperatively towards achieving a common, though distributed, goal. These aspects are:

1. *inter-process communication,* which is concerned with information exchange and synchronization of various activities undertaken by application processes;
2. *data representation,* which is concerned with representation of information being exchanged, and with ways to define alternative representations for the variety of information;
3. *data storage,* where the concern is with storage of data at possibly remote locations, and access to it;
4. *process and resource management,* which concerns ways by which application processes are declared, initiated and controlled, and the means by which such application processes acquire resources available within the OSI environment;
5. *integrity and security,* which concerns correctness and consistency of data and with access to data either during storage, exchange or processing; and
6. *program support,* which is concerned with providing an environment for program development and execution at remote locations.

While all six of the above activities have been identified to be of immediate concern to OSI, the earlier emphasis was largely on information exchange and its representation. More recently, the concerns of OSI have shifted towards providing an environment wherein application processes cooperate by accessing computing resources at remote locations.

2.1.3   Application Processes

In the above we have used the term *application process* without really defining it. During execution, users run application programs on a real system or interact with one such application program. Most of what an application program does is task dependent and has meaning only in the context of that application. However, certain aspects may have relevance to OSI. That is, an application program may exchange information with similar programs running on other systems or may cooperate with them using resources made available by the OSI environment. An application process may be viewed as the sum total of those portions of the application program which relate to the application, *per se,* and to accessing OSI resources. Thus, an application process is an element within an open system which performs information processing tasks for a particular application. A few examples may help:

1. a FORTRAN program running on a computer which accesses a database maintained at a remote computer. The remote database is also an application process. These are what one might call computerized application processes;
2. a human operating a terminal and interacting with some software or database running on a computer. This is an example of an interactive application process; and
3. a process control program executing on a dedicated machine which is directly attached to some industrial process control equipment. The control program may be termed as a physical application process.

Later we shall emphasize only those aspects of application processes that are relevant to the OSI environment.

2.1.4 The Reference Model

Figure 2.1 provides an abstract model of the OSI environment as it becomes available to application processes within open systems. Note

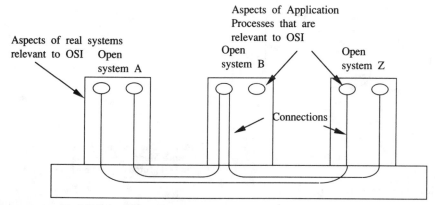

Figure 2.1 Model of the OSI environment.

that only open systems are considered within the model of the OSI environment, and within an open system only those portions of application processes that are relevant to OSI have been included in the model. Interaction between application processes takes place when they exchange information. The model, therefore, stipulates the need for a physical communication media for transmission of data. It is this abstract model which is elaborated upon by the Reference Model. In fact all of the international standards or recommendations within OSI provide varying degrees of detail about the functioning of open systems (or sub-systems) in this abstract model.

The Reference Model itself does not specify the external behavior of open systems (viz. services and protocols). It simply lays down the framework for a detailed specification of services and protocols to be supported by open systems. The major objective of the framework is to describe and crystallize the concept of *layered architecture*. Towards that, it also provides a definition of certain key elements of OSI. In the light of the architecture developed and the proposed seven layers, the Reference Model clarifies the notion of *conformity* to OSI standards. As such, the Reference Model may be viewed as the highest level of (abstract) description of standards developed within OSI. The second level of OSI description is provided by a specification of *OSI services,* and last, by *OSI protocol* specification. This relationship is illustrated in Figure 2.2. The Reference Model admits a large class of service specifications, only one of which is shown in the figure. Similarly, a service specification admits a large class of protocol specifications. Needless to say that a specification of services and protocols allows a variety of implementations.

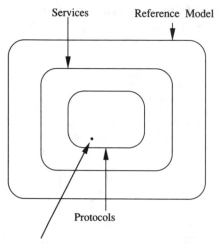

Services   Reference Model

Protocols

an implementation of a protocol

Figure 2.2 The relation between Reference Model, service specification and protocol specification.

In subsequent sections we discuss the layered architecture which provides a basis for defining the notions of service, function, protocol, and connection. Also, we discuss ways to identify various objects and develop a notation for describing data objects. The approach is somewhat formal. It is our belief that such formalism assists in understanding the distinction between what is *internal* to a system and that which is visible to other systems, between conformance issues and local issues, or between a model, a standard, and an implementation.

2.2   The Layered Architecture

In this section we discuss the layered architecture of OSI, emphasizing the point that this structure leads to a more modular approach, particularly from the viewpoint of developing standards and their implementation. The concepts of services, functions and protocols are discussed in some detail. Connections are also introduced in this section, but a more detailed discussion of connection-oriented data transfers is included in Section 2.5.

A network of interconnected systems may be viewed as just that. Such a view partitions the network vertically into a number of distinct systems that are interconnected using a physical transmission media. The view presented earlier in Figure 2.1 is similar, except that open systems are used to model real systems. The OSI Reference Model provides an alternative view of a network of systems. This model views the network in its totality, but partitions it as a series of horizontal layers (see Figure 2.3). Here, a layer cuts across the vertical boundaries of sys-

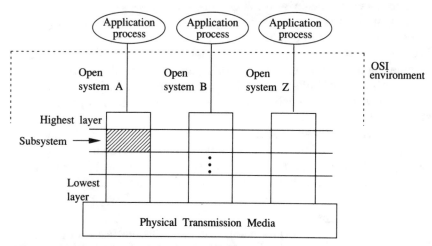

Figure 2.3 Layers and sub-systems in an OSI environment.

tems. Such a view is helpful in more than one way:

- it allows for a discussion on exchange of information between peer objects within a layer, independent of other layers,

- it allows for gradual and modular development of functionality of each layer, and

- it simultaneously allows an open system to be viewed as a succession of sub-systems, thereby permitting a modular implementation of the open system itself.

2.2.1   Layers, Services and Functions

For simplicity, a given layer is referred to as an (N)-layer, the one below it as (N−1)-layer and the one above as (N+1)-layer.[1] At the bottom we have the physical transmission media forming (0)-layer.

The succession of layers not only partitions the whole network, but it also partitions each system into a succession of *sub-systems*—a sub-system being identified (or formed) by the intersection of an open system and a layer. Sub-systems within a layer are said to be of the same *rank,* while sub-systems belonging to adjacent layers within an open system are said to be *adjacent.* Adjacent sub-systems communicate through their common boundary. Communication between sub-systems of the same rank is more complex. In fact, a major concern of OSI is to define the means to provide for such capability. Of course, communication between two adjacent sub-systems is also subject to discussion and standardization within OSI.

A sub-system is logically viewed as consisting of a number of *entities.* An entity is a representation of a process (or processes) within a computer system. It is a software or hardware module which is active, or in some cases, a manual or physical process. It can take many forms, and is capable of autonomous actions by itself, or in response to requests or commands from other entities. In this regard, the notion of an entity is very similar to that of a process in a computer system. In OSI environment, however, the entities and their inter-relationships are well structured.

Note that only those aspects that are relevant to interactions within OSI are represented as part of the entity. Thus, a layer may be viewed as consisting of a large number of entities that are spread across various open systems. At the highest layer entities model application pro-

---

[1]The standard practice in ISO documents (e.g. [ISO 7498, ISO 8509, CCITT X.200, CCITT X.210]) is to use the prefix (N) to refer to any element of layer N. In this book we avoid using this notation extensively to improve the readability by not using it explicitly where the layer referred to is clear from the context.

cesses while those below model software and hardware modules that are responsible for providing OSI services. At the bottom layer an entity allows access to the physical transmission media. An entity within an (N)-layer is referred to as an (N)-entity.

One concept that is central to the layered architecture of OSI is that of *service*. Each layer provides a different set of services to the layer above. As one moves up the layers, the set of services provided by a layer is either enhanced or improved in quality. In other words, a layer provides services to the layer above it, and also uses services provided by the lower layer, and those below. Basically, the (N)-layer adds value to the (N−1)-services, and thereby enhances the set of services it provides to the layer above or improves upon them. This it does by implementing certain *(N)-functions*.

Figure 2.4 is an illustration of the layered architecture of OSI. There the hierarchy may be looked upon recursively as:

- a layer provides services;
- part of the services are implemented as functions within the layer, while the rest are derived from (N−1)-services provided by the (N−1)-layer and those below;

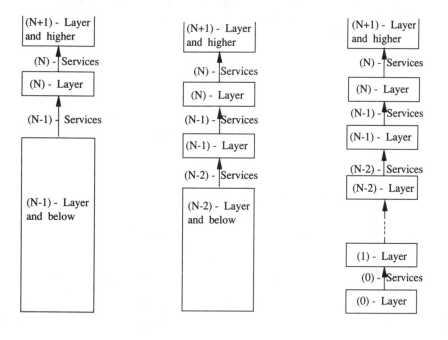

(a)   (b)   (c)

Figure 2.4 The concept of layering in OSI architecture—layers, services and functions.

- the (N−1)-services are partly implemented as (N−1)-functions in the (N−1)-layer, while others are derived from (N−2)-services, and those below. And so on.

Thus, the concept of layered architecture allows identification of different functions for implementation within various layers. This is, in fact, the usual top-down approach to designing systems. The functions to be implemented are specified in the form of services to be provided by each layer.

2.2.2 Service-Access-Points

Services made available by a layer are implemented in the form of functions in that layer and those below. Entities of the layer are responsible for implementing its functions, and similarly for the layers below. Thus, it is the entities that are ultimately the providers of services. Furthermore, it is the (N+1)-entities that are the users of (N)-services. As a consequence, a service provided by an (N)-layer may be accessed by an (N+1)-entity whenever it interacts with an (N)-entity. There are, however, restrictions on the (N)-entities with which an (N+1)-entity may interact. First, the (N)-entity and (N+1)-entity must be within the same open system. Further restrictions are specified in terms of *ser-*

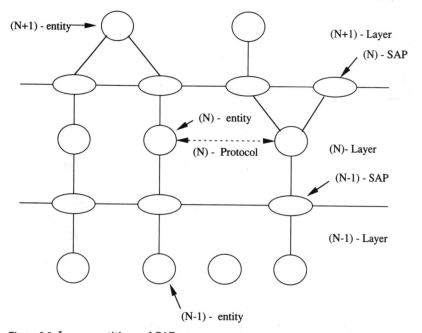

Figure 2.5 Layers, entities and SAPs.

vice-access-points. Formally, an (N)-service-access-point, or (N)-SAP, is a point at which services are provided by an entity to an (N + 1)-entity. A service-access-point is like an interface through which two entities from adjacent layers, but within the same open system, may interact with each other. In doing so, service is provided or accessed. Figure 2.5 is an illustration of the concept that services are accessible only through service-access-points. Note that:

- at most one entity is responsible for supporting a SAP;
- no more than one (N + 1)-entity may access services through an (N)-SAP at a time;
- an entity may support any number of SAPs; and
- an (N + 1)-entity may access services available at more than one (N)-SAP.

Note that the association between a user (N + 1)-entity and an (N)-SAP is not necessarily permanent. It could dynamically change.[2] The association between an entity and the SAPs at which it provides services is also not fixed.

The nature of services provided by a layer is specified in terms of the set of primitives[3] (atomic actions) that an (N + 1)-entity or an (N)-entity may issue at an (N)-SAP.

2.2.3 Protocols

A major concern of OSI is with communication between peer entities (of the same rank). For the case where peer entities reside within the same open system, there may exist a direct path or an interface between them, in which case such communication is considered to be outside the scope of OSI. In the absence of such an interface their communication is governed by procedures that are identical to those that are applicable to communication between peer entities residing in different open systems. Clearly, there exists no direct communication path between two peer entities when they reside in different open systems, except at the lowest layer, viz. the transmission media. Thus, two (N + 1)-entities wishing to communicate with each other must rely on communication services provided by the (N)-layer. This they do by accessing (N)-services at their respective (N)-SAPs, the latter being supported by two corresponding (N)-entities.

---

[2]We shall have more to say about it when we discuss *directories.*
[3]For a more detailed discussion on service primitives and their specification see Chapter 3 as well as [ISO 8509, CCITT X.210].

To provide services, the two entities themselves need to communicate with each other. Either the two (N)-entities communicate directly with each other (outside the OSI environment), or they do so using (N−1)-services. In the latter case, communication between the peer entities is governed by a set of rules and formats that each entity must adhere to in order to provide services or implement functions. This set of rules and formats (semantics, syntax, and timing) is referred to as (N)-*protocol*. This is also illustrated in Figure 2.5.

2.2.4   Connections

Two (N+1)-entities communicate with each other by accessing (N)-services made available at corresponding (N)-SAPs. One of the important services made available by an (N)-layer relates to logical *connections* that may be established by the supporting (N)-entities on behalf of the requesting (N+1)-entities. Such connections are established between corresponding (N)-SAPs. Information exchanged between (N+1)-entities flows over a connection established on behalf of the communicating (N+1)-entities.

It is quite conceivable that an (N+1)-entity may desire to communicate with a number of other (N+1)-entities at the same time. In fact, an (N+1)-entity may request establishment of a number of distinct connections with the same (N+1)-entity. As shown in Figure 2.6, such con-

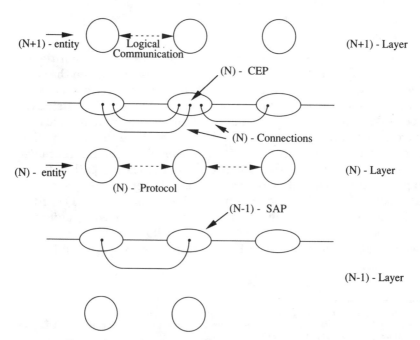

Figure 2.6   Connections and connection-endpoints.

nections may be established between the same pair of SAPs, or even between different SAPs. All connections established via the same SAP are supported by the corresponding (N)-entity. To enable the supporting (N)-entity and the attached (N+1)-entity to distinguish between various connections established through the same (N)-SAP, the notion of connection-endpoints is introduced. For each connection two *connection-endpoints* are defined, one for each end of the connection. Such an (N)-connection-endpoint ((N)-CEP) terminates an (N)-connection at an (N)-SAP. Thus, an (N)-CEP associates three objects, namely, an (N+1)-entity, an (N)-entity and an (N)-connection. A reference to a CEP by the supporting entity immediately identifies, for the (N+1)-entity, the (N)-connection,[4] and *vice-versa*.

Exchange of data between peer entities over a connection is not the only mechanism available within OSI. Information may be transferred by an (N+1)-entity to another (N+1)-entity without having to first formally establish an association. This is made possible by the use of *connection-less data transfer* services made available by the (N)-layer. This type of data transfer mechanism is discussed in Section 2.6, where we also bring out the distinction between connection-oriented data transfer and connection-less data transfer.

2.3 Identifiers

A notation for uniquely identifying objects, including entities, SAPs, and connections, is considered in this section. We also discuss techniques for maintaining correspondences between entities and the SAPs to which they are attached, or between SAPs from adjacent layers.

To be able to uniquely reference an object anywhere within the network, the OSI architecture requires that each object within the OSI have a unique identifier, or a name. Identifiers associated with entities are called *titles,* while service-access-points are identified using *addresses.* A connection is primarily identified by its endpoints using a *connection-endpoint-identifier* (CEP-identifier) for each CEP. To be sure:

- an (N)-entity has an (N)-title,
- an (N)-SAP has an (N)-address, and
- an (N)-CEP has an (N)-CEP-identifier.

In the above, the "(N)-" suggests that such identifiers have a significance that is local to the particular layer, viz. the (N)-layer. Also, notice

---

[4]Mechanisms for establishing connections, releasing connections and transferring data over a connection are discussed in Section 2.5.

that an (N)-entity has simply a title. This title is referred to as a *global-title* which is unique within the domain of the entire OSI environment. One may instead use a *local-title* to uniquely refer to an entity. But when such a reference is made the scope must be clear or obvious. Usually the scope is limited to the layer in question.

2.3.1   Titles, Addresses and Directory

As one consequence of the above, one does not refer to the *address of an entity,* but instead to that of the *title of an entity* or to the *address of a SAP* through which the entity is reachable or to which it is attached. The latter *binding* between the global-title of an (N+1)-entity and the (N)-*address* (of an (N)-SAP through which it is reachable) is in a *directory* maintained by the (N+1)-layer as part of its (N+1)-functions. Such a directory is referred to as an (N+1)-directory. Thus, an (N+1)-entity wishing to, for example, establish a connection with another (N+1)-entity may consult the (N+1)-directory to determine the (N)-address of a SAP to which the remote (N+1)-entity is attached. It may then make this address available to the (N)-entity that supports the local SAP.

In the above, we have on purpose used the term *binding* in place of *correspondence* to emphasize the fact that such bindings may change with time, and that these are not necessarily permanent. This is consistent with the fact that an (N+1)-entity may be detached from an (N)-SAP and subsequently attached to a different SAP. If, however, the bindings between (N+1)-entities and (N)-SAPs to which they are attached are permanent then one may simply use addresses to uniquely identify (N+1)-entities. The global-titles, however, permit references to entities regardless of their current location within the OSI environment.

The purpose of an (N)-directory is to maintain a listing of the bindings in existence between the titles of (N)-entities and (N−1)-addresses of (N−1)-SAPs. Such a directory may be consulted by any (N)-entity and is treated as a layer wide directory. In a dynamic environment, in which bindings change with time, the directory entries have to be updated. A number of implementation issues arise when we consider how directories may be implemented, managed, updated and accessed in an OSI environment.

2.3.2   Address-Mapping

Next, we discuss the concept of an (N)-*address-mapping,* and two different ways of implementing it (see [ISO 7498-3]). But, we first discuss an application where it is relevant for an (N)-entity to identify the (N−1)-SAP that a remote entity uses to support an (N)-SAP. Consider again the process of establishing connections between peer (N+1)-entities. For this, an (N+1)-entity makes available an address (of the (N)-SAP to which a remote (N+1)-entity is attached) to the entity that supports its local SAP. This supporting (N)-entity must now establish a connection, if necessary, with the entity that supports the remote (N)-SAP. It is truly not necessary for it to first determine its title and subsequently the (N−1)-address of the (N−1)-SAP to which the remote (N)-entity is attached. Only the latter would suffice. This is done using the (N)-address-mapping function.

The (N)-address-mapping, a function implemented within an (N)-layer, provides the mapping between an (N)-address and the (N−1)-address associated with the (N)-entity. There are two kinds of address-mapping functions that may be defined:

- *hierarchical* (N)-address-mapping; and
- (N)-address-mapping *by table.*

Hierarchical address-mapping is somewhat simpler to implement, but may only be used in a layer for which every address is mapped onto one (N−1)-address, and where such associations are permanent. In hierarchical mapping, a number of addresses are mapped onto a single (N−1)-address (see Figure 2.7). These restrictions then enable a simple mapping function. An (N)-address is composed of two parts:

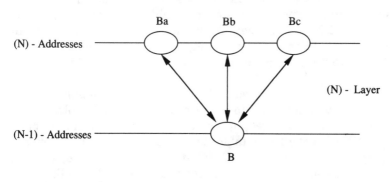

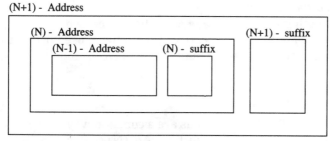

Figure 2.7 Hierarchical (N)-address-mapping.

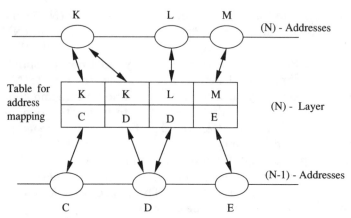

Figure 2.8 An example table for (N)-address-mapping.

- an (N−1)-address of the (N−1)-SAP which supports the (N)-entity, which in turn supports the (N)-SAP, and

- an (N)-*suffix* which uniquely identifies the particular (N)-SAP within the domain of all SAPs supported by the (N)-entity.

As such, the (N−1)-address of the supporting (N−1)-SAP may be obtained by simply stripping off the suffix from the (N)-address.

A table lists, for each (N)-address, the collection of all (N−1)-addresses to which it maps. An example of a table of address-mapping is given in Figure 2.8. Address-mapping by table permits greater flexibility, although its implementation would, in general, be more complex. None of the two restrictions mentioned in the context of hierarchical mapping are applicable.

In implementing a table-based address-mapping, the mapping within each open system may have to be defined using a local table. Such a table may be stored, managed, updated and accessed within the open system. A collection of all such tables in a layer define the complete address-mapping for the layer. A distributed implementation, such as this, raises many implementation issues that are similar to those encountered in distributed databases.

It is worth noting that within a layer either of the two address-mapping schemes may be used irrespective of the scheme used in other layers. In this regards, address-mapping in each layer is independent.

2.3.3   Identifying Connections

As noted in Section 2.2.4, connections are a common way to transfer information between peer (N+1)-entities. An (N)-connection is established on their behalf between the corresponding (N)-SAPs by the supporting (N)-entities. Each (N)-connection is terminated at each end in an (N)-*connection-endpoint.*

An (N)-*connection-endpoint-identifier* ((N)-CEP-identifier) uniquely identifies an endpoint of an (N)-connection. It allows the (N+1)-entity, attached to the (N)-SAP, and the supporting (N)-entity to distinguish a connection from other connections that may also have an endpoint within the same SAP. Thus, it is sufficient to ensure that a CEP-identifier is unique within the domain of the particular SAP. However, the OSI Reference Model insists that a CEP-identifier be unique within the scope of the attached (N+1)-entity, instead. It, therefore, views the (N)-CEP-identifier to be consisting of two parts:

1. the address of the concerned (N)-SAP, and

2. an (N)-CEP-*suffix,* which is unique within the scope of the SAP.

It is obvious that the CEP-identifiers at the two ends of a connection are distinct, even though the CEP-suffix at the two CEPs may be the same. Furthermore, the association between a CEP-identifier and the CEP is meaningful as long as the corresponding connection exists. The CEP-identifier is assigned by the supporting entity at the time of connection establishment, and loses significance with the release of the connection.

In the past, we have not referred to identifiers for connections themselves. Identification of connections is required so that the supporting entities may distinguish one connection from the others that they support. For such purposes each connection is said to have an (N)-*protocol-connection-identifier.* This identifier must be unique within the scope of the pair of supporting (N)-entities.

The OSI Reference Model recognizes the need for yet another identifier for each connection. The scope of such an identifier is, however, different from that discussed above. Each connection is additionally identified by an (N)-*service-connection-identifier.* The latter serves to bind three objects, namely, the two corresponding user (N+1)-entities and the (N)-connection. Thus, communicating (N+1)-entities are able to distinguish one connection from others, but the scope of the identifier is limited to the two (N+1)-entities.

2.4   The Nature of Data Units

This section introduces a notation for different types of data units exchanged between peer entities or between entities from adjacent layers. The discussion brings out the distinction between information exchanged only for the purposes of coordination and user-data, the latter being the focus of all communication.

Exchange of information may take place either between two peer entities or between an (N+1)-entity and an (N)-entity that are attached to the same SAP. The nature of information exchanged between a pair of entities may be classified into two types:

- user-data, and

- control information.

Transfer of *data* is the prime objective of all communication between entities. But, entities also need to exchange *control information* which enables them to coordinate their operations so as to exchange data. Examples of control information include address of destination, sequence number associated with data being exchanged, acknowledgement information. More generally, control information provides a description of the state of the entity participating in information exchange, or additionally describes user-data being exchanged.

2.4.1   Data Units

Recall that information exchange between an (N+1)-entity and an (N)-entity takes place across an interface (viz., the SAP to which the two entities are attached), while information exchange between two *peer* entities is governed by an (N)-protocol. In view of the distinction between control information and data, it is pertinent to define four different types of data units:

- *protocol-control-information:* information exchanged between peer entities to coordinate their joint operation;

- *user-data:* data transferred between (N+1)-entities for whom the (N)-entities provide services;

- *interface-control-information:* information transferred between an (N+1)-entity and an (N)-entity to coordinate their joint operation; and

- *interface-data:* data transferred from an (N+1)-entity to the supporting (N)-entity for transmission to a corresponding (N+1)-entity, or *vice-versa.*

It is often the case that data is transferred along with control information. We, therefore, require two additional definitions:

- *(N)-protocol-data-unit* ((N)-PDU): information exchanged between peer entities, which consists of control information as well as user-data; and

- *(N)-interface-data-unit:* information exchanged between an (N+1)-

entity and an (N)-entity across a SAP, which consists of control information as well as user-data.

An (N)-protocol (governing communication between peer entities) specifies the set of PDUs. It is from this set that an entity selects a relevant PDU to transfer control information and possibly data. On the other hand, a description of services does not include specification of the set of interface-data-units. Instead, it is recognized that exchange of information (in the form of interface-control-information or interface-data) between an (N+1)-entity and an (N)-entity is across an interface within an open system. It is, therefore, not subject to standardization within OSI. The definition of these information types is included within the OSI Reference Model to distinguish these from (and facilitate the definition of) (N)-service-data-units.

An (N)-service-data-unit ((N)-SDU) is interface-data whose identity is preserved from one end of a connection to the other. It is immaterial how an (N)-SDU is exchanged between a pair of (N+1)-entity and (N)-entity, as long as boundaries between SDUs are preserved. In fact, an SDU may well be exchanged in one or more interface-data, or a number of SDUs may be exchanged within an interface-data. (Also note that SDUs only contain data.)

There may be occasions when an (N+1)-entity may wish to communicate a small amount of data on a priority basis. This need is well recognized within OSI. As such, a layer may provide *expedited data transfer* service. Such a service accepts an (N)-*expedited-service-data-unit* ((N)-expedited-SDU) and transfers it over a connection possibly on a priority basis. The (N)-layer may not be in a position to guarantee its delivery within a prespecified time delay. It does, however, ensure that an (N)-expedited-SDU will not be delivered after any subsequent SDU or expedited-SDU.

Recall that a layer provides a service that enables communicating (N+1)-entities to exchange data, in fact, (N+1)-PDUs. An (N+1)-entity hands over an (N+1)-PDU to the supporting (N)-entity at the (N)-SAP (to which they are attached) in the form of an (N)-SDU. This SDU is delivered to a remote (N+1)-entity at a corresponding SAP. The manner in which such an SDU gets communicated across is, of course, governed by the protocol operating between the two entities. The sending (N)-entity treats this as user-data and forms an (N)-PDU by appending to it the relevant protocol-control-information as dictated by the protocol. This mapping of (N+1)-PDU onto an SDU and of an SDU onto a PDU is illustrated in Figure 2.9(a). Therein, we have assumed that neither segmentation, blocking, nor concatenation is performed. Other forms of mapping are discussed in the remaining part of this section.

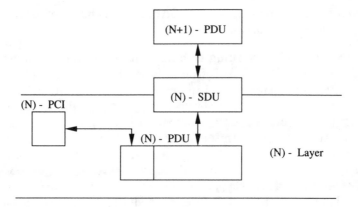

(a): Neither segmentation, blocking nor concatenation.

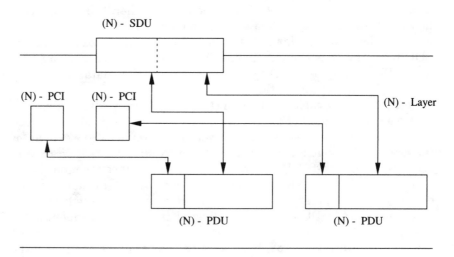

(b): Segmentation and reassembly.

Figure 2.9 Mapping between different data units in adjacent layers.

2.4.2 Segmentation, Blocking and Concatenation

The OSI Reference Model does not place any constraints on the size of data units. This is primarily to allow implementations to define their own constraints on permissible size, a decision that may be based on available buffer size, etc. To support varying length of data units, the OSI Reference Model permits a data unit to be mapped onto a number of data units, or for a number of data units to be mapped onto one data unit. Thus, one may consider the following possibilities:

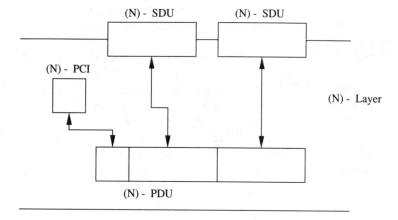

(c): Blocking and deblocking.

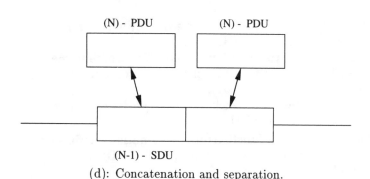

(d): Concatenation and separation.

Figure 2.9 (*Continued*)

- An (N)-SDU is segmented and subsequently mapped onto a number of (N)-PDUs;
- A number of (N)-SDUs are blocked together and mapped onto a single (N)-PDU;
- An (N)-PDU is broken down into a number of sub-PDUs, each of which is mapped onto a different (N−1)-SDU; and
- A number of (N)-PDUs are concatenated together and mapped onto a single (N−1)-SDU.

Of the four possibilities listed above, the third is recognized to be meaningless. This is so since a PDU is composed of two parts, viz. protocol-control-information and user-data. Now, if a PDU were to be broken down into a number of sub-PDUs, then, except for the first sub-PDU, none of the other sub-PDUs would have any associated protocol-control-information.

The other three forms of mapping between PDUs and SDUs are well recognized. Further, corresponding to segmenting of SDUs, or mapping them onto a number of PDUs, there is a reverse mapping, or reassembly, of the corresponding PDUs into an SDU at the other end of the connection. Similarly, mechanisms for deblocking (the reverse of blocking) of a PDU into the corresponding SDUs, and for separating (the reverse of concatenation) an (N−1)-SDU into the corresponding PDUs need to be defined. These are illustrated in Figure 2.9 and formally defined below.

1. *Segmentation* is a function performed by an (N)-entity by which it maps one (N)-SDU into multiple (N)-PDUs.
2. *Reassembly* is the reverse function (of segmentation) whereby a corresponding (N)-entity maps corresponding multiple (N)-PDUs into one (N)-SDU.
3. *Blocking* is a function performed by an entity by which it maps multiple (N)-SDUs into one (N)-PDU.
4. *Deblocking* is the reverse function (of blocking) whereby the corresponding entity maps an (N)-PDU into its corresponding multiple (N)-SDUs.
5. *Concatenation* is a function which allows an entity to map multiple (N)-PDUs into one (N−1)-SDU.
6. *Separation* is the reverse function (of concatenation) performed by a corresponding entity whereby it maps an (N−1)-SDU into its corresponding multiple (N)-PDUs.

Within a layer, it is conceivable that all three forms of mapping may be used. Segmentation is possibly the most important of these, since it allows an SDU of an arbitrary size to be transferred across a connection as a sequence of multiple PDUs, each containing a portion of the SDU. The specific mapping used will be a function of the protocol and the size of the buffers available. Blocking and concatenation permit a more efficient utilization of an (N)-connection or of an (N−1)-connection, respectively. It is worth mentioning that in the specification of an (N)-protocol there may be constraints placed on whether any of these functions can be used. Surely, two (N)-SDUs destined for different (N+1)-entities may not be blocked, or two (N)-PDUs destined to different (N)-entities may not be concatenated. Otherwise, the reverse functions of deblocking or separation cannot be carried out! It is, therefore, relevant to constrain the use of these functions to map data units that pertain to communication between the same pair of (N)-entities.

2.5   Connection-Based Data Transfer

In this section we discuss the more common approach to transfer data over an established connection. Here, we describe in some detail the procedures to establish or to release connections, aside from functions relating to data transfer that are generally preferred to be implemented.

As mentioned earlier in Section 2.2.4, two $(N+1)$-entities may communicate with each other over an (N)-connection established and maintained on their behalf by the supporting (N)-entities between the corresponding (N)-SAPs. Such a connection is, in fact, an association (however temporary) between three parties, namely, the two $(N+1)$-entities and the (N)-layer. The establishment of this association enables the two $(N+1)$-entities to, firstly, express agreement (or disagreement) on their willingness to communicate with each other. Further, while agreeing to do so, they also decide upon the syntax and semantics (viz., $(N+1)$-protocol) of all information exchanges that would take place over the connection. The process of establishing a connection also enables the communicating $(N+1)$-entities to initialize themselves to a mutually known global state so that subsequent exchanges of information may be interpreted and acted upon in accordance with the agreed $(N+1)$-protocol.

Since the (N)-layer is actively involved in establishing and maintaining the (N)-connection, the agreement includes a commitment on the part of the layer to support the connection to the extent it is able to. This is particularly so in respect of the nature of the connection and the quality of services provided. Towards the latter, the relevant entities determine for themselves as to how they can best support the connection by selecting an appropriate (N)-protocol. The supporting entities may themselves need to establish an $(N-1)$-connection (or to assign one that is already in existence) over which all communication pertaining to the particular (N)-connection takes place. Assignment of such resources, including that of message buffers, would also be done at the time of establishment of the connection.

Connection-oriented interaction between $(N+1)$-entities proceeds through three distinct phases: connection establishment, data transfer, and connection release. Data transfer may only take place once a connection has been established. The connection is preferably released once data transfer is complete since committed resources can be re-allocated for use with other connections.

2.5.1   Connection Establishment

The manner in which connections are established or released varies from layer to layer. Similarly, procedures that govern data transfers

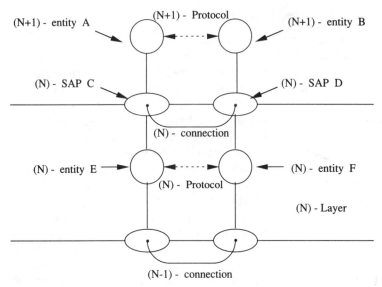

Figure 2.10 Establishment of an (N)-connection.

are dependent upon the nature of service requested or offered over the particular connection and upon the selected protocol. However, there are certain aspects that are common to all layers. These are discussed below.

Before attempting to establish a connection, the (N+1)-entity initiating the connection must know the title of the (N+1)-entity it wishes to communicate with. With that title, its (N)-address may be obtained from the corresponding directory. The connection establishment request is then initiated using the address.

The connection establishment procedure is illustrated in Figure 2.10, where an (N+1)-entity A initiates the establishment of a connection with an (N+1)-entity B. The connection is established between the corresponding SAPs C and D. It is through the attached (N)-entities E and F that the (N)-layer provides connection-oriented services at the two SAPs. The establishment procedure, typically, involves the following six steps:

1. The (N+1)-entity A, while initiating the establishment of an (N)-connection, specifies, together with the request at its (N)-SAP C, the (N)-address of the (N)-SAP D to which the responding (N+1)-entity B is attached.

2. The supporting (N)-entity E communicates the request to the (N)-entity F at the other end.

3. The (N)-entity F informs the responding (N+1)-entity B (at the (N)-SAP D) of the incoming request for connection establishment to-

gether with the (N)-address of the (N)-SAP C to which the initiating (N+1)-entity A is attached.

4. If the establishment of the (N)-connection is acceptable to the responding (N+1)-entity B, it simply informs its supporting (N)-entity F at its (N)-SAP D.

5. The (N)-entity F communicates this acceptance by the (N+1)-entity B to the (N)-entity E at the initiator's end.

6. The (N)-entity E conveys to the initiating (N+1)-entity A the acceptance obtained from the responding (N+1)-entity B.

Clearly, the two (N+1)-entities interact with the layer during the process of connection establishment. As such they may also negotiate between themselves and the layer the optional services (and their quality) to be provided over the established connection. Furthermore, since the supporting entities themselves communicate with each other, they may select the appropriate protocol to be used for subsequent data transfer.

The protocol between the two entities may permit a limited amount of user-data to be exchanged as part of connection establishment. As a consequence, the two (N+1)-entities may fix the (N+1)-protocol to be associated with subsequent data transfers.

It may be noted that the attempt to establish a connection may fail for any reason, including

- an unwillingness on the part of the responding (N+1)-entity, either because of lack of available resources, or its inability to work with the type of connection proposed by the initiating (N+1)-entity or offered by the layer; or

- an inability on the part of the layer to allocate required resources, or to provide the optional services (or their quality) requested by the initiating (N+1)-entity.

In either case, the connection establishment procedure is terminated prematurely, but not before all parties involved in the establishment process up to that stage have been informed of the failure of the attempt.

2.5.2 Multiplexing and Splitting

A major requirement of a layer that provides connections is that supporting entities should be able to communicate with each other. Either they are within the same open system and a direct (outside the OSI environment) interface exists between them, or they communicate over an (N−1)-connection. Such an (N−1)-connection, if it does not already exist, will need to be established before any connection-related communication between the entities may take place. But, in case the protocol of (N−1)-layer permits, (N−1)-user-data may be exchanged during its establishment. As a consequence, an (N)-connection could be established simultaneously with that of (N−1)-connection. Of course, before two (N−1)-entities communicate there must exist an (N−2)-connection, and so on. A physical transmission media must be available at the bottom-most layer.

Another issue related to the above is that of mapping connections onto (N−1)-connections. It is recognized, within OSI, that PDUs relating to a number of (N)-connections may be transmitted on the same (N−1)-connection, as long as the (N)-connections are supported by the same pair of (N)-entities. This is referred to as *multiplexing* of (N)-connections onto an (N−1)-connection. If multiplexing of (N)-connections is done at one end, then surely the reverse operation of *de-multiplexing* must be performed at the other end. Multiplexing may be absolutely essential in those cases where only one (N−1)-connection can be established. Further, multiplexing enables a more efficient and often more economical use of an (N−1)-connection. Figure 2.11 illustrates the concepts of multiplexing and de-multiplexing.

In contrast to the above, it is possible to map a single (N)-connection onto a number of (N−1)-connections. This function is called *splitting*. It may be useful in situations where reliability is of major concern. Even if one of the (N−1)-connections were to break down, an (N−1)-connection would still be available. Or, splitting may be used to simply obtain a higher throughput than what may be available with one (N−1)-connection. The reverse process of associating (N)-PDUs received on different (N−1)-connections with the particular (N)-connection is called *recombining*. Figure 2.12 illustrates the concepts of splitting and recombining.

The use of multiplexing or of splitting calls for implementation of a number of sub-functions within the (N)-layer. Some of these are listed below.

1. a means to identify (N)-PDUs that pertain to different (N)-connections, but which are sent as (N−1)-user-data over the same (N−1)-connection. This identification is done by associating with each PDU a protocol-connection-identifier;

2. a mechanism to schedule the transmission of (N−1)-user-data from different (N)-connections over the same (N−1)-connection. Such a mechanism would also incorporate the means to control the rate of flow of user-data originating from different (N)-connections;

3. a means to schedule the transmission of (N−1)-user-data from an (N)-connection over different (N−1)-connections; and

4. a mechanism to re-sequence (N)-PDUs, associated with an (N)-connection, in case they arrive out of sequence. The latter may be the

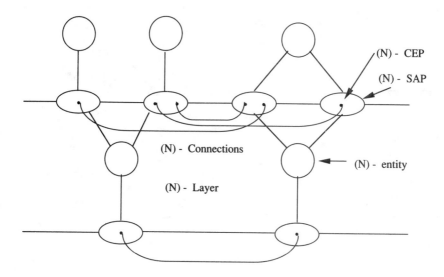

(a) The logical view.

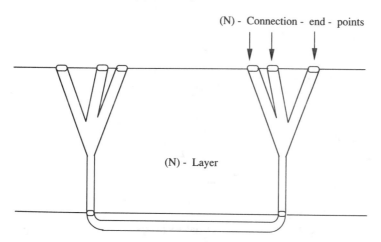

(b) Connections viewed as pipes.

Figure 2.11 The concept of multiplexing and de-multiplexing.

case when they are transmitted over different (N−1)-connections, and even though each (N−1)-connection may guarantee in-sequence delivery of (N−1)-user-data.

The first two functions are needed only if multiplexing is supported, while the latter are required only to support splitting.

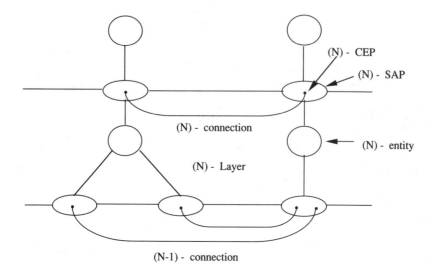

(a) The logical view.

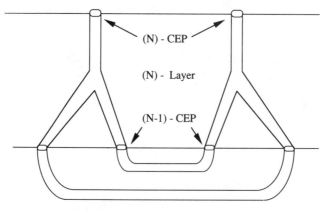

(b) Connections viewed as pipes.

Figure 2.12 The concept of splitting and recombining.

2.5.3 Connection Release

As noted earlier, a connection establishment attempt may be unsuccessful. In that case the connection is automatically released. Additionally, a connection may be released by either of the communicating (N+1)-entities, or by the supporting (N)-layer. A release procedure may be invoked by either party once the connection has been established. There are a variety of ways in which the connection may be released. The most graceful of these is where the communicating (N+1)-entities agree to release the connection by exchanging information in a manner very similar to the one described in the context of connection establishment. As part of that information exchange, the supporting entities also become aware of the connection release. Such a release procedure is termed *orderly release*.

The other variations of the release procedure are more abrupt and somewhat unilateral. As a consequence, there may be loss of user-data. Either of the (N+1)-entities may decide to release the connection. Of course, the other parties, namely, the corresponding (N+1)-entity and the two supporting entities, do participate in the process, but have very little say in it. Similarly, either of the supporting entities may terminate the connection. The latter situation may arise when, for example, an entity detects a breakdown of the supporting (N−1)-connection or congestion over it. This is, however, not to suggest that a connection must be released whenever the supporting (N−1)-connection breaks down. It is quite possible that the (N)-connection is maintained while an attempt is made to re-establish an (N−1)-connection.

It is not necessary that the supporting (N−1)-connection be released once the supported (N)-connection is released. The (N−1)-connection may continue to be maintained to support other connections that currently use it, or to support future connections.

2.5.4 Data Transfer

Once a connection has been established, user-data originating at an (N+1)-entity is made available to the supporting (N)-entity in the form of a sequence of SDUs or expedited-SDUs. These data units are then transferred to its corresponding peer entity which subsequently delivers them to the corresponding (N+1)-entity, again in the form of a sequence of SDUs and expedited-SDUs. The only constraint placed thus far is that an expedited-SDU may not be delivered after any subsequent SDU or expedited-SDU. A number of issues pertaining to the transfer of such a sequence still remain to be discussed. These include:

- regulating the rate of flow of user-data over a connection;
- guaranteed delivery of SDUs in the proper sequence;
- confirming the delivery of user-data to the destined (N+1)-entity;
- detection of errors and loss of SDUs, and recovery; and
- re-initializing the connection.

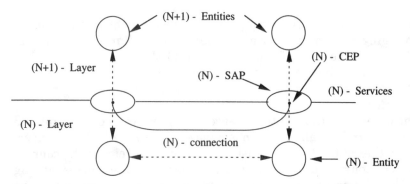

Figure 2.13 An (N)-connection viewed as a path consisting of three elements.

2.5.5 Flow Control

Our first concern is with limiting the rate at which user-data is made available to that which can conveniently be supported over a connection. However, communicating (N+1)-entities generate data at a rate dictated by the application, as well as the (N+1)-protocol they use. One scheme is to explicitly limit the rate at which user-data is generated by user (N+1)-entities to no more than a prespecified permissible rate. This scheme, however, does not dynamically adjust to changing conditions in terms of availability of communication and computing resources within the layer and those below. As such, a scheme, referred to as *flow control,* is used which dynamically limits the amount of data that is made available for transfer over a connection. The scheme recognizes that a connection may be viewed as a path consisting of three segments, as indicated in Figure 2.13.

Flow control between peer entities limits the rate at which user-data (within (N)-PDUs) is exchanged between them. This peer flow control is defined as part of the protocol. The protocol may also limit the amount of user-data that may be contained in a PDU. Similarly, at each SAP, there may exist some form of flow control on user-data exchanged between a supporting entity and the attached (N+1)-entity. The specification of the nature of such interface flow control is considered to be outside the scope of OSI, and as such implementation dependent.

Expedited-SDUs are not subject to the same flow control as are SDUs. Where necessary, a separate flow control would be applied to the transfer of expedited-SDUs.

2.5.6 Sequencing

Delivery of (N)-SDUs in the proper sequence is an important function of a layer. In its absence, the sequence of user-data delivered to the receiving (N+1)-entity may be different from the sequence of user-data obtained from the sending (N+1)-entity. This may happen for a number of reasons, including loss of user-data followed by retransmission, or user-data moving along different physical (or even logical) paths.

The mechanism to achieve in-sequence delivery of user-data is specified as part of the protocol, whenever the corresponding function is required to be implemented. Typically, user-data contained within each PDU is uniquely identified by the sending entity, so that the receiving entity can re-order the received PDUs, as necessary. This ensures that the sequence of user-data within PDUs is preserved across the segment of the connection within the layer. But that is not adequate. The sequence must also be preserved at each of the two interfaces. The latter aspect is considered to be implementation dependent and outside the scope of OSI.

2.5.7   Acknowledgements

An entity sending information may, in certain applications, wish to receive an acknowledgement from the receiver. This may be necessary if there is a finite probability of information being lost or unduly delayed during transfer. In the context of a connection, the source and destination entities are, truly, the (N+1)-entities for whom the supporting entities establish and maintain the connection. OSI, however, is primarily concerned with acknowledgements to user-data (within PDUs) exchanged between the supporting entities. The mechanism to transfer acknowledgement information is specified, again, as part of the protocol. Such a specification normally requires identification of each PDU (only the ones that contain user-data need be identified).

The OSI does, however, recognize the need for a user (N+1)-entity to exchange acknowledgement information with its peer entity. This may be covered by the (N+1)-protocol that operates between the peer entities. However, an additional mechanism is sometimes used to convey acknowledgement information between peer (N+1)-entities when they use a connection to transfer data. A receiver (N+1)-entity may request the supporting entity, at its end, that an indication suggesting *confirmation of receipt* be given at the other end to the sender (N+1)-entity. Such a mechanism is specified as part of the services that a layer may offer.

2.5.8   Error Detection and Recovery

Issues relating to preserving the sequence of SDUs across a connection and of acknowledgements are part of the larger issue of reliable data transfer. Reliability of data transfer refers to the requirement that

SDUs be communicated without any error, loss of data, or duplication, and (possibly) in the same sequence with an acceptably high probability. Such reliable transfer must take place against all odds, including noise over transmission media, lack of computing resources, limited bandwidth, or excessive delays. Breakdown of transmission media, hardware faults, faults in software design, or non-conformity to OSI standards are examples of more serious *failures*. The latter may prevent communication of data altogether.

The OSI architecture and its protocols are concerned not so much with these impairments, but with detecting the occurrence of errors and of failures. Generally, if a layer detects an error, it makes every effort to recover from it using, for example, error detecting or correcting codes and, possibly, a positive acknowledgement with re-transmission scheme. Normally, such attempts succeed, but when errors persist with high frequency, a re-initialization of the connection may be undertaken in the hope that recovery may still take place. This re-initialization, called *reset,* enables the entities to move back to a pre-defined global state. There is, however, a finite probability that some errors may go unnoticed, in that case data may be lost or duplicated. If, in spite of all efforts, the layer is unable to recover from errors it simply *signals* a failure of the connection to the user (N+1)-entities. It is then the responsibility of the user (N+1)-entities to attempt a recovery or to abandon communication altogether.

Procedures to detect errors or failures and to recover from them are specified as part of the protocol. The procedures to reset a connection are also specified. A method by which a layer signals failure to user entities is specified as part of services. Typically, the layer must also provide a reason for the failure, if it is known, and whether such a condition is temporary or permanent.

2.6   Connection-Less Data Transfer

In this section we discuss an alternative approach to data transfer without first establishing a connection. It is emphasized that connection-less data transfer protocols are relatively simple since each data unit is self contained and totally unrelated to other data units (see [ISO 7498-1]).

In the previous section we have seen how connection-oriented data transfers between two user (N+1)-entities requires the establishment of an (N)-connection before user-data may be exchanged, and that this is to be followed by a connection release. Thus, connection-oriented data transfer may be characterized as follows:

1. Each connection has a clearly distinguishable lifetime as determined by the three distinct phases of establishment, data transfer, and release.
2. The successful establishment of an (N)-connection also establishes a three-party agreement between the two user (N+1)-entities and the layer which provides the connection-oriented service. This agreement indicates their mutual willingness to exchange data.
3. As part of the connection establishment procedure, the three parties also negotiate use of certain optional services and parameter values to be associated with the connection. This enables each party to allocate resources that are required by the particular connection.
4. (N)-SAP addresses are exchanged between user (N+1)-entities and the supporting (N)-entities only during connection establishment. Subsequently, requests to transfer data over an (N)-connection (or to release it) make no reference to these addresses, but to the (N)-connection-endpoint-identifiers, one for each end.
5. (N)-service-data-units (as also (N)-expedited-SDUs) transferred over an (N)-connection are related to each other by virtue of their being transferred over the same connection. As such, it is relevant to discuss flow-controlled, or reliable transfer of a sequence of (N)-SDUs.

Connection-less data transfer, on the other hand, is the transmission of independent, unrelated (N)-SDUs from one (N)-SAP to another in the absence of a connection. To support such data transfer an (N)-layer may offer connection-less (N)-service. Figure 2.14 illustrates how an

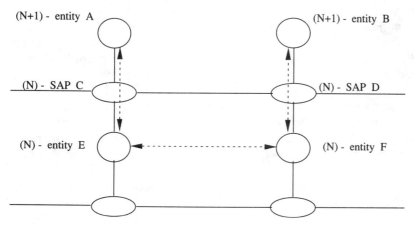

Figure 2.14 Connection-less data transfer.

(N+1)-entity A may transfer data to another (N+1)-entity B. The transfer is, typically, carried out in three steps:

1. The (N+1)-entity A passes the (N)-SDU across the local (N)-SAP C, to the supporting (N)-entity E, together with the (N)-address of the (N)-SAP to which the destination (N+1)-entity B is attached.
2. The supporting (N)-entity E transfers the (N)-user-data to the corresponding (N)-entity F which supports the (N)-SAP D, together with the addresses of the source and destination (N)-SAPs.
3. The (N)-entity F passes the (N)-SDU across the (N)-SAP D to the attached (N+1)-entity B, together with the address of the (N)-SAP C to which the sending (N+1)-entity A is attached.

The three step procedure ends with the delivery of the SDU to the destination (N+1)-entity. It is up to the receiving (N+1)-entity to act upon the received data or to simply ignore it, depending upon a number of considerations. These may include the identity of the source (N+1)-entity, the nature of data communicated, and its ability to interpret or process the received data. It is, however, expected that each communicating (N+1)-entity has some prior knowledge of each other, particularly regarding their ability to interpret (syntactically as well as semantically) the data received. Any response generated subsequently by the receiving (N+1)-entity is similarly transferred, but as far as (N)-service is concerned, without any reference to a previous data-unit.

With the request to transfer a data-unit, an (N+1)-entity may specify parameter values and options, such as transfer delay or acceptable rate of error, that are to be associated with the transfer of the particular SDU. Depending upon the manner in which the service is implemented, the supporting entity may or may not be in a position to determine whether such a request can be entertained. If it determines that the request cannot be met, then it may inform the requesting (N+1)-entity; otherwise it simply goes ahead and makes a *best* effort to transfer the data. It may even be the case that data is not delivered to the destination (N+1)-entity, and neither the sending (N+1)-entity nor the supporting (N)-entity becomes aware of this fact. The latter again depends upon how the two supporting (N)-entities communicate between themselves. To be sure, communication between the supporting (N)-entities may be connection-less or it may be over an established (N−1)-connection.

To summarize this discussion, connection-less data transfer exhibits the following characteristics:

■ Only a single interaction between a user (N+1)-entity and the supporting (N)-entity is required to initiate transmission of data. Once a request for data transfer has been made (or an (N)-SDU is delivered to the destination (N+1)-entity), no further interaction takes place between the user (N+1)-entity and the supporting (N)-entity at its (N)-SAP.

- Since a connection is not established prior to data transfer, data transfer is based on an *a priori* knowledge shared between the two communicating (N+1)-entities. Similarly, at each end, there is an *a priori* agreement between a user (N+1)-entity and its supporting (N)-entity regarding (N)-services available at the (N)-SAP. Further, since negotiation is not performed, this *a priori* knowledge or agreement is not altered.

- Each data-unit is considered to be self-contained, in that the required address information is communicated together with the data. Independence of data-units from others implies that a sequence of data-units handed over to the (N)-layer at one end may not be delivered to the destination (N+1)-entity without loss or duplication or even in the same sequence.

2.7 Summary

The main purpose of the Reference Model is to provide the framework within which open systems may interact and exchange information. The Reference Model is organized as a layered architecture where each layer is organized to provide a specific functionality. A common structure of a layer is used in the description of the Reference Model. In this chapter we have presented the basic concepts of the Reference Model and the details of the common structure assumed for the layered architecture.

In the Reference Model a layer is specified in terms of the services and the functions it provides and implements. The mechanisms for accessing the services through the SAPs are also provided. Protocols are the rules used by the entities in a layer to interact with another peer entity at a remote location. This interaction requires the establishment of a connection between the entities. A common general framework is used for the specification of these functionalities.

When a number of open systems interact using the framework of the Reference Model and the layered architecture, a large number of entities may have to interact through many connections. Identification of entities and connections has to be made so that they can be used effectively. The Reference Model not only provides for an approach to the identification as titles and addresses but also describes the directory mechanism which may be used for name translation.

When there are several open systems interconnected, they exchange information. The Reference Model provides details of how the layered architecture may be used to exchange information and data among peer entities at remote locations using facilities of lower layers. The structure of the data units is also provided. Systematic exchange of data units is provided through mechanisms of flow control, acknowledgements, etc.

In this chapter we have presented the general concepts relevant to any layer in the layered architecture. In subsequent chapters we discuss details of various layers of this architecture.

Service Definition
and Protocol
Specification

Concepts that are fundamental to giving a precise definition of services offered by a layer and specification of protocols are covered in this chapter. We also discuss techniques to model access to services and to measure quality of services. We discuss the central role played by state tables in providing a somewhat formal specification of protocol exchanges between peer entities.

3.1 Service Primitives

In this section we discuss service primitives and their types. It is shown that a complete definition of services offered by a given layer may be made in terms of a set of primitives (and their parameters) that may be issued by service-users or the service-provider. Restrictions, if any, on the sequence of primitives issued also form part of the service definition (see [ISO 8509, CCITT X.210]).

3.1.1 Service-Users and -Provider

While discussing, in Section 2.2, the layered architecture of OSI, we had emphasized the notion of *services* as being central to the concept of layering. The Reference Model discussed in Chapter 2 describes the OSI environment at the highest level, while a definition of services, as provided by each layer, enables the next level of description of the architecture of OSI.

Each layer in an OSI environment provides a step-by-step enhancement to services available to entities within the next higher layer. An (N)-layer, for instance, uses the available (N − 1)-services to implement certain (N)-functions, and thereby provides an enlarged or improved set of services to (N + 1)-entities at (N)-SAPs to which they are, respectively, attached. The implementation of the functions is embodied in the design or operation of the (N)-entities. However, the (N)-entities do need to communicate with each other, since the functions they implement relate to services that, by their very nature, are used to implement certain distributed functions. In other words, the services provided by an (N)-layer are a consequence of the joint effort of possibly several (N)-entities, and not just one entity. It is, however, true that an (N + 1)-entity may access (N)-services by interacting with the supporting (N)-entity across an (N)-SAP. Let us define the concepts of *(N)-service-user* and *(N)-service-provider.* (N + 1)-entities are each, individually, users of (N)-services while the (N)-layer (partly or wholly) is the *(N)-service-provider.* More formally, an (N)-service-user is an abstraction of an (N + 1)-entity that uses (N)-services at an (N)-SAP. That is, all details of (N + 1)-entity are not of concern, but only those aspects that are relevant to accessing (N)-services are considered while modelling an (N + 1)-entity as an (N)-service-user. Similarly, the (N)-service-provider is an abstraction of all entities within the (N)-layer, and possibly those below, that together are responsible for providing (N)-services at one or more (N)-SAPs. The internal functioning of the (N)-layer, or the layers below, is unimportant, as long as its model as a service-provider includes a description of the nature of services it provides, and of how these may be accessed. See Figure 3.1 for an illustration of the relation between (N)-service-users and the (N)-service-provider.

Our concern in this chapter is not with defining services provided by each layer in the OSI environment. These would be covered partly in

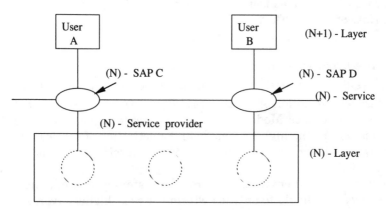

Figure 3.1 Service-users and the service-provider.

Chapter 4, but a more detailed discussion is included starting in Chapter 5. Here, as well as in Section 3.2, we discuss concepts that are somewhat fundamental to formally defining services provided by a layer.

3.1.2 Service Primitives

Interaction between an (N)-service-user and the (N)-service-provider across an (N)-SAP can be viewed as (and as such broken down into) a series of certain basic or primitive interactions. During each primitive interaction either a user passes control information or data, or both, to the service-provider, or *vice versa*. It is primitive in the sense that an interaction can be broken down in terms of these primitive interactions. Further refinement of primitive interactions may be unnecessary since an adequate description of the services provided by a layer can be given in terms of the set of available primitive interactions.

Thus, to model the permissible sequence of primitive interactions or, more generally, the nature of services provided, the concept of *service primitive* is introduced. Formally, a service primitive is an abstract, implementation-independent element of interaction between a service-user and the service-provider. It is an indivisible *atomic action* that is assumed to logically occur instantaneously. Thus a service-user or a service-provider may issue a service primitive at any time (subject to certain constraints on their sequence, to be discussed subsequently). A primitive describes an interaction only in an abstract manner, independent of how the exchange of information between interacting entities takes place at a SAP.

From an implementation viewpoint, issuing of a service primitive by a service-user, for instance, may involve a number of physical interactions over a finite time duration, each consisting of an exchange of control information or only a part of data. But the service-provider receiving the primitive will process these as a single primitive interaction, in that the service-provider does not change state *while the primitive is being issued,* or at least such change is not visible from the standpoint of the architectural description of OSI.

Some examples of service primitives are in order. A request to establish an (N)-connection, for instance, made by an (N + 1)-entity, at its (N)-SAP, to the supporting (N)-entity is an example of issuing a particular service primitive by a service-user (namely, (N + 1)-entity). Similarly, when the (N)-layer responds with a confirmation to the requesting (N + 1)-entity that the requested (N)-connection has been established, it does so by issuing a corresponding service primitive at the relevant (N)-SAP. This service primitive is issued in the direction of service-provider to service-user. Also, notice that each time a primitive is issued the state of the service-user as well that of the service-provider changes. To be sure, it is the state of the interface (namely, the (N)-SAP) that changes.

3.1.3 Types of Primitives

Recall that services provided by an (N)-layer are primarily to support some form of interaction between two (or more) user (N + 1)-entities. Typically, when a service-user issues a primitive at an (N)-SAP, the (N)-service-provider would issue a primitive at the (N)-SAP to which the corresponding (N + 1)-entity is attached. This clearly allows for one-way interaction between the communicating (N + 1)-entities through the use of primitives. This is illustrated in Figure 3.2(a), where the two primitives issued are typed as being a *request primitive* and an *indication primitive*.

Formally, a request primitive is issued by an (N)-service-user to invoke, or initiate the use of, some procedure related to the (N)-services. Similarly, an indication primitive is issued by the (N)-service-provider to indicate to the receiving (N)-service-user that a procedure has been invoked by a correspondent (N)-service-user, or by the (N)-service-provider itself. This procedure is typically used for data transfer from a user (N + 1)-entity to another.

Often, a procedure is considered to be incomplete unless there is some form of response, in the reverse direction, from the correspondent user (N + 1)-entity. Completion of such a procedure may be achieved with the correspondent user (N + 1)-entity issuing a *response primitive* in response to an indication, and the service-provider, in turn, issuing a *confirm primitive* at the (N)-SAP to which the initiating user (N + 1)-entity had earlier issued a request primitive. This is illustrated in Figure 3.2(b). Formally, a response primitive is issued by a service-user to complete, at a particular service-access-point, some procedure that had previously been invoked by an indication at the same service-access-point. A confirm primitive is issued by a service-provider, at a service-access-point, to complete the procedure that had earlier been invoked by a request primitive issued at the same service-access-point. As an example, the establishment of an (N)-connection requires that the (N + 1)-entity requesting the establishment of the connection be informed of the completion (successful or otherwise) of the establishment procedure.

It may be pointed out that there are occasions when a procedure is invoked by the (N)-service-provider because of an event occurring within the (N) layer or the one below. As an example, when the service-provider detects an error, it informs the service-users of the resulting condition. This it does by issuing an indication primitive possibly at each of the relevant (N)-SAPs, as illustrated in Figure 3.2(c).

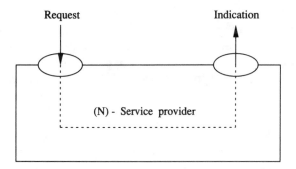

(a) Unconfirmed service

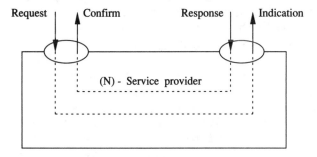

(b) Confirmed service

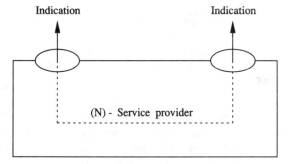

(c) Provider-initiated service.

Figure 3.2 Primitives and types of service elements.

Documents related to OSI architecture are consistent in using a notation for naming service primitives. Typically, a service primitive is referred to using three component names. These are:

- name of the layer;
- name of the service; and

- type of service primitive.

As an example, *T-DATA request* refers to a service primitive that a service-user may issue to request the transfer of user-data. Here the letter *T* refers to a specific layer—the Transport layer—within the OSI architecture, *DATA* is the name of the service, and *request* is the type of service primitive.

3.1.4 Associated Parameters

Recall that during a primitive interaction a service-user and the service-provider may exchange some information, aside from initiating a related procedure. As such, associated with each service primitive there is a collection of zero or more *parameters*. These parameters provide a mechanism to specify the nature of control information or data, or both, that may be passed by the service-user to the service-provider when it issues a service primitive, or *vice-versa*. Thus, a complete definition of services offered by a layer involves specifying not only the set of allowed service primitives, but also the parameters associated with each service primitive. As an example, a request primitive, when issued by a user (N + 1)-entity to initiate the establishment of a connection, has a number of associated parameters. These include, for instance, the (N)-addresses of the (N)-SAPs to which the communicating (N + 1)-entities are attached, (N)-user-data which needs to be communicated transparently, etc.

The values of parameters are assigned by the entity that issues the primitive, and interpreted by the entity receiving it. A definition of a parameter thus specifies the set of constants from which the parameter shall be assigned its value. This allows the receiver to associate a unique meaning with each parameter passed with the primitive. The definition, however, does not specify the representation of the parameter value, since syntactical issues pertaining to interaction across a SAP are considered to be local and implementation dependent, and as such outside the scope of OSI. Note that not all parameters associated with a primitive are considered to be mandatory. Some parameters are optional, while the presence of some parameters (or their values) may be conditioned upon one or more factors. These factors generally relate to the nature of (N)-services provided or used at an (N)-SAP to support the particular instance of communication between peer (N + 1)-entities. As an example of optional parameters, a user may include user-data in a connection request primitive. Furthermore, a complete definition of the associated parameters excludes such parameters that are believed to be totally local to the interface, or are desirable only to support an implementation. Exchange of connection–end point–identifier (its significance is local) or that of information relating to available local resources are some examples of parameters that are not explicitly specified.

3.2 Service-Elements

Services offered by a layer can be visualized to be a collection of service-elements. In this section we classify them on the basis of whether a service-element is confirmed, unconfirmed or provider-initiated, and on the basis of whether it is mandatory or optional. Constraints on values of parameters of primitives of the same service-element are discussed at length.

Services made available by a service-provider are, in fact, a collection of several individual services, called *service-elements*; and associated with each service-element there is a procedure (or a function) implemented by the service-provider. Below we list a few examples:

- connection establishment,
- connection release,
- expedited data transfer.

3.2.1 Type of Services

A procedure related to a service-element may be invoked by a service-user by issuing a corresponding request primitive. Or, once such a procedure has been invoked by the service-provider on its own initiative, it issues a corresponding indication primitive. Based on who invokes the procedure and on whether a confirm primitive is issued to signal completion of a procedure, a service-element (or its corresponding procedure) may be classified as being either an

1. *unconfirmed service-element,* which does not require an explicit end-to-end confirmation to be issued upon the completion of the procedure;
2. *confirmed service-element,* which does require an explicit end-to-end confirmation to be issued upon the completion of the procedure; or
3. *provider-initiated service-element,* where the service-provider on its own initiative invokes a procedure.

The above distinction between the various types of service-elements is graphically illustrated in Figure 3.2.

Figure 3.2, as well as the above discussion, may suggest that the primitives concerning each service-element may be issued only in accordance with a specific sequence. This is only partly true. But before discussing it, we emphasize that this aspect of sequencing of primitives is only part of the problem of defining the permissible sequences of primitives, because currently, we are concerned with sequencing primitives related to individual service-elements, rather than all the service-elements taken together. We may, thus, term this as a discussion on *intra-service sequence* of primitives, as opposed to *inter-service sequence* of primitives.

3.2.2   Intra-Service Sequence of Primitives

For each type of service-element discussed earlier, the sequence in which the four (or fewer) primitives (namely, request, indication, response, and confirm) may be issued is given in Figure 3.3. For an unconfirmed service-element, the sequence is as indicated in Figure 3.3(a). For confirmed service-elements either of the sequences given in Figure 3.3(b) or (c) may be applicable, but only one of these would be specified to be valid for a given confirmed service-element. The sequence given in Figure 3.3(d) is the one relevant for a provider-initiated service-element.

In Figure 3.3, the vertical lines distinguish the two service-users from the service-provider. A directed arrow indicates the issuing of a service primitive by a service-user or the service-provider, as the case may be. Time increases downwards, so that some timing relationship may be established between the issuing of service primitives. A directed straight arc within the vertical lines suggests a time dependency (or cause-effect relationship) between a primitive issued by a service-user at one end and the primitive issued by the service-provider at the other. The symbol tilde (~) indicates that there is no such cause-effect relationship between the primitives issued at the two ends. Certain confirmed service-elements may require that the confirmation be end-to-end (all the way up to the correspondent service-user), while for other service-elements a locally generated confirmation may be adequate. For instance a service-element related to connection establishment would typically require the confirmation to follow the sequence illustrated in Figure 3.3(b). For that matter, any service where there is a possibility of a negative response from the correspondent service-user, the required sequence is as in Figure 3.3(b).

The discussion of sequencing of primitives related to all the service-elements taken together is taken up in Section 3.3.

3.2.3   Relation between Primitive Parameters

Now that we have discussed sequencing of primitives concerning a service-element, it is relevant to discuss whether the parameters associated with the four primitives (request, indication, response and

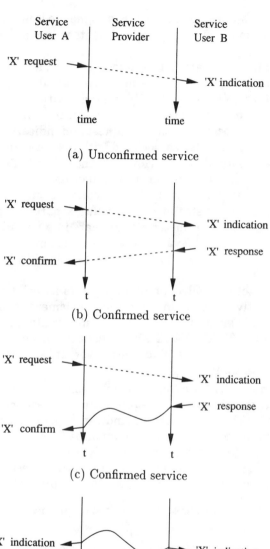

Figure 3.3 Possible sequences of primitives related to a service-element.

confirm) are related. First, one needs to identify whether the collection
of parameters is the same for all the primitives concerning a service-
element, or not. Next, if a parameter is common to two of the primitives,

request and indication, for instance, then the value assigned to it in the indication primitive may or may not be constrained by its value in the request primitive.

It is only to be expected that the parameters associated with a primitive issued at one end are also present in the primitive issued at another end. This is so since an (N)-layer basically interacts with a user (N + 1)-entity on behalf of some other user (N + 1)-entity. Invariably, the collection of parameters associated with the request and indication are the same. Similarly, the parameters associated with response and confirm primitives are generally identical. However, the collection of parameters associated with the response primitive may be substantially different from those associated with the indication primitive. Further, there is usually some constraint on the value a parameter may assume in a primitive if the parameter also appears in a preceding primitive. More often than not, the value is identical, but in many cases this value is constrained to belong to a subset determined by its value in the preceding primitive.

An example specification of the collection of parameters associated with the sequence of primitives pertaining to a service-element, and constraints on their values, is given in Table 3.1. The specification relates to the parameters of the *T-CONNECT* service-element, a service offered by a specific layer, namely, the Transport layer. It is a confirmed service-element. Note that:

1. Except for the parameter *TS User Data,* all other parameters are mandatory. *TS User Data* may or may not be present in the response primitive, even if it is present in the request and indication primitives. Its value in the indication (or confirm) primitive must be identical to that in the preceding request (or response, respectively) primitive.

2. The parameters *Calling Address* and *Called Address* are present only in the request primitive, while *Responding Address* is present in

TABLE 3.1   An Example Specification of Primitive Parameters and Constraints

Parameter	T-CONNECT			
	request	indication	response	confirm
Called Address	X	X		
Calling Address	X	X(=)		
Responding Address			X	X(=)
Expedited data option	X	X(=)	X	X(=)
Quality of service	X	X	X	X(=)
TS user data	X(U)	X(=)	X(U)	X(=)

Note:

X: mandatory parameter,

(=): parameter value is same as in previous primitive,

(U): user optional.

the response as well confirm primitives. Further, the value of each of these parameters is required to be identical to its value in the preceding primitive.

3. The parameter *Expedited Data Option* may assume either of the two values, namely, *selected* or *not selected*. Its value in an indication or confirm primitive is required to be the same as that in the preceding primitive. But its value in the response primitive is constrained by its value in the indication primitive. To be specific, if its value in the indication is *not selected,* then the only option available to the user is to assign to it a value *not selected.*

4. The value of the parameter *Quality of Service* in the confirm primitive is required to be identical to that in the response primitive. However, its value in the response (or indication) primitive is constrained to be from a subset of values determined by its value in the indication (or request, respectively) primitive. This is, in fact, a generalization of the constraints applicable to values of *Expedited Data Option,* discussed above.

3.2.4 Optional Services

Yet another classification of service-elements offered by a layer is based on whether a service-element is considered essential or simply desirable. From the viewpoint of minimizing the complexity of implementation of open systems, it is important that only a small enough set of service-elements be made mandatory. However, for many applications such a minimal set may be inadequate, in which case individual systems may choose to implement additional functions. So as to permit interconnection between open systems, an additional set of optional service-elements is defined by the OSI architecture for each layer. An optional service-element, if found to be sufficiently useful, may be supported by an individual open system, and possibly accessed by service-users within.

Formally, the following classification of service-elements is recognized by the OSI architecture:

1. *(N)-mandatory-service-element* is an element of service that must be provided as part of the (N)-service.

2. *(N)-provider-optional-service-element* is a service-element which may or may not be provided as part of the (N)-service.

3. *(N)-user-optional-service-element* is a service-element that is provided only if a user requests it and is available as part of (N)-service.

Mandatory service-elements are an essential set of (N)-services, and must be provided by the (N)-layer at each of the (N)-SAPs in each system, if such a system is to be considered as an open system. Support for provider-optional services may or may not be provided in a given system, and within a system such a service may only be provided at some of the (N)-SAPs. Thus, when two service-users interact, through their respective (N)-SAPs, an optional service may or may not be available depending upon whether the service is provided at each (N)-SAP. Furthermore, although a provider-optional service-element may be available at an (N)-SAP, the corresponding (N)-service-user may or may not opt to use the service. Although rare, even a mandatory service-element may not be used by a service-user.

A provider-optional service-element or a mandatory service-element, whose use may be negotiated by the service-users and the service-provider, is referred to as user-optional service-element. In the context of connection-oriented data transfers, the negotiation takes place at the time of connection establishment, and involves the two service-users and the service-provider.

Some examples of optional services may be relevant. Connection-oriented communication makes implementation of procedures for connection establishment and for connection release mandatory, whereas support for, for instance, expedited data transfer is generally considered provider-optional. The latter is also a user-optional service-element.

3.3 Models of Service

In this section we discuss constraints on issuing primitives that correspond to different service-elements. A state transition diagram is used to describe the permissible sequence of inter-service primitives. We also discuss the cause-effect relationship between issuing of primitives at corresponding SAPs using a queue model.

In the previous sections we have discussed the nature of primitives and their parameters, as well as the classification of service-elements based on whether a service-element is confirmed, unconfirmed, or provider-initiated. We also mentioned that only some of the service-elements are considered mandatory, while others may be optionally provided. Let us consider next, how services made available by a layer are specified. The entire service definition includes specification of the following:

1. collection of service-elements;
2. classification of each service-element based on whether it is mandatory or provider-optional, and whether it is user-optional or otherwise;
3. classification of each service-element based on whether it is confirmed, unconfirmed, or provider-initiated;
4. parameters associated with each service primitive;

5. applicable constraints on the sequence of primitives issued at a SAP;

6. a queue model, and

7. the quality of service provided.

The first four items of the service definition have been covered in some detail in the preceding sections of this chapter. For completeness, we shall give an example to illustrate the above. The two topics on inter-service sequence of primitives, and a queue model are covered in the remainder of this section. Quality of service is discussed in the next section.

Table 3.2 is an example specification of the collection of service-elements made available by a layer, and their classification. Table 3.1, for example, specifies the collection of parameters associated with the four primitives concerning the service-element *TC-establishment* of Table 3.2, and any constraints on their values (see [ISO 8072] or [CCITT X.214]). Similarly, parameters, and constraints on their values, may be

TABLE 3.2   Example Specification of Service Elements Provided by a Layer

Service element	Nature of service	Primitives
Establishment Phase		
TC establishment	confirmed and mandatory	T-CONNECT request T-CONNECT indication T-CONNECT response T-CONNECT confirm
Data Transfer Phase		
Normal data transfer	unconfirmed and mandatory	T-DATA request T-DATA indication
Expedited data transfer	unconfirmed and mandatory but user optional	T-EXPEDITED DATA request T-EXPEDITED DATA indication
Release Phase		
TC release	unconfirmed, or provider-initiated and mandatory	T-DISCONNECT request T-DISCONNECT indication

(a) Connection Oriented Services

Service element	Nature of service	Primitives
Data Transfer Phase		
Unit data transfer	unconfirmed provider and user optional	T-UNITDATA request T-UNITDATA indication

(b) Connection-less Services

specified in respect of primitives related to other service-elements. Typically, additional description, in the form of text, may be made available to indicate the semantics associated with each primitive and its parameters, or to specify any additional constraints on using an optional feature.

3.3.1   Inter-Service Sequence of Primitives

The classification of a service-element as being either confirmed, unconfirmed, or provider-initiated does suggest the sequence in which the primitives related to it may be issued. However, this description is incomplete since it does not describe the constraints, if any, on issuing service primitives that relate to all the service-elements taken together. Such constraints are incorporated as part of the specification of the set of admissible inter-service sequences of primitives.

Recall that the service-elements offered as part of the service by a layer either support connection-oriented services or connection-less data transfer services. By its very nature, connection-less data transmission is a single-access service. That is, issuing of a primitive at a SAP has no bearing on the issuing of other primitives at the same SAP. It is a different matter that when a service-user at a SAP issues a request primitive to invoke connection-less data transfer, a corresponding indication primitive may be issued at a SAP. Thus, issuing of a primitive concerning connection-less data transfer is neither constrained, nor does it constrain, the issuing of any other primitive. In other words, as far as the interface at a SAP is concerned, its state does not change with issuing of a connection-less service-related primitive. This is graphically illustrated in Figure 3.4. Therein, we have used, as an example, service primitives related to the service-element *T-UNIT-DATA* of Table 3.2(b).

In the context of connection-oriented data transfer, one may expect a number of constraints on issuing of primitives. For instance, a request for data transfer, or for connection release, has no meaning unless a connection has been established, or at the very least, the establishment of which has been initiated. But before discussing ways to specify such constraints, it is pertinent to point out that issuing of primitives concerning a connection has no bearing on issuing of primitives concern-

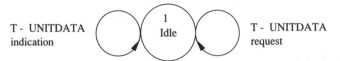

Figure 3.4 State transition diagram describing the sequence of connection-less service related primitives.

ing other connections. Since our concern is with issuing primitives at a SAP, it follows that the constraints need to be specified for each connection-endpoint (CEP), separately.

The allowed sequences of primitives concerning a connection may be specified in the form of a state transition diagram. A state transition diagram (see Figure 3.5, for example) describes a set of states. At any time instant the CEP may be in any one of the states. The diagram also defines how the CEP transitions from its current state to the next state when a service primitive is issued either by the service-user or the service-provider. For any given state of the CEP, if a transition corresponding to a service primitive is not indicated on the diagram, then either the service primitive may not be issued or, if issued, it is ignored by the receiving entity. From the viewpoint of the OSI, the CEP does not change state.

The following comments, some of which are applicable to state transition diagrams in general, are made:

1. The initial state of the CEP is denoted as *Idle*. It corresponds to the state where the establishment of the connection has not been initiated, or equivalently, the CEP has not been associated with any connection, thus far. After the connection has been released the CEP returns to the initial state.

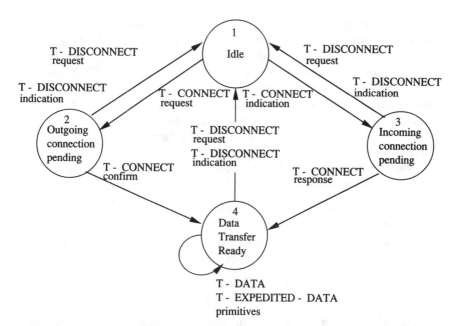

Figure 3.5 State transition diagram concerning connection-oriented primitives issued at a CEP.

2. The CEP may remain within a state for any length of time. Further, for any state of the CEP, it is not specified as to which primitive may be issued next.

3. For the given state transition diagram, it is easy to determine the entire set of admissible sequences of primitives. This set may be infinitely large.

Figure 3.5 is an example of the state transition diagram associated with the service primitives related to connection-oriented services offered by a layer, namely, the Transport layer of OSI. The following constraints are additionally implied by the state transition diagram:

1. A connection release procedure can be invoked at any time during the establishment or the data transfer phase.

2. Procedures for normal data transfer or expedited data transfer can only be initiated during the *Data Transfer Ready* state.

3.3.2   A Queue Model

Constraints on issuing (N)-service primitives discussed thus far are local to an (N)-SAP or to an (N)-CEP. For instance, they do not suggest any cause-effect relationship between issuing of request and indication primitives at two (N)-SAPs, in case of connection-less data transmission. Nor do they indicate how issuing of primitives at the two endpoint CEPs of a connection are related.

OSI documents make extensive use of a queue model to describe the operations over a connection established between two (N)-CEPs. The queue model attempts to relate the issuing of a service primitive at a CEP of a connection to primitives issued at the other CEP. Note that this is only a model, and must be used to obtain a better and a more precise understanding of the operations over the connection. It may not be taken to be a suggested implementation. Any implementation which functionally conforms to this model would be acceptable.

The queue model views an (N)-connection as a pair of queues linking its two CEPS, one for each direction of communication, as shown in Figure 3.6. Therein, it is shown that

1. each queue is a first-in-first-out data structure,

2. the queues carry *objects,* and

3. the user (N + 1)-entities attached to the corresponding (N)-SAPs (and possibly the service-provider) are able to place or remove objects.

Such a description is, however, incomplete till we have discussed the following:

1. the relationship between removing or placing objects and issuing primitives,

2. the nature of objects placed in the queues,
3. who may place objects or remove them from the queues,
4. whether the queues are truly first-in-first-out or follow some other service discipline, and
5. initialization, destruction or emptying of queues.

The issuing of connection-related primitives has a one-to-one correspondence with operations performed on the queues. Two queues are required since, in general, a connection is viewed as a channel providing two-way simultaneous (or two-way alternate) transfer of information. We discuss this correspondence in relation to Figure 3.6. Whenever a user (N + 1)-entity A (or B) issues a request or response primitive related to the particular (N)-connection at an (N)-SAP, an object is added to the tail of the outgoing queue Q1 (or Q2, respectively). However, when the service-provider issues an indication or confirm primitive at an (N)-SAP C (or (N)-SAP D), this corresponds to the attached user (N + 1)-entity removing an object from the incoming queue Q2 (or Q1, respectively). The service-provider may also add or remove objects from the two queues, but only under certain situations. For instance, the service-provider adds an object to a queue whenever it issues an indication primitive resulting from a provider-initiated

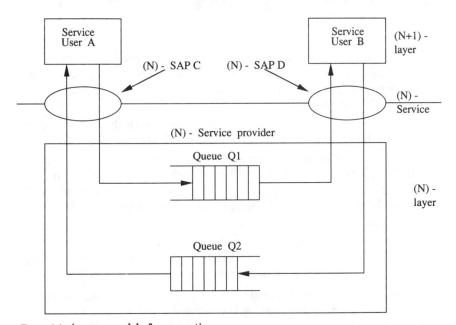

Figure 3.6 A queue model of a connection.

procedure. Generally, a service-provider rarely has an occasion to remove objects from the queues.

As for the nature of objects placed in the queues, we consider two examples. When a user (N + 1)-entity A issues a primitive to request the establishment of an (N)-connection, a *connect* object is placed in the outgoing queue. Assume that the service-provider has the resources to establish yet another connection. When the service-provider informs the other user (N + 1)-entity B of the entity A's request to establish a connection through an indication primitive, the same connect object is removed by the entity B. Similarly, when user B issues a response primitive, thereby indicating its willingness to accept the connection, this action is viewed in the queue model as a placement of a connect object in the queue from B to A, but this is a different type of connect object. The removal of this object by user A models the issuing of a confirm primitive by the service-provider.

As another example, if for some reason the service-provider is no longer able to support the (N)-connection and wishes to break it, places a *disconnect* object in each of the queues. This is equivalent to the service-provider issuing an indication primitive at each of the two CEPs.

Connect and disconnect objects are just two examples. There are objects associated with each service primitive. In some cases an object corresponding to user-data is broken down into *octets of data* with an *end marker* indicating the end of the service-data-unit. Logically, all such octets of data, up to and including the end marker, are treated as one whole.

Other aspects of the queue model are briefly discussed in the following:

1. *Initialization of queues:* A queue in the appropriate direction is created as soon as a connect object is ready to be placed, as a consequence of issuing of a request primitive corresponding to connection establishment.

2. *Destruction of queues:* A queue is destroyed with the removal of an object that corresponds to the release of the connection.

3. *Reordering of objects:* Objects are generally removed in a first-in-first-out manner. But these objects may be reordered by the service-provider. This condition may arise when an expedited-SDU is transferred on an urgent basis, or when a disconnect object or a *re-initialize* object is placed in the queue.

4. *Removal of objects by the service-provider:* In case an (N)-connection is re-initialized using a reset procedure, data already in the pipeline over the connection may be removed by the service-provider.

There is a need to precisely state the conditions under which objects may be re-ordered or removed by the service-provider, and to what extent. A table is usually given which specifies:

1. whether an object of type x may advance ahead of another object of type y, and

2. if an object of type x may advance ahead of another object of type y, then whether the object of type y may be destroyed.

See Table 3.3 for an example specification (see also [ISO 8072]). This table enables one to specify the effect of issuing primitives related to certain service-elements on procedures that have already been initiated but not completed. For example, release of a connection, or its re-initialization, has an overriding influence on SDUs in the pipeline. Further, while there is freedom to advance objects ahead of other objects, or to destroy objects, it is not mandatory to do so. A given implementation may or may not implement such functions, or even it did it may not use them to the extent feasible.

As a final remark, the queue model of service must be taken as a specification of additional constraints on issuing service primitives at CEPs of a connection. Any implementation of the service-provider and its interface with service-users must conform to the specifications implied by the queue model, but only at a functional level.

3.4 Quality of Service

In this section we discuss the notion of quality of service provided by a layer. We define a number of parameters used to quantify the quality of connection-oriented and connection-less services. The parameters

TABLE 3.3   Precedence of Objects within a Queue

Precedence over Queue Object y	Queue Object x				
	CO	OND	ETI	ET	DO
CO	-	-	-	-	Advance Destroy
OND	-	-	-	Advance	Advance Destroy
ETI	-	-	-	Advance	Advance Destroy
ET	-	-	-	-	Advance Destroy
DO	-	-	-	-	-

Note:
CO: Connect Object,
OND: Octets of Normal Data,
ETI: End-of-TSDU Indication,
ET: Expedited TSDU,
DO: Disconnect Object.

are classified on the basis of whether a parameter characterizes performance or simply specifies additional features.

The term *Quality of Service* (QOS) refers to certain characteristics of (N) services as observed by user (N + 1)-entities. These characteristics are independent of how users use these services, and instead describe only those aspects of services that are attributable solely to the service-provider. It is assumed that the pattern of usage of these services is not likely to impact the quality of services provided.

Recall that the services provided by a layer can be classified into those that support connection-less data transfer and those that are connection-oriented. We shall discuss QOS of connection-oriented data transfer services first, and later specialize the discussion to that of connection-less data transmission.

In the context of connection-oriented services, one refers to QOS of each individual connection, separately. That is, the QOS of two (N)-connections, established between two different pairs of (N)-SAPs, may be different. This allows one to balance the cost of implementation with the level of QOS provided. Further, the QOS over two connections established from the same (N)-SAP may also be different. This allows a user (N + 1)-entity to decide the level of QOS that is adequate for each of its applications, and thereby minimize the costs charged to it.

3.4.1 QOS Parameters

The specification of available or desired QOS is made in terms of parameters, called *QOS parameters*. As part of the connection establishment procedure, the three parties (namely, the two user (N + 1)-entities and the service-provider) together negotiate the values of QOS parameters. The negotiation procedure requires each user to make known the level of QOS over the connection that it desires, while the service-provider, in turn, indicates the level of QOS that it can support over a connection. Once a connection has been established, the service-provider and the service-users at the two ends have the same knowledge and understanding of the QOS provided over the connection. It must, however, be pointed out that not all parameters are negotiated, and that the procedure to negotiate differs from layer to layer. For those parameters that are not negotiated, users either have an *a priori* knowledge of their values, or determine their values using methods that are outside the scope of OSI.

A value of a QOS parameter, whether negotiated or not, remains the same through the lifetime of the connection. As one implication, a QOS parameter, once negotiated, is not re-negotiated. As another, the service-provider is committed to provide the QOS over the connection.

There is, however, no guarantee that the service-provider will maintain the original values. Minor changes are quite frequent, since these are statistical averages, any way. In fact, if the QOS were to deteriorate even substantially the service-provider is under no obligation to signal such a change in QOS to the users of the connection. It may, on its own initiative, disconnect the connection. A user, on the other hand, always has the option to disconnect the connection if it were to experience a poor QOS over the connection.

The QOS parameters may be classified along several different lines as illustrated in Figure 3.7 (see also [ISO 8348] or [CCITT X.213]). Some of the QOS parameters simply indicate availability of additional features over a connection, for example, *protection* or *priority*. These parameters are defined below:

1. *Protection* is the extent to which a service-provider attempts to prevent unauthorized monitoring or manipulation of user-data. The level of protection is specified qualitatively by selecting one of the four options:
   (*a*) no protection,
   (*b*) protection against passive monitoring,
   (*c*) protection against modification, addition or deletion, and
   (*d*) both (*b*) and (*c*), above.
2. *Priority* is concerned with the relative importance assigned to the particular connection (in relation to others) with respect to:
   (*a*) the order in which connections are to have their QOS degraded, if it becomes necessary, and
   (*b*) the order in which connections are to be released to recover resources, if it becomes necessary.

3.4.2 Performance-Related QOS Parameters

Other QOS parameters strictly measure performance during the three different phases of connection establishment, data transfer, and connection release. Table 3.4 classifies some of the parameters that are commonly encountered in the specification of QOS. In the following we give their definitions. We shall use Figure 3.8 to illustrate the delay concerning successful completion of procedures that are essential to the three different phases of a connection. Therein, it is assumed that the service-elements *CONNECT, DATA* and *DISCONNECT,* respectively, correspond to connection establishment, (normal) data transfer, and connection release.

1. *Establishment Delay* is the delay, T_{Est}, between the issuing of a CONNECT request and the corresponding CONNECT confirm. Its

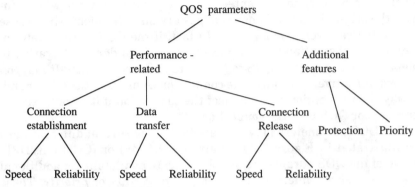

Figure 3.7 Classification of QOS parameters.

value is interpreted as being the *maximum acceptable* Establishment Delay. Note that T_{Est} includes the component, T_1, that may solely be attributed to the responding service-user (see Figure 3.8(a)).

2. *Establishment Failure Probability* is the estimated probability that a requested connection is *not* established within the specified maximum acceptable Establishment Delay, but only as a consequence of actions that are solely attributable to the service-provider. That is, the computation of the probability excludes those measurement samples where a connection establishment procedure failed as a result of the responding service-user either refusing the connection, or excessively delaying its response.

3. *Transit Delay* is the time delay, T_{Trans}, between the issuing of a DATA request and the corresponding DATA indication (see Figure 3.8(b)). The parameter is usually specified as a pair of values, a statistical average and the maximum. Only successful (namely, error-free,

TABLE 3.4 Quality of Service Parameters Related to Performance over a Connection

Phase	Performance Criterion	
	Speed	Accuracy/Reliability
Connection Establishment	Establishment Delay	Establishment Failure Probability
Data Transfer	Transfer Delay Throughput	Residual Error Rate Transfer Failure Probability Resilience
Connection Release	Release Delay	Release Failure Probability

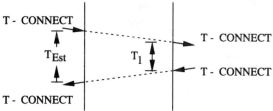

(a) Connection Establishment

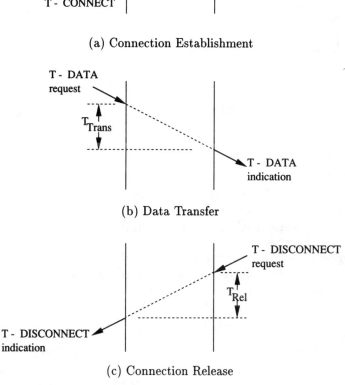

(b) Data Transfer

(c) Connection Release

Figure 3.8 Illustration of delay.

duplication-free and in the proper sequence) transfers of service-data-units (SDUs) are included in computing the average or the maximum. Further, those data transfers where a receiving service-user exercises flow control are also excluded. The computations are all based on SDUs of a fixed size of 128 octets, for example.

4. *Residual Error Rate* is the estimated probability that an SDU is transferred with error, or that it is lost, or that a duplicate copy is transferred. Its estimate may be obtained using the formula (see Figure 3.9)

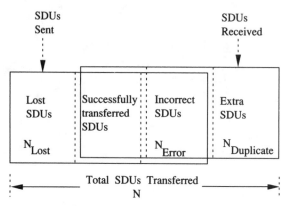

Figure 3.9 Transfer of SDUs with or without error.

$$\text{Residual Error Rate} = \frac{(N_{Error} + N_{Lost} + N_{Duplicate})}{N}.$$

In the above N_{Error}, N_{Lost}, and $N_{Duplicate}$ are, respectively, the number of SDUs that are transferred with error, those not transferred at all, or those that are duplicate SDUs. N is the total number of all SDUs transferred, successfully or otherwise.

5. *Throughput* is the maximum number of octets, contained in SDUs, that may be successfully transferred in unit time by the service-provider over the connection, on a sustained basis. It is assumed that the sending service-user is able to present SDUs to the service-provider continuously, and that the receiving service-user does not introduce delays while receiving incoming SDUs.

6. *Transfer Failure Probability* is the estimated probability that the observed performance in respect of Transit Delay, Residual Error Rate or Throughput will be worse than the specified level of performance. The failure probability is, as such, specified for each measure of performance of data transfer, discussed above.

7. *Resilience* is the estimated probability that a service-provider will, on its own, release the connection, or reset it, within a specified interval of time.

8. *Release Delay* is the delay, T_{Rel}, between the issuing of a DISCONNECT request primitive by a service-user and the corresponding DISCONNECT indication primitive by the service-provider. Its value has the interpretation of being the maximum acceptable delay in releasing the connection (see Figure 3.8(c)).

9. *Release Failure Probability* is the estimated probability that the service-provider is unable to release the connection within the specified maximum Release Delay.

3.4.3 QOS of Connection-less Data Transfers

Above we have mainly been concerned with QOS for connection-oriented services. QOS of connection-less service-elements is in fact similar, except that the concept of negotiation is not applicable, and only those QOS parameters that concern transfer of user-data have meaning. These include Protection, Transit Delay, and Residual Error Rate. The definition of these parameters is similar to those given earlier, but must be redefined using the connection-less service-element *UNIT-DATA,* for instance, in place of the service-element DATA.

3.5 Layer Functions

In this section we discuss specification of a layer protocol in terms of the collection of functions, and related procedures, to be implemented by the layer. In view of the fact that a function may be optional, protocol specification includes a description of a number of protocol classes and a mechanism for negotiation.

3.5.1 Protocol Specification

In the earlier sections we have been primarily concerned with concepts that are fundamental to defining services offered by a layer. Recall that service definitions form the second level of description of the OSI architecture (see Figure 2.2). The next and the last level of description of OSI architecture is concerned with specification of protocols that govern all communication between peer entities.

For a specified set of (N)-services, it is possible to design and implement the (N)-service-provider in a variety of ways. All such designs would meet the (N)-service requirements, but may differ in the manner in which (N)-entities cooperate with each other in making available the (N)-service. Since, in general, the available (N − 1)-services are also specified *a priori,* the implementations differ mainly in respect of procedures used by (N)-entities to implement (N)-functions. The goal of a protocol specification is to describe the form and content of all cooperation between the (N)-entities in their attempts to provide (N)-services. Such a specification would, of course, assume availability of an (N − 1)-service, and its defined properties.

3.5.2 Functions

A protocol specification is in the form of:

1. a collection of (N)-functions to be implemented,

2.   the procedure used by (N)-entities to implement an (N)-function, and

3.   the rules that govern all communication between the (N)-entities.

The collection of (N)-functions are those needed to bridge the gap between services available and those offered, and in some ways correspond to the (N)-service-elements that the layer supports. The above specification is collectively referred to as an (N)-protocol. As such, the (N)-entities are sometimes called *protocol machines* (see also Figure 3.10).

Recall that an (N)-service, provided by the (N)-layer, may be broken down into a collection of (N)-service-elements, which in turn may be classified into those that are mandatory or those that are provider-optional. Further, since the (N)-functions do correspond to the (N)-service-elements offered by the (N)-layer, an (N)-protocol classifies the (N)-functions into mandatory and optional functions. Any implementation of the protocol that claims conformance with OSI architecture and its standard protocols must implement the mandatory functions. However, use of some of the mandatory functions is subject to negotiation by the protocol machines.

Optional functions may, of course, be implemented by a protocol machine either to support optional service-elements or to efficiently utilize resources available to it. It is immaterial whether such a functionality is specifically implemented within the (N)-layer, or simply derived from the (N − 1)-service available to it. In either case, an optional function may not be activated unless each of the cooperating protocol machines implement the corresponding procedure (or have access to the corresponding (N − 1)-service-element) and agree to use it. Negotiation

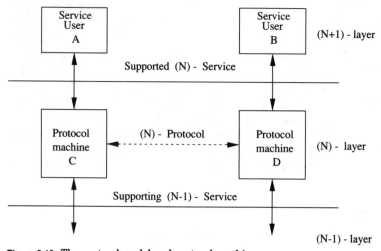

Figure 3.10 The protocol model and protocol machines.

is, of course, relevant only in the context of connection-oriented data transfers.

For connection-less data transfer services, the only set of functions needed are the ones that correspond to data transfer. These are:

- transfer of PDUs, and

- treatment of protocol errors.

It is assumed that user-data is exchanged in the form of protocol-data-units. Treatment of protocol errors, in connection-less data transfers, may simply be limited to error detection. But in the context of connection-oriented data transfers, the (N)-protocol must specify procedures to implement a wide variety of additional functions including (see Section 2.5 and [ISO 8073], for example):

- connection establishment,

- data transfer, and

- connection release.

Their implementation is considered mandatory, since these form the basis for connection-oriented services. Since a connection request may be refused by the responding service-user, a procedure corresponding to

- connection refusal

is also, typically, part of protocol specification. A number of mandatory functions, which are not as visible at the (N)-service boundary, include:

- assignment of (N)-connection to (N − 1)-connection, and

- association of received (N)-PDU to (N)-connection.

The first of these functions recognizes the fact that each (N)-connection must be mapped onto an (N − 1)-connection, while the second function ensures that each received PDU is properly identified to belong to the appropriate (N)-connection. Each connection is identified using an (N)-protocol-connection-identifier, unique within the scope of the communicating (N)-entities, or protocol machines. (See also Section 2.3.) A related procedure specifies how the communicating (N)-entities may reuse an identifier once the corresponding connection has been released. This procedure is optional and referred to as

- frozen references.

Protocols may also specify procedures for the following optional functions:

- expedited data-transfer,

- flow control,

- sequencing,

- acknowledgement, and

- error detection, reporting and recovery.

In view of the fact that a functionality may specifically be built into the (N)-layer, or it may be derived from (N − 1)-services, many of the above functions have two variants, namely, (i) *explicit variant,* and (ii) *implicit variant.* In an implicit variant of expedited data-transfer (or acknowledgement) the corresponding (N − 1)-service-element is used to expedite transfer of (N)-expedited-SDU (or to acknowledge), whenever the service is available and its use has been negotiated.

Similarly, an (N)-connection may be implicitly released by releasing the corresponding (N − 1)-connection, but only when there is a one-to-one correspondence between the (N)-connection and the supporting (N − 1)-connection, and the *lifetime* of the (N)-connection and that of the (N − 1)-connection are the same. More generally, the existence of an (N)-connection is independent of that of the supporting (N − 1)-connection(s), as shown in Figure 3.11. Therein, we have shown three commonly encountered correspondences between the lifetimes of the connections.

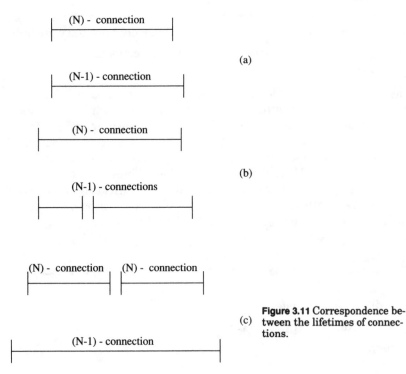

Figure 3.11 Correspondence between the lifetimes of connections.

In respect of error detection and recovery, a protocol may, in the simplest of cases, require connection release, namely,

- error release,

or provide for elaborate mechanisms for recovery. More specifically, if a supporting $(N - 1)$-connection were to fail then the protocol may require reestablishment of the $(N - 1)$-connection and subsequent

- reassignment after failure (see Figure 3.11).

Other optional functions concern mapping of (N)-connections onto $(N - 1)$-connections, namely,

- multiplexing and de-multiplexing, and
- splitting and recombining,

mapping of (N)-service-data-units onto (N)-protocol-data-units, namely,

- segmentation and reassembly, and
- blocking and de-blocking,

or mapping (N)-protocol-data-units onto $(N - 1)$-service-data-units, namely,

- concatenation and separation.

Note that a number of additional mandatory or optional functions may be defined for each given layer, but these are considered to be specific to the layer.

3.5.3 Classes of Protocols

It is often the case that implementation of an optional function is meaningful only when some related set of other optional functions are also implemented. For this reason, a protocol specification may group the optional functions together, and thereby define a number of classes of protocols, each of which includes the *kernel* (or basic) set of mandatory functions. See Table 3.5 for an example specification of protocol classes and the functions supported by each protocol class.[1] The manner in which the protocol machines negotiate the use of a particular class of protocol (and any optional function within the class) is, of course, part of specification of the (N)-protocol. This assumes that each protocol class is uniquely identified and that the *protocol identifier* is exchanged between the protocol machines during connection establishment.

---

[1]See [ISO 8073].

3.6 Protocol Specifications

This section is concerned with the detailed specification of the manner in which protocol-data-units are exchanged between communicating entities or protocol machines. PDU parameters and their encoding rules are discussed at some length. State tables may be used to specify the time when a PDU may be sent or received, as well the correspondence between such an event and issuing of a related service-primitive.

A major portion of the specification of an (N)-protocol relates to procedures required to implement the specified (N)-functions. These procedures are described in terms of the form and content of all messages exchanged between the cooperating (N)-entities. The corresponding rules include specification of the

- syntax,
- semantics, and
- timing

TABLE 3.5 Example Specification of Protocol Classes and Functions Supported

Procedure	Protocol Class				
	0	1	2	3	4
Assignment to Network Connection	*	*	*	*	*
Transfer of TPDUs	*	*	*	*	*
Connection Establishment	*	*	*	*	*
Connection Refusal	*	*	*	*	*
Normal Release	*	*	*	*	*
Association of TPDUs with TC	*	*	*	*	*
Treatment of Protocol Errors	*	*	*	*	*
Segmentation and Reassembly	*	*	*	*	*
Concatenation and Separation		*	*	*	*
Data TPDU Numbering		*	*	*	*
Expedited Data Transfer		*	*	*	*
Multiplexing and Demultiplexing			*	*	*
Flow Control			*	*	*
Error Release	*		*		
Retention of TPDUs until Acknowledged		*		*	*
Resynchronization		*		*	*
Reassignment after Failure		*		*	*
Frozen References		*		*	*
Inactivity Control					*
Checksum					*
Splitting and Recombining					*
Retransmission on Timeout					*
Resequencing					*

of all messages exchanged. On some occasions, however, a function may not require exchange of any messages at all. Instead, the protocol specifies actions to be initiated by a protocol machine. These actions take the form of issuing of primitives at the service boundary with either the (N)-layer or the (N − 1)-layer.

3.6.1 Syntax

Syntactical issues pertain to encoding of messages exchanged between (N)-entities in the form of (N)-protocol-data-units ((N)-PDUs), each of which carries (N)-protocol-control-information ((N)-PCI) and possibly (N)-user-data. A PDU is viewed as containing values of one or more parameters, called *PDU parameters*. The syntax specifies the encoding of each PDU parameter as well as the relative position it occupies within the PDU. Alternatively, the syntax specification enables a receiver to determine the value of each parameter included in the PDU by investigating the received bit sequence. Thus a PDU may contain, for instance,

- the type of PDU,
- the type of parameter,
- the length of each parameter value, and
- the parameter values.

Figure 3.12 gives an example of a PDU encoded in accordance with the syntax, a sample of which is illustrated in Table 3.6.

Syntactical issues are extremely important in the context of protocol specification since the communicating (N)-entities may reside in different open systems. This is in contrast to service definitions where issues relating to representation of service primitives and their parameters are considered to be implementation dependent, and, therefore, not subject to standardization.

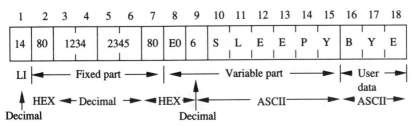

Figure 3.12 Encoding of a PDU: an example.

3.6.2 Semantics

Semantic issues, on the other hand, relate to the contents of messages communicated between (N)-entities. A specification may thus include the different types of PDUs that may be sent, and the interpretation that a receiving entity may associate with it in terms of changes in its state. Since implementation of certain functions is optional, only those PDUs that correspond to functions that have been implemented and whose use has been negotiated (and the mandatory functions) may be transmitted or received. Table 3.7 is an example specification of the set of PDUs that may be exchanged by the (N)-entities. Additionally, an (N)-protocol specifies the contents of each PDU in terms of its parameters and the values that each PDU parameter may assume. Again, as with primitive parameters, inclusion of some of the parameters is optional, and there may be constraints on the values assumed by a parameter in PDUs that correspond to the same function. Some examples of PDU parameters are:

TABLE 3.6 Syntax Specification: An Example

PDU Format in Transport Layer:

1	$2 \ldots n$	$n+1 \ldots p$	$p+1 \ldots$
LI	Fixed Part	Variable Part	User Data

LI(Length Indicator): $p - 1$

Fixed Part for Disconnect Request PDU, for example:

1	2 3	4 5	6
Code	DST-REF	SRC-REF	Reason

Code: 10000000.
DST-REF, SRC-REF: Pair of Reference Numbers.
Reason: 10000000, for example signifies disconnect requested by user.

Variable Part for Additional Information, for example:

1	2	$\ldots q$
Code	LI	Information

Code: 11100000.
LI(Length Indicator): $q - 2$.
Information: User defined additional information.

TABLE 3.7   Example Specification of PDUs Exchanged

TPDUs	Protocol Class				
	0	1	2	3	4
Connection Request	*	*	*	*	*
Connection Confirm	*	*	*	*	*
Disconnect Request	*	*	*	*	*
Disconnect Confirm		*	*	*	*
Data	*	*	*	*	*
Expedited Data		*	?	*	*
Data Acknowledgement		?	?	*	*
Expedited Data Acknowledgement		*	?	*	*
Reject		*		*	
TDU Error	*	*	*	*	*

Note:
* : PDU is always used,
? : Conditionally used.

- address,
- sequence number,
- user-data,
- acknowledgement information,
- connection identifier, and
- synchronization point number.

Table 3.8 is an example specification of the list of parameters associated with a PDU. The PDU is a *CONNECTION REQUEST TPDU* of the Transport layer protocol.

Reception by a protocol machine of a PDU

- which is outside the repertoire of the selected protocol,
- which includes an inadmissible parameter,
- which contains an invalid parameter value, or
- which cannot be decoded

is considered to be erroneous. As such the receiving protocol machine may initiate error recovery procedures that may require:

- re-transmission of the erroneous message,
- reporting of an error to the user (N + 1)-entities,
- re-initialization of the (N)-connection, or
- connection release.

3.6.3   Timing

Timing issues in (N)-protocols relate to the specification of the time when a particular PDU may be transmitted, or as to what prompts the transmission of a PDU. Generally, the protocol requires transmission of one or more PDUs and/or initiation of certain related actions when an external *event* occurs. Three distinct types of events are recognized. These are:

1.   reception of a (valid or invalid) PDU from a corresponding (N)-entity,
2.   issuing of a (request or response) primitive by a user (N + 1)-entity,
3.   issuing of an (indication or confirm) service primitive by the (N − 1)-service-provider, and
4.   time-out.

The actions taken by an (N)-entity, upon detecting the occurrence of an external event, may include one or more of the following

TABLE 3.8   Example Specification of PDU Parameters

Parameter	Parameter Length
Length Indicator	1 byte
Fixed Part	
Connection request code	4 bits
Initial credit allocation	4 bits
Destination reference	2 bytes
Source reference	2 bytes
Protocol class	4 bits
Options	
Use of extended format	1 bit
Use of Explicit flow control	1 bit
Variable Part	
TSAP identifier	variable
Maximum TPDU size	1 byte
Protocol version no.	1 byte
Protection parameters	user defined
Checksum	2 bytes
Additional options	
Use of Network expedited transfer	1 bit
Use of Receipt confirmation	1 bit
Use of Checksum	1 bit
Use of Transport expedited transfer	1 bit
Alternate protocol classes	variable
Acknowledgement time	2 bytes
Quality of service parameters	
Throughput	12 to 24 bytes
Residual error rate	3 bytes
Priority	2 bytes
Transit delay	8 bytes
Reassignment time	2 bytes
User data	variable

1. transmission of a PDU,
2. issuing of an indication or a confirm primitive at the (N)-service boundary,
3. issuing of a request or a response primitive at the (N − 1)-service boundary, or
4. starting or stopping a timer.

An (N)-protocol specifies the relation between the occurrence of events, and the actions initiated by a protocol machine using either a state transition diagram or a state table. Therein, the actions initiated by an (N)-entity are viewed as *outgoing events,* and the events initiating such actions are referred to as *incoming events.* The state table describes, for each possible state of the protocol machine,

- the incoming events that possibly cause a state change,
- the outgoing events associated with each incoming event, and
- the resulting state of the protocol machine.

Table 3.9 illustrates the specification of timing of interaction between protocol machines using a state table (see [ISO 8602]). Such a description is valid for each communicating protocol machine. Therein the outgoing event(s) and the resulting state are specified for the case when a protocol machine (in the Transport layer) is in some state, and for each incoming event. Note that each outgoing event is conditioned upon the truth value of a corresponding *predicate* P0, P1 and/or P2. The latter helps in presenting a more concise state table. A blank entry is an indication of the fact that an incoming event may not occur when the protocol machine is in the corresponding state. If an unspecified incoming event were to occur, then that would be considered to be a protocol error.

It must be pointed out that a state table description is given for the protocol as a whole, and not separately for each protocol procedure or function. Thus the state table description does take into account the interaction between all the procedures of the protocol. It is, of course, possible to abstract from the state table description the sequence of PDUs exchanged to complete a protocol procedure.

3.7 Summary

In this chapter we have described mechanisms that are used to specify a given layer, both in terms of the service it provides and the protocol it uses to realize the service. The definition of services offered by a layer can be given in terms of a collection of service primitives. Primitives are a convenient way to define an interaction between the service-provider and its users since it does not constrain its implementation in any way. Further, the OSI architecture consider representation of primitive parameters to be implementation dependent.

TABLE 3.9   State Table for Connection-less Transfer Protocol

State	Incoming Event		
	Closed	Wait Path	Transacting

TUNI.req	P0:UD
	  Closed;
	(not P0) and (not P1):
	  UD
	  Closed;
	(not P0)and P1:
	  NCON.req
	  Wait Path;		

NCON.conf		UD [1] Transacting;	
NDIS.ind		Closed;	Closed;

D-t expired			P2:Closed;
			(not P2):
			  NDIS.req
			  Closed;

UD	P0:TUNI.ind
	  Closed;
	(not P0) and P2:
	  TUNI.ind
	  Closed;
	(not P0) and (not P2):
	  TUNI.ind
	  NDIS.req
	  Closed;		

N-RESET.ind			N-RESET.rsp Transacting

Note [1]: Set disconnect timer.

Since services provided by a layer are in many ways related, a service-user and the service-provider are constrained to issue related primitives in a sequence that is consistent with a specified state transition diagram. The state diagrams for each connection are independent of other such diagrams. In this chapter we have also discussed the relation between issuing of primitives at the two service-access-points between which a connection has been established. The queue model, used to described the interaction, has been discussed in some detail.

Quality of service provided by a layer is of particular concern to each layer since it finally influences the quality of service that a user-developed application experiences. With that in mind, the definition of many parameters that characterize the quality of service have been presented.

The specification of a protocol for any layer is in terms of the procedures that each participating entity must implement. Since these entities may reside in different open systems, the specification must include a detailed description of the syntax of each protocol-data-unit exchanged between them. The procedures are best specified using a state table description. State tables are used extensively throughout standards documents, and in this book, to describe the protocols of each layer.

Note that the OSI standards for the different layers do not necessarily use all the techniques discussed to specify the layer services and its protocols. It would be an interesting exercise to develop more formal methods for specifying both services and protocols. In the technical literature there is some progress along these lines. But use of formal techniques to specify standards for each layer in the OSI architecture is likely to take some time.

4

Seven-Layer Architecture

This chapter introduces the basic structure of the OSI architecture in terms of its seven layers. The basic principles used in developing the layers are also introduced. Each layer in the OSI architecture is defined in terms of the services it offers and as a collection of required functions. The functions implemented within the layers enhance the services, in a step-by-step fashion, from those made available by the communication media to those required by user applications. This chapter also contains a brief discussion on OSI standards currently available, and their status regarding adoption by ISO and CCITT.

4.1 Introduction

The OSI architecture has been described in general terms in Chapter 2. This structure is centered around the concept of layers and has been used extensively in developing the OSI Reference Model. The Model consists of the following seven layers (see Figure 4.1):

1. the Application layer,
2. the Presentation layer,
3. the Session layer,
4. the Transport layer,
5. the Network layer,
6. the Data Link layer, and
7. the Physical layer.

The highest layer is the Application layer. It consists of Application entities[1] that co-operate with each other to provide application-related

---

[1]See Section 4.2.1 for its definition.

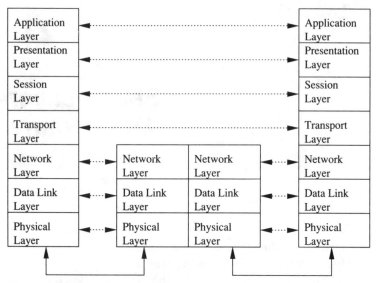

Figure 4.1 The seven layers of OSI.

services in an OSI environment. The lower layers, Physical through Presentation layers, provide services which make it possible for Application entities to communicate with each other. At the bottom, the Physical layer uses the communication media to exchange encoded bits of information.

The Application entities are the final source and destination of all data. Some of the open systems, however, simply perform the functions of relaying information from one open system to another. Such a system, therefore, implements functions included in the three lower layers only.

In any case, as one goes up the layers one notices a layer-by-layer enhancement of services provided by each layer to entities in the next higher layer. This, as discussed in Chapter 2, is made possible by implementing in each layer a set of functions required to bridge the gap between the services that it provides and the services available to it.

As can be expected, there are a variety of ways in which the OSI environment and its capability can be provided. Although the OSI Basic Reference Model (see [ISO 7498]) prescribes the use of seven layers, the same capability can, in principle, be provided by fewer than seven layers, or using more than seven layers. Further, the Reference Model defines, for each of the seven layers, the service that it provides to the next higher layer. In doing so, it implicitly specifies the collection of functions to be included in each layer. Here again, one may argue whether this is the most appropriate way of enhancing services from one layer to the next. This is equivalent to looking for alternative ways to partition the collection of functions necessary to provide OSI capabilities, and to assign them to different layers.

The above issues concerning the number of layers, and assignment of functions to each layer, have been dealt with in the Reference Model. A set of principles have been defined and repeatedly used to obtain the seven-layer OSI architecture, and to define the functionality of each layer. We shall briefly state these principles, and discuss how they relate to the design of the seven layers in the architecture. These are:

1. Have a reasonable number of layers to make the engineering task of system specification and integration no more difficult than necessary;

2. Define interfaces so that the description of services across the interface is simple;

3. Have a separate layer to handle functions which are clearly different in terms of the required processing or the supporting technology;

4. Include similar functions within the same layer;

5. Use successful experiences of the past in identifying the boundaries;

6. Create layers with well identified functions so that a layer can be modified to take advantage of technological developments in hardware or software, without changing the services of the adjacent layers;

7. Create a layer boundary where it may be useful at a later time to standardize its corresponding interface;

8. Ensure that each layer reflects a consistent level of abstraction in handling of data;

9. Permit changes to be made in the functions and protocols of a layer without affecting the other layers;

10. For each layer, have clear and well defined boundaries with only the layer above and the layer below it;

11. Permit the possibility of having sub-layers within a layer as necessary or appropriate;

12. Create, where necessary, two or more sub-layers with a common and minimal functionality to allow interface operation with the adjacent layers; and

13. Permit by-passing of sub-layers.

These principles, when applied to the problem of interconnection of open systems, lead to an identification of the seven layers. The OSI environment must permit the use of a variety of physical media and of different control procedures. Principles 3, 5 and 8, therefore, suggest the use of a separate *Physical layer* as the bottom layer in the seven-layer

OSI architecture. The Physical layer enables a user entity to transmit or receive a sequence of bits using an encoding scheme that is most suited for the particular communication media.

Each physical media, such as telephone lines, offers a different set of data transmission characteristics, for example, channel capacity, bit error rate, and propagation delay. It, therefore, requires special techniques to transmit data between two neighboring nodes in order to tolerate high error rates, or to take advantage of long propagation delays, as in the case of satellite channel. Similarly, reliable media, such as fibre-optic cables, require data link control procedures that are different from those used over telephone lines or satellite channels. Different techniques for data link control have been developed and used over a variety of physical communication media. Application of principles 3, 5 and 8, above, suggests the use of a separate *Data Link layer* on top of a Physical layer.

In an open system the topology for system interconnection may be quite different, and may, therefore, require that some systems act as intermediate relay nodes while others act as final source and destination of data. As a consequence, and using principles 3, 5, and 7, the use of a *Network layer* on top of the Data Link layer becomes necessary. This layer provides an end-to-end communication path between open systems using appropriate routing techniques and relaying.

In order to provide a reliable and efficient data transport service between computer systems, a *Transport layer* above the Network layer becomes essential. This is also consistent with principles 2, 5 and 6. As a result the higher layers are no longer concerned with issues relating to transportation of data across the network. Further, as suggested by principle 7, an interface corresponding to the Transport layer services may at a later date be subject to standardization.

Clearly, there is need to organize, manage and synchronize interaction between Application entities. These functions are all related and quite different from those encountered earlier in the lower layers. Application of principles 3 and 4 results in the definition of a *Session layer* on top of the Transport layer. Similarly, issues concerning representation of user information exchanged between Application entities are clearly distinct from those addressed by other layers. A *Presentation layer* is, therefore, included in the OSI architecture so that an Application entity in an open system may use locally defined syntax and still be able to communicate with every other peer entity.

The main purpose of the OSI is to permit users to implement distributed applications across a network of open systems. The *Application layer* provides a number of OSI services, for example, *association control, reliable transfer, message handling.*[2] The collection of

---

[2]These and other applications are discussed in Chapters 9 through 14.

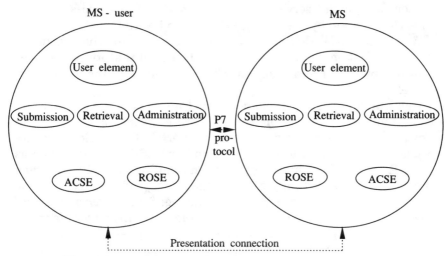

Figure 4.2 The sub-layers of the Application layer.

protocols required to support such services are implemented as sub-layers of the Application layer. A subset of Application sub-layers is shown in Figure 4.2.

4.2 Description of Layers

Below, we present a brief description of the nature of services provided by each layer and the functions required to be implemented to support the services. We distinguish those functions that are optional from those that are mandatory.

4.2.1 The Application Layer

The Application layer is the highest layer of the OSI architecture, and permits application processes to access OSI capabilities. The purpose of the layer is to serve as a window between correspondent application processes so that they may exchange information in the open environment. The description of the Application layer makes use of three definitions.

An *Application entity* is a model of those aspects of an application process that are significant from the viewpoint of accessing OSI capabilities. It consists of one *user element* and a set of *Application service elements*. Each Application service element uses the underlying OSI communication services to provide a specific application-level service, *reliable transfer* or *message handling,* for instance. Unlike services provided by the lower layers, application-related services are not provided to any higher layer and, therefore, do not have access points attached to them. Application service elements themselves use services provided by each other and by the lower, Presentation layer.

A user element is that part of an application process which models a user's application program, but only to the extent that it uses services provided by the Presentation layer and the required Application service elements.

Application layer services and related protocols are classified into two groups, *Common Application Service Elements (CASE)* and *Specific Application Service Elements (SASE)*. CASE elements are commonly required by user elements and by SASE elements, whereas a SASE element is included as part of an Application entity only when the application specifically requires the corresponding service. Some examples of the latter are message handling, *file transfer* and *virtual terminal* access. On the other hand, *association control, reliable transfer* and *remote operations* are common application services which are typically used by SASE elements. Association control, for instance, enables its users to negotiate and establish the communication environment between Application entities. Once that is done protocol-data-units concerning user elements and Application service elements may be exchanged.

Functions implemented within the Application layer are very much dependent upon the service provided by each service element. But there are a number of functions that are commonly found in most Application layer protocols. These include:

1. identification of communicating Application entities,
2. determination of their access rights and user authentication,
3. negotiation of the "abstract syntax" of Application protocol and user data,
4. the use of lower layer services, and
5. error detection and notification.

4.2.2 The Presentation Layer

The Presentation layer is responsible for the appropriate representation of all information communicated between Application entities. It covers two aspects, the structure of user data, and its representation during transfer in the form of a sequence of bits or bytes. Note that the Presentation layer is only concerned with the syntax and its logical structure, not with the meaning given to it by Application entities.

A notation, called *Abstract Syntax Notation (ASN)*, for defining the structure of Application protocol-data-units and of user information is available. It enables a sending entity to represent information using a syntax that is local to the open system. This syntax may differ from the one used to store the information in another system or during transfer between the systems. The main functionality of the Presentation layer, therefore, is to transform information from its local representation to the one used during transfer, or vice versa. It thereby relieves Application entities from issues related to representation of information.

To support the above, the Presentation layer implements the following functions:

1. connection establishment, and its termination,
2. negotiation and possibly re-negotiation of the abstract syntax of Application protocol-data-units,
3. syntax transformation including data compression, if required, and
4. data transfer.

A number of services provided by the Session layer are also transparently made available by the Presentation layer. That is, for such services no additional functionality is built into the Presentation layer itself, except to map the service requests onto corresponding Session services.

4.2.3   The Session Layer

The main functionality of the Session layer is to provide Presentation layer entities with the means to organize exchange of data over a connection either in the full-duplex or half-duplex mode of communication. That is, depending upon the application, user entities may decide to take turns to transfer data. It also enables users to release a connection so that there is no loss of data during a release operation. In fact, the connection release may even be negotiated, in which case a user entity retains the option to reject a connection release.

Synchronization points, when established in the stream of data exchange, enable the two users to structure their communication in the form of *dialogue units.* It thereby enables them to resynchronize data exchange to an earlier synchronization point. Resynchronization may be useful in case of errors or, more generally, to reset the connection to an earlier defined environment. The Session layer also allows users to define an *activity.* Activities are another way of providing structure to data exchange between users. Aside from starting or ending an activity, a user may interrupt the activity in the midst of communication and later resume it.

In order to support the above services, the Session layer implements the following functions:

1. connection establishment and its maintenance,
2. orderly connection release, which may optionally be negotiated,
3. normal data transfer, which may be half-duplex or full-duplex,

4. typed data transfer, which is not subject to restrictions imposed by the half-duplex mode of communication,
5. expedited data transfer, which is not subject to flow control restrictions,
6. establishment of synchronization points and resynchronization,
7. activity management, and
8. reporting of exceptional conditions.

4.2.4 The Transport Layer

While the Network layer, and those below, provide a path for data transfer between host computers, the Transport layer provides a facility to transfer data between Session entities in a transparent, reliable and cost-effective manner. It is the responsibility of this layer to optimize the use of Network services and ensure that the quality of Transport services is at least as good as that requested by the Session entities.

The Transport layer protocol has end-to-end significance, and is therefore implemented in host computers only. The protocol makes use of the available Network services and is, therefore, not concerned with issues of routing, etc. In view of the fact that the characteristics and performance of the Network service may vary substantially, a variety of Transport protocols are available to ensure that the service that it provides is largely independent of the underlying communication network. At one extreme, whenever the Network layer provides a reliable service (that is, acceptably low error rates and low failure probability), the functions implemented within the Transport layer are limited to:

1. connection establishment and its maintenance,
2. normal and expedited data transfer, and
3. error detection and reporting.

But, if the Network service is such that user data may be corrupted, lost, duplicated or delivered out of sequence, then the Transport layer protocol must detect errors and recover from them. Functions that are additionally implemented are:

1. error detection and recovery, and
2. end-to-end sequence control of protocol-data-units.

In order to transfer data in a cost-effective manner and to match user requirements in terms of the quality of Transport service, the Transport layer uses one or more of the following functions:

1. multiplexing or splitting of Transport connections onto Network connections,
2. end-to-end flow control, and
3. segmentation, blocking and/or concatenation.

4.2.5 The Network Layer and Below

The basic purpose of the Network layer, and those below, is to provide data transfer capability across the communication sub-network. The required functions are, as a consequence, specific to the communication sub-network and must be implemented by each open system in the sub-network, including *intermediate systems*. Intermediate systems are capable of routing and relaying information between possibly dissimilar communication sub-networks. Thus, the Network layer relieves Transport layer entities from all concerns regarding sub-network topology and their interconnection, and regarding routing and relaying through one or more sub-networks.

The Network layer provides the means to establish, maintain and terminate Network connections between open systems. It specifies the functional and procedural means to transfer user data between Transport entities over a Network connection. A Network connection may involve messages to be stored and later forwarded through several communication sub-networks. In order to suitably relay user data from the source host to the destination computer through one or more sub-networks, a route must be determined either centrally or in a distributed manner. Messages must also be routed within each sub-network through which the connection is established.

The major set of functions required to be implemented by a connection-oriented Network layer protocol includes:

1. connection establishment and its maintenance,
2. multiplexing and possibly splitting,
3. re-initialization, or *reset,* of connection,
4. addressing, routing and relaying,
5. normal and expedited data transfer,
6. sequencing and flow control,
7. error detection, notification and possibly recovery.

Alternatively, the Network layer may provide connection-less data transfer service, in which case the only significant set of functions built into the Network layer is data transfer, routing and relaying. Segmentation may also be used to ensure that Network protocol-data-units can be accommodated within buffers maintained by the Data Link layer.

The purpose of the Data Link layer is to provide functional and procedural means to establish, maintain and release connections between Network entities and to transfer user data. This layer is also responsible for detection and possible correction of errors occurring over the Physical connection. Connection-oriented Data Link services are supported by the following functions:

1. connection establishment and release,

2. splitting of Data Link connections,

3. delimiting and synchronization of protocol-data-units,

4. error detection and recovery, and

5. flow control and sequenced delivery.

Alternatively, a Data Link layer may simply support connection-less data transfer capability. In that case each service-data-unit is transferred independently of all other service-data-units. Such a Data Link layer requires a minimal set of functions to be implemented.

The Physical layer provides mechanical, electrical, functional and procedural means to establish, maintain and release physical connections and for bit transmission over a physical medium. The services provided to the Data Link entities include connection establishment and in-sequence transmission of bits over a data circuit. The Physical layer may, alternatively, provide connection-less data transfer capability, as in the case of local area networks.

4.3   OSI Layer Standards

While the Basic Reference Model (see [ISO 7498]) discusses the OSI architecture in its totality, the detailed development of each layer in the architecture requires a careful study of solutions to fundamental problems posed for each layer. The outcome of each study takes the form of service and protocol standards for a layer. These standards are previewed in this section.

A number of organizations, in particular CCITT, ISO, IEEE and ECMA, have been developing standards for the six bottom layers, Physical layer through Presentation layer, and for different applications of the Application layer. These organizations work independently, but have cooperated with each other by adopting many of each other's standards as their own. This has not only cut down the time and cost of development of OSI standards, but has led to the development of a consistent and compatible set of standards for the seven layers.

For the layers, Physical layer through Presentation layer, a standard typically consists of two documents, one for service definition while the other covers protocol specification. These documents may make references to one or more related documents as well. Standards for Transport, Session and Presentation layers literally fit into this document structure. The situation regarding the lower layers is different since several options are available to a designer regarding the choice of communication media, sub-network topology and their interconnection, and whether the Network service is connection-oriented or connection-less. Note that, particularly because of options concerning Network service and protocol, multiple Transport layer protocols may have to be defined so that the Transport service is uniformly identical across the entire network.

Application layer standards are also differently documented. There may be several documents concerning a single application. Two of these documents, again, relate to service definition and to protocol specification. The other documents discuss related concepts and the application itself. In some cases, such as message handling, more than one services may be defined to cater to a variety of users or equipment.

Tables 4.1 and 4.2 summarize the related standards documents for each layer from ISO and CCITT.[3] For most layers, ISO and CCITT standards are identical except for editorial changes. Such standards are termed as *co-standards*. The co-standards, in general, permit interoperability between implementations conforming to ISO and CCITT standards.

Figure 4.3, and similarly Figure 4.4, describe the constraints on the use of a higher layer protocol in conjunction with a lower layer service (see also [CCITT X.220]). These constraints are, in fact, part of the protocol specification since each protocol must explicitly state the service it expects of the supporting lower layer.

It may be pointed out that not all the standards documents, referred to above, are accepted as standards by ISO. Some of the documents may still be at the stage of Draft International Standard (DIS) or even Draft Proposal (DP). These documents are, therefore, subject to minor changes, if not major ones.

---

[3]ISDN and FDDI standards are mentioned in the tables only briefly since the emphasis in the book is more on higher layers.

TABLE 4.1   ISO Documents Pertaining to Each Layer (Documents Are Numbered as, for Example, ISO 9545)

Layer	Service Documents	Protocol Documents	Other Documents
Application layer			9545
Association control	8649	8650	-
Reliable transfer	9066-1	9066-2	-
Remote operations	9072-1	9072-2	-
CCR	9804	9805	-
Directory services	9594/3	9594/5	9594/1, /2, /4, /6, /7, /8
Message handling	10021-4, -5	10021-6	10021-1, -2, -3, -7
File transfer	8571/3	8571/4	8571/1, /2
Virtual terminal	9040	9041	9646, 2022
Presentation layer	8822	8823	8824, 8825
Session layer	8326	8327	-
Transport layer	8072	8073,8602	-
Network layer	8348	8878, 8473	8208, 8648, 8880, 8881, 9068, 9542
Data Link	8886	8802	7776
Physical layer	10022	-	8802

TABLE 4.2   CCITT Documents Pertaining to Each Layer (Documents Are Numbered as, for Example, Recommendations X.217)

Layer	Service Documents	Protocol Documents	Other Documents
Application layer			-
Association control	217	227	-
Reliable transfer	218	228	-
Remote operations	219	229	-
CCR	-	-	-
Directory services	511	519	500, 501, 509, 518, 520, 521
Message handling	411, 413	419	400, 402, 403, 407, 408, 420
File transfer	-	-	-
Virtual terminal	-	-	-
Presentation layer	216	226	208, 209
Session layer	215	225	-
Transport layer	214	224	-
Network layer	213	223	25, 75, 121
Data Link	212	-	25
Physical layer	211	-	21, 21(bis)

4.4   Summary

In this chapter we have introduced the seven layers that constitute the OSI architecture. The rational for structuring the architecture in this manner has been presented. The functions implemented within each layer have also been described. A more detailed discussion on the services provided by each layer and the protocol required to do so is the topic of the rest of this book. Several documents are required to precisely define the functionality of each layer. The overall structure of the documents, and their interrelationships, has been described in this chapter. A comparison of these standards across ISO and CCITT has also been presented.

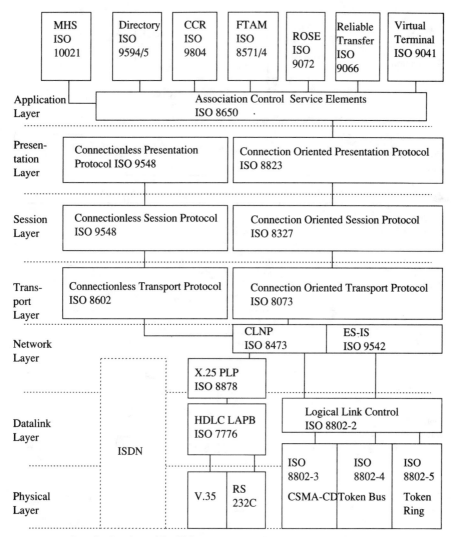

Figure 4.3 Standards adopted by ISO.

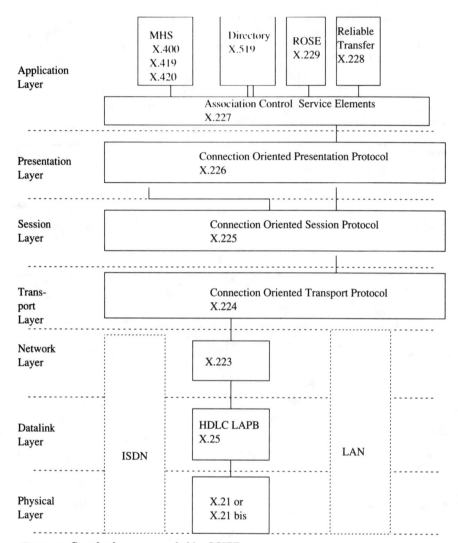

Figure 4.4 Standards recommended by CCITT.

The Network Layer
and Below

This chapter is concerned with a discussion of the three bottom layers of the seven-layer OSI architecture, that is the Network, Data Link, and Physical layers. Taken as a whole, the three layers offer to entities in the Transport layer a service using which they may exchange user data. The Transport entities, residing in the end systems, are not concerned as to how packets containing user data are routed through the physical communication network, and how such a network is accessed.

The three layers are treated together in one chapter in order to bring out the dependency of the corresponding protocols upon each other. Further, these protocols are heavily dependent upon the physical media and the switching/routing techniques used within a network. The emphasis here, however, is on Network layer services and protocols, and how they relate to protocols used to access a real network. Also contained herein, is a discussion of local area networks and of internetworking using gateways that permit interconnection of two or more networks, and perform protocol conversion, where necessary.

5.1 The Communication Subnetwork

Let us consider the physical structure of the computer communication network in terms of its functional components first. Formal definitions of terms used to model real objects, including an end system, a communication subnetwork and a relay system (a gateway, for example) are given.

5.1.1 End Systems

A computer communication network is a collection of *real end systems,* that support user application processes, and one or more physical com-

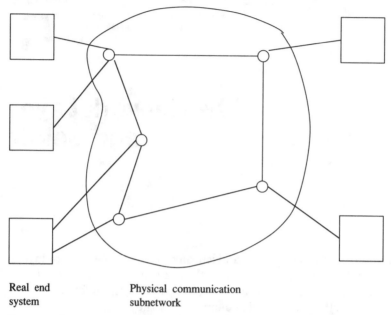

Real end   Physical communication
system   subnetwork

Figure 5.1 A computer communication network.

munication networks (see Figure 5.1). A real end system transfers data
to other real end systems using the data transfer facility provided by the
communication network. This interaction with the communication network is governed by a protocol that is specific to the interface between
the real end system and the communication network. From the viewpoint of the OSI architecture, only those aspects of the real end system
that concern communication with the network or with other real end
systems are of interest. This abstraction of the real end system will simply be referred to as an *end system,* or *ES.* Formally, an end system is
an abstraction of a system that hosts user applications. Such a model includes the protocol that it uses to access the communication network,
and protocols that concern communication with *other* end systems.

5.1.2 Subnetworks

The physical communication network is a collection of equipment and
physical media, viewed as one autonomous whole, that interconnects two
or more real end systems. Such a network may be a public or a private
network. Further, it may be a wide area or local area network. The term
real subnetwork is used to denote the physical communication network.
From the viewpoint of the design of the Network layer, the internal
working of the real subnetwork is unimportant. What is of significance

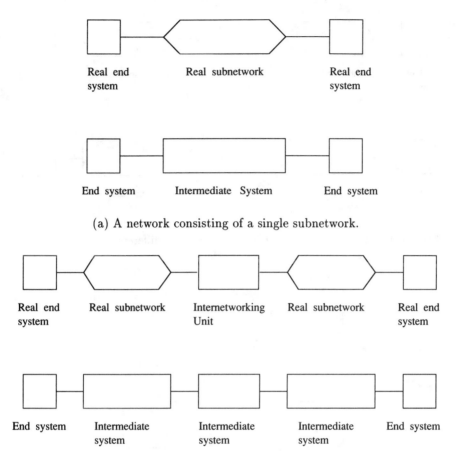

(a) A network consisting of a single subnetwork.

(b) A network consisting of two subnetworks connected using a relay system.

Figure 5.2 An abstract model of a computer communication network.

is the interface[1] that it offers to end systems so that information may be exchanged across the network. Using this interface an end system may access subnetwork resources to establish connections or to simply transfer information to other end systems. Thus, from the viewpoint of OSI architecture, the entire real subnetwork can be viewed as one whole without concern for its internal details. In OSI terminology, the real subnetwork is simply referred to as a *subnetwork*. Figure 5.2(a) illustrates this. At the very least, the subnetwork enables an end system to transfer data across the subnetwork to another end system.

---

[1]Recommendations X.21 and X.25 and IEEE 802.3, etc. are example interfaces standardized by CCITT and IEEE, respectively.

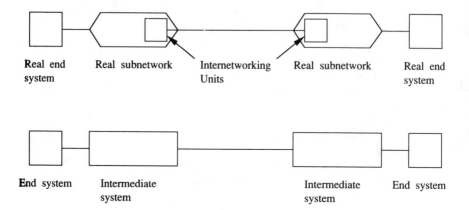

(c) A network of subnetworks, each implementing different access protocols at its interfaces.

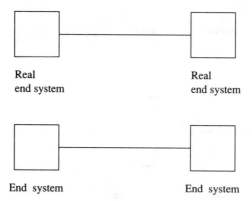

(d) A network where end systems are directly connected.

Figure 5.2 (*Continued*)

5.1.3 Internetworking

A communication network may be formed by interconnecting two or more similar, or dissimilar, communication subnetworks. From the viewpoint of OSI architecture, a designer may view the interconnected network as one subnetwork or as two (or more) distinct subnetworks that are interconnected. Two subnetworks are interconnected using an equipment whose primary function is to (selectively) relay information from one subnetwork to another and to perform protocol conversion, where necessary (see Figure 5.2(b)). A Network layer gateway is one example. In the world of communication such an equipment is called an *Interworking Unit*[2] (*IWU*). Obviously, when an IWU interconnects two subnetworks, it must be able to access both subnetworks so that data, received over a subnetwork, can be forwarded to an end system connected to the other subnetwork (or to another IWU). Thus, aside from relaying, an IWU must perform protocol conversion if its interfaces with the two subnetworks are different. In OSI terminology, the term *relay system* is used to abstract the functions of relaying and of protocol conversion in an IWU.

The function performed by an IWU is similar to that of any real subnetwork, except that the protocols at the two interfaces of the IWU may be different. This aspect is not fundamental enough to distinguish between real subnetworks and interworking units. A subnetwork may also offer different interfaces to hosts or to other subnetworks, depending upon their communication requirements (see Figure 5.2(c)). Thus, from the viewpoint of OSI architecture, real subnetworks and IWU are treated alike, and are also referred to as *Intermediate Systems*. Formally, an Intermediate System (IS) is an abstraction of equipment and/or communication media which performs the function of relaying (and routing) of information to end systems or to other intermediate systems. This abstraction takes the form of an access protocol specified for each interface. From this perspective, an end system does not perform any relay functions.

Finally, two real end systems may be directly connected using a communication link, or possibly through a shared media (as in local area networks, for example). The network and its model are illustrated in Figure 5.2(d). The important point to be noted is that a subnetwork based on a shared medium does not perform a relay function within the subnetwork.

The initial portion of this chapter is concerned more with a discussion of protocols in the context of end systems that are connected using a single subnetwork. Later, in Sections 5.8 and 5.9, we discuss Network layer protocols that allow different subnetworks to be interconnected via relay systems.

5.2   The Network Layer and Below: A Model

In this section we discuss a model of the three bottom layers of the OSI architecture. This model is used to describe the functions of routing and relaying of user data through the Network layer (and those below). Characteristics of data transfer, irrespective of whether it is connec-

---

[2]IWU is also referred to as Network Layer Gateway.

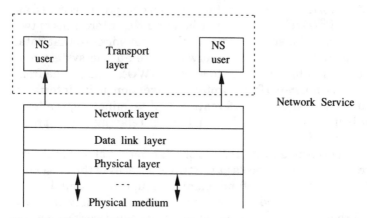

Figure 5.3 The Network Service provider and its users.

tion-oriented or connection-less, are discussed. Further, we take a close look at the structure of an Intermediate system to highlight the relationship between routing and relaying and the three layers of protocols.

5.2.1   User-Provider Model of Network Service

A model of the Network layer together with the two bottom layers, the Data Link and Physical layers, is given in Figure 5.3. The Network layer offers to entities in the Transport layer a capability by which they may exchange data across the physical subnetwork, without concern for how it is actually routed or relayed through the subnetwork. Entities within the Network layer and those below coordinate their operations to provide a service, called *Network Service* (*NS*). Together, the Network entities (and those below the Network layer) are modelled as the *Network Service Provider* (*NS Provider*). Since the next higher layer is the Transport layer, the users of the Network service are Transport entities residing in end systems. As such, a Transport entity is called a *Network Service User* (*NS User*).

We now elaborate upon the model of the Network layer and those below. The Network service is provided at interfaces, termed *Network Service Access Points*[3] (*NSAPs*). Transport entities that wish to use the Network service are bound to one or more NSAPs, as shown in Figure 5.4.

---

[3]See Chapter 2 for additional discussions on service access points.

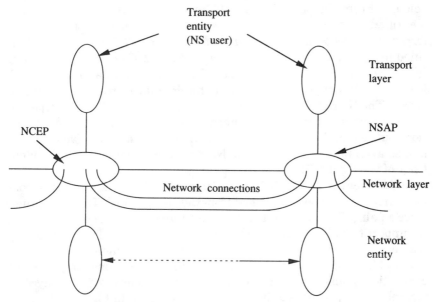

Figure 5.4 Network service access points and connection end points.

The Network Service may be connection-oriented, in which case two Transport entities must establish a connection before data can be transferred. The connection is preferably released soon after data transfer is complete. Or, the Network service may be connection-less. In connection-less Network service, a Transport entity simply makes available user data to the NS provider, together with the *address* of an NSAP to which the destination Transport entity is attached. The NS provider then appropriately routes packets through the subnetwork(s) to the destination NSAP. A packet, or more precisely a *Network Protocol Data Unit,* consists of user data and the addresses of both the source NSAP and destination NSAP. The source NSAP address may be used by the destination Transport entity to determine the identity of the source Transport entity. These addresses constitute only a part of the packet header, better known as *Protocol Control Information.*

5.2.2 Network Connections

A similar approach is used by the Network layer to establish a connection on behalf of a pair of Transport entities (see Figure 5.4). Such a connection is formally termed *Network Connection* (or *NC*). Once a connection is established, packets containing user data do not explicitly carry the address of source and destination NSAPs. Instead, they carry information that uniquely identifies the connection to which the data belongs. From the point of view of Transport entities, a connection is identified by its end points, one in each NSAP. These are formally referred to as *Network Connection End Points,* or *NCEPs,* and are identified using, what are formally termed, *Network Connection End Point Identifiers (NCEP Identifiers).* Each NCEP identifier has a local significance, in that it is unique within the domain of the corresponding NSAP. The NCEP Identifiers are assigned at the time of connection establishment, and remain unchanged during the lifetime of the connection. Subsequently, during the data transfer phase, a Transport entity makes available user data to the NS provider, together with the identifier of the local NCEP.

NCEP Identifiers also help to distinguish between a number of connections that may be established from the same NSAP. This is required since a pair of Transport entities may establish a number of connections to support transfer of unrelated streams of data. Or, a Transport entity may establish an independent connection with a number of Transport entities. The NS provider is invariably capable of supporting multiple connections, subject of course to availability of resources, primarily storage related. These possibilities are also illustrated in Figure 5.4.

Within the Network layer, a connection is identified by the supporting Network entities in end systems, and in intermediate systems, by an identifier which has a significance that is local to the communicating Network entities (see Figure 5.4). This identifier, termed *Network Protocol Connection Identifier,* is assigned during connection establishment. Further, at each end of the connection, a one-to-one onto mapping of the NCEP Identifier and the Network Protocol Connection Identifier is maintained by the supporting Network entity.

5.2.3 Data Transfer Characteristics

We now give an overview of the characteristics of data transfer capability provided by the Network layer. Irrespective of whether data transfer is connection-oriented or connection-less, the service offered to a Transport entity is characterized as being end-to-end, transparent, and independent of the underlying communication media. We discuss these below.

1. *End-to-end data transfer* is made possible through the use of intermediate system, that is, subnetworks and/or relay systems, which together are responsible for appropriately relaying and routing user data through the network and delivering it to the destination end system. The *address* of the destination end system is provided by the source end system. Addressing is one of the important issues concerning the Network layer and shall be discussed later in this chapter.

2. *Transparency of data transfer* refers to the fact that the Network layer (and those below) do not place any constraint on the contents of user data, since user data is not interpreted by the Network layer.

3. *Independence from the underlying media* implies that NS *users* are neither concerned with the characteristics of the underlying transmission media, nor with the protocol used to access the subnetwork(s). It is a different matter that the decision to provide a Network service, which is connection-oriented or simply connection-less (or perhaps both), may depend upon the communication media and the subnetwork protocol. Further, the quality of the Network service[4] is, to a large extent, dependent upon the subnetwork.

5.2.4 Intermediate Systems: A Model

We now take a look at the three bottom layers that together are responsible for providing data transfer capability through the Network layer. More specifically, we present a model of an Intermediate system, and thereby highlight the functions implemented at the Network, Data Link, and Physical layers. We also discuss the relationship between routing and relay functions in an Intermediate system and Network layer protocols.

Consider the simpler case where end systems are connected using an Intermediate system which offers identical access to all end systems.[5] This situation, earlier modelled in Figure 5.2(a), is elaborated in Figure 5.5 to show the three distinct layers, and the context of routing and relay functions. The end systems have entities in the Transport layer and those above. An Intermediate system, on the other hand, aside from implementing protocols at the three layers, also implements routing and relay functions. As is clear from the figure, user data received from an end system over an interface is processed by the subnetwork and relayed to another interface. It is subsequently forwarded to the destination end system.

The upper triangle in the Intermediate system, *Routing and Relaying,* is more than a simple software module. It is, in fact, a representation of the entire physical subnetwork consisting of switching nodes, transmission media, and protocols that are totally internal to the subnetwork. From the viewpoint of OSI architecture, it is adequate to abstract the subnetwork as simply implementing a routing and relay function, and providing interfaces to end systems.

---

[4]See Sections 5.7 and 3.4.

[5]A good example of this situation is a wide area subnetwork with an implementation of X.25 protocol.

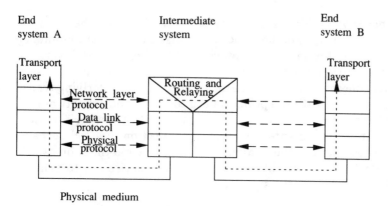

Figure 5.5 Elaboration of the structure of an Intermediate System.

The design of the Intermediate system can be further elaborated, as in Figure 5.6. The two Network layer entities within the Intermediate system interface with each other using a protocol, the specification of which is outside the scope of the OSI environment.

Note that Network layer entities within an Intermediate system do not provide any service. As a consequence, within an Intermediate system, there are neither NSAPs nor Network connection end points. Thus, a Network connection, logically, extends from an NCEP, in an NSAP in an end system, to an NCEP in another end system. As discussed earlier in this section, communicating Network entities identify a connection using a Network Protocol Connection Identifier which has local significance only. Thus, one of the functions implemented by Network entities in Intermediate systems is to maintain a correspondence between the two identifiers used to identify the same connection, but over the two interfaces.

A Network entity, whether it is in an end system or an Intermediate system, uses Data Link services made available at a *Data Link Service Access Point* (or *DLSAP*). This it does to transfer *Network Protocol Data Units* across the interface to a corresponding Network entity. Similarly, a pair of Data Link entities, one each in an end system and an Intermediate system, uses Physical layer services made available at *Physical Service Access Points*[6] (or *PhSAPs*).

---

[6]Services and example protocols concerning the Data Link and Physical layer are discussed in Sections 5.3 through 5.6. Network services and protocols are discussed in Sections 5.7 onwards.

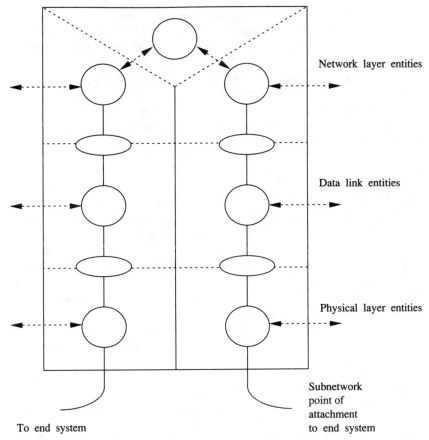

Figure 5.6 Entities within an Intermediate system and their interfaces.

5.2.5 Subnetwork Access Protocol

The protocols at the three bottom layers specify the procedure that should be used by entities in end systems to access the routing and re-laying capability of the subnetwork. This collection of protocols is also called Subnetwork Access Protocol or simply *SNAcP*. The SNAcP may, of course, vary from one subnetwork to another. For example, CCITT's X.25 protocol specifies the interface a host computer must use to es-tablish a network layer connection with another host. This connection is routed through a packet-switched subnetwork. The CCITT's X.21 protocol, on the other hand, provides for a Physical layer connection across a circuit-switched network. Similarly, a local area network pro-vides connection-less or connection-oriented data transfer between end systems over a shared communication channel.

These examples also serve to highlight a related issue concerning the design of a Network protocol capable of supporting the desired Network service. Often, and particularly in private networks, the SNAcP is quite adequate. For instance, X.25 protocol can be used to provide connection-oriented Network service (see Sections 5.7, 5.8). But, in other cases, an additional sub-layer will have to be added to provide the Network service. These cases arise particularly when two or more subnetworks are interconnected possibly using a relay system. These are discussed in Section 5.9.

5.2.6 Subnetwork Address

Figure 5.6 also brings out the interface between a Physical entity, in an end system, and the physical medium that it accesses to transmit/receive a stream of encoded bits to/from the subnetwork. There is no service access point associated with the physical medium. Instead, the physical interface between the real end system and the real subnetwork is modelled as a *Subnetwork Point of Attachment* (or *SNPA*). It is the physical interface at which data transfer capability of the subnetwork is available to a real end system. As an example, a host computer may physically interface with a communication subnetwork though a modem connected to one of its RS 232C ports. The modem is modelled as a point of attachment.

Subnetwork Points of Attachments are identified by an address, termed *Subnetwork Point of Attachment Address,* or *Subnetwork Address* for simplicity. Subnetwork Addresses are used to route Network layer packets within the subnetwork and to deliver them to the appropriate end system, relay system or another subnetwork. In the context of public data networks, a DTE[7] Address is used to identify an SNPA. The Subnetwork Addresses are assigned by the subnetwork administration. Their scope, however, is local to the subnetwork and outside the OSI environment.

Subnetwork addresses must be distinguished from NSAP Addresses. The NSAP addresses are used to identify Network service access points, whereas a Subnetwork Address identifies the physical interconnection between a subnetwork and an end system. It is a different matter that there may be a correspondence between the NSAP Address and a Subnetwork Address. Such a mapping must be flexible enough to accommodate multiple NSAPs in an end system and at-

---

[7]In public data networks, a host computer or a data terminal is referred to as a *Data Terminal Equipment,* or *DTE.*

TABLE 5.1 Assignment of NSAP Addresses

IDI format	AFI (decimal value)	IDI (no. of decimal digits)	DSP (max. length)
X.121	36	14	24 digits
	37	14	9 octets
ISO DCC	38	3	35 digits
	39	3	14 octets
Local	48	0	38 digits
	49	0	15 octets
	50	0	19 ISO 646 char.
	51	0	7 National char.

tachment of an end system to one or more subnetworks using a number of physical links. Thus, in general, the mapping between NSAP addresses and Subnetwork Addresses may be many-to-many. In the simplest of cases an NSAP address may be mapped one-to-one onto a Subnetwork Address.[8]

While assignment of NSAP addresses may be done in one of several ways, a hierarchical structure permits interoperability between open systems, while retaining control over the assignment of addresses by local administrations. This structure is briefly described below.

The ISO document [ISO 8348 DAD 2] specifies, at the highest level, that an address may conform to any one of the several available standards, including CCITT's X.121, ISO DCC, and LOCAL (see also [CCITT X.121]). At the next level, X.121, for example, may specify the country codes and perhaps a network identifier. The latter may be viewed as identifying the *Initial Domain* within which the remaining part of the NSAP address is unique. At lower levels, the assignment of addresses is domain specific, and may be specified (hierarchically) in terms of location, machine, etc. Thus, each NSAP address is composed of at least three parts (see also Table 5.1).

1. The *Address and Format Identifier* (*AFI*) specifies the structure of the address. More specifically, the two AFI digits encode the particular standard that is used (X.121, ISO DCC, local, etc.), and the format (octets, digits, ISO 646 or National characters) of the domain specific part of the address.

2. *Initial Domain Identifier,* or *IDI,* specifies the initial domain within which the NSAP address must be unique. When X.121 is used,

---

[8]A print server connected to a network, for example.

for example, the 14 digit IDI field specifies the country code (3 digits), the network number (1 digit) and the 10 digit DTE address. If a local addressing scheme is used, the IDI is absent. The 3 digit IDI in an ISO DCC specification is a country code.[9]

3. Assignment of the *Domain Specific Part,* or *DSP,* is a local matter, as long as they are unique. The DSP is a sequence of either octets or digits (see Table 5.1).

We give below two examples, conforming to X.121 and Local (respectively):

1. Using X.121 Specification:

    AFI: 36 (X.121, Decimal)

    IDI: 310 5 1234567890 (USA, 5th Network, Machine Number)

    DSP: 1234567890123456 (Access Point)

2. Using Local Specification:

    AFI: 50 (Local, ISO646 Characters)

    DSP: EDU& EnR& IITD005& abc (Education, Network Name, Location, SAP)

A concept closely related to NSAP addresses is that of *Network Protocol Address Information* (or *NPAI*). It is, in fact, the encoding of an NSAP address as specified by the particular Network layer protocol. For instance, a sequence of digits may be encoded as a sequence of octets, each octet being formed from two 4-bit binary-coded digits.[10]

The next few sections are concerned with services and protocols of the Physical and Data Link layers. Network service and protocols are discussed in Section 5.7, onwards.

5.3   Physical Layer Services and Protocols

In this section we discuss the service offered by the Physical layer to Data Link entities. Protocols that use an available transmission facility in order to support a physical connection are covered using example protocols, including RS 232C, X.21, and IEEE 802.3.

---

[9]There is no relationship between routing and assignment of NSAP addresses. However, a routing scheme may take advantage of information contained within an NSAP address.

[10]The maximum number of digits (or octets) specified in Table 5.1 is such that the total number of octets required to encode an NSAP address is no more than 20 (see [ISO 8348 DAD 2]).

5.3.1 A Model of the Physical Layer

A model of the Physical layer is presented in Figure 5.7. It brings out the fact that the Physical layer service, formally termed *Physical service,* or *PhS,* is used by Data Link entities, irrespective of whether they reside in end systems or in Intermediate systems. As such, Data Link entities are also referred to as *Physical service users,* or *PhS users.*

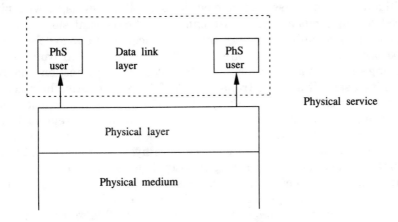

(a) Physical service users and providers.

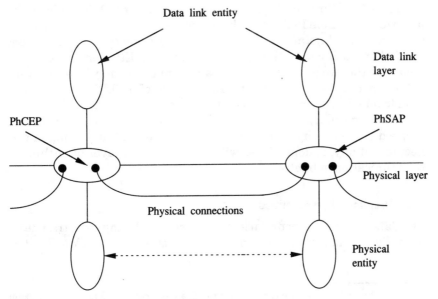

(b) PhSAPs and Physical layer.

Figure 5.7 A model of the Physical layer.

Physical services are provided to its users at service access points, termed *Physical Service Access Points,* or *PhSAPs.*

The Physical layer provides to its users an ability to send or receive a stream of bits (or more generally symbols) over a physical transmission medium. Physical service users are not concerned with how a bit is encoded in the form of an electrical (or optical) signal before transmission. As such, the design of Data Link protocols can be carried out without concern for issues like modulation, voltage levels, or with pin-level description of a physical attachment to the transmission medium.

The other capability provided by the Physical layer has to do with *activating* or *deactivating* a connection. This is no different from establishing or releasing a connection. Activation of a connection ensures that if a user initiates the transmission of a stream of bits, the receiver at the other end is ready to receive them. The process of activation may require that resources, both processing and transmission related, be reserved for exclusive use by this connection. Deactivation of a connection releases all resources for use by other Physical connections. Figure 5.8 illustrates how a Physical connection is mapped onto a communication path or *data circuit.* In some cases the path may consist of more than one data circuit, interconnected using a *Physical layer* relay system.[11] The relay system or its operation is not visible to the communicating Physical entities.

A Physical connection is established on behalf of PhS users between two PhSAPs.[12] Since multiple connections may be established by a PhS user from the same PhSAP, each connection is identified by a *Physical Connection End-Point Identifier,* or a *PhCEP Identifier.* There is one PhCEP for each end of the connection. The PhCEP Identifiers associated with the two end points of the same connection may be (or may not be) distinct. This is so since the significance of a PhCEP identifier is local to a PhS user and the service provider (the local Physical layer entity, in particular). Within the Physical layer, each connection is mapped onto one physical transmission medium. Multiplexing of connections, if any, is done either within the Physical layer or within the communication subnetwork.

5.3.2 Service Characteristics

The data unit whose boundaries are preserved during data transfer is a bit. Such a data unit is referred to as *Physical Service Data Unit,* or

---

[11]In case Physical entities are connected through a circuit-switched network, for example.

[12]It is possible to have multi-point connections as well, in which case the connection is established between a number of PhSAPs.

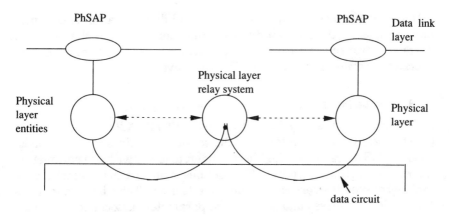

(a) Logical view of relay operation.

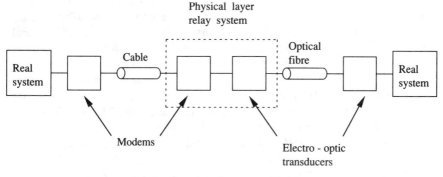

(b) Real view of relay operation.

Figure 5.8 Physical connection using a data circuit through a Physical layer relay system.

PhSDU.[13] Further, bits are delivered in-sequence although there is no guarantee that the bits would be delivered unaltered. Some bits may not be delivered at all, while others may be duplicated. Flow control may be exercised by PhS users over and above the agreed rate of data transmission. Further, synchronization of transfer of a bit stream, when required, is the responsibility of the Physical layer and not that of the users. However, frame-level or character-level synchronization, where required, is performed by the PhS users.

---

[13]In cases where data transfer is parallel, the PhSDU consists of n bits. In other cases the PhSDU is a symbol which is either a bit or a delimiter. The delimiter is used to delimit a data link frame, as in IEEE standard 802.5 (see [IEEE 802.5]).

Data transfer over a connection may be full-duplex, half-duplex or perhaps simplex.[14] Over a half-duplex connection, which of the two PhS users may transmit a data bit at a particular time is determined by the users themselves, and not by the Physical layer protocol.

5.3.3 Service Primitives

A description of the Physical service (see [CCITT X.211], [ISO 10022], [IEEE 802.3]) is given in terms of the service primitives that may be issued by PhS users and/or the PhS provider, together with the parameters associated with each primitive. This defines in an abstract manner the interface between the service provider and its users. Table 5.2 summarizes the service primitives and some of the parameters associated with each primitive. Note that parameters of primitives concerning connection activation or deactivation have not been completely specified (see [ISO 10022]). But, it is certain that these will include addresses of the source and destination PhSAPs, aside from parameters that allow data rate selection and negotiation of the class of Physical service. Classes of Physical service may be defined in terms of whether data transfer is serial or parallel, synchronous or asynchronous, full-duplex or half-duplex, etc.

It may be pointed out that connection activation service is an unconfirmed service, in that the PhS user initiating the activation is not made aware of whether the connection has been established. Further, if a full-duplex connection is required to be established, then the responding PhS user must activate the connection in the reverse direction. Data transfer service is also an unconfirmed service. However, deactivation of a connection can be initiated by either user or by the Physical layer itself. Thus, deactivation service is both unconfirmed as well as provider-initiated. Further, deactivation of the connection takes place for each direction independently.

---

[14]In OSI terminology, these are also referred to as *two-way simultaneous, two-way alternate* and *one-way*, respectively.

TABLE 5.2 Physical Layer Service Primitives and Their Parameters

Service	Primitive	Parameters
Connection Activation	Ph Activate request	(see Note 1)
	Ph Activate indication	(see Note 1)
Data Transfer	Ph Data request	user data
	Ph Data indication	user data
Connection Deactivation	Ph Deactivate request	none
	Ph Deactivate indication	none

Note 1: Parameters concerning connection activation have not been completely specified. The list may include source and destination PhSAP Addresses, quality of service parameters, and selection of a class of service.

The service offered by the Physical layer in local area networks is connection-less. That is, data transfer may be initiated without first activating a connection (see [IEEE 802.3, IEEE 802.4, IEEE 802.5]). These standards also define additional service primitives whose significance is local. These primitive are used to simply indicate the outcome of a primitive issued earlier by the local user.

There may be a number of constraints imposed by the service specification on the sequence in which a user and the service provider may issue primitives at a PhSAP. These are usually given in the form of a state transition diagram (see [ISO 10022] for more details). The specification also indicates the correspondence between events occurring at the two end points of a connection. This correspondence is illustrated in Figure 5.9. The figures are self-explanatory. Not all possibilities are indicated in the figure. But note, from Figure 5.9 (e), that if Ph-Data request and Ph-Deactivate request are issued by the two users at the same time, then the data bit is *not* discarded since deactivation of the connection is in the reverse direction.

Errors may occur during data transmission in two different ways. First, a bit may be altered, duplicated, or lost. The Physical layer protocol does not detect such errors. The other form of error relates to a breakdown in the physical communication path. When that happens, the Physical layer simply reports this condition to its users.

5.3.4 Physical Layer Protocols

We briefly discuss some protocols to illustrate data transfer over a physical medium. The protocols considered here are EIA's RS 232C and CCITT's Recommendation X.21 (see [McNam 82,CCITT X.21]). These protocols specify standard interfaces for connecting a host/terminal equipment, also called DTE, to a communication subnetwork. These interfaces provide for serial baseband communication, and do not permit multiplexing. The IEEE 802.3 standard is also covered briefly.

A comparison of some of the characteristics of the three protocols is given in Table 5.3. These characteristics reflect in some ways the different contexts in which these protocols are applicable. RS 232C, one of the oldest and most popular interfaces, is particularly suited for connection-oriented, character mode, asynchronous communication over short distances at relatively low data rates. A data terminal typically uses an RS 232C to interface with a host computer or to a modem to access a switched/leased circuit. The greatest disadvantage of RS 232C interface is its limitation in terms of speed and distances. A subsequent EIA standard RS 449, together with RS 422A and 423A, has overcome these limitations at the cost of increasing the number of connector pins or circuits (see [McNam 82]).

The X.21 interface is particularly suited for use over digital switched networks. It provides for connection-oriented, full-duplex,

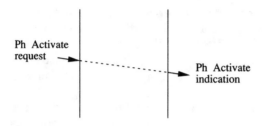

(a) Connection activation.

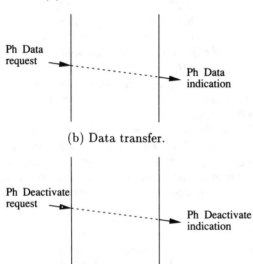

(b) Data transfer.

(c) Connection deactivation (user initiated).

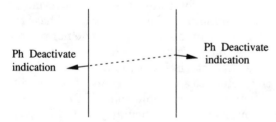

Figure 5.9 Some typical sequences of primitives issued at the two end points of a connection.

(d) Connection deactivation (provider initiated).

synchronized transfer of a stream of bits. It uses a fewer number of circuit (up to 8), but provides extensive control of the physical connection, including transmission of address information to the DCE so that an end-to-end connection can be established through a switched network. As such, it could be used to interface with a local DCE, remote DCE through a switched network, or to connect two DTEs. In

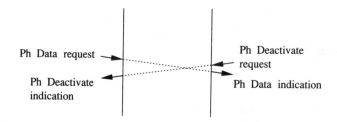

(e) Simultaneous data transfer and deactivation by user.

Figure 5.9 (*Continued*)

TABLE 5.3   Characteristics of Some Physical Layer Protocols

Characteristics	RS 232C	X.21	IEEE 802.3
Connection oriented	yes	yes	no
Data rate	up to 19.2 kbps	up to 9600 bps	10 Mbps
Synchronous	asynchronous (usually)	synchronous	synchronous
Duplex	full-duplex	full-duplex	half-duplex (shared medium)
Encoding scheme	NRZ	NRZ	Manchester
Connector	25	15	15
No. of circuits used	9 to 16	6 to 8	9 or 10

the latter case, it may be used, in conjunction with a Network layer protocol, to provide Network layer services to Transport entities in end systems. IEEE 802.3 is a standard which covers more than just the Physical layer. It provides for connection-less data broadcast from a host, or a relay system, to all systems that are connected directly over a local area network. Data transfer is synchronous and half-duplex. The coaxial-cable based bus is shared by all systems that are connected to the network using CSMA/CD multiple access scheme. This function is implemented as part of the Data Link protocol. Addressing and frame-delimiting are also functions that are part of the Data Link layer.

5.4   Data Link Service

Data Link services include establishment and maintenance of a data link between Network entities in neighboring systems. Over such a link, users can transfer data reliably and without concern for framing, addressing, and detection and recovery from transmission errors. Two

Data Link protocols, X.25 LAPB and IEEE 802.2 (together with IEEE 802.3), are discussed in later sections, with a view to illustrate how a Data Link can be maintained over a Physical connection.

5.4.1   A Model of Data Link Layer

Figure 5.10 is a model of the Data Link layer and the service that it offers to its users. Users of the *Data Link service* are Network entities residing in end systems or in Intermediate systems. They are, as such, referred to as *Data Link service users,* or *DLS users.* The Data Link layer, together with the Physical layer below, is responsible for providing the service. These layers are thus modelled as the *Data Link service provider,* or simply *DLS provider.* Data Link service is provided at, what is called, *Data Link service access point,* or *DLSAP.* A DLS user is attached to one or more DLSAPs, and can be identified using the address of a DLSAP to which it is attached, or simply *DLSAP address.*

Data Link service is generally connection-oriented (see [CCITT X.212, ISO 8886.2], and [IEEE 802.2]). But in some cases it may simply be connection-less. In either case, data transfer is transparent to the Data Link layer. That is, user data is not constrained in any manner by the Data Link layer.[15] Further, characteristics of the Physical layer and of the transmission medium are not visible to the DLS users. A *Data Link Connection* (or simply *DLC*) is established by the Data Link layer between two DL service access points on behalf of two DLS users. Each connection is identified by its end points, also called *DL Connection End Points,* one for each end of the connection. A DLC end point is identified by a *DLC End-Point Identifier,* the significance of which is local to the DLS user and the DLS provider. It may, however, be pointed out that usually there is only one Data Link connection established between a pair of DLS users (see [CCITT X.25]). This DLC is able to support a number of Network connections.

A *Data Link Service Data Unit* (or simply *DLSDU*) is a sequence of bits, or bytes, transferred from one DLSAP to another with its two boundaries preserved. There may be a constraint on the maximum size of the DLSDU. Thus, one of the major concerns of the Data Link is to suitably delimit, and perhaps segment, DLSDUs so that these can be transferred from one DL entity to another. Other major functions of the Data Link layer include addressing, error detection and recovery, and flow control. Error recovery and flow control are meaningful only when

---

[15]In a byte-oriented Data Link protocol, user data is constrained to be a sequence of ASCII characters (see for example [Tanen 88]). In a bit-oriented protocol there is no constraint whatsoever (see [ISO 7776]).

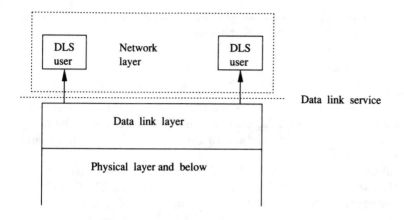

(a) Data Link service users and provider.

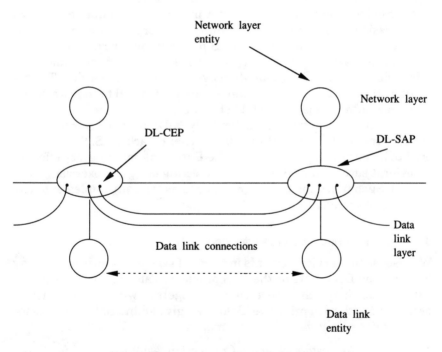

(b) DLSAPs, connections and DLCEPs.

Figure 5.10 A model of the Data Link layer, service access points and connection end points.

the service is connection-oriented. We shall discuss these soon after we have reviewed Data Link service primitives.

5.4.2   Data Link Service

The Data Link layer provides to its users the capability to establish or release a connection. Once a connection has been established between two DLSAPs, an attached DLS user may issue a primitive to the Data Link layer to transfer (normal) data, in the form of DLSDU, to the corresponding DLS user.

Normal data transfer may be slowed down due to flow control, exercised either within the Data Link layer or by DLS users. The Data Link layer may provide an additional mechanism by which a user may request urgent transfer of an *Expedited DLSDU* of a fixed maximum length. This is useful in case users wish to exchange control information outside the flow controlled normal data stream.

A connection may, conceivably, run into difficulties due to frequent transmission errors or from its inability to interpret an incoming *protocol data unit*. In that case the DLS provider simply *resets* (or re-initializes) the data link. Similarly, either user may reset the connection, if it so desires. In any case, all data over the link is discarded. The resulting status of the Data Link connection is identical to that which existed soon after connection establishment.

Over local area networks, particularly, a Data Link layer *may* only support connection-less data transfer. There, each DLSDU is considered to be unrelated to all others. The Data Link makes every effort to transfer it successfully, but without detecting errors, or exercising flow control. Such functionality, when required, is typically implemented by the Transport layer.

5.4.3   Service Primitives and Parameters

We discuss the service elements in terms of service primitives that may be issued by DLS users or the DLS provider. Table 5.4 lists the primitives concerning each service element, together with the parameters associated with each primitive. Below, we give additional comments for each service primitive and its parameters.

1. *Connection establishment:* Connection establishment is a confirmed service, and is available only when DLS is connection-oriented. During establishment, the two DLS users and the DLS provider negotiate the use of optional service elements, if available (see Table 5.5). The optional service elements are expedited data transfer and error reporting. The DLS users and the DLS provider also negotiate the quality of service to be provided over the connection. The quality of ser-

TABLE 5.4   Data Link Services and Their Parameters

Service	Primitive	Parameters
Connection Establishment	DL-CONNECT request	see Table 5.5
	DL-CONNECT indication	see Table 5.5
	DL-CONNECT response	see Table 5.5
	DL-CONNECT confirm	see Table 5.5
Connection Release	DL-DISCONNECT request	Reason
	DL-DISCONNECT indication	Originator, Reason
Normal Data Transfer	DL-DATA request	user data
	DL-DATA indication	user data
Expedited Data Transfer	DL-EXPEDITED-DATA request	user data
	DL-EXPEDITED-DATA indication	user data
Connection Reset	DL-RESET request	Reason
	DL-RESET indication	Originator, Reason
	DL-RESET response	
	DL-RESET confirm	
Error Reporting	DL-ERROR-REPORT indication	Reason
Data Transfer (connection-less)	DL-UNIT-DATA request	see Table 5.6
	DL-UNIT-DATA indication	see Table 5.6

vice parameters include throughput and transit delay. Other parameters, not related to performance, are protection and priority. (See Section 3.4 for details.) The above discussion suggests that the requirements specified by the initiating DLS user may not match those required by the responding user. Or, these may not be supported by a provider. In either case, connection is not established. This situation results in primitive sequences shown in Figure 5.11(b) and (c). Refusal to accept or to support a connection is indicated by issuing a *DL-DIS-CONNECT* primitive.

Commenting upon other parameters of *DL-CONNECT* primitives, the Responding Address is usually the same as the Called Address.

TABLE 5.5   Parameters of the DL-Connect Primitives

Parameter	DL-Connect request	DL-Connect indication	DL-Connect response	DL-Connect confirm
Called Address	X	X		
Calling Address	X	X		
Responding Address			X	X
Expedited Data Selection	X	X	X	X (=)
Quality of Service	X	X	X	X (=)
DLS User Data	X	X (=)	X	X (=)

Note: (=): The parameter value is equal to its value in preceding primitive.

Further, some Data Link protocols may not permit User Data to be included in DL-CONNECT primitives.

2. *Connection release:* DL-DISCONNECT service is both unconfirmed as well as provider-initiated. Further, when a connection is released, all data in transit is discarded. Preferably, users must ensure that there is no data in transit before issuing a DL-DISCONNECT request, unless a user or the provider is forced to do so due to errors. The parameters *Originator* and *Reason* obviously specify whether the release is initiated by a user or the provider, and the reason, if known. The value of the parameter Originator is one of *DLS User, DLS Provider,* or *Unknown.* The value of the parameter Reason depends upon the value of Originator. Example values of Reason are *Connection rejection, DLSAP unreachable, permanent condition, Disconnection, abnormal condition,* and *Reason unspecified.* Figure 5.12(a), (b) and (c) illustrate the release of a connection by a DLS user, the DLS provider, or by both simultaneously.

3. *Normal data transfer:* Normal data transfer is an unconfirmed service (see Figure 5.12(d)). But, within the layer, Data Link entities may acknowledge the receipt of *Data Link Protocol Data Units* that contain user data. In other words, a user can be assured that its DLSDU will be delivered without errors, unless the connection is reset or released.

4. *Expedited data transfer:* When available, the use of the service is negotiated during connection establishment. Expedited DLSDUs are sent on an urgent basis, and are subject to flow control different from that applicable to normal user data. (See Figure 5.12(e) for an illustration of the use of *DL-EXPEDITED DATA* primitives.)

5. *Connection reset:* The service is a confirmed service. A reset may also be initiated by the DLS provider. The net effect is to discard all data in transit. The parameters Originator and Reason identify the source and the reason for doing so. If the value of the Originator parameter is *DLS Provider,* then the value of Reason parameter is one of *Data Link flow control congestion* or *Data Link error.* If Originator is DLS User, then the value of *Reason* parameter is *User Synchroniza-*

TABLE 5.6   Parameters of the DL-Unitdata Primitives

Parameter	DL-Unitdata request	DL-Unitdata indication
Called Address	X	X (=)
Calling Address	X	X (=)
Quality of service	X	
DLS User Data	X	X (=)

Note: (=): The parameter value is equal to its value in preceding primitive.

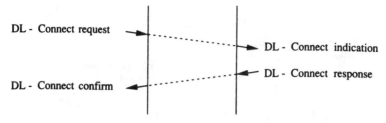

(a) Successful connection establishment.

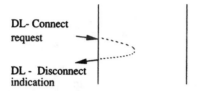

(b) Connection rejected by the DLS provider.

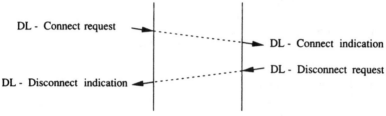

(c) Connection rejected by the other DLS user.

Figure 5.11 Example use of DL-Connect primitives.

tion. Figure 5.12(f) and (g) illustrates the sequences of primitives for situations where the two DLS users, or a user and the DLS provider, issue a *DL-RESET* primitive at about the same time.

6. *Error reporting:* The optional Error Report service is used by the service provider to inform a user that an error has occurred. This error may result in the loss of one or more DLSDUs. Currently, most Data Link protocols simply reset the connection, instead of reporting the error and proceeding. This service is provider-initiated, and is illustrated in Figure 5.12(h).

7. *Connection-less data transfer:* In local area networks, particularly, the Data Link may simply provide connection-less data transfer. A DLSDU is made available to the service provider together with a Calling and a Called Address. The quality of service expected of the Data Link layer is also specified. Again, this service is unconfirmed. Within the layer, Data Link entities may *not* acknowledge the receipt

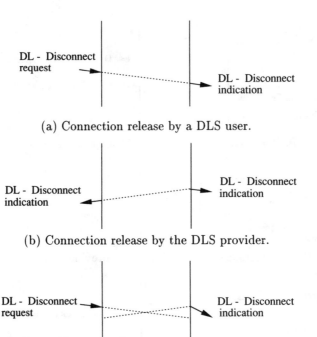

(a) Connection release by a DLS user.

(b) Connection release by the DLS provider.

(c) Connection release simultaneously by a user and the provider.

(d) Normal data transfer.

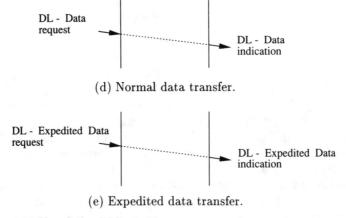

(e) Expedited data transfer.

Figure 5.12 Use of other DLS primitives: some examples.

of a protocol data unit containing a DLSDU. Figure 5.12(i) illustrates the use of corresponding primitives.

Figures 5.11 and 5.12 give some idea of how the use of a Data Link service involves issuing of primitives at the two service access points. A formal model which specifies the interaction at the two DLSAPs is given in

(f) Connection reset by the two users simultaneously.

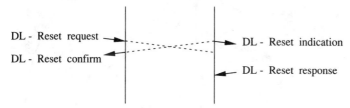

(g) Connection reset by a DLS user and the DLS provider simultaneously.

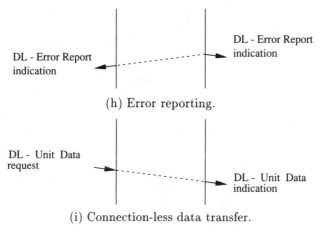

(h) Error reporting.

(i) Connection-less data transfer.

Figure 5.12 (*Continued*)

[ISO 8886.2] (see also [CCITT X.212]). The model is based on two queues between the two DLSAPs, one for each direction of data transfer.[16] It specifies in an abstract manner the cause-effect relationship between the interactions at the two service access points. It does not, however, specify the constraints, if any, upon issuing of primitives by a user or the service provider at a given DLSAP. Such constraints are formally specified using a state transition diagram (see Figure 5.13(a)).

---

[16]See Chapter 3 for a more complete and general description of queues used to model interaction between service users and the provider at two service access points.

This diagram is applicable to each connection end point separately. Clearly, from the figure, a connection goes through the three phases of establishment, data transfer, and release. Data transfer can take place only when the connection is in *data transfer* phase. But, disconnection

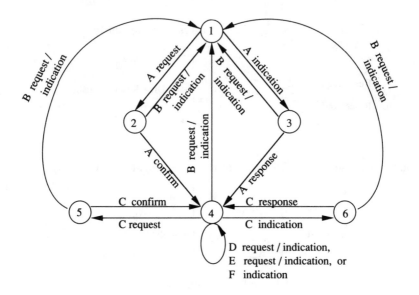

(a) Connection-oriented service.

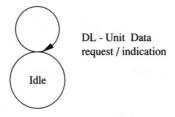

DL - Unit Data
request / indication

(b) Connection-less service.

Notes:

State description	Primitives
1. Idle	A. DL Connect
2. Outgoing connection pending	B. DL Disconnect
3. Incoming connection pending	C. DL Reset
4. Data transfer ready	D. DL Data
5. User-initiated reset pending	E. DL Expedited Data
6. Provider-initiated reset pending	F. DL Error Report

Figure 5.13 State transition description of a Data Link connection end point.

can be initiated from any state. This diagram may also be used to determine the outcome of issuing of service primitives by the users simultaneously. For instance, if a local user issues a DL-RESET request, while the other issues a DL-DISCONNECT, the result is a connection release. The corresponding state transition diagram for connection-less Data Link service is given in Figure 5.13(b).

5.5   Data Link Protocols

Instead of discussing Data Link protocols in general terms, we concentrate on two Data Link protocols, viz. CCITT's X.25 LAPB and IEEE's 802.2 and 802.3. These protocols broadly cover both wide area and local area networks.

5.5.1   Functions

A Data Link protocol is a specification of the functions that are implemented to bridge the gap between the available Physical layer service and the Data Link service. The functions include:

1. addressing,
2. frame delimiting,
3. error detection, recovery and sequencing,
4. flow control, and
5. protocol error detection and notification.

Aside from processing information, Data Link entities exchange *DL protocol data units (DLPDU)*, which contain user data as well as *protocol control information*. The major portion of a protocol specification relates to the syntax (format), semantics and the timing of DLPDUs. A DLPDU may be sent by a Data Link entity to its peer entity in response to:

1. a user issuing a service primitive at a DLSAP,
2. receipt of a DLPDU from its peer entity,
3. an event occurring within the Data Link entity, or
4. an event notified by the lower PhS provider in the form of a service primitive.

When one of such events occurs, the Data Link entity may simply issue a service primitive either at the corresponding DLSAP or PhSAP, or initiate some activity which is local to the entity itself. Figure 5.14 illustrates these cases. Note that "Timer" and its operations are internal to the Data Link entity, whereas "Physical connection failure" is an event signalled by the lower Physical layer. We now discuss some of the functions and their implementation.

Frame-delimiting is a function that enables Data Link entities to delimit the start and end of a DLPDU. A portion of the protocol control information, a *start delimiter* and an *end delimiter,* is used to enclose the remaining PDU (see Figure 5.15). Since the entire DLPDU is transferred transparently over the Physical medium, one must ensure that a portion of the enclosed PDU is not interpreted as a delim-

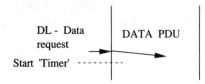

(a) User issues a primitive.

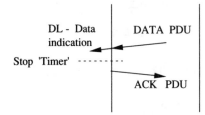

(b) Receipt of a DL PDU.

(c) Event occurs within the DL-entity.

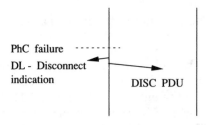

Figure 5.14 Occurrence of incoming events and resulting actions: an illustration.

(d) Event notified by the Physical layer.

iter. In X.25 protocol, the start and end delimiter is a *flag*. Transparency of user data is ensured by *bit-stuffing* the remaining PDU (see [CCITT X.25]).

5.5.2   Error Detection, Recovery and Sequencing

Error detection, recovery and *sequencing* functions are all concerned with ensuring that DLSDUs are delivered to the receiver entity without error. Recall that transfer of a sequence of bits over the physical medium is prone to transmission errors. Further, since processing capability and buffer space is always finite, a receiver may not be able to buffer all incoming DLPDUs. In spite of these limitations, DLSDUs must be delivered without alteration in their contents, loss, or duplication, and in the proper sequence.

There are a number of approaches to error detection and recovery, but the one most frequently employed is based upon error detection and re-transmission. If a PDU is known to have been corrupted by noise it is simply discarded. A discarded PDU can now be treated in a manner identical to that when it is lost. Transmission errors can be detected by computing a checksum on the PDU and transmitting it as part of the PDU itself. Thus, a checksum is considered to be a part of the protocol control information. The choice of a checksum algorithm is based upon the characteristics of transmission error. For example, a *Cyclic Redundancy Checksum* (or *CRC*) is considered ideally suited for detecting burst errors.[17] Further, the generation of a CRC, or its interpretation, can be conveniently done in hardware.[18]

Lost PDUs can be recovered using one of several protocols, based on re-transmissions. Once a PDU is known to have been lost, it is simply re-transmitted. Thus detection of loss of PDUs becomes a major concern. In most protocols, the responsibility of ensuring that a PDU has been delivered to the corresponding Data Link entity rests with the sender. The receiving Data Link entity is expected to acknowledge the receipt by sending an appropriate *acknowledgement*. Acknowledgement PDUs are themselves not acknowledged. Thus, if an acknowledgement does not arrive within a predefined interval (because either the original PDU or the corresponding acknowledgement PDU is lost), the initiator simply re-transmits the original PDU. Of course, this may

---

[17]X.25 Data Link protocol recommends the use of a 16 bit checksum based upon the generator polynomial $P(x)=x^{16}+x^{12}+x^5+1$. IEEE 802.3 suggests the use of a 32 bit checksum [IEEE 802.3].

[18]For a detailed discussion on CRC and other checksum algorithms see [Tanen 88].

Flag	Other header information and user data	Flag	Flag	

Note : Flag = '01111110'

Figure 5.15 Frame delimiting in X.25 Data Link protocol.

result in duplication sometimes. Thus, a protocol is needed that can recover from lost or duplicated PDUs.

5.5.3 Alternating-Bit Protocol

Below, we discuss the *alternating-bit* protocol that forms a basis for most protocols, including *window protocols*. Elsewhere in the literature the protocol is also called *stop-and-wait* protocol (see [Tanen 88]). For simplicity, we shall consider reliable transfer of PDUs that carry user data, but only in one direction. Such a PDU shall be referred to as a *Data PDU*. A PDU sent as acknowledgement is called *Ack PDU*. Further, the Data Link entity which sends Data PDUs is called the *sender*, whereas the entity which receives Data PDUs, and sends Ack PDUs, will be termed the *receiver*. The Physical layer is assumed to support full-duplex transfer of PDUs. PDUs are received in the proper sequence, but may be lost. No upper bound is assumed on the delay in transferring a PDU.

Each Data PDU is sequentially numbered modulo-2. Similarly, an Ack PDU carries the sequence number, 0 or 1, of the Data PDU being acknowledged. The sender maintains a timer, which is started soon after a Data PDU is sent. It is stopped as soon as an outstanding Data PDU is acknowledged by the receiver. When the timer runs out, the Data PDU is re-transmitted, and the timer restarted. Sample PDU transmissions are shown in Figure 5.16, covering four different situations, viz.:

1. error-free and timely transfer of Data and Ack PDUs,
2. the Data PDU is lost,
3. the Ack PDU is lost, and
4. delay in acknowledging the Data PDU.

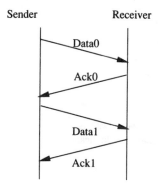

(a) PDUs are transferred error-free and without delay.

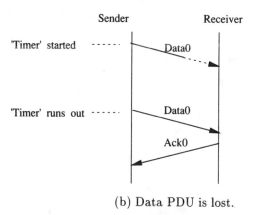

(b) Data PDU is lost.

Figure 5.16   The alternating-bit protocol: an illustration.

These basically show that the alternating-bit protocol is capable of detecting and recovering from lost or duplicated Data and Ack PDUs.

5.5.4   Window Protocols

The major limitation of the alternating-bit protocol is throughput. The initiator entity has to wait until the outstanding Data PDU is acknowledged, before it can send another Data PDU. To circumvent this limitation, Data PDUs are numbered using a modulo-n numbering scheme. The sender may transmit up to (n − 1) Data PDUs without receiving an Ack. On the other hand, the receiver accepts numbered Data

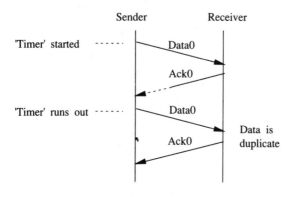

(c) Ack PDU is lost.

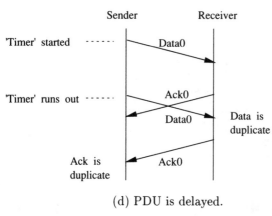

(d) PDU is delayed.

Figure 5.16 (*Continued*)

PDUs in sequence only. An Ack PDU is then interpreted as an acknowledgement to all Data PDUs numbered up to but not including the sequence number it carries. If an Ack to a Data PDU is delayed, the sender re-transmits the lost PDU, and all subsequent PDUs. Re-transmissions could also have been initiated if the receiver sends back a *Reject* PDU whenever it receives an out-of-sequence Data PDU. Such a scheme is called *Go-back n* window protocol.

The alternative to it is the *Selective-Repeat* window protocol. It permits a receiver to buffer out-of-sequence Data PDUs. The Ack PDU continues to have the same interpretation. The Reject PDU, however, invokes re-transmission of the rejected Data PDU alone. Further, the sender may have up to $(n/2)$ outstanding frames. Figure 5.17 illustrates the two window protocol schemes. In each case, a Data PDU is assumed lost. In Go-back n scheme the sender re-transmits all unacknowledged

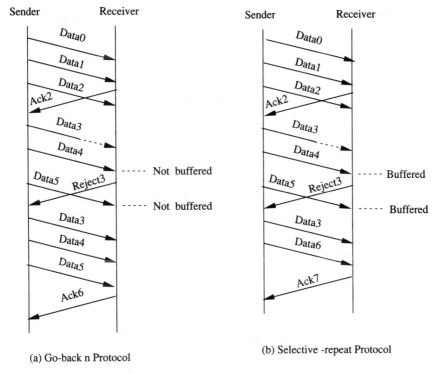

(a) Go-back n Protocol

(b) Selective -repeat Protocol

Figure 5.17 Illustration of a window protocol.

Data PDUs, whereas in Selective-Repeat protocol, the sender re-transmits only that Data PDU which is lost. The Selective-Repeat protocol requires that (n/2) buffers be available to the receiver, and is more suited for implementation over noisy channels.[19]

The X.25 Data Link protocol, which is based upon HDLC protocol, recommends the use of a Go-back n window protocol with n = 8 or 128 (see [CCITT X.25] and [ISO 7776]). The logical link control sub-layer in local area networks (see [IEEE 802.2]) suggests the use of data link procedures that are also based on HDLC protocol.

5.5.5   Other Functions

Flow Control function ensures that a receiving entity is not swamped by Data PDUs. This function is partly implemented in the window protocol since a receiver may delay acknowledgement to incoming Data

---

[19]For a more detailed discussion see [Tanen 88].

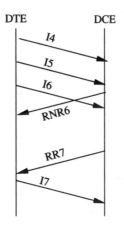

Notes:
I: Information frame containing user data
RNR: Receive Not Ready
RR: Receive Ready
The number x with RR/RNR PDU acknowledges all data PDU numbered upto, but excluding x.

Figure 5.18 Flow control procedure in X.25 Data Link protocol.

PDUs. Additionally, a Data Link protocol may define DLPDUs that allow a receiver entity to indicate to the sender its ability or inability to receive more Data PDUs. This is illustrated in Figure 5.18, where *Receiver Ready PDU and Receiver Not Ready PDU* are assumed to be available, as in X.25 Data Link protocol.

Connection establishment is relatively straightforward. Figure 5.19 illustrates the establishment of a balanced-mode connection using *SABM* and *UA* PDUs.[20] This is, in fact, the recommended procedure in X.25 Data Link protocol. Note that a full-duplex connection is established, as a consequence. Further, in a balanced mode, reset or release of the connection affects both directions of communication simultaneously. As a consequence, the role of the two communicating entities is not that of master-slave, but that of peer entities.

Protocol error detection and notification is yet another function built into the protocol, primarily with a view to detect errors from which recovery within Data Link is not possible. These include errors due to incompatible or incorrect implementations, or errors due to

[20]These are abbreviations for *Set Asynchronous Balanced Mode* and *Unnumbered Acknowledgement,* respectively.

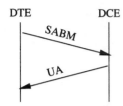

Figure 5.19 Procedure for Data Link establishment in balanced-mode operation of X.25.

malfunction. When such an event is detected, the Data Link layer simply resets or releases the connection, depending upon whether the error is transient or permanent.

Each Data Link connection is mapped onto a Physical layer connection. As such, multiplexing is not performed within the Data Link layer. Thus, once a connection has been established, a corresponding DLPDU need not carry any address information or connection identifier.[21] Splitting of a Data Link connection over a number of Physical connections is permissible. In fact, Recommendation X.25 defines a *multilink* protocol that may take advantage of multiple physical circuits, where available. In case of local area networks, all DLPDUs must carry source and destination addresses. The latter address ensures that the DLPDU will be received, buffered and analyzed by the intended receiver(s) only.

5.6   Local Area Networks

The Data Link layer in local area networks is sub-divided into two sub-layers, called *Media Access Control* layer (or *MAC*) and *Logical Link Control* layer (or *LLC*). This is illustrated in Figure 5.20. As discussed in Sections 5.2 and 5.3, the Physical layer in local area networks provides connection-less data transfer service over a shared physical medium. Each Data Link entity has equal access to this medium, and all transmissions are broadcast over the medium. However, only the addressed receiver(s) may buffer incoming PDU. The mechanism used to coordinate access to the medium by all contending systems on the network is called *media access control* scheme. Other functions implemented within the MAC sub-layer include frame-delimiting, addressing, and error detection.

Thus, the MAC layer may be viewed as a sub-layer that provides a service using which LLC entities may transfer a protocol data unit

---

[21]In case of a multi-point Physical connection, each DLPDU carries either a source or a destination address. This aspect is in fact carried over in the specification of X.25 Data Link protocol, where each frame contains an address.

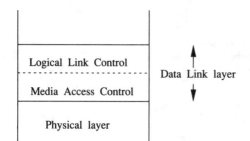

Figure 5.20 Sub-layers in local area networks.

without being concerned with how to access the broadcast medium, or with frame-delimiting, addressing, and error detection. The Logical Link Control layer uses this service to provide a connection-less or both connection-less and connection-oriented Data Link service. If the service is connection-oriented, flow control, error recovery and resequencing functions are implemented by LLC entities.

5.6.1 Media Access Control Sub-Layer

Depending upon the physical characteristics of the medium and the topology of the network, a number of media access control schemes have been developed and standardized. Figure 5.21 shows the relation between the three commonly used MAC layer protocols and the LLC protocol. Notice that the LLC protocol can use any MAC layer protocol. Each MAC layer is a specification of the media access scheme together with that of the physical and electrical interface with the transmission medium.

Table 5.7 summarizes the major differences between the three MAC layer specifications. Below we consider the contexts in which each protocol is particularly suited. A network based upon CSMA/CD scheme

TABLE 5.7   A Summary of the Specification of IEEE's MAC and Physical Layer Standards

Characteristics	IEEE 802.3	IEEE 802.4	IEEE 802.5
Channel Access	CSMA/CD bus	Token-passing bus	Token ring
Data rate	10 Mbps	1, 5, 10 Mbps	1, 4 Mbps
Trunk cable	50 ohm co-axial	75 ohm co-axial	twisted pair
Topology	omnidirectional bus	omnidirectional/ directional bus	ring
Baseband/broadband	baseband	both	baseband
Bit-level encoding	Manchester	Manchester/ modulation	differential Manchester

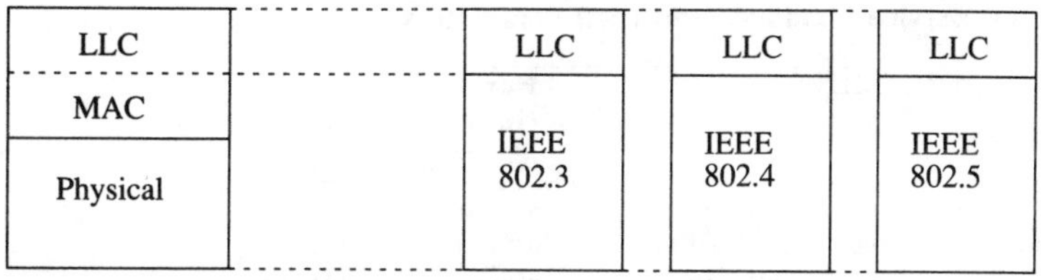

LLC		LLC	LLC	LLC
MAC		IEEE 802.3	IEEE 802.4	IEEE 802.5
Physical				

Figure 5.21   IEEE 802 standards and their relation to OSI layers.

over a 10 Mbps co-axial cable[22] is particularly suited in those environments where the volume of traffic is low and minimum channel access delay is desirable. There is, however, no upper bound on the access delay, which implies that it may not be suited for real time applications, specially if the volume of traffic is high.

Applications that require a high throughput, and are not as particular about access delay, may benefit from the use of a 4 Mbps ring that uses Token-passing channel access scheme (see [IEEE 802.5]). An upper bound on the delay can be computed and enforced.

The IEEE 802.4 standard has provision for a variety of transmission rates and media. The most interesting, perhaps, is its implementation over a broadband CATV cable based bus. It offers multiple high speed channels, some of which may be used to carry voice or video signals. The channel access scheme is token-passing which, as before, offers high throughput and bounded delay. It is, therefore, suited for real time applications, including factory automation.

5.6.2   Logical Link Control Sub-Layer Services

The LLC sub-layer offers to Network entities two *classes* of service. *Class 1* service is connection-less, and is relevant to those applications that do not require error-free or flow-controlled transfer of user data. *Class 2* service is both connection-oriented and connection-less. The standard IEEE 802.2, however, defines these classes in terms of *types* of operations. *Type 1* operation is simply connection-less data transfer, whereas with *Type 2* operation a balanced-mode connection is required to be established before data transfer can take place.

There are some important differences in the specification of the service that the LLC layer offers to Network entities from those discussed earlier in Section 5.4. A summary of LLC service primitives and their

---

[22]This is sometimes referred to as *Ethernet* (see [IEEE 802.3]).

TABLE 5.8   LLC Service Primitives and Their Parameters

Service	Primitives	Parameters (in addition to source, destination addresses)
Connection Establishment	L-Connect request L-Connect indication L-Connect confirm	service class service class, status service class, status
Data Transfer	L-Data-Connect request L-Data-Connect indication L-Data-Connect confirm	user data user data status
Release	L-Disconnect request L-Disconnect indication L-Disconnect confirm	- reason status
Reset	L-Reset request L-Reset indication L-Reset confirm	- reason status
Flow control	L-Flow-Control request L-Flow-Control indication	amount of data amount of data
Connection-less Data Transfer	L-Data request L-Data indication	user data, service class user data, service class

parameters is given in Table 5.8. First, note that there is no *response* primitive at all. That is, in any confirmed service, connection establishment or reset for instance, the responding Network entity does not issue a primitive in response to an *indication* primitive. Of course, the responding LLC service user is simply informed of the operation. But, a *confirm* primitive issued to the initiating LLC service user is based on the acknowledgement received from the remote LLC entity. Figure 5.22 illustrates the sequence of primitives that are issued in order to establish, reset or disconnect a connection, or to transfer data. Note that connection establishment, reset, disconnection *and data transfer* are confirmed services. It may be pointed out that the *Status* information provided in a confirm primitive has remote significance.

The other major difference is that expedited data transfer and error reporting are not supported. Instead, users may authorize the LLC layer to receive only a specified amount of data. There is, however, no correspondence between the Flow-Control request and Flow-Control indication primitives (as one may have expected). These are independent service primitives, and have local significance only. Lastly, connection-less data transfer is unconfirmed, but a confirm primitive, with local significance, is issued.

5.6.3 Logical Link Control Sub-Layer Protocol

The functions implemented in Class 2 service, and the corresponding procedures, are similar to those of X.25 Data Link layer. A major dif-

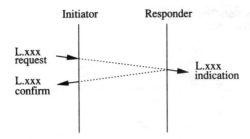

(a) Connection establishment, reset, disconnection or connection-oriented data transfer.

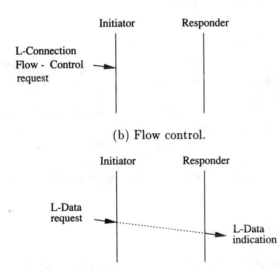

(b) Flow control.

(c) Connection-less data transfer.

(Note: Above it is assumed that a service is not initiated simultaneously by two users or a user and the LLC layer.)

Figure 5.22 Sequence of LLC service primitives.

ference between the two is in the modulus used to sequentially number Data PDUs and, as a consequence, in the PDU formats. The Data PDUs are numbered modulo-128, which is basically a recognition of the fact that the protocol is for use over high speed networks where it is desirable to have as many outstanding Data PDUs as possible, subject to buffer availability.

An LLC PDU carries addresses of the source and destination LLC service access points. These are in addition to MAC layer addresses. But, as with X.25 protocol, only one data link may be established be-

TABLE 5.9   Connection-Oriented and Connection-Less Network Service Elements

Connection-oriented	NC establishment
	Normal data transfer
	Receipt Confirmation (optional)
	Expedited data transfer (optional)
	NC Reset (optional)
	NC release
Connection-less	Unitdata transfer

tween a pair of LLC entities, unless each entity supports services at more than one service access point.

5.7   Network Services

Let us consider the details of the Network service. Both connection-oriented and connection-less services are discussed in this section, whereas Network protocols are discussed in Sections 5.8 and 5.9. The model of the Network layer, in terms of NS users and NS provider, was presented in Section 5.2 (see also Figure 5.3). A formal definition of Network objects, including NSAPs, Network connections, NCEPs, and NCEP Identifiers was also given (see Figure 5.4). The discussion in this section is mainly concerned with Network service primitives and with their parameters.

5.7.1   Connection-Oriented Service Elements

Table 5.9 summarizes the service elements available to NS users. Connection-oriented Network service is a collection of service elements that allow its users: (a) to establish or release connections, (b) to transfer data transparently (either normally or on an urgent basis), (c) to acknowledge the receipt of normal data, or (d) to re-initialize a connection.

1. *NC Establishment:* An NS user may establish a Network connection (NC) with another NS user. The address of the NSAP to which the *responding* NS user is attached is assumed to be known to the *initiating* NS user. During NC establishment, an NS user may request, and negotiate with the other NS user and the NS provider, the quality of service to be provided over the NC.

2. *NC Release:* Either NS user may unilaterally and unconditionally release the NC once a connection has been established, or even during the establishment phase. As one consequence, any user data currently in transit may not be delivered, and discarded. Alternatively, a connection may be released by the NS provider, if it determines that it is

no longer possible to support the connection, either due to breakdown or deterioration in the quality of service.

3. *Normal Data Transfer:* NS users may exchange data, in the form of *Network Service Data Units* (or *NSDUs*) consisting of an integral number of octets, such that the boundaries between NSDUs and their contents are preserved at the two ends. A receiving NS user may control the rate at which an NS user sends data.

4. *Receipt Confirmation:* By itself, when an NSDU is delivered to the destination NS user, the NS provider does not confirm its delivery to the initiating NS user. If the users so desire, and if the Receipt Confirmation service is provided by the Network layer, an NS user may acknowledge the receipt of an NSDU.[23]

5. *Expedited Data Transfer:* Transfer of a limited amount of user data on an urgent basis may be requested by an NS user. But, this service is available only when the NS users agree to use it and the NS provider agrees to provide it. Further, the transfer of Expedited-NSDUs may be subject to a similar, but distinct, flow control by a receiving NS user.

6. *Reset:* A reset, or a re-initialization, of the established connection may be initiated by either NS user or by the service provider, provided the service is available and its use has been negotiated at the time of establishing the connection. The net effect is to restore the connection to a state where there is no data within the network. All data with Network entities or in transit is discarded. From the NS users viewpoint, the service may be used to resynchronize their states, in case they detect errors within the Transport layer.

5.7.2 Connection-less Service Element

Connection-less data transfer, on the other hand, does not require the establishment of a connection prior to data transfer. Thus, the only available service element relates to *Connection-less Data Transfer.* An NS user may transparently transfer an NSDU, of a fixed maximum length, to another NS user. The address of the NSAP, to which the receiving NS user is attached, is provided by the sending NS user. Each NSDU is sent independent of other NSDUs together with the address of the source and destination NSAP. While initiating the transfer, the sending NS user may request a desired quality of service that the NS provider must associate with the transfer. The NS provider is expected to make every attempt to deliver the message, correctly and timely.

---

[23]This is very similar to the D bit facility in X.25 Network layer protocol, which allows users to acknowledge receipt of messages.

TABLE 5.10   Connection-Oriented and Connection-less Network Service Elements

Service element	Primitives	Parameters
NC establishment (confirmed)	N-Connect request N-Connect indication N-Connect response N-Connect confirm	see Table 5.11 see Table 5.11 see Table 5.11 see Table 5.11
Normal data transfer (unconfirmed)	N-Data request N-Data indication	user data, confirm request user data, confirm request
Receipt Confirmation (unconfirmed)	N-Data-ACK request N-Data-ACK indication	- -
Expedited data (unconfirmed)	N-Expedited-Data request N-Expedited-Data indication	user data user data
NC Reset (confirmed and provider-initiated)	N-Reset request N-Reset indication N-Reset response N-Reset confirm	reason originator, reason - -
NC release (unconfirmed and provider-initiated)	N-Disconnect request N-Disconnect indication	see Table 5.12 see Table 5.12
Unitdata transfer (unconfirmed)	N-Unitdata request N-Unitdata indication	see Table 5.13 see Table 5.13

There is no guarantee, however, that the data would be delivered correctly, or delivered at all.

To summarize the discussion thus far, the specification of the NS does not define any classes of Network services, except to distinguish between the two forms of data transfers, viz. connection-oriented and connection-less, and to indicate that expedited data transfer and receipt confirmation service elements are optional (see Table 5.9).

5.7.3   Service Primitives and Parameters

Table 5.10 is a summary of the primitives associated with each element of the Network service. The table also indicates whether a service is unconfirmed, confirmed or provider-initiated. Note, that NC Release is unconfirmed as well as provider-initiated, whereas NC Reset is confirmed and provider-initiated. Normal data transfer is unconfirmed, but users may acknowledge receipt of data using the unconfirmed Receipt Confirmation service. Table 5.10, together with Tables 5.11, 5.12 and 5.13, list the parameters of the primitives. We shall briefly discuss these.

1. The *Calling* and the *Called Addresses* of the *N-CONNECT* primitives refer to the addresses of the NSAPs to which the initiating and the responding NS users are attached. More often than not, the *Responding Address* in the corresponding response and confirm primi-

TABLE 5.11   Parameters of the N-Connect Primitives.

Parameter	N-Connect request	N-Connect indication	N-Connect response	N-Connect confirm
Called Address	X	X (=)		
Calling Address	X	X (=)		
Responding Address			X	X (=)
Receipt Confirmation Selection	X	X	X	X (=)
Expedited Data Selection	X	X	X	X (=)
Quality of service	X	X	X	X (=)
User Data	X (C)	X C(=)	X (C)	X C(=)

Note: (=): The value of the parameter must be the same as that in the preceding primitive.
C: The presence of the parameter is conditional.

TABLE 5.12   Parameters of the N-Disconnect Primitives.

Parameter	N-Disconnect request	N-Disconnect indication
Originator		X
Reason	X	X
Responding Address	X(C)	X (C=)
User Data	X	X (=)

Note: See note in Table 5.11.

TABLE 5.13   Parameters of the N-Unitdata Primitive.

Parameter	N-Unitdata request	N-Unitdata indication
Called Address	X	X (=)
Calling Address	X	X (=)
Quality of service	X	X
User Data	X	X (=)

Note: See note in Table 5.11.

TABLE 5.14   Possible Values for Parameters Receipt Confirmation/Expedited Data Selection

Different cases	N-Connect request	N-Connect indication	N-Connect response	N-Connect confirm
case 1	use	use	use	use
case 2	use	use	no-use	no-use
case 3	use	no-use	no-use	no-use
case 4	no-use	no-use	no-use	no-use

tive is identical to the Called Address. However, in case of re-direction or generic addressing the value of Responding Address may be the address of the NSAP to which the connection has been established or should be established by the Calling NS user entity.

2. N-CONNECT parameters, *Receipt Confirmation Selection* and *Expedited Data Selection* parameters enable NS users and the NS provider to negotiate the availability, and use, of the corresponding optional service elements. The negotiation procedure, for each selection, is such that if either one of the users or the provider does not agree to its availability or its use then the service is not used. This results in four different combinations, listed in Table 5.14.

3. While a number of quality of service parameters have been defined, only *Throughput* (for forward and reverse directions, separately) and *Transit Delay* (applicable to both directions) are negotiated. The value of each quality of service parameter is specified using a variety of sub-parameters, as indicated in Table 5.15. The table illustrates an example resulting in successful negotiation.

4. The parameters, *originator* and *reason,* may be used to convey the source (NS user or NS provider) of disconnection and the reason, if known. The parameter, *Responding Address,* relevant only when a connection request is refused by the corresponding user, conveys the address of the NSAP from which the *N-DISCONNECT* was issued. The address may be different from the Called Address, in case of re-direction or generic addressing.

TABLE 5.15   Example Values (in bits/sec) for Sub-Parameters of Throughput, for Example

Sub-parameter	N-Connect request	N-Connect indication	N-Connect response	N-Connect confirm
target	9600			
lowest acceptable	1200	1200		
available		4800		
selected			2400	2400

5. User data in N-CONNECT primitives is optional. Further, while it is specified as one of the parameters in N-DISCONNECT primitives, it may not be available in some networks. When an implementation supports transfer of user data in N-CONNECT or N-DISCONNECT primitives, its length is limited.

6. Once a Network connection has been established, at each end the NS user and the NS provider refer to it using an NCEP Identifier. This identifier is assigned by the NS provider at the time of connection establishment and made known to the local NS user. Since it has local significance, the identifier does not appear as a formal parameter of N-CONNECT primitives.

5.7.4 Sequence of Service Primitives

For each service element separately, Figure 5.23 gives a typical sequence in which corresponding service primitives are issued by NS users and the NS provider. The fact that these sequences are at all possible is, clearly, not suggested by Table 5.10. A formal model of the Network service is required which provides details on constraints, if any, on the interactions that take place between an NS user and the NS provider. Later we shall discuss the relation between interactions taking place at two corresponding NSAPs.

Figure 5.24(a) describes the constraints on issuing connection-oriented service primitives at an NSAP. These constraints are applicable separately for each NSAP and for each NCEP. Further, for a given state of the NCEP, if a transition corresponding to a service primitive is not indicated on the diagram, then that service primitive may not be issued. It also defines how the NCEP transitions from its current state to the next state when a service primitive is issued. Note that the NCEP may remain within a state for any length of time. The particular transition that it makes depends only upon the primitive issued.

Figure 5.24(b) is a state transition description of the constraints applicable to issuing of primitives, but corresponding to connection-less data transfer. Clearly, the diagram suggests no constraints, whatsoever. This is understandable since each interaction at an NSAP is independent of every other interaction.

5.7.5 A Queue Model of Network Service

From Figure 5.23, when a primitive is issued at an NSAP, for a specific connection, a corresponding primitive is subsequently issued by the NS provider at the other end of the connection. A model is, therefore, required to specify such a correspondence between interactions at two

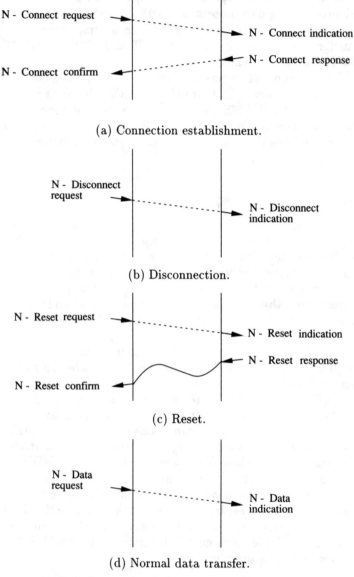

(a) Connection establishment.

(b) Disconnection.

(c) Reset.

(d) Normal data transfer.

Figure 5.23 Typical sequences of primitives.

NCEPs.[24] Such a model, based on queues, was earlier described in Chapter 3. The application of that model to Network service is described here (see [ISO 8348, CCITT X.213]). This model is only an abstraction,

---

[24]Or at two NSAPs in case of connection-less data transfer.

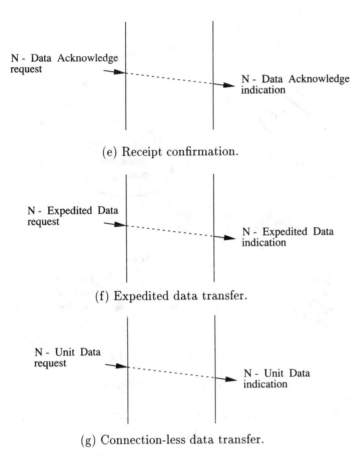

(e) Receipt confirmation.

(f) Expedited data transfer.

(g) Connection-less data transfer.

Figure 5.23 (*Continued*)

and may only be used to guide an implementation of the Network layer.

We first consider connection-oriented Network service. Figure 5.25 illustrates the queue model of an NC. Two queues (one for each direction of communication) are associated with each NC. An interaction between an NS user and the NS provider at an NCEP results in a queue object being added to the outgoing queue, or an object being deleted from the incoming queue. There are no restrictions on placing objects in the queue, or on removing them, except those that follow from the constraints suggested by the state transition diagram of Figure 5.24.

When a request/response primitive is issued, a corresponding queue object is added by the user to the outgoing queue. The NS provider may also place objects in either queue. The latter corresponds to initiation of a *provider-initiated* service-element. Removal of an object from the incoming queue by a user, corresponds to issuing of an indication/con-

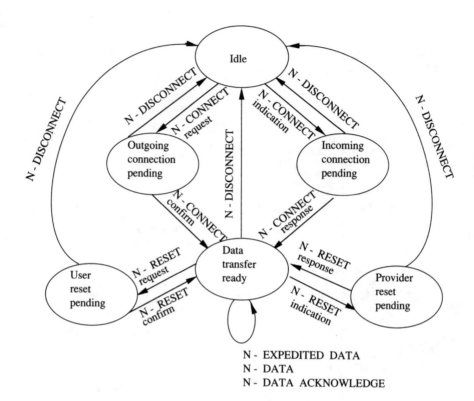

N - EXPEDITED DATA
N - DATA
N - DATA ACKNOWLEDGE

Note: N-DISCONNECT, N-DATA, N-EXPEDITED-DATA, and N-DATA ACKNOWLEDGEMENT are request or indication primitives.

(a) Connection-oriented services.

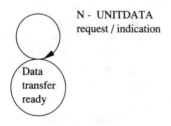

N - UNITDATA
request / indication

(b) Connection-less services.

Figure 5.24 State description of permissible primitive sequences at an NCEP/NSAP.

firm primitive by the NS provider. Normally, an object is removed First-In-First-Out by the NS user. But, the NS provider may alter the sequence of objects in the queues, or delete objects. The latter two queue operations correspond, respectively, to expediting transfer of user data, or to discarding user data that may be in transit.

The objects that may be placed by an NS user in an outgoing queue are:

1. Connect objects,
2. Octets of Normal Data,
3. End-of-NSDU,
4. Expedited NSDUs,
5. Data Acknowledge,
6. Reset objects, and
7. Disconnect objects.

The NS provider may place the following objects in a queue:

1. Disconnect objects,
2. Reset objects, and
3. Synchronization mark.

Whenever an N-CONNECT, N-DISCONNECT, N-EXPEDITED-DATA, or N-DATA-ACK request or response primitive is issued, a corresponding object is either added to the outgoing queue, or is removed in case the primitive is an indication or confirm primitive. In case of N-

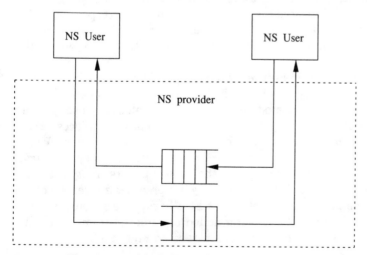

Figure 5.25 The queue model of a Network connection.

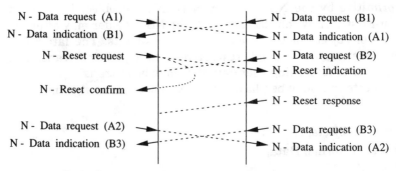

Figure 5.26 Desired separation of user data across a connection reset.

DATA primitives, a string of objects, consisting of *Octets of Normal Data* and terminated by an *End-of-NSDU* object, is placed (or removed) when an N-DATA request is issued (or when an N-DATA indication is received). This approach to model (normal) data transfer service is useful since flow control can be discussed in terms of the number of user data octets, rather than the number of normal NSDUs. Needless to say, an N-DATA request primitive is said to have been issued only with the placement of the corresponding End-of-NSDU. Similarly, with the removal of an End-of-NSDU, the corresponding N-DATA indication is said to have been issued.

The model concerning N-RESET primitives is somewhat complicated. Once the connection has been reset, all data in transit in the two directions must be discarded. Figure 5.23(c) illustrates one of the sequences in which reset primitives is issued. But, as illustrated in Figure 5.26, user data made available to the Network layer before a reset procedure is initiated may be delivered to the corresponding user. The queue model, therefore, introduces the object, *synchronization mark,* to ensure that proper synchronization takes place within the Network layer.

Initiation of a reset procedure by the NS provider results in placing a reset object followed by a synchronization mark in each queue. Issuing of an N-RESET request is modelled as being equivalent to a user placing a reset object in the outgoing queue, while the NS provider places a reset object followed by a synchronization mark in the other queue. A user cannot remove a synchronization mark from a queue. If a synchronization mark is at the head of the queue, the queue appears empty to a user. It can be removed by the NS provider only if it precedes a reset object. As with other primitives, issuing of an N-RESET response or confirm primitive results in a reset object being added or removed from the queue. User-initiated reset procedure is illustrated[25] in Figure 5.27.

---

[25]The figure assumes that a reset object may destroy objects, Octet of normal data and End of NSDU. See Table 5.16.

TABLE 5.16 Reordering and Deletion of Objects from Queues

Preceding object	Expedited NSDU	Data Acknowledge
Octets of Normal Data	yes	yes
End of NSDU	yes	yes
Expedited Data		yes
Data Acknowledge	yes	

(a) Queue objects that may advance ahead of other objects.

Preceding object	Reset	Disconnect
Connect		yes
Octets of Normal Data	yes	yes
End of NSDU	yes	yes
Expedited Data	yes	yes
Data Acknowledge	yes	yes
Reset		yes
Synchronization mark	yes	yes

(b) Queue objects that may delete other objects.

The two queues are created and associated with the particular pair of NCEPs as soon as an N-CONNECT request primitive is issued by an NS user. The queues are initialized to being empty. A queue is destroyed as soon as a Disconnect object is removed from it by an NS user, or deleted by the NS provider.

Queue objects are removed from a queue by an NS user in First-In-First-Out discipline. However, some objects, Expedited Data and Data Acknowledge, may be moved ahead of some of the other objects. A Reset or Disconnect object may also move ahead of other objects, but they do so by destroying them. Details concerning re-ordering and deletion of queue objects are given in Table 5.16. The latter in some ways models the specification that an Expedited NSDU may be transferred on an urgent basis, or that when a connection is reset all data in transit must be discarded.[26]

5.7.6 Connection-less Data Transfer

In the context of connection-less data transfer service, a queue model relates issuing of an N-UNITDATA request primitive at an NSAP to issuing of N-UNITDATA indication at the corresponding NSAP. As an aid to understanding the model, consider the pair of NSAPs, (A, B). To this pair of NSAPs, a queue may be permanently associated from the NSAP A to NSAP B. When an N-UNITDATA request primitive is is-

---

[26]When a Disconnect object deletes a Connect object, it deletes itself as well. As an example application of this specification, if the NS provider were to reject an attempt to establish an NC, then the attempt is aborted.

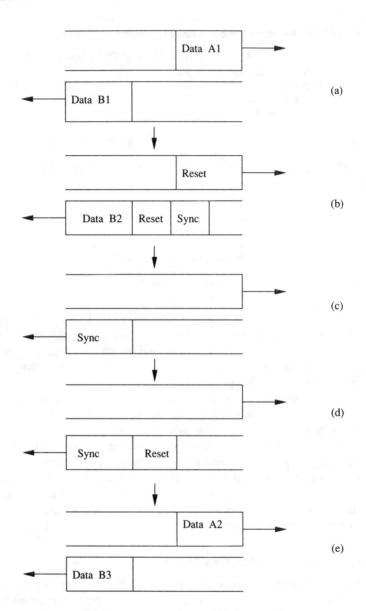

Note: In (b) Data B2 is deleted by the Reset object, and in (d), the Sync object is deleted by the Reset object.

Figure 5.27 A queue model of the Reset procedure.

sued at NSAP *A,* a *Unitdata* object is inserted at the tail of the outgoing queue. Removal of a Unitdata object from the queue by the attached
NS user corresponds to issuing of an N-UNITDATA indication primitive by the NS provider at the corresponding NSAP. The NS provider
may *not* add any object to the queue. Thus, the only type of objects in
the queue are Unitdata objects. Normally, objects are removed from the
queue in First-In-First-Out order. However, the NS provider may discard objects, duplicate objects, or re-order the Unitdata objects. That is,
there is no guarantee that data contained in UNITDATA primitives
will be delivered, or that it will be not be duplicated or re-ordered.

5.8   Network Layer Protocols

In this section we discuss the use of X.25 protocol to support connection-oriented Network service. We cover both wide area and local area
networks, but limit ourselves to a network consisting of one subnetwork only. Internetworking issues are covered in the next section together with protocols that support connection-less Network service.

   In the last section we have discussed Network services, whereas the
earlier sections covered Data Link and Physical layer services and the
protocols required to provide these services. Recall that the Data Link
service is available to Network entities in neighboring systems,
whereas the Network service is provided across the network to
Transport entities in end systems. The Network layer protocol, however, is implemented by Network entities that reside in end systems as
well as in the Intermediate system, a term used to abstract a subnetwork. For simplicity, we assume that there is only one subnetwork connecting all systems, and that the subnetwork access protocol (or
SNAcP) is the same for each interface (see also Section 5.2).

5.8.1   X.25 Packet-Level Protocol

We have already seen that the Network service may be connection-oriented or connection-less. Further, the Data Link service may also be
connection-oriented or connection-less. We first discuss a protocol for
providing connection-oriented Network service using a connection-oriented Data Link service. It is based on CCITT's Recommendation X.25
(see Figure 5.28) and is a specification of a subnetwork access protocol
that allows Network entities in end systems (also called *packet-mode
DTEs*) to interface with a packet-switched subnetwork. The access protocol at the Network layer is connection-oriented. That is, using X.25
protocol, Network entities in end systems can establish connections between themselves. Each connection is end-to-end, although the ex-

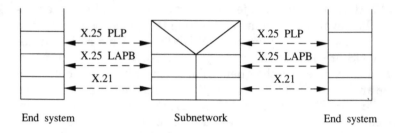

End system   Subnetwork   End system

Note: PLP = Packet - level protocol.

Figure 5.28 Subnetwork access protocol: X.25.

change of protocol data units is only between an end system entity (or DTE) and the subnetwork (or DCE). It is, of course, the responsibility of the subnetwork to maintain correspondence between the two segments of the connection, and thereby, relay the semantics of each PDU across the subnetwork.

Before discussing the details of the X.25 protocol, it is important to point out that in the case of wide area networks, the Network layer X.25 protocol assumes the availability of a Data Link connection established in conformity with X.25 link access procedure (balanced or unbalanced LAP). Therefore, all X.25 Network layer Protocol Data Units are transferred as user data in Information frames of the link access procedure.

Figure 5.29 illustrates the procedure for establishment, release and re-initialization of connections, and for data transfer (both normal and expedited). Note that these figures do relate sending or receiving of PDUs[27] to issuing of service primitives, although such a specification is not part of X.25. This relation can only be established once it is clear that X.25 protocol can be used to provide connection-oriented Network service. Discussion of packet parameters is also postponed to the next sub-section. Below, we comment upon these procedures, and other characteristics of the X.25 Packet Level Protocol, also known as *X.25 PLP*.

1. X.25 protocol provides a means to simultaneously maintain a number of connections, called *virtual calls* or *permanent virtual circuits.* Each virtual call goes through a call establishment, data transfer, and call clearing phase. It may also be reset. Permanent virtual circuits, on the other hand, are established on a permanent basis with-

---

[27]PDUs are referred to as *packets* in X.25 terminology.

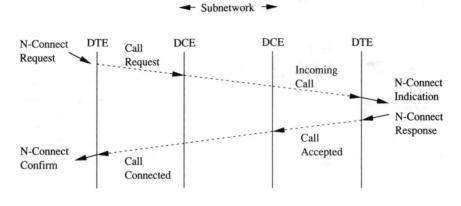

(a) Connection establishment.

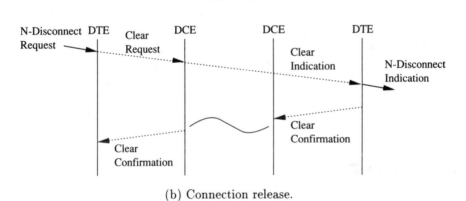

(b) Connection release.

Figure 5.29 X.25 protocol procedures.

out going through a formal establishment procedure. These may only be reset, but never cleared. Each virtual call or permanent virtual circuit is identified by a *Logical Channel Number (LCN)*, which serves the purpose of a connection protocol identifier. The LCN is carried as a parameter in each X.25 PDU (see Tables 5.17 and 5.18, for instance). Further, all virtual calls and permanent virtual circuits are possibly multiplexed onto a single Data Link connection.

2. During connection establishment Network entities in the two end systems and the subnetwork negotiate, on a per connection basis, the values of a number of connection-related parameters, and the use and availability of certain optional services. The negotiations can broadly be divided into two categories. Negotiations take place between Network

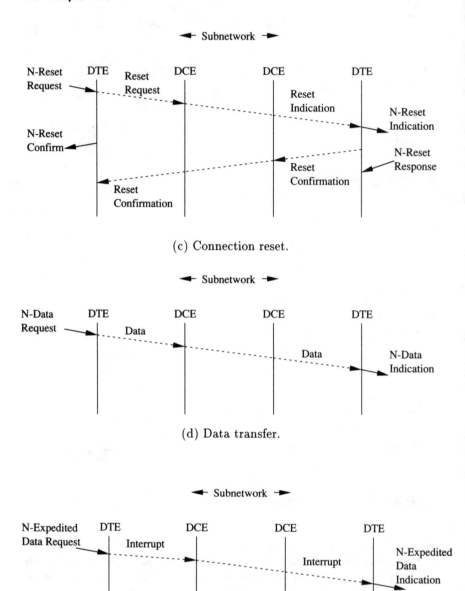

(c) Connection reset.

(d) Data transfer.

(e) Expedited data transfer.

Figure 5.29 (Continued)

TABLE 5.17   Contents of *Call Request* or *Incoming Call* packets in X.25 protocol

General format identifier (xx01)	Logical channel group number
Logical channel number	
Packet type identifier (00001011)	
Calling DTE address length	Called DTE address length
Called DTE address ...	
Calling DTE address ...	
Facilities length	
Facilities ...	
Call user data ...	

entities and have significance for subnetwork entities as well. These include end-to-end acknowledgement, reverse charging, flow control parameters, and fast select facility. (Some of these will be discussed shortly.) The second category includes facilities using which Network entities in end systems negotiate, or simply convey, the value of parameters. Use of Expedited data transfer is one such example. Most of these parameters are passed as optional *facility* parameters (see Table 5.17).

3. Acknowledgements in X.25 may have an end-to-end significance (see Figure 5.29(d)). Or, the significance of an acknowledgement may be local to the host-subnetwork interface. The (so-called) D-bit is used to negotiate this facility during connection establishment, or to request an end-to-end acknowledgement. Either way, acknowledgements are carried in the $P(R)$ field of *User Data* or *Receive Ready* packets, among others (see Tables 5.17 and 5.18).

4. Expedited data transfer is supported by the protocol, and is known as an *Interrupt* facility in X.25 terminology. Its use is negotiated between Network entities in end systems alone.

TABLE 5.18   Contents of *User Data* Packets in X.25 Protocol

General format identifier (QD01)		Logical channel group number	
Logical channel number			
$P(R)$	M	$P(S)$	0
User data ...			

5. X.25 protocol has the added provision for a *fast-select* facility. This permits a *calling* end system to request establishment of a connection with an option to the *called* end system entity to reject the connection. But, in doing so, the two end systems can exchange limited amounts of user data in both directions. Of particular interest to us is the fact that use of fast select service permits inclusion of user data in *Call Accepted/Connected* and *Clear Request/Indication* packets as well.

6. Flow control of user data across an interface (and as a consequence over the end-to-end connection) can be achieved firstly by negotiating, on a per connection basis, an appropriate value for the window size and packet size. Further, Network entities may also use *Receive Ready* and *Receive Not Ready* packets to limit the number of incoming User Data packets.

7. Segmentation is an important function performed within the Network layer. The procedure to perform segmentation (and reassembly) is specified by the X.25 protocol in terms of an *M-bit sequence* of packets. Each packet contains one segment of user data with an indication of whether the packet is the last packet in the sequence, or not. This information is carried in the *M-bit* of User Data packets.

8. The *Restart* procedure in X.25 protocol may be used by a Network entity in an end system or the subnetwork to initialize or re-initialize an interface. The consequence of restarting an interface is to clear all existing virtual calls, and to reset all permanent virtual circuits across the interface. This procedure is invariably used soon after a data link connection has been established or re-initialized.

9. Finally, there are some differences between the 1980, 1984 and the proposed 1988 versions of CCITT's Recommendation X.25. These differences may be significant from the viewpoint of using the protocol to provide connection-oriented Network service (see discussion below).

Above, we have highlighted some of the key features of the X.25 packet level protocol. In the next section we discuss the applicability of the protocol to providing a connection-oriented Network service, discussed earlier in Section 5.7.

5.8.2 Connection-Oriented Network Service using X.25 Protocol

We now consider using X.25 protocol to support connection-oriented Network service. Since X.25 protocol is basically connection-oriented, all aspects concerning connection management and data transfer over it are supported. What remains to be seen is whether X.25 protocol procedures and packet formats are adequate to convey the semantics of Network service primitives and to support negotiation of optional services. Below, we discuss these issues as also the mapping of Network service primitives onto transmission and reception of X.25 packets.

To provide connection-oriented Network service, the X.25 subnetwork must support fast select service and the following facilities:

1. Throughput Class Negotiation,
2. Minimum Throughput Class Negotiation,
3. Transit Delay Selection and Indication,
4. End-to-End Transit Delay Negotiation,
5. Calling Address Extension,
6. Called Address Extension, and
7. Expedited Data Negotiation.

By using the fast select service, one is merely providing an extended packet format, so that user data may be communicated during connection establishment or release. Further, the above facilities permit additional (and optional) parameter values to be communicated so that negotiation may take place. Permanent virtual circuits have no role in providing the Network service. A restart operation may be initiated by the subnetwork or by an end system. Its consequence is, however, the same as that of clearing a virtual call.

Figures 5.29 and 5.30 illustrate the correspondence between issuing service primitives and exchange of packets between Network entities in end systems and the subnetwork. Table 5.19 summarizes the mapping of parameters of N-CONNECT primitives onto different fields of the corresponding packets. (For more details see [CCITT X.223].) Note that:

1. Maintaining the correspondence between a Network connection and a virtual call is a local issue. What is significant is that a logical channel number enables the pair of Network entities at an interface to uniquely identify a virtual call.

TABLE 5.19   Mapping of the Parameters of N-Connect Primitives

Parameters	Field or Facility
Called Address	Called DTE Address field
	Called Address Extension facility
Calling Address	Calling DTE Address field
	Calling Address Extension facility
Responding Address	Called DTE Address field
	Called Address Extension facility
Receipt Confirmation Selection	General Format Identifier
Expedited Data Selection	Expedited Data Negotiation facility
QOS Parameter Set	Throughput Class Negotiation facility
	Minimum Throughput Class Negotiation facility
	Transit Delay Selection and Indication facility
	End-to-end Transit Delay Negotiation facility
NS User Data	Calling or Called User Data field
	(Fast Select facility)

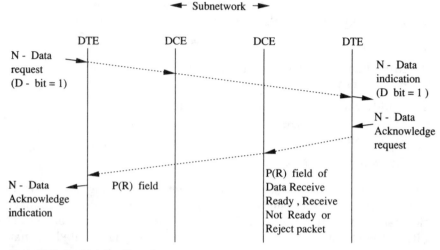

Figure 5.30 Receipt Confirmation.

2. The service parameters Calling and Called NSAP addresses are encoded as *Calling* and *Called DTE Addresses*[28] provided the NSAP addresses can be deduced from the DTE addresses. This is the case when the Domain Specific Part of the NSAP addresses is absent (see also Section 5.2.6), or equivalently, when only one NSAP is served by the Subnetwork Point of Attachment (SNPA). In that case, an NSAP address is the same as its DTE Address. Otherwise, when two or more NSAPs are served by an SNPA, the NSAP addresses are encoded using *Calling* and *Called DTE Address Extension* facilities, together with Calling and Called DTE Addresses. Further, since we are currently concerned only with a single subnetwork, the DTE addresses are directly obtainable from the Initial Domain Identifier portion of the NSAP Address.

3. There is no X.25 packet which specifically conveys the semantics of N-DATA ACKNOWLEDGE primitives. A variety of X.25 packets carry acknowledgement information in the form of a $P(R)$ value. When a sender entity receives a $P(R) = (x + 1)$, it is an acknowledgement to all User Data packets sequentially numbered up to and including x. Whether this acknowledgement is local or end-to-end depends upon whether the sender had requested an end-to-end acknowledgement with the User Data packet numbered x. If it is an end-to-end acknowledgement, the Network entity issues an N-DATA ACKNOWLEDGE indication primitive. At the remote receiver end, the Network entity delays sending an acknowledgement to a packet numbered x, until the

---

[28]These addresses, in fact, constitute the *Network Protocol Address Information.*

corresponding NS user issues an N-DATA ACKNOWLEDGE request primitive. Needless to say, if an NSDU is segmented into a number of User Data packets, then end-to-end acknowledgement is sent only after the NSDU has been completely delivered and an N-DATA ACKNOWLEDGE request issued by the user.

It is not a coincidence that the X.25 packet level protocol (X.25 PLP) can be used directly to provide a connection-oriented Network service. In fact, the specification of the Network service and the design of the current version (1984) of X.25 PLP have considerably influenced each other. The earlier (1980) version of the protocol is deficient, particularly regarding packet formats. As a consequence, it is unable to directly provide connection-oriented Network service, unless additional procedures are defined so that NS primitive parameters can be supported. In other words, a thin layer of protocol is required to be implemented by each end system that wishes to support connection-oriented Network service. This layer of protocol is referred to as a *convergence protocol,* and is specified in [ISO 8878]. By definition, a convergence protocol implements those additional functions that are essential to providing the Network service, but are missing from the subnetwork access protocol.

Note that, as with 1984 version of X.25, availability of fast select facility is optional. But, the convergence protocol, discussed here, may be implemented even when fast select facility is not available. In the absence of fast select facility and limited support for packet parameters, user data and many other parameters cannot be transmitted as part of Call Request or Call Clear packets. Thus, some of the parameters of N-CONNECT and N-DISCONNECT primitives are carried as user data in User Data packets. Figure 5.31 illustrates the procedures for call establishment when the supporting subnetwork access protocol is the 1980 version of X.25. Note that while the X.25 call through the subnetwork is established much earlier, the end-to-end NC is established only after the semantics of N-CONNECT primitives and their parameters have been conveyed. Further, the Q-bit is used to distinguish such User Data packets from those that carry user data contained in N-DATA request/indication primitives. It may also be pointed out that the convergence protocol does not support expedited data transfer service, primarily because the 1980 version permits only one byte of user data in Interrupt packets. N-DATA ACKNOWLEDGE service is supported only when the use of D-bit facility is successfully negotiated.

5.8.3   Use of X.25 Protocol over a LAN

We now discuss the use of X.25 packet level protocol over a local area network. The X.25 PLP may be used as a Network layer protocol over

X25 (1980) Subnetwork

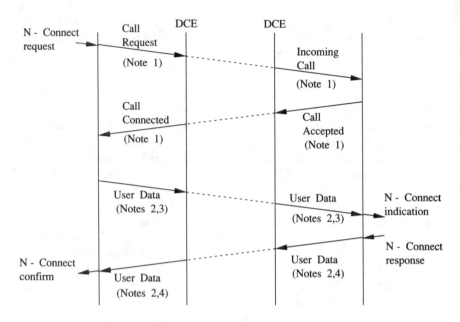

Note 1: It carries the "Continuation" parameter in its User Data field.
Note 2: The Q-bit is 1.
Note 3: User Data field is encoded as "N-CR packet" containing QOS parameters, Called/Calling Address Extensions, and User Data from N-Connect Request primitive.
Note 4: User Data field is encoded as "N-CC packet" containing QOS parameters, Called Address Extension, and User Data from N- Connect Response primitive.

Figure 5.31 Alternative procedure for NC establishment without using fast select facility of X.25 (1980 version).

the Logical Link Control layer in a local area network environment (see [ISO 8881.3]). As discussed earlier in Section 5.6, the LLC service permits users (X.25 PLP entities, in this case) to carry out connection-less data transfer (known as Type 1 LLC operation) or connection-oriented data transfer (also known as Type 2 LLC operation). We shall mainly emphasize the use of X.25 PLP over a Type 2 LLC operation. Its use over a Type 1 LLC operation is also possible except that the Data Link may lose a packet, once in a while. Additional procedures would then have to be specified to resolve this problem.

Recall that X.25 PLP is a subnetwork access protocol at the Network layer. It permits an end system (or DTE) to use the relay facility of the

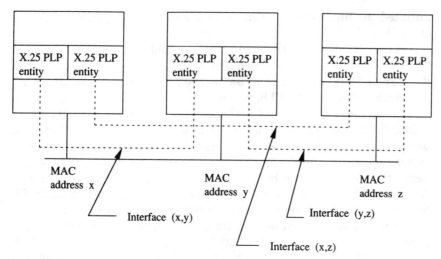

Figure 5.32 Use of X.25 PLP over a local area network.

subnetwork. This mode of X.25 PLP operation is necessarily asymmetric. That is, the Network entity in an end system operates as a DTE, while the Network entity in the subnetwork operates as a *DCE*.[29] Such is not the case in a LAN, although it is a subnetwork just like any other. The distinction arises because all packets over one interface are mirrored at the other end (see Figure 5.32). A recent modification to X.25 PLP (see [ISO 8208]) permits the protocol to be used for interfacing two DTEs. With this modification the X.25 PLP can be made to operate in a local area network as if each pair of end systems is directly connected, or in a DTE-DTE mode.

Operation of the X.25 PLP in a DTE-DTE mode raises the issue of selection of Logical Channel Number by the two DTEs from a common pool of available numbers. This problem becomes acute when the two DTEs (more or less) simultaneously attempt a call establishment and use the same Logical Channel Number. This results in, what is termed, *Call Collision*. When the protocol is used in DTE-DCE mode, the collisions are resolved in favor of the DTE. Thus, in the case of local area networks, asymmetry can be introduced by requiring that one of the two DTEs takes the role of a DCE, but only for the purpose of selecting Logical Channel Numbers and resolving Call collisions. When the Data Link protocol supports Type 2 operation, the role of DCE is assigned soon after the Data Link connection is established. The station which

---

[29]An abbreviation for Data Circuit-terminating Equipment.

initiated the link establishment assumes the role of a DTE, while the other that of a DCE.

It is important to note that virtual calls established between station A and station B are totally independent of virtual calls that exist between the station A and a station C. That is, the assignment of a logical channel number to a virtual call between stations A and B has no bearing on logical channel numbers of virtual calls between station A and C.

Clearly, a Data Link connection between the two DTEs must exist before a virtual call can be established. As a consequence, a LAN station is required to simultaneously maintain a number of Data Link connections, one for every other station. Because of resource constraints, it is desirable that each Network entity disconnect its Data Link if it determines that the link does not currently support any virtual call.

The Subnetwork Point of Attachment of a LAN station refers to the physical interface between the station and the broadcast channel. Each station is, therefore, identified by its MAC layer station address. For each station on the LAN, the Network service is available at one or more NSAPs, each identified by a distinct NSAP address. Further, addresses exchanged in Call establishment packets are Calling and Called DTE Addresses. The Calling and Called Addresses are instances of the Network Protocol Address Information (NPAI), specific to the use of X.25 PLP. The correspondence between the Called NSAP Address (in the N-CONNECT primitives) and the Called DTE Address (in Call establishment packets) is maintained, as before, by the Network Directory. And, so it is between Calling NSAP and DTE Addresses. Similarly, given a DTE Address, the Network Directory gives the SNPA Address, which in this case is a MAC layer station address.

5.9   Internetworking Protocols

In this section we re-consider internetworking issues from the viewpoint of Network layer protocol. The design of a Network layer protocol is complex since the access protocols used over individual subnetworks may be different or may not fully support the Network service. As a consequence, an internetwork may require a sub-layer of convergence protocol to be implemented to support end-to-end communication. We discuss a protocol that supports connection-less Network service across an internetwork of dissimilar subnetworks. Internetworking of LANs and WANs that use X.25 PLP is also covered in some detail.

5.9.1   Introduction

A communication network may be formed by interconnecting two or more similar, or perhaps dissimilar, communication subnetworks.

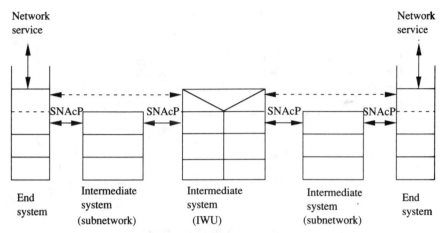

Figure 5.33 Internetworking of subnetworks using an Internetworking Unit.

Although it is transparent to users, it is helpful to consider an inter-network as consisting of distinct subnetworks. It, thereby, enables one to study addressing, subnetwork access protocols and their conversion, where necessary. While it is possible to directly interconnect two net-works with identical subnetwork access protocols to form one internet-work, we shall assume that the two subnetworks are connected using a network layer gateway, or an Inter-Working Unit (IWU) to be precise (also see Figure 5.2(b)).

Figure 5.33 illustrates an internetwork of two subnetworks, con-nected using an IWU. The subnetwork access protocols for the two sub-networks are not necessarily the same. It is important, at this stage, to verify whether the access protocols are rich enough to support all ele-ments of the Network service. Provided, each access protocol is able to directly support the required Network service, the design of the network layer protocol may be simplified (see Section 5.9.2, below). Otherwise, additional procedures need to be defined in the form of a convergence protocol, as was the case with using the 1980 version of X.25 protocol. The two available approaches are discussed in Section 5.9.3.

5.9.2 Interconnection of X.25 Networks

Below we discuss interconnection of subnetworks whose access proto-cols, though not identical, are able to support all elements of the Network service. In particular, we consider interconnection of X.25 (1984 version) based on local area and wide area subnetworks. We have already seen that X.25 (1984 version), as an access protocol, is capable of supporting connection-oriented Network service, and that it can be

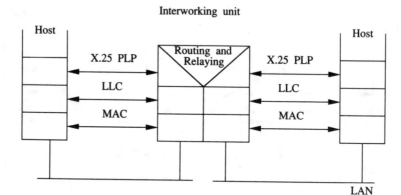

(a) LAN-LAN interconnection.

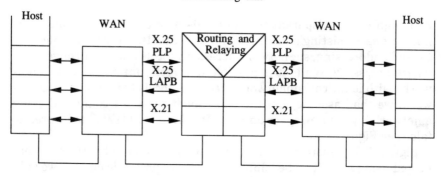

(b) WAN-WAN interconnection.

Figure 5.34 Interconnection of X.25 based LANs and WANs.

implemented over local or wide area networks. It is, therefore, to be expected that an interconnection of X.25 subnetworks using gateways could provide connection-oriented Network service to users in end systems. Figure 5.34 illustrates, respectively, LAN-LAN, WAN-WAN and LAN-WAN interconnections. Clearly, the protocols used at the physical and data link layers on the two sides of the IWU are independent of each other. Further, the operation of X.25 PLP protocols on the two sides is also independent, except that as part of its relay function the IWU relays the events occurring on one subnetwork to the other subnetwork. For example, when a station on subnetwork 1 needs to establish a Network connection with a machine connected to subnetwork 2, an X.25 virtual call is established between a station and the IWU

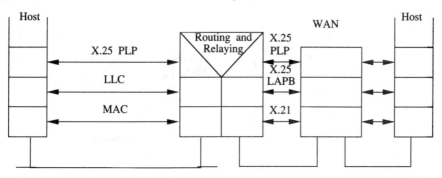

(c) WAN-LAN interconnection.

Figure 5.34 (*Continued*)

across each subnetwork. The IWU (gateway), on its part, relays each event on a virtual call onto the other. Thus from the viewpoint of NS users in end systems, the concatenation of two X.25 virtual calls appears as one X.25 virtual call which can then effectively support the end-to-end Network connection. (See also [ISO 8881.3].)

In the context of wide area public data networks, it is desirable to implement the IWU as two half-gateways, as illustrated in Figure 5.35. This, to some degree, solves the problem of distributed ownership and maintenance of gateways. In such cases, one may use CCITT's X.75 access protocol to link the two gateways (see [CCITT X.75]). The X.75 protocol is very similar to X.25 access protocol, except that it is symmetric. Note that X.25 PLP protocol defines an interface between a DTE and a DCE, which is inherently asymmetric. Symmetry is introduced by requiring that whenever there is a conflict in choosing a logical channel number, the two gateways abort the attempt to simultaneously establish a virtual call. Further, since the two gateways are directly connected, the call establishment procedure is considerably simplified.

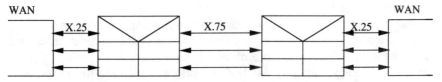

Figure 5.35 Interconnection of X.25 subnetworks using X.75 based half-gateways.

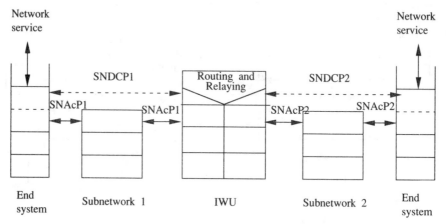

Figure 5.36 Hop-by-hop harmonization: use of a convergence protocol across each subnetwork to support Network service.

5.9.3 Convergence Protocols

Hop-by-hop harmonization. Consider now the case where the internetwork is formed using two subnetworks, but where the access protocol of at least one subnetwork cannot support the required Network service. Figure 5.36 illustrates the situation. One obvious approach to providing end-to-end Network service is to install a sub-layer of protocol over each deficient access protocol. Such a sub-layer of protocol, called *convergence* protocol, implements functions that are essential to provide the required Network service, but are missing from the native access protocol. (In Figure 5.36 the convergence protocols are denoted as SNDCP1 and SNDCP2.) The approach here is similar to the one used to provide connection-oriented Network service using X.25 (1980 version). The context this time, however, is internetworking. As such the convergence protocol is implemented by end systems as well as the gateway. The approach is also referred to as *hop-by-hop harmonization,* and may be used irrespective of whether the subnetwork access protocol is connection-oriented or connection-less, and whether the Network service is connection-oriented or connection-less. Note that the convergence protocols used over each subnetwork are independent. It is the gateway which relays the semantics of events from one subnetwork to another.

As one application of hop-by-hop harmonization, consider providing connection-oriented Network service across an interconnection of two X.25 based subnetworks, one of which uses the 1980 version of X.25 protocol. Clearly, one may use the convergence protocol, discussed earlier, over this subnetwork to provide end-to-end connection-oriented

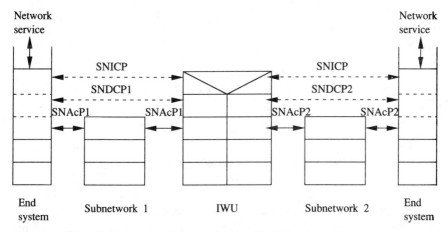

Figure 5.37   Use of an internetwork protocol to provide Network service.

Network service. No such protocol need be implemented over the subnetwork which uses the 1984 version of X.25 recommendation.

Internetwork protocols.   An alternative approach to internetworking requires that a sub-layer of protocol be defined and implemented across the entire internetwork. The protocol is called *Subnetwork Independent Convergence Protocol* (or *SNICP*), and is illustrated in Figure 5.37. Obviously, as the name implies, before such a protocol is defined and implemented, it must be ensured that the service available to it is independent of the access protocols of individual subnetworks, and uniform across the internetwork. In case an individual subnetwork is unable to provide the required service element, then a *Subnetwork Dependent Convergence Protocol* (or *SNDCP*) is implemented over and above its access protocol.

Clearly, using the internetwork protocol approach, the convergence protocol is implemented in two sub-layers. The upper sub-layer is concerned with providing the required Network service, whereas the lower sub-layer tries to iron out the differences between the access protocol of each subnetworks. This approach also simplifies the design of gateways. That is, the gateway simply relays (and routes) the semantics across subnetworks with the sole purpose of supporting the intermediate service required by the subnetwork independent SNICP.

As an example of the application of internetwork protocol, consider the interconnection of two networks, using an X.25 (1984 version) subnetwork. Figure 5.38 suggests a protocol stack that may be used to support connection-less Network service across the internetwork. The

CLNP
LLC Type 1
IEEE 802.x

LAN Host

CLNP	CLNP
	SNDCP
	X.25 PLP
LLC Type 1	X.25 LAPB
IEEE 802.x	X.21

IWU

CLNP
SNDCP
X.25 PLP
X.25 LAPB
X.21·

WAN Host

Figure 5.38 A suggested protocol stack for use over LAN-WAN interconnection.

subnetwork independent SNICP used across the internetwork is the Internetwork Protocol [ISO 8473], discussed later in this chapter. The protocol is capable of directly providing connection-less Network service (see Section 5.7.2). It uses the connection-less Data Link service separately provided over the LAN. The subnetwork dependent convergence protocol used over the X.25 subnetwork enables, for instance, a local gateway to send data in connection-less mode to a remote system connected to the internetwork via the X.25 subnetwork.

5.9.4   Connection-less Network Protocol

The connection-less network protocol (or *CLNP*) is also referred to as an *Internetwork Protocol,* and is intended to be implemented by end systems to provide end-to-end connection-less Network service (see Figure 5.39). It may be used across one subnetwork, or an interconnection of a

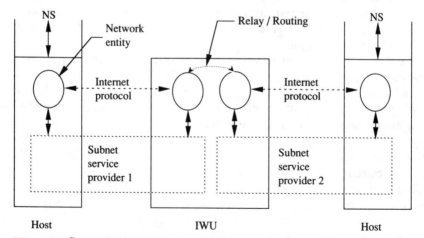

Figure 5.39 Connection-less Internetwork Protocol.

number of subnetworks. Further, it assumes the availability of connection-less data transfer service across each subnetwork. Such a capability
is made available, for instance, by the LLC (Class 1) service in local area
networks, or by an SNDCP protocol running over an X.25 network.

Table 5.20 lists the only services it assumes of the underlying subnetworks. Note that addresses are subnetwork points of attachments,
whose significance is local to each subnetwork. Therefore, it is the responsibility of intermediate IWUs (Network entities, to be sure) to suitably route information through the internetwork, either based upon
routing information that they generate from the given NSAP addresses, or based upon routing information already contained within
the protocol data units (or *PDUs*).

Below we discuss some of the more significant functions implemented by the internetwork protocol (see also Figure 5.39):

1. *Lifetime Control* of PDUs: This function requires that a CLNP
PDU be discarded by an intermediate Network entity, if it is known
that it has been in the internetwork for a sufficiently long time. This
feature helps to simplify the design of a Transport layer protocol that
ensures error-free connection-oriented data transfer across the internetwork. The maximum lifetime of CLNP PDUs is determined using an
estimate of the maximum end-to-end transfer delay.

2. *Segmentation* of PDUs: While the maximum size of user data in
an N-UNITDATA request primitive is 64512 octets, it is rarely the case
that an underlying subnetwork access protocol (or a convergence protocol on top of it) supports such large PDUs. Therefore, the Internetwork protocol permits an NSDU to be transferred as a sequence of
segmented PDUs with the same sequence number (or *Data Unit
Identifier*). Since the segmented PDUs may be transferred through a
number of intermediate subnetworks, each supporting a different maximum permissible PDU size, intermediate IWUs may further segment
the received PDU segments. However, reassembly of PDUs takes place
only at the destination end system.

3. *Routing* of PDUs: Once a CLNP PDU has been composed, the
sending Network entity determines the *next* Network entity to which
the PDU must be sent, as well as the underlying subnetwork to be used

**TABLE 5.20 Subnetwork Service Primitives and
Parameters**

Primitives	Parameters
UNITDATA request/indication	Source SNPA Destination SNPA Quality of Service User Data

to reach the entity. This determination is based upon the Source and Destination NSAP addresses, provided by the NS user as part of N-UNITDATA request primitives. The Network entity may be identified by its *title* or the address of the point of its attachment to the corresponding subnetwork. The underlying subnetwork service is then invoked to transfer the PDU across the subnetwork. Each intermediate Network entity similarly transfers the received PDU to the next (or destination) Network entity.

There is, however, an optional procedure whereby the source Network entity determines either a complete, or partial, route. This route is specified as a sequence of Network entity titles. Each intermediate Network entity must still determine the subnetwork over which it forwards the PDU and the SNPA address of the next Network entity.

The specification of the CLNP protocol, however, gives enough flexibility to the implementors to choose from a collection of subsets of the protocol depending upon the characteristics of the internetwork. For instance, where the Internetwork consists of only one subnetwork, the *Inactive Subset* of the protocol may be implemented where none of the functions described above are available. However, when each subnetwork of the internetwork is capable of supporting large enough PDUs, one may implement the *Non-segmenting Subset* of the protocol where, as the name implies, PDUs are not segmented at all. PDU lifetime control must necessarily be performed. The third option is to implement the full protocol. (For more details, and a description of other optional functions, see [ISO 8473].)

We end the discussion on Internetwork protocol with a figure describing the transfer of an example NSDU supplied by a connection-less NS user. Figure 5.40 illustrates its transfer using the full protocol. The initially composed CLNP PDU is segmented into two PDUs, each of which is then transferred over the two subnetworks. Routing is independently performed by the intermediate IWU as well. The figure also shows the correspondence between issuing of service primitives at the two layer boundaries, and transferring of PDUs within the two sub-layers.

5.10   Summary

The bottom three layers of the OSI architecture are used by Transport entities for providing data transport service across a subnetwork or a collection of connected subnetworks. All characteristics of the physical media and of network interconnection are hidden from Transport layer entities when they use the Network services described in this chapter.

The Physical layer is the lowest layer of the OSI architecture. It provides to its users an ability to send and receive a stream of bits over a

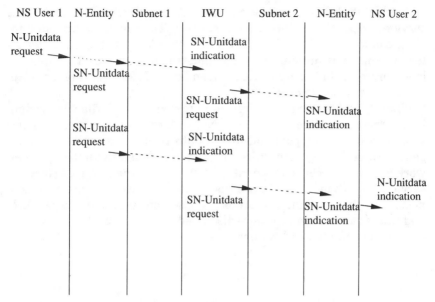

Figure 5.40 Transfer of segmented CLNP PDUs over subnetworks.

physical transmission medium. The Physical service provided by this layer is presented in terms of service primitives that may be issued by Data Link entities. Examples of a protocol at this level include RS 232C, X.21 and IEEE 802.3.

Data Link services include establishment and maintenance of a data link between Network entities in connected neighboring systems. Users may transfer data reliably and without concern for framing, addressing, and detection and recovery from transmission errors over Physical links. Services provided by this layer include connection establishment, connection release, normal data transfer, expedited data transfer, connection reset, error reporting, and connection-less data transfer. Examples of Data Link Protocols include CCITT's X.25 LAPB and IEEE's 802.2 and 802.3. These protocols provide for addressing, frame delimiting, error detection, recovery and sequencing, flow control, and protocol error detection and notification.

The technology used on local area networks requires that the functions of the data link layer be divided into two sub-layers: media access control layer and logical link control layer. Most of the local area networks use a shared medium which must be accessed first before any data transfer can begin. Access to the medium can be controlled using any one of the available media access control schemes. The logical link layer provides the other functions of the data link layer.

The Network layer provides connection-oriented or connection-less services to entities in the Transport layer. The functions provided include connection establishment, connection release, normal data transfer, receipt confirmation, expedited data transfer, and reset. A Network layer protocol, based upon Recommendation X.25, was presented in this chapter in some detail.

When several communication subnetworks with similar or dissimilar characteristics are connected, a Network connection may span a few subnetworks. To support end-to-end data transfer capability, convergence protocols may be required particularly when the native subnetwork access protocol is not capable of supporting the required Network services, or when two or more dissimilar subnetworks are interconnected. In this context, two protocols based on Recommendation X.75 and Internetwork Protocol were discussed. These, respectively, support connection-oriented and connection-less Network services.

6

The Transport Layer

While the Network layer, and those below, provide a path for data transfer between communicating *end* systems, the Transport layer is primarily responsible for providing end-to-end services and ensuring that such communication is largely error-free. In this chapter, we discuss the nature of Transport level services, and the variety of protocols necessary to bridge the gap between the services provided by the Network layer and those desired of the Transport layer. Connection-less Transport services and the required protocol are also discussed.

6.1 The Transport Layer

This section is an overview of the nature of services provided by the Transport layer. We also discuss, briefly, the nature of Network services assumed to be available to the Transport layer. The different classes of protocols are also listed.

The Transport layer is situated between the Network layer and the Session layer (see Figure 6.1). While the Network layer spans the entire collection of open systems, the Transport layer, and those above, have components that are implemented only in *end* open systems, that is, systems where applications are implemented. This is so since all interactions within the Transport layer are end-to-end. Exchange of information between peer Transport entities is made possible by the end-to-end data transfer service provided by the Network layer. The services provided by the Transport layer to user-entities in the Session layer are called *Transport service* (see [ISO 8072, CCITT X.214]). These services ensure efficient and reliable data transfer between Session entities, independent of the underlying communication network or media (see Figure 6.1).

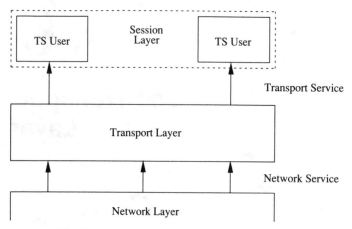

Figure 6.1 The Transport service, its users and the provider.

6.1.1 Data Transfer Characteristics

Elements of the Transport service may be classified into those that are *connection-less* services and those that are *connection-oriented*. In either case, data transfer service may be characterized as being:

1. end-to-end,
2. transparent,
3. independent of the underlying communication media,
4. varied in quality of service,
5. (possibly) reliable, and
6. efficient or optimized.

Let us consider these characteristics.

1. End-to-end data transfer capability is largely derived from the Network service characteristics (see Chapter 5).

2. Transparency of information transfer refers to the fact that the Transport layer places no constraints on the message contents or its coding.

3. Independence from the underlying communication media implies that the users of the Transport service do not experience a difference in the quality of service (or QOS) of Transport service as a result of changes in the Network service or its quality. The QOS of the Network service are substantially dependent on the transmission media used, as well as upon the networking technique employed.

4. The Transport layer may provide a variety of *quality of service.* Provision is thus made for Transport service users (or TS users) to request and to negotiate, among themselves and with the Transport layer, the desired QOS of Transport service. The QOS may be characterized in terms of throughput, transit delay, residual error-rate, and failure probabilities.

5. Provision of *reliable* data transfer facility implies that data will be transferred error-free, loss-free, duplication-free, and possibly in the proper sequence. This functionality may sometimes be derived from the Network service. If not, functions and protocols are defined and implemented as part of the Transport layer to achieve reliability of data transfer. The extent to which reliability is ensured is limited, but is consistent with the negotiated quality of Transport service.

6. Efficiency of data transfer is another major requirement of the Transport service. That is, the Transport service is required to provide the desired QOS by suitably (in fact, optimally) using available Network layer services and other resources. For instance, multiplexing and splitting are particularly relevant in the context of connection-oriented Transport service.

6.1.2 Transport Connections

In the context of Transport services, Session entities are its users, while the Transport layer, and those below, are the provider of Transport service. These services are made available by the TS provider at *Transport-service-access-points* (or TSAPs) to the attached TS users. Transport services may be classified into those that are connection-oriented or connection-less data transfer services, either or both of which may be offered by the Transport layer. Connection-oriented services assume that data transfer can begin only after a connection has been established between the TSAPs, to which the corresponding TS users are attached. Such a connection is referred to as *Transport Connection, or TC.*

A TC is established between two TSAPs on behalf of the attached TS users. Surely, there may exist a number of TCs at a TSAP. Further, there may even exist more that one TC between the same pair of TSAPs. The use of *T-Connection-end-points* (or TCEPs) allows one to distinguish between the various TCs established at the same TSAP. At a TCEP, the TS user and the supporting Transport entity refer to the corresponding TC using a distinct *TCEP-identifier.* Thus, corresponding to each TC, there is an associated pair of TCEP-identifiers, one for each end of the TC. Note, these identifiers need not be the same, since their significance is only local (see Figure 6.2).

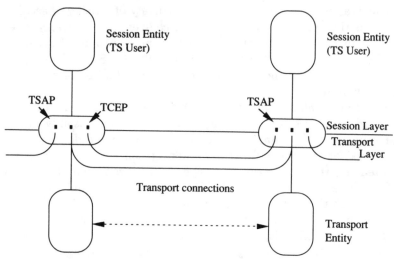

Figure 6.2 A Transport Connection, and its end points.

6.1.3 Connection-Oriented Services

Connection-oriented Transport service includes service-elements to establish or release connections, or to transfer data transparently. Data is normally transferred in the form of *Transport-service-data-units* (or TSDUs). These services are summarized below:

1. TC Establishment: A TS user may establish a TC with another TS user. The address of the TSAP to which the *responding* TS user is attached is assumed to be known to the *initiating* TS user. During TC establishment, a TS user may request, and negotiate with the other TS user and the TS provider, the quality of service to be provided over the TC.

2. TC Release: Either TS user may unilaterally and unconditionally release the TC during its establishment, or subsequently. As one consequence, any data currently in transit may not be delivered, and destroyed.

3. Normal Data Transfer: TS users may exchange data, in the form of TSDUs consisting of an integral number of octets, such that the boundaries between TSDUs and their contents are preserved. The Transport layer may control the rate at which a TS user sends octets of data. Note, that the Transport layer controls the rate of octets of data sent, rather than the rate of TSDUs.

4. Expedited Data Transfer: A limited amount of user data my be transferred by a TS user in the form of Expedited-TSDU. But, this service being provider-optional as well user-optional, is available only if

the TS users agree to use it and the TS provider agrees to provide it. Further, the transfer of Expedited-TSDUs may be subject to a similar, but distinct, flow control by the Transport layer.

6.1.4 Connection-less Services

Connection-less data transfer services, on the other hand, do not require the establishment of a connection prior to the data transfer (see [ISO 8072 AD 1]). Thus, the only service-element available relates to *Connection-less Data Transfer*. A user may transparently transfer a TSDU, of restricted length, to a TS user. The address of the TSAP, to which the receiving TS user is attached, is known to the sending TS user. Each TSDU is sent independent of other TSDUs. While initiating the transfer, the sending TS user may request the desired quality of service that the TS provider must associate with the transfer.

To summarize the discussion thus far, specifications of the TS does not define any class of Transport services, except to distinguish between the two forms of data transfer, viz. connection-oriented and connection-less, and to indicate that expedited data transfer service is optional (see Table 6.1).

6.1.5 Network Services Assumed

In order to provide Transport service, the Transport layer uses the available Network service. The available Network service quality may in some cases be comparable, or even identical, to the Transport service it provides. In that case, the design and the implementation of the Transport layer and its protocol is relatively simple. But when the Network layer provides minimum functionality, or is poor in quality, the Transport layer is fairly complex. In other words, the Transport layer implements those Transport functions that are necessary to bridge the gap between the Network service available to it and the Transport service which it offers.

Two types of Network services may be available. These are, again, connection-oriented and connection-less Network services. It should be

TABLE 6.1 Connection-Oriented and Connection-less Transport Service Elements

Connection-oriented	TC establishment
	Normal data transfer
	Expedited data transfer(Optional)
	TC release
Connection-less	Unit data transfer

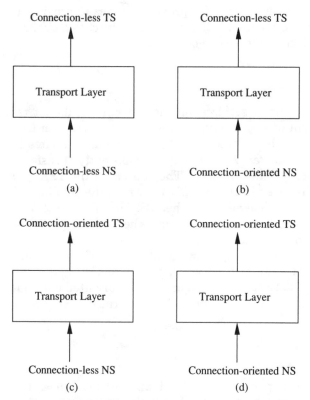

Figure 6.3 Mapping Transport service onto Network service.

possible to build a Transport layer using either of the Network services. In fact, four different combinations seem feasible (see Figure 6.3):

1. The Transport service is connection-less, and uses connection-less Network service.

2. The Transport service is connection-less, but uses connection-oriented Network service.

3. The Transport service is connection-oriented, but uses connection-less Network service.

4. Finally, the Transport service is connection-oriented, and uses connection-oriented Network service.

All four possibilities are recognized within the OSI architecture as a part of its specification of the Transport layer.[1] The most commonly made available services are connection-oriented.

[1]While ISO recognizes the need for both connection-oriented and connection-less Transport service, CCITT has standardized protocols to support connection-oriented Transport service using connection-oriented Network service only (see [CCITT X.224]).

6.1.6   Classes of Transport Protocols

In view of the fact that the Transport layer may support either connection-oriented or connection-less services, and that the nature of available Network service may differ, a variety of Transport level protocols may be defined. Further, the Network service may also differ in quality and the optional connection-oriented services. Thus, aside from defining a Transport protocol for connection-less Transport service (see [ISO 8602]), five different classes of connection-oriented Transport protocols have been defined. These differ primarily on the basis of the range and quality of connection-oriented Transport services that the layer provides, and the quality of connection-oriented Network service (see [ISO 8073,CCITT X.224]). Additionally, a protocol is defined for providing connection-oriented Transport service using a connection-less Network service (see [ISO 8073 DAD 2]). We list the different classes of Transport protocols that have been defined within the OSI architecture.

1. Protocol for providing connection-oriented Transport service using connection-oriented Network service. The five different classes are:
   (a) *Class 0:*   Simple Class,
   (b) *Class 1:*   Basic Error Recovery Class,
   (c) *Class 2:*   Multiplexing Class,
   (d) *Class 3:*   Error Recovery and Multiplexing Class, and
   (e) *Class 4:*   Error Detection and Recovery Class.
2. Protocol for providing connection-less Transport service using connection-less *or* connection-oriented Network service.
3. Protocol for providing connection-oriented Transport service with error detection and recovery using connection-less Network service. This is, in fact, a variation of the Class 4 protocol mentioned above.

These protocols are discussed in detail in later sections of this chapter.

6.2   Service Primitives

From a TS user's viewpoint, the most important description of the Transport service is the collection of service primitives, their associated parameters, and any constraints on issuing or receiving the primitives. These are discussed in this section (see also [ISO 8072, ISO 8072 AD 1]).

6.2.1   Available Primitives

The collection of service primitives that a TS user may issue or receive correspond to the set of service-elements supported by the Transport layer. Table 6.2 lists, for each service-element listed in Table 6.1, the

associated service primitives. Both connection-oriented as well as connection-less Transport services are covered. The table also indicates
whether the service-element is:

confirmed,

unconfirmed, or

provider-initiated.

Note that the service-element *TC Establishment* is, as usual, confirmed, and that *TC Release* is both unconfirmed as well as provider-
initiated. All other service-elements are unconfirmed. For each
service-element separately, the typical sequence in which the corresponding service primitives may be issued by the concerned TS users
and the TS provider are given in Figure 6.4. The fact that these sequences are at all possible is not suggested by Table 6.2. A queue model
of the Transport service, discussed later in Section 6.4, provides details

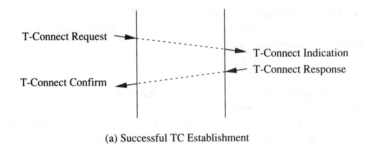

(a) Successful TC Establishment

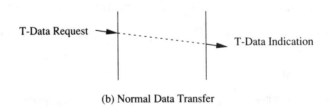

(b) Normal Data Transfer

(c) Expedited Data Transfer

Figure 6.4 Typical sequences pertaining to each service-element of the Transport
service.

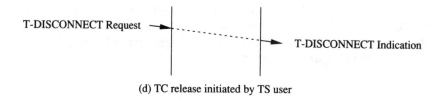

(d) TC release initiated by TS user

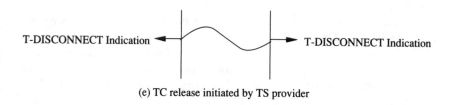

(e) TC release initiated by TS provider

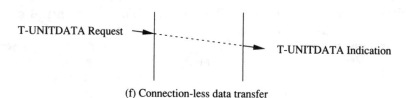

(f) Connection-less data transfer

Figure 6.4 (*Continued*).

TABLE 6.2   Transport Service Primitives

Service element	Nature of confirmation	Primitives
Unit data transfer	unconfirmed	T-UNITDATA request T-UNITDATA indication

(a) Connection-less data transfer.

Service element	Nature of confirmation	Primitives
TC establishment	confirmed	T-CONNECT request T-CONNECT indication T-CONNECT response T-CONNECT confirm
Normal data transfer	unconfirmed	T-DATA request T-DATA indication
Expedited data transfer	unconfirmed	T-EXPEDITED DATA request T-EXPEDITED DATA indication
TC release	unconfirmed, or provider-initiated	T-DISCONNECT request T-DISCONNECT indication

(b) Connection-oriented service primitives.

on the interactions that take place between the TS users and the provider. In the next sub-section we discuss constraints, if any, on issuing a service primitive at a TSAP (in the context of connection-less data transfers) or at a TC end point.

6.2.2   Sequence of Connection-Oriented TS Primitives

In the context of connection-oriented data transfer services, the definition of TS imposes certain constraints on issuing TS primitives by TS users or by the TS provider. These constraints are applicable separately for each connection. That is, issuing of a service primitive pertaining to a connection is in no way constrained by the state of any other connection. Thus, the OSI architecture defines, for each TCEP, a state transition diagram that describes the entire collection of states of a TCEP. It also specifies, for each state, the allowable set of service primitives that may be issued (see Figure 6.5(a)). An identical state transition diagram is applicable to the other corresponding TCEP.

For a given state of the TCEP, if a transition corresponding to a service primitive is not indicated on the diagram, then that service primitive may not be issued, or if issued it shall be ignored. It also defines how the TCEP transitions from its current state to the next state when a service primitive, related to the particular TC, is issued. Also note that the TCEP may remain within a state for any length of time, and the particular transition it makes depends only upon the primitive issued.

6.2.3   Description of State Transitions

Though not suggested by the state transition diagram of Figure 6.5(a), the *T-CONNECT* request primitive may be issued by a TS user at any time. Even if a connection is already in existence, the TS provider initiates the establishment of yet another TC. One may view this as follows: the TS provider has the capability to establish a (fixed) number of TCs from a TSAP, and each corresponding TCEP is initially assumed to be in a state of being *idle*. When a T-CONNECT request primitive is issued by the TS user (or when a T-CONNECT indication primitive is issued by the TS provider), one of the idle TCEPs is selected, and associated with the connection being established. The state of the TCEP as a consequence changes. When a TC is released, the corresponding TCEP moves to the *idle* state. This TCEP is now available to support yet another TC. Additional comments on the state transition diagram of Figure 6.5(a) are given below.

1. The procedure to establish a TC may be unsuccessful if the responding TS user rejects an incoming connection request, made by

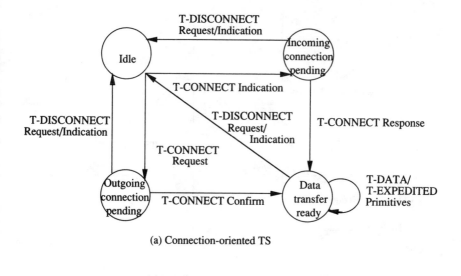

(a) Connection-oriented TS

Idle   T-UNITDATA
        Request/Indication

(b) Connection-less TS

Figure 6.5 State transition description of constraints on issuing of primitives.

the TS provider on behalf of the initiating TS user. This is indicated in Figure 6.6(a). The responding TS user may reject the connection for a variety of reasons including its inability to interwork with the initiating TS user, or lack of resources, or failure of negotiation for the quality of service or optional service-elements.

2. As illustrated in Figure 6.6(b) the TC Establishment procedure may terminate prematurely before its completion if the TS provider itself were to reject the establishment of the connection for any reason. These include lack of resources, responding TS user is unknown, or its inability to support the requested QOS or optional services.

3. The procedure to release the connection may be initiated at any time by either TS user or by the TS provider with a view to disconnect the established TC or to abandon the TC establishment procedure. Note that since an identical state transition diagram is applicable at each TCEP, the procedure may even be initiated simultaneously by a TS user at one end, and the other TS user or the TS provider at the other end (see Figure 6.6(c), (d)).

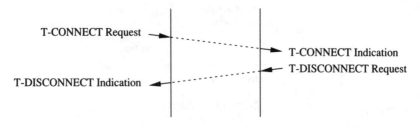

(a) Rejection of TC establishment by TS user

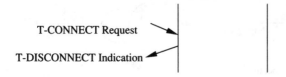

(b) Rejection of TC establishment by TS provider

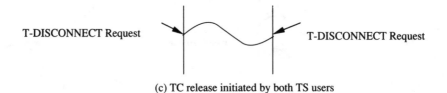

(c) TC release initiated by both TS users

(d) TC release initiated by TS user and TS provider

Figure 6.6 Additional sequences pertaining to TS primitives.

4. Since the state transition diagram of Figure 6.5(a) does not place any constraint, within *Data Transfer Ready* state, on issuing of *T-DATA* or *T-EXPEDITED DATA* primitives, both (normal) data transfer and expedited data transfer are *two-way simultaneous* data transfer services. These services are invoked using, respectively, T-DATA request and T-EXPEDITED DATA request primitives, but only after a TC has been established.

5. TS provider makes every attempt, consistent with the QOS negotiated, to preserve the integrity, sequence, and boundaries of TSDUs (normal as well as expedited) being transferred. Although the TS

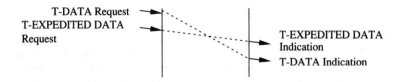

(e) Transfer of TSDU and Expedited TSDU

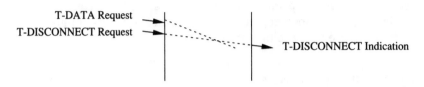

(f) Loss of data when TC release initiated by sending TS users

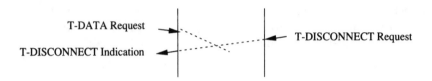

(g) Loss of data when TC release initiated by receiving TS user

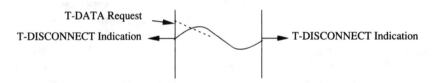

(h) Loss of data when TC release initiated by TS provider

Figure 6.6 (*Continued*)

provider may not attempt to transfer Expedited TSDUs on a priority basis, it does guarantee that an Expedited TSDU will not be delivered after any subsequently submitted normal TSDU or Expedited TSDU (see Figure 6.6(e)). This is discussed in greater detail as part of the queue model of TS, in Section 6.4.

6. Issuing of *T-DISCONNECT* request or indication by the TS provider or by a TS user may result in a TSDU, or Expedited TSDU, not being delivered. This is depicted in Figure 6.6(f) to (h). (See also the discussion on a queue model in Section 6.4.)

6.2.4   Sequence of Connection-less TS Primitives

A similar, though much simpler, description is available for connection-less data transfer primitives. Since connection-less data transfer is a single access service, the corresponding state transition diagram is defined for each TSAP (see Figure 6.5(b)). Clearly, from the state transition diagram, there are no constraints imposed upon issuing of connection-less service primitives. Further, issuing of a connection-less service primitive does not in any way influence the issuing of a connection-oriented service primitive.

6.3   Primitive Parameters

A specification of service primitives requires that each of its parameters be listed together with the range of values it may take. There may, however, be additional constraints on values assigned to them. In this section we discuss the parameters associated with each TS primitive, both connection-less as well as connection-oriented.

6.3.1   Parameter Values

Associated with each primitive, there is a set of none, one, or more parameters. The parameters of the various primitives associated with a particular service-element are not necessarily the same. Thus, a parameter p, for instance, may be present in a request primitive, but may be absent from the corresponding indication primitive. Furthermore, some of the parameters are optional, while the presence of another parameter may depend upon the value of one or more parameters in a preceding primitive, or upon whether certain optional services have been selected or not.

Aside from specifying the collection of parameters for each service primitive, a layer standard also specifies the data types of each parameter, and the meaning to be associated with its assigned value. The standard does not, however, specify the coding of the parameters, since that is an issue that relates to the design of an interface between a service-user and the service-provider.

When a parameter is common to two or more service primitives pertaining to the same service-element, the values assigned to the parameter may be constrained by the value assigned to the parameter in a preceding primitive. For instance, the value of a parameter p in an indication primitive may be required to be assigned a value that is "less than or equal" to its value in the corresponding request primitive.

The parameters associated with each TS primitive are given in Tables 6.3 to 6.7. The primitives are grouped together so that parame-

TABLE 6.3 Parameters of T-CONNECT Primitives

Parameter	T-CONNECT			
	request	indication	response	confirm
Called Address	X	X		
Calling Address	X	X(=)		
Responding Address			X	X(=)
Expedited data option	X	X(=)	X	X(=)
Quality of service	X	X	X	X(=)
TS user data	X(U)	X(=)	X(U)	X(=)

Note:
X: mandatory parameter,
.(=): parameter value is same as in previous primitive,
(U): user optional.

TABLE 6.4 Parameters of the T-DATA Primitive

Parameter	T-DATA	
	request	indication
TS user data	X	X(=)

Note: see also Table 6.3.

TABLE 6.5 Parameters of the T-EXPEDITED-DATA Primitive

Parameter	T-EXPEDITED DATA	
	request	indication
TS user data	X	X(=)

Note: see also Table 6.3.

TABLE 6.6 Parameters of the T-DISCONNECT Primitive

Parameter	T-DISCONNECT	
	request	indication
Reason		X
TS user data	X(U)	X(=)

Note: see also Table 6.3.

TABLE 6.7 Parameters of the T-UNITDATA Primitive

Parameter	T-UNITDATA	
	request	indication
Calling Address	X	X(=)
Called Address	X	X(=)
Quality of service	X	X
TS user data	X	X(=)

Note: see also Table 6.3.

ters of primitives pertaining to the same service-element may be discussed at the same time. Below we discuss the interpretation of some of the parameters, and make additional comments as necessary.

6.3.2 T-CONNECT Primitive Parameters

Parameters of the T-CONNECT primitives are listed in Table 6.3. Note that the parameters *Calling Address* and *Called Address* refer to the addresses of TSAPs to which the initiating TS user and the intended responding TS user are bound. Typically, the *Called Address* would be obtained by the initiating TS user from the Session layer directory or by using its mapping function. Further, since there is no notion of *redirection* (see Chapter 5), the parameter *Called Address* in a T-CONNECT indication primitive is required to be the same as that in the corresponding T-CONNECT request primitive. Other comments follow:

1. As of now, the actual TS user responding to a connection request must be the TS user, the address of which is specified in *Called Address*. But note that there is a distinct *Responding Address* parameter in the T-CONNECT response and confirm primitives, which is the address of the TSAP to which the responding TS user is, in fact, attached. This suggests that in the future *generic addressing* may be used, in which case the two *Responding Address* and *Called Address* may be different.

2. The *Expedited Data Option* parameter allows the two TS users to negotiate the use of expedited data transfer facility. Note that the value of the parameter in the T-CONNECT indication primitive is identical to its value in the corresponding request primitive. Similar constraints also apply to the value of the parameter in response and confirm primitives. This suggests that the TS provider plays a passive role in the negotiation. Since the negotiated value is known to the TS provider, it must provide expedited data transfer service, if it provides it and the users negotiate its use. If expedited data transfer service is unavailable the TS provider rejects the connection establishment request.

3. The *quality of service* parameter is, in fact, a collection of a number of sub-parameters, one for each measure of QOS. Performance-related QOS parameters of the TS are (see Chapter 3 for their definitions):

- TC Establishment Delay,
- TC Establishment Failure Probability,
- Throughput,
- Transit Delay,
- Residual Error Rate,
- Transfer Failure Probability,
- TC Resilience,

- TC Release Delay, and

- TC Release Failure Probability.

Features of the connection that may be negotiated include:

- TC Protection, and

- Priority.

4. While the value of a QOS parameter in the T-CONNECT request primitive may be any one of the defined values, the value of the parameter in other primitives are constrained by its value in the preceding primitive. To be specific, its value in the confirm primitive must be identical to its value in the response primitive. Further, the parameter value in the response primitive may be the same as its value in the corresponding indication primitive, or *poorer*. Similarly, its value in the indication primitive can be no better than its value in the request primitive (except in case of TC Protection). This, in fact, is a mechanism to specify the negotiation procedure. The initiating TS user specifies the desired level of QOS in the request primitive, while the TS provider may agree to provide a poorer level of service. The responding TS user still has the option to lower the QOS by suitably assigning values to QOS parameters. In effect, the negotiation procedure determines the lowest level of quality of service that is desired or available.

5. The set of possible values for each QOS parameter (and its default value, if any) are normally specified at the time of installation of the TS provider. In some implementations, the value of each parameter may be fixed, in which case negotiation of the QOS parameter value is not required.

6. The parameter *TS User-Data* is user-optional. When present the number of octets is at least 1, but no more than 32. Such information is transferred transparently, and may be used by the responding TS user to determine for itself whether it should accept the incoming connection. Further, the quality of service associated with this transfer of user-data has no relation to the negotiated QOS.

6.3.3 Parameters of Other Connection-Oriented Primitives

The following comments are made regarding the parameters of other connection-oriented primitives, listed in Tables 6.4 through 6.6:

1. The parameter *TS User-Data* is mandatory in both T-DATA and T-EXPEDITED DATA primitives. The parameter is optional in a T-DISCONNECT request primitive. Its value in an indication primitive is necessarily the same as its value in the corresponding request primitive.

2. There is no restriction on the number of octets of user-data in a T-DATA primitive, since user-data may anyway be broken down into a

number of packets (viz., segmented). However, in a T-EXPEDITED DATA primitive, user-data is limited to 16 octets, while in a T-DIS-CONNECT primitive it is limited to 64 octets. This is so, since segmentation is not applicable to transfer of expedited data, or to connection release.

3. User-data (as provided in a request primitive) is transferred transparently over the TC and delivered in an indication primitive. User-data in a T-DISCONNECT primitive may not be delivered in case the release procedure is simultaneously initiated either by the TS provider or by the corresponding TS user.

4. The parameter *Reason* is contained only in the T-DISCONNECT indication primitive, and is used to indicate to the receiving TS user the originator of the release procedure. In case the originator is the TS provider, it also indicates the reason why the release procedure was initiated. But when the originator of the release procedure is a TS user, additional information may be included by the TS user in the form of TS User-Data.

6.3.4　The Parameter TCEP Identifier

The parameter *TCEP-Identifier* is used by the TS provider and the attached TS user to uniquely identify the TC at one end of a connection. The manner in which such an identifier is assigned a value, and its use, is an issue that is local to the interface and as such implementation dependent. Therefore, its specification is not covered by the OSI architecture. But surely, with issuing of every primitive there is a parameter associated with the identifier.

6.3.5　Parameters of T-UNITDATA

Table 6.7 lists the parameters of the T-UNITDATA primitives used to transfer data on a connection-less basis. The parameters *Calling Address* and *Called Address* refer to the addresses of TSAPs to which the sending and receiving TS users are attached. The addressing mechanism is the same as that used in connection-oriented data transfers. The *quality of service* parameter is a list of sub-parameters, viz.

- Transit Delay,

- Protection from Unauthorized Access, and

- Residual Error Rate.

Their definitions are the same as those for connection-oriented data transfer. The values of the QOS parameters are not negotiated. However, a TS user, as a part of its *a-priori* knowledge, is aware of the quality of service that a TS provider is capable of providing. How such knowledge is acquired is outside the scope of OSI architecture specification. Inclusion of *TS-User-Data* is mandatory. The number of octets is not limited by the service specification. It may, however, be constrained by an implementation.

6.4   A Model of Transport Service

A model of the Transport service describes, in a somewhat formal manner, the interactions that take place at one TSAP (or at a TCEP), and relates these to the interactions that result at another corresponding TSAP (or TCEP). This model is only an abstraction, and may only be used to guide an implementation of the Transport layer.

6.4.1   A Queue Model of Transport Connection

The queue model of a TC relates issuing of TS primitives at a TCEP with issuing of TS primitives at the corresponding TCEP at the other end of the connection. Figure 6.7 illustrates the queue model of a TC. (It is very similar to that of a Network Connection (see Chapter 5).) Two queues (one for each direction of communication) are associated with each TC. An interaction between a TS user and the TS provider at a TCEP results in a queue object being added to the outgoing queue, or an object being deleted from the incoming queue. There are no restrictions on placing objects in the queue, or on removing them, except those that follow from the constraints suggested by the state transition diagrams of Figure 6.5.

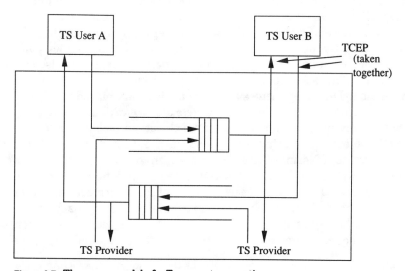

Figure 6.7 The queue model of a Transport connection.

In case a request or a response primitive is issued by a TS user, a corresponding queue object is added to the outgoing queue. The TS provider may also place objects in either queue. This corresponds to the initiation of a provider-initiated service-element. When an object is removed from the incoming queue, it corresponds to issuing of an indication or confirm primitive by the TS provider. Normally, an object is removed in a First-In-First-Out order by the TS user.

The TS provider may, under certain situations, alter the sequence of objects in the queues, or even delete one or more of these objects. The two queue operations correspond, respectively, to expediting user data, or to discarding user data in case of simultaneous release of the connection by the two users, or by a user and the TS provider.

6.4.2 Queue Objects

The objects that may be placed by a TS user in an outgoing queue are:

1. Connect objects,
2. Octets of Normal Data,
3. Indication of End-of-TSDU,
4. Expedited TSDUs, and
5. Disconnect objects.

The TS provider may only place a *Disconnect object* in the queues. Placing of a *Connect object* represents the issuing of a T-CONNECT request or response primitive. Similarly, issuing of a T-CONNECT indication or confirm primitive by the TS provider is represented in the queue model by removal of a Connect object from the incoming queue. An *Expedited TSDU,* or a *DISCONNECT object,* when placed in a queue, or removed from a queue, similarly represents the issuing of a corresponding request or an indication primitive. From the viewpoint of the model, each queue object is not only identifiable, but it also carries with it information contained in the primitive.

In case of T-DATA primitives a string of objects are placed in a queue or removed from a queue. These are *Octets of Normal Data* followed by (without interruption by any other queue object) an *Indication of End-of-TSDU* object. The latter, as the name suggests, terminates the string of Octets of Normal Data. This approach to model the service-element (normal) Data Transfer is convenient, since flow control can then be discussed in terms of the number of user data octets, rather than the number of normal TSDUs.[2] Additionally, the approach avoids having to make any assumption on how a TSDU is segmented. Further, a T-DATA request primitive is said to have been issued only with the

---

[2]The capacity of each queue is not constrained by the service specification. An implementation may, however, impose a limit on the number of Octets of Data that may be entered into the queue.

placement of the corresponding Indication of End-of-TSDU. Similarly, with the removal of an Indication of End-of-TSDU, the corresponding T-DATA indication is said to have been issued. As a consequence, issuing of a T-DATA primitive may be considered as an atomic action.

6.4.3 Creation and Destruction of Queues

The two queues are created and associated with the particular pair of TCEPs as soon as a T-CONNECT request primitive is issued by a TS user. The TSAPs are those identified by the Calling Address and Called Address. The queues are initialized to being empty. Thereafter, a Connect object (representing the issuing of a T-CONNECT request primitive) is placed in the outgoing queue by the initiating TS user. A queue is destroyed (or becomes dissociated) as soon as a Disconnect object is removed from it by a TS user, or deleted by the TS provider.[3]

6.4.4 Re-ordering and Deletion of Objects

Queue objects are removed from a queue by a TS user primarily in a First-In-First-Out order. However, some objects may be moved ahead of others. Expedited Data objects may move ahead of Octets of Normal Data and an Indication of End-of-TSDU. Similarly, a Disconnect object *may* move ahead of other queue objects. In fact, when a Disconnect object is moved ahead of others, it does so by deleting them. This corresponds to an initiation of a TC Release procedure.

There is, however, an exception to the above. When a Disconnect object deletes a Connect object, it deletes itself as well. In other words, if the TS provider were to reject an attempt to establish a TC, then the attempt is aborted half way, and the TS user at the Called Address would neither receive a T-CONNECT indication nor a T-DISCONNECT indication.

6.4.5 Connection-less Data Transfer

The queue model of connection-less data transfer service relates issuing of a T-UNITDATA request primitive at a TSAP with issuing of a corresponding T-UNITDATA indication primitive at a TSAP, the address of which is specified as the value of the parameter *Called Address* in the request primitive. As an aid to understanding the model, consider an arbitrary ordered pair of TSAPs, (A, B). To this pair of TSAPs, a queue may be permanently associated from TSAP A to TSAP B. When a T-UNITDATA request primitive is issued at TSAP A, a *Unitdata* object is inserted at the tail of the outgoing queue. When a Unitdata object is removed from the queue by the attached TS user, this action

---

[3]In the context of a Transport layer there is no concept of the queues being re-initialized.

corresponds to issuing of a T-UNITDATA indication primitive by the TS provider at the corresponding TSAP. The TS provider may *not* add any object to the queue. Thus, the only type of objects in the queue are Unitdata object.

Normally, objects are removed from the queue in a First-In-First-Out order. However, the TS provider may discard objects, duplicate objects, or re-order Unitdata objects. That is, there is no guarantee that data contained in UNITDATA primitives will be delivered or that it will be not be duplicated or re-ordered.

6.5   Transport Protocols

Since there is a great variability in the Transport service to be provided and the Network service that may be available, a number of classes of Transport protocols are defined. In this section (and subsequent ones), we discuss protocols required for connection-oriented as well as connection-less Transport services (see also [ISO 8073, ISO 8602] and [CCITT X.224]).

The responsibility of providing Transport services, described earlier, lies with the TS provider. Since its TS users are spread across open systems, implementation of a TS provider is in the form of a collection of cooperating *Transport entities*. Communication between Transport entities residing in different open systems must conform to a set of rules and procedures, so that there is no ambiguity in interpreting received messages. These rules are specified as a part of a Transport protocol . Further, communication between Transport entities requires that there be available some Network service, using which data units of the Transport protocol may be exchanged.

From the viewpoint of standardization, aspects of communication that are open and subject to standardization are those that are related to services and to protocol only. A protocol standard specifies in a detailed manner the semantics and syntax of all messages communicated between peer entities. Syntactical issues are important in the context of protocol specification, since a receiver must decipher from the received bits and bytes the message being encoded. The mapping of service primitives onto messages communicated is equally important, but only from the viewpoint of ensuring that a protocol achieves the goals of providing the defined Transport service(s). Similarly, specification of the manner in which a Transport entity uses the available Network service enables a common view of how Transport protocol data units are transferred.

6.5.1   Network Services

Recall, from Sections 6.1 and 6.2, that connection-oriented Transport service includes the following service elements:

1. TC Establishment,
2. TC Release,
3. Normal Data Transfer, and optionally
4. Expedited Data Transfer.

To provide these services, the Transport layer implements a number of functions that are necessary to bridge the gap between the Transport service it provides and the available Network service. Flow control, multiplexing, segmentation, error detection and recovery, and expedited data transfer are some example functions that may be implemented by the Transport layer. The range of functions to be implemented depends not only upon whether or not expedited data transfer service is to be provided, but also upon the availability of certain optional Network layer services and their quality.

The Network layer may provide either connection-oriented or connection-less data transfer service. Below, we list the elements of the Network service that are assumed to be available to the Transport layer. (In the following NC refers to a Network Connection (see also Chapter 5).)

Connection-oriented NS

1. NC Establishment,
2. NC Release,
3. Normal Data Transfer,
4. NC Reset, and optionally
5. Expedited Data Transfer, and
6. Data Acknowledgement.

Connection-less NS

1. Connection-less Data Transfer.

It is assumed that Expedited Data Transfer and Data Acknowledgement services are optionally provided, and that their use is negotiated in providing connection-oriented TS. Further, a protocol for *connectionless* TS does not make use of NC Reset, Data Acknowledgement, and Expedited Data transfer services.

6.5.2   Types of Network Connection

The quality of connection-oriented NS is largely characterized in terms of the *residual error rate* and the *frequency of occurrence of signalled failures* over a Network connection. As discussed in Chapter 3, residual error rate is the estimated probability that user data is transferred with error, that it is lost, that a duplicate copy is delivered, or that these are delivered out-of-sequence. Frequency of signalled failures is similar to *resilience*. The difference is that only *signalled* NC release or reset are considered while computing the frequency of signalled failures. Based on this characterization, an NC may be classified as one of the following types:

Type A: A network connection with an acceptably low residual error rate and an acceptably low rate of signalled failures.

Type B: A network connection with an acceptably low residual error rate, but which has an unacceptably high rate of signalled failures.

Type C: A network connection which has an unacceptably high residual error rate.

From the viewpoint of Transport layer protocol design, a high residual error rate is considered to be far more serious, thereby requiring a fairly complex protocol to carry out error detection and recovery. Thus, it is immaterial whether a Type C network connection has a low frequency of signalled failures or not. Further, the design of Transport protocol for use over a connection-less NS is likely to be as complex as the one that uses a Type C network connection, since they both exhibit similar error characteristics.

6.5.3   Protocol Classes

In view of the above classification of Network services (and of network connections), and the fact that Expedited Data service is optional, a variety of Transport protocols have been defined. These are:

1. protocols for providing connection-oriented Transport service using connection-oriented NS. Depending upon the type of connections available, either one or more of the following five classes of protocols may be implemented:
   (a) *Class 0:*   Simple Class (TP0),
   (b) *Class 1:*   Basic Error Recovery Class (TP1),
   (c) *Class 2:*   Multiplexing Class (TP2),
   (d) *Class 3:*   Error Recovery and Multiplexing Class (TP3), and
   (e) *Class 4:*   Error Detection and Recovery Class (TP4).
2. protocol for providing connection-oriented Transport service using a connection-less Network service.
3. protocol for providing connection-less Transport service using connection-less or connection-oriented Network service.

6.5.4 Connection-Oriented Transfer Protocols

We shall first discuss the five different classes of Transport protocols that use connection-oriented NS.

TP0—Simple class protocol. This class of protocol may only be implemented when a Type A network connection is available. As such its implementation is relatively simple, but it provides for minimum functionality, including:

1. connection establishment (with negotiation of TPDU size),
2. data transfer with segmentation and reassembly of TSDUs,
3. reporting and treatment of protocol errors, and
4. implicit release of TC, and
5. error release of TC in case of NC reset or release.

TC Release is specifically not implemented as part of the Transport Protocol, but is derived from the supporting NS. To be sure, the lifetime of a TC is directly related to that of the supporting NC. This mechanism is also referred to as *implicit variant* of *normal* TC Release procedure. Whenever a T-DISCONNECT request is issued by a TS user, the NC Release procedure is initiated. As a consequence, it is not possible to multiplex a number of TCs over an NC. There is, thus, a one-to-one correspondence between a TC and an NC. The other variant, where TPDUs are exchanged between Transport entities to release the TC, is called *explicit* variant of normal TC release. A TC may also be released when a protocol error is detected (as a consequence of NC reset or NC release), a function known as *Error Release,* or when a connection establishment request is turned down by the responding Transport entity (also called *Connection Refusal*).

Flow control is not explicitly part of the TP0 protocol. Any flow control exercised over the corresponding NC is visible to the user of the TC. As such, Expedited Data transfer service is not provided as part of TS. The collection of functions needed to support this protocol are listed in Table 6.8, and discussed in the next section.

TP1—Basic error recovery class protocol. This protocol may be implemented only when a Type B network connection is available, that is, where the frequency of signalled failures is unacceptably high. It extends Class 0 features by:

1. recovery from NC reset and release,
2. storage of TPDUs until acknowledged,
3. explicit release of Transport connection,

TABLE 6.8   Applicable Procedures to Each Protocol Class

Procedure	Protocol Class				
	TP0	TP1	TP2	TP3	TP4
Assignment to Network Connection	*	*	*	*	*
Transfer of TPDUs	*	*	*	*	*
Connection Establishment	*	*	*	*	*
Connection Refusal	*	*	*	*	*
Normal Release	*1)	*	*	*	*
Association of TPDUs with TC	*	*	*	*	*
Treatment of Protocol Errors	*	*	*	*	*
Segmentation and Reassembly	*	*	*	*	*
Concatenation and Separation		*	*	*	*
Data TPDU Numbering		*2)	*3)	*	*
Expedited Data Transfer		*	*	*	*
Multiplexing and Demultiplexing			*	*	*
Flow Control			*	*	*
Error Release	*		*		
Retention of TPDUs until Acknowledged		*		*	*
Resynchronization		*		*	*
Reassignment after Failure		*		*	*
Frozen References		*		*	*
Inactivity Control					*
Checksum					*
Splitting and Recombining					*
Retransmission on Timeout					*
Resequencing					*

Note:
1) Implicit release
2) Normal PDU numbering
3) Normal and extended PDU numbering

4. concatenation and separation, and

5. TPDU numbering and resynchronization.

The most important distinction between Class 1 and Class 0 protocols is that the Transport Connection and its supporting NC have independent lifetimes. That is, the TC is explicitly released whenever desired, while the supporting NC may or may not be released. Further, and as its name implies, the protocol incorporates mechanisms to recover from signalled failures. Upon disconnection of the supporting NC, the Transport layer attempts to establish yet another NC. A resynchronization procedure is initiated to ensure loss-free, duplication-free, in-sequence delivery of TS user data. An identical resynchronization procedure is invoked when the NC resets. The resynchronization procedure is totally transparent to the TS user. (Note that the protocol is unable to *detect* occurrence of errors.)

The first requirement of the error recovery procedure is that Transport-PDUs (or TPDUs) containing data must be numbered.

Further, TPDUs containing user data must be retained by the sender till they are acknowledged by the receiver. One variant, known as *confirmation of receipt,* of the acknowledgement procedure uses the N-DATA-ACKNOWLEDGE service, if available. The other variant uses an acknowledgement function specifically implemented as part of the TP1 protocol, and is known as the AK variant of acknowledgement. Its implementation is mandatory, while the former variant may only be used if the corresponding N-DATA-ACKNOWLEDGE service is available and its use has been negotiated by the two Transport entities at the time of connection establishment.

As with TP0 protocol, flow control is not explicitly implemented as a part of the Class 1 protocol. However, the Network level flow control is visible over the TC. Expedited transfer of user data is achieved either using an available Network layer expedited data transfer service, or by transferring, on a priority basis, TPDUs containing user Expedited data. The latter uses normal data transfer facility over the supporting NC. The two variants are, respectively, called *network express* and *network normal* variants of Expedited Data Transfer.

TP2—Multiplexing class protocol. This class of protocol, used over a Type A NC, is similar to Simple Class (Class 0) protocol, except that a number of TCs may be multiplexed onto a single NC. Necessarily then, a number of *additional* functions must be implemented, including:

1. explicit release of TC,
2. explicit flow control,
3. expedited data transfer,
4. TPDU numbering and acknowledgement, and
5. concatenation and separation.

Implementation of flow control function is mandatory, but its use by the Transport entities is negotiable. In case two TCs are multiplexed onto an NC, and flow control is not used over one of them, then the throughput over the other TC may be substantially poorer. Flow control requires that each TPDU containing user data be numbered. But such TPDUs need not be retained since their delivery is guaranteed by the Type A NC. Similarly, implementation of expedited data transfer function is mandatory. It may, however, not be used if use of flow control is not negotiated.

Recovery from errors is unnecessary, since the supporting NC provides acceptable residual error and signalled failure characteristics. If a protocol error is detected, then the corresponding TC is released (as is the case with TP0 protocol).

TP3—Error recovery and multiplexing class protocol. This class of protocol combines the functionality of both Class 1 and Class 2 protocols. It is used with Type B Network Connections. It provides for multiplexing as well as error recovery from signalled failures. Flow control and expedited data transfer are an essential set of functions to be implemented, and must be used to support Transport services.

TP4—Error detection and recovery class protocol. Class 4 Error Detection and Recovery protocol is applicable when the supporting NC is of Type C, where the residual error rate is higher than the acceptable limit. In other words, TPDUs may be lost, corrupted with errors, duplicated, reordered, or unduly delayed, during transit between the communicating Transport entities. Further, the supporting NC may be reset or released, although such failures are signalled. The Class 4 protocol as a consequence is extremely complex. Aside from implementing certain functions, discussed earlier in the context of other protocols, the protocol incorporates mechanisms for error detection, retransmission of TPDUs, and resequencing. These functions are similar, though more complex than those that are employed at the data link layer to ensure reliable communication between entities over a point-to-point link.

It extends Class 3 features by:

1. inactivity control,
2. checksum,
3. splitting and recombining, and
4. control of PDUs regarding loss, duplication and sequencing errors.

The set of functions applicable to Class 4 protocol is listed in Table 6.8. A more complete discussion of this protocol must wait till we have specifically discussed each function (see Section 6.6).

Consider the five classes of protocols discussed above, it is evident that the protocols are increasingly complex, although there is no strict hierarchy in terms of functions employed. Further, within each *class* of protocols there are a number of options that are negotiated at the time of connection establishment.

6.5.5   Connection-less Transfer Protocol

This protocol specifies the procedures necessary to provide connection-less data transfer service between two TS users. The procedures, aimed at moving a user TSDU from one TSAP to another, are extremely simple, since the supporting Transport entities do not have to ensure reliable delivery of user data. Further, since connection-less data transfer service is on a per TSDU basis, these procedures do not relate transfer of one TSDU with another. As a consequence, procedures for acknowledgement, flow control, multiplexing, error recovery, etc. are not relevant.

The connection-less data transfer protocol may either use the available connection-less Network service or connection-oriented Network service. As such the protocol defines two variations of a procedure to transfer Transport layer protocol-data-units, one for each type of available Network service. Error detection may optionally be carried out to enable a receiving Transport entity to detect, and thus discard, TPDUs that contain transmission errors.

6.6 Connection-Oriented Protocol

In the preceding section reference was made to a number of functions, for example, flow control, multiplexing, etc. But there are many more needed to implement the different classes of connection-oriented protocols. In this section we discuss each function and the associated procedure.

With each function, there is an associated procedure which specifies the details of all communications that take place between peer Transport entities, and how such communication is affected using an available Network service. As to when a function is invoked, is not of particular concern here. There may be a correspondence between issuing of TS primitives and invoking of these procedures. This correspondence is partly specified as part of state table description of each protocol (see Section 6.8). For instance, when a TS user issues a T-EXPEDITED DATA request primitive, the supporting Transport entity invokes the expedited data transfer procedure. On the other hand, multiplexing is used within the Transport layer to provide efficient and cost-effective data transfer service.

6.6.1 Transport-Protocol-Data-Units

Each procedure describes communication between Transport entities in terms of TPDUs exchanged between them. It specifies the contents of each TPDU and the interpretation that a receiving Transport entity associates with each TPDU and its parameters.

The collection of TPDUs required to implement each class of connection-oriented Transport protocols is listed in Table 6.9. Note that some of the TPDUs are used only when certain options are negotiated in protocol Classes 1 and 2. The encoding of TPDUs is discussed in Section 6.9.

The following functions are commonly used in all classes of protocols that support connection-oriented TS and use connection-oriented NS. We shall discuss the related procedure for each of these:

1. Assignment to Network Connection,
2. Transfer of TPDUs,
3. Connection Establishment,
4. Connection Refusal,
5. Connection Release,
6. Association of TPDUs with TC,

TABLE 6.9   Applicable TPDUs for Each Protocol Class

TPDUs	Protocol Class				
	TP0	TP1	TP2	TP3	TP4
CR: Connection Request	*	*	*	*	*
CC: Connection Confirm	*	*	*	*	*
DR: Disconnect Request	*	*	*	*	*
DC: Disconnect Confirm		*	*	*	*
DT: Data	*	*	*	*	*
ED: Expedited Data		*	NF	*	*
AK: Data Acknowledgement		NRC	NF	*	*
EA: Expedited Data Acknowledgement		*	NF	*	*
RJ: Reject		*		*	
ER: TPDU Error	*	*	*	*	*

Note:
*: TPDU is always used,
NF: not available when non-explicit flow control is selected,
NRC: not available when receipt confirmation is selected.

7.   Treatment of Protocol Errors, and

8.   Segmentation and Reassembly.

6.6.2   Assignment to Network Connection

Each Transport connection is supported using a Network connection. That is, TPDUs concerning a TC are sent over an NC assigned to it. This assignment of a TC is made at the time of TC establishment. The procedure for *Assignment to Network Connection* enables a pair of communicating Transport entities to use the same NC to support all communication pertaining to a TC. The Transport entity which initiates the TC establishment procedure is the one responsible for assigning the TC to an NC. The assignment can, however, only be made to an NC which the initiating Transport entity *owns*. That is, the NC to which the TC is assigned must have been established upon a request from the initiating Transport entity. The responding Transport entity becomes aware of the assignment when it receives a TPDU requesting the establishment of a TC (that is, a CR TPDU) over the assigned NC.

The above suggests that there is a one-to-one correspondence between a TC and its supporting NC. Such is not the case. If multiplexing is used, then a number of TCs may be assigned to the same NC. Similarly, when splitting is permitted, a TC may be assigned to a number of NCs. Also note that in those classes of protocols where recovery from network disconnection is possible, a TC may be reassigned to a different NC (see the procedures for *Reassignment after Failure,* below).

6.6.3   Transfer of TPDUs

Each TPDU communicated between Transport entities is transferred over an NC, to which the TC is assigned, using Normal Data transfer or Expedited Data transfer service. These services are, of course, accessed using N-DATA or N-EXPEDITED DATA primitives. Unless network express variant of the procedure Expedited Data transfer is used, all TPDUs are sent as NS user data in N-DATA primitives. In Class 1 protocol, expedited TS user data may be sent using the Expedited Data transfer service provided by the Network layer. This is, however, subject to availability and negotiation by the communicating Transport entities.

6.6.4   Connection Establishment

This procedure relates to the establishment of a Transport connection between a pair of supporting Transport entities. The initiating Transport entity sends a *CR* TPDU, to which the responding Transport entity responds with a *CC* TPDU if it accepts the establishment of the TC (see Figure 6.8(a), (b)). These TPDUs are sent using N-DATA primitives over the assigned NC. If, however, the responding Transport entity cannot accept the connection, it responds with a *DR* TPDU, signifying a disconnection request (see also the discussion on *Connection Refusal*[4]).

A number of parameters are included in each of CR and CC TPDUs. Prominent among these are:

1. Calling and Called TSAP Addresses (optional, in case the NSAP Addresses uniquely identify TSAPs),
2. Source and destination reference numbers, which are used to identify a Transport connection,
3. Initial Credit allocation in case flow control is used,
4. Proposed or selected values of negotiable parameters, and
5. User data, if any.

Identifying TC. A Transport connection is identified using a pair of *reference* numbers, one chosen by each communicating Transport entity. This identifier is, in fact, a *Transport protocol-connection-identifier* (see Section 2.3), and has significance which is local to the communicating Transport entities. The initiating Transport entity chooses a *source* reference number (called *SRC-REF*), but assigns a value of 0 to *DST-REF* (a destination reference number) before sending the CR TPDU. The re-

---

[4]Note, in protocol Class 4, the accepting Transport entity considers the connection to have been established only after its CC TPDU has been acknowledged (see *Retention of TPDUs until Acknowledged,* below).

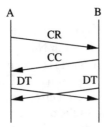

(a) Successful establishment in protocols classes 0 through 3

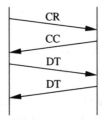

(b) Successful establishment in protocol class 4

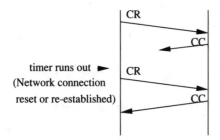

(c) Multiple attempts at establishment in protocol classes 0 through 3

Figure 6.8 Connection establishment.

sponding Transport entity chooses a value for the other reference number just before sending the CC TPDU. Subsequently, whenever a TPDU containing the parameters SRC-REF and/or DST-REF is sent, SRC-REF has the value of the reference number assigned by the sending Transport entity at the time of connection establishment. Similarly, DST-REF is assigned the value of the reference number chosen by the receiving (or destination) Transport entity.

The range of values of reference numbers, and the mechanism for choosing one, is not specified by the protocols, except to limit its code to 16 bits. A reference number may be reassigned to another TC, once the

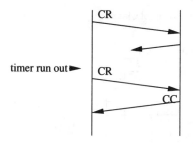

(d) Retransmissions of CR TPDU in protocol class 4

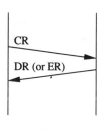

(e) Connection Refusal   **Figure 6.8** (*Continued*).

TC has been released *and* it is reasonably clear that no TPDU concerning the released TC is anywhere in the network (see *Frozen References*).

Negotiation of protocol class and options. During connection establishment a number of parameters are negotiated, including:

1. protocol class,
2. use of optional functions or their variants, including window size, and use of expedited data transfer and checksums,
3. maximum TPDU size, and
4. quality of service parameters, such as throughput and security.

The choice of protocol class is primarily dictated by TS user requirements in terms of optional services, quality of service, and by the type of available network connection. The Transport entity proposes a preferred protocol class and possibly some alternatives, while the responding Transport entity either totally rejects the connection establishment or selects a protocol class, depending upon its view of TS user requirements and available resources. Table 6.10(a) to (c) specifies the valid alternative protocol classes for each preferred class, and the responses that are valid for each preferred or alternative protocol class. For sure, an alternative protocol class may not be higher in number than the one preferred. Further, if the preferred class is Class 2 protocol then Class 1 protocol may not be an alternative. The responding Transport entity may select any of the proposed protocol classes. In addition, if Class 1 is a proposed protocol then Class 0 protocol may be se-

TABLE 6.10   Valid Alternatives and Responses in Protocol Class Negotiation

Preferred Class	Alternative Class				
	0	1	2	3	4
0					
1	yes				
2	yes				
3	yes	yes	yes		
4	yes	yes	yes	yes	

(a) Valid alternative classes.

Preferred Class	Alternative Class				
	0	1	2	3	4
0					
1	0,1				
2	0,2				
3	0,2,3	0,1,2,3	2,3		
4	0,2,4	0,1,2,4	2,4	2,3,4	

(b) Valid responses when alternatives are proposed.

Preferred Class	Valid response
0	0
1	0,1
2	2
3	2,3
4	2,4

(c) Valid responses when no alternatives are proposed.

lected, and similarly when Class 3 or 4 is proposed, Class 2 protocol may be selected by the responding Transport entity.

A number of optional functions and/or their variants are also negotiated at the time of connection establishment. These are listed in Table 6.11 which also indicates, for each option, the protocol classes in which its negotiation is relevant. If the initiator proposes to use the option,

TABLE 6.11   Applicable Variants (or Options) for Each Protocol Class

Option	Protocol Class				
	0	1	2	3	4
Use of receipt confirmation		x			
Use of network expedited variant		x			
Non-use of explicit flow control			x		
Non-use of checksum					x
Use of extended format (Note 1)			x	x	x
Transport expedited data transfer		x	x	x	x

Note 1. Modulo 2^7 is used in normal format for data PDU numbering and modulo 2^{31} is used in extended format.

then the responder may or may not accept it, otherwise it has no option. Note that selection of Expedited Data Transfer service is relevant only in protocol classes 1 through 4, and that its selection is based on user requirements. Selection of Receipt Confirmation and of network expedited variant, in Class 1 protocol, determines how the available NS is used in implementing Transport layer protocol. Use of checksums, explicit flow control, and of extended format fixes the particular manner in which the selected class of protocol is operated. There may be additional constraints on how a responder selects an optional parameter in case the initiator proposes use of a mandatory function or its variant.

Maximum TPDU size and certain quality of service parameters, including throughput, transit delay, priority, and residual error rate are negotiated during connection establishment. *Version number* and *retransmission time* (see discussion on *Reassignment after Failure,* and *Resynchronization,* below) are selected by the Transport entity initiating the TC establishment.

In protocol Classes 0 through 3, it is recommended that a timer be maintained to track the time that has elapsed since a CR TPDU was last sent. In case a CC or DR TPDU is not received before the timer runs out, a fresh attempt may be made, but not before the supporting network connection has been disconnected and the TC reassigned (in protocol Classes 0 and 1), or reset (in Classes 2 and 3). The reference number used as SRC-REF may be re-used but only after it has been frozen for some time to avoid duplication of CR TPDU. The latter is relevant only in protocols where error recovery is possible, that is, Classes 1 and 3. In effect, the earlier connection is abandoned, and establishment of a new connection is attempted (see Figure 6.8(c)).

In Class 4 protocol, where the possibility of a TPDU being lost is relatively higher, a mechanism is available to re-transmit the lost CR TPDU and to handle duplicate CR or CC TPDUs. The supporting network connection need not be reset or disconnected, nor is there a need to use a fresh source reference number (see Figure 6.8(d)).

6.6.5 Connection Refusal

A Transport entity may refuse connection establishment for one of many reasons, including its inability to support another connection, inability to support the desired class of protocol or options, inability to interpret the incoming CR TPDU and/or its parameters, or refusal on the part of the TS user to accept the incoming TC. The Transport entity does so by transmitting either a *DR* TPDU or an *ER* TPDU (the latter in case of errors or when Class 0 is the preferred protocol) together with the reason, if available. The two TPDUs signify, respectively, Disconnection Request and Error. (See Figure 6.8(e).) The value of the SRC-REF in the DR TPDU is 0, while in an ER TPDU it is totally absent. The receiving

Transport entity uses the value of DST-REF to relate the incoming TPDU with the particular TC. On receiving the ER or DR TPDU, the initiating Transport entity assumes that the connection has been released.

6.6.6 Connection Release

A TC upon establishment may be released, in Class 0 protocol, by simply disconnecting the supporting NC. This procedure is referred to as the *implicit* variant of connection release. However, in protocol Classes 1 through 4 where either multiplexing is admissible or where error recovery is feasible, a TC release is initiated by a Transport entity by sending a DR TPDU. The receiving Transport entity considers the connection as closed once it has responded with a *DC* TPDU, signifying Disconnection Confirmation. (See Figure 6.9.) The supporting NC may, if necessary, be disconnected using NS primitives. Additional comments follow:

1. Upon release of a TC, each Transport entity may be required to freeze the reference number that it had earlier assigned to the TC. In protocol classes 0 and 2, where it is not mandatory to do so, an implementation may, in fact, freeze the reference numbers.

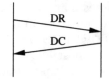

(a) Initiated by either T-entity

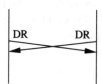

(b) Initiated by both T entities, simultaneously

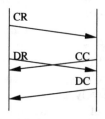

Figure 6.9 Normal release of connection.

(c) Release initiated during connection establishment

2. Since the TC may be released, either at the request of a TS user or because of failure of the supporting NC,[5] the reason, if available, is made known to the TS user(s).

6.6.7   Association of TPDUs with TC

Normally, a Transport entity, upon receiving an NSDU (or an Expedited-NSDU) over an NC would have no difficulty in associating the enclosed TPDU with the corresponding TC. However, two other procedures make this association complex. These are multiplexing (valid in protocol Classes 2 through 4), and concatenation (valid in protocol Classes 1 through 4). Thus, a Transport entity must first separate out the concatenated TPDUs from the received NSDU, and later associate each individual TPDU with the corresponding TC. Certain additional difficulties arise at this point. First, if the received NSDU cannot be separated (due to a protocol error at the Transport layer or at the Network layer), then surely the NC is reset, or it may even be released. Then, over each Transport connection assigned to the NC, the procedure to handle a signalled failure is initiated.

Once individual TPDUs have been separated out, their association with a TC is primarily based on a *Transport protocol-connection-identifier*. This identifier, as mentioned earlier in this section, is the paired reference numbers, viz. (SRC-REF, DST-REF). In fact, the DST-REF contained in the received TPDU is used, in most cases, to associate the TPDU with the TC.[6] There are two additional difficulties in using this scheme. These relate to the following.

1. The TPDU may be received over an NC to which the corresponding TC is not currently assigned. In such a case, reassignment of TC onto a different NC is presumed.

2. At the time the TPDU is received, the TC may have already been released, but only from the viewpoint of the receiving Transport entity. In that case a TPDU is returned that confirms the release of the corresponding TC, or the received TPDU is ignored.

6.6.8   Treatment of Protocol Errors

A *protocol error* occurs whenever a Transport entity receives a TPDU which can be associated with a particular Transport connection, but

---

[5]The latter is applicable only in Class 0 and Class 2 protocols (see *Error Release* procedure, below).
[6]Except in protocol Classes 0 and 1 where there is a one-to-one correspondence between a TC and the supporting NC.

which the Transport entity is unable to interpret or which it considers to be invalid. For instance, in protocol Class 2, reception of a numbered data TPDU which is out of sequence is considered erroneous, since it assumes that the supporting network connection is error-free. However, in protocol Classes 1 and 3 reception of a duplicate data TPDU is not treated as a protocol error since a network reset will most likely result in duplication of data TPDUs (see the procedure for *Resynchronization,* below). There reception of a data TPDU which implies loss of data TPDU is surely considered to be a protocol error. In protocol Class 4, recovery procedures are available to handle occurrence of such events, and are, therefore, not considered to be protocol errors.

Whenever a protocol error is detected, the associated TC may be released by the Transport entity which detects the error. Or, it may inform the correspondent Transport entity of the occurrence of the protocol error by sending an ER TPDU, and wait for the TC to be released by the other entity. The ER TPDU contains the *reject cause* of why the TPDU was considered invalid. Additionally, a part or whole of the rejected TPDU may be included in the ER TPDU. In some implementations, the supporting network connection may, instead, be reset or even released. In the latter case, all Transport connections currently assigned to the NC are affected. The specific action to be taken by the Transport entities is not specified by the protocol. It is considered to be an implementation issue.

6.6.9 Segmenting and Reassembling

Segmenting (and its inverse procedure, reassembling) is available for use in all classes of protocols. As a concept, it enables Transport entities to segment and map a TSDU (containing TS user data) into a number of *DT* (for data) TPDUs. These are communicated, uninterrupted by any other DT TPDU from the same TC. The last DT TPDU of such a sequence carries an indication of *End of TSDU.*

We now discuss the following procedures, each of which is applicable to protocol classes 1 through 4:

1. Concatenation and Separation,
2. Data TPDU Numbering, and
3. Expedited Data Transfer.

Subsequently, we discuss procedures that are relevant to protocol Classes 2, 3 and 4, viz.

1. Multiplexing and De-multiplexing, and
2. Flow Control.

6.6.10 Concatenation and Separation

Recall, from Chapter 2, that *concatenation* is a function whereby the Transport layer maps a number of TPDUs onto a single Network-service-data-unit (NSDU). The Transport layer protocol specification, however, restricts the use of concatenation to only protocol Classes 1 through 4. Further, no more than one of CR, CC, DR, DT, and ED TPDUs may be included in the set of concatenated TPDUs. This is so since each such TPDU contains variable length user data, and the scheme to encode TPDUs does not include a parameter that specifies the length of user data. Thus, a Transport entity receiving an NSDU is able to separate the concatenated TPDUs only when either of these is the last TPDU to be concatenated.

Any number of AK, EA, RJ, ER, and DC TPDUs may be concatenated together, provided they pertain to different Transport connections. The reason, again, is simple. Concatenation, as a concept, does not restrict the sequence in which TPDUs are placed in the NSDU, whereas over a TC, it is important to transfer two TPDUs in the proper sequence.

6.6.11 Data TPDU Numbering

This procedure is essential to any class of protocol that implements flow control and/or recovery from errors, that is, Classes 1 through 4. Only DT TPDUs are numbered. The numbering is modulo-128, the first DT TPDU being numbered 0. An extended format is also available, wherein numbering is modulo-(2^{31}).

6.6.12 Expedited Data Transfer

This facility is available to TS users only when the supporting transport entities use either of Classes 1 through 4 protocols. The TS user data provided in a T-EXPEDITED DATA request primitive is sent within an *ED* TPDU. A Transport entity receiving an ED TPDU acknowledges it by sending across an EA TPDU.[7] (No more than one ED TPDU may, at any time, remain unacknowledged.) Typically, it is the responsibility of the Transport layer to expedite the transfer of ED TPDU by placing it ahead of other DT TPDUs in the outgoing queue. In that case, it uses the normal data transfer service made available by the Network layer. However, in protocol Class 1, the Transport layer may additionally use expedited data transfer service when made available by the Network layer, and its use has been negotiated.

---

[7]In Class 4 protocol, ED TPDUs are also numbered modulo-128 (or 2^{31}).

6.6.13   Multiplexing and Demultiplexing

These procedures, used only in protocol Classes 2, 3 and 4, enable several Transport connections to share a Network connection at the same time. But, two Transport connections, each conforming to a different class of protocol, may not be multiplexed onto the same Network connection. The decision to whether to multiplex Transport connections or not is taken by the Transport entity initiating the establishment of a Transport connection. (Of course, it may assign a TC only to a Network connection which it owns.) Such a decision is primarily based upon the quality of service expected over the Transport connection, availability of resources, and the cost of providing the service.

6.6.14   Flow Control

This procedure, used to control the rate of flow of user data contained in DT TPDUs, is applicable to protocol Classes 2 through 4. In protocol Classes 0 and 1, flow control as applicable to the Network layer is the one experienced by DT TPDUs, whereas in other classes of protocol, an additional mechanism is available to control the flow of user data separately over each Transport connection. In protocol Class 2, the use of flow control procedure is negotiated.

Unlike the Data Link layer, where, aside from using a "moving window" mechanism, a receiver entity may declare its inability to accept additional data PDUs by sending a "Receiver Not Ready" PDU, the procedure used at the Transport layer is based solely upon a *variable size* moving window at the sender's end. This mechanism is referred to as a *credit* mechanism, where the receiver occasionally updates the sender's window by specifying its *lower window edge* and the number of *credits*. A credit, by definition, is the maximum number of DT TPDUs that the sender may send with an associated sequence number starting with the lower edge of the window. The *upper window edge* is, by implication, the lower window edge plus the number of credits. The Transport entity receiving DT TPDUs updates the sender's window by sending an *AK* TPDU (for acknowledgement) with its parameters *YR-TU-NR* and *CDT* set to the lower window edge and the number of credits, respectively. The value of YR-TU-NR is, in fact, the sequence number of DT TPDU that the receiver next expects to receive. Initially, when the Transport connection is established, the lower window edge at each end is set to 0, and the initial credits are exchanged as part of CR and CC TPDUS.

In all classes of protocol, the lower window edge may not be moved back. And, at any time, the actual number of credits available to a sender may even be reduced to 0, if it were to receive an AK TPDU which acknowledges all DT TPDUs for which credits were available (see Figure 6.10(a)). Further, in protocol Class 2 alone, the upper edge may

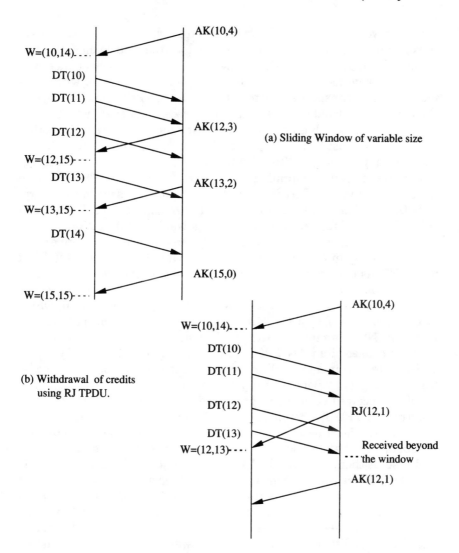

(a) Sliding Window of variable size

(b) Withdrawal of credits using RJ TPDU.

Notes:

W(l,u): Window with l and u as lower and upper edges.

AK(l,s): Acknowledgements with l as lower edge and s as window size.

DT(i): Data with i as sequence number.

Figure 6.10 Flow control using credit mechanism.

not be moved backwards. However, in protocol Classes 3 and 4, a receiver may subsequently "withdraw" credits from the sender, thereby moving the upper window edge backwards. Mechanisms for doing so are different for protocol Classes 3 and 4. As one implication of withdrawing credits, a Transport entity may receive a DT TPDU which is beyond the transmitter window, or a sender may receive an acknowledgement for a DT TPDU which is beyond its current window (see Figure 6.10(b)).

In protocol Class 3, a Transport entity may send an *RJ* TPDU (for reject), with parameters YR-TU-NR and CDT corresponding, respectively, to the sequence number of the next expected DT TPDU and to the allowed number of credits. An RJ TPDU may be sent to simply reduce the number of credits or to invite re-transmission of DT TPDUs in case of signalled failure of the supporting Network connection.

In protocol Class 4, a Transport entity may indicate its receiver status by sending an AK TPDU containing updated values of YR-TU-NR and CDT. As one consequence, the upper edge of the sender's window may be moved back or forward. There is, however, one difficulty that arises due to the nature of the underlying Network connection, which is assumed to be of Type C. That is, over such a connection TPDUs contained in NSDUs may be lost, duplicated, or re-sequenced. No great harm is caused if an AK TPDU is lost or duplicated. But, if two AK TPDUs are sent in a particular order, then these must be processed by the receiving Transport entity in the same order. Or, if the second AK TPDU is received earlier and processed, then the sender must ignore the first AK TPDU, when it arrives subsequently. It is, therefore, proposed that, where necessary, AK TPDUs may be assigned sequence numbers,[8] so that the sender may re-sequence incoming AK TPDUs and process them accordingly. In many instances, where an AK TPDU moves the lower window edge forward by at least one place, or where it increases the number of credits available to the sender, an AK TPDU may be assigned the sequence number 0, which is as good as not assigning any sequence number. But, whenever an AK TPDU actually withdraws credits without moving the lower window edge, it must be assigned a sequence number greater than the sequence number assigned to the last AK TPDU.

6.6.15   Error Release

The error release procedure is relevant only to protocol Classes 0 or 2. In these protocols no procedure is available to recover from signalled

---

[8]Note, the sequence number associated with an AK TPDU is a 16-bit number. Further, the specification of Class 4 protocol uses the term *sub-sequence number,* instead.

TABLE 6.12   Acknowledgement of TPDUs

Retained TPDU	Variant	Acknowledgement
CR	both	CC, DR, or ER TPDU
DR	both	DC or DR TPDU
CC	confirmation of receipt	N-DATA ACKNOWLEDGE indication, RJ DT, ED or EA TPDU
CC	AK	RJ, DT, AK, ED or EA TPDU
DT	confirmation of receipt	N-DATA ACKNOWLEDGE indication
DT	AK	AK or RJ TPDU
ED	both	EA TPDU

failure of the Network connection. As such, whenever the Network connection resets or disconnects, the supported Transport connection(s) are released.

The procedures, listed below, are used in protocol Classes 1 and 3, and each allows recovery from signalled failures of the supporting Network connection. The procedures for Frozen References and Retention of TPDUs until Acknowledged are also applicable to Class 4 protocol. There, reassignment and resynchronization are handled somewhat differently.

1.   Retention of TPDUs until Acknowledged,

2.   Resynchronization,

3.   Reassignment after Failure, and

4.   Frozen References.

6.6.16   Retention of TPDUs until Acknowledged

Recovery from signalled failure of the Network connection, or from lost or corrupted TPDUs, requires that a Transport entity be able to retransmit a TPDU. As such, in protocol Classes 1, 3, and 4, a TPDU of the type CR, CC, DR, DT, or ED must be retained until it is acknowledged by the corresponding Transport entity. Table 6.12 lists the type of TPDU that may be used as an acknowledgement to each retained TPDU. (In Class 1 protocol, when use of Confirmation of Receipt variant of acknowledgement has been agreed upon, an N-DATA ACKNOWLEDGE indication, corresponding to an N-DATA request containing the retained TPDU (or to a subsequent one), may be used in lieu of an AK TPDU.)

6.6.17   Reassignment after Failure, and Resynchronization

The two procedures are together used over a T-Connection, in protocol Classes 1 and 3, once the supporting Network connection to which it is assigned is disconnected. But, when the Network connection is simply reset, the Transport connection is not reassigned. Instead, the pair of communicating Transport entities resynchronize themselves by exchanging status information.

A distinction is made between the two communicating Transport entities. The Transport entity which initiates the establishment of the Transport connection is called the *initiator,* whereas the other Transport entity is called the *responder.* The primary responsibility of reassignment lies with the initiator, while the responder passively participates in the process. If the procedure(s) cannot be completed within a prespecified time interval (typically 2 min. or less), then the Transport connection is released. Towards this, the initiator maintains a timer *TTR* (for example, time to try reassignment/resynchronization), while the responder maintains the timer *TWR* (for example, time to wait for reassignment/resynchronization). Their values are specified by the initiator in the CR TPDU at the time of connection establishment.

Typically, when an N-DISCONNECT indication is received, the initiator Transport entity reassigns the Transport connection to a different Network connection, starts the TTR timer and initiates the resynchronization procedure (also called *active* resynchronization). As part of resynchronization, it transmits any unacknowledged ED TPDU, followed by an RJ TPDU containing the parameters YR-TU-NR and CDT. The latter reflects the current status of the initiator as a receiver of DT TPDUs. It subsequently awaits the reception of an RJ TPDU. When that happens, both reassignment as well as resynchronization procedures are considered complete. Subsequently, it may begin (re-)transmission of all available DT TPDUs.

The responder, on the other hand, having received an N-DISCONNECT indication, starts the TWR timer and awaits reception of an ED or RJ TPDU from the initiator. This is referred to as *passive* resynchronization. From the received TPDU, the responder is able to identify the Network connection to which the Transport connection has been reassigned. Subsequently, the responder transmits any unacknowledged ED TPDU, followed by an RJ TPDU containing, therein, its current receiver status. If the TPDU received earlier is an RJ TPDU, then it considers the reassignment and resynchronization procedures to have been successfully completed. It may then transmit all available DT TPDUs. Figure 6.11 illustrates resynchronization, as described thus far.

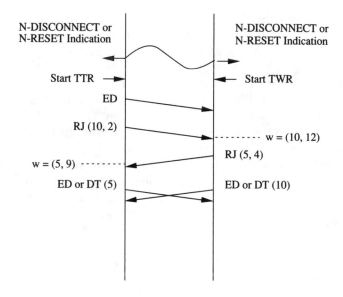

Note: See also Figure 6.10

Figure 6.11 Resynchronization procedure.

If the timer, TTR or TWR, were to run out at either end, then the procedures are unsuccessfully terminated, and the TC is considered released. Further, instead of disconnection, had the Network connection been reset, the reassignment of Transport connection does not take place.

The above description assumes that the Transport connection, prior to reassignment or resynchronization, is in a data transfer state, and that neither Transport entity had initiated the release procedure.[9] When such is not the case, resynchronization enables the Transport entities to establish the Transport connection, or to release the connection.

6.6.18   Frozen References

The concept of freezing a reference number (or disallowing its use for a certain duration) after the corresponding Transport connection has been released is relevant only to protocol Classes 1, 3 and 4. This is nec-

---

[9]By exchanging RJ TPDUs, each Transport entity becomes aware of the receiver status of the other. This aspect of the procedure is called *data* resynchronization.

essary, since a TPDU bearing the same reference number may arrive long after the corresponding TC is considered to have been released. First, while one Transport entity may assume that the Transport connection has been released, the corresponding Transport entity may continue to believe otherwise. Next, even when the TC is known to the communicating Transport entities to have been released, a duplicate TPDU may still be in transit over a Network connection. Thus, in these classes of protocol, a reference number may not be re-used (or *frozen*) for the time duration TWR, a duration considered to be long enough to ensure that an NSDU would have been delivered or destroyed.

The following procedures, applicable only to Class 4 protocol, are discussed below:

1. Inactivity Control,
2. Checksum,
3. Splitting and Recombining,
4. Re-transmission on Timeout, and
5. Re-sequencing.

6.6.19   Inactivity Control

The procedure *inactivity control* enables a Transport entity to detect release of a Transport connection in case such an event is not signalled by the corresponding Transport entity (or by the Network layer). Corresponding to each Transport connection, a Transport entity maintains a timer, I, which tracks the time that has elapsed since a TPDU was last received. If the timer runs out, the Transport entity initiates the release procedure. It is, therefore, suggested that, in case no user data is available for transmission, a Transport entity transmit an AK TPDU at regular intervals, to prevent unintentional release by the corresponding Transport entity.

6.6.20   Checksum

Use of the *checksum* procedure enables Transport entities to detect errors in communicating TPDUs with a high probability. Conceptually, this procedure is similar to the procedure employed at the Data Link layer to detect transmission errors. The algorithm used to compute the checksum parameter is, however, different. For a given TPDU, including its two checksum octets, the following conditions must be satisfied:

$$\sum a_i = 0, \ \sum i a_i = 0$$

In the above a_i is the decimal equivalent of the i-th octet, and the arithmetic is modulo-255. If the receiving Transport entity detects a checksum error in the received TPDU, it may totally ignore the TPDU.

The implementation as well as use of this procedure in Class 4 protocol is optional. The use of the procedure is negotiated at the time of connection establishment. There is, however, a requirement that a CR-TPDU, with Class 4 as the preferred protocol, must include the checksum parameter. This suggests that a Transport entity, that supports Class 4 protocol, must implement it, at least to the extent of sending a CR TPDU with the checksum included.

6.6.21 Splitting and Recombining

Protocol Classes 2 through 4 support multiplexing of Transport connections over a supporting Network connection. Class 4 protocol, additionally, permits *splitting* of a Transport connection over a number of Network connections. That is, a Transport connection may be simultaneously assigned to a number of Network connections, and TPDUs pertaining to the Transport connection may be sent over each Network connection. Splitting may be used with a view to achieve a higher throughput over the Transport connection, or to provide greater resilience against failure of Network connection(s). Use of this procedure, however, requires that TPDUs received over different Network connections be properly re-sequenced (see *Re-sequencing,* below).

6.6.22 Re-transmission on Timeout

Recall that a TP4 protocol assumes that the supporting Network connection is of Type C. That is, the rate at which residual errors (checksum error, loss, duplication, and re-ordering) occur is unacceptably high, with the added possibility that a TPDU sent over a Network connection may be unduly delayed. Therefore, Class 4 protocol requires that a TPDU, for which an acknowledgement is long overdue, be re-transmitted. As such, each Transport entity maintains a timer, *T1,* which tracks the time that has elapsed since an unacknowledged TPDU was last (re-)transmitted. (See Table 6.12, and the earlier discussion on Retention of TPDUs until Acknowledged.) If the timer runs out repeatedly, N times, the Transport entity may release the Transport connection.

Whether the timer T1 is maintained on a per Transport connection basis (that is, one for every connection), or on a per TPDU basis is implementation dependent. Further, it is for the Transport entity to determine whether all, or simply the first, unacknowledged DT TPDUs are re-transmitted when the timer runs out. Note that this latter issue arises only in the case of DT TPDUs, since no more than one TPDU of any other type may be outstanding. In view of the fact that the receiving Transport entity accepts DT TPDUs that are out of sequence, such an option is meaningful.

6.6.23   Re-sequencing

In any protocol that permits re-transmission of DT TPDUs, or which supports splitting, numbered DT TPDUs must be re-sequenced to ensure loss-free,, duplication-free, and in-sequence delivery of user data. If a Transport entity receives an out-of-sequence DT TPDU (but within the current transmit window), it may accept it but may not deliver it to the TS user until it has received all in-sequence DT TPDUs. Further, since DT TPDUs may traverse different Network connections, out-of sequence reception of a DT TPDU does not necessarily imply loss of DT TPDU (as such, RJ TPDUs are not applicable to Class 4 protocol). If a DT TPDU does get lost, the sending Transport entity would soon re-transmit it.

To summarize, the TP4 protocol, as it pertains to reliable data transfer, is truly a *Positive Acknowledgement with (periodic) Re-transmissions* protocol, where the window size at the transmitter end is subject to control by the receiver. Further, the receiver window overlaps the transmitter window.

There is one additional feature of Class 4 protocol. This attempts to counter the problem of delayed arrival of DT TPDUs, and re-ordering of DT TPDUs. The DT TPDUs are sequentially numbered using a modulo-128 (or -2^{31}). In Class 4 protocol a sequence number may not be re-used for a time duration L, where L is an upper bound on the maximum time between the transmission of a TPDU and receipt of an acknowledgement to it. This is equivalent to freezing a sequence number for a certain time duration, thereby ensuring that a duplicate copy of a previous DT TPDU is not erroneously delivered in place of a fresh DT TPDU. As one consequence, in applications requiring high throughput, one may need to use a modulo-2^{31} numbering scheme.

This completes the discussion of all procedures that are relevant to the five classes of connection-oriented Transport protocols. These protocols assume the availability of a connection-oriented Network service. ISO has also defined a Transport protocol that resembles Class 4 protocol, but uses a connection-less Network service. For details see [ISO 8073 DAD 2]. In the next section we discuss a protocol for providing connection-less Transport services.

6.7   Connection-less Protocol Procedures

In Section 6.5, we briefly discussed the protocol for providing connection-less data transfer service using either connection-less or connection-oriented Network service. In this section we discuss procedures that are relevant to this protocol (see reference [ISO 8602]).

6.7.1   Transport-Protocol-Data-Units

Only one type of TPDU is defined for connection-less Transport protocol, viz. *UD* TPDU (for Unitdata). Such a TPDU primarily contains user data provided by a TS user in the form of TSDU in a T-UNITDATA request primitive. Aside from the TSDU, the source and destination TSAP addresses, and optionally a Checksum parameter, are also included. The TSAP addresses are also provided as part of T-UNITDATA request primitive.

6.7.2   Transfer of TPDUs

A UD TPDU is transferred by a Transport entity to the relevant peer Transport entity using connection-less or connection-oriented data transfer service provided by the Network layer. This selection of Network service is based upon the availability of these services, and the quality of service requested by the TS user (as part of T-UNIT-DATA primitive). Quality of service parameters include transit delay, protection from unauthorized access, cost, and residual error rate. A connection-less Network service is likely to offer better delay and cost characteristics while a connection-oriented Network service offers, in general, a smaller residual error rate.

In either case, the sending Transport entity uses its address mapping function to determine the source and destination NSAP addresses from the given TSAP addresses. Further, depending upon the requested quality of service, a Transport entity may or may not include a checksum parameter in the UD TPDU. If residual error rate is of particular concern then the checksum parameter may be included. A receiving Transport entity discards the TPDU if it determines that the TPDU is erroneous. No positive (or negative) acknowledgement is sent by the receiving Transport entity, nor is there any confirmation provided by the supporting Network layer.

Using connection-less network service.   In case connection-less data transfer service is used, the UD TPDU is sent as NS user data (or NSDU) using N-UNITDATA service primitives. If the size of the UD TPDU exceeds the acceptable maximum NSDU size, the sending Transport entity may abandon transfer of UD TPDU, altogether.

Using connection-oriented network service.   A UD TPDU is sent as NS user data using N-DATA service primitives, but only after a Network connection has been established. If the attempt to establish a Network connection fails, or if it disconnects prior to issuing an N-DATA primitive request, then the transfer of UD TPDU is abandoned by the Transport entity. (It is a local matter whether the TS user is informed of such an event, or not.) Once data transfer is complete (successfully or otherwise), the supporting Network connection may be released by either Transport entity. The Transport entities communicating a UD TPDU, of course, have no need to reset the Network connection. However, if a reset occurs, they simply respond to an N-RESET indication with an N-RESET response.

6.7.3 Checksum

Computation of the checksum parameter is identical to that encountered in the context of Class 4 connection-oriented Transport protocol (see Section 6.6, above).

6.8   State Table Description of Protocols

In this section, a somewhat formal approach is taken to describe a protocol. A state table may be used to describe how a Transport entity interacts with its peer Transport entities, as well as with a TS user and the Network service provider. The Transport entity is viewed as a finite state machine whose state changes whenever events are caused by other entities. In doing so, it also causes events to occur at other entities.

6.8.1   Communicating Finite State Machines

In the discussion so far the attempt has been to describe Transport layer protocols using informal text. A more precise description of the protocols may be given, provided the two communicating Transport entities are viewed as a pair of *finite state machines*. Each finite state machine is, at any time, in some particular state; and the state may change whenever an *event* occurs. For instance, the state of a finite state machine may change when it receives a T-CONNECT request from the corresponding TS user.

The finite state machines interact with each other and with other entities external to the Transport layer. The external entities are, of course, the two TS users and the NS provider. A finite state machine interacts with another finite state machine, or an external entity, by causing an event, *an outgoing event,* to occur at another machine or an external entity. Further, a finite state machine processes events, *incoming events,* that occur as a consequence of actions of the other finite state machine, or an external entity (see Figure 6.12). In other words, when a Transport entity sends a DT TPDU, it is causing an event to occur at its peer Transport entity. The receiving peer Transport entity processes the incoming event and initiates certain actions. In particular, it issues a T-DATA indication at its TSAP. As another example, when a TS user issues a T-DISCONNECT request at its TSAP, an event occurs at the corresponding finite state machine (the supporting Transport entity), which may subsequently send a DR TPDU. Similarly, the NS provider may cause events to occur at a finite state machine, or process events caused by a finite state machine.

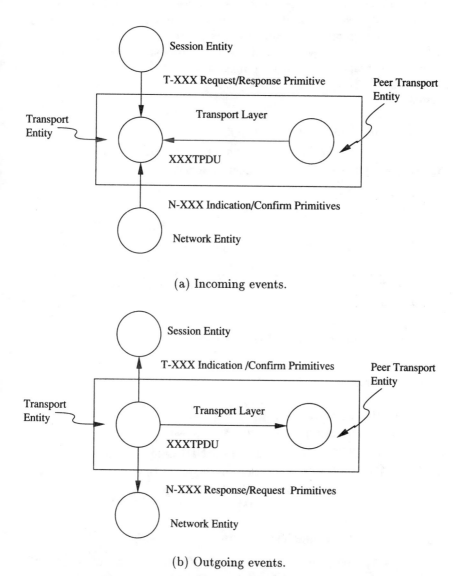

(a) Incoming events.

(b) Outgoing events.

Figure 6.12 Interactions between finite state machines and other entities.

Since the concern here is to specify the layer protocol, we shall be concerned only with processing of incoming events by the finite state machines, and with outgoing events caused by these finite state machines. It is irrelevant as to how and when an external entity causes an event to occur in a finite state machine, or how, and with what consequence, an external entity processes an event occurring within itself.

To summarize, each Transport entity is viewed as a finite state machine, and its state changes with the occurrence of an incoming event. Further, with every transition a finite state machine there may be an associated outgoing event. Below we list, for example, the set of incoming events, outgoing events, and the applicable states for a finite state machine corresponding to the connection-less Transport protocol.

States

1. Communication Closed (or CLOSED),
2. Waiting for Network Connection (or WAIT PATH), and
3. Waiting for Network Disconnection (or TRANSACT).

Incoming events

1. T-UNITDATA request received (or TUNI.req),
2. N-CONNECT confirm received (or NCON.conf),
3. N-DISCONNECT indication received (or NDIS.ind),
4. Disconnect Timer expired (or D-t expired),
5. UD TPDU received (or UD), and
6. N-RESET indication (or N-RESET.ind).

Outgoing events

1. Send UD TPDU (or UD),
2. Issue N-CONNECT request (or NCON.req),
3. Issue N-DISCONNECT request (or NDIS.req),
4. Issue T-UNITDATA indication (or TUNI.ind), and
5. Issue N-RESET response (or N-RESET.rsp).

6.8.2   State Table Description

To specify a given protocol, it is necessary to list the set of admissible states of each finite state machine, the collection of incoming and out-

TABLE 6.13 State Table for Connection-less Transport Protocol

State	Incoming Event		
	Closed	Wait Path	Transacting
TUNI.req	P0:UD Closed; (not P0) and (not P1): UD Closed; (not P0) and P1: NCON.req Wait Path;		
NCON.conf		UD [1] Transact;	
NDIS.ind		Closed;	Closed;
D-t expired			P2:Closed; (not P2): NDIS.req Closed;
UD	P0:TUNI.ind Closed; (not P0) and P2: TUNI.ind Closed; (not P0) and (not P2): TUNI.ind NDIS.req Closed;		
N-RESET.ind			N-RESET.rsp Transact

Note [1]: Set disconnect timer.

going events, and the relation between them. This relation is specified in terms of actions taken (that is, outgoing events initiated) by a finite state machine when it processes an incoming event in a particular state, and the state to which the finite state machine transitions as a consequence. Such a description is presented in the form of a table, called *state table*. Table 6.13 is a state table description of the connection-less Transport layer protocol. Therein, a table entry for each pair, (current state, incoming event), specifies the outgoing event(s) initiated by the finite state machine and its resulting state. For example, the table entry, in Table 6.13, corresponding to (WAIT PATH, NCON.conf) requires that the Transport entity transmit a UD TPDU and move to the state TRANSACT, if it receives an N-CONNECT confirm primitive in the state Waiting for Network Connection.

Often, it is necessary to further qualify the incoming event and/or the current state in case the transition to be made and the outgoing events to be initiated depend upon the current selection of classes, options, or upon values of parameters received in a TPDU or a service primitive. Such conditions are referred to as *predicates*. In the context of connection-less data transfer protocol, the following predicates are defined:

Predicates

1. P0: Connection-less Network service,
2. P1: Connection-oriented Network service, but requires a new connection,
3. P2: Connection-oriented Network service, where multiplexing is available.

To illustrate the notion of predicates and their use in state tables, consider the table entry corresponding to (CLOSED, TUNI.req). It suggests that in case

1. A connection-less Network service is used: the Transport entity transmits a UD TPDU, and remains in the CLOSED state;
2. A connection-oriented Network service is used and a connection is available: the Transport entity transmits a UD TPDU and remains in the CLOSED state; or
3. A connection-less Network service is not used, but a new connection is required: the Transport entity issues an N-CONNECT request and moves to the state WAIT PATH.

Additional actions, if any, are specified wherever necessary. In the example above, a timer, pertaining to receiving an N-DISCONNECT indication, is started by a Transport entity, if it were to receive an N-CONNECT confirm primitive in the state WAIT PATH.

Invariably, there are a number of blank entries in the table. If, in the corresponding state, an incoming event occurs, then it surely is unexpected. The specific action to be taken, as a consequence, is not specified by the table. In some cases it may be interpreted as a protocol error, in which case the text prescribes the remedial actions to be initiated by the Transport entity. In other cases, the Transport entity simply ignores the incoming event.

The state table is an overall description of the protocol. Details regarding specific parameter values, encoding of TPDUs and other actions are, however, not included in the tables, but may be obtained from the text of the state transition diagram. Further, any doubt or conflicting interpretation of the standard is resolved by consulting the text, rather than the state table.

6.8.3   Connection-less Transport Protocol

The connection-less Transport protocol that uses a connection-oriented Network service or connection-less Network service was discussed in Section 6.7. A state table description of it is given in Table 6.13. (Also, see the earlier discussion in this section.)

6.8.4   Connection-Oriented Transport Protocols

Recall, from Sections 6.5 and 6.6, that five different classes of protocol for connection-oriented data transfer are available. Protocol Classes 0 and 2 use a Type A Network connection, and have no facility to recover from failure of the Network connection. Protocol Classes 1 and 3 support recovery from failure of the assumed Type B Network connection. Class 4 protocol uses a Type C Network connection, which has an unacceptable rate of residual errors. In view of the similarity (or dissimilarity) of the assumed type of Network connection, three separate state tables are provided (see the document [ISO 8073]). These cover, respectively,

1. Protocol Classes TP0 and TP2,
2. Protocol Classes TP1 and TP3, and
3. Protocol Class TP4.

6.9   Encoding of TPDUs

As mentioned earlier, a protocol not only specifies the messages to be exchanged, but also their encoding to enable correct interpretation of the message and the parameters contained therein. The collection of TPDUs, as applicable to connection-oriented Transport service is given in Table 6.9 (see also Section 6.7). In this section, we discuss the structure used to encode TPDUs and their parameters.

The encoding of a TPDU is illustrated in Figure 6.13(a), where it is shown that a TPDU is encoded using a *Header* and optionally user data. The header itself consists of a *Length Indicator, a Fixed Part,* and optionally a *Variable Part*. The Length Indicator specifies the number of octets in the Fixed Part and the Variable Part, if present. The Fixed Part consists of an octet of *TPDU Code,* which specifies the TPDU being communicated, and a variable number of octets that are fixed for each type of TPDU. (See Figure 6.13(b), for an example encoding of a DR TPDU, where octets 2 through 7 constitute the Fixed Part.)

The Variable Part of the header contains the encoding of a variable number of parameters and their associated values. Any parameter

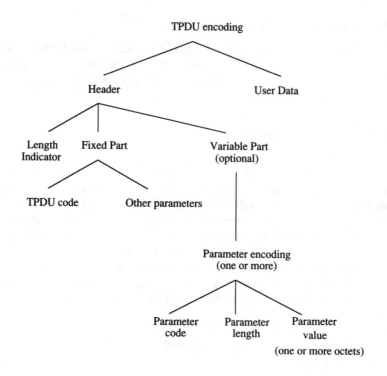

(a) Encoding of TPDU's

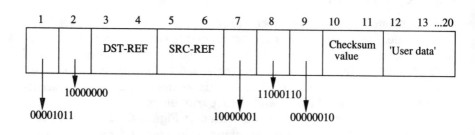

(b) Example Encoding of DR TPDU

Figure 6.13 Encoding of TPDUs.

from a given list of parameters may be included in the Variable Part. A parameter is encoded using three fields, viz. *Parameter Code, Parameter Length Indicator,* and a *Parameter Value.* The Parameter Code is specific to each parameter, while the Parameter Length Indicator indicates the length (in octets) of the Parameter Value field. The Parameter Value is specified in one or more octets. (In the example given in Figure 6.13(b), octets 8 through 11 encode the *Checksum* parameter.) The Variable Part is typically used to encode those parameters of a TPDU that are infrequently included in the TPDU.

User data must be present in certain TPDUs, for example, DT TPDU or ED TPDU, whereas it may not be included in some others (for example, in a DC TPDU). For most TPDUs it is optional, as in DR TPDU. Note that the start of the User Data field can always be identified from Length Indicator in the Header. In the following, we make additional comments regarding encoding of certain parameters of the TPDUs.

1. In some cases, for example in an AK TPDU, part of the TPDU Code may be used to encode the CDT (credits) parameter.
2. For each TPDU, the optional parameters that may be included in the Variable Part are separately specified. Further, inclusion of an optional parameter may be dependent on the selection of certain options or class of protocol. For example, a checksum parameter may only be included when use of checksum procedure in a Class 4 protocol has been agreed to.
3. There is a limit on the number of optional parameters that may be included in the Variable Part, as implied by the length of the Fixed Part and the available 8 bits to encode the Length Indicator.
4. For each parameter (optional or otherwise), the protocol defines the range of admissible values and the interpretation to be associated with each value. For example, in Figure 6.13(b), octet 7 refers to the Reason parameter, and its value "10000001" is interpreted as *Remote Transport Entity is Congested.*

6.10 Summary

The Transport layer consists of functions that are implemented in end systems only. The data transfer service that it provides is, therefore, end-to-end, and largely independent of the underlying transmission media and network interconnections. The Transport service is generally connection-oriented, although ISO considers the need for connection-less Transport service as well. The use of connection-less Transport service is not anticipated in the near future, however. The greatest advantage resulting from connection-oriented Transport service is that data transfer is reliable, efficient, and of the desired quality of service. As a consequence, entities in the higher layers are relatively free of such concerns.

The complexity of the Transport protocol is very much dependent upon the type of available Network service and its quality. Therefore, a variety of Transport protocols have been considered in this chapter.

We have, however, concentrated upon the five different protocols which are used to provide connection-oriented Transport service and use connection-oriented Network service. The specific class of protocol to be used further depends upon the characteristics of the supporting Network layer connection, expressed in terms of residual error rate and failure probability.

A formal description of the protocols is often presented in terms of state tables. Such a description is presented where the two communicating Transport entities are treated as a pair of finite state machines. The state table description of the protocol for connection-less protocols has been discussed in some detail.

The Transport layer provides services to support Session layer protocol, which is presented in the next chapter.

The Session Layer

The main functionality of the Session layer is to provide Presentation entities with the means to organize exchange of data over a connection, to negotiate release of the connection, or to place synchronization points in the stream of data. The latter enables users to structure their communication in the form of a series of dialogue units, and to subsequently resynchronize data exchange in the event of errors. Synchronization points also allow users to define an activity that may be interrupted and later resumed. These services, and the necessary protocols, are discussed in this chapter.[1]

7.1 Introduction

This section is an introduction to the nature of services provided by the Session layer, as well as an overview of the protocol it uses to bridge the gap between the service it provides and the Transport service it uses.

The Session layer is situated between the Transport layer and the Presentation layer. As with the Transport layer, subsystems corresponding to the Session layer are present only in those open systems where Application entities reside. As such, all interactions between Session entities are end-to-end, and are made possible by the services provided by the Transport layer (see Figure 7.1).

The Session layer, together with the layers below, provides services, called *Session service (SS)*, to its user entities in the Presentation layer, and thereby, to the Application entities. These services are accessible by a Presentation entity at a *Session service-access-point (SSAP)*, to which it is attached. As such, a Presentation entity attached to an SSAP is also referred to as an *SS user,* while the Session layer, together with layers below, is called the *SS provider.* Further, the Session ser-

---

[1]See also [CCITT X.215], [CCITT X.225] or [ISO 8326], [ISO 8327].

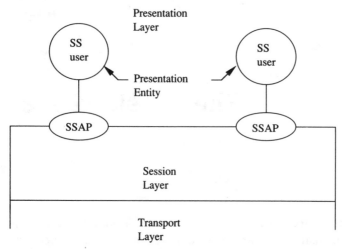

Figure 7.1 The Session layer.

vice is connection-oriented. That is, two Presentation entities may exchange data only after a connection has been established between the SSAPs, to which they are, respectively, attached. Such a connection is called a *Session connection.*

7.1.1   Session Connections

A Session connection is established by the Session layer between two SSAPs on behalf of the attached Presentation entities. The Presentation entity requesting the establishment of a Session connection provides to the Session layer the address of the SSAP, to which the responding Presentation entity is attached. Such an address may have been obtained using the directory or the address mapping function of the Presentation layer. Since there may exist a number of connections between an SSAP and other SSAPs, each Session connection is identified by its end point. Such an identifier is called *Session-connection-end-point identifier (SCEP-identifier).* Thus, for each connection there is an associated pair of SCEP-identifier, one for each end of the connection. An SCEP-identifier allows the Session service provider and the attached Presentation entity to uniquely identify (or refer to) the connection. (See Figure 7.2.)

7.1.2   Data Transfer Characteristics

Data transfer over a Session connection is end-to-end and reliable, a characteristic largely derived from the connection-oriented Transport

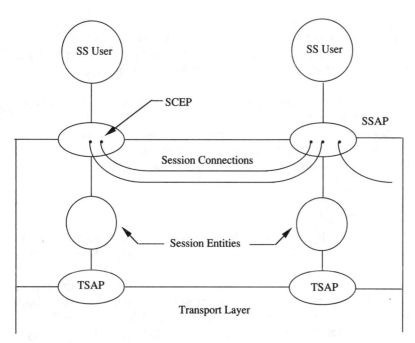

Figure 7.2   Session connections, SSAPs and SCEP identifiers.

service. Additionally, data is transferred transparently and independent of how the underlying Transport connection is set up or maintained. However, the quality of data transfer service over a Session connection, in respect of throughput, delay, etc., is to a great extent dependent upon the quality of Transport service. In other words, the quality of Session service requested by an SS user determines the quality of service required of the Transport service. Further, a Session connection exhibits the following additional characteristics:

1. Interaction between two users over a Session connection may be *organized*. That is, the users cooperate between themselves to determine as to who may initiate certain operations over the connection at any given time. Operations that are subject to such control are half-duplex data transfer, orderly release, and synchronization.[2] As to how such a decision is arrived at is not the concern of the Session layer. The SS provider simply enables transfer of control over the connection from one user to the other.

2. *Synchronized* data transfer refers to an ability on the part of users to structure their exchanges in the form of a series of *dialogue units*. All

---

[2]These concepts are discussed in greater detail in the following sections.

data exchanges within a dialogue unit are totally separated from those that take place in other dialogue units. Using services made available by the Session layer, users may identify the start and end of a dialogue unit, and resynchronize their data exchanges, when necessary. (See also Section 7.2.)

3. Users may structure their communication in the form of an *activity*. Many of the data transfer operations have meaning only within an activity. The most important characteristic of an activity is that it may be interrupted and resumed subsequently, either during the life time of the current Session connection or a fresh one.

7.1.3 Services

Services provided by the Session layer may be broken down into a number of individual service elements. Connection establishment, data transfer, and connection release are similar to those associated with any connection-oriented service. There are, however, some differences in connection release and data transfer services, primarily since both these services are subject to being organized. Additional service elements are required to support synchronized data transfer and resynchronization. It may, however, be pointed out that provision of service to support organized or synchronized data transfer is not mandatory on the part of the Session layer, and, even if provided, the users may or may not negotiate their use.

In view of the fact that data transfer, connection release, or synchronization may be subject to mutual control by the users, the notion of *functional units* is defined. A functional unit is a logical grouping of related service elements, and is based on the fact that whenever a particular service element is selected, selection of other service elements from the same group is essential. This enables users and the SS provider to negotiate on the basis of functional units rather than individual service elements. Functional units are discussed in Section 7.4, after a discussion of the concepts of organized data transfer and synchronization, and their related service primitives.

7.1.4 Assumed Transport Services

As mentioned earlier, the quality of service over a Session connection is largely determined by the quality of service made available over the supporting Transport connection. As one consequence, the Session layer assumes that data is transferred over a Transport connection reliably, that is, error-free, loss-free, duplication-free, and in-sequence (see Figure 7.2). Or, at the very least, the frequency of occurrence of errors is acceptably low. Such an assumption is critical since within the Session layer there is no mechanism available for error detection or recovery. In fact, if the Transport connection fails, then the supported Session connection is disconnected (or *aborted*) by the Session layer. Therefore, it is critical that the probability of failure of a Transport connection be low.

Transport service elements corresponding to connection establishment, (normal) data transfer, and release are assumed to be available, while provision of expedited data transfer is optional. The latter simply affects how some of the Session layer protocol-data-units are transferred over a Transport connection.

7.1.5 Session Layer Protocol

Given the nature of Transport service, discussed earlier in Chapter 6, the Session layer protocol implements those functions that allow SS user entities to organize and/or synchronize data transfer. As such, there is only one class of Session layer protocol, within which a number of options are available. These options pertain to various functional units, including half-duplex data transfer, synchronization, negotiated release, etc.

Functions of error detection and recovery, resequencing, flow control, etc. are of little importance in the context of Session layer, since each Session connection is mapped onto a relatively error-free Transport connection. If a Transport connection fails, or if a protocol error is detected, then the corresponding Session connection is aborted. It is for the SS users to re-establish a Session connection and resynchronize exchange of data. The latter would be feasible, provided an *activity* is in progress. (Activity concepts are discussed in Section 7.3.) Maintenance of the history of an activity is also the responsibility of the SS users. Again, the Session layer protocol allows activities to be started, ended, interrupted, resumed or even abandoned. The Session layer protocol is discussed in detail in Section 7.6.

7.2 Organized and Synchronized Data Transfer

Organized data transfer refers to a service provided by the Session layer, whereby a pair of SS users, in a cooperative manner, determine who may initiate certain operations related to a Session connection, at a given time. These operations relate to (normal) data transfer, orderly release, synchronization, and to activity management. These concepts, together with that of synchronization, are discussed in this section.

7.2.1   Half Duplex Data Transfer

(Normal) data transfer may either be full duplex (two way simultane-ous) or half duplex (two way alternate). In the latter case, at any time, at most one SS user has exclusive rights to initiate transfer of data over the connection. To enable SS users to transfer control over the connec-tion, the notion of a *token,* or more precisely a *data token,* is defined.

1. If, at the time of connection establishment, half duplex data trans-fer has been negotiated, then the data token is said to be *available.*
2. Otherwise the token is *not available,* in which case there exists no constraint on an SS user issuing data transfer primitives. But, if the token is available, then, at any time, it is either
   (a) *assigned* to one of the users, or
   (b) *not assigned* to either.

In the former case, 2(a), only the user to whom the data token is as-signed, may initiate data transfer by issuing an S-DATA request prim-itive. The latter case, 2(b), may arise when the token is being transferred by a user to the other. Figure 7.3 illustrates half duplex data transfer between SS users. Note that the service element *S-DATA* is unconfirmed.

Soon after a connection has been established, and if the data token is available, then it may be assigned by the initiating SS user to itself, or

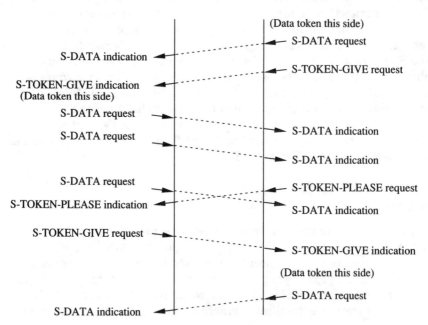

Figure 7.3 Half duplex data transfer and exchange of data tokens.

to the other SS user. The initiating SS user may, if it so chooses, leave it to the responding SS user to assign the data token. Subsequently, the SS user, to which the data token is currently assigned, may *give* the token to the corresponding user using the service element *Give Tokens*. Or, an SS user may even request the corresponding SS user to transfer the token to it using the service element *Please Tokens*. Exchange of data token between SS users, using the primitives *S-TOKEN-GIVE* and *S-TOKEN-PLEASE,* is shown in Figure 7.3.

7.2.2 Negotiated Release

Yet another operation that is subject to being organized is connection release. Three different connection release procedures are available. These are *User Abort, Provider Abort,* and *Orderly Release.* User Abort and Provider Abort are service elements,[3] where an SS user or the SS provider may unilaterally abort the connection, respectively. The other parties involved are at best informed of its release. Note that, as a consequence, data in transit may be lost or destroyed.

Orderly release, on the other hand, involves a two way interaction between the two SS users, as well as the SS provider, before the connection is released. This ensures that data in transit is delivered before the connection is released. See Figure 7.4(a) for an illustration, where it is assumed that the service *Orderly Release* is confirmed, and that the associated service primitive is *S-RELEASE.* Orderly release has two important characteristics. These are:

1. either SS user may initiate orderly release of the connection, and

2. an SS user responding to the connection release has *no* option but to accept the release of the connection.

Instead, the SS users may agree at connection time to alter these characteristics of orderly release by making available a *release token* and, thereby, subject orderly release to be controlled by the current assignment of the release token. This form of connection release is called *negotiated release,* wherein the SS user, to which the release token is currently assigned, has exclusive right to release the connection. The corresponding SS user has, in that case, the right to refuse the release of the connection. See Figure 7.4(b). The management of release token is similar to that of the data token. (For details see Section 7.4.)

A Session layer is required to provide all three forms of disconnection. It may or may not implement functions to support negotiated release. Further, selection of half duplex data transfer and that of negotiated release are totally independent. But, for any given selection

---

[3]Very similar to those encountered in some of the lower layers.

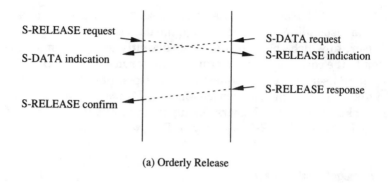

(a) Orderly Release

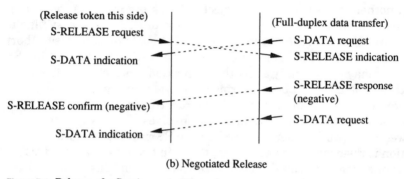

(b) Negotiated Release

Figure 7.4 Release of a Session connection.

of these services, additional constraints on issuing corresponding service primitives are implied. These are discussed later in Sections 7.4 and 7.5.

7.2.3 Dialogue Units and Major Synchronization Points

As mentioned earlier, SS users may structure their communication in the form of a series of *dialogue units*. Each dialogue unit is identified by a pair of *major synchronization points*. That is, with the insertion of a major synchronization point, the current dialogue unit is ended, and a new dialogue unit started. Figure 7.5 illustrates the relation between a dialogue unit and major synchronization points. The most important characteristic of a dialogue unit is that all data transfers within a dialogue unit are totally separated from those belonging to a previous dialogue unit as well as from those in the following dialogue unit. We shall shortly illustrate the separation of data belonging to two successive dialogue units.

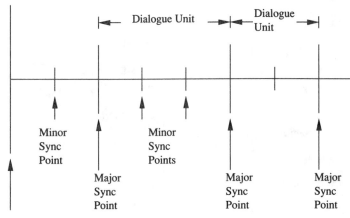

Figure 7.5 Dialogue units and synchronization points.

Whenever negotiated successfully, the Session layer provides services using which users may insert major synchronization points. This service, termed *Major Synchronization,* is also subject to token control. That is, during connection establishment a *major token* becomes available and is assigned to *an* SS user. Subsequently, it may be transferred back and forth using the service elements, Give Tokens and Please Tokens. At any time, the SS user, to which the major token is assigned, may initiate the insertion of a major synchronization point. Since Major Synchronization is a confirmed service, both SS users as well as the Session layer are party to the insertion of a synchronization point.

To illustrate how a dialogue unit separates data, we shall assume (normal) data transfer to be full duplex. Figure 7.6 illustrates the insertion of two major synchronization points in the stream of data, thereby, defining a dialogue unit. It is assumed, therein, that the service primitive associated with Major Synchronization is *S-SYNC-MAJOR*. Note, from Figure 7.6, that both users are able to associate transfer of each user data with the same dialogue unit. In other words, their view of data transferred within a given dialogue unit is identical. It should also be clear that such would not have been possible if the major synchronization service was unconfirmed. Further, in case data transfer is half duplex, the separation of data between dialogue units is even more obvious.

Each major synchronization point has an associated serial number, called *synchronization point serial number.* Serial numbers are assigned by the SS provider, but their association with synchronization points is made known to both the users. This allows SS users to subse-

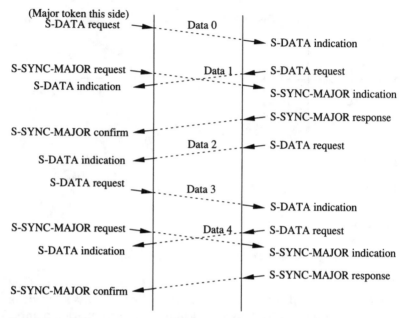

Note: Data 2, Data 3, Data 4 transfers take place within the same dialogue unit.

Figure 7.6 Data transfer within a dialogue unit.

quently make a reference to a major synchronization point, and resume communication from that point onwards, if found necessary. Or, it may be to restore the communication environment that existed at the time the major synchronization was inserted. We shall have more to say about *resynchronization,* later in this section.

7.2.4 Minor Synchronization Points

Minor synchronization points are used by Presentation entities to further structure their communication, but *within* a dialogue unit. (See Figure 7.5.) Here again, the users determine when minor synchronization points are to be inserted. Further, the semantics to be associated with each minor synchronization point is user determined. The Session layer simply enables their insertion. Unlike major synchronization points, insertion of a minor synchronization point does not necessarily separate data transfers that have taken place prior to the insertion of a minor synchronization point from those that take place subsequently. This is particularly so when data transfer is *full* duplex. We shall discuss separation of data transfers shortly.

Placement of minor synchronization points is also subject to control by the users. That is, whenever the corresponding service, *Minor Synchronization,* is negotiated during connection establishment, a *minor token* becomes available and is assigned to one of the users. The service element Give Tokens and Please Tokens may be used to transfer the minor token, and thereby give control of who may insert minor synchronization points.

Strictly, negotiation of the service elements, Half Duplex, Negotiated Release, Minor Synchronization, and Major Synchronization, may take place independently. If, however, two or more of these services are negotiated, then additional constraints are imposed on which user may issue a corresponding request primitive. In particular, a user may request insertion of a minor synchronization point only if it has the minor token *and* the data token.[4]

Each minor synchronization point is similarly identified by a synchronization point serial number. The serial number is, again, assigned by the Session layer, and its association with the minor synchronization point made known to the SS users.

Figure 7.7 illustrates separation of data transfer before and after the placement of a minor synchronization point. Therein, it is assumed that the service Minor Synchronization is a confirmed service, with the associated primitive termed *S-SYNC-MINOR.* Although the service is confirmed, a responding SS user may delay its confirmation, or not confirm it at all. In case data transfer is half duplex then, irrespective of whether the minor synchronization point is confirmed or not, there is complete separation of data. In case data transfer is full duplex, these are separated in their respective directions, provided the minor synchronization point is confirmed immediately. As such, minor synchronization points are particularly useful in structuring data transfers, either when data transfer is half duplex, or when minor synchronization is confirmed.

7.2.5 Synchronization Point Serial Numbers

As indicated earlier, the SS provider identifies each synchronization point by a serial number, and makes this association known to the users whenever a major or minor synchronization point is inserted. Further, it is the responsibility of the Session layer to maintain the current state of the dialogue unit. Therefore, the Session layer maintains a set of variables for each established connection. These are:

---

[4]Provided the data token is available.

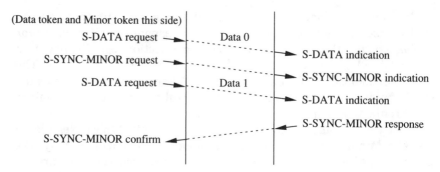

(a) Half-duplex data transfer

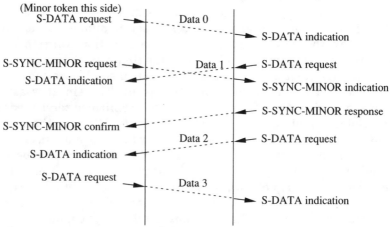

(b) Full-duplex data transfer

Figure 7.7 Data separation across minor synchronization points.

1. V(M) is the serial number to be used to number the *next* minor or major synchronization point.

2. V(A) is the least serial number associated with a synchronization point, confirmation to which is expected from an SS user.

3. V(R) is the serial number to which resynchronization (with the restart option) is permitted. (It is one more than the serial number of the last confirmed major synchronization point.)

4. V_{sc}. Whenever true, it implies that the *corresponding* SS user may issue a response primitive corresponding to insertion of a

minor synchronization point. The value of V_{sc} is not relevant when $V(M) = V(A)$.

Truly, only one set of variables need to be maintained to record the current status of the dialogue unit for each connection. But, since V_{sc} makes a specific reference to an SS user, two sets of variables are used to model the current state, one for each interface with an SS user. The values of these variables at the two ends are updated as and when primitives are issued at their respective ends. But, surely the values of the state variables at the ends must be consistent. Further, note that variables $V(A)$ and V_{sc} are simply concerned with ensuring that an SS user responding to insertion of a *minor* synchronization point does so without errors. The status of the dialogue unit is truly described by the variables $V(M)$ and $V(R)$. As such we shall only concentrate on the variables $V(M)$ and $V(R)$.

We now discuss the operations on these variables resulting from connection establishment, and insertion of minor and major synchronization points. The SS users and the SS provider, while negotiating the use of minor and/or major synchronization services, also agree upon the initial serial number, s_0, to be associated with the first synchronization point. Upon connection establishment, the following assignments are made at each connection end point (the value of V_{sc} is immaterial since $V(A) = V(M)$):

$$V(M) \Leftarrow s_0,$$

$$V(R) \Leftarrow 0.$$

Figure 7.8 illustrates the assignment of new values to these variables when a Session connection is established, or when a minor or major synchronization point is placed.

After a major synchronization point is placed

$$V(M) \Leftarrow V(M) + 1,$$

$$V(M) \Leftarrow V(M).$$

But, when a minor synchronization point is placed, only

$$V(M) \Leftarrow V(M) + 1$$

It is a matter of interpretation as to whether a synchronization point is identified by the old value of $V(M)$ or the updated one. It seems more convenient to use the old value to identify a synchronization point, and

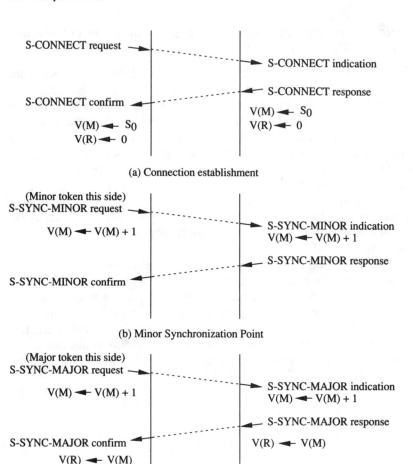

(a) Connection establishment

(b) Minor Synchronization Point

(c) Major Synchronization Point

Figure 7.8 Insertion of synchronization points.

the new value of $V(M)$ may be used to refer to the communication environment after the synchronization point has been inserted.

7.2.6 Resynchronization

Although rare, the possibility of occurrence of an error, either within the Session layer or in logical communication between the two users, cannot be ruled out. (See Section 7.4 for a discussion on *exception reporting*.) Or, users may wish to restore the environment that may have existed earlier.[5] To handle such requirements, SS users may initiate a resynchronization procedure that allows them to set the state of their communication to a defined state. Such a state may be the last confirmed major synchronization point, or a subsequent minor synchronization point. That is, using S-RESYNCHRONIZE primitives, SS users may resynchronize to any synchronization point within the current dialogue unit. In other cases, users may even define a new state, if the current dialogue unit is to be abruptly terminated, and a new one started. As such, three different forms of resynchronization are defined. These are referred to as *options*, and are discussed below:

1. *The Restart Option:* The restart option enables SS users to resynchronize communication to a synchronization point, previously defined. Such a point may be the last major synchronization point or a (confirmed or unconfirmed) minor synchronization point placed within the current dialogue unit. While making the request, the initiating SS user identifies the serial number, s_1, of the synchronization point to which communication is to be resynchronized. s_1 is constrained to be $V(R) \leq s_1 \leq V(M)$. Once resynchronization is complete,

$$V(M) \Leftarrow s_1.$$

$V(R)$ remains unchanged. See Figure 7.9 for an illustration of resynchronization using S-RESYNCHRONIZE primitives with the Restart option. Subsequently, it is for the SS users to restore communication to the numbered synchronization point.[6]

2. *The Abandon and Set Options:* These options also permit SS users to resume communication from an agreed point, but after the current dialogue unit has been terminated. In terms of the net effect, once resynchronization is complete,

$$V(M) \Leftarrow s_1,$$

$$V(R) \Leftarrow 0,$$

where s_1 is the synchronization point serial number passed by/to the SS user as a parameter of the corresponding request primitive. If the abandon option is used, s_1 is the next available serial number, provided by the SS provider, while the serial number is provided by an SS user in case of set or restart options. (See Figure 7.10 for an illustration of resynchronization using the abandon option.) This state is similar to

---

[5]For an application of resynchronization to restore the syntax of user information, see Chapter 8.

[6]Any resulting re-transmission or use of a restored context is transparent to the SS provider.

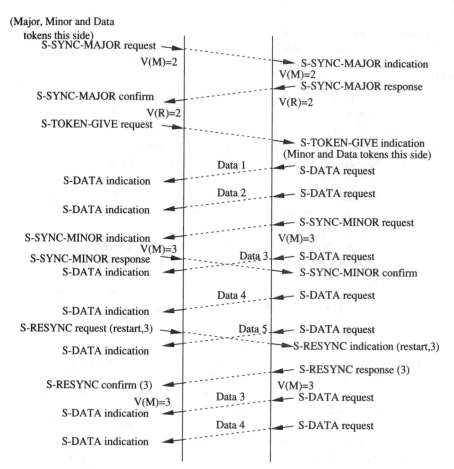

Note: S-RESYNC parameters are Resynchronize Type (optional), Synchronization point serial
number

Figure 7.9 Resynchronization using the restart option.

the one reached once a connection has been established. In such re-
spects, therefore, there does seem to be a similarity between the two options. The difference between the two is in respect of the serial number
to be associated with a future major or minor synchronization point.[7]

Whether or not users abandon the current dialogue unit, and thereby disregard all communication within it, is a matter of semantics to be
determined by the users, by mutual agreement. One possible use of

---

[7]With the set option, the serial number specified by the user is arbitrary, as long as it is
within the allowed range, 0 through 999999.

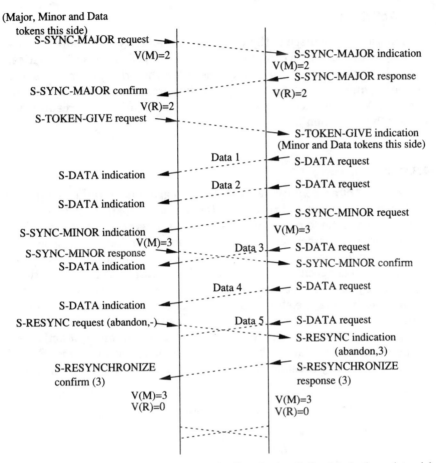

(Major, Minor and Data tokens this side)

Note: S-RESYNC parameters are Resynchronize Type (optional), Synchronization point serial number

Figure 7.10 Resynchronization using the abandon option.

resynchronization, with the set option, is for users to resynchronize to any of the previously established major synchronization points.

With resynchronization, data currently in the pipeline may be destroyed, or *purged*. In fact, one of the uses to which resynchronization service may be put is to purge the Session connection of all data. This is best done using the restart option. Further, with resynchronization, the available tokens are reassigned by mutual negotiation between the users. Also, resynchronization service may be used by an SS user to destructively assign tokens to itself.

7.3   Activities

In this section we discuss the concept of an activity and show its usefulness in structuring a computation in the form of a series of activities, several of which may be started, one after the other, over the same Session connection. Or, an activity may be spread over a number of connections. We also discuss changes in state information that result from associated operation.

7.3.1   Introduction

The concept of an *activity* permits users to give an overall structure to their communication by bracketing data exchanges, and to use an alternative mechanism to resynchronize, when necessary. The duration of an activity may be associated with some computation being performed by the users in a cooperative manner. (See Figure 7.11 for an illustration.) An activity has specifically to be *started* and *ended*. At any time, there may be at most one activity in progress. However, once an activity is ended, another may be started over the same Session connection. An activity may even be *interrupted* and subsequently *resumed*.[8] This permits, at least conceptually, a pair of users to initiate a number of activities, while ensuring that at most one activity is active at any time. Surely then, each activity must be identified separately, so that a unique refer-

---

[8]For instance, as a consequence of an error being detected by an SS user or signalled by the SS provider.

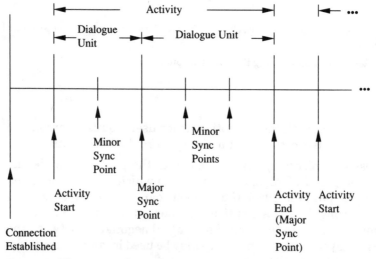

Figure 7.11 The concept of an activity.

ence to an activity may be made subsequently, when it needs to be resumed. Such an identifier is referred to as an *activity identifier*.

The concept of activity may be used in conjunction with minor and/or major synchronization services as well as with resynchronization. That is, an activity may be further structured to be composed of a number of successive dialogue units. However, related operations are then limited to occur only within an activity (see Figure 7.11). Users may insert minor as well as major synchronization points, and resynchronize their communication within a dialogue unit in a manner very similar to that discussed earlier. To allow resynchronization across dialogue units, a user may interrupt the activity and subsequently resume the activity at any of the confirmed minor or major synchronization points. See Figure 7.12 for an illustration.[9]

The most important distinction between the two mechanisms for structuring data exchanges—dialogue units and activities—is that, unlike a dialogue unit, an activity may spread over a number of Session connections. An activity may be interrupted over a connection and subsequently resumed over a different connection. Clearly, to make this possible each Session connection needs to be identified. Such an identifier is called *Session Connection Identifier*. It permits the two users to uniquely refer to an old connection and, within it, to an activity using its activity identifier. We shall have more to say about these identifiers, subsequently. Suffice it to state at this point that all such identifiers are totally transparent to the Session layer, and that their scope is limited to the two users.

7.3.2 State Variables

To ensure that certain operations are initiated only within an activity, the Session layer maintains a variable, V_{act}, which indicates whether an activity is currently in progress, or not.

The Session layer uses this variable in conjunction with variables defined earlier to record the status of each connection in respect of synchronization points and activities. We now discuss the consequence of issuing primitives related to the five different service elements concerning activity management on the variable V_{act} as well as $V(M)$, $V(A)$ and $V(R)$. The related service elements are *Activity Start, Activity End, Activity Interrupt, Activity Resume,* and *Activity Discard*. The last service element enables users to simply discard a current activity, perhaps with a view to discontinue computation or to subsequently start it all over again.

---

[9]See Section 9.3.3 for use of activities in structuring exchange of information.

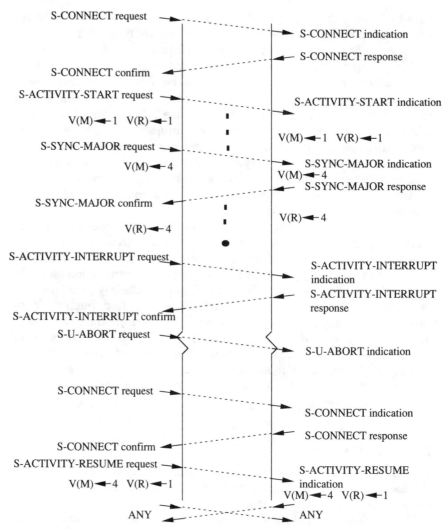

Figure 7.12 Resuming an activity after interrupting it.

The operations on the variables upon completion of each procedure are summarized in Table 7.1, where s_1 is the serial number of a synchronization point to which users synchronize upon resumption of the activity. Note, that within an activity users may place minor or major synchronization points. As a consequence, values of $V(A)$, $V(M)$, and $V(R)$ may be updated. Users may resume an activity from any of the confirmed minor or major synchronization points.

As before, services related to management of an activity are subject to token control. The token in this case is the same as major token, ex-

TABLE 7.1   Assignment of Values to Variables
during Activity Related Operations

Session service	Operations
Connection Establishment:	$V_{act} \Leftarrow false$
Activity Start:	$V_{act} \Leftarrow true,$ $V(M) \Leftarrow 1,$ $V(R) \Leftarrow 1.$
Activity End:	$V_{act} \Leftarrow false,$ $V(M) \Leftarrow V(M) + 1,$ $V(R) \Leftarrow V(M).$
Activity Interrupt:	$V_{act} \Leftarrow false.$
Activity Resume:	$V_{act} \Leftarrow true,$ $V(M) \Leftarrow s_1 + 1,$ $V(R) \Leftarrow 1.$
Activity Discard:	$V_{act} \Leftarrow false.$

cept that it is renamed as *major/activity token*. Thus, the SS user to
which the major/activity token is currently assigned may issue primitives to start, end, interrupt, resume or abandon the activity. This
token becomes available whenever Major Synchronization and/or those
related to activities are negotiated during connection establishment.
Further, the token may be transferred between the users using the services Give Tokens and Please Tokens.

As a last remark, the services Activity End, Activity Interrupt, and
Activity Discard are confirmed, whereas Activity Start and Activity
Resume are unconfirmed.

7.4   Session Services

In this section we discuss Session services, classifying them according
to whether a given service is mandatory or optional. For each service,
a number of additional services may be required to support the service.
Such requirements are specified in the form of functional units.
Additionally, the OSI architecture defines a number of service subsets
which are currently believed to be useful. These are discussed in some
detail (see also [CCITT X.215] or [ISO 8326]).

7.4.1   Mandatory Services

In the previous two sections we have discussed a number of concepts
related to Data transfer, connection release, and synchronization.
Therein, we also made reference to a number of related services, many
of which are optional. Services that must be implemented and used in
conjunction with optional services are

1. Connection establishment,
2. (Normal) data transfer,
3. Orderly release,
4. U-Abort, and
5. P-Abort.

A few comments may be helpful at this point. First, during connection establishment, a number of parameters, including the set of services to be used, are negotiated between the two users and the Session layer. Normal data transfer is full duplex, unrestricted by the availability of data token. Lastly, orderly release is also not subject to control by the current assignment of the release token.

7.4.2 Functional Units

The mandatory services, discussed above, are clubbed together in the form of a *Kernel functional unit*. A functional unit is a logical grouping of related service elements, and is based on the fact that whenever a particular service element is selected, selection of other service elements from the same group is essential. This enables users and the SS provider to negotiate on the basis of functional units rather than individual service elements. Negotiated release, for instance, is meaningful only when use of the services Give Tokens and Please Tokens is also negotiated. Therefore, the functional unit *Negotiated Release* includes both services Give Tokens and Please Tokens. See Table 7.2 for its definition as well as that of other functional units. Note that no additional service need be negotiated in order to provide for full duplex data transfer, whereas to support half duplex data transfer users need to negotiate the use of Half Duplex functional unit in addition to the Kernel.

The table also lists services required to support expedited data transfer, minor synchronization, major synchronization, resynchronization, and activities. Expedited Data transfer service[10] permits users to transmit a limited amount of data on an expedited basis. Its use may be desirable since normal data is subject to flow control at the Transport layer. As usual, Expedited Data transfer service is unconfirmed. Typed Data transfer, Capability Data transfer and Exception reporting are discussed below.

7.4.3 Typed and Capability Data Transfers

Typed Data transfer allows users to exchange data that is not subject to control by assignment of the data token. This service is particularly

---

[10]If Expedited Data transfer service is not made available by the Transport layer, then the Session layer does not provide this service to its users.

**TABLE 7.2   Functional Units and Their
Associated Service Elements**

Functional unit	Service(s)
Kernel	Session connection Normal data transfer Orderly release User-Abort Provider-Abort
Negotiated Release	Orderly release Give token Please token
Half Duplex	Give token Please token
Duplex	none, additionally
Expedited Data	Expedited Data transfer
Typed Data	Typed Data transfer
Capability Data	Capability Data transfer
Minor Synchronization	Minor synchronization Give token Please token
Major Synchronization	Major synchronization Give token Please token
Resynchronization	Resynchronization
Exception Reporting	Exception by provider Exception by user
Activity Management	Activity start Activity resume Activity interrupt Activity discard Activity end Give token Please token Give control

useful when half duplex data transfer is negotiated, in which case either user may transfer data using the Typed Data transfer service, irrespective of the current assignment of data token. Caution must be exercised while using typed data transfer, since separation of typed data transfer is not guaranteed by the Minor Synchronization and Resynchronization services.

Capability Data transfer, on the other hand, allows users to transfer a limited amount of data when an activity is *not* in progress. Its use may only be negotiated when the Activity functional unit has also been selected, but independent of whether half duplex data transfer and minor synchronization are selected or not. Further, a Capability Data transfer request may be made only by that SS user to which major/activity token is currently assigned, in addition to data and minor tokens, if available.

7.4.4   Exception Reporting

Whenever the SS provider or an SS user detects an error, or encounters a difficulty in operating the Session connection, an *exception* is said to occur. For example, if a protocol error is detected within the Session layer, it is the responsibility of the Session layer to inform the SS users of the error condition. Such an error is presumed to be relatively minor and non-persistent, in that it is possible for SS users to recover from it using resynchronization. Similarly, an SS user may detect a procedural error that pertains to communication between the users, or to the computation being carried by the users in a distributed manner. In either case, the occurrence of an exception must be *reported* to the other user, so that recovery may be initiated.[11]

The Session layer, optionally, provides two distinct services, viz. *Provider Exception Reporting* and *User Exception Reporting*. As suggested by their names, the former service allows the SS provider to report the occurrence of an exception. User Exception Reporting service is used by an SS user to convey the nature of an exception to the corresponding SS user and to request it to initiate error recovery.

The use of these services is negotiated in the form of a functional unit, *Exception Reporting,* but only in conjunction with half duplex data transfer. Further, if use of activities is also negotiated, then exceptions may only be reported when an activity is in progress. Aside from the above, there is no constraint on the SS provider issuing a related indication primitive. But, only the SS user to which the data token is *not* assigned may report an exception. In either case, the responsibility of initiating a recovery lies with the SS user to which the data token *is* assigned.

Once an exception is reported, no meaningful communication is possible until recovery is initiated by the user. A number of mechanisms are available to recover from an error condition, the most prominent amongst these being resynchronization and activity interrupt (the latter followed by activity resumption). See Figure 7.13 for an illustration of recovery from an exception condition. These mechanisms, of course, may be used only when the corresponding functional units have been negotiated. Otherwise, the user initiating error recovery may either abort the Session connection or simply transfer the data token. The latter assumes that the user reporting an exception does so simply to obtain the data token. (There is, however, a more elegant way of obtaining a token, viz. using Token Please service.)

---

[11]See Section 9.3.3 for its use in reliable transfer.

(Minor and Data tokens this side)

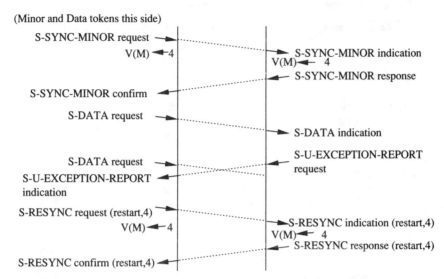

Note: S-RESYNC parameters are Resynchronize Type (optional), Synchronization point serial number

Figure 7.13 Exception reporting and recovery using resynchronization.

7.4.5 Service Primitives

Table 7.3 lists the services that may be provided by the Session layer together with their corresponding service primitive names. It characterizes each service according to whether a service is mandatory or optional, and whether it is confirmed, unconfirmed, or provider-initiated.

7.4.6 Token Management and Constraints

We are now ready to discuss the management of tokens and the constraints they impose upon issuing primitives. A total of four tokens are defined:

1. data token,
2. release token,
3. minor token, and
4. major/activity token.

A token becomes available whenever the corresponding service is negotiated. During connection establishment, an available token may be assigned by the initiating user to itself or to the other user. Alternatively, it may let the responding user make the assignment. Subse-

TABLE 7.3   Session Services and Their Primitives

Service elements	Type of service	Mandatory/Optional
S-CONNECT	confirmed	mandatory
S-RELEASE	confirmed	mandatory
S-U-ABORT	unconfirmed	mandatory
S-P-ABORT	provider-initiated	mandatory
S-TOKEN-GIVE	unconfirmed	optional
S-TOKEN-PLEASE	unconfirmed	optional
S-CONTROL-GIVE	unconfirmed	optional
S-DATA	unconfirmed	mandatory
S-EXPEDITED-DATA	unconfirmed	optional
S-TYPED-DATA	unconfirmed	optional
S-CAPABILITY-DATA	confirmed	optional
S-SYNC-MINOR	confirmed	optional
S-SYNC-MAJOR	confirmed	optional
S-RESYNCHRONIZE	confirmed	optional
S-U-EXCEPTION-REPORT	unconfirmed	optional
S-P-EXCEPTION-REPORT	provider-initiated	optional
S-ACTIVITY-START	unconfirmed	optional
S-ACTIVITY-RESUME	unconfirmed	optional
S-ACTIVITY-INTERRUPT	confirmed	optional
S-ACTIVITY-DISCARD	confirmed	optional
S-ACTIVITY-END	confirmed	optional

quently, a token may be reassigned by a user by issuing the service primitive *S-TOKEN-GIVE* request. Or, its re-assignment may be requested by a user by issuing *S-TOKEN-PLEASE* request primitive. Which user may issue these primitives is determined by the current assignment of the various tokens. Table 7.4 specifies these constraints. All available tokens may be re-assigned simultaneously using the service *S-CONTROL-GIVE*. But this service is available only when the Activity functional unit has been negotiated.

Since there are no constraints imposed by the assignment of tokens on issuing S-RESYNCHRONIZE primitives, any user may re-assign a token (forcibly) using resynchronization service. Further, since resynchronization attempts may collide, re-assignment of tokens can be negotiated during resynchronization.

7.4.7   Service Subsets

The OSI architecture defines a number of service *subsets,* which today are believed to be useful from the viewpoint of Session layer implementation and negotiation of functional units. These are

TABLE 7.4   Constraints Imposed by Assignment of Tokens

Service elements	Tokens that must be assigned to the initiating user
S-CONNECT	-
S-RELEASE	all available tokens (see Note 1)
S-U-ABORT	-
S-P-ABORT	-
S-TOKEN-GIVE	the particular token
S-TOKEN-PLEASE	not the particular token
S-CONTROL-GIVE	all available tokens
S-DATA	Data token, if available
S-EXPEDITED-DATA	-
S-TYPED DATA	-
S-CAPABILITY-DATA	Major token, and Data and Minor tokens, if available
S-SYNC-MINOR	Minor token, and Data token, if available
S-SYNC-MAJOR	Major token, and Data and Minor tokens, if available
S-RESYNCHRONIZE	-
S-U-EXCEPTION-REPORT	not the Data token
S-P-EXCEPTION-REPORT	-
S-ACTIVITY-START	Major token, and Data and Minor tokens, if available
S-ACTIVITY-RESUME	Major token, and Data and Minor tokens, if available
S-ACTIVITY-INTERRUPT	Major token
S-ACTIVITY-DISCARD	Major token
S-ACTIVITY-END	Major token, and Data and Minor tokens, if available

Note 1: A responding user may reject the release of connection only if the release token is available, but assigned to the initiator.

1. *Basic Combined Subset (BCS),*
2. *Basic Synchronized Subset (BSS),* and
3. *Basic Activity Subset (BAS).*

The functional units that comprise each subset are listed in Table 7.5. Note that

1. Expedited data transfer has not been included in any of the subsets.
2. Full duplex data transfer is included only in the Basic Combined Subset.
3. Major Synchronization and Resynchronization functional units are

TABLE 7.5   Subsets and Their Definition

Functional unit	BCS	BSS	BAS
Kernel	yes	yes	yes
Negotiated Release		yes	
Half Duplex	yes	yes	yes
Full Duplex	yes	yes	
Expedited Data			
Typed Data		yes	yes
Capability Data			yes
Minor Synchronization		yes	yes
Major Synchronization		yes	
Resynchronization		yes	
Exceptions			yes
Activity Management			yes

not part of the Basic Activity Subset. As such, resynchronization may only be carried out using Activity Interrupt and Activity Resume services.

7.4.8   Parameters

Each service primitive has an associated list of parameters. One is particularly concerned with:

1. the meaning to be associated with each parameter,
2. the possible set of values that a parameter may take,
3. whether a given parameter is mandatory, optional, conditional, or totally absent, and
4. whether there is any relationship between the values of a parameter in two or more primitives related to the same service.

We shall not discuss every parameter of each service primitive. Instead, we concentrate only upon those that are unique to the Session layer or its services. These include Synchronization Point Serial Numbers, Session Connection Identifier, and Activity Identifier.

Synchronization point serial number.   The parameter *synchronization point serial number* is exchanged with almost every service primitive that has anything to do with either placement of a synchronization point, resynchronization, or activity management, including

S-SYNC-MINOR,

S-SYNC-MAJOR,

TABLE 7.6   Assignment of Synchronization Point Serial Number

Service Primitive	Synchronization point serial number assigned by			
	Request	Indication	Response	Confirm
S-SYNC-MINOR	provider	provider (=)	user	provider (=)
S-SYNC-MAJOR	provider	provider (=)		
S-RESYNCHRONIZE (restart)	user	provider (=)		
S-RESYNCHRONIZE (abandon)		provider	user	provider (=)
S-RESYNCHRONIZE (set)	user	provider (=)	user	provider (=)
S-ACTIVITY-START				
S-ACTIVITY-RESUME	user	provider (=)		
S-ACTIVITY-INTERRUPT				
S-ACTIVITY-DISCARD				
S-ACTIVITY-END	provider	provider (=)		

S-RESYNCHRONIZE,

S-ACTIVITY-RESUME,

S-ACTIVITY-END, and

S-CONNECT.

For one, the value of synchronization point serial number is between 0 and 999999, both inclusive. Usually, for most parameters, it is readily evident as to who, an SS user or the SS provider, assigns a value to it. For instance, it is the user that provides a value to each parameter in a request or response primitive. In contrast to this, the value of the synchronization point serial number in a request primitive may, in some cases, be provided by the SS provider. Table 7.6 indicates as to which entity assigns a value to synchronization point serial number. (See also Figures 7.8 to 7.10, Figure 7.12 and Figure 7.13.) Note, in some cases the parameter may not be present at all.

Session connection identifier.   The parameter *Session connection identifier* is optionally included in the following service primitives:

S-CONNECT, and

S-ACTIVITY-RESUME.

This parameter allows users to identify an earlier connection in case an activity is interrupted, and subsequently resumed after a break in the connection. Recall that the scope of Session connection identifier is limited to the two users, and is, therefore, totally transparent to the

Session layer. The Session layer service specification simply indicates that the identifier is composed of four fields:

1. Calling SS user reference number (64 octets),
2. Called SS user reference number (64 octets),
3. Common reference (64 octets), and
4. Additional reference information (4 octets).

For the purpose of discussion, we may ignore additional reference information. The common reference may, for instance, be the date and time of connection establishment. The calling and called references are assigned individually by the two users. The fact that 64 octets are available to encode each user reference, implies that this field may be used to encode a variety of user related information, including possibly user identity, location, and the nature of computation.

Activity identifier. An *Activity identifier* is associated with an activity at the time it is started, so that subsequently a reference to it may be made, in case the activity is to be resumed. Once resumed, an activity is assigned a new identifier. As far as the Session layer is concerned, this parameter is encoded using 6 octets. More than that, the Activity identifier is totally transparent to the Session layer.

7.5   A Model of Session Service

The Session service available to users may be described (somewhat) formally in a variety of ways. In this section we look at sequencing of primitives pertaining to each service, independent of other services. Then, the constraints on issuing primitives, all of them taken together, are discussed using a state transition diagram, or, equivalently, a state table. Some of these constraints relate to resolving collisions that occur as a consequence of primitives being issued by the two users at the two connection end points. Lastly, we discuss the quality of Session service.

7.5.1   Intra-Service Sequence of Primitives

A service primitive issued by an SS user at one end point of a connection generally results in a corresponding primitive being issued by the SS provider at the other connection end point. Thus, for each service, a typical sequence in which service primitives are issued is primarily determined by whether a service is confirmed, unconfirmed or provider-initiated. From Table 7.3, it is relatively simple to determine such sequences. (Also see figures later in this chapter.)

We shall simply make observations in respect of some of the Session services. First, issuing of an S-CONNECT request primitive by a user should be interpreted as a request to establish yet another Session connection. If a connection establishment attempt is rejected by the SS provider then it simply issues an S-CONNECT confirm with the *result* parameter set to "rejected by the provider" together with the reason. Surely, no corresponding indication primitive is issued at the called service-access-point.

Although Minor Synchronization is a confirmed service, a responding SS user is not required to explicitly confirm it using an S-SYNC-MINOR response. A response by a user to a subsequent S-SYNC-MINOR (or S-SYNC-MAJOR) indication primitive confirms all outstanding minor synchronization points. As a final comment, some of the sequences may be disrupted in case collision with other primitives occurs.

7.5.2 State Transition Description

Allowable sequences in which primitives may be issued at a service-access-point, but relating to a Session connection, are usually given in the form of a state transition diagram. But, the Session service primitives being so varied, the constraints are, instead, specified in the form of a state table. A state table description of the Session service includes

1. the different states of a Session connection, for example, *Wait for S-CONNECT confirm,*
2. the collection of events, initiated by either a user or a service provider. As an example, issuing an S-RELEASE indication constitutes an event,
3. the set of events that may take place in each state of the Session connection. For instance, within the state *Wait for S-CONNECT confirm* only an S-CONNECT confirm primitive may be issued, whereas in *Wait for S-RELEASE confirm,* a large variety of service primitives may be issued,
4. the state of the connection resulting from the occurrence of an admissible event, and any associated condition that must be tested before a state change occurs. For example, in the *Data transfer* state, an event corresponding to issuing an S-SYNC-MAJOR request causes the state to change to *Wait for S-SYNC-MAJOR confirm.* But this change occurs
   (a) provided data and minor tokens, if available, and major/activity token, are assigned to the user, and
   (b) *either* the Activity functional unit has not been negotiated or, if negotiated, an activity is currently in progress,
5. the additional house-keeping operations that need to be performed, for example, assignment of values to variables V_{sc}, or $V(M)$.

The condition, mentioned in 4. above, may formally be specified as

TABLE 7.7   An Example State Table Description of the Session Service

Event		States	
	...	Data transfer	...
...	...	...	...
S-SYNC-MAJOR request	...	if condition P is true, then assign suitable values to $V_{sc}, V(A), V(M)$; and change state to "Await S-SYNC-MAJOR confirm"	...
...	...	...	...

(Note: P is defined in the text.)

$$P: (not(FU(ACT)) or \ V_{act}) and I(dk) and I(mi) and II(ma) = true.$$

In the above, V_{act} is the variable defined earlier in Section 7.3, and

1. $FU(x) = true$ provided the functional unit x has been negotiated. $x = ACT$ refers to the Activity functional unit.
2. $I(x) = true$ provided the token x is either not available, or if available, then it is currently assigned to the user. In the above, dk and mi refer to, respectively, data and minor tokens.
3. $II(ma) = true$ provided the token is available and it is currently assigned to the user. In the above, ma refers to the major/activity token.

Table 7.7 illustrates a portion of the state table description of a Session connection. The complete state table can be found in references [ISO 8326] or [CCITT X.215]. One of the important issues resolved by the state table relates to collisions. These occur when primitives are issued by the two users more or less simultaneously, or by a user and the SS provider.

7.5.3   Collisions

A collision occurs when a user, having issued an S-RESYNCHRO-NIZE request primitive, for instance, receives an indication primitive other than the expected S-RESYNCHRONIZE confirm primitive. As one example, it may receive an S-RESYNCHRONIZE *indication*. The latter may be a consequence of the other user issuing an S-RESYN-CHRONIZE request primitive. Collisions are resolved by the service provider. See Figure 7.14 for its illustration. There, it is assumed that the two resynchronization attempts use different options, viz. restart

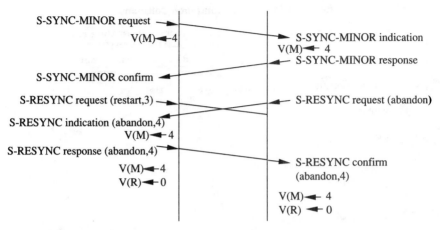

Figure 7.14 Occurrence of collisions and their resolution.

and abandon. The collision is resolved in favor of a resynchronization with the abandon option.

Collisions may occur whenever a user is waiting for any of the following services to complete:

1. resynchronization,
2. activity interrupt,
3. activity discard, and
4. recovery from an exceptional condition.

Instead, it may receive (or, in fact, is about to receive) an indication primitive pertaining to resynchronization, activity interrupt or discard, or to an exception report. Collisions are resolved by the service provider in favor of an abort, activity discard, activity interrupt, or resynchronization (listed in order of decreasing favor). Table 7.8 illustrates the rules used to resolve collisions between resynchronization attempts by users, but using different options. The table may be interpreted as follows: if a user is waiting to receive, for example, an S-RESYNCHRONIZE confirm primitive with the restart option, then the procedure that it initiated is terminated in favor of a resynchronization attempt with a set or abandon option by the other user.

Surely, it is possible for the two users to initiate a resynchronize procedure with the same option. In that case, collision is resolved in favor of the user which initiated the connection establishment procedure in the first place. If the option, however, is restart then the request with the lower synchronization point serial number takes precedence.

TABLE 7.8   Rules for Resolving Resynchronization Collisions

An SS user waiting for an	may receive from the provider an S-RESYNCHRONIZE indication with an option		
	restart	set	abandon
S-RESYNCHRONIZE (restart) confirm	yes	yes	yes
S-RESYNCHRONIZE (set) confirm		yes	yes
S-RESYNCHRONIZE (abandon) confirm			yes

7.5.4   Quality of Service

The quality of Session service refers to the characteristics of a Session connection as visible to its users. These are properties that can solely be attributed to the Session layer. In reality, user behavior is bound to affect these characteristics to some degree or the other. For instance, a user may delay its response to an incoming connection. In that case, the delay would be in excess of the expected connection establishment delay. The quality of Session service is specified in terms of a number of parameters, some of which relate to performance issues, including delay, throughput, failure probability. Others describe certain features available to the users over a connection.

Yet another classification of the parameters is based on whether the value of a parameter is negotiable or fixed. Parameters whose values are negotiated during connection establishment are

1. Performance related parameters:
   (a) Residual error rate,
   (b) Throughput, and
   (c) Transit delay,
2. Service features:
   (a) Protection,
   (b) Priority,
   (c) Extended control, and
   (d) Optimized dialogue transfer.

Many of these parameters were defined earlier in Section 3.4. *Extended control* of a connection is an optional feature that enables a user to initiate certain primitives, even when the network is congested. When the network is congested, the Session layer typically applies some form of back pressure, and thereby prevents a user (or users) from issuing any primitive other than those that are aimed at recovery. Primitives that fall in this category are Resynchronization, User-Abort, Activity Interrupt and Activity Discard.

Optimized dialogue transfer, if negotiated, allows the Session layer to use an extended form of concatenation to transfer certain Session protocol data units. For example, this permits two or more protocol data units containing user data to be concatenated with a protocol data unit corresponding to Give Tokens.

The negotiation procedure differs from parameter to parameter, but only in respect of details concerning assignment of parameter values by the parties involved. The SS user initiating the establishment of a connection proposes, in an S-CONNECT request primitive, the *desired* value for each parameter, and in some cases the *lowest acceptable* as well. The SS layer, if it is not in a position to provide the desired quality, or the lowest acceptable level of quality of service, may simply reject the connection request. Otherwise, it informs the responding user entity of the *available* quality of service by issuing a corresponding indication primitive. If the available quality is adequate, the responding SS user simply specifies the *agreed* quality of service in a response primitive. The agreed values of parameters are communicated to the initiating SS user by the SS provider in an S-CONNECT confirm primitive.

As for parameters whose values are not negotiated, users do become aware of them, somehow or the other. Possibly, these are documented, or their values may be interrogated using procedures that are local to an interface. But, these values are the same for the two users. During the operation of a connection, it is quite conceivable that the quality of service, both in respect of negotiable parameters as well as others, may deteriorate. If that is the case, the SS provider is not obliged to indicate this to the users. Eventually, if the quality of service deteriorates considerably, a user or the service provider may abort or release the connection.

7.6 Session Protocol

We now discuss procedures used within the Session layer to provide Session services.[12] Recall that the Transport layer simply provides services for end-to-end connection establishment, termination, normal data transfer and optionally expedited data transfer. Therefore, the Session layer is required to implement a variety of functions in order to close the gap between Transport services and Session services. Aside from using a Transport connection to establish (or terminate) a Session connection, it must maintain state information concerning synchro-

---

[12]See also [CCITT X.225] or [ISO 8327].

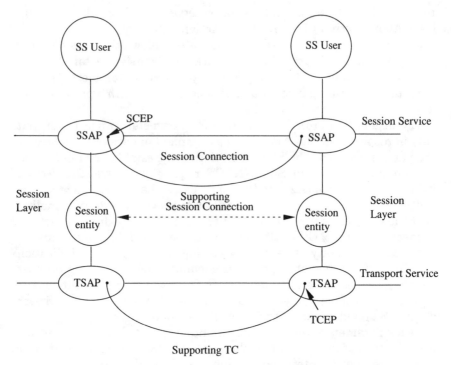

Figure 7.15 Model of the Session layer concerning a single Session connection.

nization points and activities[13] and update the same each time a minor or major synchronization point is placed, resynchronization occurs, or an activity related service element is initiated. Further, the Session layer must ensure that interaction between SS users and the SS provider is consistent with the current distribution of available tokens.

7.6.1 Session Protocol Data Units

Needless to say, that an important function of the Session layer is to convey the semantics of its interaction with an SS user over the connection to the other user. Figure 7.15 gives a model of the Session layer as it concerns a single Session connection. The interaction between a Session entity and the corresponding SS user is via service primitives. The two supporting Session entities interact with each other by exchanging *Session Protocol Data Units (SPDUs)* over a logical connec-

---

[13]See Sections 7.2.5 and 7.4.2. for a list of related variables.

tion that they establish between themselves to support the particular connection between the two SS users.

Exchange of SPDUs between the two entities is governed, both in respect of semantics and syntax, by the Session protocol. The protocol also specifies the event(s) that causes an SPDU to be sent, or the actions to be taken by a Session entity when it receives an SPDU. For instance, when an SS user issues an S-CONNECT request, its supporting Session entity, sends a *CONNECT* SPDU to the corresponding remote Session entity. Further, when the remote Session entity receives a CONNECT SPDU, it issues an S-CONNECT indication primitive to the corresponding SS user. The responding SS user's response is conveyed through an *ACCEPT* or *REFUSE* SPDU, depending upon whether the value of the *Result* parameter in the S-CONNECT response primitive is "accepted" or "rejected by SS user." Figure 7.16 illustrates the use of CONNECT, ACCEPT and REFUSE SPDUs in connection establishment. The figure illustrates three different cases corresponding to:

1. successful establishment,
2. rejection by the responding Session entity, and
3. rejection by the responding Session user.

Table 7.9 lists the SPDUs that are associated with each Session service primitive.[14] This association of SPDUs with service primitives immediately suggests the sequence of events that take place when a Session service is initiated by a user or the Session layer itself. Some of the other procedures are illustrated in Figure 7.17, including data transfer, resynchronization, and provider-initiated abort.

7.6.2 Connection Initialization

During connection establishment, several aspects concerning procedures to be used subsequently are negotiated. Depending upon the procedure, the negotiation may take place between the two SS users alone, the two supporting Session entities, or between all four entities. We shall first consider:

---

[14]Note that
1. There is no acknowledgement SPDU associated with a service that is not confirmed. The exception to this is the abort procedure, where the supporting Session entity may acknowledge an abrupt termination, particularly if the supporting Transport connection is be re-used.
2. The responding Session entity may send any of the two SPDUs in response, thereby completing the procedure either successfully or otherwise.
3. In case of provider-initiated services, only S-P-ABORT and S-P-EXCEPTION REPORT indication primitives are defined.

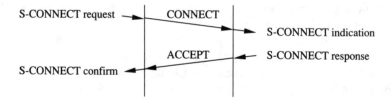

(a) Successful connection establishment.

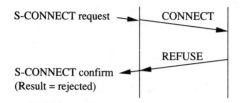

(b) Connection refused by responding Session entity.

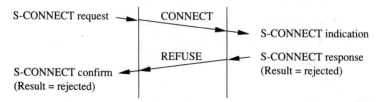

(c) Connection refused by responding SS user.

Figure 7.16 Use of CONNECT, ACCEPT, and REFUSE SPDUs in connection establishment.

1. assignment of Session Connection Identifier,
2. assignment of Activity Identifier, where applicable, and
3. initial assignment of available tokens.

As noted earlier (see Section 7.4.8), Session Connection and Activity Identifiers are totally transparent to the SS provider (that is, to Session entities), and are, therefore, negotiated between the two users alone.[15]

Assignment of available tokens is also negotiated between the two users, but the Session layer makes a record of the assignment. It does so to later ensure that SS users issue related primitive in accordance with constraints imposed by the token assignment (see Table 7.4).

Now, consider those parameters that are negotiated between SS users and the supporting Session entities. These include:

---

[15]These and other parameters are, in fact, negotiated between Application entities.

TABLE 7.9   Mapping of Session Service Primitives onto SPDUs

Service elements	SPDU associated with request, indication primitives	Associated ACK or reject SPDU
S-CONNECT	CONNECT	ACCEPT or REFUSE
S-RELEASE	FINISH	DISCONNECT or NOT FINISHED
S-U-ABORT	ABORT	ABORT ACCEPT
S-P-ABORT	ABORT	ABORT ACCEPT
S-TOKEN-GIVE	GIVE TOKENS	-
S-TOKEN-PLEASE	PLEASE TOKENS	-
S-CONTROL-GIVE	GIVE TOKENS CONFIRM	-
S-DATA	DATA	-
S-EXPEDITED-DATA	EXPEDITED DATA	-
S-TYPED-DATA	TYPED DATA	-
S-CAPABILITY-DATA	CAPABILITY DATA	CAPABILITY DATA ACK
S-SYNC-MINOR	MINOR SYNC POINT	MINOR SYNC ACK
S-SYNC-MAJOR	MAJOR SYNC POINT	MAJOR SYNC ACK
S-RESYNCHRONIZE	RESYNCHRONIZE	RESYNCHRONIZE ACK
S-U-EXCEPTION-REPORT	EXCEPTION DATA	-
S-P-EXCEPTION-REPORT	EXCEPTION REPORT	-
S-ACTIVITY-START	ACTIVITY START	-
S-ACTIVITY-RESUME	ACTIVITY RESUME	-
S-ACTIVITY-INTERRUPT	ACTIVITY INTERRUPT	ACTIVITY INTERRUPT ACK
S-ACTIVITY-DISCARD	ACTIVITY DISCARD	ACTIVITY DISCARD ACK
S-ACTIVITY-END	ACTIVITY END	ACTIVITY END ACK

1. Functional units, and
2. Initial Synchronization Point Serial Number.

User requirements of functional units are proposed by the initiating SS user in parameter *Session Requirements* of S-CONNECT request primitive. The Session protocol assumes that both supporting Session entities are capable of providing the services implied by the proposed functional units. In other words, the initiating and responding entities are free to reject the connection establishment, in case either of them does not implement related functions (see Figure 7.16(b)). Provided the two Session entities support the functional units, the proposed list of

(a) User initiated data transfer.

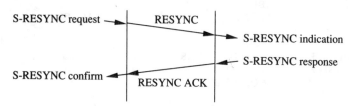

(b) Resynchronization.

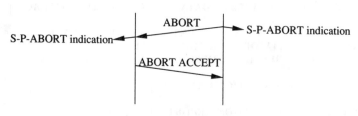

(c) Provider initiated abort.

Figure 7.17 Sequence of SPDU transmissions: some examples.

functional units is indicated to the responding SS user, who in turn makes a counter proposal of functional units that it wishes to use. The applicable set of functional units is determined by the intersection of the two proposals.

Synchronization point serial number, or equivalently the value of variable $V(M)$, has significance only for when one or more of the following functional units has been negotiated:

1. Minor and/or Major synchronization,
2. Resynchronization, and
3. Activity management.

In that case, the Synchronization Point Serial Number is initialized as follows:

1. If the Activity management functional unit has been selected, the synchronization point serial number is not initialized. Instead, it is initialized to 1 whenever an activity is "started" (see Table 7.1).

2. Otherwise, $V(M)$ is initialized to the value returned in the parameter, *Initial Synchronization Point Serial Number,* of S-CONNECT response primitive, or for the initiator in the ACCEPT SPDU.

Negotiation of the particular Session protocol to be used is clearly of concern only to the supporting Session entities. Therefore, each Session entity sends, to its peer entity, a list of protocol versions that it is capable of supporting. The negotiated version is the one with the largest version number (an integer) present in the two lists. Currently versions 1 and 2 of the Session protocol are available. These versions refer to the 1984 and 1988 versions of CCITT's Session protocol (see [CCITT X.225]).

Session entities also determine between themselves the manner in which an underlying Transport connection is used to support the Session connection. At any time, there is a one-to-one correspondence between the Session connection and the supporting Transport connection. In other words, multiplexing or splitting functions are not used by the Session layer protocol. Instead, a Transport connection may be used to support another Session connection, but only after the former Session connection has been terminated.[16] Thus, at the time of Session connection establishment, it is not necessary to establish afresh a Transport connection if there already exists a connection. Such a connection

1. is between a pair of TSAPs, to which the respective Session entities are attached, and
2. the quality of service of the available Transport connection is comparable to those requested by the initiating SS user.

The Address of the *Called TSAP* is obtained using the address mapping function of the Session layer. This function also provides a *Called Session Selector,* used by the responding Session entity to uniquely identify the particular SSAP within the domain of the Called TSAP. A similar procedure is used to obtain, from the given *Calling SSAP Address,* the *Calling TSAP Address* and the *Calling Session Selector.* While the Calling and Called TSAP Addresses are used to establish a supporting Transport connection, the Calling and Called Session Selectors are communicated as parameters in the CONNECT SPDU.

There are other characteristics of the Transport connection that are of particular relevance to the Session protocol. These include

1. availability of Expedited Data transfer service over the Transport layer, and

---

[16]When a Session connection is terminated, the underlying Transport connection is also terminated, unless the Session entities agree to "re-use" it.

2. the maximum TSDU size.

Their values are negotiated at the time of Transport connection establishment. The procedure for doing so is, of course, given by the Transport service specification. We shall simply discuss the implication this has on the manner in which the Transport connection is used to convey SPDUs.

7.6.3 Use of Available Transport Service

Since the Transport service is limited to connection establishment, termination, and normal and expedited data transfer, and since the lifetime of the underlying Transport connection may be beyond that of the Session connection, it is evident that all SPDUs concerning the particular Session connection are sent as normal TSDUs. In case use of Expedited Data transfer over the Transport connection is negotiated, then *ABORT* and *ABORT ACCEPT* SPDUs are sent as Expedited TSDUs.[17]

As one consequence of the above, it may be necessary to negotiate an appropriate value of the maximum size of TSDUs that can be supported. Its negotiation is, clearly, between the two Session entities and the TS provider. The negotiation is done independently for each direction of data transfer, and follows the procedure laid out by the Transport service specification (see also Chapter 6). If a maximum TSDU size is negotiated successfully then, by implication, the two Session entities also agree to segment an SSDU (*Session Service Data Unit*), provided the length of its corresponding SPDU exceeds the negotiated maximum TSDU size. Obviously, each SPDU so constructed after segmentation must contain an indication of whether it contains the first, last or an intermediate segment of the corresponding SSDU. SSDUs from S-DATA, S-TYPED DATA, and other primitives are all subject to segmentation.

Concatenation of a number of SPDUs onto a single TSDU is required of every implementation of the Session protocol. Of course, it is always desirable to build such a feature into a protocol. But, the design of the Session protocol is such that concatenation (in its usual sense) is necessary to support both segmentation and *Extended Concatenation*. The latter feature is optional, and it is here that one is truly able to effi-

---

[17]The protocol specifies the use of a *PREPARE* SPDU only when Transport level Expedited Data transfer service is negotiated. It is used to notify the imminent arrival of certain SPDUs related to major synchronization, resynchronization, and activity management. The PREPARE SPDU is also sent as an Expedited TSDU.

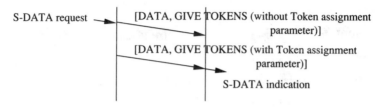

Note: The concatenation is shown as [SPDU1, SPDU2]

Figure 7.18 Segmentation and concatenation: an illustration.

ciently utilize the supporting Transport connection. Figure 7.18 illustrates the use of concatenation and segmentation in transferring a large SSDU.

7.7   Encoding of SPDUs

In this section we consider encoding of SPDUs. In doing so we also consider a number of SPDU parameters, and the possible values each may assume. The encoding scheme is structured, and may be viewed as an introduction to the encoding rules used at the Presentation layer, and discussed in Chapter 9.

7.7.1   SPDU Structure

An SPDU, together with its parameters, consists of the following fields:

1. the *SPDU Indicator* field, which identifies the type of SPDU,
2. the *Length Indicator* field, which indicates the length of the associated parameter field,
3. the *SPDU Parameter* field, which, if present, encodes one or more parameters, and
4. the *User Information* field, if defined for the SPDU and present.

These fields must appear in the order given above. The SPDU Parameter field itself consists of one or more:

1. *Parameter Group units,* each of which encodes a group of parameters, and
2. *Parameter units,* each of which encodes a single parameter.

See Figure 7.19 for an illustration of the above structure, as well as that of a Parameter Group unit and a Parameter unit, defined shortly. A Parameter Group unit contains

SPDU structure:

| SPDU Indicator | Length Indicator | SPDU Parameter (*) | User Information (*) |

SPDU Parameter structure:

| Group Parameter Unit (+) | Parameter Unit (+) |

Group Parameter Unit structure:

| Group Parameter Indication | Length Indicator | Parameter Unit (+) |

Parameter Unit structure:

| Parameter Indication | Length Indicator | Parameter Value (*) |

Notes:
(*): optional,
(+): zero, one or more number of occurrences.

Figure 7.19 The structure of SPDUs.

1. the *Group Indicator* field, which identifies the group of parameters being encoded,

2. the *Length Indicator* field, which indicates the length of the encoding of parameter in the group, and

3. one or more Parameter units, if present.

A Parameter unit is similarly structured, and consists of the following three fields:

1. the *Parameter Indicator* field, which identifies the parameter being coded,

2. the *Length Indicator* field, which indicates the length of the following parameter value, and

3. the *Parameter Value,* if present.

Lastly, the User Information field is encoded transparently. Its length may be determined from the length of the received SPDU and the length of earlier fields. Note that the value of Length Indicator may even be 0. Further, a parameter or a group of parameters may not be coded at all, unless it is stated to be mandatory, or (in the case of a Parameter Group unit) at least one parameter value is present. A detailed example of a resulting SPDU structure is given in Figure 7.20.

7.7.2 Encoding of Fields

We shall briefly describe the coding of each of the above fields with a view to present a complete example of encoding of an SPDU. The SPDU

CONNECT SPDU structure	Encoding of CONNECT SPDU
SPDU Indicator	13
Length Indicator	actual length
Group Parameter Indicator	1
Length Indicator	actual length
Parameter Indicator	10
Length Indicator	≤ 64
Parameter Value	Calling SS User Reference
Parameter Indicator	11
Length Indicator	≤ 64
Parameter Value	Common Reference
Parameter Indicator	12
Length Indicator	≤ 4
Parameter Value	Additional Reference
Group Parameter Indicator	5
Length Indicator	actual length
Parameter Indicator	19
Length Indicator	1
Parameter Value	Protocol Options
Parameter Indicator	21
Length Indicator	4
Parameter Value	TSDU Maximum Size
Parameter Indicator	22
Length Indicator	1
Parameter Value	Version Number
Parameter Indicator	23
Length Indicator	6
Parameter Value	Synchronization Point Serial Number
Parameter Indicator	26
Length Indicator	1
Parameter Value	Token Setting Item
Parameter Indicator	20
Length Indicator	2
Parameter Value	Session User Requirements
Parameter Indicator	51
Length Indicator	≤ 16
Parameter Value	Calling Session Selector
Parameter Indicator	52
Length Indicator	≤ 16
Parameter Value	Called Session Selector

Note: Some of the parameters have not been included (see [CCITT X.225] or [ISO 8327]).

Figure 7.20 Encoding of the CONNECT SPDU.

Indicator, Group Indicator and Parameter Indicator fields are each 1 octet long, and encode a decimal number in the range 0 through 255 using binary encoding. A decimal code is assigned by the Session protocol for each SPDU, Group Parameter unit and Parameter unit. As examples:

1. the CONNECT SPDU has an associated SPDU Indicator of 13,

2. the group parameters, *Session Connection Identifier* and *Connect / Accept Item,* have a Group Indicator of 1 and 5, respectively, and

3. the parameters, *Token Setting Item* and *Session User Requirements,* have a Parameter Indicator of 26 and 20, respectively.

The Length Indicator is either between 0 and 254, in which case 1 octet is used to binary code the length, or it is between 255 and 65535, in which the Length Indicator is 3 octets long and is coded as 1111 1111 followed by the 16 bit binary representation of the length in integer.

The value of each parameter is coded as per rules that are specific to the particular parameter and its possible values. We shall discuss some of these shortly, in the context of the CONNECT SPDU.

7.7.3 Encoding of CONNECT SPDU: An Example

Figure 7.20 illustrates the encoding of a typical CONNECT SPDU. Note that there are two Parameter Group units, followed by three Parameter units. The two Parameter Group units, in turn, encode 3 and 5 Parameter units, respectively. The coding of SPDU Indicator, Group Indicator and some of the Parameter Indicators is consistent with the discussion above. We shall briefly discuss the Parameter units and the coding of their values.

The coding of values corresponding to the three components of *Session Connection Identifier* is determined by SS users themselves. Therefore, these parameter are communicated transparently. The coding of the two Parameter units, *Calling* and *Called Session Selectors,* is specified not by Session protocol but by the directory function.

The coding of the five parameters in the group Connect/Accept Item is discussed below.

1. *Protocol Option* (1 octet): Currently, the only option defined relates to Extended Concatenation. Bit 1 is set to 0 or 1, depending upon whether its use is proposed or not. The other 7 bits are set to 0, for instance.

2. *Maximum TSDU size* (4 octets): It is encoded as 16-bit binary representations of two decimal numbers. Each number represents the proposed maximum TSDU size for forward or reverse direction of data transfer.

3. *Version Number* (1 octet): Currently two versions of Session protocol are available (see [CCITT X.225]). These are numbered as 1 and 2, respectively. Bit 1 (and similarly bit 2) is used to indicate whether version 1 is supported or not. Other bits are not used, currently.

4. *Initial Synchronization Point Serial Number* (at most 6 octets): The serial number may be 6 digits long. Each digit is encoded as 0011 xxxx, where xxxx is the BCD code of the corresponding digit.

5. *Initial Token Setting* (1 octet): Two bits are used to assign each of the four tokens. For instance, bits 8 and 7 are assigned 00, 01, or 10 if the release token is assigned to "initiator side," "responder side," or "responder chooses," respectively.

6. *Session User Requirements* (2 octets): The 16 bits may be used to propose use of a corresponding functional unit. Of course, only 11 functional units have been currently defined. Bits 12 through 16 are, therefore, not used.

7.8 Summary

The Session layer implements a variety of functions which Presentation entities, and ultimately Application entities, may use to structure their communication. Three different methods for structuring interaction have been discussed in this chapter. These are based upon minor and major synchronization points and activities. Since synchronization points are numbered, user entities can use these to resynchronize communication to an earlier point. Activities permit interaction between users to continue even if the supporting Transport connection fails.

Half duplex data transfer and orderly or negotiated release are other functions implemented by the Session layer. The latter ensures that transit data is not lost when Session layer is disconnected.

The operation of half duplex data transfer, negotiated release, placement of synchronization points, and management of activities are controlled by the availability and current assignment of corresponding tokens. These controls and the exchange of tokens are discussed in detail in this chapter.

A detailed description of Session services, including service primitives and their parameters is given. We have also discussed constraints on issuing service primitives at an SSAP.

The Session layer protocol specifies the procedures for realizing different Session services. For the first time, the protocol is relatively unconcerned with issues of reliability and efficiency of data transfer, since these issues have been adequately addressed in the design of the Transport layer. The majority of the Session protocol relates to management of synchronization points, activities, and related tokens.

In the next chapter, we discuss issues that concern representation of user information. Many of the Session services are transparently made available to Application entities by the Presentation layer as well.

8

The Presentation Layer

The main functionality of the Presentation layer is to provide for suitable transformation of the syntax of all data exchanged between Application layer entities. This ensures that the data exchanged can be interpreted appropriately by the two Application layer entities, while permitting each Application entity to represent information using a local syntax.

8.1 Introduction

This section is an introduction to services provided by the Presentation layer. In particular, it covers issues that concern representation of information exchanged between Application entities. Presentation layer protocol is also briefly discussed.

8.1.1 Representation of Information

Recall, from earlier chapters, that issues concerning end-to-end, reliable and cost-effective data transfer have already been resolved at the Transport layer. The Session layer ensures that such transfer is organized and/or synchronized. As such, major issues concerning data transfer have already been taken up and resolved by the Session layer, and those below. What remains to be discussed is representation of information exchanged between Application entities.

All along, data exchanged between users of a given service has taken the form of a string of bits (or octets). But, given the fact that the users exchange a variety of information, the problem of representing user data is non-trivial. Either each Application entity itself encodes user information in a manner that is well understood by its peer entity, or this problem is solved by placing a separate layer—the Presentation layer—between the Session layer and the Application layer. The latter approach is adopted by the architecture of Open Systems Interconnection.

The Presentation layer, together with the lower layers, provides *Presentation Service (PS)*. Using this service Application entities may transfer information without concern for how information is represented. This is illustrated in Figure 8.1, where it is shown that two communicating Application entities, sometimes referred to as *PS users,* access these services at *Presentation service access points (PSAPs)* to which they are attached. The sending Application entity hands over user information to the Presentation layer using a representation scheme that is *local* to its interface with the Presentation layer. (The Presentation layer, together with the layers below, is referred to as *PS provider.*) The PS provider ensures that the user information is made available to the corresponding PS user using a representation that is also local to its interface, and possibly different from the former.

8.1.2 The Abstract Syntax

Aside from transferring information from one user to the other, the Presentation layer carries out translation from one scheme of representation to another. To do so, it must clearly be aware of the structure of user information. Obviously, this structure must also be known to the two communicating users for them to be able to associate a definite meaning with the information communicated.

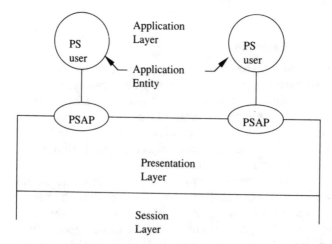

Figure 8.1 The Presentation Service Provider and its users.

Thus, the structure of user information must be unambiguously defined, and made known to the two users as well as the PS provider. The structure of user information may be either simple, for instance, an integer, a character, or an octet. Or, it may be more complex, in that it is defined in terms of a number of components each of which is either simple or complex, for example, a string of characters, a record of values, or a sequence of records. The structure of user information is known as an *abstract syntax,* and may be defined using the *Abstract Syntax Notation One (ASN.1),* which itself is a standard (see reference [ISO 8824,CCITT X.208]). Data structures and the notation for defining these are discussed in Section 8.2.

8.1.3 The Transfer Syntax

Above, we have made no mention of how the PS provider encodes user information and then transfers it from one user to the other. Figure 8.2 is a model of the Presentation layer, where it is shown that the supporting Presentation entity encodes the information into a string of bits (or octets) using a particular scheme and transfers the coded string of bits to its peer Presentation entity. The scheme used to encode user information must be known to its peer Presentation entity as well. The Presentation entity, which receives the encoded user information, may decode the information content and hand it over to the corresponding user. The *encoding scheme* is known as the *transfer syntax.* Together, the abstract syntax and the transfer syntax are known as the *presentation context.*

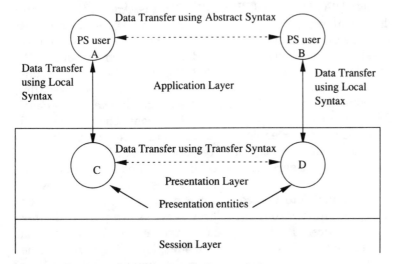

Figure 8.2 Data transfer using presentation services.

Schemes for encoding user information whose structure is defined using the Abstract Syntax Notation have been standardized, and are available in reference [ISO 8825, CCITT X.209]. These are discussed at some length in Section 8.3.

To summarize the discussion thus far, user information that needs to be communicated must be structured. This structure, or the abstract syntax, must be known to, or negotiated between, the PS users as well as the PS provider. Further, the transfer syntax used to encode data consistent with the abstract syntax must be negotiated between the supporting Presentation entities.

8.1.4 Presentation Services Characteristics

The Presentation layer provides services by which a presentation context can be negotiated between the concerned parties. This usually takes place at the time of connection establishment. In fact, at connection establishment, the concerned parties negotiate a *set* of presentation contexts. Furthermore, using available Presentation services it is possible for PS users to dynamically change the set of defined presentation contexts that are currently active. In case the presentation context set is empty, then a default context is used to encode user information. The default context may also be negotiated at connection establishment. In the absence of any such negotiation, a default context is always available, which is known *a-priori* to all communicating Presentation entities and Presentation service users.

The above implies that the Presentation service is connection oriented (see references [ISO 8822, CCITT X.216]). That is, Application entities may exchange information only after a connection has been established between PSAPs to which they are respectively attached. Such a connection is called a *Presentation connection*. Between a given pair of PSAPs, there may exist zero, one or more Presentation connections at any time. Such connections may be distinguished from each other by associating with each connection a pair of *Presentation-connection-end-point-identifiers (PCEP-identifiers)*, one for each end of the connection. The significance of a PCEP-identifier is, as usual, local. As such, the two PCEP-identifiers of a connection may or may not be distinct.

Aside from providing services to establish a connection, transfer normal data, and to abort a connection, the Presentation layer provides services to add and delete a presentation context from the currently defined set of presentation contexts. These services are part of Context Management services. It also provides to the Application entities all those services that the Session layer provides, including normal or negotiated release, placing of minor and major synchronization points, resynchronization, activity management, transfer of normal data in half duplex mode, transfer of typed data, capability data, and expedited data, as well as exception reporting. Resynchronization and activity management operations restore the defined context set to that which existed at some specified earlier time.

8.1.5 Data Transfer Characteristics

The majority of characteristics of data transfer over a Presentation connection are derived from those of the supporting Session connection. Surely, data transfer is end-to-end, reliable, and possibly organized and/or synchronized. Further, the quality of Presentation service is closely tied to that of the supporting Session service. The characteristics of data transfer specifically contributed by the Presentation layer relate to representation of user information. Once a presentation context has been negotiated, PS users may transfer data without concern for how such data is represented and transferred. User data may be transferred as normal data, typed data, expedited data, capability data or as part of certain operations including abort, release, resynchronization, etc. But, not all user data is subject to the currently defined presentation context set. User data contained in expedited data transfers, is *always* encoded using a default presentation context.

8.1.6 Assumed Session Services

As discussed above, the Presentation layer basically enhances the Session service made available to it, by adding primitives that enable Application entities to define or to delete presentation contexts. Aside from those that are mandatory, the Session layer may make available a number of optional services including those related to half duplex data transfer, negotiated release, expedited data transfer, synchronization, typed data transfer, capability data transfer, activity management, and exception reporting. If one or more of these are not provided, then the Presentation layer is unable to support corresponding services. Furthermore, since context management services are dependent upon the use of typed data transfer service, it is important that the Session layer provide typed data transfer service to enable the Presentation layer to permit context definition and deletion.

As for the quality of service of the PS, it is completely determined by that of the Session service.

8.1.7   Presentation Layer Protocol

For most part, the Presentation layer protocol directly maps the Presentation layer primitives onto the corresponding Session layer primitives, except for primitives that permit context definition or deletion (for details see [ISO 8823] or [CCITT X.226]). Thus, at least at a conceptual level the Presentation layer protocol is relatively simple. The complexity of the protocol essentially lies in negotiating the currently active set of presentation contexts.

From an implementation point of view, the Presentation layer protocol may be quite complex, mainly because of two reasons. First, the algorithm required to encode user information, belonging to a variety of abstract syntax or applications, must be implemented. Secondly, the protocol machines that model the Presentation layer protocol support a large number of service primitives.

8.2   The Abstract Syntax

Information may be exchanged between two Application entities provided its structure is well defined and made known to each other. This structure, also known as the abstract syntax, conveys the organization of user data, and thereby enables them to associate a meaning with the received data. Further, the abstract syntax specifies the structure of user information, independent of how it is to be represented for the purpose of transmission.

Representation issues are equally important, but may only be discussed once the abstract syntax is well understood. Towards that, an algorithm needs to be specified using which one may represent any instance of the abstract syntax. One such algorithm is discussed in the next section.

8.2.1   Data Types and Values

The abstract syntax may be defined in a variety of ways, but the one discussed here uses the notation standardized within the framework of OSI (see references [ISO 8824] or [CCITT X.208]). Definition of an abstract syntax is based upon the idea of a *data type,* as distinguished from a value. The idea behind specifying a value is to distinguish it from other possible values. The collection of all values, including the one being distinguished, defines a data type, or simply a *type*. One specific instance of it is a *value*. This is no different from the concept of abstract data types encountered in programming languages. A data type may be simple, or it may be complex. In the latter case the data type is defined in terms of a number of simpler data types, perhaps recursively. We give below a few examples of data types:

```
PDU ::= SEQUENCE {
    COUNT 1    INTEGER         42
    UNIT 1     BITSTRING       43
    DataType1  BOOLEAN         44
    NAME 1     IA5 String      4 18-22, 25
    DATA 1     OCTETSTRING     47
}

UNIV. ISO 646 STRING
```

EmployeeNoType	::=	INTEGER	
SocialSecurityType	::=	INTEGER	
EmployeeRecord	::=	SET	
		{	
		name	ISO646STRING
		address	ISO646STRING
		idNumber	EmployeeNoType
		}	

8.2.2 Tags

The notation used above to specify a data type is very similar to that encountered in many of the programming languages. There is, however, a particular inadequacy of all such notations. Once an instance of the data type is assigned a value and subsequently encoded for transmission, it is generally not possible to decode the received data and associate the same with its corresponding data type. Thus, a data type needs to be identified with a *tag* to allow unambiguous decoding of the received data. The tag may be explicitly or implicitly assigned to a data type. A data type defined according to the Abstract Syntax Notation is implicitly assigned a tag. But, in order to distinguish between two data types with the same implicit tag, one has to assign a tag explicitly, as would be required for EmployeeNoType and SocialSecurityType. Such is also required of the types associated with name and address, since the SET construction allows the components to be optional, and to appear in any order.

A tag is composed of possibly two components: a class identifier, and a nonnegative number. Four different classes are defined by the Abstract Syntax Notation: *UNIVERSAL, APPLICATION, PRIVATE,* and *CONTEXT.* A number identifies the particular data type within the class.

8.2.3 Classes of Tags

The UNIVERSAL tags, assigned only by the standard which defines the Abstract Syntax Notation, are assigned to certain commonly used data types, or to commonly used mechanisms for constructing or defining data types. As their name implies, UNIVERSAL tags have global significance, in that no other data type or construction mechanism may be assigned the same tag. The UNIVERSAL tags are not explicitly stated, they are implied by the keyword identifying the data types or the construction mechanism. For example, the data type INTEGER has a tag UNIVERSAL 2, while the construction mechanism SET has the tag UNIVERSAL 17. Other UNIVERSAL tags are listed in Table 8.1.

Tags from the APPLICATION class are assigned by other standards,

TABLE 8.1   Universal Tags and Their Assignment

UNIVERSAL tag	Assignment
0	reserved
1	BOOLEAN
2	INTEGER
3	BITSTRING
4	OCTETSTRING
5	NULL
6-15	not assigned
16	SEQUENCE and SEQUENCE-OF
17	SET and SET-OF
18-22, 25	CHARACTER SET STRING
23, 24	TIME
26, and beyond	not assigned

including those pertaining to the Application layer. Two tags within an application may not be the same. Assuming that the data types defined in the example above relate to a particular application, their tags may be assigned as follows:

```
EmployeeNoType        ::=   [APPLICATION 1]   INTEGER
SocialSecurityType    ::=   [APPLICATION 2]   INTEGER
EmployeeRecord        ::=   [APPLICATION 0]   SET
                            {
                            name              ISO646STRING
                            address           ISO646STRING
                            idNumber          EmployeeNoType
                            }
```

From its assignment, the tag APPLICATION 0 also uniquely identifies the construction mechanism SET used to define the data type, EmployeeRecord. Thus, in all future references, the tag UNIVERSAL 17 for the SET construction may be made IMPLICIT to enable a more compact encoding of values of the type EmployeeRecord.

The PRIVATE tags are assigned by specific users (or user groups), and their scope is again limited only to the particular abstract syntax.

Tags from the CONTEXT class are used freely to distinguish between the components of a structured data type. For example, the data type EmployeeRecord may be redefined to remove the ambiguity concerning name and address that currently exists, as follows:

```
EmployeeRecord      ::=   [APPLICATION 0]   SET
                          {
                          name              [0] ISO646STRING
                          address           [1] ISO646STRING
                          idNumber          [2] EmployeeNoType
                          }
```

Now, if within a value of the type EmployeeRecord, a value for name and/or address were to be specified, then the context-sensitive tags [0] and [1] enable decoding of their values.

8.2.4   An Example of an Abstract Syntax

Below we give a fairly detailed example of the specification of an abstract syntax purely for the purpose of illustration.

EmployeeRecord	::=	[APPLICATION 0]	IMPLICIT SET
		{	
		employeeName	[0] NameType,
		jobTitle	[1] JobTitleType,
		idNumber	EmployeeNoType,
		dateHired	[3] DateType,
		nameOfSpouse	NameType,
		childrenInfo	[5] IMPLICIT SEQUENCE OF ChildInfoType DEFAULT {}
		}	
NameType	::=	[APPLICATION 1]	IMPLICIT SEQUENCE
		{	
		firstName	ISO646STRING,
		midInitial	ISO646STRING,
		lastName	ISO646STRING,
		}	
JobTitleType	::=	ISO646STRING	
EmployeeNoType	::=	INTEGER	
DateType	::=	[APPLICATION 2]	IMPLICIT ISO646STRING
		– YYYYMMDD	
ChildInfoType	::=	SET	
		{	
		childName	NameType,
		birthdate	[1] DateType
		}	

In the following a number of comments are made with a view to help understand the structure and the notation used to specify the abstract syntax, and to indicate various equivalent ways of defining the data types. This abstract syntax will also be used to illustrate the standard encoding procedure.

1. In all instances an identifier has been associated with a component of a structured data type, for instance, jobTitle and idNumber. The identifiers truly do not have any significance. They only help a human user to better understand a syntax definition.

2. Table 8.2 lists the various data types defined above and, for each data type, the associated *list* of tags. Note that EmployeeNoType, JobTitleType, ChildInfoType and the types of idNumber, firstName, midInitial, and lastName are the only data types which have a UNIVERSAL tag. The reason is that these data types have not been reassigned a tag as part of the above definition.

TABLE 8.2 · Data Types and Their Tags for the Example Syntax

Data Type	Tags	Implicit Tags
EmployeeRecord	APPLICATION 0	UNIV. SET
(type of) employeeName	CONTEXT 0,	UNIV. SEQUENCE
	APPLICATION 1	
(type of) jobTitle	CONTEXT 1,	
	UNIV. ISO646STR.	
(type of) idNumber	UNIV. INTEGER	
(type of) dateHired	CONTEXT 3,	
	APPLICATION 2	UNIV. ISO646STR.
(type of) nameOfSpouse	APPLICATION 1	UNIV. SEQUENCE
(type of) childrenInfo	CONTEXT 5	UNIV. SEQUENCE OF
NameType	APPLICATION 1	UNIV. SEQUENCE
(type of) firstName	UNIV. ISO646STR.	
(type of) midInitial	UNIV. ISO646STR.	
(type of) lastName	UNIV. ISO646STR.	
JobTitleType	UNIV. ISO646STR.	
EmployeeNoType	UNIV. INTEGER	
DateType	APPLICATION 2	UNIV. ISO646STR.
ChildInfoType	UNIV. SET	
(type of) childName	APPLICATION 1	UNIV. SEQUENCE
(type of) birthDate	CONTEXT 1,	
	APPLICATION 2	UNIV.ISO646STR.

3. The construction SET used to define EmployeeRecord type permits a value which is an unordered collection of at most one value for each of the listed component data types. The SEQUENCE construct requires that one value for each component type be listed in the specified order. The SEQUENCE OF construct, used to define the type of childrenInfo, describes a data value which is an ordered collection of none, one or more values of the data type specified, in this case ChildInfoType.

4. A data type may either be *simple* or *structured*. Data types that are simple are also called primary types. In the above, the primary types used are INTEGER and ISO646STRING, defined as part of ASN.1 (see also [ISO 646]). The ISO646STRING is a sequence of none, one or more number of characters from the IA5 character set. Also, note that EmployeeNoType is a primary data type, whereas the type of jobTitle is structured. The important distinction is that with the assignment of a tag, one is necessarily defining a structured data type.

5. Note that none of the component data types in the definition of NameType have been assigned a tag. Here, it is unnecessary since the SEQUENCE construct insists that a value corresponding to each component data type be present in a value of NameType. A similar observation may be made regarding the definition of EmployeeRecord, but here the reason is different. Firstly, the type of employeeName is tagged, whereas that of nameOfSpouse is not. Next, the type EmployeeNoType is totally different from that of the other components of EmployeeRecord.

6. A value of childrenInfo may or may not be present in a record of a given employee. If not present, then the default value is an empty sequence, thereby implying that the employee has no children.[1]

7. The use of the keyword IMPLICIT in the definition of EmployeeRecord, (the type of) childrenInfo, NameType and DateType only suggests that, if necessary, the implicit UNIVERSAL tag corresponding to the SEQUENCE construct or ISO646STRING may not be encoded.

8. Comments (as in DateType) may be inserted in the definition of an abstract syntax. These comments obviously have no significance from the viewpoint of machine interpretation.

The documents [ISO 8824] or [CCITT X.208] on Abstract Syntax Notation describes in detail the formal notation for specifying an abstract syntax. It is not our intention to discuss this notation. Later in this chapter, while discussing the Presentation protocol, we shall make references to the syntax used to exchange Presentation layer protocol-data-units.

8.3   The Transfer Syntax

The abstract syntax of information exchanged between two communicating Application entities must be made known to the Presentation layer, so that supporting Presentation entities may appropriately determine an encoding scheme to represent it during transfer. The encoding algorithm, also known as the *Transfer Syntax,* is negotiated only between the Presentation entities that support the particular connection. One such transfer syntax is discussed below. It corresponds to the one specified by the OSI architecture for use together with the Abstract Syntax Notation One (see [CCITT X.209] or [ISO 8825]).

The encoding of a value of a given data type consists of three or four components, each of which is one or more octets: *identifier, length, contents,* and perhaps *end-of-contents.* Often, octets corresponding to end-of-contents field are absent, unless the length indicator requires that it be present to delimit the contents field. The four fields are discussed below.

8.3.1   Tag Identifier

The *identifier* octets encode the tag class and number of the associated data type. The encoding of the identifier is given in Table 8.3.

The identifier octets for some of the data types discussed in Section 8.2, are given in Table 8.4. If the tag number is between 0 and 30, one identifier octet is adequate to encode the tag. Additional octets are required to specify the tag number in case it is 31 or more. A data type

---

[1]This is distinct from the situation where information on an employee's children is unavailable.

TABLE 8.3   Encoding of a Tag Class and Number: Leading Octet

Bits	Value	Interpretation
bits 8 and 7	00	Universal class
	01	Application class
	10	Context-specific
	11	Private class
bit 6	0	Primitive data type
	1	Constructed data type
bits 5 through 1	11111	Tag number is 31 or more
	xxxxx	Binary representation of tag number

Note: Bit 8 is the most significant bit, and bit 1 is the least significant.

TABLE 8.4   Encoding of Tags: an Example

Data type	Tag	Identifier octets
Employee Record	APPLICATION 0	01100000
JobTitleType	UNIVERSAL 22	00010110
(type of) jobTitle	CONTEXT 1	10100001

whose tag is, for example, APPLICATION 180, the three identifier octets would be 01111111 10000001 00110100, where bit 8 of the second and third octets indicate whether at least one identifier octet follows the current octet, or not, and x is 0 or 1.

8.3.2   Length of Contents

The *length* octet specifies the number of octets in the contents field. There are three distinct cases:

1. The data type is primitive, in which case the length specifies the exact number of octets in the contents field,

2. The data type is constructed, but the encoding of data value is unavailable at the current time. Here the length field is encoded to suggest that end-of-contents octets are present and will be used to delimit the contents field, and

3. The data type is constructed, and the encoding for contents field is available. Here the sending Presentation entity has the option to either specify the length explicitly, or delimit the contents field with end-of-contents octets.

If the number of octets in the contents field is less than or equal to 127, then one octet is adequate, otherwise 2 or more octets are required to specify the length. The encoding of the leading length octet is given in Table 8.5. In Table 8.6 the examples illustrate the encoding of the length field.

TABLE 8.5 Encoding of the Length Field: Leading Octet

Bits	Value	Interpretation
bits 8 through 1	0xxxxxxx	Number of octets is less than 128, binary encoded
	10000000	End-of-contents octet is present
	11111111	Not used
	1xxxxxxx	Number of subsequent octets in the length field, binary encoded

TABLE 8.6 Encoding of the Length Field: Some Examples

Length	Encoding
18	00010010
180	10000001 10110100
1048	10000010 00000100 00011000
unknown	10000000

The *end-of-contents* octets, if present, are encoded as two zero octets. The question of ensuring transparency would be discussed shortly.

8.3.3 Encoding of Contents Field

The *contents* field, consisting of zero or more octets, is used to encode the actual data value. This encoding depends upon its data type. If the type being encoded is primary, then it directly encodes the data value. Otherwise, if the type is constructed, then each component is encoded in a manner similar to the one being discussed, that is, recursively using the 4-tuple (identifier, length, contents, end-of-contents).

The OSI standards specify the encoding of the contents field for each of the primary data types, as well as for those that are constructed. Below we discuss the encoding of some of these.

1. A value of type BOOLEAN is encoded as (00)H if the value is FALSE, and as a non-zero octet, otherwise.

2. An integer is encoded as one or more octets using Two's complement binary representation using a minimum number of octets. For example, – 25 is encoded as 11100111, or (E7)H, but not as (FF E7)H.

3. Consider now the encoding of a value of type OCTETSTRING. If the entire string of octets is available, then it may be treated as one long string of octets whose length is known and indicated in the length field. The encoding of the octets is straightforward. But, when it is necessary to encode one part of the string at a time, then the string is viewed as constructed. The end-of-contents indicator is then used to delimit the construction. Each substring is transferred as a component with its own identifier, length, contents, and possibly end-of-contents

octets. To illustrate the above, consider the transfer of the OCTET-STRING (0F 1E 2D 3C 4B 5A 69 78)H. It may be encoded as (using hexadecimal notation):

Identifier	Length	Contents
04	08	0F 1E 2D 3C 4B 5A 69 78

or as two substrings (0F 1E 2D)H followed by (3C 4B 5A 69 78)H:

Identifier	Length	Contents			End-of-Contents
24	0C	00			00
		Identifier	Length	Contents	
		04	03	0F 1E 2D	
		Identifier	Length	Contents	
		04	05	3C 4B 5A 69 78	

4. A similar scheme may be used to encode a BITSTRING. Here, additionally, one needs to indicate the number of significant bits in the last octet. All data transfers, however, are of an integral number of octets.

5. A character string of the type ISO646STRING is encoded very much like an octet string, but after mapping each character onto an octet using the IA5 7-bit character encoding scheme. Bit 8 is set to zero.

6. A value of a data type that has been tagged is treated as constructed. As such the contents field consists of encoding of the base encoding. For example, a value 'J. T. SMITH' of the type [APPLICATION 4] ISO646STRING is encoded as follows:

Identifier	Length	Contents		
64	0D			
		Identifier	Length	Contents
		16	0B	'J. T. SMITH'

However, if the data type is tagged using an IMPLICIT keyword, [APPLICATION 4] IMPLICIT ISO646STRING, for example, then its encoding would be

Identifier	Length	Contents
44	0B	'J. T. SMITH'

As can be observed, the use of IMPLICIT enables one to encode a value more compactly.

7. As a last illustration of encoding of the contents field, consider the construction of the type SET. Its encoding is constructed. The contents field then consists of the complete encoding of each component of the data value. The detailed example below illustrates this.

8.3.4   A Detailed Example

We shall close the discussion on Transfer syntax by giving a detailed example. Consider the following value of the data type Employee-Record, discussed earlier in Section 8.2:

```
{
 employeeName        { firstName           "Mary",
                       midInitial          "N",
                       lastName            "McBeth"      },
 dateHired           "19691018",
 idNumber            52,
 jobTitle            "Manager",
 nameOfSpouse        { firstName           "Tim",
                       midInitial          "",
                       lastName            "BARRY"
                     },
 childrenInfo        {{childName           {firstName    "Jane",
                                            midInitial   "T",
                                            lastName     "McBeth"
                                            },
                       birthDate           "19801115"
                     }                      }
}
```

Its encoding, as per the transfer syntax discussed above, is given in Table 8.7. All octets are given in hexadecimal notation, except for character strings.

Identifiers, such as dateHired, are not coded. They are given above to assist the reader in identifying the various components of the value. The actual string of octets transferred is

60 62 A0 13 61 11 16 04 'Mary' 16 01 'N' 16 06 'McBeth' A3 0A 42 08 '19691018' 02 01 34 A1 07 'Manager' 61 0E 16 03 'Tim' 16 00 16 05 'Barry' A5 21 31 1F 61 11 16 04 'Jane' 16 01 'T' 16 06 'McBeth' A1 0A 42 08 '19801115'

8.4 Presentation Services

In this section we discuss services that the Presentation layer makes available. This enables Application entities to transfer information using a syntax of their choice. The applicable collection of abstract syntax may be agreed to at the time of connection establishment, and perhaps changed subsequently. Service primitives, and their parameters, are discussed in this section. The protocol required to support the service is discussed in the next section. For details on Presentation services, see [ISO 8822] or [CCITT X.216].

Recall that an abstract syntax is a definition of a collection of the data types used to describe the information exchanged between two Application entities. In other words, it describes the structure of Application protocol-data-units exchanged over a Presentation connection. Each abstract syntax is identified by a name, so that PS users and the PS provider may uniquely refer to it. The Presentation entities supporting the connection negotiate between themselves the transfer syntax to be used to encode user information consistent with the abstract

TABLE 8.7   Encoding of the Example Abstract Syntax

Id	Le	Co								
60	62	Id	Le	Co						
		A0	13	Id	Le	Co				
				61	11	Id	Le	Co		
						16	04	'Mary'		
						Id	Le	Co		
						16	01	'N'		
						Id	Le	Co		
						16	06	'McBeth'		
		Id	Le	Co						
		A3	0A	Id	Le	Co				
				42	08	'19691018'				
		Id	Le	Co						
		02	01	34						
		Id	Le	Co						
		A1	07	Id	Le	Co				
				16	07	'Manager'				
		Id	Le	Co						
		61	0E	Id	Le	Co				
				16	03	'Tim'				
				Id	Le	Co				
				16	00					
				Id	Le	Co				
				16	05	'Barry'				
		Id	Le	Co						
		A5	21	Id	Le	Co				
				31	1F	Id	Le	Co		
						61	11	Id	Le	Co
								16	04	'Jane'
								Id	Le	Co
								16	01	'T'
								Id	Le	Co
								16	06	'McBeth'
						Id	Le	Co		
						A1	0A	Id	Le	Co
								42	08	'19801115'

(Note: Id=Identifier, Le=Length, Co=Contents.)

syntax. Successful negotiation of the compatible transfer syntax results in an association between the abstract syntax and the transfer syntax. This association is referred to as a *Presentation context*. From the users' point of view, only the abstract syntax, and not the transfer syntax, is of any significance.

8.4.1   Defined Context Set

Over a given Presentation connection, and at any given time, one or more Presentation contexts may be required to cater to a variety of user information. This gives rise to the notion of a *defined context set* (*DCS*), which is the set of presentation contexts currently applicable to exchange of (almost) all user data.

An abstract syntax name is used to identify an abstract syntax so that its use and support for it may be negotiated between the three parties, viz. the two Application entities and the PS provider. During data transfer between supporting Presentation entities, the abstract syntax name is not specifically used, thereby implying that the tag is the only means available to a receiving Presentation entity to determine the applicable abstract syntax, and within that its data type. Thus, each data type must be assigned a tag so that it is unique within the defined context set, or its Presentation context is determinable from the tag of the enclosing data type.

8.4.2 Default Context

Earlier we mentioned that the defined context set is applicable to transfer of all user information. There is, however, one exception. User data contained in expedited data transfer primitives is encoded using a *default context*. If at any time the defined context set is empty, then the default context applies to user information contained in other service primitives as well. In the absence of a negotiated default context, Application entities use an abstract syntax for which there is a-priori agreement between the PS users. In that case, the Presentation layer transfers it transparently, perhaps, as a string of octets.

Both the defined context set and the default context are negotiated at the time of connection establishment. The defined context set may subsequently be altered using P-ALTER CONTEXT primitives. The default context may not be changed once the connection has been established.

8.4.3 Information Transfer

User information may be transferred as User Data parameter of (almost) any service primitive. It must, however, conform to either one of the contexts from the current defined context set, or to the default context. The following rules apply (see, however, the discussion below on Context Management and Context Restoration services):

1. User data in P-EXPEDITED DATA primitives must conform to the default context.

2. If the defined context set is empty, then the applicable context for all user data is the default context.

3. If the defined context set is non-empty, then user data in every primitive other than P-EXPEDITED DATA conforms to one or more of the contexts from the defined context set.

Below, we discuss the procedure for establishment of a Presentation connection. The emphasis, however, is on negotiation of Presentation contexts. Subsequently, we discuss procedures to alter or to restore a defined context set.

8.4.4 Context Establishment

The Presentation layer provides services using which Application entities may initially define the set of Presentation contexts, and subsequently modify it. The defined context set, to be initially applicable, is negotiated during connection establishment. The interface with the PS provider enables the initiating user to identify one or more abstract syntax to be supported by the PS provider. The connection establishment procedure is successful provided:

1. the PS provider is capable of supporting the default context and some, if not all, of the named abstract syntax using an appropriate transfer syntax,

2. the responding service user at the other end agrees to the proposed default context and, partly or wholly, to the proposed defined context set, and

3. together, the Presentation layer and the supporting Session layer are able to provide the required services.

If either of these conditions is not satisfied, then the establishment of the connection is unsuccessful. The three possibilities, indicated in Figure 8.3, correspond to:

1. successful Presentation connection establishment,

2. connection establishment refused by the PS provider, and

3. connection establishment refused by the responding PS user.

The P-CONNECT service is confirmed.[2] Table 8.8 lists the parameters of the P-CONNECT primitives. We briefly discuss each of these parameters.

1. The *Calling* and the *Called Presentation Addresses* are as usual PSAP addresses. The Called Presentation Address is mapped by the Presentation layer, using the address mapping function, to obtain a Called Session Address of a SSAP to which the supporting Session connection must be established. The Responding Address is present in the response and confirm primitives only if a PSAP address other than the Called Presentation Address should be used to re-establish

---

[2]Note when a P-CONNECT request is simultaneously issued at two PSAPs for connection establishment between the same pair of PSAPs, then these attempts relate to two distinct Presentation connections.

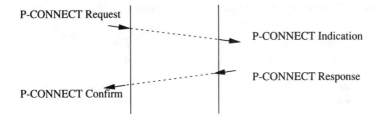

(a) Successful Establishment

(b) Establishment rejected by the PS provider

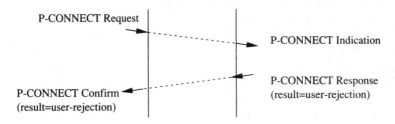

(c) Establishment rejected by PS user

Figure 8.3 Establishment of a Presentation connection.

a Presentation connection. This is helpful in case of generic addressing or in redirection.

2. Whenever present, *Presentation Context Definition List* contains one or more items. Each item consists of two components, a *Presentation context identifier* and an *abstract syntax name*. The Presentation context identifier has significance only for the local PS user and the PS provider. It is assigned by the initiating PS user

TABLE 8.8   Parameters of the P-CONNECT Primitives

Parameter name	P-CONNECT			
	Req	Ind	Resp	Conf
Calling Presentation Address	R	R		
Called Presentation Address	R	R		
Responding Presentation Address			O	O
Presentation Context Definition List	O	O(=)		
Presentation Context Definition Result List		O	O	O(=)
Default Context Name	O	O(=)		
Default Context Result			O	O(=)
Mode	R	R(=)		
Quality of Service	S	S	S	S
Presentation Requirements	O	O(=)	O	O(=)
Session Requirements	S	S	S	S
Initial Synchronization Point Serial Number	S	S	S	S
Initial Assignment of Tokens	S	S	S	S
Session Connection Identifier	S	S	S	S
User Data	O	O(=)	O	O(=)
Result			R	R

(Note: Req=request, Ind=Indication, Resp=Response, Conf=Confirm.)

and interpreted by the PS provider. In all future references to a Presentation context only the context identifier is used.

Similarly, the responding PS user and the PS provider use a Presentation context identifier, which is perhaps different. The correspondence between the two identifiers is established by the supporting PS entities.

3. The *Presentation Context Definition Result List* is again a list of one or more items, each of which indicates acceptance or rejection of the corresponding context in the proposed Presentation Context Definition List. Each value represents either *acceptance, user-rejection* or *provider-rejection.* Further, if a proposed context is rejected by the PS provider (as indicated in an indication primitive), then the PS user may *not* accept the particular context.

4. The *Default Context Name,* if present, identifies the abstract syntax to be used as the default abstract syntax. The *Default Context Result* is an indication of the acceptance or rejection by the responding PS user. If the proposed default context is not acceptable to the PS provider, it simply issues a P-CONNECT confirm primitive, and terminates the connection (as in Figure 8.3(b)).

5. The parameter *Mode* may take the value *normal* or *X.410 (1984).* The latter mode is highly restrictive in terms of availability of Presentation contexts, but is adequate to support CCITT's X.400 based messaging system (see [CCITT X.400a] through [CCITT X.420] and Chapter 11). With this mode of operation, there is no

need to negotiate a defined context set or a default context. User data concerning this application is assumed to be of the type OCTET STRING.

6. Through *Presentation Requirements,* a user may specify the list of optional functional units[3] of the Presentation service that it requires. Three functional units are defined:

   (a) The *Kernel* functional unit, which is always available. It permits transfer of user information consistent with an abstract syntax from the prevailing defined context set.

   (b) The *Context Management* functional unit, additionally enables a user to add or delete a context to/from the defined context set.

   (c) The *Context Restoration* functional unit, when used together with Context Management, enables a user to request that the defined context set be restored to a defined context set prevailing at an earlier time. Restoration is carried out as part of session resynchronization and activity management.

7. Information exchanged as *User Data* in P-CONNECT primitives may be expressed in any Presentation context listed in the Presentation Context Definition List or, if the Definition List is absent, in the default context. If the abstract syntax used is not supported by the PS provider, then user data cannot be transferred. In that case, the connection establishment attempt is terminated by the service provider. Further, if the context used is unacceptable to the responding PS user, it may reject the connection. Or, it may simply ignore the user data.

8. The *Result* parameter, present only in P-CONNECT response and confirm primitive, indicates whether or not the connection has been successfully established. It may take one of the three values, viz. *acceptable, user-rejection,* or *provider-rejection.* It, thereby, suggests to the initiating Application entity the cause of rejection.

9. The parameters, including *Session Requirements, Quality of Service, Initial Synchronization Point Number, Initial Assignment of Tokens,* and *Session Connection Identifier,* are directly mapped onto parameters supplied within corresponding S-CONNECT primitives (see Chapter 7). Recall, a Presentation connection is supported by an underlying Session connection.

8.4.5 Context Alteration

Once a connection is established, one or more presentation contexts may be added or deleted. This may be necessary to reflect the changing

---

[3]A functional unit is a collection of service elements, the use of any one of which makes sense only when other service elements from within the functional unit are also available.

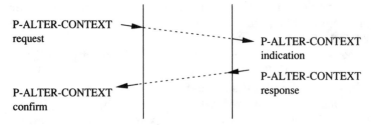

Figure 8.4 Changing the set of defined Presentation contexts.

requirements of the Application entities, as time progresses. This is illustrated in Figure 8.4. The use of the confirmed service P-ALTER CONTEXT enables users to request addition or deletion of one or more Presentation contexts to or from the defined context set.[4]

Table 8.9 lists the parameters of P-ALTER CONTEXT primitives.

1. The parameters *Presentation Context Addition List* and *Presentation Context Addition Result List* are similar to corresponding parameters in P-CONNECT primitives, except that instead of defining a new context set, PS users and the PS provider negotiate the use of additional Presentation contexts.

2. The *Presentation Context Deletion List* is a list of one or more *identifiers* of Presentation contexts that are currently part of the defined context set, but are now proposed to be deleted. The corresponding result list contains the response of the responding PS user.

3. *User Data,* if any, in the request and indication primitives must conform to the defined context set existing before the P-ALTER CON-

---

[4]This service is optional, and is offered as part of Context Management functional unit of the Presentation service.

TABLE 8.9 Parameters of the P-ALTER-CONTEXT Primitives

Parameters	P-ALTER CONTEXT Req	Ind	Resp	Conf
Presentation Context Addition List	O	O(=)		
Presentation Context Deletion list	O	O(=)		
Presentation Context Addition Result List		O	O	O(=)
Presentation Context Deletion Result List			O	O(=)
User Data	O	O(=)	O	O(=)

Note: See the note in Table 8.8.

TEXT request primitive is issued. But, User Data in the corresponding response and confirm primitives must conform to the defined context set that prevails after it has been updated by the responding user. Updating of the defined context set occurs with the issuing of the P-ALTER CONTEXT response primitive. If, at any time before or after the alteration, the defined context set is empty, then User Data conforms to the default Presentation context.

8.4.6   Context Restoration

Once a defined context set is changed using P-ALTER CONTEXT service element, it is possible to restore the defined context set to that prevailing at some earlier point of time. This is possible only when the Context Restoration functional unit has been selected at the time of connection establishment.[5] We now discuss Presentation service elements that may be used for the purpose. These are:

1. P-RESYNCHRONIZE,

2. P-ACTIVITY START,

3. P-ACTIVITY END,

4. P-ACTIVITY DISCARD,

5. P-ACTIVITY INTERRUPT, and

6. P-ACTIVITY RESUME.

P-RESYNCHRONIZE is a confirmed service element. It is indirectly mapped onto the corresponding S-RESYNCHRONIZE primitives. Its parameters (see Table 8.10) are identical to those of the S-RESYNCHRONIZE, except for *Presentation Context Identification List* parameter, present only in the indication and confirm primitives. Each item of the list is a context identifier. The list, as a whole, indicates to

---

[5]Of course, context restoration has meaning only when the Context Management functional unit has also been selected.

TABLE 8.10   Parameters of P-RESYNCHRONIZE Primitives

Parameter name	Req	Ind	Resp	Conf
Resynchronization Type	S	S		
Synchronization Point Serial Number	S	S	S	S
Tokens	S	S	S	S
Presentation Context Identification List		C		C
Use Data	U	C(=)	U	C(=)

Note: See the note in Table 8.8.

the PS users the contents of the resulting defined context set *after* restoration is complete.

The defined context set to which the connection is restored is determined by the parameter *Synchronization Point Serial Number* used in P-RESYNCHRONIZE primitives. The parameter *Resynchronization Type* must be either *restart* or *set*. Further, the defined context set is restored to the set prevailing at a minor or major synchronization point, the serial number of which (plus 1) appears as the parameter. Of course, such a synchronization point must have been established within the current activity, if applicable. In other cases the defined context set is either restored to the set defined at connection establishment, or remains unchanged (see [CCITT X.216] or [ISO 8822] for more details). Figure 8.5 illustrates the restoration of the defined context set to an earlier major synchronization point.

To discuss restoration of the defined context set using P-ACTIVITY primitives, we need the concept of *inter-activity defined context set* (*IADCS*). This is the defined context set that is applicable when no activity is in progress. To begin with, it is identical to that which has been defined at the time of connection establishment. Subsequently,

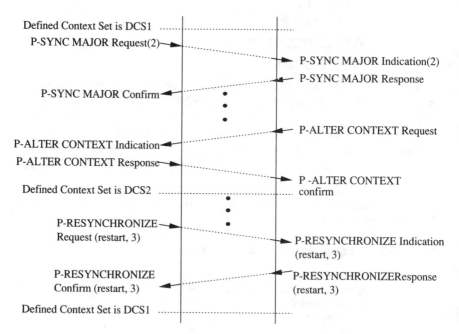

Note- The parameter(s) of P-Sync Major is Synchronization Point
Serial Number, and of P-Resynchronize are Synchronization Point
Serial Number, and optionally Resynchronization Type

Figure 8.5 Restoration of the defined context set using P-RESYNCHRONIZE primitives: an example.

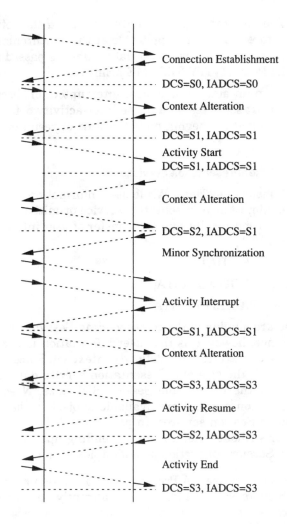

Note- DCS is Defined Context Set, IADCS is Inter-Activity Defined Context Set

Figure 8.6 Restoration of the defined context set using P-ACTIVITY primitives: an example.

alterations made to the defined context set, but outside an activity, are reflected as changes in the inter-activity defined context set. Thus (see Figure 8.6):

1. Addition and deletion of contexts within an activity are localized, and are applicable only as long as the activity is not *interrupted, discarded,* or *ended.*

2. The context applicable at the beginning of an activity is the inter-activity defined context set applicable at the time the activity is *started.*

3. When an interrupted activity is *resumed* the defined context set is restored to the one applicable at the synchronization point within the activity, but whose serial number is passed as a parameter in the P-ACTIVITY RESUME primitives.

4. When an activity is ended, interrupted, or discarded the defined context set is restored to the inter-activity defined context set prevailing at the beginning of the start or resumption of the activity.

8.4.7 Other Presentation Services

Data transfer primitives. While user information may be transferred as part of almost any Presentation service primitive, the following service elements specifically support transfer of user information:

1. P-DATA,

2. P-TYPED DATA,

3. P-EXPEDITED DATA, and

4. P-CAPABILITY DATA.

These are similar to the corresponding Session service elements. The difference, however, is that user information is encoded using an applicable context from the defined context set. Since segmentation is not permitted, the size of a Presentation service data unit is determined solely by the permissible Session SDU size. Needless to say, these Presentation services are available subject to the provision of corresponding Session services. In particular, P-DATA service is available with or without token control depending upon whether data transfer over a Session connection is half duplex or not.

Connection release. A Presentation connection may be terminated by its PS users or by the PS provider abruptly,[6] or in an orderly manner. The corresponding Presentation service primitives are:

1. P-U-ABORT,

2. P-P-ABORT, and

3. P-RELEASE.

Primitives concerning P-RELEASE service are mapped directly onto the corresponding Session service primitives. As such, rules governing P-RELEASE primitives are the same as those concerning S-RELEASE primitives. Further, the Presentation connection is released simultaneously with release of the supporting Session connection.

Synchronization and token management. The remaining Presentation services are also derived directly from those made available by the

---

[6]Perhaps resulting in loss of user information.

Session service. This allows a PS user to effectively access these Session services. The PS provider, on its part, simply passes the semantics of the primitives onto corresponding Session primitives. The Presentation services that fall in this category include:

1. P-TOKEN GIVE, P-TOKEN-PLEASE, and P-CONTROL GIVE,

2. P-SYNC MINOR and P-SYNC MAJOR, and

3. P-U-EXCEPTION REPORT and P-P-EXCEPTION REPORT.

Constraints, if any, on issuing Presentation service primitives are discussed in the next section. Further, since most of the Presentation service primitives are directly (or indirectly) mapped onto corresponding Session service primitives, these are more or less identical to those specified by the Session service and its protocol (see [ISO 8326, ISO 8327] and Chapter 7). We shall, therefore, limit the discussion to P-ALTER CONTEXT primitives for which there are no corresponding constraints implied by the Session protocol. In the next section, we also consider collision of P-ALTER CONTEXT primitives with other primitives, and the manner in which collisions are resolved particularly in respect of the resulting defined context set.

8.5 Presentation Protocol

The Presentation protocol specifies the functions required to be implemented by the Presentation layer in order to close the gap between Presentation services and those made available by the Session layer. A quick comparison between the two services immediately reveals that these functions are basically related to negotiation of the use of one or more Presentation contexts, and to encoding of user information in an appropriate transfer syntax. We, therefore, discuss in this section protocol procedures for establishment of the initial defined context set and default context, context alteration and context restoration. For details see [ISO 8823] or [CCITT X.226].

8.5.1 Introduction

The Presentation protocol specifies, for a given Presentation connection, the cause-effect relationship between issuing of Presentation service primitives at a given PSAP and the exchange of *Presentation Protocol-Data-Units* (*PPDUs*) between the two supporting Presentation entities (see Figure 8.7). The supporting Presentation entities are also called *Presentation protocol machines.*

The correspondence between PPDUs and the Presentation service primitives is summarized in Table 8.11. The semantics of PPDUs is additionally defined in terms of PPDU parameters, and whether these are derived from (or determine) the parameters of the corresponding

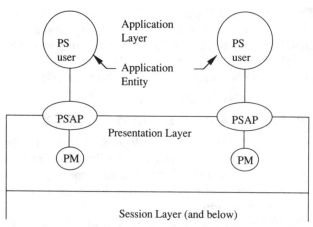

Figure 8.7 Model of the Presentation service provider.

TABLE 8.11 Mapping between Presentation Primitives, PPDUs and Session Primitives

Presentation primitives	PPDUs	Session primitives
P-CONNECT	CP, CPA, CPR	S-CONNECT
P-U-ABORT	ARU	S-U-ABORT
P-P-ABORT	ARP	S-U-ABORT
P-ALTER CONTEXT	AC, ACA	S-TYPED DATA
P-TYPED DATA	TTD	S-TYPED DATA
P-RESYNCHRONIZATION	RS, RSA	S-RESYNCHRONIZE

Note: See also Table 8.12.

primitives. The protocol specification is incomplete, unless the protocol also specifies the manner in which Presentation entities use the supporting Session service to send and receive PPDUs. This is specified in the form, once again, of a mapping between PPDUs and Session service primitive (see Table 8.11).

Since many of the Presentation services are derived directly from those made available by the Session service provider, the protocol does not define corresponding PPDUs in respect of these services. Instead, the protocol specifies a direct mapping between related primitives and corresponding Session service primitives. (These are summarized in Table 8.12.) In such cases, there is a one-to-one correspondence between parameters of Presentation service primitives and those of Session service primitives. The only difference is in respect of the parameter, User Data. User Data is encoded using a negotiated transfer syntax before it is handed over to the Session layer.

We now discuss connection establishment procedure which also establishes the initial defined context set and permits a number of other

TABLE 8.12   Direct Mapping of Some Presentation Primitives onto Corresponding Session Primitives

Presentation primitives	Session primitives
P-DATA	S-DATA
P-EXPEDITED DATA	S-EXPEDITED DATA
P-CAPABILITY DATA	S-CAPABILITY DATA
P-RELEASE	S-RELEASE
P-TOKEN GIVE	S-TOKEN GIVE
P-TOKEN-PLEASE	S-TOKEN-PLEASE
P-CONTROL GIVE	S-CONTROL GIVE
P-SYNC MINOR	S-SYNC MINOR
P-SYNC MAJOR	S-SYNC MAJOR
P-U-EXCEPTION REPORT	S-U-EXCEPTION REPORT
P-P-EXCEPTION REPORT	S-P-EXCEPTION REPORT
P-ACTIVITY START	S-ACTIVITY START
P-ACTIVITY END	S-ACTIVITY END
P-ACTIVITY INTERRUPT	S-ACTIVITY INTERRUPT
P-ACTIVITY DISCARD	S-ACTIVITY DISCARD
P-ACTIVITY RESUME	S-ACTIVITY RESUME

Note: See also Table 8.11.

agreements to be reached between the concerned users and supporting entities.

8.5.2   Connection Establishment

The connection establishment procedure is used to establish a connection between two communicating Presentation entities, and as a consequence, between the supported PS users (or Application entities). The procedure specifies the use of *CP, CPA,* and *CPR* protocol data units.[7] Figure 8.8 illustrates the resulting three different possibilities,[8] corresponding to

1. successful connection establishment,

2. connection is rejected by the responding Presentation entity, and

3. connection is rejected by the responding PS user.

A connection is successfully established provided negotiation in respect of each of the following is successful:

1. defined context set,

---

[7]For *Connect Presentation, Connect Presentation Accept,* and *Connect Presentation Reject,* respectively.

[8]There is a fourth possibility, where the initiating Presentation entity does not send a CP PPDU, perhaps because it is unable to support one or more features of the requested connection. In that case it rejects the connection by issuing an appropriate P-CONNECT confirm primitive. In the discussion that follows, we assume that the initiating Presentation entity does go ahead with connection establishment.

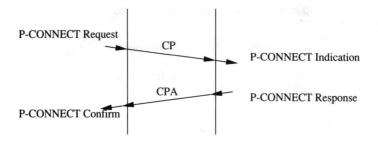

(a) Successful establishment

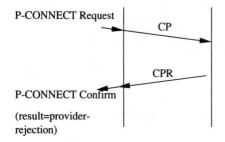

(b) Establishment rejected by the PS provider

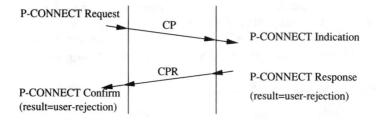

(c) Establishment rejected by the PS user

Figure 8.8 Exchange of CP, CPA, CPR PPDUs in connection establishment.

2. default context,

3. Presentation functional units and Session services, and

4. version of the Presentation protocol.

The negotiation generally take place between the four entities, viz. the two PS users and the two supporting Presentation entities. But, clearly, the version of the Presentation protocol is of concern only to the Presentation entities. Further, use and availability of Session services is determined by the Session layer as well. The negotiation procedure for each of these is necessarily different. We shall, however, emphasize negotiation of Presentation contexts alone.

The negotiation procedure for the defined context set is described below.

1. For each abstract syntax requested by its PS user, the initiating Presentation entity indicates to its peer entity, in a CP PPDU, a list of transfer syntaxes it is capable of supporting.

2. The responding Presentation entity indicates, in the indication primitive it issues to the corresponding PS user, those abstract syntaxes that it can (or cannot) support.

3. The responding PS user indicates to its supporting Presentation entity those abstract syntaxes that it can use. This it does by issuing a P-CONNECT response primitive.

4. The responding Presentation entity sends out a CPA or a CPR PPDU indicating, therein, the selection of a transfer syntax for each accepted abstract syntax. For each abstract syntax not accepted, it conveys the source of rejection. A reason is provided if the abstract syntax is rejected by the responding Presentation entity itself.

Above, we have assumed that no entity may accept an abstract syntax if it has already been rejected by another entity. Table 8.13 illustrates an example. Each item of the Presentation Context Definition List is

TABLE 8.13 An Example of Negotiation of a Defined Context Set

Primitive or PPDU	Presentation Context definition list	Presentation Context definition result list
P-CONNECT request	$\{(S1, 1),$ $(S3, 3),$ $(S5, 5)\}$	-
CP PPDU	$\{(S1, 1, T11),$ $(S3, 3, T31, T32),$ $(S5, 5, T51, T52)\}$	-
P-CONNECT indication	$\{(S1, 1),$ $(S3, 3),$ $(S5, 5)\}$	{provider-rejection, acceptance, acceptance}
P-CONNECT response	-	{provider-rejection, acceptance, user-rejection}
CPA PPDU	-	{(provider-rejection, limit exceeded), (acceptance, T32), user-rejection}
P-CONNECT confirm	-	{provider-rejection, acceptance, user-rejection}

assumed to be of the form (Si, j) or (Si, j, Tk) depending upon whether it is a parameter of a service primitive or that of a corresponding PPDU. Further, Si is an abstract syntax name, j is an integer context identifier, and Tk is a list of one or more transfer syntax names.

Negotiation of the default context is relatively simple. It is assumed that the default context requested by the initiating PS user is acceptable to the supporting Presentation entity. If the responding Presentation entity is unable to support the proposed default context, it rejects the connection attempt by sending a CPR PPDU while also indicating the source, *provider-rejection,* and the reason, *default context not supported.* In that case it does not issue a P-CONNECT indication primitive (see Figure 8.8(b)). If the responding PS user rejects the default context, the responding Presentation entity responds similarly, except that this time the value of the CPR PPDU parameter, *Default Context Result* is *user-rejection* (see Figure 8.8(c)).

Use and availability of the proposed Presentation functional units is negotiated between the user and supporting entities. As discussed earlier, the Kernel functional unit is always available. However, availability of Context Management and Context Restoration functional units depends upon whether the Presentation entities have access to the implied Session services, including Typed Data transfer, Resynchronization, and Activity Management. Further, even though the Presentation layer may support these functional units, the responding PS user may find little use for them. Its response is conveyed in a CPA PPDU.

The need for Presentation services that are directly mapped onto corresponding Session services is determined by the PS users themselves. The supporting Presentation entities, on their part, simply mirror the availability of required Session services in the corresponding parameters of CP and CPA PPDUs.

Negotiation of the protocol version to be used by the Presentation entities to support the particular connection requires that the initiating Presentation entity indicate a list of different versions of the protocol it is capable of supporting. The responding Presentation entity selects one of the proposed versions. If none is acceptable, it simply sends a CPR PPDU with a list of protocol versions that it can support.[9]

As a final remark, the negotiation procedure is such that it results in the smallest set of proposed features of the connection that are acceptable to the concerned entities. If the resulting connection, as characterized by the negotiation, is not acceptable to the initiating PS user, it may simply release (or perhaps abort) the connection.

Connection related PPDUs are conveyed by the initiating or responding Presentation entity in S-CONNECT primitives. Specifically,

---

[9]This information may be used in network planning to later ensure compatibility of protocol versions.

the CP PPDU is transferred by the initiating Presentation entity in S-CONNECT request/indication primitives. Similarly, CPA and CPR PPDUs are mapped onto S-CONNECT response/confirm primitives. Most of the parameters are, together, mapped onto the User Data field of S-CONNECT primitives. The exceptions are PSAP addresses, and those that directly concern the supporting Session connection.[10] Each address of a PSAP, whether Calling, Called or Responding, is broken down into its two constituent parts, viz. *Presentation Selector* and *Session Address*. The Presentation Selector uniquely identifies the particular PSAP reachable through the supporting SSAP. Therefore, the Calling, Called or Responding Session Address is directly mapped onto the corresponding SSAP address parameter of Session primitives, whereas the selector part is conveyed as one component of User Data.

Needless to say, the Presentation connection is established simultaneously with the supporting Session connection. If the responding Presentation entity or the Presentation entity rejects the Presentation connection, the supporting Session connection is also not established. The responding Presentation entity, aside from conveying the CPR PPDU through the S-CONNECT response primitive, also sets the *Result* parameter in the S-CONNECT response primitive to the value *rejected by SS user* (see also Chapter 7).

8.5.3 Context Alteration

The P-ALTER CONTEXT service, when invoked by a PS user, results in the exchange of *AC* and *ACA* PPDUs[11] between the supporting Presentation entities. It, thereby, permits Presentation entities to negotiate a suitable transfer syntax to be used for each context proposed to be added, or delete those contexts that are agreed to by the PS users. The exchange of PPDUs is illustrated in Figure 8.9, together with their rela-

---

[10]For instance, Initial Synchronization Point Serial Number, Initial Assignment of Tokens, and Session Connection Identifier.

[11]For *Alter context* and *Alter context acknowledgement*, respectively.

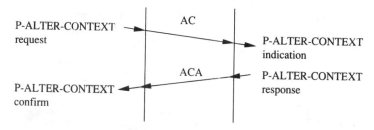

Figure 8.9 Illustration of the use of AC and ACA PPDUs.

tion with issuing of P-ALTER CONTEXT primitives. It is assumed, as in connection establishment, that the initiating Presentation entity is able to support each Presentation context proposed to be added to the defined context set. As for deletion of Presentation contexts, Presentation entities simply convey the proposal or the response from one user to another. See Table 8.14 for an illustration of negotiation of the contexts to be deleted. It is assumed that each item of the *Presentation Context Deletion List* is an identifier of a context proposed to be deleted.

The procedure to add one or more contexts to the defined context set is identical to that discussed earlier as part of the connection establishment, but with one important difference. The P-ALTER CONTEXT procedure may be simultaneously initiated by the two users over the same connection. This results in a collision, the two possibilities for which are illustrated in Figure 8.10. The collision is resolved by treating the two alterations independently, and ensuring that changes in the defined context set due to a procedure become effective:

1. for the responding side when the corresponding response primitive is issued or received, and

2. for the initiating side when the corresponding confirm primitive is issued or received.

The resulting defined context set, as a consequence, is the accumulation of agreed changes in the two alterations. Note that the result is the same, irrespective of which of the two is processed first. This is significant since the defined context set at the two ends must be identical.[12]

---

[12]If the same context is proposed to be deleted by the two users, then a Presentation entity (or PS user) may receive a proposal (or a confirmation) to delete a context which has earlier been deleted by it.

TABLE 8.14   Deletion of Presentation Context: an Example

Primitive or PPDU	Presentation Context deletion list	Presentation Context deletion result list
P-ALTER CONTEXT request	{1, 2, 4}	-
AC PPDU	{1, 2, 4}	-
P-ALTER CONTEXT indication	{1, 2, 4}	-
P-ALTER CONTEXT response	-	{acceptance, acceptance, user-rejection}
ACA PPDU	-	{acceptance, acceptance, user-rejection}
P-ALTER CONTEXT confirm	-	{acceptance, acceptance, user-rejection}

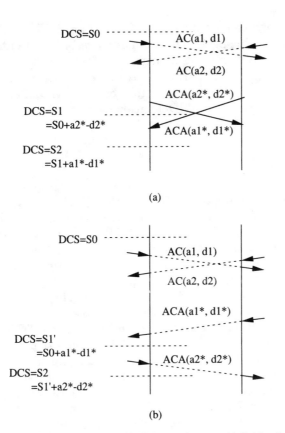

(a)

(b)

Note- Parameters of AC and ACA PPDU shown above are (definition list, deletion) or corresponding result list.

Figure 8.10 Collision of context alteration.

When a collision occurs, there may also occur a conflict in assigning an identifier to a context proposed to be added, unless each Presentation entity uses a different identifier space. Therefore, the protocol requires that the Presentation entity which initiated the connection use odd integers to identify Presentation contexts. The other Presentation entity assigns even integer identifiers to Presentation contexts that it proposes to add. Obviously, at the time of connection establishment each context in the proposed defined context set must be assigned an odd integer identifier.

A Presentation entity conveys the AC and ACA PPDUs as User Data parameters in S-TYPED DATA request/indication primitives over the supporting Session connection. As one consequence, a PS user invoked P-TYPED DATA request primitive is first mapped onto a PPDU, TTD[13]

---

[13]For Transfer Typed Data.

in this case, and then conveyed as User Data in an S-TYPED DATA primitives (see also Table 8.11). Thus, when a Presentation entity receives an S-TYPED DATA indication primitive, it first analyzes the initial few octets of its User Data parameter to determine the PPDU type. Depending upon the PPDU type and its abstract syntax, it subsequently identifies the values of PPDU parameters.

8.5.4   Context Restoration

Restoration of the defined context set occurs soon after the completion of a procedure corresponding to P-RESYNCHRONIZE or activity management primitives. We discuss the procedure concerning resynchronization first. Normally, a P-RESYNCHRONIZE primitive would be directly mapped onto the corresponding S-RESYNCHRONIZE primitive. But, such is not the case since Presentation entities, sometimes, do need to exchange the list of resulting Presentation contexts. Therefore, two PPDUs are defined by the protocol. These are RS and RSA PPDUs,[14] and each has the parameter *Presentation Context Identifier List,* in addition to those required by the S-RESYNCHRONIZE primitives. Thus, a P-RESYNCHRONIZE request primitive is first mapped onto an RS PPDU and later conveyed using an S-RESYNCHRONIZE primitive (see Table 8.11). Similarly, a P-RESYNCHRONIZE response primitive is mapped onto an RSA PPDU, which in turn is conveyed through an S-RESYNCHRONIZE response primitive. The parameter, Presentation Context Identifier List, is mapped onto one part of the User Data parameter in the Session primitive.

The procedure for context restoration is illustrated in Figure 8.11. The actual restoration of defined context set takes place:

1. for the responding Presentation entity (and PS user) when it receives an RS PPDU, and

---

[14]For Resynchronize and Resynchronize Acknowledgement, respectively.

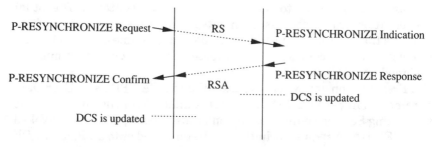

Figure 8.11 Exchange of resynchronization related PPDUs: an example.

2.   for the initiating Presentation entity (and PS user) when it receives the corresponding RSA PPDU.

The initiating Presentation entity updates the defined context set based upon the Presentation Context Identifier List that it receives as part of the RSA PPDU. The responding Presentation entity, however, uses the corresponding list from the received RS PPDU to align its context set with that of the sender, in case of restoration to an earlier minor/major synchronization point. Otherwise, they restore the context set to that existing at the time of connection establishment. The latter is the case when a synchronization point is not proposed or resynchronization is not possible.

It may be pointed out that the resynchronization procedure disrupts any context alteration procedure if simultaneously initiated by any other user.

Restoration of the defined context set also occurs when an activity related procedure is initiated by a PS user. From Table 8.12, note that every activity related Presentation primitive is directly mapped onto the corresponding Session primitive. To keep the discussion short, we simply add that restoration of the defined context set occurs with the issuing of:

1.   request or indication primitives related to P-ACTIVITY START or P-ACTIVITY RESUME services, or

2.   response or confirm primitives related to the confirmed P-ACTIVITY END, P-ACTIVITY INTERRUPT, or P-ACTIVITY RESUME services.

Further, issuing of ACTIVITY INTERRUPT or DISCARD related primitives disrupts other services, particularly context alteration. Other activity related procedures may not be initiated once context alteration is in progress.

8.6 Summary

The Presentation layer addresses the issue of representation of data exchanged by Application layer entities. The Presentation service is such that Application entities may transfer information without concern for how information is represented so that it can be properly interpreted by its peer entity. The supporting Presentation entities are responsible for translating information from the representation scheme used locally by the sending entity to that used by the receiving entity. Between themselves, Presentation entities use a transfer syntax which is capable of representing information which is consistent with the agreed abstract syntax. Together, the abstract syntax and the transfer syntax define a Presentation context.

Presentation services include establishment of a connection, data transfer, and connection release. Additionally, the layer provides services for maintaining and using a set of defined presentation contexts. Context management services include context alteration and context restoration.

9

Common
Application
Services

In this chapter we discuss Application layer services that are commonly used by other applications. These include establishment of an association with peer entities in the Application layer, reliable information transfer, remote operations, and services that ensure atomicity of remote operations. Other applications, for instance directory access, file transfer, message handling and virtual terminals, are discussed starting Chapter 10.

9.1 Application Layer Structure

The broad structure of the Application layer is described in this section. Concepts that are fundamental to this layer, including those of Application processes, Application entities and their composition in terms of Application service elements are discussed in this section. The manner in which each Application entity is described is also covered in some detail.

9.1.1 Application Processes

The Presentation layer, discussed in Chapter 8, provides a capability to users so that information may be exchanged between them without concern for its representation, or its transfer. Within the Application layer there exist *Application Processes* that use this capability to process information in a distributed manner. Physically, an Application process is a collection of one or more user-developed application programs and communication software. It is through the communication software that the ultimate user or an application program gains access to services offered by the OSI environment (see [ISO 9545]).

An Application process may directly interface with the Presentation layer. In that case it must include protocol modules to:

1. initialize communication with its peer Application processes,

2. establish an appropriate Presentation context, and

3. transfer files or messages as necessary, etc.

Alternatively, a user program may include an instance of available modules that support commonly required application-related services like those of establishing an application association, file transfer, program compilation and execution at a remote site, or electronic mail. Such a module is referred to as an *Application Service Element* (*ASE*).

An Application service element is an integrated set of functions which together provide one or more application-related communication capabilities. These capabilities are available to user-developed programs and to other Application service elements included in the same Application process. The capability provided by an Application service element is defined in a manner very similar to that used to specify the service provided by a layer below. Its realization is again specified by a protocol. The protocol may specify use of Presentation services directly and/or those provided by other Application service elements contained within the Application process.

The OSI architecture suggests that a number of Application service elements be implemented in the Application layer. An Application process may then use services provided by corresponding modules to communicate with its peer processes. This approach alleviates the need, on the part of users, to design and implement a number of additional software modules. Further, users need only be concerned with their specific application, and with its interface with Application service elements. As a consequence, an Application process consists of a user program, an instance of each Application service element that it requires, and interfaces between them.

In abstract terms, an Application process is a representation of those elements of a real system which perform information processing for a particular application. Depending upon the nature of the application, an Application process may communicate with one or more other Application processes residing in different open systems. In the latter case, two things are obvious. Application processes must have access to (OSI) communication capabilities, and they must share the same view of how such capabilities are to be used and for what purpose.

9.1.2 Application Entities

Open Systems Interconnection is primarily concerned with aspects that relate to interaction between Application processes residing in

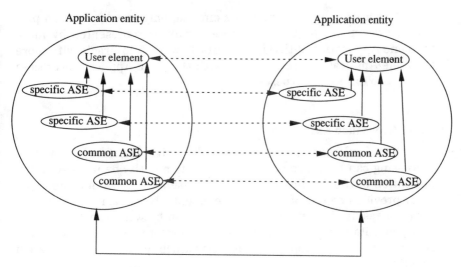

Figure 9.1 Application entity and its elements.

possibly different systems. The notion of an *Application entity* (*AE*) is, therefore, defined. An Application entity is a model of those aspects of an Application process that are concerned with its interaction with other Application processes. Such a model views a user program, together with its interface with Application service elements that it uses, as a *User Element*. An Application entity is, therefore, composed of a collection of one or more Application service elements that a user element accesses to perform distributed processing of information.

Figure 9.1 illustrates the configuration of an Application entity, and how its service elements interface with each other and with services provided by the Presentation layer.

A user element is a model of the particular service that an Application process makes available to, for instance, human users, other programs, or devices that are outside the OSI environment. As such, the OSI architecture does not address issues relating to the design of the user element, except to insist that its interface with the Presentation layer (or with Application service elements) conforms to the standards. As an example, the software which carries out local processing and provides an interface to a local bank teller is specific to the application. It is, therefore, not covered by the model. But, in order to gain access to a remote file storage, the process must interact with a service element that supports file transfer capability. The latter aspect is subject to modelling within the OSI framework. File transfer capability is, therefore, included as an Application service element as part of a corresponding Application entity.

An Application entity represents one and only one Application process. However, an Application process may be represented by more than one Application entities, particularly when it interacts with more than one Application processes, or with the same Application process but for two different purposes.

9.1.3   Application Association

Just as an Application process needs to be activated before information processing can begin, so must an Application entity be invoked. Each invocation of the Application entity represents the use of some capability provided by one of its service elements. Necessarily then, an invocation results in some form of interaction between the Application entity and its peer entity. There must, therefore, exist an association between the pair of Application entities. Such an association is called *Application association.*

An Application association between two Application entities is a relationship (however temporary) between them which not only establishes the common communication environment initially, but provides a basis for coordinating interactions between them. The environment, for instance, defines what capabilities are available in terms of Application service elements, and the nature of user data to be communicated using these capabilities[1]. Thus, the aspects that are negotiated at the time of association establishment are the:

Application Context, and the *Abstract Syntax.*

The Application Context is the common environment shared by the two communicating Application entities. It essentially comprises of the list of Application service elements, and the particular capabilities that each service element provides. The latter is particularly significant if there are optional facilities provided by an Application service element, or if the required protocol permits a choice in using certain procedures.

The Abstract Syntax is a specification of the syntax of Application PDUs that are communicated (ultimately) over a supporting Presentation connection. It consists of the abstract syntax of PDUs that relate to the various Application service elements that comprise the Application entity, and of information communicated between the user elements.

9.1.4   Application Service Elements

As a matter of judgement, Application service elements (ASEs) are subdivided into two groups, viz.:

---

[1]An association differs from a connection (as defined in Chapter 2) in that the Application layer does not provide services to any higher layer. Instead, it provides services to user elements that are part of the Application layer itself. In every other respect an association is similar to a connection.

common Application service elements (CASE), and

specific Application service elements (SASE).

The common ASEs provide services that may be used by a user element, a common ASE or a specific ASE. Four common ASEs are currently defined. These are:

1. *Association Control service element (ACSE)*, which enables a user to establish or terminate an Association between Application entities,

2. *Reliable Transfer service element (RTSE)*, which enables reliable transfer of information between peer entities,

3. *Remote Operations service element (ROSE)*, which permits users to initiate operations at a remote site, and

4. *Commitment, Concurrency and Recovery services (CCR)*, which enable users to recover from a failure during execution of a task using commit or rollback procedures.

The common Application service elements are discussed in the remaining sections of this chapter. Other Application service elements also provide services that may be used by a variety of Application service elements as well as by a user element. These services are not as generic, and are, therefore, useful only in specific instances. Directory services are discussed in Chapter 10, whereas Message Handling Systems are covered in Chapter 11. File transfer, access and management services are discussed in Chapter 12, followed by a discussion of Virtual Terminal protocols. Other Application service element, including Job transfer and Manipulation, are briefly covered in Chapter 14. In future, one may expect a number of standard ASEs to be developed, including those useful to specific user-groups or applications.

9.2 Association Control Services

As discussed in the previous section, a common Application service element (ASE) is a collection of modules, which provides a service to a user element or to other ASEs of the same Application entity. The Association Control service element (ACSE) is discussed in this section (see [CCITT X.217], [CCITT X.227] or [ISO 8649], [ISO 8650]).

9.2.1 Application Context

The concept of an *Application Association* is central to the discussion of Application layer services. Its main purpose is to establish the correct environment for information exchange, viz. negotiation of the *Application context*, the set of required Presentation contexts, and the set of required Presentation layer functional units. The Application context is a specification of the set of Application service elements used by communicating Application entities, together with related options. When used, the Association Control service element is always included in the Application context (see [ISO 8649])[2].

The negotiated Presentation context set includes the abstract syntax required to convey protocol data units (PDUs) of all Application service elements specified in the Application context, including ACSE, and the user element. Such PDUs are called *Application PDUs* or simply *APDUs*.

Yet another purpose of establishing an association is to properly identify the source and destination Application entities. Application entities are referred to by names (or titles, to be exact). An Application entity title (*AE title*) is composed of an Application process title (*AP title*) and an *AE qualifier*. The latter uniquely identifies the particular Application entity which models (perhaps) only a part of the Application process. Further, since there may be multiple invocations of the same process, it is necessary to distinguish one invocation from the others. An Application entity is, therefore, identified by:

1. AP Title,

2. AE Qualifier,

3. AP-Invocation-Identifier, and

4. AE-Invocation-Identifier.

The directory function may be used to map an Application entity title onto the address of a unique Presentation service access point (PSAP) to which the target Application entity is attached. The responsibility of doing so is that of ACSE-user (see Figure 9.2).

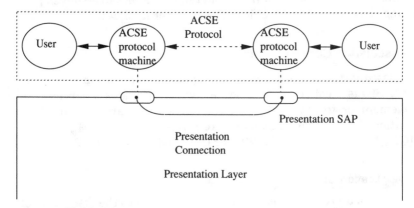

Figure 9.2 Model of Association Control service element and its users.

---

[2]In fact, it is expected that the ACSE service element will be included in all Application context specifications.

TABLE 9.1   Association Control Service Primitives

Service	Service Primitives	Type of Service
Association Establishment	A-ASSOCIATE	Confirmed
Normal Release	A-RELEASE	Confirmed
Abnormal Release	A-ABORT	Unconfirmed
	A-P-ABORT	Provider-initiated

9.2.2   ACSE Services

Services included in ACSE are those of:

1. association establishment,

2. orderly or negotiated termination of the association, which ensures that there will be no loss of information in transit, and

3. user-initiated or provider-initiated abrupt termination of the association, which may result in loss of information during transit.

Negotiated termination permits a responding user to either accept or reject a termination of the association. Orderly release, on the other hand is not subject to availability of release token (see also Chapters 7 and 8). The correspondence between the above service elements and ACSE service primitives is given in Table 9.1. With termination of the association, the negotiated Application and Presentation contexts are no longer valid. These must be re-negotiated if the association is re-established.

9.2.3   ACSE Protocol

ACSE services are realized using two protocol machines, one for each communicating Application entity. The protocol for Association Control[3] specifies that each Application association be mapped one-to-one onto a Presentation connection established between PSAPs to which the Application entities are attached (see Figure 9.2). The protocol describes the different ACSE-APDUs that convey the semantics of ACSE service primitives, and as to how ACSE-APDUs are transferred using Presentation layer services. The correspondence is summarized in Table 9.2.

The interaction between ACSE protocol machines and their use of Presentation services is illustrated in Figures 9.3 and 9.4. Note that the Application association and the supporting Presentation connection are established simultaneously. The *AARQ* and *AARE* APDUs[4],

---

[3]See [CCITT X.227] or [ISO 8650].

[4]For Application Associate Request and Application Associate Response, respectively.

TABLE 9.2   Correspondence between ACSE Service Primitives, Associated ACSE-APDUs and Their Transfer Using Presentation Services

Service Primitive	Associated ACSE-APDUs	Presentation Service(s) that carries ACSE-APDU
A-ASSOCIATE	AARQ	P-CONNECT service
	AARE	P-CONNECT service
A-RELEASE	RLRQ	P-RELEASE service
	RLRE	P-RELEASE service
A-ABORT	ABORT	P-U-ABORT service
A-P-ABORT		P-P-ABORT service

respectively, convey the semantics of *A-ASSOCIATE* request/indication and response/confirm primitives. These APDUs are transferred using corresponding P-CONNECT primitives. Similarly, APDUs corresponding to orderly or negotiated release of the association, *RLRQ* and *RLRE*[5], are carried by P-RELEASE primitives. The supporting Presentation connection is released simultaneously with release of Applica-

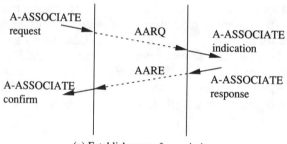

(a) Establishment of association

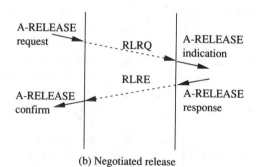

(b) Negotiated release

Figure 9.3 Exchange of ACSE-APDUs to support ACSE services.

---

[5]For Release Request and Release Response, respectively.

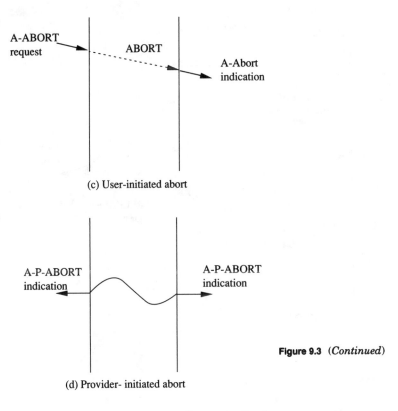

(c) User-initiated abort

(d) Provider- initiated abort

Figure 9.3 (*Continued*)

Presentation Service

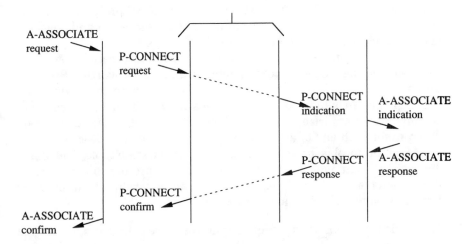

(a) Establishment of an association

Figure 9.4 Transfer of ACSE-APDUs over a Presentation connection.

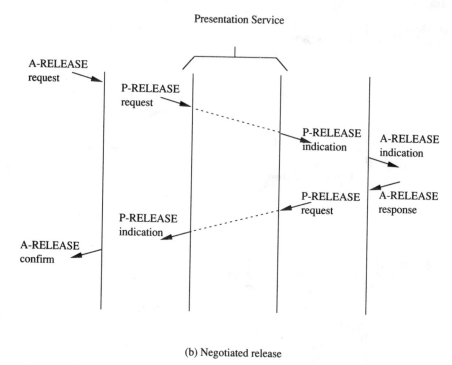

(b) Negotiated release

Figure 9.4 (*Continued*)

tion association. Clearly, from Figure 9.4, the ACSE protocol requires access only to the Kernel functional units of Presentation and Session layers, in addition to normal data transfer.

Figures 9.3 and 9.4 describe only a typical interaction between ACSE-users, the ACSE protocol machines and the supporting Presentation service provider. They makes little reference to constraints on the sequence in which ACSE primitives may be issued. These constraints are summarized in Figure 9.5 in the form of a state transition diagram for each end of an Application association. The description of the ACSE protocol is, however, given in terms of a state table. The table describes the changes in the state of the ACSE protocol machine and the actions that it initiates whenever an external event occurs. External events which influence the state are:

1. receipt of ACSE service request and response primitives,

2. receipt of Presentation layer service indication and confirm primitives containing ACSE-APDUs.

The actions which a protocol machine initiates as a consequence are:

Presentation Service

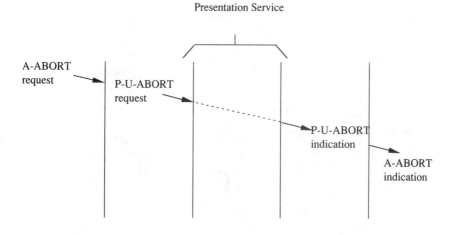

(c) User-initiated abort

Presentation Service

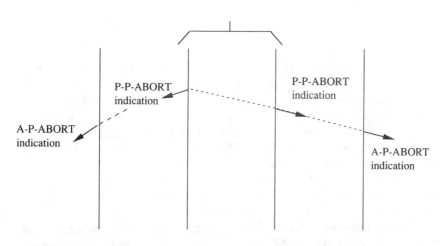

(d) Provider-initiated abort

Figure 9.4 (*Continued*)

1. issuing of ACSE service indication or confirm primitives, and
2. issuing of Presentation layer service request or response primitives, which in many instances carry ACSE-APDUs as user data.

Once an instance of Association Control service element is included in the Application context, a user element, or another Application service

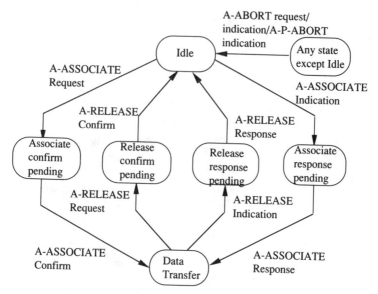

Figure 9.5 Constraints on issuing ACSE service primitives at one end of an Application association.

element included within the Application entity, does not need to access Presentation services to establish, terminate or abort a connection. Other Presentation services may be directly accessed. For instance, APDUs concerning commitment protocol are transferred using P-DATA primitives. Similarly, the file-related Application service element, *FTAM,* may access P-ALTER-Context services to update the required Presentation context.

Before concluding the discussion on ACSE services and its protocol, we briefly discuss the parameters of ACSE service primitives and their correspondence with the contents of ACSE-APDUs. Table 9.3 summarizes the parameters of A-ASSOCIATE primitives. The parameters of corresponding AARQ and AARE APDUs are best described by their abstract syntax, given in Table 9.4.

Note that a large number of parameters of A-ASSOCIATE primitives are directly mapped onto parameters of P-CONNECT primitives, since these do not appear in the AARQ or AARE APDUs (see also Chapter 8). Titles of Application entities are communicated as parameters of the AARQ and AARE APDUs. The PSAP addresses, obtained using the directory function, are used to ensure that the Presentation connection is established between the right pair of PSAPs to which the Application

TABLE 9.3 Parameters of the A-ASSOCIATE Primitives

A-ASSOCIATE Parameters	Carried by
Called AE Title	AARQ APDU
Calling AE Title	AARQ APDU
Responding AE Title	AARE APDU
Mode	
Application Context Name	AARQ, AARE APDUs
User Information	AARQ, AARE APDUs
Result	AARE APDU
Result Source	AARE APDU
Diagnostics	AARE APDU
Calling PSAP Address	P-CONNECT primitives
Called PSAP Address	P-CONNECT primitives
Responding PSAP Address	P-CONNECT primitives
Presentation Contexts Definition List	P-CONNECT primitives
Presentation Contexts Result List	P-CONNECT primitives
Default Presentation Context Name	P-CONNECT primitives
Default Presentation Context Result	P-CONNECT primitives
Presentation Requirements	P-CONNECT primitives
Session Requirements	P-CONNECT primitives
Quality of Service	P-CONNECT primitives
Initial Synchronization Point	
Serial Number	P-CONNECT primitives
Initial Assignments of Tokens	P-CONNECT primitives
Session Connection Identifier	P-CONNECT primitives

TABLE 9.4 Abstract Syntax of AARQ and AARE APDUs

```
AARQapdu   ::=   SEQUENCE
{
protocolVersion              [0]    BIT STRING,
applicationContextName       [1]    OBJECT IDENTIFIER,
calledAETitle                [2]    ANY,
callingAETitle               [6]    ANY,
implementationInformation    [29]   ImplementationDataType,
userInformation              [30]   ApplicationDataType
}
```

```
AAREapdu   ::=   SEQUENCE
{
protocolVersion              [0]    BIT STRING,
applicationContextName       [1]    OBJECT IDENTIFIER,
result                       [2]    INTEGER,
resultSourceAndDiagnostics   [3]    DiagnosticsInformation,
respondingAETitle            [4]    ANY,
implementationInformation    [29]   ImplementationDataType,
userInformation              [30]   ApplicationDataType
}
```

entities are attached. The Application Context Name identifies the set of Application service elements that constitute the initiating (and responding) Application entity.

The AARQ and AARE APDUs have *Implementation Information* as an additional parameter, whereas this parameter is not present in the corresponding ACSE primitives. This implies that the significance of the information is local to the two communicating ACSE protocol machines.

For the particular association, ACSE services may be operated in one of two *modes:*

1. *normal* mode, or
2. *X.410-1984* mode.

The normal mode allows ACSE users to take full advantage of both ACSE and Presentation services. On the other hand, the X.410-1984 mode of operation permits ACSE users to communicate with a peer Application entity that directly uses the Presentation and Session services as specified in [CCITT X.410]. The latter is particularly useful if the ACSE service is used to support 1988 version of Message Handling System. In X.410-1984 mode, none of the ACSE APDUs are defined or transferred. The semantics of ACSE service primitives are directly mapped onto Session layer primitives as defined by the CCITT standard X.410 (1984 version). The Application context and Presentation contexts are not negotiated either.

9.3 Reliable Transfer Services

In this section we discuss a Common Application Service which provides reliable transfer of protocol data units defined by an application. This service is provided in the form of *Reliable Transfer Service Elements* (see [CCITT X.218], [CCITT X.228] or [ISO 9066-1], [ISO 9066-2]. It may be used by a variety of applications, including Remote Operations Services and Message Handling Systems, for instance.

9.3.1 Introduction

In Sections 9.1 and 9.2 we have seen that communication between two Application processes is represented in terms of communication between the pair of corresponding Application entities. Such communication can be established and supported using Presentation layer services, alone. But, as illustrated in Figure 9.1, Association Control services may be used to establish or release an Association, while transferring protocol-data-units using Presentation layer services directly.

In many applications, communication between the two entities may also be required to be reliable. That is, each *Application Protocol Data*

Unit (APDU) must be transferred without loss, duplication or re-sequencing in spite of failures in the underlying layers or in end-systems. Such a capability is provided by *Reliable Transfer Service Elements (RTSEs)*.

A capability to transfer user data reliably is also provided by the Transport layer. However, the Transport protocol is capable of recovering from loss, duplication or re-sequencing of user data as it moves through the network, as also from failure of Network connections. Reliable Transfer service, on the other hand, provides for recovery from failure of the supporting Application Association (or the underlying Presentation connection) resulting from an end-system failure. It also recovers from any residual loss or duplication of user data.

Reliable transfer of Application PDUs is carried out without the specific involvement of its user(s). Thus, if an Application PDU is lost or duplicated by the Presentation layer, the Reliable Transfer protocol is able to detect it and recover from it. Similarly, if there is failure of one of the end systems, as a consequence of which the Association is aborted, the Reliable Transfer protocol re-establishes the Association and resumes transfer of Application PDUs. The RTSE protocol uses *minor synchronization points* and *activities* to structure communication of all Application PDUs. These procedures are transparent to the RTSE service users. Of course, if the protocol is unable to re-establish the Association, or if it encounters un-recoverable errors on its own, it will abort the Association and inform the users accordingly. Needless to say that, in the absence of Reliable Transfer services, the application protocol itself may be designed to detect and recover from such failures.

An application which requires reliable transfer of Application PDUs must include the Application Service Elements, RTSE, in its Application Context, together with Association Control Service Element (ACSE). The composition of an Application Entity (AE) which includes RTSE as an Application Service Element (ASE), and the interaction between the AEs is shown in Figure 9.6. The User Element accesses the RTSE element for the establishment, release or abort of the supporting Application Association, and for (reliable) transfer of its APDUs.

On its part, the RTSE elements use ACSE services to establish, release, or abort an Application Association. But, for transfer of APDUs, the RTSE elements directly use Presentation services. It may be pointed out that once the ACSE and RTSE have been included in the Application Context, access by User Elements to ACSE and Presentation services is precluded. Note that, in general an AE comprises of a number of ASEs, including ACSE and RTSE. For instance, in a Message Handling System (MHS) an AE corresponding to a Message Transfer Agent includes an ASE that permits interaction with other Transfer Agents. The AE also includes an ASE through which User Agents gain access to MHS capability (see Section 11.7).

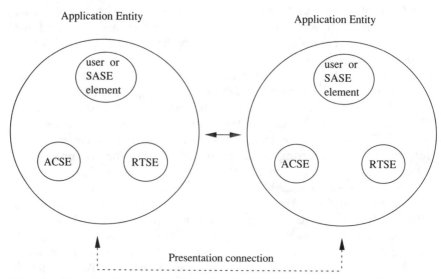

Figure 9.6 Interaction between Application entities which use RTSE service elements.

Before moving on to discuss RTSE services, we would like to draw a distinction between the variety of PDUs that are transferred over the supporting Presentation connection. Application PDUs are defined by the ACSE protocol, RTSE protocol, other ASE protocols, and the user defined application. In this section, APDUs defined by the RTSE protocol and those defined by user ASEs and the application are of particular interest. These are, respectively, referred to as *RTSE APDUs* and *RTSE-user APDUs*. The role of the RTSE service is to transfer RTSE-user APDUs reliably.

9.3.2　RTSE Services

Reliable Transfer services are listed in Table 9.5, together with an indication of whether a given service is confirmed, unconfirmed, or provider-

TABLE 9.5　Reliable Transfer Services

Service	Type of service	Function
RT-OPEN	Confirmed	Association establishment
RT-CLOSE	Confirmed	Association release
RT-TRANSFER	Confirmed	Data transfer
RT-TURN-PLEASE	Un-confirmed	Token request
RT-TURN-GIVE	Un-confirmed	Token transfer
RT-U-ABORT	Un-confirmed	User-initiated abort
RT-P-ABORT	Provider-initiated	Provider-initiated abort

initiated. From the viewpoint of specification, RTSE services may be described rather simply, since they provide services that are mapped onto those provided by ACSE and Presentation layer. However,

1. transfer of RTSE-user APDUs is reliable,

2. transfer of an RTSE-user APDU may not be initiated unless transfer of all previous RTSE-user APDUs is complete, and

3. transfer of RTSE-user APDUs is either in one direction only, or it is half-duplex.

Since transfer of RTSE-user APDUs is half-duplex (or simplex), the concept of *Turn* is introduced. The Turn is assigned to one of the two RTSE-users, at any time. The assignment may be changed dynamically by agreement between the two users. The RTSE-user that possesses the Turn may request data transfer. Also, an RTSE-user must possess the Turn to release the supporting Association. The concept of Turn is very similar to that of a *token,* introduced in Chapter 7 while discussing Session services. The difference, however, is that a Turn is an aggregate of all available tokens.

Service primitives.   We are now in a position to discuss the services. Figure 9.7 illustrates the transfer of RTSE-user APDUs using RTSE services in half-duplex mode.

1. The *RT-OPEN* service enables an RTSE-user to request the establishment of an Application Association with another named Application entity. The Application entity making the request is called *Association-initiating AE,* whereas the other AE is called *Association-responding AE.* As part of the establishment procedure, the Application Context as well as the Presentation contexts are negotiated. Necessarily, RT-OPEN is a confirmed service (see Figure 9.7).

2. The *RT-TRANSFER* service enables a user possessing the Turn to reliably transfer an RTSE-user APDU over an established Association, provided all RTSE-user APDUs earlier submitted to the RTSE service provider have been transferred. The RTSE-user issuing the corresponding request primitive is called the *sending RTSE-user,* while the peer user is called *receiving RTSE-user.* This service is also a confirmed service, but with a difference. The RTSE service provider delivers the APDU to the receiving RTSE-user, but does *not* expect a corresponding RT-TRANSFER response from it. An RT-TRANSFER confirm primitive is, however, issued to the RTSE-user soon after (see Figure 9.7).

3. The service, *RT-TURN-PLEASE,* enables a user to request the Turn, provided the user, itself, does not possess the Turn. Whether, the RTSE-user receiving the request agrees to give the Turn, is determined

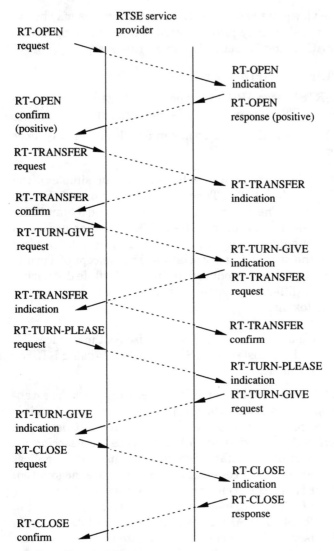

Figure 9.7 Use of RTSE services to transfer user APDUs in half-duplex mode.

by the application. In particular, a parameter, *priority* is defined, the significance of which is application dependent and transparent to the RTSE service provider. The need to possess the Turn may arise on two counts. First, the user may wish to transfer RTSE-user APDUs (see Figure 9.7). Or, the requesting user may wish to release the connection[6]. In the latter case, the requesting user must be the Association-initiating RTSE-user.

4. The *RT-TURN-GIVE* service may be used by an RTSE-user to give the Turn to the peer user. Obviously, it may do so provided the user possesses the Turn (see Figure 9.7).

5. The service, *RT-CLOSE,* is used to release the Association. The user making the request must be the Association-initiating user, and must also possess the Turn. The Association release is a confirmed service. It, therefore, does not disrupt the transfer of RTSE-APDUs (see Figure 9.7).

6. The *RT-U-ABORT* service may be used to abruptly abort the Association. It may result in a PDU transfers being disrupted. The service may be invoked by either RTSE-user.

7. The *RT-P-ABORT* service is initiated by the RTSE service provider to inform the RTSE-users of its inability to maintain the Association, because of errors from which it is not possible to recover. Surely, when the corresponding primitives are issued, transfer of user data may be disrupted.

Service parameters. Parameters of RTSE primitives are summarized in Table 9.6. The parameter, *Dialogue Mode,* is used to specify whether transfer of RTSE-user APDUs is half-duplex or in one direction. In either case, the parameter, *Initial Turn* specifies the initial assignment of Turn to one of the RTSE-users.

TABLE 9.6 Parameters of RTSE Primitives

Service	Parameters
RT-OPEN	Dialogue Mode, Initial Turn, User Data, Application Protocol (see also Note 1)
RT-CLOSE	User Data (see also Note 2)
RT-TRANSFER	RTSE-user APDU, Transfer Time, Result
RT-TURN-PLEASE	Priority
RT-TURN-GIVE	-
RT-U-ABORT	User Data
RT-P-ABORT	-

Note 1: ACSE and Presentation services related parameters, including Mode, Result, Result Source.
Note 2: ACSE related parameters, including Reason.

---

[6]The request to obtain the Turn is synonymous with requesting all available tokens, from the viewpoint of the Session service.

There are a number of other parameters of RT-OPEN primitives, but these parameters are identical to those of A-ASSOCIATE primitives of ACSE service. The RTSE user issuing the RT-OPEN request primitive may specify the *mode* of operation[7] for the RTSE service and the supporting protocol. It may be operated in *normal* mode (as defined by the 1988 version of [CCITT X.218], [CCITT X.228]) or in *X.410-1984* mode (as defined in [CCITT X.410]). This selection permits the implementation to be compatible with earlier implementations of RTSE services, and thereby enables inter-working of current (1988) versions of Message Handling Systems with those conforming to 1984 standards (see [CCITT X.400b]).

The parameters related to ACSE and Presentation layers are directly mapped onto the corresponding A-ASSOCIATE primitives. Aside from Mode, the parameters, *Result, Result source* and *User Data,* are of particular interest. The parameter, Result, indicates whether the Association is successfully established or not. If the Association has been rejected, then the Result source parameter indicates the source of rejection, viz. ACSE-user (in this case it would be RTSE service provider or the RTSE-user), ACSE service provider, or Presentation service provider.

User Data may be present in RT-OPEN request/indication primitives as well as in RT-OPEN response/confirm primitives. Their values must conform to an abstract syntax specified by the particular application. The syntax must be known to the RTSE protocol layer, since it encodes User Data as part of an RTSE APDU corresponding to RT-OPEN operations. User Data contained in RT-U-ABORT primitives must similarly conform to the same abstract syntax.

User Data in RT-TRANSFER or RT-CLOSE primitives again conforms to the abstract syntax specified by the application. This time, however, User Data may be encoded by the RTSE-user, and is handed over to the Presentation layer for its proper representation using the necessary transfer syntax. Thus, User Data in RT-TRANSFER or RT-CLOSE primitive may conform to any one of the abstract syntaxes named by the application.

The parameter, *transfer time,* in an RT-TRANSFER primitive is used by the RTSE-user to specify the time before which the RTSE service provider must ensure successful transfer. The parameter, *Result,* is present in a RT-TRANSFER confirm primitive to indicate to the user whether the RTSE-user APDU has been transferred or not. As dis-

---

[7]In X.410-1984 mode of operation, many of the other parameters are absent. The Application Context and Presentation Context Definition List are not specified. Instead, only the Application protocol name is specified.

cussed earlier, the parameter, *Priority,* in an RT-TURN-PLEASE request primitive is an indication by an RTSE-user to suggest the urgency that it associates with its request to possess the Turn.

There are few constraints on the sequence in which the RTSE service primitives may be issued. Of course, an Application Association must have been established before any other primitive may be issued, except that RT-U-ABORT or RT-P-ABORT primitives may be issued at any time, even while the Association is being established. But, the most significant constraints relate to issuing of RT-CLOSE, RT-TRANSFER, RT-TURN-PLEASE, and RT-TURN-GIVE primitive. As discussed earlier, a RT-CLOSE, RT-TURN-GIVE or RT-TRANSFER request primitives may be issued only if the user possesses the Turn, while RT-TURN-PLEASE request primitive may be issued only if the user does not possess the Turn. Further, a user may not issue a second RT-TRANSFER request primitive, or surrender the Turn, till it has received a confirm primitive corresponding to an earlier RT-TRANSFER request.

9.3.3 RTSE Protocol

The RTSE protocol defines the procedures used by RTSE service elements to establish, release or abort an Application Association, or to reliably transfer RTSE-user APDUs. It also handles reassignment of the Turn. The procedures are implemented in the form of a finite state machine, also called *RTSE Protocol Machine (RTSE PM).* Each RTSE PM interacts with:

1. an RTSE-user, by issuing or receiving RTSE service primitives,

2. ACSE and Presentation service providers, by issuing and receiving corresponding service primitives, and

3. its peer RTSE protocol machine, by exchanging RTSE APDUs.

This interaction is illustrated in Figure 9.8. The RTSE protocol defines the cause-effect relationship between these interactions. It, thereby, describes the method by which RTSE services are realized using RTSE APDUs. The protocol also describes the manner in which the underlying services (both ACSE and Presentation services) are used to exchange RTSE APDUs between the protocol machines. The abstract syntax of RTSE APDUs is specified using an ASN.1 notation (see [CCITT X.228] and [ISO 9066-2]).

The RTSE protocol is discussed below, starting with a discussion of how RTSE-user APDUs are transferred. This is followed by a discussion of procedures for establishing, releasing, or aborting an Application Association. Error reporting and recovery procedures are also discussed.

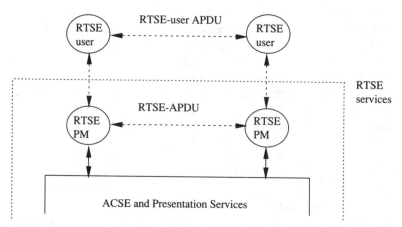

Figure 9.8 A model of the interaction between RTSE protocol machines.

Transfer of User APDUs.   Figure 9.9 illustrates the procedure used by RTSE protocol machines to transfer an RTSE-user APDU[8]. Transfer of each RTSE-user APDU is considered to be an *activity* as defined in the Session layer (see also Chapter 7). Thus, transfer of each RTSE-user APDU is preceded by the *start* of an activity. The sending RTSE PM uses the P-ACTIVITY-START primitives to start an activity. An RTSE-user APDU is transferred in a TRANSFER APDU of the RTSE protocol. The TRANSFER APDU, itself, is send as user data in a P-DATA request/indication. The activity is *ended* by the sending protocol machine. It uses P-ACTIVITY-END request primitive to indicate the end of APDU transfer. The receiving protocol machine, after securing the received RTSE-user APDU, delivers it to the corresponding RTSE-user in an RT-TRANSFER indication primitive. It then issues a P-ACTIVITY-END response. The resulting confirm primitive received by the sender is an indication of the fact that the APDU has been delivered to the RTSE-user. It may be mentioned that each activity is separately identified using an *Activity Identifier*.

The parameters, *Transfer Time* and *Result* of RT-TRANSFER primitives are local to the sending RTSE protocol machine. If the sending machine does not receive the P-ACTIVITY-END confirm primitive within the stipulated Transfer Time, then it simply discards the current transfer attempt, and indicates to the RTSE-user that it could not transfer the RTSE-user APDU.

---

[8]It is assumed that its size is acceptably small, and that segmentation of the APDU is not required.

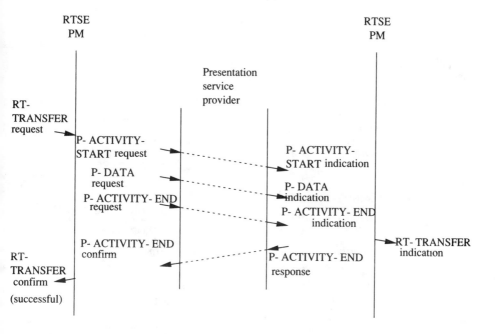

Note: P-DATA contains TRANSFER APDU as user data.

Figure 9.9 Transfer of RTSE-user APDUs.

If the size of the RTSE-user APDU is large, its segmentation may be necessary. Further, since the RTSE protocol machines must detect errors and recover from them, it is essential that transfer of each APDU segment be suitably identified and acknowledged by the receiving RTSE PM. The procedure to do so is called *checkpointing,* and is illustrated[9] in Figure 9.10. It is based upon placing *minor synchronization points* after the transfer of each segment of the RTSE-user APDU.

Except for the last segment of the RTSE-user APDU, following the transfer of each segment, the sending RTSE PM places a minor synchronization point. Each synchronization point has an associated serial number, and must be explicitly confirmed by the receiving RTSE PM. At any time, however, there may be a number of unconfirmed synchronization points. The maximum number of unconfirmed (or outstanding) synchronization points is called *window size*[10]. Its value is

[10]In Figure 9.10 the window size is assumed to be 2.

[9]The figure assumes that no errors occur during transfer of the APDU.

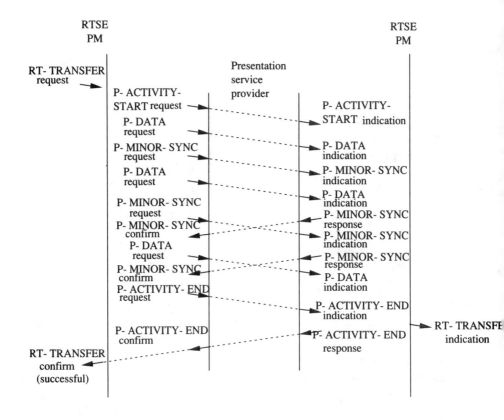

Note: P-DATA contains TRANSFER APDU as user data.

Figure 9.10 Transfer of RTSE-user APDU using checkpointing.

negotiated at the time of Association establishment. At that time the peer RTSE PMs also negotiate the maximum size of an APDU segment which may be sent as user data in a P-DATA request/indication primitive. The maximum APDU segment size is also called *check-point size*.

The procedure for re-assignment of Turn is relatively simple, and is illustrated in Figure 9.11. The RTSE protocol defines the RTSE APDU, *TURN PLEASE,* to carry the semantics of RT-TURN-PLEASE primitives. This is necessary because the TURN PLEASE APDU must carry the parameter, *Priority.* The APDU is communicated as user data in P-TOKEN-PLEASE primitives. The RT-TURN-GIVE request/indication primitives, on the other hand, are mapped directly onto P-CONTROL-GIVE service of the Presentation layer. Note that when the P-CON-TROL-GIVE service completes, all tokens (in this case *data, minor, activity* and *release* tokens of the underlying Session layer) are transferred to the receiving side.

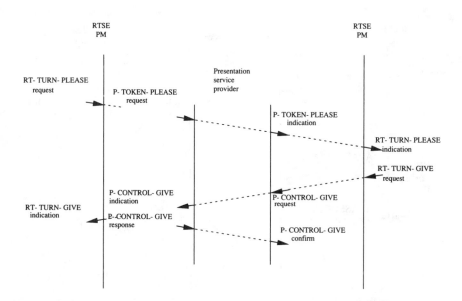

Note: P-TOKEN-PLEASE contains TURN-PLEASE APDU as user data.

Figure 9.11 Re-assignment of Turn.

Association management. We now discuss the procedure used by RTSE protocol machines to establish, release or abort an Application Association. Figure 9.12 illustrates the procedures for establishment (successful or unsuccessful) of an Association and its release. It is shown that the semantics of RT-OPEN request and indication primitives is conveyed in the RTSE APDU, *OPEN REQUEST*, whereas that of RT-OPEN response and confirm primitives is conveyed in either *ACCEPT* or *REJECT* APDUs. The latter depends upon whether or not the Association is accepted by the responding RTSE-user and the responding RTSE PM. In Figure 9.12 the first attempt is rejected by the responding RTSE PM, perhaps because it is too busy.

The RTSE APDUs, OPEN REQUEST, ACCEPT and REJECT, are communicated using the underlying A-ASSOCIATE primitives. This mapping of RTSE service primitives onto RTSE APDUs and/or the underlying services is summarized in Table 9.7. The RT-CLOSE primitives do not have a corresponding RTSE APDU. Their semantics is simply mapped onto A-RELEASE primitives. This is possible since RT-CLOSE primitives have User Data as the only parameter, which can be conveyed in the user data field of A-RELEASE primitives.

The procedures for Association abort are illustrated in Figure 9.13. The semantics of RT-U-ABORT primitives is conveyed in a *ABORT*

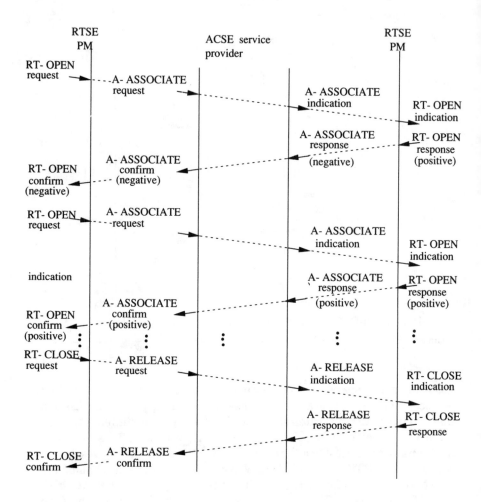

Note: A-ASSOCIATE primitives carry OPEN REQUEST, ACCEPT or REJECT APDUs as user data.

Figure 9.12 **Establishment and release of an Application Association.**

APDU. The same APDU, ABORT, is also used by an RTSE PM to carry out provider-initiated abort. This may be necessary to indicate to its peer protocol machine that it is aborting the Association because it has encountered errors from which it is not possible to recover.

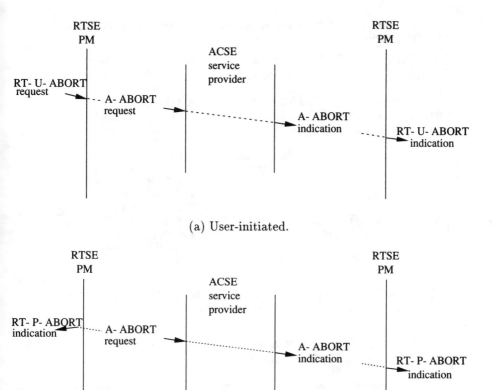

(a) User-initiated.

(b) RTSE service provider initiated.
Note: A-ABORT primitives carry ABORT APDU as user data.

Figure 9.13 User-initiated and provider-initiated Association abort.

Table 9.8 summarizes the parameters of the RTSE APDUs (see also Table 9.6). The parameter, dialogue mode, in OPEN REQUEST APDU is derived from the corresponding RT-OPEN request/indication primitive. But, the parameter, Initial Turn, is mapped by the RTSE protocol machine onto the parameter, *Initial Assignment of Tokens,* of the underlying Session service.

The parameter, *Session Connection Identifier,* is only used if the Application Association is being re-established by the communicating RTSE protocol machines. Such a need arises if the underlying Presentation connection fails. The parameter identifies the earlier (failed) connection which is required to be linked with the connection now

TABLE 9.7   Mapping of RTSE Services and Procedures onto RTSE APDUs and Underlying Services

RT service primitive	RTSE APDU	Lower layer primitives
RT-OPEN req/ind	OPEN REQUEST	A-ASSOCIATE req/ind
RT-OPEN resp/conf	ACCEPT	A-ASSOCIATE resp/conf
RT-OPEN resp/conf	REJECT	A-ASSOCIATE resp/conf
RT-CLOSE req/ind	-	A-RELEASE req/ind
RT-CLOSE resp/conf	-	A-RELEASE resp/conf
RT-TRANSFER request	-	P-ACTIVITY-START req/ind
	TRANSFER	P-DATA req/ind
	-	P-MINOR-SYNC req/ind
	-	P-MINOR-SYNC resp/conf
RT-TRANSFER ind/conf	-	P-ACTIVITY-END req/ind
	-	P-ACTIVITY-END resp/conf
RT-TURN-PLEASE req/ind	TURN PLEASE	P-TURN-PLEASE req/ind
RT-TURN-GIVE req/ind	-	P-CONTROL-GIVE req/ind
RT-U-ABORT req/ind	ABORT	A-ABORT req/ind
RT-P-ABORT ind	ABORT	A-ABORT req/ind

being established. This ensures that transfer of RTSE-user APDUs will continue uninterrupted.

Error recovery.   Transfer of user APDUs, as described above, may not succeed for several reasons, including:

1. the sending or receiving RTSE protocol machines may detect an error during transfer of a user APDU (that is, during an activity),

2. the underlying Presentation layer may indicate occurrence of an exceptional condition by issuing a P-P-EXCEPTION REPORT which, note, may only occur during an activity (see Section 7.4.4),

3. an RTSE protocol machine may detect an error outside an activity, or

4. the underlying ACSE service provider may abort the Application Association.

TABLE 9.8   Parameters of RTSE Protocol Data Units

RTSE APDU	Parameters
OPEN REQUEST	Checkpoint Size, Window Size, Dialogue Mode, User Data, Session Connection Identifier, Application Protocol
ACCEPT	Checkpoint Size, Window Size, User Data, Session Connection Identifier
REJECT	Refuse Reason, User Data
ABORT	Abort Reason, Reflected Parameters, User Data
TRANSFER	User Data
TURN PLEASE	Priority

Within an activity, the sending RTSE protocol machine initiates error handling and subsequent recovery. Thus, if a receiving RTSE protocol machine detects an error, it reports the same to the sending RTSE protocol machine by issuing a P-U-EXCEPTION-REPORT request primitive. Depending upon the severity of the problem detected by it, or indicated to it by the receiving RTSE protocol machine, the sending RTSE protocol machine may initiate any one of the error handling and recovery procedures. The error handling and recovery procedures are also carried out in case the Presentation service issues a P-P-EXCEP-TION-REPORT indication primitive.

Figure 9.14 illustrates three different error handling and recovery procedures. Common to all of these is the error handling scheme, *transfer discard*, used to abruptly terminate the current transfer of a user APDU.

1. In case the error reflects duplication of transfer, then after the transfer has been discarded, the sending RTSE protocol machine issues an RT-TRANSFER confirm primitive with the value of parameter, *Result*, as *successful* (see Figure 9.14(a)). The transfer discard procedure uses the Activity Discard service made available by the Presentation layer.

2. If the receiving or sending RTSE protocol machines is (temporarily) unable to send or receive a user APDU, the sending RTSE protocol machine, after discarding the current transfer, confirms to the sending RTSE-user completion of RT-TRANSFER service, but with *no success,* as in Figure 9.14(b).

3. In other cases, particularly when none of the minor synchronization points have been confirmed, it may be desirable to discard the transfer and later retry its transfer, as illustrated in Figure 9.14(c).

If a less severe form of error is detected by an RTSE protocol machine, and at least one of the minor synchronization points has been confirmed, then the sending RTSE protocol machine may interrupt the transfer, and subsequently resume its transfer. The procedure uses the activity-related interrupt and resume services offered by the Presentation layer. This is illustrated in Figure 9.15. Since each activity is identified, the receiving protocol machine is able to correlate the resumed activity with the one interrupted.

If during APDU transfer, a severe form of error is detected, the RTSE protocol machine may abort the underlying Association, and then attempt to re-establish the Association[11], as shown in Figure 9.16. The

---

[11]This procedure may also be necessary, if a receiving RTSE protocol machine receives a P-ACTIVITY-DISCARD indication, but only after it has delivered the received user APDU to the RTSE user.

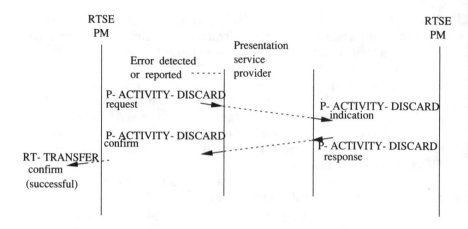

(a) Discard resulting in successful transfer.

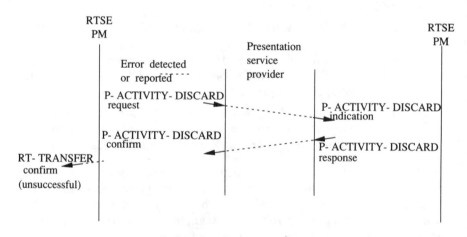

(b) Discard resulting in unsuccessful transfer.

Figure 9.14 Error handling and recovery using the discard procedure.

OPEN REQUEST APDU used to re-establish the Association carries with it the *Old Session Connection Identifier*. The identifier may be used by the responding RTSE protocol machine to treat the current Association essentially as a continuation of the old one. It is also used,

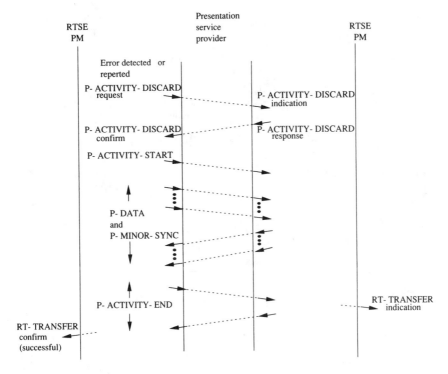

(c) Discard and retry resulting in successful transfer.

Figure 9.14 (*Continued*)

together with the *Old Activity Identifier,* to resume the activity so that transfer of the interrupted (in fact aborted) user APDU may continue.

If the underlying ACSE service provider aborts the Association, either within an activity or outside, then the Association-initiating RTSE protocol machine re-establishes the Association, as discussed above. But, the transfer of user APDU is resumed only if the Association was earlier aborted during an activity.

In case, an RTSE protocol machine is simply not able to support the Association, or is unable to recover from failures, it aborts the Association by sending an ABORT APDU, and gives an RT-P-ABORT indication to the concerned RTSE user, as in Figure 9.13(b).

As a last comment, RTSE services are used extensively by Remote Operations Service Elements (see Section 9.4), as well in implementing the protocols of Message Handling Systems (see Chapter 11).

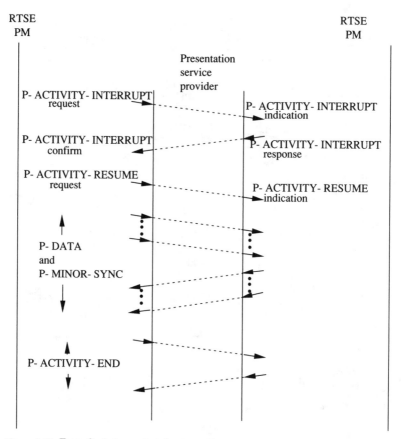

Figure 9.15 Transfer interrupt and resumption.

9.4 Remote Operations

In this section we discuss services that are useful in applications where interactions between processes is structured in the form a sequence of remote operations. Remote operations are performed by an Application entity upon specific requests from another Application entity. *The Remote Operations Service Elements (ROSE)* provide such a capability to user elements. We discuss below the related concepts, services and protocols.

9.4.1 Introduction

In an OSI environment, communication between two Application processes is represented in terms of communication between the two corresponding Application entities (*AE*). They use Presentation services

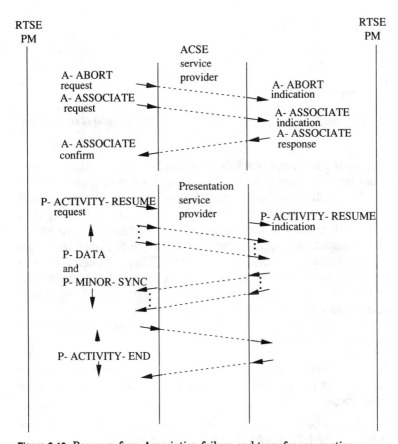

Figure 9.16 Recovery from Association failure and transfer resumption.

together with Association Control and Reliable Transfer services. In the latter case, the service elements RTSE and ACSE are also included in the definition of the Application entities. The application APDUs may be conveyed using Presentation, Association Control or Reliable Transfer services.

In many applications, however, communication between processes is interactive, and simply involves a sequence of operations performed by one AE upon request from another (remote) AE. A model of the environment which uses remote operations is given in Figure 9.17, where an Application entity, AE1 for instance, requests an operation to be performed. Entity AE2 attempts to perform the operation and reports back the outcome of the attempt in the form of a *result reply* or an *error reply,* depending upon whether the attempt succeeded or failed.

operation request

AE1

client

AE2

server

reply (result/error)

Figure 9.17 A model of remote operations.

Not every operation requires that the Application entity that performs the operation respond back with a reply (result or error). In certain cases, the Application entity may be required to return a result only, in which case it must be presumed by the requesting entity that the operation will complete successfully. In other cases, where no results are anticipated, the Application entity may be required to return an error indication, only in case the operation failed. Conceivably, one may even define operations where no response is expected from the entity performing the operation. Remote operations may, thus, be classified on the basis of whether a result and/or error reply is expected or not.

Remote operations may also be classified based upon the *operation modes.* The two modes are defined below:

1. *synchronous mode,* where an Application entity does not invoke an operation till a reply to the previous similar operation has been received[12], and

2. *asynchronous mode,* where an Application entity may invoke an operation without waiting for a reply to previous operations.

The above characterizations of remote operations give rise to five different *Operation Classes.* These are summarized in Table 9.9. Note that each operation has an associated Operation Class, and must be agreed to, *a priori,* by the communicating Application entities. Thus,

TABLE 9.9   Operation Classes

Operation Class	Mode	Reply
Class 1	Synchronous	result *or* error
Class 2	Asynchronous	result *or* error
Class 3	Asynchronous	error
Class 4	Asynchronous	result
Class 5	Asynchronous	-

---

[12]It is obvious that in synchronous mode of a remote operation, a result or error reply to a corresponding request for remote operation must be sent by the Application entity performing the operations.

TABLE 9.10   Classes of Association Based upon
Which Application Entity May Invoke the Remote
Operations

Association Class	Application entity which may invoke remote operations
Class 1	initiating AE
Class 2	responding AE
Class 3	initiating or responding AEs

for a given operation, the two entities are well aware of the expected response from the entity performing the operation, and the mode which an entity uses to request execution of an operation.

The *Remote Operations Service Elements* (*ROSE*) (see [CCITT X.219] and [CCITT X.229] or [ISO 9072-1] and [ISO 9072-2]) have been included within the framework of OSI to facilitate the design and specification of applications which require remote operations. The corresponding services, discussed shortly, enable a user element in an AE to request an operation, or to respond with a result reply or error reply. The ROSE protocol conveys the semantics of remote operations to the peer Application entity using the available lower layer services.

The specification of ROSE services requires that before remote operations are invoked by the user element or another ASE, an Association between the two communicating Application entities must be established. As part of Association establishment, the two Application processes also agree to include ROSE elements while defining the Application context, as well and to use the specific set of remote operations.

As before, an AE initiating the establishment of an Association is referred to as the *Association-initiating AE,* whereas the AE responding to the Association request is termed *Association-responding AE.* The description of ROSE services permits both Application entities to invoke remote operations. However, there are a number of applications where the relation between the initiator and the responder is that of client-server. The server performs operations upon request from a client Application entity. The ROSE service specification, therefore, defines three classes of Association. These are summarized in Table 9.10. Note that Association Class 1 permits only the client AE to establish an Association and subsequently invoke a sequence of remote operations. (Of course, the client and the server are free to use any of the Operation Classes to define remote operations.)

9.4.2   Specification of Remote Operations

As an example of remote operations, consider a hypothetical electronic mail system, shown in Figure 9.18. The mail-server and the mail-user

Figure 9.18 An electronic mail system.

are application processes, and are also referred to as *objects.* The collection of permissible operations is, for example, listed in Table 9.11. The name of each operation suggests its semantics. Because of the asymmetric nature of the application, it is necessary to specify as to which of the two objects may invoke a given operation. In the above example, except for *change-parameters,* all the other operations can be invoked *either* by the mail-server *or* a mail-user, but not both. The operation change-parameters can be invoked by either process.

It is also useful to club together related operations into one or more subsets of operations, as shown in Table 9.11. These subsets are termed *ports.* A port is conceptually a point through which an Application process interacts with other Application processes using operations from the subset. Therefore, each port is of a certain *type.* Two application processes may interact only though a pair of ports of the same type. In the above example, the mail-server and the mail-user have ports of three different types, submission, delivery and register. But, from the above description, it is unclear whether two mail-servers, for instance, can interact with each other through the ports. Obviously, such is not the case with these ports. Thus, it is also necessary to specify the role of each application process with respect to each port, that it supports. This role is defined in terms of whether an associated object or process acts as a *supplier* or as a *consumer* of services. For the above example, the role of a mail-server (and of a mail-user) with respect to each port is given in Table 9.12. Each port in this case is asymmetrical since the role of an object is that of a supplier or that of a consumer, but not both. If a port is asymmetric, then an object with the role of a supplier can interact through the port with an object with the role of a consumer. This then implies that the mail-user, above, may interact only with a mail-server through any of the three ports. But two mail-

**TABLE 9.11   Operations in an Hypothetical Mail
System**

Port	Operation(s)	Who may invoke
submission	submit mail	mail user
delivery	mail delivery	mail server
	mail ack	mail server
	delivery control	mail user
control	register	mail user
	change parameters	mail server or mail user

TABLE 9.12   The Role of Each Application
Process Concerning Its Ports

Object (or process)	Ports	Object's role
mail-server	submission	supplier
	delivery	supplier
	control	supplier
mail-user	submission	consumer
	delivery	consumer
	control	consumer

servers, or two mail users, may not interact with each other using any of the three asymmetric ports.

Consider the addition of a port, called *transfer,* to the mail-server. The port supports *mail-transfer* and *ack-transfer* operations that can be used by two mail-servers to move mail and acknowledgements through the network. Such a port is necessarily symmetric so that the operations can be invoked by any mail-server.

Thus, a complete description of the operations may be given in terms of:

1.   the ports that each Application process supports,

2.   for each port the role of each process either as a supplier, consumer, or both,

3.   the permissible operations at each port and as to who, a consumer or supplier, may invoke the operation.

For the example discussed above, see Tables 9.12 and 9.13. Note that the specification of which object(s) can invoke an operation is independent of the object, itself. Instead, it is based upon the *role* of object.

Consider the detailed specification of each operation. Each separately identified remote operation is specified using a notation that is independent of how an operation is realized using underlying services. The specification includes:

1.   the data type of the parameter, also known as *argument,* to be con-

TABLE 9.13   Port Specification in Terms of
Permissible Operations, and Who May Invoke Them

Port	Supplier invokes	Consumer invokes
submission		submit mail
delivery	mail delivery	delivery control
	mail ack	
control	change parameters	change parameters
		register

TABLE 9.14   Example Definition of Operations and Errors

Operation identifier	Request data type	Result data type	Error condition
op1	ud-type1	ud-type2	error1, error2
op2	ud-type3		error1, error3

(a) Example operations.

Error identifier	Error data type
error1	error-data-type1
error2	error-data-type2
error3	error-data-type3

(b) Example errors.

veyed as part of the remote operation request to the corresponding Application entity,

2. the data type of the parameter (if any), also known as *result,* to be conveyed to the Application entity initiating the remote operation, in case the remote operation is performed successfully, and

3. a list of possible error conditions that may be encountered. Each error condition is separately identified together with the data type of an associated parameter. The latter may be used to convey additional information.

Example definitions of two operations and related error conditions are given in Table 9.14. Note that *op1* is of Operation Class 1, whereas *op2* is of Class 2. The error condition, *error1,* may occur when either of the two operations is performed.

While the above notation to specify an operation is independent of the underlying services, realization of an operations using ROSE services is fairly straightforward, and is discussed below.

9.4.3   Bind/Unbind Operations

Before an Application process invokes an operation, it must *bind* the ports that it proposes to use with matching ports of another Application process. The process initiating the Bind operation is called the *initiating* object, whereas the process responding to a Bind request is called *responding* object. As discussed earlier, two ports, one from each of the initiating and responding objects, match provided they are of the same type and one process acts as a supplier while the other as a consumer. Or both could simultaneously act as a supplier and a consumer. A Bind operation, if it completes successfully, ensures that the two processes have a common view of their roles concerning each port through which they interact, and of the related operations. A formal specification of a Bind operation includes:

1. the list of ports of the responder object to be bound, and the requested role of the responder,

2. a detailed specification of the parameters conveyed during the Bind operation.

An *Unbind* operation, may be used by the initiating object to Unbind the listed ports of the responder. Here again, the notation for specifying an Unbind operation is similar to that used to define Bind operations. Note that the specification of Bind and Unbind operations is independent of how these operations are realized.

We now discuss the detailed specification of the parameters conveyed during a Bind (or an Unbind) operation. A Bind operation is specified by the application again using a notation that permits a variety of implementations. The discussion below, however, assumes that the Bind (and Unbind) operations are realized using the Association Control services[13]. The Bind operation is mapped onto the A-ASSOCIATE primitives of ACSE services, whereas the Unbind operation is mapped onto the A-RELEASE primitives.

The specification of a Bind operation includes:

1. the data type of the parameter to be conveyed as user-data in the A-ASSOCIATE request or indication primitives,

2. the data type of the parameter to be conveyed as user data in the A-ASSOCIATE response or confirm primitives, in case the Association is established successfully, and

3. the data type of the parameter to be conveyed as user-data in the A-ASSOCIATE response or confirm primitives, in case the Association is not established.

The data types, are determined by the application protocol which invokes remote operations. The application protocol also supplies the values to the above parameters, together with those to be associated with other parameters of A-ASSOCIATE primitives.

The Unbind operation is similarly specified by the application protocol. It is, however, mapped onto the A-RELEASE primitives.

The use of the notation Bind or Unbind and for remote operations permits development of applications, independent of how these operations are mapped onto the underlying service elements. Thus each

---

[13]Alternatively, Reliable Transfer Services (see [CCITT X.218], [ISO 9066-1] or Section 9.3) may be used to map Bind or Unbind operations.

AE1   AE2

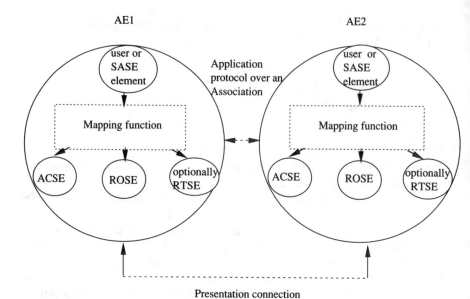

Presentation connection

Figure 9.19 The model of an AE that uses remote operations.

Application entity contains a module that maps the Bind/Unbind (and remote operations) onto the available service elements.

Whereas the Bind and Unbind operations are mapped onto Association Control services, the remote operations may be directly mapped onto ROSE service elements. The resulting structure of an AE which uses ROSE services is given in Figure 9.19. There, it is illustrated that the user element of an Application entity maps its operations onto ACSE services or onto ROSE services. The Application Context must, therefore, include the ACSE, ROSE and other Application Service Elements needed by the user element.

TABLE 9.15   ROSE Services and Their Parameters

Service	Type	Parameters
RO-INVOKE	unconfirmed	Operation-Class, Operation-ID, Invocation-ID, User-data, Priority
RO-RESULT	unconfirmed	Operation-ID, Invocation-ID, User-data, Priority
RO-ERROR	unconfirmed	Error-ID, Invocation-ID, User-data, Priority
RO-REJECT-U	unconfirmed	Invocation-ID, Reject-reason, Priority
RO-REJECT-P	provider-initiated	Invocation-ID Reject-reason, Returned-parameters

9.4.4   ROSE Services

The Remote Operations Service Elements permit users (a user element of an Application entity, through a mapping function) to request execution of an operation, to furnish results, or to report errors. The collection of services available as part ROSE elements are listed in Table 9.15, together with their parameters (see [CCITT X.219] or [ISO 9072-1]). Note that ROSE services are unconfirmed services, except for the provider-initiated *RO-REJECT-P* service (see Figure 9.20). The semantics of the services and their parameters are now discussed. Later, we discuss their use in implementing example operations, op1 and op2, from Table 9.14.

The *RO-INVOKE* service is used by an ROSE-user to request (or *invoke*) execution of an operation, identified by the value of the parameter, *Operation-ID*. The associated User Data may be used as input data to perform the requested operation. Each invocation of an operation is separately identified in *Invocation-ID* (an integer), so that a subsequent response from a ROSE-user can be correlated with the particular invocation. The associated *Operation Class* parameter enables the ROSE-user, performing the operation, to suitably respond with a result or error reply, or to not respond at all.[14]

The *RO-RESULT* and *RO-ERROR* primitives enable the ROSE-user performing the requested operation to furnish a result or error reply. In both cases, the user provides the Invocation-ID of the related RO-INVOKE primitive, together with user-data (to be interpreted as results or as error information, as the case may be). The RO-RESULT also identifies the remote operation, whereas the RO-ERROR identifies the error condition in the parameter *Error-ID*.

The *RO-REJECT-U* service may be used by a ROSE-user to reject a request to perform an operation (earlier submitted in the form of RO-INVOKE indication). Or, it may also be used to reject a reply (in the form of RO-RESULT or RO-ERROR indication). There are several reasons why a ROSE-user may reject a request or a reply. Request for a remote operation that has not been agreed to, indication of an unrecognizable error condition in a reply, or inclusion of parameters that cannot be interpreted are some of the reasons for invoking the RO-REJECT-U service. The reason for rejecting the received indication primitive is conveyed to the peer user element in the parameter *Reject reason*. This parameter describes whether the rejection is due to an RO-INVOKE, RO-RESULT, or RO-ERROR, as well as the specific difficulty faced by the user.

---

[14]The parameter *Priority* specifies the priority to be accorded by the ROSE protocol in sending a related protocol data unit. In some cases, this may be of marginal significance.

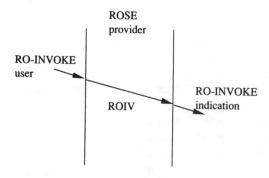

(a) RO-INVOKE service.

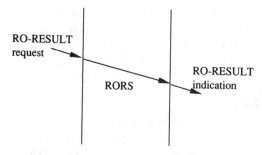

(b) RO-RESULT service.

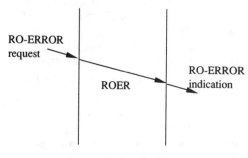

Figure 9.20 ROSE services and their mapping onto ROSE protocol-data-units.

(c) RO-ERROR service.

The *RO-REJECT-P* service may be initiated only by the ROSE service provider. It may do so to advise the ROSE-user(s) that a previously issued RO-INVOKE request (or RO-RESULT or RO-ERROR request) is unlikely to be conveyed to its peer entity due to protocol errors. The parameter *Returned parameters* contains a copy of the parameters of the rejected ROSE primitive.

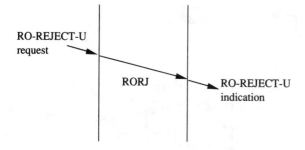

(d) RO-REJECT-U service.

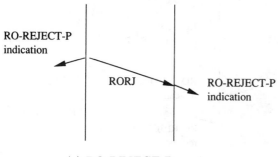

(e) RO-REJECT-P service.

Figure 9.20 (*Continued*)

Figure 9.21 illustrates the use of ROSE services in implementing remote operations. We have used the operations, op1 and op2, of Table 9.14 to show how remote operations of different classes can be mapped onto ROSE services.

There are no constraints on issuing ROSE primitives, except that they can be issued only after a Bind operation has been successfully performed and before an Unbind. Of course, they must also be consistent with the agreed Association Class and Operation Class. That is, an RO-RESULT or RO-ERROR can only be issued in response to an outstanding (for which a reply is awaited) RO-INVOKE primitive of an appropriate Operation Class. Similarly, an RO-REJECT-U primitives can be issued only in response to outstanding RO-INVOKE, RO-RESULT, or RO-ERROR primitives. The RO-REJECT-P primitive can be issued by the service provider in response to any request primitive.

Issuing of a ROSE primitive does not disrupt any other outstanding ROSE primitive, except that receipt of an RO-REJECT-P indication signifies that an indication primitive corresponding to the user-initi-

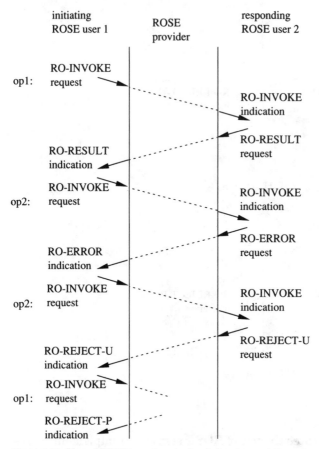

Figure 9.21 Use of ROSE services to implement remote operations.

ated ROSE request primitive will not be issued by the ROSE service provider to its peer user element.

9.4.5　ROSE Protocol

The protocol used to support ROSE services is relatively very simple. It essentially describes the collection of *ROSE Application protocol-data-units (ROSE APDUs)* used to convey the semantics and parameters of ROSE service primitives. This mapping of ROSE primitives onto ROSE APDUs is given in Table 9.16, and illustrated in Figure 9.20, above. The protocol also specifies that the ROSE APDUs are carried as user data in P-DATA primitives[15].

---

[15]As an alternative, PDUs may be transferred using Reliable Transfer Services ([CCITT X.218]).

TABLE 9.16   Mapping of ROSE Primitives onto ROSE Protocol Data Units

ROSE primitives	ROSE APDUs
RO-INVOKE	ROIV
RO-RESULT	RORS
RO-ERROR	ROER
RO-REJECT-U	RORJ
RO-REJECT-P	RORJ

It may be recalled that the ROSE protocol does not, by itself, map Bind/Unbind operations onto the ACSE services. It does, however, take note of the fact, whenever the Association (and by implication, the supporting Presentation connection) is successfully established, released or aborted.

9.5   Concurrency, Commitment and Recovery

In systems involving permanent (or even semi-permanent) data storage, consistency of stored information is of prime importance. That is, if two or more related operations are to be carried out on a file, for instance, then either each operation executes successfully and the resulting changes made permanent, or the file is left unaltered in case any operation fails. The last step, whereby a processor makes the change permanent, is referred to as a *commit* operation. An operation may fail either because it is invalid, or resources required for its execution are unavailable, or the processor itself fails. The need for consistency of data storage requires that the sequence of operations be viewed as an *atomic action* which either succeeds or fails. Figure 9.22

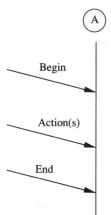

Figure 9.22 Sequence of commands to a processor to execute an atomic action.

illustrates the sequence of commands issued to the processor to execute an atomic action. In case an operation fails, the processor aborts the execution. Such an abort is also referred to as a *rollback* (for details see [ISO 9804], [ISO 9805] and [Berns 87]).

9.5.1 Commitment

The situation is more complex in distributed applications, where two or more Application entities, possibly residing in two different open systems, cooperate to manipulate a shared or distributed data base. At the end of processing (and necessary communication), not only must the cooperating entities be sure that the data base is consistent, but all entities must be aware of the final state of the data base. We shall illustrate the complexity of the problem using a few examples.

Consider an application where an Application entity A requests execution of an atomic action by another entity B (see Figure 9.23(a)). Once the request has been received, the entity starts its execution. The atomic action either succeeds or fails. If it succeeds, the entity B commits all changes to the data base made thus fax, otherwise it leaves the database unaltered. However, the initiator is unaware of the outcome, unless the fact is specifically made known to entity A, as shown in

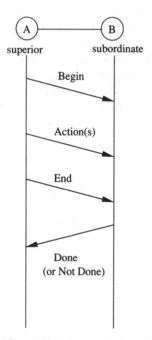

Figure 9.23 Sequence of messages to an entity to execute an atomic action.

(a) Processing is by one single entity.

Figure 9.23(a). The initiator of an atomic action is called the *superior,* while the responder entity is called *subordinate.* It is under the direction of the superior that a subordinate entity processes requests and sends back a report on the outcome.

In the second example, an atomic action is viewed as a distributed task to be executed by two subordinate entities, B and C (see Figure 9.23(b)). The exchange of messages illustrated in Figure 9.23(a) is now shown to be inadequate in ensuring consistency of the data base dis-

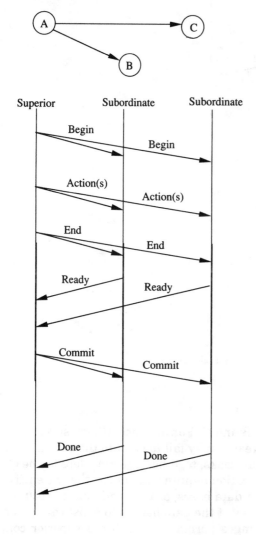

(b) Processsing may be distributed over two subordinates.

Figure 9.23 (*Continued*)

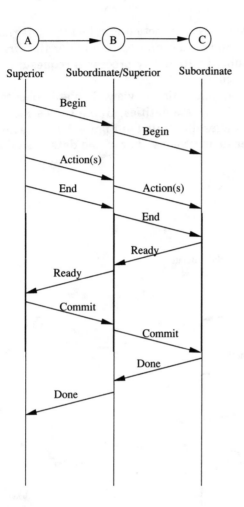

(c) Processing may be further subdivided by a subordinate

Figure 9.23 (*Continued*)

tributed over the two sites, B and C. For instance, B may successfully execute the operation, whereas C may fail to execute the sub-task due to some failure. If the two sub-tasks, together, are considered to be one atomic action, then the application requires that either the two entities successfully operate on their data bases, or they both abort execution. One way to ensure consistency of the data base is to insist that an entity does not make the changes permanent, until the superior commands it to do so. Note that the superior entity is the only entity which is in a position to determine whether the changes can be committed or rolled back. Of course, before issuing a commit command, the superior entity A ensures that both entities, B and C, have succeeded in their operation and are ready to update their data bases permanently. In the event a subordinate entity is unsuccessful in executing its operations, it should inform the superior. The superior in turn, commands all subordinate entities to restore data to its original state.

The last example has to do with an entity A initiating an atomic action at entity B. Successful completion by entity B, in turn, may require that a sub-sequence of operations be executed by a third entity C. (See Figure 9.23(c).) Here, entity B is a subordinate of entity A, as well as a superior of entity C. In such a situation, the sequence in which commit (or rollback) operation is executed is of particular interest. Typically, when entity C is ready to commit, it informs its superior, entity B, which in turn informs the initiating entity A of its readiness to commit. Entity A may now request commitment of updates by entity B and by its subordinates, as applicable. In case of failure, at entity B or C, entity A would be obliged to request a rollback[16].

9.5.2 Atomic Actions

Formally, an atomic action is a sequence of operations performed by a distributed application with the property that it is controlled by a unique Application entity, and that parts of it may be executed by two or more communicating entities. Further, the atomic action either completes successfully, or terminates without any change in the state of the data storage controlled by participating entities.

The atomic action may be modelled as a rooted tree with two or more nodes, as illustrated in Figure 9.24. Each node of the tree models a participating Application entity. The root node A is also called the *master* entity, and determines whether the atomic action is subsequently committed or aborted. Each branch of the tree models the superior-subordinate relationship between entities, discussed earlier. Such a relationship is also called a *CCR (or Commitment, Concurrency and Recovery) relationship*. For example, the entity A partitions the atomic action into two sub-tasks to be executed concurrently by the subordinates B and C. Each of these sub-tasks is an atomic action in its own right. Further, entity C assigns execution of a portion of its sub-task to its subordinate D. This again is an atomic action in so far as it concerns the pair of entities C and D. Needless to say, that successful execution of the entire atomic action is dependent upon successful execution of each sub-task, or equivalently of each sub-atomic action.

---

[16]Note that entity A need not be aware that part of the processing is done by a third entity.

Above, we have assumed that entities corresponding to each node in the tree are distinct. Such need not be the case. That is, nodes A and D, from the example of Figure 9.24, could conceivably be a model of the fact that the same Application entity not only controls the entire atomic action, but is also acting as a subordinate entity executing a part of the task assigned to the instance C of an Application entity. The distinction between two or more instances can be made based on the knowledge that each branch of the tree (or a CCR relationship) uses a distinct Application association. Further, what constitutes an atomic action is determined solely by the application. In fact, the corresponding tree may be constructed dynamically based upon the current location of data and availability of other resources.

9.5.3 Application Failure

Before discussing the protocol to handle commitment or rollback we describe the nature of failures that may be encountered in a distributed application. Two types of failures are recognized. The first type, due to failure of an Application entity, may result in loss of *unsecured* stored data. Subsequently, after execution of a local recovery procedure, the failed Application entity may be restored. However, secured data, typically on a reliable disk, is assumed to be available. When applying commit procedures, it is assumed that data to be manipulated by a subordinate as part of an atomic action is stored on a secure medium. Such data is called *bound data*, since it is *bound* to the atomic action. Changes, if any, to the bound data are also stored on a secure medium together with *atomic action data*. The latter includes a description of the Application association, the atomic action, concurrency controls

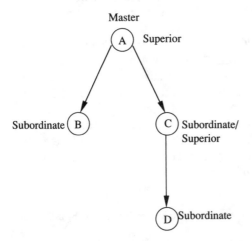

Figure 9.24 An atomic action tree.

(discussed shortly), and pointers to bound data. Subsequently, when a commit operation is performed, the old copy is released and the update made permanent. In case a rollback to the original state of bound data is performed, additional resources acquired during the execution of the atomic action are released.

Communication breakdown is the second type of failure. Such failure causes loss of data in transit only. The Application association may be re-established and communication restarted. A restart procedure will enable Application entities to resynchronize communication to the beginning of the atomic action (or to an intermediate checkpoint). The restart procedure may be used in case of failure of an Application entity.

9.5.4 Concurrency

While discussing atomic actions and their execution, it is quite conceivable that two or more atomic actions may concurrently attempt to manipulate the same data. In such a situation, commitment of an atomic action becomes more complex, since not only do their actions modify the data simultaneously, but either of them may decide to rollback their computations. Concurrency controls, imposed by an implementation, must therefore ensure that:

1. data bound to an atomic action is not changed other than by the atomic action, itself, and

2. if an atomic action, to begin with, uses data that is subject to rollback (as part of another atomic action), then it is not committed until and unless the other atomic action commits.

One simple way to implement concurrency control is to install locks (or prevent access) on all data that is bound to an atomic action, and to release them when a commit or rollback occurs. More efficient ways to implement concurrency control are available (for more details see [Berns 87]). Such controls are, however, transparent to a user of CCR services.

9.5.5 CCR Services

Commitment, concurrency, and recovery procedures are optionally supported by an open system implementation in the form of a set of common Application service elements, called CCR elements. CCR services, when available, may be used to ensure atomicity of interactions in a distributed application. A user, or another Application service element included within the Application entity, which requires CCR services must include CCR elements in the Application context that it negotiates at the time of establishing an association with its peer user. Figure 9.25 illustrates access to CCR services, and the fact that CCR

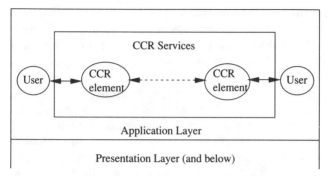

Figure 9.25 CCR services and its use by other elements.

elements themselves use Presentation services to implement the CCR protocol. Each CCR relationship requires a *distinct* Application association to be established between a superior and its subordinate entities. Further, over an Application association, there may not be more than one atomic action in progress at any given time. In this respect, nesting of atomic actions is currently not supported.

The two phase commit procedure may now be discussed. The collection of CCR service primitive available to a user are listed in Table 9.17, together with an indication of whether a service element is confirmed or not. Figure 9.26 illustrates the typical sequence in which CCR service primitives are issued to start execution of an atomic action or to terminate it, leading to either a commit or rollback operation[17].

The execution of an atomic action consists of two phases, with the first phase ending with the subordinate indicating its readiness to commit (using *C-READY* primitives) or its inability to progress further (using *C-REFUSE* primitives). The second phase consists of a commit (or rollback) operation. Further, as indicated in the figure, the superior may optionally issue a *C-PREPARE* request primitive to solicit a response in the form of either a C-READY indication or C-REFUSE indication primitive. Where a C-PREPARE is not issued, the Application determines the event that prompts the subordinate to indicate its ability to commit, or otherwise.

Figures 9.27 and 9.28 illustrate the use of these primitives in situations where three instances of Application entities are involved in execution of an atomic action. For each, the tree model of the atomic action is also given. Note how the primitives issued by the root entity propagate down the tree. Those issued by the subordinates propagate towards the root of the tree. A superior is forced to rollback if any of its subordinates indicates an inability to proceed.

---

[17]See [ISO 9804], for constraints on the sequence in which service primitives may be issued.

TABLE 9.17   CCR Service Primitives

Service	Primitive	Type of Primitive	Parameter(s)
Initiation	C-BEGIN	Unconfirmed	atomic action identifier, branch identifier, atomic action timer user data
Indication of Termination	C-PREPARE	Unconfirmed	User data
Offer of Commitment	C-READY	Unconfirmed	User data
Refusal of Commitment	C-REFUSE	Unconfirmed	User data
Commitment	C-COMMIT	Confirmed	-
Rollback	C-ROLLBACK	Confirmed	-
Restart	C-RESTART	Confirmed	resumption point, atomic action identifier, branch identifier, restart timer, user data

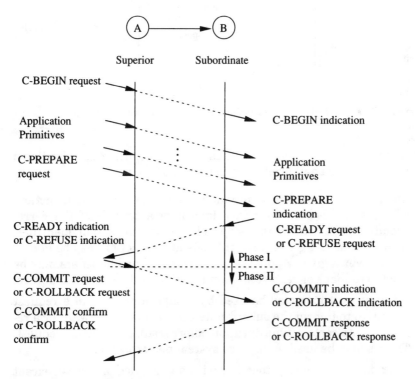

Figure 9.26 Illustration of the two phase procedure.

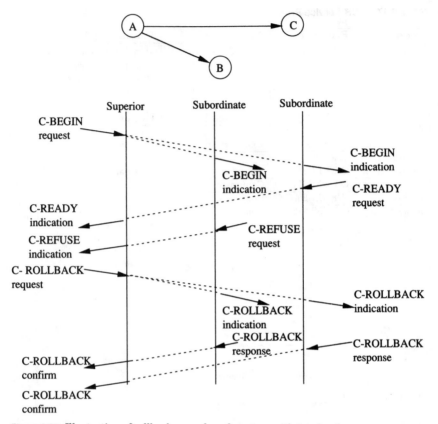

Figure 9.27 Illustration of rollback procedure for a tree with two levels.

The parameters associated with each CCR primitive are also listed in Table 9.17. We shall briefly discuss some of these.

1. *Atomic action identifier* uniquely identifies an atomic action, whereas the *branch identifier* identifies a branch of the corresponding tree within the scope of the atomic action identifier. Although, at any given time, only one atomic action may be in execution over a given Application association, the identifiers may be used to rollback or restart an atomic action in the event of a failure.

2. An optional timer may be used by a superior entity in a request primitive to inform the subordinate that it intends to wait for a response for a certain time duration before issuing a rollback request. Timers may be used to improve system performance.

3. User data may be sent together with any service primitive, except *C-COMMIT* and *C-ROLLBACK*. The Presentation context applica-

ble to user data is established at the time of establishment of the supporting association. It may subsequently be modified using Presentation services.

4. The parameter *resumption point* will be discussed shortly, together with the restart procedure.

9.5.6 Restart Procedure

Rollback of the atomic action is not the only option available to cooperating entities in case failures occurs. Either Application entity may attempt a *restart* of the atomic action, in the hope that execution of the atomic action may still progress. Whether the restart is to resynchronize the state to the beginning of the atomic action, or to an intermediate point is specified as a parameter *resumption point* of the primitive

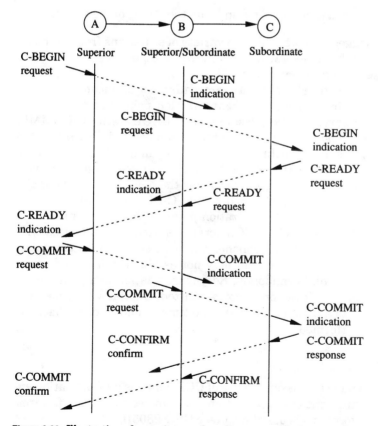

Figure 9.28 Illustration of commit procedure for a tree with three levels.

C-RESTART request. When a C-RESTART *request* is issued by a superior entity, then the parameter may assume a value *action, commit,* or *rollback,* whereas its value in the primitive, when issued by a subordinate, may be *action,* alone. In a C-RESTART *response* primitive, the value of the parameter when issued by a subordinate may be *done, retry-later, refuse,* or *action.* If a superior issues the response primitive, the resumption point may only be *action.* These values have the following interpretation:

1. the value *action* is used to request, or to agree to a request, to a restart to the beginning;

2. the values *commit* and *rollback* are a used by the superior to request a subordinate to end the atomic action;

3. the value *done* indicates that the subordinate has no record of the atomic action—either due to failure or because the atomic action has already been committed or rolled back; and

4. the values *refuse* or *retry-later* indicate the status of the subordinate.

The above suggests that there are a variety of situations from which recovery is feasible, some of which are shown in Figure 9.29. The figures are quite self explanatory.

In addition to the above restart procedure, an application may establish checkpoints (or minor synchronization points) and resynchronize as necessary. In fact, issuing of *C-BEGIN* and C-COMMIT primitives establishes a *major* synchronization point. A C-ROLLBACK service initiates a resynchronization to the major synchronization point established at the time of establishing the association. From such a viewpoint, a restart either synchronizes the operations to the major synchronization point, established by the C-BEGIN primitive, or establishes a new major synchronization point in case a commit or rollback takes place. Thus, if the CCR service is used in conjunction with another protocol that also establishes minor and/or major synchronization points, then the application may not establish minor and major synchronization points randomly. Resynchronization to a point before the start of an atomic action is not permitted. Similarly, one may not resynchronize to a point earlier than the time a commit or rollback operation was performed.

9.5.7 CCR Protocol

Thus far, we have discussed the use of CCR services by Application entities in commitment of atomic actions, and in recovery from failures. The CCR protocol is discussed next (see [ISO 9805]).

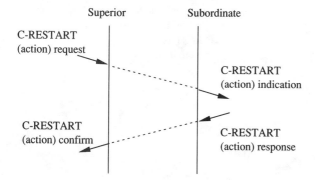

(a) Successful restart to the beginning of atomic action.

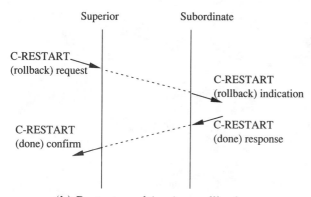

(b) Restart resulting in a rollback.

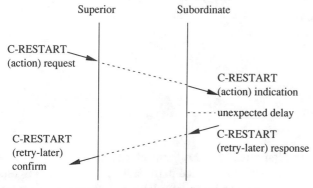

(c) Restart to be tried later.

Figure 9.29 Illustration of the restart procedure.

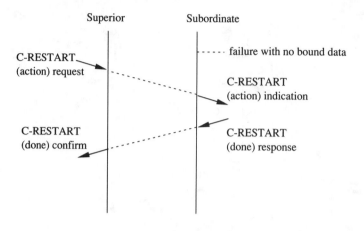

(d) Unsuccessful restart.

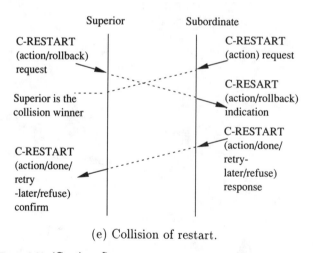

(e) Collision of restart.

Figure 9.29 (*Continued*)

The protocol is implemented in the form of two protocol machines which interpret, and respond to, service primitives issued by users (see Figure 9.30). To enable users to interact with each other, the protocol machines exchange information between themselves. This they do in the form of *CCR Application protocol data units* (*CCR APDUs*).

Exchange of CCR APDUs between the protocol machine enables the semantics of CCR service elements to be conveyed between the users. The CCR protocol specifies, in unambiguous terms, the actions that a protocol machine takes when it receives:

1. a CCR service request or response primitive, or
2. a CCR APDU from the corresponding protocol machine (contained in a Presentation service indication or confirm primitive).

In response to any of the above incoming events, the action taken by a protocol machine is to issue (or transfer):

1. a CCR service indication or confirm primitives, or
2. a CCR APDUs to the corresponding CCR protocol machine (contained in a Presentation service request or response primitive).

Of course, the specific action, or the sequence of actions, is dependent upon the current state of the protocol machine, as well as upon the parameters of the service primitive or APDU received. The specification is in the form of a state transition table, which also specifies the state to which the protocol machine transitions. We shall not specifically discuss the table. Instead, we illustrate in Figure 9.31 the procedure associated with each CCR service. The CCR APDUs are listed in Table 9.18.

The abstract syntax of CCR APDUs is specified by the CCR protocol. The Presentation context required to support the syntax must be negotiated at the time of the establishment of the Application association. The Presentation context for CCR APDUs may not be deleted at any time unless a user is later able to include it using P-CONTEXT DEFINE service.

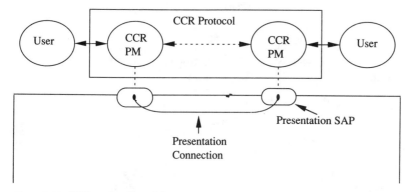

Figure 9.30 CCR protocol machines.

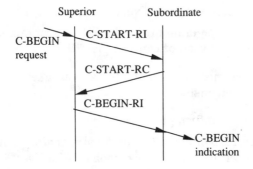

(a) Initiation.

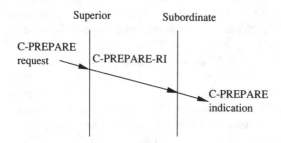

(b) Indication of termination.

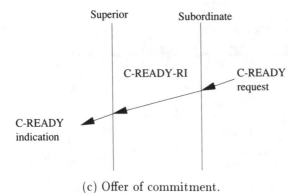

(c) Offer of commitment.

Figure 9.31 Ilustration of exchange of the CCR APDUs for each service element.

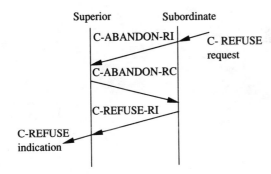

(d) Refusal to commit.

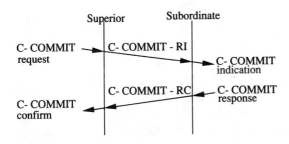

(e) Commitment.

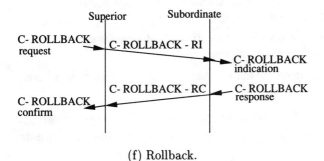

(f) Rollback.

Figure 9.31 (*Continued*)

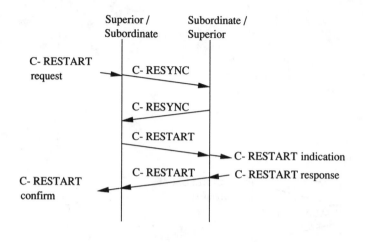

(g) Restart.

Figure 9.31 *(Continued)*

The CCR APDUs are transferred by the protocol machines using Presentation and Session functional units[18]. These include:

Presentation kernel,

Session kernel,

Typed data,

Major synchronization, and

Resynchronization.

The use of Presentation services to transfer CCR APDUs is also given in Table 9.18. Note that:

1. some of the CCR APDUs are transferred as user data in a P-TYPED DATA primitive,

2. a major synchronization point is established whenever an atomic action is started or committed, and

3. resynchronization takes place in case the atomic action is refused or rolled back, or during a restart operation.

As noted earlier, while discussing ACSE services in Section 9.2, all tokens are assigned to the initiator of the association. Since an atomic

---

[18]Session layer services are transparently made available through the Presentation layer.

TABLE 9.18 CCR APDUs and Their Parameters

Service	Protocol data unit	Parameter(s) of APDUs	Presentation service which carries APDUs
Initiation	C-BEGIN-RI	atomic action identifier, branch identifier, atomic action timer, user data	P-SYNC-MAJOR request/indication
	C-BEGIN-RC	-	P-SYNC-MAJOR response/confirm
Termina-tion	C-PREPARE-RI	user data	P-TYPED-DATA request/indication
Offer to commit	C-READY-RI	user data	P-TYPED-DATA request/indication
Refusal to commit	C-REFUSE-RI	user data	P-RESYNC (abandon) request/indication
	C-REFUSE-RI	-	P-RESYNC (abandon) response/confirm
Commit	C-COMMIT-RI	-	P-SYNC-MAJOR request/indication
	C-COMMIT-RC		P-SYNC-MAJOR response/confirm
Rollback	C-ROLLBACK-RI	-	P-RESYNC (abandon) request/indication
	C-ROLLBACK-RC	-	P-RESYNC (abandon) response/confirm
Restart	C-RESTART-RI	atomic action identifier, branch identifier, restart time, resumption point, user data	P-RESYNC (restart) request/indication
	C-RESTART-RC	resumption point, user data	P-RESYNC (restart) response/confirm

action may be started by either Application entity, the superior must obtain the major synchronization token before starting an atomic action. It retains control over it as long as the atomic action has not been committed or rolled back. Minor synchronization and other tokens may be exchanged as dictated by the application. However, all tokens must be passed back to the superior whenever an atomic action is refused or rolled back.

Collisions may occur at any time during the execution of an atomic action. As an example, consider the situation where a superior issues a C-ROLLBACK request primitive. At about the same time, the subordinate issues a C-REFUSE request primitive. The CCR protocol specifies that in such an event the protocol machine corresponding to the superior entity should ignore the incoming *C-REFUSE-RI* APDU and await a response to the *C-ROLLBACK-RI* APDU that it transmitted earlier. Figure 9.32 illustrates the collision and its resolution by the CCR protocol machines.

More generally, the protocol specifies as to which of the two—the superior or the subordinate—is the winner, and the actions to be initiated by the winner. For more details see the state table description of CCR protocol machines in [ISO 9805].

9.6   Summary

The Application layer is designed to offer a rich set of application-related services, called Application service elements. This is necessary if we wish to support a variety of distributed applications. Depending upon the particular application, users may selectively incorporate into the design of an Application process those Application service elements that are necessary for Application process to communicate with its peer process(es). From the viewpoint of OSI, an Application process is modelled as an Application entity. This model is the basis for defining the structure of the Application layer.

An Application association forms the basis for communication between two Application entities. Once established, the identity and the structure of communicating Application entities becomes known to them. The structure of an Application entity is also known as the Application context. Association control service elements enable Application entities to establish or terminate an association. At the time of its establishment, Application entities also negotiate the set of required Presentation and Session layer services, together with the Presentation context necessary to represent APDUs that are exchanged between the Application entities and between end-users.

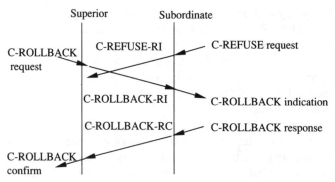

Figure 9.32 Handling of collisions by CCR protocol.

In this chapter, we have also discussed three other common Application service elements. These are:

1. Reliable Transfer service elements (RTSE), which enables reliable transfer of information between peer entities,

2. Remote Operations service elements (ROSE), which permit users to initiate operations at a remote site, and

3. Commitment, Concurrency and Recovery services (CCR), which enable users to recover from a failure during execution of a task using commit or rollback procedures.

Basic concepts relating to each Application service element are discussed in this chapter. The available service primitives and the corresponding protocols have been covered in some detail. Before any of the protocols can be implemented, one must ensure that the required set of Session and Presentation layer services are available. Each of the above Application element requires that Association control services be available. Remote operations protocol may optionally use Reliable Transfer services.

Directory Services

In this chapter we discuss the architecture of a Directory and its logical representation in the form of a tree. We discuss the services available to a user to access (read, search, or modify) directory information, and the protocol that maps these service elements onto lower layer services. Related issues of authentication and distributed directory are also discussed in this chapter.[1]

10.1 Introduction

A *Directory* holds information on a collection of objects in the real world. The information is structured so as to permit Application processes to read, search or modify information concerning one (or several) objects. Such a capability to access information can be very useful in applications which require, for instance, name-to-address translation, or which simply seek related information on people or equipment. In particular, OSI applications need to determine the address of the Presentation service access point through which an Application entity can be reached, and the *title* of which is known. OSI network management protocols could also use a directory to access information on various network resources, including gateways, or other servers. Determination of an electronic mail address of a given individual is also made possible using a similar directory.

More formally, a directory is a collection of open sub-systems which cooperate between themselves to hold information about a variety of

---

[1]For more details, see [CCITT X.500], [CCITT X.501], [CCITT X.509], [CCITT X.511], [CCITT X.518], [CCITT X.519], [CCITT X.520] and [CCITT X.521] or [ISO 9594-1] through [ISO 9594-8]. Reference in this chapter is primarily made to CCITT documents, there being a one-to-one correspondence between them and ISO documents.

objects. The users of the directory include human users as well as computer programs. A program is an embodiment of another Application service element or of a user element of an Application entity. Users can read, search, or modify information concerning one or more named objects. Of course, each user must possess the necessary permission to perform the operation. From the OSI viewpoint, each user is represented as a *Directory User Agent (DUA)*, while the directory is itself composed of one or more cooperating *Directory Service Agents (DSAs)*. Permissible operations on a directory are modelled as *directory services,* and made available to DUAs at well-defined service access points (see Figure 10.1).

10.2 Directory Information Base

We now discuss the structure of the information stored in a directory (see also [CCITT X.500,CCITT X.501]). For the present, we assume that the directory is not distributed.[2] The information held in a directory is collectively known as a *Directory Information Base (DIB)*. It is composed of a number of *directory entries*. Each entry stores information about an object, and is made up of one or more *attributes* of the object. The collection and type of attributes stored in an entry is dependent upon the *object class* to which the object belongs. An object class is an identified collection of objects which share certain common characteristics. As such, each object class is described in terms of a common set of attributes (*attribute types,* to be more precise). Some or all attributes may be optional.

An object class may, itself, be a *sub-class* of some other object class, in which case objects from the sub-class share an additional set of characteristics. Thus, entries concerning objects belonging to a sub-class contain an additional set of common attributes.

---

[2]It is expected that the directory will be widely distributed across networks, organizations, and open systems. We discuss this aspect later in this chapter.

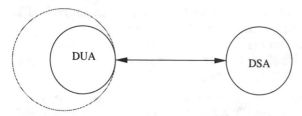

Figure 10.1 Model of directory user and service agents.

10.2.1 Entry Attributes

Each entry in the DIB contains one or more attributes that describe the object class(es) to which the corresponding object belongs. Once its object class(es) is known, the set of remaining attributes and their values can be interpreted.

An attribute, itself, is composed of two component, viz. *attribute type* and a list of *attribute values* (see Figure 10.2). An example of a Directory Information Base is illustrated in Figure 10.3 in the form of a linear list of entries. Therein, the object represented by the entry P1 belongs to three object classes, that is, *country, organization,* and *organization-person.* The object class organization-person is a sub-class of object class *person.* Its associated attributes, therefore, include *common-name, surname,* and *title.*

Table 10.1 lists several object classes, together with related mandatory and optional attributes. These classes, and many more, have been defined[3] to facilitate the development of additional object classes and attributes by organizations as and when required by specific applications. The classes *top* and *alias* will be discussed shortly after an introduction of the *tree* representation of DIB. Further, the attribute types *country-name, description* and *search-guide,* etc. are described formally in [CCITT X.520] using the ASN.1 notation (see [CCITT X.208] and Chapter 8).

10.3 Directory Information Tree

Given the above definition of the DIB and the structure for an entry, one may maintain a directory in the form of a flat file containing a list

---

[3]For more details on the description of these and other object classes see [CCITT X.521].

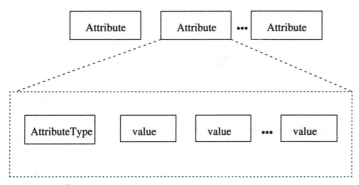

Figure 10.2 Structure of information stored in an entry.

Entry-ID	List of classes	Corresponding attribute values
O1	organization	ABC Inc.
L1	organization, locality	ABC Inc.; York, NY
L2	organization, locality	ABC Inc.; Boston, MA
C1	country	US
O2	country, organization	US; XYZ Labs.
P1	country, organization, organization-person	US; XYZ Labs.; V. Good Feller, Feller, MTS
P2	country, organization, organization-person	US; XYZ Labs.; Mr. Nice Guy, Guy
O3	country, organization	US; Ice Corp.
P3	country, organization, organization-person	US; Ice Corp.; AB Clark, Clark, Biggy
D1	country, organization, device	US; Ice Corp.; BigVaxHost
L3	locality	Hawaii, USA
O4	locality, organization	Hawaii, USA; IIIT, Nowhere

Note: *entry-ID*, above, is used only for the purpose of discussion, and future reference.

Figure 10.3 Contents of a Directory Information Base, stored in the form of a list of entries.

TABLE 10.1   Some Standard Classes of Objects, Together with Related Attributes

Object Class	Sub-class of	Mandatory attributes	Optional attributes
country	top	country-name	description, search-guide
locality	top	-	locality-name, etc.
organization	top	organization-name	business-category, etc.
person	top	common-name, surname	description, telephone-no, etc.
organization-person	person	-	title, etc.
device	top	common-name	description, serial-number, etc.
Application-entity	top	common-name, presentation-address	description, Application-context, etc.
top	-	-	-
alias	-	aliased-object-name	-

of entries, where each entry stores the set of classes to which the corresponding object belongs, and the required attributes. Since the number of entries can be very large, such a structure is not efficient, both from the viewpoint of storage and access. Fortunately, directory information naturally reflects a hierarchical relationship between objects. It is this hierarchy that is exploited in maintaining the directory as a tree.

Thus, a directory is organized in the form of a (rooted) tree, called *Directory Information Tree (DIT)*. A Directory Information Tree is illustrated in Figure 10.4, where each vertex, other than the root, represents an entry corresponding to an object. It is expected that vertices nearer the root of the tree will represent objects belonging to large classes, countries or organizations for instance, whereas leaf vertices will represent people, equipment or Application entities.

10.3.1 Directory Names

Each entry in the tree is, therefore, not required to store the complete list of object class(es) and sub-classes to which the corresponding object belongs (and by implication, the corresponding attributes). Some of the object classes to which an object belongs are implied by the position the entry occupies in the tree. The derived classes and related attributes are those of the parent vertex, and recursively of all ancestors in the tree. The object corresponding to a given entry belongs to the class(es) listed in the entry, as well as to the class(es) of the object represented by its parent entry, and so on. Further, attributes of the object stored

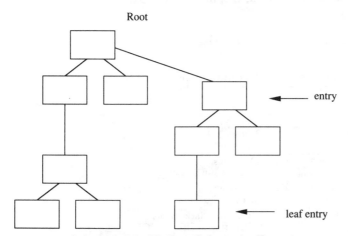

Figure 10.4 Structure of the Directory Information Tree.

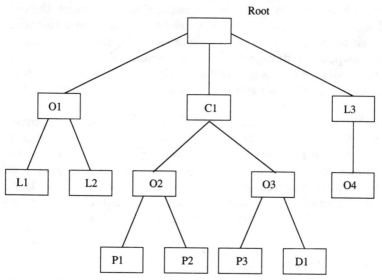

Figure 10.5 Directory Information Tree: an example.

in an entry are also the attributes of each object represented by a child entry.

In Figure 10.5, for example, the applicable classes of the entry P1 are those of O2 and C1 as well. Thus, the entries, corresponding to the DIB of Figure 10.3, store information as shown in Table 10.2. Put differently, by virtue of the position of the entry P1, the organization-person, P1, belongs to the organization, O2, in country, C1.

TABLE 10.2   Information Stored in Entries of the DIT: an Example

Entry-ID	List of classes	Attribute values
Root	top	-
O1	organization	ABC Inc.
L1	locality	York, NY
L2	locality	Boston, MA
C1	country	US
O2	organization	XYZ Labs.
P1	organization-person	V. Good Feller, Feller, MTS
P2	organization-person	Mr. Nice Guy, Guy
O3	organization	Ice Corp.
P3	organization-person	AB Clark, Clark, Biggy
D1	device	BigVaxHost
L3	locality	Hawaii, USA
O4	organization	IIIT, Nowhere

Notice, from Figures 10.4 and 10.5, the inclusion of an extra entry corresponding to the root of the tree. The entry at the root of the DIT tree is of class *top*, with no associated attribute. The class, top, is also considered to be the super-class of all objects represented in a DIT. Thus, each object may be treated as not only belonging to class(es) listed in the entry, and its ancestors, but also to the class top.

The definition of classes and the tree structure allows great flexibility in designing the DIT. For instance, the DIT of Figure 10.5 stores information on various *localities*, L1, L2, within a given organization, O1, as well as information on the organization, O4, within the locality, L3. Further, objects of two different classes can be represented as child entries of a given entry. In Figure 10.5 child entries, P3 and D1, of entry O3 correspond to classes organization-person and *device*. However, some constraints on structuring the tree are necessary to reflect the natural hierarchy exhibited in different directories. These constraints are specified at the time of defining the object classes. Some constraints from [CCITT X.521] are summarized in Table 10.3.

Each object in the directory has a name. This permits a user to uniquely identify an object and obtain relevant information on the object. These names may, however, not be unique, as discussed below. The name of an *object* is more formally known as *distinguished name*.[4] It consists of a sequence of *relative distinguished names* (*RDNs*). Each RDN uniquely identifies an entry, relative to its parent entry. Assume that the distinguished name of an object corresponding to an entry, E, is $x_1, x_2, ..., x_{i-1}, x_i$. Then $x_1, x_2, ..., x_{i-1}$ is the distinguished name of the object represented by its parent entry. And x_i is the RDN of the object represented by the entry, E, itself. Thus every initial sub-sequence of a distinguished name also is a distinguished name of an object represented by an ancestor entry. In this respect the name of the object rep-

---

[4] These are also called Directory Names, sometimes.

TABLE 10.3 Constraints on Structuring Information in a DIT Based upon Object Classes

Object Class	Must be an immediate sub-class of any one of
country	top
locality	top, country, locality, organization, organization-unit
organization	top, country, locality
person	(no constraints)
organization-person	organization, organization-unit
device	organization, organization-unit
Application-entity	organization, organization-unit

resented by the root of the directory tree is *null*. Thus, an RDN is used to distinguish one child entry from all other child entries of a given entry.

An RDN is specified using a set of *Attribute Value Assertions (AVAs)*, each of which must evaluate to *true* when determining whether a given entry has the particular RDN. Each AVA is an assertion consisting of a pair (attribute type = value). Thus, in order to evaluate a given AVA, one simply matches the value[5] of the attribute stored in the entry with that supplied in the AVA. The set of AVAs used to form an RDN is, of course, dependent upon the application, but must include those attributes that naturally enable one to distinguish two objects of the same class.

Consider the DIT of Figure 10.5 and the corresponding entries from Table 10.2. The attributes whose values are listed in the table may be used to define the RDNs for each of the objects. For example,[6] an RDN for O2 may be (organization-name = XYZ Labs.). The distinguished name of O2 is, as a consequence, the sequence of RDNs of entries starting with the root and leading to the entry O2, viz. [(country-name = US); (organization-name = XYZ Labs.)]. The RDNs and the distinguished names of the objects in Figure 10.5 can similarly be obtained (see also Table 10.2).

For each object represented in the tree, there is one entry. However, there may be one or more additional *alias* entries in the tree. An alias entry is used to provide an alternative name for the object, thereby reflecting an alternative relationship to other objects. For instance, an organization may be spread over a number of locations. One possibility is to then include the organization as a child entry of each concerned locality, as illustrated in Figure 10.6. The figure also shows one method of modelling a multi-location organization. Note that an alias entry is always a leaf node. Further, aliases of an alias entry are not permitted.

An alias entry is of object class *alias* with one attribute, *aliased-object-name* whose value points to the entry where its attributes are stored. Its type is the same as that of a distinguished name.

10.4   Authentication

One of the uses to which the directory can be put is to authenticate a user's identity. Further, since the directory holds information on various objects, it must itself be protected from unauthorized access. The

---

[5]If there are more than one values of the attribute stored in the entry, only the one designated to be the *distinguishing value* is used for evaluating an AVA.

[6]In respect of entries concerning objects P1, P2, P3 one could use the *surname* and/or the *common-name*.

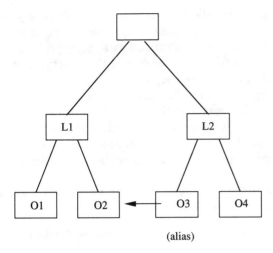

(alias)

Figure 10.6 Aliases: an example.

extent to which two users make their communication secure depends upon the application. This in turn determines the level of security one builds into the system. Surely, when a user accesses the directory, both the DSA as well as the DUA must be sure of each other's identity. (Authentication is also relevant when two DSAs communicate with each other.)

Two approaches are proposed in [CCITT X.509], both of which provide different levels of authentication of a requester's identity. The second approach also ensures that requests can only be interpreted by the intended recipient. The first approach, also called *simple authentication,* requires a user to furnish not only its distinguished name, but also a *password* which may be checked against a value stored in the directory. The stored value is an encrypted form of the user's password, to prevent users from reading it. This scheme, obviously, provides limited security.

10.4.1 Public Key Encryption

The second approach, also called *strong authentication,* is based upon the use of *public key encryption.*[7] It involves the use of a pair of distinct but complementary keys, a *secret key* and a *public key.* The identity of a user (say user A) can be authenticated, if it can be determined that user A possesses its secret key, A_s. For another user (say user B) to authenticate the identity of user A, it must possess the public key of user A, A_p. (We shall shortly discuss at least one secure way by which user B can obtain the public key of A.)

---

[7]See [CCITT X.509,Rives 78] for more details.

A scheme based upon the above is called *Digital Signature*. Basically, user A sends to B a message with its signature appended to the message. The signature consists of a message obtained by applying a (one-way) hashing function, h, to the information, *info*, and then encrypting the hashed information using its secret key, A_s, to obtain *signature* = X $(h(info); A_s)$. Here $X(I;k)$ is the encryption function, where information I is encrypted using the key, k. The message that A sends to B then consists of [A,*info*,*signature*]. User B decrypts the received *signature* using the same function X, but using the key A_p to obtain $X(signature;A_p)$. It then compares[8] it with $h(info)$ to determine whether the user sending the message is one claimed.

An encrypted message, sent by user A to another user B, is also called *token*. A token consists of the following:

1. the name of the sender, A, and the encryption algorithm used by A to obtain the signature;
2. information that is subject to user A's signature, which may include:
   (*a*) the time of generation of the token, and the time when its validity expires,
   (*b*) a random number or a sequence number to prevent replay,
   (*c*) name of the recipient, B,
   (*d*) additional information subject to user A's signature, for example, encryption algorithm used to encrypt confidential data, and
   (*e*) confidential data obtained using the public-key, B_p; and
3. user A's signature, obtained by encrypting a hashed version of the above information using an encryption algorithm mentioned in 1. above, and A's secret key, A_s.

User B decrypts the last portion using A's public key, and compares it with a hashed version of information, and thereby authenticates the origin of the message.

If confidential data is included, such data can only be interpreted by the intended recipient, B. The recipient uses its secret key, B_s to decrypt the confidential data. The confidential data, for instance, may be an encryption key itself, used to encrypt data in subsequent data transfers.

Public-key encryption can also be used to obtain the public key of any user, but from a trusted agent whose public key is well known. Such an agent may well be the directory itself, and is referred to as an *authority*. It is assumed that the public key, D_p, of the authority corresponding to a encryption algorithm is well known. Upon request from any

---

[8]It is a property of public key encryption that $X(X(I;k_s);k_p) = I$, and that the roles of the keys, k_s and k_p can be interchanged.

user, the authority, D, issues a *certificate* which contains a verified copy of the public key of A, A_p. This certificate can be decrypted by any user who has the public key, D_p, of the source, D. The certificate is made up of:

1. the name of the authority, D, and the encryption algorithm used to encrypt the certificate,

2. the time duration for which the certificate is valid,

3. the name of the user, A, the public-key algorithm used by A, and its public-key, A_p, and

4. a hashed and signed copy of the above information using the authority's own secret key, D_s.

If such a certificate is obtained by A and sent to another user B, or directly obtained by user B, then user B can use the well known public key of D to verify the signature of D, and thereby verify subject A's public key. This, of course, assumes that users A and B are served by the same authority D.

The strong authentication scheme, therefore, suggests the use of public key encryption system, described above, to obtain the public key of a user, and authenticate the identity of the sender. A user certificate, together with a message token, is also called *strong credentials* of a user. Note that the above procedure ensures integrity of data which is also signed, because of the use of the hash function. (For more details and other forms of authentication see [CCITT X.509].)

10.5   Directory Services

10.5.1   Directory Operations

A directory provides three different sets of operations [CCITT X.511], viz. *read-access, search-access,* and *modify-access.* These correspond to three different types of ports,[9] and may be used to limit a user's access to only those operations that are permitted by its access rights. The specific operations included within each port are listed in Table 10.4. Both DUA and the DSA support such ports. The role of DUA and of DSA with respect to each port is listed in Table 10.5. The operations which a DUA or a DSA may invoke in their role as a supplier or consumer of directory services are listed in Table 10.6. As a consequence,

---

[9]For a discussion on the concept of ports and the role of objects as supplier or consumer see Section 9.4 and [CCITT X.407].

TABLE 10.4   Directory
Operations

Ports	Operation
read-access	read
	compare
	abandon
search-access	list
	search
modify-access	add entry
	remove entry
	modify entry
	modify RDN

a DUA may only interact with another DSA. If two DSAs are to interact with each other, they may *not* do so through any of these ports. Further, the operations may only be invoked by the DUA, whereas a DSA simply responds to user request for operations. These operations and their required arguments are discussed below.

1. The *read* operation is used to obtain information concerning a named entry. More specifically, the operation causes the values of some or all attributes to be returned. The DUA is required to identify the attributes of interest.

2. A *compare* request is similarly aimed at a particular entry in the DIT, and can be used to verify whether an attribute value supplied by the user matches the one stored in the entry. As an example, this facility can be used to check the user's own password. The attribute value itself may not be accessible for a read operation. Even if it can be read, it may not be interpretable since the stored value may be in an encrypted form.

3. The operation, *list,* causes the directory to return a list of immediate child entries of a named DIT entry. Specifically, the DIT returns the RDN of each child entry.

4. The operation, *search,* as it name implies, permits a user to obtain information on several entries within a sub-tree of the DIT. Specifical-

TABLE 10.5   The Role of Each Application Process
Concerning Its Ports

Object (or process)	Ports	Object's role
DSA	read-access	supplier
	search-access	supplier
	modify-access	supplier
DUA	read-access	consumer
	search-access	consumer
	modify-access	consumer

TABLE 10.6 Port Specification in Terms of Permissible Operations and Role of DSA and DUA

Port	Supplier invokes	Consumer invokes
read-access	-	read, compare, abandon
search-access	-	list, search
modify-access	-	add entry, remove entry, modify entry, modify RDN

ly, the attribute values of only those entries are returned which satisfy a certain property. The property is specified by the user in the form of a *filter,* discussed below.

5. An *abandon* request can only be made when one of the above operations is outstanding. It causes the directory to stop processing an earlier request and to provide all available results. The DSA is, of course, free to discard the results so far available to it.

6. An *add entry* operation permits the user, with appropriate access rights, to add a leaf entry (as a child) of a named entry. The entry to be added may either be an alias entry or it may correspond to a real object. A repeated use of this service will permit addition of an entire subtree to the DIT.

7. The *remove entry* operation causes the directory to delete the named leaf entry from the DIT.

8. One or more attribute values in a named entry can be changed using the *modify entry* operation. Attributes can also be added or deleted. Further, one or more values of an attribute may be removed, added or changed. It may also be used to change an alias entry, thereby referencing a different object entry in the DIT. Before carrying out any change, the directory ensures that the resulting tree remains consistent with the schema used to design the DIT. That is, the resulting attribute types must be consistent with the object class, and their values with the attribute data types.

9. The operation *modify RDN* causes the RDN of a named leaf entry to be changed. A different RDN is provided by the user in the form of changes to the list of attribute types that determine the RDN, and/or their distinguishing values. It does imply that part of the entry information may also change, as a consequence.

10.5.2 Bind/Unbind Operations

The directory operations discussed above are abstract remote operations.[10] Before the operations can be invoked, the directory user (or

---

[10]See Section 9.4 and [CCITT X.407].

DUA) must establish a binding between its ports with corresponding ports in a DSA. Subsequently, after accessing the directory, the binding must be released (also known as *unbinding*) by the user. In the context of directory services, these are called *Directory-Bind* and *Directory-Unbind* operations. These operations are mapped onto the A-ASSOCIATE and A-RELEASE primitives of Association Control Service Elements. The Directory-Bind, and similarly Directory-Unbind, operation is specified in terms of the data type of the parameter to be conveyed as user-data in the:

1. A-ASSOCIATE request or indication primitives,

2. A-ASSOCIATE response or confirm primitives, in case the Association is established successfully, and

3. A-ASSOCIATE response or confirm primitives, in case the Association is not established.

These parameters are, respectively, called *argument, result,* and *bind-error* parameters. The operation Directory-Unbind has no parameters. The Directory-Bind operation has the following parameters:

1. *user-credentials,* which allows the directory to establish the user's (or DUA's) identity. A number of options are available, depending upon the level of security built into the directory. The lowest level of security requires the user's distinguished name and a password. The highest level of security ensures that communication between the DUA and the DSA is both secure and authenticated (see also the discussion on authentication, above).

2. *version number, v1988,* for example.

If the Directory-Bind operation succeeds, a result will be returned. The result parameters and their syntax are identical to that of the argument parameters. Should the bind operation fail, a bind-error is returned together with the reason. A Directory-Bind operation may fail due to unavailability of the DSA or inability of the DSA to authenticate the identify of the DUA.

10.5.3 Parameters

We now discuss the parameters associated with the directory access operations. A directory operation is specified in terms of (see also Section 9.4):

1. the data type of the argument to be conveyed as part of the remote operation request to the DSA (Directory Service Agent),

2. the data type of the result to be conveyed to the DUA which initiated the particular directory access, in case the remote operation is performed successfully, and

3. a list of possible error conditions that may be encountered. (Each error condition is separately identified together with the data type of an associated parameter.)

The parameters associated with the read operation, as well as others, are listed in Table 10.7. We briefly discuss some of these parameters. In the read operation, the parameter, *object-name,* is the distinguished name of the object entry, from which information is requested. If the name is that of an alias, then it is substituted by the object's distinguished name stored in the alias entry.[11] The parameter, *entry-information-selection,* indicates a selection of the attributes whose type, and perhaps values, are requested in the read (or some other) operation.

---

[11]In other operations, if the entry referenced was an alias entry, then the object-name of the affected entry is returned as part of the result parameters.

TABLE 10.7   Argument and Result Parameters of Directory Operations

Operation	Argument parameters	Result parameters
read	object-name entry-information-selection common-arguments	entry-information common-results
compare	object-name attribute-value-assertion common-arguments	matched common-results object-name
abandon	invoke-ID	-
list	object-name common-arguments	object-name set-of-RDNs
search	base-object-name filter entry-information-selection common arguments	object-name set of entry-information
add entry	object-name set of attributes common-arguments	-
remove entry	object-name common-arguments	-
modify entry	object-name set of entry-modifications common-arguments	-
modify RDN	object-name RDN-changes common-arguments	-

The parameter *common-arguments* is a set of parameters commonly used with a number of directory operations. It optionally includes:

1. *service-controls,* which may be used to indicate
   (a) priority level for the operation,
   (b) a time limit during which the operation must complete,
   (c) a maximum number of entries to be searched or listed,
   (d) the scope of the search, and
   (e) whether chaining (see Section 10.6) is allowed, preferred, or prohibited;
2. *security parameters* ensure that communication between the requesting DUA and the DSA is secure. It includes information which may be used to verify the user's identify, the identity of the DSA, and integrity of the argument (or result) parameters; and
3. the distinguished name of the requesting DUA.

The parameter, *invoke-ID,* of the abandon operation, is an identifier associated with an earlier operation which is to be abandoned. This parameter is assigned by the directory protocol at the time of invoking a remote operation, and made available to the directory user, for later reference.

The parameter, *filter,* is a logical expression of one or more attribute value assertions.[12] It is used in a search operation to specify the entries that are of interest, and whose attributes are sought. The search space is relative to the entry whose *base-object-name* is supplied in a search operation.

The parameter, *set of attributes,* of the add-entry operation is the information to be stored in the entry to be added. The *set of entry-modifications,* used in a modify entry operation, is a selection of attributes, together with any relevant values, and the nature of modifications (add, delete, or modify attribute or value).

We now discuss the result parameters of the directory operations. The parameter *common-results* includes the security parameters discussed earlier, and whether the entry that was finally referenced is an alias entry or the one pointed to by an alias. *Entry-information* is the information (attribute types, and possibly their values) returned by the directory in response to a read or search operation. The *matched* parameter with a value true is returned if the corresponding attribute-value-assertion, in a compare operation, evaluates to true.

Errors that may potentially occur when a DSA attempts to perform a directory operation are listed in Table 10.8, together with *a* possible

---

[12]More generally, an assertion could test whether a given string is a sub-string of a string-valued attribute of an entry, or whether a supplied value satisfies a less-than or greater-than relationship.

TABLE 10.8   Error Types and One of the Suggested Causes

Error Condition	A suggested cause
abandoned	in response to an abandon request (not quite an error)
abandoned-failed	no such operation may be outstanding
attribute-error	there may be no such attribute for the named entry
name-error	an invalid syntax may have been used
referral	refers the user to other access points or to another DSA
security-error	the user does not possess the required access rights
service-error	the DSA is busy or unavailable
update-error	an update is inconsistent with the class of the object

cause for the error condition. Not all errors are relevant to each operation, but many of them are. Whenever an error condition is indicated, the exact nature of the error together with additional information is provided by the DSA to the user.

10.6   Distributed Directory Operation

Above, we have discussed the directory and its operations from the viewpoint of its logical tree structure and the (abstract) service it offers. This view assumes that the directory is modeled as one DSA which stores the entire DIT and provides services to user DUAs through a number of access points. However, it is expected that the directory would store large amounts of data, and pertaining to a wide variety of objects. In any case, one does expect a number of directories to be implemented, which should be able to inter-operate with each other.

The directory architecture (see [CCITT X.518]) permits a directory to be implemented as a collection of one or more DSAs, where each DSA stores only a portion of the DIB (or DIT), also known as a *DIB fragment*. This construction of the directory is referred to as a *Distributed Directory*. Figure 10.7 illustrates implementation of a directory as a distributed directory consisting of a number of DSAs. It provides access to DUAs through its different DSAs. Each DSA is responsible for processing directory operations submitted to it at an access point that it supports.

To a user accessing the directory, it is transparent whether the directory is distributed or not. In other words, a user may access the directory from any of the DSAs without concern for which particular DSA stores the relevant information. Further, the requested operation may reference any object, as long as it is within the DIB. From the viewpoint of the directory, the DSAs collectively (and cooperatively) provide the same access capability to all the users, irrespective of which DSA (or access points) is used by the DUA. Therefore, when a user requests an operation concerning an entry, the concerned DSA may find the entry

Directory

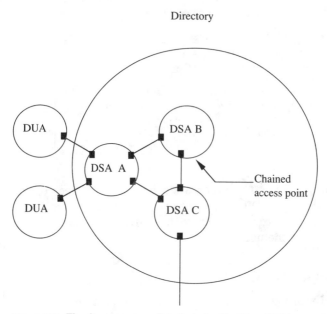

Figure 10.7 The directory as a distributed collection of DSAs.

to be outside its DIB fragment, since the DSA maintains only a portion of the DIB. In that case, the DSA may refer the user to another DSA, which is perhaps capable of performing the operation. This is illustrated in Figure 10.8(a). Such a response by the DSA to a user request is called *referral*.

As an alternative, the DSA may submit the requested operation to that DSA, which it believes can perform the operation successfully. This mechanism of forwarding[13] the operation request to another DSA is called *chaining*. Therefore, each component DSA of the directory should preferably be able to communicate with every other DSA through one or more additional ports. These ports are different from those accessed by DUAs, since they support a different set of operations (between peer DSAs). Such ports are called *chained ports*. (See Figure 10.8(b).)

Referral can also be used by a DSA in response to a chaining request from another DSA in case it is unable to forward the request to another DSA (see Figure 10.8(c)).

---

[13]*Multicasting* (sequential, or in parallel) is yet another method available to a DSA to process a request that it cannot perform. In case it is not able to determine the identity of DSA most capable of performing the operation, the DSA simply broadcasts the operation to a selected few DSAs.

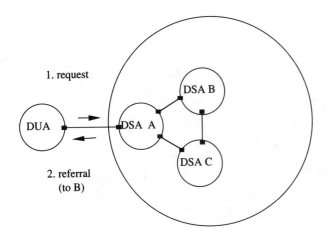

(a) Referral to another DSA.

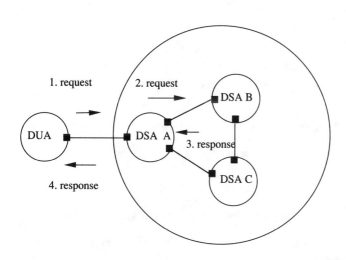

(b) Chaining.

Figure 10.8 Different modes of interaction between DSAs and the DUA.

A DSA, not capable of performing the requested operation, is required to use chaining, unless a user prefers referral or prohibits use of chaining, or where chaining is technically (see Figure 10.8(d)) or administratively not feasible. In all such cases, the DSA simply makes a referral to the concerned DSA.

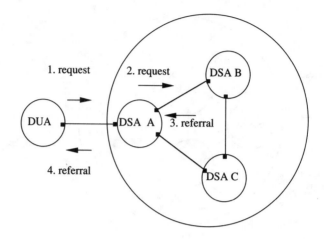

(c) Internal referral within the directory.

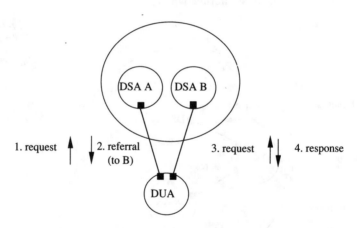

(d) Distributed directory where the DSAs do not support chaining.

Note: The numbers reflect the sequence in which messages are exchanged between the DSAs and the DUA.

Figure 10.8 (*Continued*)

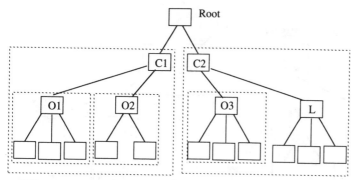

Figure 10.9 Partitioning of the Directory Information Tree.

The structure, shown in Figure 10.8 may, in fact, be the simplest mechanism available to integrate a number of sub-directories, particularly in the initial stages of development of an integrated directory.

10.6.1 Directory Management Domain

The directory as a whole is managed by an authority, called the *Directory Management Domain (DMD)*. The DMD is responsible for the design of the DIB (and the structure of the corresponding DIT), together with a definition of object classes, attribute types, and attribute value syntax. It also ensures that the directory is at all times consistent with this *schema*.

In case the directory is distributed, the DMD also determines the partitioning of the DIB and the mapping of DIB fragments onto DSAs. The partitioning of the DIB can be done in several ways, perhaps based upon (sub-) classes of objects, as shown in Figure 10.9 (in terms of corresponding sub-trees of the DIT). A sub-tree of the DIT is also referred to as a *naming context,* and identified by the distinguished name of the root of the corresponding sub-tree.

The mapping of DIB fragments onto DSAs can be achieved in several ways, one of which is shown in Figure 10.10. The figure illustrates the fact that a DSA may store a number of DIB fragments or DIT sub-trees, which may or may not share the same parent object. Each DSA is aware of the naming contexts (the sub-trees) that it holds, and their relation to the overall DIT structure. It is also aware of the naming contexts of one or more other DSAs. This information can then be used by a DSA to determine whether it can perform the requested operation from a DUA or DSA. But if the concerned entry (or entries) is outside its naming contexts, then the DSA is able to identify a DSA capable of performing the operation.

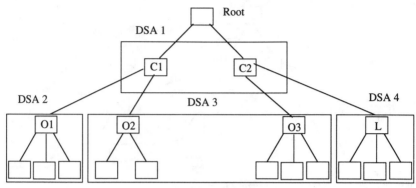

Figure 10.10 Mapping of sub-trees of DIT onto DSAs.

The distributed directory structure requires a specification of the services (or remote operations) offered by a DSA to other DSAs through the chained ports. These operations are similar to those available at a DSA-DUA interface. They differ mainly in respect of argument and result parameters conveyed as part of operations. For more details, see [CCITT X.518].

10.7   Directory Protocols

We now discuss the protocol used to support directory services (see also [CCITT X.519]). There are two protocols, *Directory Access Protocol* to support access to directory services, and *Directory Systems Protocol* which supports abstract operations at chained access points. We shall only discuss the access protocol.

A DUA and a DSA are each Application processes, but modeled as Application entities from the viewpoint of the OSI architecture. The Application service elements specifically supported by the directory protocol are read-access, search-access, and modify-access. Thus any Application process which uses directory operation must include these service elements as well as ROSE and ACSE service elements.[14] These service elements are used by the directory to implement Directory-Bind, Directory-Unbind, and directory access operations.

The directory access protocol uses the ACSE services to support Directory-Bind and Directory-Unbind operations. The operation, Directory-Bind, is directly mapped onto the A-ASSOCIATE primitives, with the following correspondence between the parameters of A-ASSOCIATE primitives and the Directory-Bind operation:

---

[14]See Sections 9.4 and 9.2.

1. The Application Context includes ACSE, ROSE, Directory-Bind, Directory-Unbind, read-access, search-access, and modify-access.

2. The Presentation context definition list includes the abstract syntax associated with ROSE and ACSE protocols and the abstract syntax of attributes stored in various entries, and argument/result parameters of directory operations.

3. The arguments of the Directory-bind operation are mapped onto the user-data parameter of A-ASSOCIATE request/indication primitives, whereas result or error parameters, depending upon whether or not the bind operation is successful, are mapped onto the user-data field of A-ASSOCIATE response/confirm primitives.

4. The directory access protocol requires only the Kernel and Duplex functional units of the Session service.

The Directory-Unbind operation is mapped onto the A-RELEASE primitives. It is expected that the release operation will always succeed.

Directory related operations are mapped onto ROSE services (see Section 9.4) which support the request/reply paradigm of remote operations. Specifically, the directory protocol specifies the use of ROSE Operation Class 2 (asynchronous, and with a result or error reply) and Association Class 1 (where only the DUA may invoke ROSE operations) procedures.

Thus when a user element requests an operation, say to read a directory entry, the protocol machine in the DUA invokes a remote operation, RO-INVOKE, with an Operation-ID of 1 (for read[15]). The DSA returns the results by invoking RO-RESULT operation or RO-ERROR operation, depending upon the outcome. Figure 10.11 illustrates the mapping of directory read operation onto ROSE operations.

10.8 Summary

Directory services are considered to be an extremely important Application layer service. It provides support to a number of other Application service elements, and may also be used in distributed applications to provide access to a variety of information concerning individuals, objects, activities, or institutions. One of the very important applications of a Directory system is to authenticate the identity of a sender or receiver of information.

A Directory is by definition a collection of directory entries each of which stores one or more attributes of the corresponding object. The

---

[15]Each operation, read, compare, etc., is separately identified by an integer value. Similarly, each error condition has an integer Error-ID.

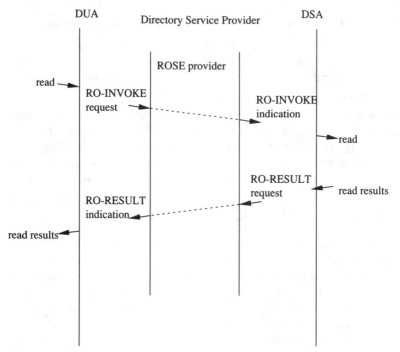

Figure 10.11 Mapping of directory operations onto ROSE operations.

collection may be logically structured in the form of a rooted tree, thereby ensuring that an entry may be accessed efficiently. The logical Directory Information Tree structure has been discussed in some detail in this chapter.

The Directory service is based upon an asymmetric relationship between a Directory user and the Directory server. The service available to a user includes read-access, search-access, and modify-access. These services are modelled in the form of abstract remote operations. This approach ensures that its service can be specified in a fairly compact manner. The supporting protocol, therefore, suggests the use of Remote Operations service elements to implement Directory operations. While the Directory operations are discussed in fair detail, the Directory protocol is only briefly discussed.

A Directory is generally regarded to be a store-house of a variety of information, and can thus be expected to become very large. Therefore, the Directory architecture allows the Directory to be implemented in the form of a number of Directory servers, each capable of referring or chaining access requests to each other. Further, the architecture is quite flexible. That is, the mapping of the sub-trees of the Directory

Information Tree onto Directory Service Agents is not necessarily one-to-one.

As a final remark, even though a Directory is implemented as a distributed directory, such a distribution may or may not be visible to a user. Transparency, to a large extent, depends upon the availability of a DSA to chain access requests to other DSAs.

11

Message Handling Systems

In this chapter we discuss Message Handling Systems, which support one of the most important applications of computer networks, electronic mail. We discuss the architecture of the system in terms of functional sub-systems, services offered by the system, and the protocols required to support the application. We also discuss the message structure when the system is used for inter-personal message communication.

11.1 Introduction

Electronic messaging, particularly inter-personal messaging, is an important application of computer networks. In the context of OSI, this application is supported by a *Messaging Handling System (MHS)*. The MHS enables users (people and computer programs) to exchange messages on a store-and-forward basis (see Figure 11.1). It also permits messages to be stored within the MHS till such time a user wishes to retrieve his/her messages. The MHS system, described in a series of

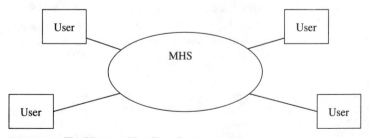

Figure 11.1 The Message Handling System and its users.

documents,[1] referred to by *X.400,* caters to a wide variety of applications, some of which are discussed below.

A message may be simultaneously sent for delivery to a number of users who have direct access to the MHS. The user originating the message either provides the names (or addresses) of individual users, or a list of user names in the form of a *distribution list.* The MHS architecture also provides for sending messages through the network for delivery to users who do not have direct access to the MHS, but using other services including Telex, FAX and postal services.

The message content is not limited to a string of bits, bytes or characters. It may even be a voice, video or FAX message, but suitably encoded for message transfer and delivery. Such messages are called *multi-media messages.* In either case, the message is transparently delivered by the MHS system to the intended user, except when the user originating the message requests format conversion to take into account differences in terminal devices. The need for format conversion can, instead, be determined by the MHS based upon its knowledge of the recipient's terminal capabilities.

There is also a provision in MHS for a user to determine, *a priori,* whether it is possible for the MHS to convey a message to a named user, or not. Such a user request is called *probe.* Depending upon the application, a user may request that the delivery of a message (or its non-delivery) be confirmed by the Message Handling System. The response of the MHS system to a message transfer or probe request is contained in a *delivery report.*

The current (1988) version of MHS, goes far beyond simple acknowledgement to message delivery. It now incorporates a variety of features that ensure secure communication of messages between users and the MHS, and between users themselves. As a consequence, the MHS can now be used to support a number of applications, where confidentiality and integrity of message transfer and authentication of the identity of communicating entities are important. For such purposes, it relies heavily upon the use of Directory services (see Section 10.5).

Inter-personal message communication is likely to continue to be a major application of MHS and its capabilities. As such, the MHS architecture also defines the abstract syntax of inter-personal messages, and the services available to human users (see [CCITT X.420]). Inter-personal messaging may be even more effective if the MHS service is

---

[1]The documents [CCITT X.400a], [CCITT X.402], [CCITT X.407], [CCITT X.411], [CCITT X.413], [CCITT X.419] and [CCITT X.420] cover all aspects of MHS, including its architecture, services and protocols and inter-personal messaging. The corresponding documents are [ISO 10021/1] through [ISO 10021/7]. However, in this chapter, reference is primarily made to CCITT documents, alone.

available on a world-wide basis. It is, therefore, expected that the MHS would ultimately be a world-wide service involving a number of inter-connected public and private MHS systems.

Finally, before discussing the architecture of MHS and related services and protocols, we note that there are some differences between the 1984 (see [CCITT X.400b]) and 1988 versions. However, the 1988 specification of the MHS system does provide for inter-working with systems conforming to 1984 version.

11.2 MHS Architecture

A model of the MHS, together with its major components, is shown in Figure 11.2. A message submitted by a user, through its *User Agent,* is transferred transparently through the *Message Transfer System* to the named user. The recipient is also connected to the MHS through its own User Agent, or through other means. A User Agent *(UA)* is an Application process in an open system which enables a user to access MHS capabilities, including submission of messages (or probes) and to take delivery of messages and reports. From the OSI architecture view-point, the user is modeled as the User element of the Application entity, and is thus identified by the corresponding UA. There is, as a consequence, exactly one UA per user.[2]

---

[2]There may be different types of UAs, depending upon whether the UA directly or indirectly accesses the MTS. Further, a UA may itself provide for additional services, Interpersonal Messaging, for instance (see Section 11.8).

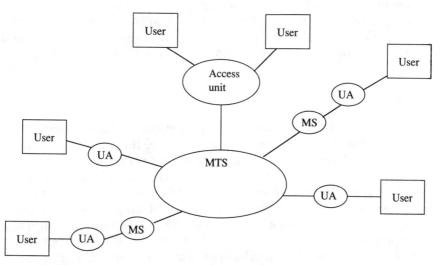

Figure 11.2 The Message Handling System and its components.

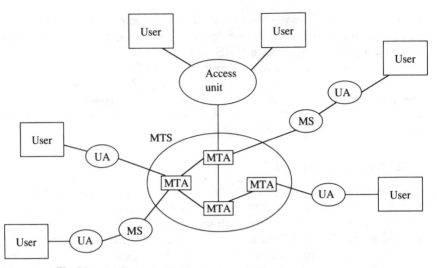

Figure 11.3 The Message Transfer System and its architecture.

11.2.1 Message Transfer System

The Message Transfer System (MTS) is a collection of Application processes collectively responsible for conveying messages between UAs, as well as probes and reports between UAs and the MTS. The MTS is a store-and-forward communication network consisting of one or more *Message Transfer Agents*. (See Figure 11.3.) Each Message Transfer Agent (*MTA*) is capable of receiving messages from UAs or from other MTAs, and storing them. It may subsequently deliver the stored message to a connected UA if the message is destined to the corresponding user, or forward the message to another MTA depending upon the route selected. Within an MTS there may be any number of MTAs, and each MTA may be connected to none, one or more UAs and MTAs.

11.2.2 Message Store

An MTA performs a number of other functions, including routing, authentication checks, message conversion, etc. But the one function it does *not* perform is to store messages so that users may retrieve messages and process them at their convenience. Such a function is implemented in the form of a *Message Store (MS)*, also shown in Figure 11.2. A Message Store is an Application process which provides an alternative method to interface a UA with the MTS. Aside from enabling users to submit messages and probes to the MTS, the MS takes delivery of messages (and reports) on behalf of the user from the MTS. Further, it permits the user to selectively retrieve messages, store them, and process them as and when it is convenient for the user to do so. Conceptually, there is one MS per UA.

The interface between a UA and its corresponding MS enables a user to submit messages (or probes) to the MTS, and to retrieve messages and reports. The services provided by the MTS to an MS are identical to those provided to a UA directly connected to the MTS. As one consequence, a user may be identified by the UA or the MS through which its UA is connected.

The functional unit, *Access Unit (AU)*, enables users with access to other forms of communication systems, Telex, FAX, or even postal services, to gain access to MHS capabilities. The interface between the MTS and an AU is different. Its specification is dependent upon the nature of the secondary communication network and the services it offers to its users.

From the viewpoint of implementation, there are a number of ways in which the MHS system can be configured for a given application. Some of these are shown in Figure 11.4. An MHS can be configured using a mix of stand-alone systems, each implementing a function, or as systems where two or more functional units (UA, MS, and MTA) are co-located. It may also include systems with a number of identical Application processes that cater to multiple users. The system, F, for instance, combines the functions of MTA, MS and UA, and provides MHS capabilities to a number of users.

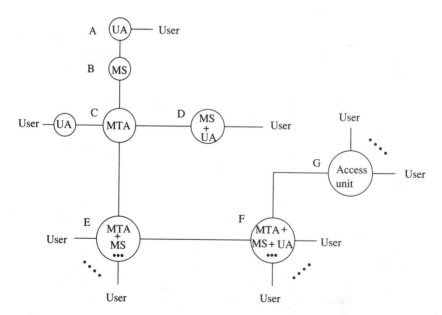

Figure 11.4 An MHS that uses a variety of systems, with co-located functions.

11.2.3   Management Domains

From the viewpoint of organization, an MHS system may comprise a number of interconnected, independently managed, messaging systems, also called *Management Domains.* A management domain *(MD)* consists of an MTS, together with none, one or more UAs either connected directly or through message stores. Such a management domain is managed independently by a single authority in respect of naming and addressing of users, and routing and security of messages. Since messages may be transferred from one management domain to another, the interface between management domains must be consistent. Figure 11.5 illustrates a global MHS which spans more than one country, organization or an administration.

11.2.4   Naming and Addressing

As discussed above, there is a one-to-one correspondence between a user, UA and, where applicable, a message store. Thus, when a UA, or an MS, submits a message for transfer, it identifies the intended recipient(s) of the message by name. When the MTS delivers a message to a user, it identifies the originator of the message also by its name. In the MHS architecture, a *name* is an *O/R Name* (short for *Originator/Recipient*

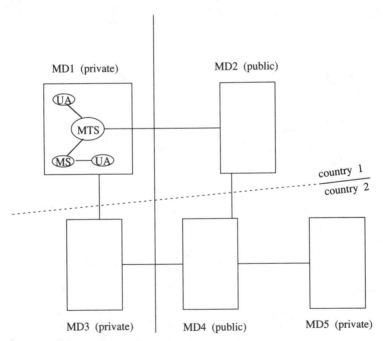

Figure 11.5 Interconnected set of management domains.

Name), and consists of an *O/R Address,* or *Directory Name,* or both. There is a one-to-one correspondence between the O/R Address and the Directory Name. This correspondence is stored in a Directory[3] in the form of an entry, one for each user. Each entry is identified by the user's Directory Name.[4] One of the user attributes stored in the entry is the O/R Address. From an MHS user's viewpoint, the Directory Names are more *friendly,* whereas the MTS internally uses O/R Addresses to route and to deliver messages.

A user may provide a Directory Name or an O/R Address, or both. If only the Directory Name is made available, the MTS can determine the O/R Address, using a directory *read* operation. The O/R Address uniquely identifies the UA (or an MS) with which a user is associated. In case the user can only be accessed through some other communication system, then the O/R Address is the Telex, FAX, or postal address.

An O/R Name is also used to identify a list of potential recipients of a message. Such a list is termed *Distribution List (DL).* A distribution list is a list of O/R Names, where an O/R Name can, recursively, be a distribution list itself. Each distribution list has a corresponding entry in the directory, with two attributes. The first attribute lists its members using O/R Names. The second attribute is its O/R Address. An O/R Address of a distribution lists is the address of the MTA where the distribution list is to be *expanded* to determine the collection of intended recipients. A user must, therefore, provide the Directory Name of the distribution list.

11.2.5 Information Objects

Three types of information objects may be conveyed through the MHS, viz. *messages, probes,* and *reports.* Messages are the primary objects that users wish to convey between themselves. A message consists of two parts, the *envelope* and *contents,* as shown in Figure 11.6:

1. The contents of a message are conveyed transparently by the MTS, except for its *conversion* to account for different terminal types

---

[3]See Chapter 10.

[4]The Distinguished Name of the entry is, in fact, the user's Directory Name.

Envelope

Content

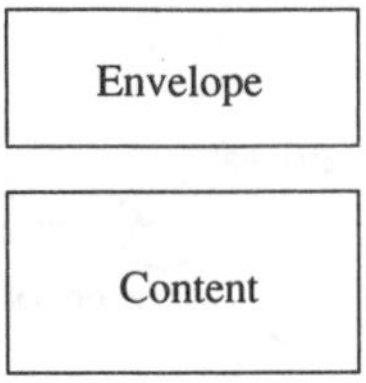

Figure 11.6 The message structure.

and/or transmission or delivery media. Such a conversion may be explicitly requested by the originating user or implicitly determined by an MTA, based upon known characteristics of the recipient's terminal.

2. The envelope is composed of several pieces of information, including the O/R Names (Directory Names or O/R Addresses) of the originating user and intended recipients, a summary of past actions concerning the message, routing information, and a characterization of the contents. The contents are characterized using identifiers for its *content type* and its *encoding* (the latter denotes the medium and format, IA5 or Group 3 FAX, for example).

The second type of information object conveyed by the MHS is a *probe*. A probe is very similar to a message, except that it only consists of an envelope, and not the contents. A user, before submitting a message for delivery to a user, may submit a probe to the MHS to determine whether it is possible to send a message characterized by the envelope. A probe is handled by the MTS in a similar manner, except that it is neither delivered nor is a distribution list expanded.

A *report* is generated by an MTA, in response to a message (or a probe), and conveyed to the originating user. It contains information on the outcome of attempts made by the MTS to deliver the message or the probe. A report may either indicate delivery, non-delivery, export (in case of delivery using non-MHS means), affirmation, non-affirmation, or the fact that the message has been handed over for expansion of the distribution list. Further, in response to a message or probe, the MTS may deliver several reports, particularly when the message/probe is intended for several recipients.

11.3 MTS Services

Before describing the abstract services provided by the MHS, we briefly discuss some of the operations performed by each functional unit in the MHS. Figure 11.7 illustrates the transfer of a message from an *originating* user to a *recipient* user. Such a transfer requires a number of steps, each involving the movement of the message to the next functional unit. When a user wishes to send a message to its peer, it makes the message available to its UA. This step is called message *origination*. Subsequently, the UA *submits* the message to an MTA within the

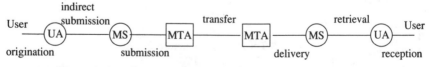

Figure 11.7 Transmission of messages through an MHS.

MTS. It is the responsibility of the MTS to move the message across the MTS, by *transferring* it from one MTA to the next MTA, depending upon the selected route. Ultimately, the MTS *delivers* the message to a UA. A user is then said to have *received* the message.

In case an originating user (or UA) accesses the MTS capability through an MS, submission of a message by the UA to the MS is said to be *indirect submission*. It is the MS that finally submits the message to the MTS. Further, if a recipient UA takes delivery through an MS, the message may be *retrieved* at any time. If a message is submitted (or delivered) through an Access Unit which supports non-MHS systems, the message is said to have been *imported* (respectively, *exported*).

A probe also undergoes similar transmittal steps, except that a probe is neither delivered, retrieved nor received. Reports are generated in response to message delivery or probes, but only upon request by the originating user. Transmission of a report is very similar, except that reports originate within the MTS.

11.3.1 MTS Abstract Operations

We now discuss the capabilities provided by the Message Transfer System to User Agents or to Message Stores. These capabilities are described in terms of remote abstract operations that a UA (or an MTA) may invoke. The operations are performed by an MTA, acting on behalf of the MTS (or respectively, by the UA acting on behalf of the user).

Figure 11.8 models the service provided by the MTS. Both the MTS and an MTS-user[5] are modeled as objects that interact with each other through *ports*. A port defines the permissible operations that are available to the objects, either as a *supplier* of corresponding services or as its *consumer*.[6] The grouping of operations into those available at different ports is given in Table 11.1.

---

[5]The is either an MS or a UA, while the MTS provides service through one or more MTAs.

[6]See Section 9.4 for a discussion on ports and the concepts of supplier and consumer.

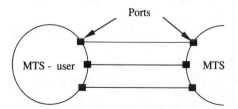

Figure 11.8 A model of the interaction between the MTS and an MTS-user.

TABLE 11.1   MTS Operations

Ports	Operation
submission	message submission probe submission cancel deferred delivery submission control
delivery	message delivery report delivery delivery control
administration	register change credentials

TABLE 11.2   The Role of MTS and MTS-User Concerning Its Ports

Object (or process)	Ports	Object's role
MTS	submission delivery administration	supplier supplier supplier
MTS-user	submission delivery administration	consumer consumer consumer

TABLE 11.3   Specification of Operations in Terms of the Role of MTS and MTS-Users

Port	Supplier invokes	Consumer invokes
submission	submission control	message submission, probe submission, cancel deferred delivery
delivery	message delivery, report delivery	delivery control
administration	change credentials	change credentials, register

Table 11.2, on the other hand, characterizes each port in terms of the role assumed by the corresponding object, MTS or MTS-user. As shown therein, the MTS is viewed as a supplier of corresponding services, while an MTS-user acts as a consumer. This does not, however, imply that the operations can be invoked by an MTS-user alone. Table 11.3 lists the operations that each object may invoke, but in their role as a supplier or as a consumer.

In effect, the MTS and an MTS-user may interact with each other through one or more ports, since the ports are asymmetrical and their roles are complimentary. It also implies that two MTS-users may not interact directly with each other through any of the ports. They may do so only through an MTS. Similarly, if two MTAs are required to interact with each other, then ports (and operations) of a different type will be needed. Furthermore, except for *change credentials,* all other operations may be invoked by an MTS-user *or* the MTS. Both, the MTS and the MTS-user, may invoke the operation, change credentials.

11.3.2 MTS Bind/UnBind

The MTS service specification requires that before any of the operations, listed above, can be invoked, the MTS-user (or the MTS) bind the ports that it uses with corresponding ports of the MTS (respectively, MTS-user). Subsequently, after accessing MTS services, the binding must be released by the object which initiated the bind operation. These operations are, respectively, called *MTS-Bind* and *MTS-Unbind,* and may be mapped onto the A-ASSOCIATE and A-RELEASE primitives of Association Control Service Elements. If an MTS-Bind operation is successful, then:

1. an underlying Association is established between the MTS-user and the MTS, with each one of them aware of the identity and access rights of each other,

2. the required Association context is established, which includes service elements corresponding to the three ports, ACSE, ROSE and possibly RTSE,

3. the correspondence between the ports of the MTS and of the MTS-user is known, together with an understanding of which of the two may invoke each operation,

The MTS-Bind operation, and similarly MTS-Unbind operation, is specified in terms of the data type of the parameters to be conveyed as user-data in the:

1. A-ASSOCIATE request or indication primitives,

2. A-ASSOCIATE response or confirm primitives, in case the Association is established successfully, and

3. A-ASSOCIATE response or confirm primitives, in case the Association is not established.

These parameters are, respectively, called *argument, result,* and *bind-errors.*

The operation, MTS-Unbind has no parameters. The MTS-Bind operation has the following argument parameters:

1. Initiator's *O/R Name.*

2. *Initiator-credentials,* which allows the responder to authenticate the initiator's identity. If only simple authentication is used, then the initiator's Directory Name and a password are adequate. If strong authentication is used then the parameter consists of a (bind) *token* and

optionally a *certificate* (see also Section 10.4). The bind token allows the responder to authenticate the initiators identity using digital signature. The associated public key of the initiator may be derived from the authenticated certificate, or obtained directly by the responder.

3. *Security context,* which is a list of descriptive labels that suggest the manner in which information objects are to be handled by users and the MHS. A label identifies the security classification (classified, etc.), privacy mark (in-confidence, etc.) and security category (commercial, etc.).

4. *Messages waiting,* which indicates the number of messages waiting for delivery. This parameter is present only when the MTS initiates the bind operation.

If the MTS-Bind operation succeeds, a result will be returned. The result parameters and their syntax are identical to those of the argument parameters, except that security context parameter is not present. If the MTS-Bind operation fails, a bind-error is returned together with the reason. There are several reasons why an MTS-Bind operation may fail, inability of the responder to authenticate the identify of the initiator, for example.

11.4   MTS Operations

We now discuss MHS operations, listed earlier in Table 11.1, together with their parameters.[7] An MHS operation is specified in terms of (see also Section 9.4):

1. the data type of the argument to be conveyed as part of the operation request,

2. the data type of the result to be returned, in case the MHS operation is performed successfully, and

3. a list of error conditions together with the type of information returned with each error.

11.4.1   Submit Operations

Message submission.   The operation, *Message submission,* may be invoked by a user to request transfer and delivery of a message to one or more MTS-users. Successful completion of the operation only signifies that the message has been accepted by the MTS. A successful delivery can only be confirmed by a delivery report from the MTS. We discuss its argument and result parameters. These are listed in Table 11.4.

---

[7]See also [CCITT X.411].

TABLE 11.4 Argument and Result Parameters of Message Submission

Argument parameters	Result parameters	Errors
originator	submission identifier	submission control violated
recipient (s)	submission time	service not subscribed
priority	MTA certificate	originator invalid
conversion	proof of submission	recipient improperly specified
delivery time	content identifier	inconsistent request
delivery method		security error
physical delivery mode		unsupported function
report request		remote bind error
security		
contents		

1. The parameter, *Recipient(s)*, consists of a list of intended recipients and distribution lists. The MTS may additionally specify an alternate recipient for each intended recipient. Further, an alternate recipient may also be assigned by the recipient, itself, or by the MTS. The originating MTS-user has the option to allow or prohibit substitution of recipient names.

2. *Conversion*-related parameters allow a user to explicitly specify a conversion of the message format. Further, it may allow or disallow any implicit conversion even when the MTS determines that a conversion is necessary for the message to be delivered.

3. *Delivery time* arguments allow a user to request the MTS to defer delivery of a message to a specified time, or to place a limit on the time before which the message must be delivered.

4. Since a message may be delivered using non-MHS media, the user has the option to specify the physical delivery mode to be used to deliver the message, or to prohibit physical delivery.

5. *Report request* parameter is used to request a delivery report and to specify its nature.

6. *Security* related parameters include the originator's certificate and a message token. The message token is used by the MTS to authenticate the origin of the message. It uses the originator's certificate to obtain a verified copy of user's public key. Further, the message token can also be used to send confidential information, and whose integrity is not compromised. Using other security parameters, an MTS user may request a proof-of-submission (from the MTS) and proof-of-delivery (to the recipients).

7. *Contents* parameters include *content identifier,* an indication of the *content type* (inter-personal message, for example), the *type of encoding* (g3-facsimile, for example), and the contents themselves.

Notice that each parameter discussed above is truly a collection of a number of parameters. Many of these parameters (and sub-parameters) are optional, except for *originator, recipients, report request, content type,* and *contents.*

If the operation, message submission, is performed successfully, the MTS returns a result reply with the result parameters, listed in Table 11.4.

1. *Message submission identifier* uniquely identifies the submission request, and may be used later to refer to this submission when a delivery report is given to the MTS-user, or by the MTS-user itself in a subsequent request to cancel its (deferred) delivery.

2. *Content identifier* identifies the contents in the corresponding message submission request.

3. *Message submission time* is the time the message was submitted to the MTS.

4. *Originating MTA certificate* contains the MTA's public key, using which the originating MTS-user may authenticate the origin of the result reply. The originating MTA is the one with which the MTS-user interfaces, and is also the one that acts on behalf of the MTS.

5. *Proof of submission* parameter provides the MTS-user with a proof that the identified message was indeed submitted, and at the stated time. The proof is of the form, message submission identifier and time, together with the MTA's signature.

There are several reasons why a message submission may fail, some of which are briefly discussed below:

1. the MTS-user may not have the permission (temporarily) to submit messages, or may not have subscribed to the particular operation,

2. the originator's O/R Name may be invalid, or the submission may fail an authentication test,

3. one or more recipients may have been improperly identified,

4. there may be inconsistency in assigning values to optional parameters, or

5. one or more functions that are critical to complete message delivery may have been requested, but are not available.

Probe submission.   The operation *Probe submission* is used by an MTS-user to determine whether or not a message can be transferred and delivered to one or more recipient users, if a message were to be submitted. Again, successful completion of the probe submission operation only signifies that the MTS has undertaken to carry out the probe. The probe consists of determining whether each named recipient in the probe submission is a valid MTS-user or not. It also determines whether there would be any major obstacle to the delivery of a message to the named users. In the case of a distribution list, the probe simply determines whether the list can be expanded or not.

The parameters of the probe operation are identical to those of message submission, except that there are no contents. Instead, a *content length* is specified. As a consequence, some of the other parameters are also absent, *delivery time* for instance. Further, the result parameter and the possible errors are also similar to those of message submission.

Cancel deferred delivery. The operation, *cancel deferred delivery,* enables an MTS-user to request the MTS to abort the deferred delivery of a previously submitted message. The MTS-user identifies the message whose delivery is to be cancelled by its *submission identifier* assigned by the MTS earlier at the time of message submission. A result reply is sent by the MTS upon successful completion of the operation, but without any parameters. This operation may, however, not succeed if the message has already been delivered, or the message submission identifier is not valid.

Submission control. The operation, *submission control,* may be invoked by the MTS to temporarily limit the operations that an MTS-user may invoke at the submission port. The MTS-user may, as a consequence, defer its message and probe submissions till the restrictions have been removed. The restrictions remain in force till submission control operation is re-invoked or the underlying Association is released. The arguments of the submission control operation permit the MTS to specify:

1. restrictions, if any, on invoking submission of messages and probes,

2. the lowest priority of the message acceptable to the MTS,

3. permissible maximum length of the message contents, and

4. permissible security context.

Unless a security violation is perceived by the MTS-user, the operation will succeed, and a result reply would be returned with an indication of the number of messages and probes waiting to be submitted at the user's end. The user, thereby, suggests the urgency with which the MTS must remove the restrictions.

11.4.2 Delivery Operations

Message delivery. Message delivery is invoked by the MTS to deliver a message to an MTS-user. The related argument parameters are to a large extent derived from those of the corresponding message submission, but may additionally contain:

1. delivery identifier, delivery time, and the time of the corresponding message submission,

2. originator's O/R Name, the intended recipient's O/R Name, if it is different from the MTS-user's name, together with the reason for redirection of the message,

3. security parameters, but which relate to the particular interface between the MTS and the message recipient (a proof of delivery may be requested by the MTS), and

4. the contents of the message. Messages are transferred transparently, except when format conversion is carried out by the MTS upon request by the originating MTS-user, or when implicitly determined by the MTS.

The result reply sent by the MTS-user includes its certificate and a proof-of-delivery, which is, in fact, an encrypted function of a hashed version of the delivery identifier, delivery time, and content identifier. The latter provides a proof to the MTS that the message was indeed delivered to the recipient MTS-user. The operation may, however, fail in case the MTS-user is unable to authenticate the MTA (acting on behalf of the MTS), or if it violates any of the controls that a user may have imposed on the MTS concerning delivery of messages to it.

Report delivery. A *report delivery* operation is invoked by the MTS to acknowledge to the MTS-user the outcome of a previous message or probe submission. In case of message submission, it indicates delivery or non-delivery of the message to one or more recipients. For a probe, it indicates whether or not a message, if submitted, could be delivered to the named recipient(s). In case of a distribution list, it simply indicates whether or not it can be expanded. Corresponding to a message or a probe submission, there may occur none, one, or more reports, each of which contains a delivery or probe report concerning one or more recipients. The report delivery operation may fail in case delivery controls are in effect or if the user is unable to authenticate the MTA.

The argument parameters of a report delivery operation indicate, among other things:

1. whether the report concerns a message or a probe, and the corresponding message or probe submission identifier,

2. for each recipient, whether the message has been delivered or not, and if so the time of delivery. Otherwise, a reason for not being able to deliver the message is given (*conversion not supported*, for example).

3. the content identifier, in case of a message, and

4. security parameters, which includes the reporting MTA's certificate and information concerning authentication of the origin of the report.

A result reply is returned by the MTS-user upon successful completion of the operation. It contain no parameters.

Delivery control. *Delivery control* is similar to submission control, except that this time it is the MTS-user that temporarily restricts the MTS from invoking operations. First, the MTS may not be allowed to invoke message delivery and/or report delivery. Even if the MTS may invoke message delivery operation, it may be restricted to messages whose contents are, for instance, of a certain type and limited in length.

A result reply to a delivery control operation contains an indication of the deliveries pending with the MTS. More specifically, the parameters consist of the number of messages and reports, together with a brief characterization of their contents. The operation may, however, not succeed if there is a security violation, or if the controls now placed are inconsistent with the parameter values set at the time of registration of the user with the MTS.

11.4.3 Administration-related Operations

Delivery control operation restricts delivery of messages and reports, but only as long as the underlying Association remains established or till delivery control is re-invoked. The operation *register,* on the other hand, enables an MTS-user to register itself as a valid user and set parameter values on a long term basis. These values are held by the MTS till they are changed by a re-invocation of the register operation. These parameters concern delivery operations. The values of these parameters are, in fact, conveyed as arguments in a register operation. They include user's name and address,[8] acceptable content type and encoding, maximum content length, and alternate recipient, if any.

The operation, *change credentials,* may be invoked by an MTS-user or the MTA (on behalf of the MTS) to change its own credentials. If simple credentials are used, then a new password, together with an old password, are sent as arguments. But if strong credentials are used, the argument consists of the new certificate and the old certificate. These certificates are issued by a trusted authority. The operation may not succeed in case the old or new certificates are incorrectly specified or are unacceptable.

11.5 Distributed MTS Operation

The MTS comprises a collection of a number of MTAs, which cooperate with each other to provide MTS services, earlier discussed in Section

---

[8]User's address is a Presentation address, TSAP address, or an X.121 address.

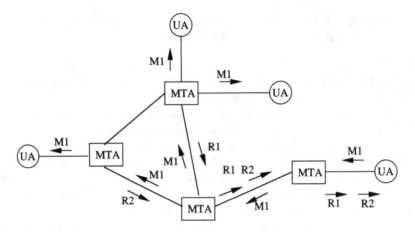

Note: M1 = message, R1 = report to M1, R2 = report to M1.

Figure 11.9 Transfer of messages and reports through the MTS.

11.3. Not only do the MTAs provide user access to MTS services, they are also responsible for moving messages, probes, and reports within the MTS. Further, it is the MTAs that perform the functions of report generation, format conversion, routing, expansion of distribution lists, and redirection of messages. For more details on the functions and the events that cause such functions to be executed, see [CCITT X.411].

A message, probe, or report may be transferred several times from one MTA to another, before it reaches its destination, as shown in Figure 11.9. Further, if a message (or a probe) is addressed to multiple recipients served through different MTAs, then multiple copies of the message (or probe) are created, whenever it is determined that the message (or probe) be sent along different paths.

Corresponding to each message, and if the originating MTS-user requests a delivery confirmation, a delivery report is generated by the MTA which delivers the message to its recipient(s). If an MTA delivers the message to a number of recipients, it generates only one delivery report. A delivery report is generated by an MTA if it determines that it is not possible to deliver the message, either to an attached recipient or to an adjacent MTA capable of delivering the message. Since messages may be delivered to recipients attached to different MTAs, a number of reports may be generated, all of which must be sent to the MTA, to which the originating MTS-user is attached. Along the path to the originating MTA, reports generated by different MTAs are *not* combined by an intermediate MTA (see also Figure 11.9).

11.5.1 MTA Operations

MTAs are again viewed as objects with ports. Some of the ports are precisely those using which users access MTS services. These are

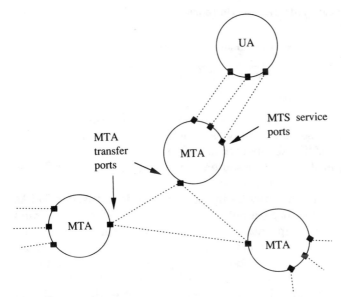

Figure 11.10 Ports of an MTA.

submission, delivery, and administration ports. MTAs have another type of port, called *transfer port*. Transfer ports are accessible from other MTA objects only (see Figure 11.10). Such a port is symmetric and permits MTAs to transfer messages, probes or reports to one another. A detailed specification of the ports is given in Tables 11.5 to 11.7. As a consequence, an MTA may invoke a transfer operation at any MTA. It is also required to perform a transfer operation when requested to do so by another MTA.

Surely, before any of the operations can be invoked, the transfer

**TABLE 11.5   MTA
Transfer Operations**

Port	Operations
transfer	message transfer
	probe transfer
	report transfer

TABLE 11.6   The Role of MTAs Concerning Its Ports

Object	Ports	Object's role
MTA	submission	Note 1
	delivery	Note 1
	administration	Note 1
	transfer	supplier, consumer

Note 1: See Table 11.2.

TABLE 11.7   Specification of Operations in Terms of the Role of MTA

Port	Supplier invokes	Consumer invokes
transfer	message transfer probe transfer report transfer	message transfer probe transfer report transfer

ports of the two MTAs must be bound using an *MTA-Bind* operation. The underlying Association may be released later using an *MTA-Unbind* operation. These operations are similar to MTS-Bind and MTS-Unbind operations discussed earlier in the context of MTS services and their access by MTS-users.

The transfer operation may be invoked by either of the two MTAs. The argument and result parameters of message transfer, probe transfer and report transfer operations are, respectively, similar to those of message submission (or delivery), probe submission and report delivery. They do, however, carry additional parameters that mainly concern relaying of information between MTAs (either within the MTS, or across management domains). The most important of these is the parameter *trace information* carried with a message, probe or report.

11.5.2   Trace Information

Trace information is a documentation of the actions performed by each MTA (and on a global scale by each MTS) as transfer takes place from one MTA to another. A trace consists of a sequence of trace elements, each of which is a record of actions performed by an MTA. Before forwarding a message, probe or a report, the MTA adds a trace element to the sequence. The element consists of, for instance,

1. the MTA's name supplying the trace element,

2. the arrival time of the object,

3. the routing action taken by the MTA, *relayed* for instance,

4. time when a delivery deferment was started, if relevant,

5. message conversion, if applicable,

6. redirection, if applicable,

7. expansion of distribution list, if applicable, and

8. loop detection, if encountered.

The OSI architecture gives a detailed description of the functionality of the MTA, and its inter-working with other MTAs in terms of modules and procedures (see [CCITT X.411]).[9] However, we shall only describe the protocol that supports MTA operations in Section 11.7.

---

[9]Such a description may even be taken to be a model of an implementation of an MTA.

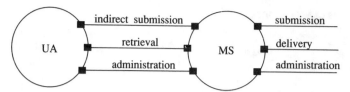

Figure 11.11 The Message store and its ports.

11.6 Message Store and Its Services

MTS services, discussed in Section 11.3, are those offered by the MTS to an MTS-user. The user can access the MTS either through a User Agent or through a *Message Store (MS)*. The latter provides the user with a capability to store incoming messages and delivery reports. The MS offers to the user (acting through its UA) services that reflect this capability. It permits the user to subsequently retrieve them at his convenience.

11.6.1 MS Operations

A model of an MS, acting in an intermediary role between a UA[10] and the MTS is shown in Figure 11.11. Its description is given in terms of operations that the MS or the corresponding MS-user (or a UA, for instance) may invoke or perform. First, an MS and the MS-user are each modeled as objects. The MS supports a variety of operations, grouped into five different types of ports (see Table 11.8). The three ports, that is, submission, delivery, and administration, are used to access MTS services. At its other two ports, *indirect submission* and *retrieval,* as well as administration port, the MS provides services to MS-users.

---

[10]The UA, acting as an MS-user, is different from a UA that directly accesses MTS services.

TABLE 11.8 MS Operations

Ports	Operation
submission	Note 1
delivery	Note 1
administration	Note 1
indirect submission	Note 2
retrieval	summarize
	list
	fetch
	delete
	MS-register
	alert

Note 1: See Table 11.1.
Note 2: Same as those at *submission* port.

TABLE 11.9   The Role of MS and MS-User Concerning Its Ports

Object	Ports	Object's role
MS	submission	consumer
	delivery	consumer
	administration	supplier, consumer
	indirect submission	supplier
	retrieval	supplier
MS-user	indirect submission	consumer
	retrieval	consumer
	administration	consumer

TABLE 11.10   Specification of Operations in Terms of the Role of MS and MS-Users

Port	Supplier invokes	Consumer invokes
submission	Note 1	Note 1
delivery	Note 1	Note 1
administration	change credentials register	change credentials register
indirect submission	Note 2	Note 2
retrieval	alert	summarize, list, fetch, delete, MS-register

Note 1: See Table 11.3.
Note 2: Same operations as for submission port.

An MS-user, on the other hand, supports only those ports that it requires to interact with the MS, that is, indirect submission, retrieval and administration ports. The role of the MS, and of the MS-user, with respect to each port is given in Table 11.9. Table 11.10 specifies which of the two, MS or MS-user in their role as supplier or consumer, may invoke a given operation. The port indirect submission, by definition, is of the same type as submission. The administration port is in fact the same as before, except that the MS acts both as a supplier of services and as a consumer. Thus, operations that an MS-user invokes at these two ports are immediately mapped onto operations at corresponding ports through which the MS accesses MTS services. We, therefore, discuss the operations concerning retrieval only.

Note that except for the operation, *alert,* all operations can only be invoked by the MS-user. Operations such as *summarize, list, fetch,* etc. may be invoked at user's convenience.

11.6.2   Message Information Base

At least conceptually, the MS stores each incoming message or report in a *Message Information Base,* which consists of a list of entries. An

TABLE 11.11   Example Contents of a Message Information Base

Sequence Number	New (N) or Listed (L)	Message (M) or Report (R)	Priority	Originator, ...
2	L	M	normal	guess-who, ...
3	L	R	-	that-guy, ...
11	N	M	low	my-pal, ...
12	N	M	urgent	the-chairman, ...

entry is conceptually similar to an entry in a Directory Information Base (see Section 10.2). Each entry, identified by a sequence number, contains a number of attributes concerning, for instance,

1. whether the entry corresponds to a message or a report,

2. whether the entry is new or has been listed earlier but not processed as yet by the user, and

3. associated priority, content type, originator, contents, etc.

(See Table 11.11, for an example of a Message Information Base.) We are now in a position to discuss retrieval operations.

1. The operation *summarize* returns a summary count of messages and reports that are currently in the information base of the MS, but which satisfy a certain property, based on priority, for instance.

2. The operation *list* is used to search through the Message Information Base for messages and/or reports that satisfy a search criteria, based upon content type, originator, for instance. The MS returns the values of the desired attributes of these messages or reports.

3. A *fetch* operation is used to return a particular message or a report from the Message Information Base. A user may specify the attributes of the entry that should be displayed.

4. A *delete* operation is used to delete messages and reports from the Message Store.

5. The *MS-register* operation is a combination of the operations, *register* and *change credentials,* encountered earlier while discussing MTS services.

6. An *alert* operation is invoked by the MS to alert the user of any incoming messages or reports.

One of the features offered by the MS is that of automatic processing of incoming messages and reports. The two actions that are of particular interest are automatic forwarding of those messages or reports that satisfy certain constraints, and alerting the user of any incoming mail, again belonging to a certain class. The MS uses the alert operation, discussed above. Users may define additional actions and acti-

Figure 11.12 MHS protocols.

vate them by registering them with the MS using the register operation, discussed above.

11.7 MHS Protocols

Above, we have discussed services and operations concerning three different pairs of MHS objects, that is:

1. MTA (acting on behalf of the MTS) and an MTS-user (which may be a UA or an MS),

2. MS and an MS-user (a UA, in particular), and

3. two MTAs.

Interactions between the above pairs of objects are also shown in Figure 11.12. As a consequence, three different protocols are required.[11] These are (the numbers indicated with each protocol are traditional names assigned to the protocols):

1. MTS Access Protocol (P3),

2. MS Access Protocol (P7), and

3. MTS Transfer Protocol (P1).

We discuss these protocols and the mapping of corresponding Application protocol-data-units (APDUs) onto services provided by the lower layers and other Application Service Elements (ASEs).

In the OSI environment, communication between Application processes is represented in terms of communication between corresponding Application entities. An Application entity is composed of one or more ASEs, each of which directly or indirectly supports a specified functionality to a *user-element*. The user-element is a model of the human user or a computer program that uses MHS services. The ASEs provide access to MHS services. The collection of ASEs is also called the *Application context*, and is common to the two Application entities.

11.7.1 MTS Access Protocols

Figure 11.13 models Application entities corresponding to an MTS-user object and the MTS (in fact, the MTA acting on behalf of the MTS).

---

[11]There is another protocol, called IPMS access protocol (P2), to support Inter-personal Message System (IPMS). The IPMS system is discussed in Section 11.8.

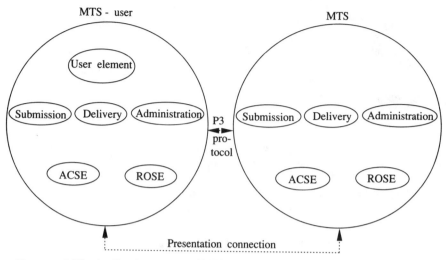

Figure 11.13 The Application context of MTS protocol.

It is assumed that Remote Operations Service Elements (ROSE) are available to support MTS services. They provide the request/reply paradigm required by the MTS operations available at different ports. Mapping functions are used to map MHS operations onto services provided by ROSE primitives. The service elements, submission, delivery, and administration, are, in fact, the functions that map operations of corresponding ports. Specifically, the MTS Access Protocol specifies the use of Class 2 (asynchronous, with result/reply) ROSE operations. Thus, when a user submits a message for transfer across the MTS, the protocol machine in a UA (or an MS) invokes the RO-INVOKE service with an Operation-ID[12] of 3 for message submission. The MTS returns a result by invoking a RO-RESULT service or RO-ERROR service, depending upon the outcome of message submission. Figure 11.14 illustrates the mapping of MTS message submission onto ROSE operations.

The ACSE service element is used to support MTS-Bind and MTS-Unbind operations. The Application context includes submission, delivery, administration, ACSE, and ROSE. As an alternative, RTSE service elements may be used by the ROSE protocol to reliably transfer Application PDUs. If such is the case then MTS-Bind and MTS-Unbind operation are mapped onto RT-OPEN and RT-CLOSE services, respectively. Other MHS operations continue to be mapped onto ROSE services, but the underlying services used by ROSE elements is RTSE services, rather than Presentation services.

---

[12]Each operation, message submission, probe submission, etc., is separately identified by an integer value. Similarly, each error condition is identified by an integer Error-ID.

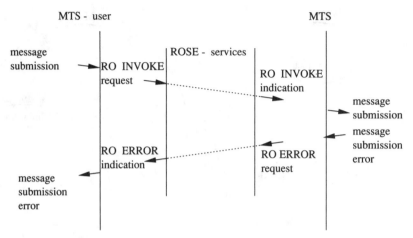

Figure 11.14 Mapping of MTS operations onto ROSE operations.

11.7.2 MS Access Protocol

The MS Access Protocol is similar to the MTS Access Protocol. The applicable Application context is shown in Figure 11.15. MS-Bind and MS-Unbind are mapped onto ACSE services, whereas MS operations are mapped onto ROSE service elements. Again, as an alternative, one may use RTSE to support MS-Bind and MS-Unbind operations and ROSE services.

11.7.3 MTS Transfer Protocol

The MTS Transfer protocol is, however, different. MTA operations are mapped onto the RTSE services, rather than ROSE services. This is

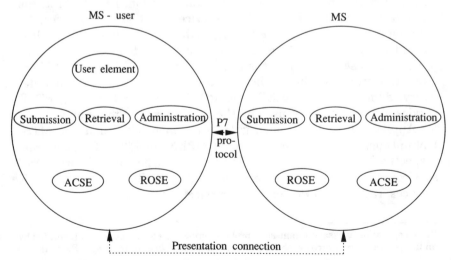

Figure 11.15 The Application context of MS Access protocol.

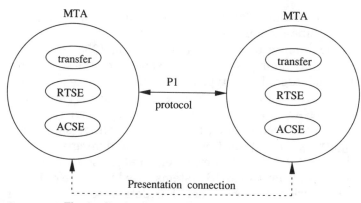

Figure 11.16 The Application context of MTA protocol.

primarily because MTA operations do not have any associated result parameter or error conditions to be returned by the MTA performing the operation. As a consequence, a simple but reliable transfer service is adequate to convey the semantics of the operation and its argument. Thus, the Application context of the MTS Transfer protocol includes ACSE, RTSE, and of course, the service elements corresponding to the transfer operations (see Figure 11.16). The ASE, transfer, embodies the mapping of transfer operations onto RTSE services. The MTA-Bind and MTA-Unbind are mapped onto RT-OPEN and RT-CLOSE services, which themselves require ACSE services. The semantics of a transfer operation and their parameters are carried in RT-TRANSFER request/indication primitives. RT-TURN-PLEASE and RT-TURN-GIVE services are used to turn the half-duplex channel around to permit MTAs to invoke other operations.

The RTSE protocol, itself, has undergone some change from its 1984 version to the current 1988 version (see [CCITT X.410], [CCITT X.218], and [CCITT X.228]). As far as its use by MHS protocol is concerned, the difference lies mainly in the way the supported application is identified. Instead of simply stating the name of the application, the 1988 version requires that the Application context and the *Presentation context definition list* be provided.

Presentation and session services required. In the three protocols, above, the Presentation context definition list includes the abstract syntax associated with ACSE, the syntax of abstract MHS operations, and the abstract syntax of messages, probes, and reports. The abstract syntax of ROSE and RTSE protocol-data-units is included wherever necessary.

The Session layer requirements are limited to the Kernel functional unit together with full-duplex transfer capability, in case ROSE APDUs are directly mapped onto Presentation layer. Otherwise, if

RTSE is used, the Session layer is required to provide the Basic Activity Subset of functional units.

There are some differences between the 1984 and 1988 versions of the MHS. These relate mainly to explicit constraints on the size of various parameters, additional data type definitions to include new ones, and additional optional parameters. Further, a user's O/R Name may now be a Directory Name rather than an O/R Address. Security related parameters have now been defined to provide for either simple authentication or strong credentials. Confidentiality and integrity of data transferred through the MHS can now be ensured. In spite of the upgrade, it is still possible for two MHS systems based upon the different versions to inter-work with each other. For details see Annex B of [CCITT X.419].

11.8 Interpersonal Messaging System

A Message Handling System can be used by human users to exchange messages or documents of any type. On the other hand, it can be tailored so that it is convenient for users to exchange business-related or personal correspondence. Such a system is called *Interpersonal Messaging System (IPMS)*. Below, we describe the system, together with its user interface and the structure of messages exchanged between human users.

11.8.1 Interpersonal Message

The structure of the *contents* field in a message submitted by a UA (on behalf of a user) to the MTS is not specified by the MHS. The IPMS system gives a structure to the contents field. Two types of messages may be exchanged between users, viz.,

1. an *interpersonal message,* which carries a user message, and

2. an *interpersonal notification,* which acknowledges the receipt of an interpersonal message.

An interpersonal message, illustrated in Figure 11.17, consists of a number of heading fields and the *body.* The heading fields together provide a rich set of options to a user. Each *interpersonal message (IPM)* optionally carries (among other fields):

1. an IPM identifier,

2. an IPM identifier, to which *this* IPM is a reply,

3. the *subject* of this IPM,

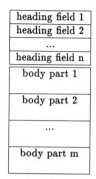

Figure 11.17 An interpersonal message.

4. the name of the user originating the IPM,

5. the name of the user on whose behalf the IPM is being sent,

6. a list of names of *primary* recipients, together with a request for reply and/or a request to notify the receipt of the IPM,

7. a list of *copy* recipients, who are to receive a copy of the IPM,

8. a list of *blind-copy* recipients, who are to receive a copy of the IPM, but whose identity is not made known to the other recipients,

9. a list of *reply* recipients, to whom a reply to this IPM may be sent,

10. *expiry* time, before which the IPM must be delivered,

11. *reply time,* before which a reply is expected,

12. *importance* (low, normal, high) associated with the IPM, and

13. *sensitivity* of the message contents, *personal, private,* or *company-confidential.*

The *body* of the IPM itself consists of one or more *body-parts.* Since each body-part may be encoded differently, the body-part indicates the encoding of the information, *text, voice, video, g3-facsimile,* or *encrypted,* for instance. Further, user data is preceded by a set of parameter values, for instance, number of pages, or encryption algorithm.

An IPM is sent as part of the *content field* of an MTS message, and delivered (hopefully) to a User Agent corresponding to each of the primary, copy, and blind-copy recipients, named in the IPM. Although a message may be delivered successfully to a UA, it may be either *discarded* or *forwarded* to another recipient. An IPM may be discarded due to its arrival after the expiry time, for instance. In both cases, the action (discard or forward) is generally performed automatically. As a consequence, a *non-receipt notification* is sent to the originator of the IPM, provided a corresponding request is contained in the received IPM.

common-field 1
common-field 2
...
common-field l

receipt *or* non-receipt field 1
receipt *or* non-receipt field 2
...
receipt *or* non-receipt field p

Figure 11.18 Structure of an interpersonal notification.

11.8.2   Interpersonal Notification

If an IPM is successfully received by an intended recipient, a *receipt notification* is sent provided the originator had requested it in the subject IPM. The IPM in response to which a notification is sent is called the *subject* IPM, and the notification is called *Interpersonal Notification* (*IPN*). The structure of an IPN is given in Figure 11.18. Both *receipt* and *non-receipt* notifications carry a common set of parameters, which includes:

1. the identifier of the subject IPM,

2. the name of the user originating the IPN,

3. the name of the original recipient, on whose behalf the IPN is being sent, and

4. an indication of whether the received IPM underwent code conversion.

A receipt IPN also carries with it the time when the subject IPM was received, and whether the notification is generated manually or automatically. A non-receipt IPN, on the other hand, carries with it the reason for non-receipt of the subject IPM, and additional information concerning why it was discarded or forwarded, as the case may be.

11.8.3   IPMS Operations

Figure 11.19 is a model of the IPMS system from the viewpoint of a user. Each IPMS-user is viewed as an object, and has three ports, each of which supports several operations, listed in Table 11.12. Similarly, the IPMS is also viewed as an object supporting corresponding ports.

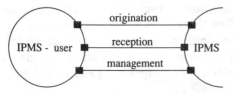

Figure 11.19 The interpersonal messaging system.

TABLE 11.12 IPMS Operations

Port	Operations
origination	originate probe originate IPM originate receipt IPN
reception	receive report receive IPM receive receipt IPN receive non-receipt IPN
management	change auto discard change auto forward change auto acknowledge

TABLE 11.13 The Role of IPMS and IPMS-User

Object	Ports	Object's role
IPMS-user	origination reception management	consumer consumer consumer
IPMS	origination reception management	supplier supplier supplier

Its role is, however, that of a *supplier* of services, whereas the IPMS-user acts as a *consumer* of services (see Table 11.13). The operations can only be invoked by the IPMS-user, whereas the IPMS performs them upon request. The details of each of the operations and the corresponding arguments and result parameters and error conditions are available in [CCITT X.420].

The resulting structure of the IPMS and its interface with users is given in Figure 11.20. There, it is shown that IPMS services are, in fact, provided by the UA that corresponds to the user. Of course, the UA may access MTS services either directly or through an MS. Thus, a UA, aside from supporting ports through which IPMS services are accessible by its users, also has ports through which *it* accesses MTS or MS services. As a consequence, many of the IPMS operations are directly mapped onto operations that a UA invokes on the MS or the MTS. In particular, all *origination* operations are mapped onto submission operations, and *reception* operations are a consequence of a message delivery operation. The operation *receive report,* however, is derived from report delivery operation.

As a last comment, the IPMS services may be integrated with Message Store capabilities to build an integrated message processing and communication system supporting a variety of business functions.

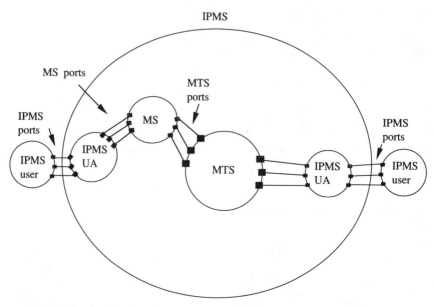

Figure 11.20 The functional units comprising the IPMS.

11.9   Summary

In this chapter we have discussed Message Handling Systems which support electronic mail, which is believed to be the most important application of computer networks. The MHS architecture models the user in the form of a User Agent (UA), which interfaces with the Message Transfer System (MTS) either directly or through a Message Store (MS). The latter provides a capability for storing incoming messages to be subsequently retrieved at his/her convenience. If an MS is used as an intermediate device to interface a UA with an MTS, then the design of the UA is necessarily different. The MTS interface is, however, independent of whether the MTS user is an MS or a UA.

The MTS is capable of communicating messages to one or more named users. Additionally the MTS provides the following capabilities:

1. By sending a probe, a user may determine whether it is possible for the MTS to convey a message to a named user, or not.

2. A user may request that delivery of a message (or a probe request) be confirmed in a delivery report.

3. A message may be simultaneously sent to a number of users, whose names or addresses are listed in a distribution list.

4. Messages may be sent through the network for delivery to users who do not have direct access to the MHS, except through other networks, including Telex, FAX and postal services.

5. The message content is not limited to a string of bits, bytes or characters. A multi-media message may contain suitably encoded voice, video or FAX messages.

6. Transfer of messages can be made secure. Public key encryption techniques can be used to authenticate both the sender as well the receiver.

7. Message handling can additionally be made reliable. That is, a sender or a receiver, at each stage, is unable to repudiate the fact that it had sent (or received) the message.

8. Integrity of message contents during transfer or processing can also be ensured.

These capabilities of the MHS have been discussed at length in this chapter.

The MTS provides services to an MS or a UA, while an MS provides services only to a UA. These services are specified in terms of abstract operations that may be invoked between corresponding ports of MTS, MS or UA. Aside from discussing the operations and their arguments, naming and addressing issues have also been covered in some detail.

Distributed operation of the MTS is made possible by interconnecting a number of Message Transfer Agents (MTAs). Communication between MTAs is also described using the concepts of abstract operations that are invoked across a different set of ports, specifically meant for transfer of messages, probes, or reports.

From the viewpoint of its architecture, an MHS is formed using three types of systems—MTAs, MSs, and UAs. This does not imply that an implementation must realize these logically distinct functions in physically separate systems. A system, for instance, may combine the functionality of an MTA, multiple MSs and (correspondingly) multiple UAs. Each pair of MS and UA corresponds to an MHS user.

The above MHS architecture gives rise to three different types of protocols:

1. MTS Access protocol which supports the abstract operations between an MS (or a UA) and the MTS,

2. MS Access protocol, which supports abstract operations between an MS and a UA, and

3. MTS Transfer protocol, which supports transfer operations between MTAs.

These protocols have been discussed briefly. The emphasis, however, has been on Application service elements that each MHS protocol requires.

Interpersonal Messaging System (IPMS) extends the capability provided by an MHS in several ways. It allows a human user to not only prepare messages for transmission, but also to process received messages and reports in a variety of ways. The basic idea of the IPMS system is to provide user-friendly interface to human users.

12

File Transfer, Access and Management

In this chapter we discuss the concepts relating to transfer, access and management of files located at a remote site. A Virtual Filestore is an abstract model of a real filestore and its interface with a user. This model has been used extensively to discuss File Transfer Access and Management services and its protocols.

12.1 Introduction

In a stand-alone computer system, a user typically has access only to the local file storage system. With interconnection of a number of computer systems into a network, where each system supports a possibly different type of file storage, it is desirable that a user be able to access any specified filestore, and with the same ease. The Application service element, *File Transfer, Access and Management (FTAM)*, provides to the users a uniform mechanism to access and manage a file storage anywhere within the network. This service is provided without the need for substantial change in the design or implementation of existing file systems or user interfaces (see [ISO 8571/1] through [ISO 8571/4]).

A user, or a user element, interacts with a real filestore through an FTAM Application service element. The FTAM service that it provides is accessed using a standard interface. If there are differences in the way users issue commands to access or manage different filestores, then these differences are concealed from the users by using a mapping which is local to the user's end. A real filestore is similarly accessible only through an FTAM Application service element. Differences, if any, in the standard interface and the interface provided by a real filestore are again resolved using a local function. This is illustrated in Figure

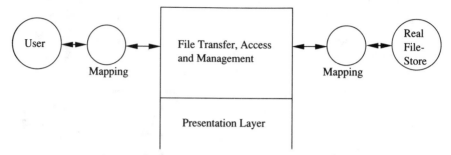

Figure 12.1   Access to real filestore using FTAM services.

12.1, where a user is shown to access a real file storage at a remote site using the standard FTAM service. The specification of the mapping is based upon the actual interface provided to a user, or to a filestore. It is, therefore, considered to be outside the scope of OSI architecture.

The FTAM service is asymmetric, in that two types of FTAM service users are recognized, the filestore and the filestore user. The filestore user is the one that initiates all transfer, access and management operations, and is, therefore, referred to as the *initiator*. A real filestore, on the other hand, responds to such requests, and is referred to as the *responder*. FTAM services available to a user, in the role of an initiator, may be invoked by a human user, a program which processes a queue of submitted file operations, or by a user-developed program (see [ISO 8831], for example). Similarly, FTAM services available to a user in the role of a responder may be accessed by a user-developed application program.

12.2   The Virtual Filestore

The description of the FTAM service is based upon the concept of a *Virtual Filestore*. It is an abstract model for describing files, file storage systems and file-related operations (see [ISO 8571/2]). A real filestore is an organized collection of files, together with a description of

1. the attributes of each existing file, and
2. the attributes relating to the current activity on each file.

A Virtual Filestore is an abstraction of the above description of a real file storage in terms of

1. a standard set of *file attributes* which are globally visible to all initiators of filestore operations,
2. a standard set of *activity attributes* which store the current state of operations initiated by a user,

3. a standard set of operations on files as a whole and on its contents, and

4. standard form(s) of organizing information within files and the manner in which data objects within a file may be addressed.

This method of describing a filestore allows differences, if any, between implementations of file storage systems to be absorbed using a mapping from each individual real filestore onto a virtual filestore. Differences in the way a file storage is accessed by users or user programs can similarly be absorbed by mapping user commands onto the set of abstract operations defined by the Virtual Filestore.

A Virtual Filestore may be accessed by a user or a program through FTAM service elements. The FTAM environment envisages interaction between a user, known as the initiator, and the identified virtual filestore, acting as a responder.[1] This interaction permits transfer of a named file (or a part of it) from the filestore to the user, or vice versa. A file may *not* be transferred between two filestores directly, except through an intermediate filestore user. The FTAM service also permits management of files within a named filestore, as well as operations on the contents of a named file. The interaction is described in terms of service primitives that an initiating user or a responding filestore may issue (or process) at its interface with the corresponding Application entity containing an instance of FTAM Application service elements.

Management or transfer of a file, or access to its contents, is possible only after an *Application association* has been established between the two Application entities representing the user and the filestore. Subsequently, a file operation may be initiated, but only after a named file has been *selected*. Note that a user may work with a number of files consecutively as long as the association is alive, but may not operate on two or more files at the same time.

12.2.1 File Access Structure

A file is a collection of related data objects. This relation between the objects may be sequential, hierarchical, network or relational. The FTAM standard currently defines Virtual Filestores that support only the *hierarchical* model of files. In a hierarchical model, a file is viewed as a rooted ordered tree, with at most one *Data Unit (DU)* associated with each node. Figure 12.2 illustrates the structure of a file. Further,

1. there may or may not be a Data Unit associated with a node,

2. each node is assigned to a specific *level* of the tree,

---

[1]Both, the filestore and filestore user are identified by the title of their respective Application entities.

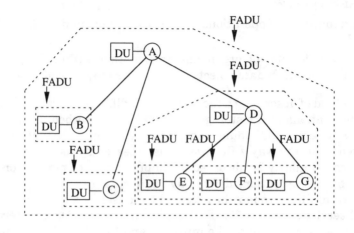

(a) Hierarchical.

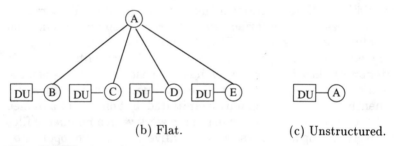

(b) Flat.   (c) Unstructured.

Figure 12.2 File access structures.

3. a child node is not necessarily assigned to the next level, and

4. optionally, each node has a unique name assigned to it.

This view of the internal organization of a file is also referred to as its *file access structure*. The exact nature of the Data Unit is not constrained by the Virtual Filestore definition. However, the data type of the Data Units must be unambiguously specified and made known to the FTAM service elements so that file contents may be communicated across open systems using an appropriate Presentation context.

As an alternative, a file may be viewed as one *File Access Data Unit* (*FADU*), which comprises a Data Unit associated with the root node and an ordered set of none, one or more subtrees. Each subtree is itself a FADU (see Figure 12.2). Using this approach, it is possible to allow access to the file as a whole or to any portion of the file. In particular, any FADU within the file may be accessed.

A number of special cases of the hierarchical access structure have been identified. Of particular interest are those cases which permit a user to view a file as a *flat* or *unstructured* file. Figures 12.2 (b) and (c) illustrate these file access structures. In a flat access structure, the tree consists of two levels. There is no Data Unit associated with the root node, but a Data Unit is associated with each leaf node. The file with an unstructured organization consists of a single node with an associated Data Unit. These access structures are helpful in modelling a file consisting of a sequence of records, or if it has a structure not covered by the hierarchical structure.

12.2.2   The Presentation Structure

Clearly, transfer of a file or that of its components takes place using Presentation layer services. Thus, each file and its components must have an identified Presentation context. There are two aspects to the Presentation context. First, the abstract syntax relating to the file structure must be known. Since this structure is pretty much standardized, its abstract syntax is given using ASN.1 notation in [ISO 8571/2] (see also [ISO 8824]). The abstract syntax of the Data Units is, however, application dependent, and must be made known to the Presentation layer before file transfers can take place. The abstract syntax of the file and its contents is, in fact, stored as a file attribute with each file.

For the purposes of transfer, a file, or more generally a FADU, is traversed in pre-order (see [Horow 87]), and the resulting sequence of Data Units, together with the structuring information, is conveyed to the Presentation layer by the corresponding FTAM Application service elements. The transfer of each Data Unit takes place using its corresponding transfer syntax.

Since the concept of Virtual Filestores permits flexibility in defining the file structure and the type of its contents, it seems desirable that some standard types of files be developed. This will encourage an early development of FTAM services. A few standard types of files, better known as *document types,* have been proposed. These are summarized in Table 12.1. Additionally, user groups are free to develop their own document types.

12.2.3   File Management

Aside from defining the file access and Presentation structure, the Virtual Filestore environment specifies a relatively complete set of operations that may be performed on a file, or its contents. Actions pertain-

TABLE 12.1   Definition of Some Document Types

Document type	Access structure	Contents type
Unstructured text file	Unstructured	CHOICE {Printable String, IA5 String, Graphic String, etc.}
Sequential text file	Sequential flat	CHOICE {Printable String, IA5 String, Graphic String, etc.}
Unstructured binary file	Unstructured	OCTET String
Sequential binary file	Sequential flat	OCTET String

ing to a file as a whole are referred to as file management operations. These operations are summarized in Table 12.2, and include file creation or deletion, and changing or reading of attributes of a file. Whenever a file is created, it is implicitly selected for any further action. Similarly, if a file is deleted, then it is automatically considered to have been deselected. Once a file has been selected, its attributes may be read or changed.[2] Further, the selected file is required to be opened before its contents can be accessed. Clearly, the file must be closed and subsequently deselected, once file management and file access is complete.

12.2.4   File Access

A number of operations are available to manipulate the contents of an opened file. These are termed *file access operations,* and are summarized in Table 12.3. These actions operate on a FADU as a whole, or on one or more Data Units associated with a FADU. The FADU to be *read, inserted, replaced, extended* or *erased* is identified either explicitly or implicitly. If no FADU is identified at the time of requesting an operation, then the FADU currently pointed to is assumed to be the one affected. After the operation is completed, the FADU identified by the pointer may change, as indicated in Table 12.3 (see also Figures 12.3(a) and (b)).

---

[2]*File attributes* are discussed in greater detail, below.

TABLE 12.2   Operations on a File as a Whole

File operation	Brief description
Create	create a new file and establish its attributes
Select	select a file for actions by the initiator on the file or its contents
Change attributes	change the file attributes, replacing scalar or vector values or adding (or deleting) values to a set valued attribute
Read attributes	read the values of requested attributes
Open	open the file for file access operations on its contents
Close	close the file, thereby preventing further file access operations
Delete	delete and de-select a file
Deselect	de-select a file, thereby preventing further file operations

TABLE 12.3. Operations on File Contents

Access operation	Brief description	FADU located after operation
Locate	locate the FADU	as specified
Read	locate and read a FADU	unchanged
Insert	create a new FADU and insert it as a child or sister	see Figure 12.3, below
Replace	replace entire FADU or Data Unit with root of FADU	unchanged
Extend	extend Data Unit with root of FADU	unchanged
Erase	erase the FADU	next FADU in pre-order traversal

The operation *Locate* is used to locate a specified FADU. Either a FADU is identified using a name, or it is located relative to another FADU or the file as a whole. The latter is, however, possible only when a tree-traversal scheme is defined. The traversal scheme used in this context is again the pre-order tree traversal scheme. As an example,

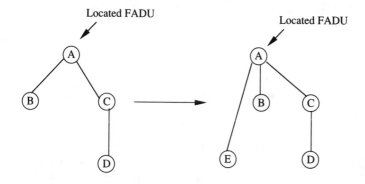

(a) Insert FADU E as a child of A

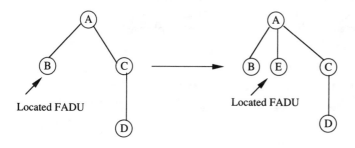

(b) Insert FADU E as a sister of FADU B

Figure 12.3 An example of Insert a FADU, using pre-order traversal sequence.

TABLE 12.4   Operations to Locate a FADU

Locate mechanism	Brief description
first	first FADU in the file for which Data Unit exists
last	last FADU in the file
previous	the FADU preceding the current FADU
current	no change
next	the FADU following the current FADU
begin	to the beginning of the file; no FADU is located
end	to the end of the file; no FADU is located
node name	the child node identified by the node name
sequence of	the FADU identified by the complete path from
node names	the root of the file
node number (n)	the n-th FADU in the pre-order traversal sequence

the tree of Figure 12.2 will be traversed in the sequence A, B, C, D, E, F, G. As a consequence, one may now refer to a FADU as the *first, last, current, next,* or the *previous* FADU. These and other methods for locating a FADU are summarized in Table 12.4. *begin* and *end* do not specifically locate a FADU, but are useful since the *next* FADU after the *begin* is the *first* FADU, and *previous* FADU before the *end* is the *last* FADU.

12.2.5   Access Context

The operation, *read,* may be used to locate a FADU and to read its contents. Whether or not the data actually read and transferred includes structuring information and/or the Data Units associated with nodes in the sub-tree, depends upon the *Access Context,* specified by the user together with the operation. The notion of access context is used to limit the scope of an operation involving transfer of information. It, thereby, permits users to have a simpler view of the affected FADU.

An access context defines the sub-set of Data Units in a FADU that are accessed, and whether information on the structure of the FADU is transferred. Seven different access contexts have been defined. These are summarized in Table 12.5. As an explanation, using Access

TABLE 12.5   Definition of Access Contexts

Access context	Data Units accessed	Structuring information	Visible access structure
HA	all	yes	hierarchical
HN	none	yes	hierarchical
FA	all Data Units	no	flat
FL	Data Units at a given level	no	flat
FS	Data Unit with the root	no	flat
UA	all Data Units	no	unstructured
US	Data Unit with the root	no	unstructured

Context *HA*, all Data Units within the addressed FADU, together with a description of the structure of the sub-tree, are transferred. The information transferred is such that it can be used to reconstruct the original FADU, including its hierarchical structure. In access contexts, *FA, FL,* or *FS,* while the sub-tree structure is not transferred, the identity of all Data Units and their contents is preserved during data transfer. It, therefore, allows the transferred information to be interpreted only as a flat file. Using the access context, *UA,* the contents of all Data Units are merged together. The only interpretation then available is that of an unstructured file. Using access context, *US,* the Data Unit associated with the root only is transferred.

12.2.6 File Attributes

File attributes are identifiable properties of a file, considered as a whole. These include *filename, date and time of creation* (or of last modification or of last read access), *identity of creator* (or that of the user who last modified it or read it), *current filesize* (or future permissible limit), and *account.* The values of a number of file attributes are assigned at the time of file creation. Subsequently, these may be modified either automatically by the filestore or specifically by a user. File attributes are *global.* That is, if two users select a file concurrently, then the same value for each attribute is read by the concurrent users.

Each file attribute is either a scalar, a vector, or set-valued. The type of value (or that of a component of a vector or set) is defined by the Virtual Filestore standard. For some of the attributes, the type is defined by the individual filestores. The type is, however, limited to printable characters, sequence of octets, boolean, integers, date and time (as per ISO standard). In other cases, the FTAM standard defines a named set of values using enumeration. Further, in those cases where a real filestore does not support a particular file attribute, the value returned is *cannot be determined.*

The number of file attributes is large. We, therefore, discuss some of the more significant ones.

1. The attribute *filename* is a *vector* of printable characters. However, the OSI architecture does not interpret its components. For that matter, it does not specify how the various components of the vector, filename, are to be mapped onto the components of the filename defined by the real filestore. The determination of the access path to a file in a real filestore from the components of a filename defined within the Virtual Filestore environment is implementation dependent.

2. The attribute *Permitted Actions* indicates the range of actions that a user may perform on the contents of the file, and the order in which the file may be accessed for each permitted action. For example, a read

operation may be permitted in either pre-order traversal order, reverse pre-order, or both.

3. *Access Control* attribute is a set of values, each of which describes the allowable actions that an identified user may perform. The allowable actions are specified as a boolean vector whose elements indicate whether *read, insert, change attribute,* etc. are permitted. Optionally, access to the file by each user is controlled through the use of user identity, access password, and user location. As an example, the value of Access Control may be set to

(11000000, user1,pw1,loc1), (10000000, user2,pw2),...

That is, *user1* may read or insert into the file provided he/she knows the password, *pw1,* and establishes the association from location, *loc1,* whereas *user2* may read the file contents only, but from any location (see also the discussion on *Activity Attributes,* below).

4. The file attribute, *Contents type,* specifies the abstract data type of the file contents and the structuring information necessary to convey the complete structure and semantics during transfer of the file or its contents. For instance, the Contents type may be specified using a document type identifier.

12.2.7 Activity Attributes

Activity attributes of a file reflect the state of its association with the user. The attributes include *Identity of Initiator, Password, Location of Initiator,* and *Requested Access.* The Requested Access attribute is a vector of requests for specific actions on the selected file, including read, insert, change attribute, etc. The four attributes, together, are matched with the attribute Access Control of the selected file before access is permitted. The other activity attributes are discussed below.

1. The attribute, *Active Contents type,* is a scalar attribute which identifies the Contents type to be used during the current file access. The requested contents type may match the corresponding file attribute, Contents Type, or it may be *simpler.* That is, a user may prefer to view a hierarchical file as either a flat or an unstructured file. Similarly, a flat file may be viewed as an unstructured file, if the user so prefers.

2. The attribute, *Current Concurrency Control,* indicates whether or not the user has exclusive or shared access to the file when it perform a particular operation. Shared access to the file depends upon the capability of the filestore to support concurrency. In particular, Current Concurrency Control indicates the restrictions on concurrent access that the initiator has requested. The four concurrency control options are:

(a) *not required,* where the user does not require access,
(b) *shared access,* thereby permitting other users to gain access concurrently,
(c) *exclusive access,* in which case the user has exclusive access to the file, and
(d) *no access,* in which case no user has access to the file.

Concurrency options are stated for each file access or management operation. Whether or not a user is permitted to exercise a particular option for an operation, depends upon the *concurrency access term,* stored as part of the file attribute, Access Control.

12.3 FTAM Services

We are now in a position to discuss FTAM services which may be used by a filestore user to interact with a filestore. The model of FTAM services is presented in Figure 12.4, where it is assumed that the two users of FTAM services are, respectively, a filestore user and a filestore, or in general, application programs. FTAM services are made available by an Application entity containing an instance of FTAM service elements. The interface between a filestore user (or a filestore) and the FTAM service provider is a standard one. It is described in terms of a set of primitives that an FTAM service user may issue or process. A primitive issued at one end of the supporting association results in a corresponding primitive being issued at the other end. It, thereby, enables service users to interact with each other. Since each primitive has a number of associated parameters including user data, users can exchange application-related information using FTAM service primitives (see [ISO 8571/3]).

12.3.1 FTAM Service Primitives

Table 12.6 lists the primitives available to users of the FTAM service. Note that a number of FTAM services may be invoked by the initiator

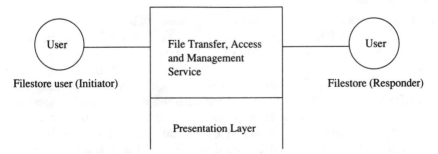

Figure 12.4 File service provider and its users.

TABLE 12.6   FTAM Service Primitives

Service primitive	Type of service	Requested by
F-INITIALIZE	Confirmed	Initiator
F-TERMINATE	Confirmed	Initiator
F-U-ABORT	Unconfirmed	Either
F-P-ABORT	provider-initiated	service-provider
F-SELECT	Confirmed	Initiator
F-DESELECT	Confirmed	Initiator
F-OPEN	Confirmed	Initiator
F-CLOSE	Confirmed	Initiator
F-CREATE	Confirmed	Initiator
F-DELETE	Confirmed	Initiator
F-READ-ATTRIB	Confirmed	Initiator
F-CHANGE-ATTRIB	Confirmed	Initiator
F-READ	Unconfirmed	Initiator
F-WRITE	Unconfirmed	Initiator
F-DATA	Unconfirmed	Sender
F-DATA-END	Unconfirmed	Sender
F-TRANSFER-END	Confirmed	Initiator
F-LOCATE	Confirmed	Initiator
F-ERASE	Confirmed	Initiator
F-BEGIN-GROUP	Confirmed	Initiator
F-END-GROUP	Confirmed	Initiator
F-RECOVER	Confirmed	Initiator
F-CHECK	Confirmed	Sender
F-CANCEL	Confirmed	Either
F-RESTART	Confirmed	Either

(the filestore user) only. Of course, data may be transferred by either the filestore user or the filestore itself, but only upon a request from the filestore user. Note that the association may be abruptly terminated by a service user, or by the FTAM service provider. Table 12.6 also indicates whether an FTAM service element is confirmed, unconfirmed, or provider-initiated. Except for data transfer and abort primitives, all services are confirmed. Later, we shall see how data transfer is indirectly confirmed.

12.3.2   Regimes

Clearly, one can expect a number of constraints to be present on the sequence in which FTAM service primitives may be issued. For instance, a filestore may be accessed only after an association has been established between Application entities representing the initiating user and the responding filestore. Further, the contents of a file may be transferred only after the file has been selected and opened for access.

Constraints on the sequence in which file transfer, access or management primitives can be issued by FTAM users are described in terms of a *nest* of *regimes,* illustrated in Figure 12.5. A regime, by def-

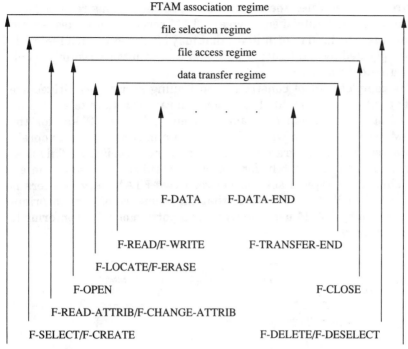

Figure 12.5 Regimes.

inition, is a state of the association during which some contextual information remains valid. Four different regimes are identified:

1. *FTAM regime,* which exists as long as the Application association is alive,
2. *file selection regime,* during which the file upon which operations are performed is implied,
3. *file open regime,* during which the negotiated Presentation context and concurrency controls remain valid, and
4. *data transfer regime,* during which the specifications for data transfer are valid.

During an FTAM regime, a number of files may be selected consecutively, and within a file selection regime, the file may be opened and closed several times. As long as a file remains open, multiple transfers may be initiated, although consecutively.

FTAM services may be invoked at any time by the initiator or the responder, as the case may be, but only within a particular regime. A regime is established by the collection of primitives issued in the past.

Figure 12.5 illustrates the relation between the various regimes, and how a regime is established when an FTAM service user issues certain primitives. The kind of primitives that may be issued in each regime is also suggested by the figure. Additional constraints on issuing primitives are now discussed.

The complete set of constraints on issuing service primitives are best specified using a state transition diagram or a state table. A simplified state transition diagram is given in Figure 12.6(a) for the FTAM association as a whole. This diagram may be refined to obtain the corresponding diagram for each end of the association. This is illustrated in Figure 12.6(b) for the phase resulting in connection establishment. A typical session between two FTAM service users is illustrated in Figure 12.7. Note that the sequence of service primitives issued by FTAM users to transfer a portion of a file conforms to the state diagram.

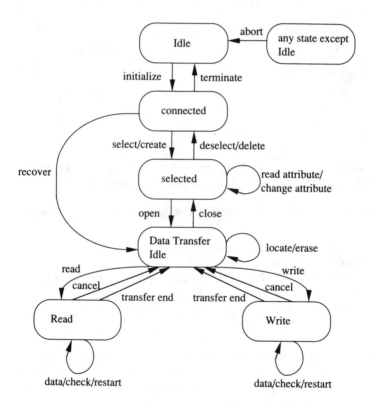

(a) FTAM association.

Figure 12.6 State transition diagrams.

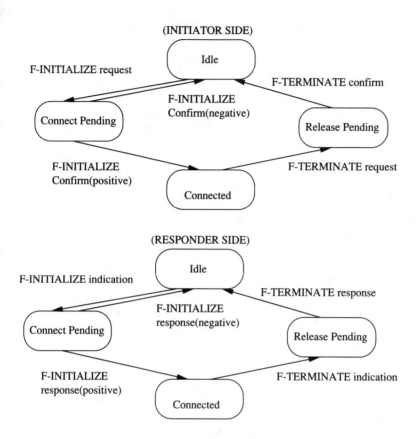

(b) State transitions during connection establishment.

Figure 12.6 (*Continued*)

12.3.3   FTAM Functional Units and Service Classes

The example, given in Figure 12.7, assumes that the FTAM service supports, what is termed as, *File Access Class* of service. Three distinct classes[3] of services have been identified by the FTAM standard. One or more of these may be supported by an FTAM implementation. The three classes are:

1. *File Transfer Class,* which enables a filestore user to read or write a complete file,

---

[3]The class, *File Transfer and Management class,* has also been defined. It is, as the name suggests, a combination of the two classes.

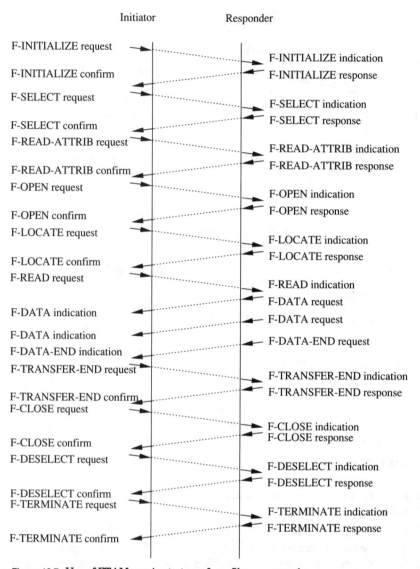

Figure 12.7 Use of FTAM service to transfer a file: an example.

2. *File Access Class,* which permits a user to additionally address any FADU within a file and to read, write, or erase it, and

3. *File Management Class,* which enables a user to create or delete a file, or to read file attributes and possibly modify them.

Each class is defined in terms of a collection of *functional units,* some of which are mandatory while others may be supported optionally. A functional unit is a logical grouping of related service elements. For

TABLE 12.7 FTAM Service Primitives and Functional Units

Functional unit	Service primitives
Kernel	F-INITIALIZE, F-TERMINATE, F-U-ABORT, F-P-ABORT, F-SELECT, F-DESELECT
Read	F-READ, F-DATA, F-DATA-END, F-TRANSFER-END, F-CANCEL, F-OPEN, F-CLOSE
Write	F-WRITE, F-DATA, F-DATA-END, F-TRANSFER-END, F-CANCEL, F-OPEN, F-CLOSE
File access	F-LOCATE, F-ERASE
Limited file management	F-CREATE, F-DELETE, F-READ-ATTRIB
Enhanced file management	F-CHANGE-ATTRIB
Grouping	F-BEGIN-GROUP, F-END-GROUP
Recovery	F-RECOVER, F-CHECK, F-CANCEL
Restart data transfer	F-RESTART, F-CHECK, F-CANCEL

instance, the read functional unit includes support for the following service primitives:

1. *F-READ* primitives, which may be used by a filestore user to request a read operation,

2. *F-DATA* primitives, which may be used by a sender (a filestore or a filestore user) to transfer data,

3. *F-DATA-END* primitives, which may be used by the sender to signal the end of data transfer, and

4. *F-TRANSFER-END* primitives, which may be used by a filestore user to acknowledge completion of a read or write operation.

Table 12.7 describes the services available as part of each functional unit, while Table 12.8 summarizes the definition of FTAM service classes in terms of mandatory and optional functional units. Note that:

1. File contents, or more precisely a FADU, may not be accessed using File Management Class.

TABLE 12.8 Definition of Classes of FTAM Services

Functional Unit	Transfer Class	Access Class	Management Class
Kernel	Yes	Yes	Yes
Read and Write	either or both	Yes, both	None
File Access	No	Yes	No
Limited management	optional	optional	yes
Enhanced management	optional	optional	optional
Grouping	Yes	optional	yes
Recovery	optional	optional	No
Restart	optional	optional	No

2. The capability to address, locate or erase an arbitrary FADU within a file is available only within File Access Class of service.
3. File management operations, including creation or deletion of files and reading or modifying file attributes, are always part of the File Management Class, whereas these are optionally available in other classes.
4. File Transfer Class permits users to transfer an entire file. Further, the initiator must *group* its requests to simultaneously establish a number of regimes, including the open file regime, or to delete previously established regimes. Requests that are grouped together are processed and responded to as one group. The entity supporting FTAM services concatenates the corresponding Application protocol-data-units and sends them across as one service data unit over the supporting Presentation connection. Figure 12.8 illustrates the opening of a file using the primitives *F-GROUP-BEGIN* and *F-GROUP-END*.

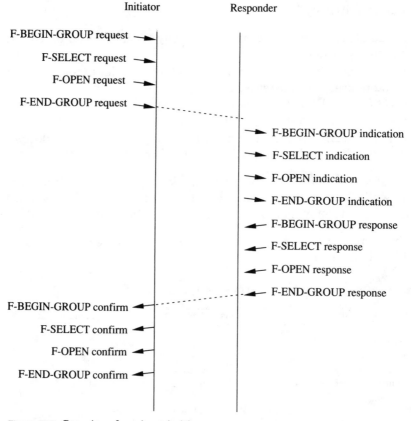

Figure 12.8 Grouping of service primitives.

The availability and use of the various classes of service, and the functional units within the preferred class, are negotiated at the time of association establishment.

12.3.4 Error Recovery and Restart

Even though reliability of data transfer is assured by the Transport layer, the possibility of occurrence of errors within the host (filestore user or the filestore itself) cannot be ruled out. As such, two *types* of data transfer services have been identified by the FTAM standard:

1. *User-correctable file service,* where the responsibility of error detection and of recovery is that of the user, and

2. *Reliable file service,* where error detection and recovery is carried out by FTAM service provider. This procedure is totally transparent to the user.

Figure 12.9 illustrates the difference. The more basic user-correctable file service is directly available to the users, together with services that enable a user to recover from errors. Optionally, a sub-layer may be added on top of it to provide reliable file service. In the latter case, service elements related to error detection and recovery are unavailable to the users.

With user-correctable file service, a filestore user may request recovery to the beginning of a file open regime or to the beginning of a data transfer operation. Alternatively, the sender or the receiver may request restart of data transfer to any agreed upon checkpoint, as long as data transfer is in progress. Checkpoints (or minor synchronization points, using Session layer terminology) may be inserted during data transfer by the sender, and acknowledged by the receiver. These services may be accessed using the primitives *F-RECOVER, F-CANCEL,*

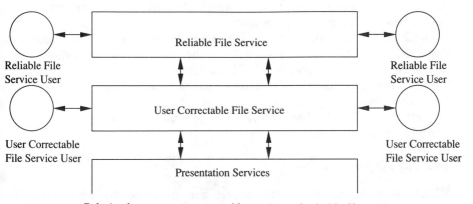

Figure 12.9 Relation between user correctable service and reliable file service.

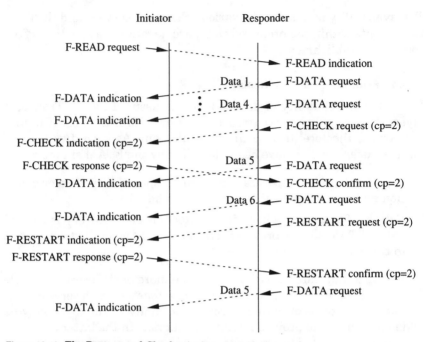

Figure 12.10   The Restart and Checkpointing procedure.

F-RESTART, and *F-CHECK,* respectively. Figure 12.10 illustrates the restart procedure together with checkpointing.

An alternative procedure is available to handle errors during file transfer. In case the error is not recoverable by FTAM service users, a user may issue an F-CANCEL request primitive to cancel a data transfer operation. F-CANCEL primitive may be issued as long as the transfer of file data is in progress. Once a sender signals the end of data transfer, it may not abandon data transfer (see Figure 12.11). Similarly, a receiver may not issue an F-CANCEL request primitive, once it has confirmed receipt of data.

The F-RECOVER primitives allow users to recover from a breakdown of an Application association. Once the Application association is re-established, users may issue F-RECOVER primitives to restore the file open regime that existed during an earlier association. As one implication, whenever a file open regime is established, a record of the current regime is stored so that recovery is feasible in case of a breakdown of the association.

12.4   FTAM Protocol

FTAM services, as discussed above, are provided by an FTAM Application service element (*ASE*). Interaction between two FTAM service users is made possible only when each user includes an FTAM ASE

Initiator (Superior)   Responder (Subordinate)

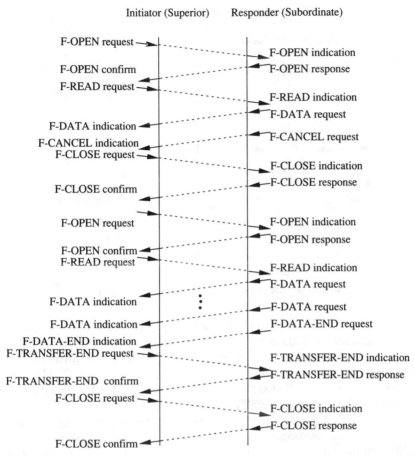

Figure 12.11 Use of F-CANCEL primitives to recover from errors during data transfer.

within its Application entity. Communication between the two FTAM ASEs is governed by the FTAM protocol. The protocol defines the syntax, semantics and timing of exchanges of *FTAM Application protocol-data-units* (*FTAM APDUs*). Therefore, each FTAM ASE is viewed as a protocol machine which implements the specified protocol[4] (see Figure 12.12). FTAM APDUs convey the semantics of the interaction between FTAM service users and the FTAM ASEs (and thereby, convey the semantics of communication between the two FTAM service users).

12.4.1 FTAM APDUs

Viewed differently, the FTAM protocol specifies the correspondence between issuing of FTAM service primitives at the two ends of an

_____

[4]For more details see [ISO 8571/4].

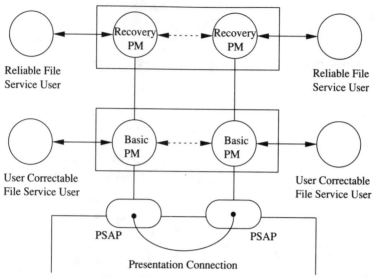

Figure 12.12 A model of the FTAM service provider in terms of protocol machines.

Application association and exchange of FTAM APDUs between the protocol machines. This correspondence is summarized in Table 12.9. For instance, whenever a user issues an *F-SELECT* request (or response) primitive, the semantics is conveyed between the FTAM protocol machines in *F-SELECT request* (or *response*) APDU. In the case of *F-DATA,* for instance, no FTAM APDU is defined.

Clearly, FTAM APDUs may be transferred only over an established Application association. The latter, in turn, is supported by a Presentation connection. Therefore, the FTAM protocol assumes the availability of Association Control Service Elements (ACSE) and a set of Presentation services. Presentation services that are specifically required to support the various FTAM functional units are listed in Table 12.10. Provided that these services are available, FTAM APDUs are transferred as user data in ACSE and Presentation services. This correspondence is also summarized in Table 12.9. Note that a protocol machine may issue additional Presentation service primitives to either alter the set of defined Presentation contexts or to exchange *minor* synchronization token.

12.4.2 FTAM Initialization

The establishment of an Application association, or equivalently an FTAM regime, is illustrated in Figure 12.13. The *F-INITIALIZE request* and *F-INITIALIZE response* APDUs are constructed by the re-

TABLE 12.9   Mapping of FTAM Primitives onto FTAM APDUs, and Use of Lower Layer Services to Transfer FTAM APDUs

FTAM primitive	FTAM APDU	Supporting service
F-INITIALIZE req./ind.	F-INITIALIZE request	A-ASSOCIATE req./ind.
F-INITIALIZE resp./conf.	F-INITIALIZE response	A-ASSOCIATE resp./conf.
F-TERMINATE req./ind.	F-TERMINATE request	A-RELEASE req./ind.
F-TERMINATE resp./conf.	F-TERMINATE response	A-RELEASE resp./conf.
F-U-ABORT req./ind.	F-U-ABORT request	A-ABORT req./ind
F-P-ABORT ind.	F-P-ABORT request	A-ABORT req./ind.
F-xxx req./ind. (see Note)	F-xxx request see Note	P-DATA req./ind.
F-xxx resp./conf. (see Note)	F-xxx response (see Note)	P-DATA resp./conf.
F-OPEN req./ind.	F-OPEN request	P-DATA req./ind., and P-ALTER-CONTEXT resp./conf.
F-OPEN resp./conf.	F-OPEN response	P-DATA req./ind., and P-ALTER-CONTEXT req./ind.
F-READ req./ind.	F-READ request	P-DATA req./ind., P-TOKEN-GIVE req./ind.
F-WRITE req./ind.	F-WRITE request	P-DATA req./ind.
F-DATA req./ind.	-	P-DATA req./ind.
F-DATA-END req./ind.	F-DATA-END request	P-DATA req./ind.
F-RECOVER req./ind.	F-RECOVER request	P-DATA req./ind., and P-ALTER-CONTEXT resp./conf.
F-RECOVER resp./conf.	F-RECOVER response	P-DATA req./ind., and P-ALTER-CONTEXT req./ind.
F-CHECK req./ind.	F-CHECK request	P-SYNC-MINOR req./ind.
F-CHECK resp./conf.	F-CHECK response	P-SYNC-MINOR resp./conf.
F-CANCEL req./ind.	F-CANCEL request	P-RESYNCHRONIZE (abandon) req./ind.
F-CANCEL resp./conf.	F-CANCEL response	P-RESYNCHRONIZE (abandon) resp./conf.
F-RESTART req./ind.	F-RESTART request	P-RESYNCHRONIZE (restart) req./ind.
F-RESTART resp./conf.	F-RESTART response	P-RESYNCHRONIZE (restart) resp./conf.

Note: F-xxx represents F-SELECT, F-DESELECT, F-CREATE, F-DELETE, F-READ-ATTRIBUTE, F-CHANGE-ATTRIBUTE, F-CLOSE, F-BEGIN-GROUP, F-END-GROUP, F-LOCATE, F-ERASE, and F-TRANSFER-END.

spective protocol machines from parameters supplied within the corresponding F-INITIALIZE request or response primitives. These are then communicated using A-ASSOCIATE primitives. The mapping of parameters of F-INITIALIZE primitives onto parameters of A-ASSO-CIATE primitives is summarized in Table 12.11.

TABLE 12.10   Presentation Services Required to Support FTAM Functional Units

FTAM Functional Unit	Presentation Functional Units
Kernel	Kernel
	Duplex data transfer
Read and Write	Minor synchronization
	Resynchronization
	Context management
File Access	-
Management	-
Grouping	-
Recovery	Minor synchronization
	Context management
Restart	Minor synchronization
	Resynchronization

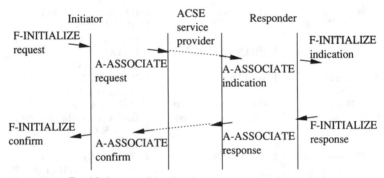

Figure 12.13 Establishment of Application association between FTAM ASEs.

The FTAM protocol maps the titles of Application entities representing the filestore and its user, as well as PSAP addresses, onto corresponding parameters of A-ASSOCIATE primitives. Further:

1. The Application context name identifies the list of Application service elements that constitute the communicating entities. In this case, it must include FTAM and ACSE service elements.

2. The abstract syntax of FTAM and ACSE protocols and that of files and their contents are included in the Presentation context definition list.

3. The Presentation and Session requirements are derived from the class of FTAM service requested by the users and the proposed FTAM functional units.

4. The initial synchronization point serial number is 1, and the minor token is initially assigned to the initiator of the association, that is, to the filestore user.

TABLE 12.11   Mapping of Parameters of F-INITIALIZE Primitives onto A-ASSOCIATE Parameters

A-ASSOCIATE parameter	relation to F-INITIALIZE parameters	Value, if un-related
Called AE Title	= Called AE Title	
Calling AE Title	= Calling AE Title	
Responding AE Title	= Responding AE Title	
Calling PSAP Address	= Calling PSAP Address	
Called PSAP Address	= Called PSAP Address	
Responding PSAP Address	= Responding PSAP Address	
Mode		normal
Application Context Name		FTAM
Presentation Contexts Def. List	Contents types	and FTAM, ACSE
Presentation Contexts Result List	Contents types	and FTAM, ACSE
Presentation Requirements		Context management
Session Requirements	from FTAM functional units	
Quality of Service	from Communication QOS	
Initial sync. point serial no.		1
Initial Assignments of Tokens		initiator
Default Presentation Context Name	-	-
Default Presentation Context Result	-	-
Session Connection Identifier	-	-
User Information	initiator, password, account, etc.	
Result, result source, diagnostics	from Result	

12.4.3   Other FTAM Protocol Procedures

The FTAM protocol requires a number of other Presentation services, including duplex data transfer to support even a minimal set of FTAM services. Recall that FTAM protocol machines may support one or more classes of FTAM services and some of the optional functional units. Part of the decision to support optional classes and functional units, and the type of FTAM service, is based upon the availability of additional Presentation layer services. These are minor synchronization, resynchronization, token exchange and context management services.

In Figure 12.14, we illustrate the use of other Presentation services to open a file, transfer data, and to subsequently close the file. The fig-

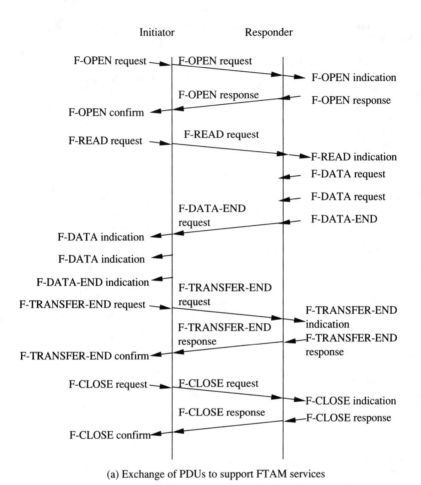

(a) Exchange of PDUs to support FTAM services

Figure 12.14 Illustration of protocol exchanges to open a file and transfer data.

ure also shows details on how *F-OPEN request* and *response* APDUs are transferred using P-DATA primitives over a Presentation connection. When a file is opened for subsequent data transfer, the defined Presentation context set may have to be updated to ensure Presentation layer support for the abstract syntax of file contents. Thus, the responding FTAM protocol machine alters the defined Presentation context set to include the one that is required to support transfer of file contents. This procedure is, however, transparent to the users. The users must, while requesting a file to be opened, specify the type of file contents. Also note that an FTAM user receives a confirmation to the F-OPEN request primitive only after the appropriate Presentation context has been included. A similar procedure is followed when the file is closed.

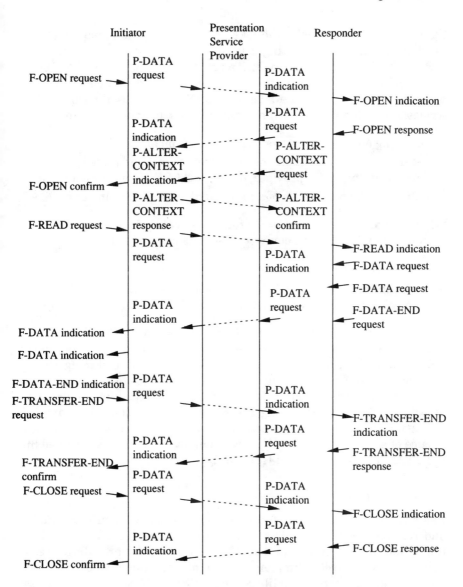

(b) Use of Presentation Services to exchange FTAM APDUs.

Figure 12.14 (*Continued*)

Transfer of file data is handled somewhat differently. There is no F-DATA request APDU, as one might expect. Instead, F-DATA primitives are directly mapped onto P-DATA primitives. Alternatively, file data may be piggybacked onto other FTAM APDUs, for example, *F-DATA-END request* APDU, as shown in Figure 12.14. Further, the initiator may have to transfer the token corresponding to minor synchronization, in case checkpointing is used.

Having briefly discussed how exchange of APDUs between FTAM protocol machines enables users to interact with each other, we now look at a formal specification of the FTAM protocol. The protocol formally describes, for each protocol machine, the actions to be taken by it upon:

1. receiving a request or response primitive from an FTAM service user,
2. receiving an indication or confirm primitive issued by the Presentation service provider, or by the ACSE service provider, and
3. detecting the occurrence of a local event, an error for instance.

Whenever an event occurs, the protocol machine depending upon its current state, initiates a sequence of actions consisting of:

1. issuing of an FTAM service indication or confirm primitive, and/or
2. exchange of FTAM APDUs by issuing a Presentation (or ACSE) service request or response primitive.

Subsequently, the protocol machine may change state. The specific sequence of actions to be taken depends also upon the value of parameters contained within service primitives or APDUs, including those processed in the past. The latter requires each protocol machine to maintain and update state information pertaining to the Application association and the supporting Presentation connection. The state information to be retained by each protocol machine, as well as the sequence of actions to be taken by it when an event occurs, is specified in the FTAM protocol standard [ISO 8571/4].

12.4.4   Error Recovery Procedures

The FTAM protocol covers both types of services, viz. user-correctable and reliable file services. The model used to describe the protocol is that given in Figures 12.9 and 12.12. The protocol for providing a reliable file service involves implementation of a sub-layer which uses the underlying user-correctable file service.

The error detection and recovery procedures required to provide a reliable file service are illustrated in Figure 12.15. Part (a) illustrates the exchange of FTAM APDUs to restart communication from a previously inserted checkpoint. Note that F-CHECK primitives are directly mapped onto corresponding P-SYNC-MINOR primitives, whereas F-RESTART primitives are mapped onto P-RESYNCHRONIZE (Restart) primitives. There are no FTAM APDUs that correspond to F-CHECK primitives. Figure 12.15(b) illustrates the use of user-correctable file

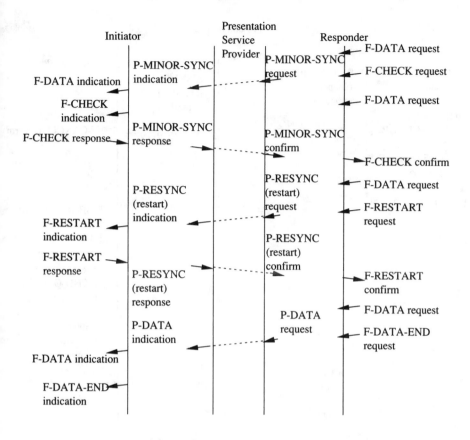

(a) User correctable file service.

Figure 12.15 Error recovery procedures.

service by the sub-layer above to recover from an error. Note, no additional APDUs are defined for this sub-layer.

12.5 Summary

File transfer capability between computer systems is, again, an important application of computer networks. It is perhaps next only to electronic mail. Unlike other protocols, for instance FTP running over TCP/IP, the OSI version permits access to and manipulation of portions of a file located in a remote filestore. Further, attributes of a given file may also be manipulated by a remote user.

Not only does the FTAM protocol permit users to access filestores located on different types of machine, its design allows access to different types of file systems. The user interface is also not standardized. That

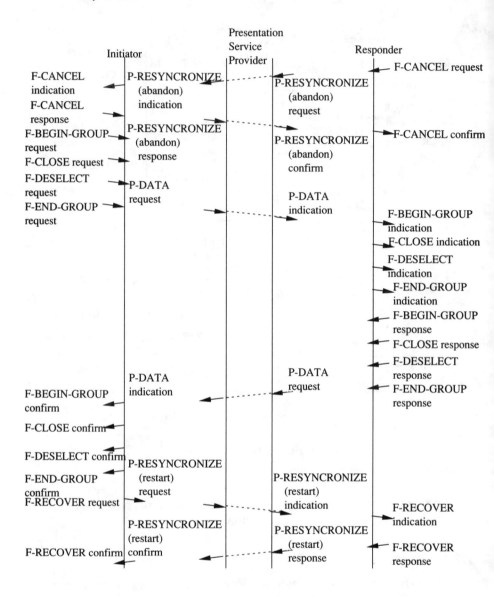

(b) Reliable file service.

Figure 12.15 (*Continued*)

is, a user may access FTAM capability using a variety of interfaces. As a consequence, a user may continue to use the same old interface to access a variety of filestore. Thus, a filestore implementation is totally transparent to a user. Similarly, a given filestore can be accessed by users connected to a wide variety of systems. In other words, the user interface is also transparent to the filestore.

The concept of a virtual filestore is central to ensuring transparent operation between the filestore and its user. A virtual filestore is an abstract model of a filestore. This model is described in terms of the file structure, file attributes and the permissible operations on files or its contents. Given such a model for describing a real filestore, the task of designing FTAM service has been considerably simplified. From the viewpoint of a person implementing a filestore so that it can be accessed by remote users as well, the major concern is to map existing user interface and filestore commands onto FTAM services. The FTAM protocol is such that the semantics of interaction between an FTAM user and an FTAM protocol machine can be conveyed to the user at the other end.

In this chapter we have discussed in detail the concept of virtual filestore and the services provided by an FTAM implementation. The FTAM protocol has been discussed using several illustrations involving exchange of FTAM protocol data units. For more details on the subject the reader is referred to the standards documents, [ISO 8571/1] through [ISO 8571/4].

13

Virtual
Terminal
Protocols

The Virtual Terminal service and its supporting protocol (see [ISO 9040] and [ISO 9041]) allow a variety of terminals to communicate with different applications running in host computers on a network. It uses the concept of a *Virtual Terminal,* which permits applications to be developed so that they are largely independent of the type of terminal it communicates with. This approach is substantially different from the one followed using CCITT's Recommendations X.3, X.28, and X.29.[1] In this chapter, ISO's Virtual Terminal service and protocol are discussed after an overview of the approach based upon Recommendations X.3, X.28, X.29.

13.1 Introduction

Over a computer network, a terminal may access any computer on the network. Similarly, an application program running on a host computer may be used by a variety of terminals over the network. If each application supports only one type of terminal, and each terminal is limited in its ability to emulate only one type of terminal, then terminal access to applications would be severely restricted. As one solution to the problem, each application could be written, or perhaps re-written, to support a large variety of terminals. Or, a terminal could be designed so that it is capable of emulating a variety of terminal classes. In both cases, the effort required is tremendous, which is one reason why these approaches have achieved limited success.

Alternatively, one may consider developing applications that offer a generic terminal interface that is largely independent of the users terminal(s) and their characteristics. Similarly, the design of a terminal

---

[1]See [CCITT X.3,CCITT X.28,CCITT X.29].

could be simplified, without compromising on its ability to interface with different applications, if it is capable of mapping the generic terminal characteristics onto its (input/output) devices. A terminal with a generic set of characteristics is called a *Virtual Terminal,* and the approach based on it is called the *virtual terminal approach.*[2]

The *parametric* approach, on the other hand, assumes a fixed type of terminal. Some of its parameters, particularly those relating to the physical transfer of data to (or from) the terminal and its display, may be controlled by the application or the terminal. It, therefore, provides limited flexibility in terms of the kind of terminals that may communicate with applications in other hosts. Terminal access to hosts using the parametric approach, but conforming to CCITT's Recommendations X.3, X.28, X.29 is described below.

13.2   Parametric Approach Using PAD

Recommendations X.3, X.28, X.29, also known as *XXX protocols,* define a set of protocols that may be used to establish a connection between a (character-mode, asynchronous) dumb terminal and a host computer over a network which conforms to CCITT's X.25 protocol. As shown in Figure 13.1, a terminal is connected to the network through a *Packet Assembler/Dissembler (PAD).* The PAD, as well as the host, are directly connected to an X.25 network. The fundamental operation performed by the PAD is, as its name suggests, to assemble a string of characters into a packet and to transmit the same to the remote host over the packet-switched data network. Similarly, it disassembles an incoming packet into a string of characters and delivers the same to the local terminal.

Recommendation X.28 defines procedures used by a terminal:

1. to establish a connection with the PAD (and indirectly with a named remote host),

---

[2]Note that the concept of Virtual Terminal is very similar to that of *Virtual Filestore* discussed earlier in Chapter 12.

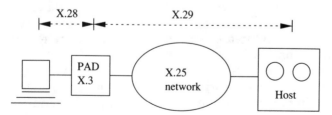

Figure 13.1 Use of Recommendations X.3, X.28, X.29 in providing remote terminal access.

2. to exchange user data with the PAD, which is transparently conveyed to (or from) the remote host, and

3. to exchange control information with the PAD.

Exchange of control information with the PAD permits a user terminal to read or alter a set of *PAD parameters*. These parameters stored in the PAD allow a terminal user (or an application program running in the remote computer) to configure the PAD operation so that the available terminal is able to communicate with the host and the application program.

Table 13.1 gives a partial list of PAD parameters specified by Recommendation X.3. Note that the PAD parameters may also be used to define the manner in which certain built-in PAD functions are used for presenting information to the user terminal, *Data forwarding* and *Line folding*, for instance. The parameters may be altered by the user terminal before or after the connection has been established. As an alternative, a consistent set of parameter values may be assigned and stored in the PAD in the form of one or more *profiles*. A suitable profile may then be selected at the time of connection establishment.

The protocol used for communication between the PAD and the application program is defined in Recommendation X.29. It, similarly, specifies the procedure used by a PAD to establish a connection with a host, or to exchange user data. Using X.29 procedures, a host may read or alter PAD parameters in much the same manner as a user does from a terminal. The X.29 protocol uses an X.25 virtual call (see Chapter 5) to transfer user data as well as control information in X.25 *User Data* packets. In particular, the *Q-bit* is used to distinguish user data ($Q = 0$) from control information ($Q = 1$).

The above approach supports a very limited class of terminals, viz. TTY-mode terminals, primarily because the terminal characteristics covered by the parameters is itself very limited. In order to provide greater flexibility, the number of parameters as well as their nature

TABLE 13.1   A Partial List of PAD Parameters

X.3 Parameter	Brief description
Echo control	Controls echo by the terminal
Data forwarding	Characters to be used as a signal to assemble and forward data
Idle timer delay	Idle time after which data is assembled and forwarded
Device control	Allows flow control by PAD using *XON/XOFF* characters
Break signal	Defines PAD action upon receiving *Break* signal
Line folding	Folding of line to terminal after a number of characters
Binary speed	Indicates line speed of terminal
Line-feed insertion	Controls insertion of line-feed character after carriage return
Line delete	Character used to signal line delete
...	

would have to be expanded or altered considerably. The other disadvantage is that access to an X.25 network is required.

13.3   Virtual Terminal Approach

The virtual terminal approach enables a terminal and an application to interact with each other through a virtual terminal, thereby permitting development of applications that are largely independent of the terminal characteristics. From the viewpoint of OSI, communication between two Application processes, or between an Application process and a terminal process,[3] is viewed as an Application layer function. Therefore, support for virtual terminal capability is provided as an Application layer service.

A virtual terminal (*VT*) is an abstraction of a terminal and consists of a standardized set of abstract information objects, each with a permissible set of operations. Communication between a real terminal and an application is conceptually viewed as operations resulting in a modification of the information objects, as shown in Figure 13.2. Together, the information objects and their definition are called *Conceptual Communication Area (CCA)*. Access to the CCA is controlled by a *Command Interpreter* or *VT service provider,* which provides processes with a means to modify and read the contents of CCA. The Application process maps the information contained in CCA and the permissible operations onto the terminal characteristics it assumes. Similarly, the terminal

---

[3]The terminal process is also an Application process. Therefore, the virtual terminal approach may also be used for communication between two Application processes or between two terminals.

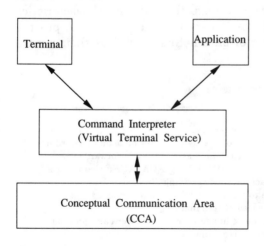

Figure 13.2 Virtual Terminal approach: a model.

process maps the virtual terminal onto its display, keyboard, mouse, etc. As a consequence, an application need not be conscious of the physical terminal characteristics and its operating procedures.

Since over a network the terminal process and the Application process generally reside in different open systems, a copy of the CCA must be maintained locally by each communicating process. The two copies, of course, must present a consistent view of their contents to the processes. To update the two copies consistently, and thereby convey the semantics of interaction between the terminal and the application, they communicate using a Virtual Terminal service. This view is illustrated in Figure 13.3, where it is also shown that the Command Interpreter of Figure 13.2 is realized using the *VT-service* and local mapping functions. An image of the CCA is maintained at each end, and may be updated or read using the local mapping function. From the viewpoint of Virtual Terminal service, a mapping function together with the corresponding (terminal or application) process is viewed as a *VT-service user*.

13.3.1 Basic Class Virtual Terminal

The Virtual Terminal Service and its realization using a VT protocol have been developed as standards within the OSI framework (see [ISO 9040] and [ISO 9041]). In order to support an ever increasing variety of terminals and applications, a number of classes of virtual terminals may be defined. Currently, however, only the Basic Class of VT is de-

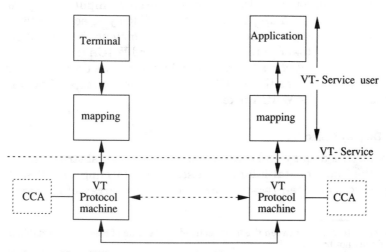

Figure 13.3 Use of VT-service to access the CCA.

TABLE 13.2   ISO's classification of virtual terminals.

Class	Data Type of elements	Display dimensions	Example of real terminal
Basic class	character	1, 2, or 3	TTY, screen-mode scroll mode
Basic class (extended)	character	2 or 3	data entry
Image class	photographic	2, or 3	Fax
Graphic class	geometric	2 or 3	graphic
Mixed mode class	character, photographic, and geometric	2 or 3	workstation

fined. ISO classifies terminals into several classes. These classes together with their characteristics are shown in Table 13.2. The Basic Class is capable of supporting character-mode terminals, where the characters are arranged in a one-, two- or three-dimensional array structure, respectively corresponding to a *line, page,* or a *book.*

The Basic class VT service supports two modes of interaction between its users, *Synchronous* mode and *Asynchronous* mode.[4] The synchronous mode (*S-mode*) supports two-way alternate interaction between the two VT-service users. It supports one *display object,* and any number of *control objects*[5] each of which is accessible by the two VT-service users. The display object, and possibly one or more control objects, are subject to access control by the *Write Access Variable* (*WAVAR*) token.

In the Asynchronous mode of communication, two display objects and any number of control objects are available for manipulation by the two users. At any time a user may update the display object associated with it. Access to control objects, if any, may or may not be controlled. Two access control tokens are defined, *WACI* and *WACA* (respectively, for *Write Access Connection Initiator* and *Acceptor*). The user initiating the *VT-Association* owns the WACI token whereas the responding VT-service user owns the WACA token.

13.3.2   Display Objects

We now discuss display and control objects. These are abstract objects and are the fundamental information structures forming the CCA. A display object is a one-, two- or three-dimensional array of elements,

---

[4]The mode of interaction between the users is fixed at the time of association establishment, and may not be changed.

[5]Display and Control objects are part of the Conceptual Communication Area, and will be discussed shortly.

each of which may be assigned a character value[6] and a secondary attribute, such as emphasis (bold, underline, etc.), foreground color, background color, and font. As an initial aid to understanding, one may view a display object as a virtual keyboard, display monitor, or a printer.

Associated with each display object there is a *display pointer* which identifies a particular array element. The semantics of the pointer is determined by the application, and is therefore not standardized. It may or may not correspond to a *cursor* on a user terminal. An operation on the pointer results in moving it to another array element. These operations are also controlled by access rights. The permissible operations on the display pointer are listed in Table 13.3. Assuming a three dimensional display object, with the current pointer location at (x,y,z), the pointer moves to

1. $(x + 1,y,z)$ using *implicit addressing,* whenever an update operation takes place on the current element (x,y,z),

2. (a,b,c) using *absolute explicit addressing,*

3. $(x + p,y + q,z + r)$, using *explicit addressing relative* to the current pointer location, or

4. (a,b,c), where a,b,c are determined relative to the current position and specified using a macro-operation. The details are summarized in Table 13.3.

There are a number of constraints on moving the pointer, particularly when a *window* corresponding to the display object is defined. For

---

[6]It is better known as character-box graphic element.

TABLE 13.3 Addressing Operations on a Display Object

Addressing operation	Parameters supplied	Resulting pointer location
Implicit	-	$(x + 1, y, z)$
Explicit (absolute)	(a, b, c)	(a, b, c)
Explicit (relative)	(p, q, r)	$(x + p, y + q, z + r)$
Explicit (macros):		
start	-	$(1, 1, 1)$
start-y	-	$(1, 1, z)$
start-x	-	$(1, y, z)$
next x-array	-	$(1, y + 1, z)$
next y-array	-	$(1, 1, z + 1)$
previous x-array	-	$(1, y - 1, z)$
next y-array	-	$(1, 1, z + 1)$
previous y-array	-	$(1, 1, z - 1)$

TABLE 13.4   Update Operations on Display Objects

Update operation	Parameters
text	character
repeat text	range-of-address, character-string
attribute change	secondary-attribute, range-of-address
erase	range-of-address, change-secondary-attribute

each dimension in the display object, a window size is specified. The upper edge of the current window is then defined by the position of the last array element that has been assigned a primary attribute using a *text* or *repeat text* operation (see the discussion below). The lower bound is determined with respect to this upper bound, and by the window size in each dimension. As a consequence, the window moves forward whenever a text insertion takes place beyond the upper edges of the window. Further, the window may not move backwards at all. The display pointer may be moved anywhere within the window or beyond the upper edges. If the window size is 0 along a dimension, then the pointer may not be moved backwards in that particular dimension.

The array elements may be manipulated in a number of ways. An array element is either implicitly or explicitly identified. The display pointer is affected in case of the first two operations.

1. A *text* operation results in the assignment of the specified character to the array element pointed to by the current pointer location.

2. A *repeat text* operation results in a range of array elements being updated with a string of characters (the latter is repeatedly used to fill the elements, as necessary).

3. An *attribute change* operation results in a range of array elements being assigned a secondary attribute specified in the operation.

4. An *erase* operation un-assigns the character assigned to each array element within the specified range of array elements, and possibly the associated secondary attributes.

The above operations are summarized in Table 13.4, together with their arguments.

Table 13.5 gives an example of a display object defined for possible use in A-mode (asynchronous, or two-way simultaneous) communication. Note that:

1. the display object, named DA, may be updated by the user process which owns the write access token, WACA;

2. the two-dimensional display object is truly a sequence of lines, each consisting of up to 80 characters;

TABLE 13.5   Definition of a Display Object: An Example

Display object parameter	Value
Name	DA
Access control	WACA
Dimensions	2
x-dimension:	
bound	80
addressing	higher only
absolute	no
window	0
y-dimension:	
bound	unbounded
addressing	higher only
absolute	no
window	0
Erase capability	no
Repertoire assignment	par-1
Font assignment	device-dependent
Foreground color assignment	device-dependent
Background color assignment	device-dependent

Note: par-1 is a parameter with an un-assigned value.

3. the window size is 0. Therefore, the display pointer may only be moved in the forward direction on the same line, or to the next line. Further, an erase operation is not permitted;

4. the repertoire assignment consists of a set of displayable and control characters. It is specified using an escape sequence which uniquely specifies the set of displayable and control characters (see [ISO 2022]). The default repertoire is <ESC> 2/8 4/0 which consists of ISO 646 characters. The 8-bit transparent character set is designated by <ESC> 2/5 2/15 4/2. In Table 13.5 the repertoire is not assigned. A value must be assigned before the display object can be used to define a virtual terminal.

While the semantics of display objects are not explicitly defined in the OSI framework, a display object is the primary means of transferring information between the users. Depending upon the write access controls, a user may write into its elements, while the other user may read its contents. For instance, the output from a keyboard may be written into the display object, and subsequently read by the application process user. Similarly, the output from an application, once written into a display object, may be displayed on a real terminal display. The mapping of information contained in a display object onto a real device is defined by the user process and stored in a *de-*

vice object. This mapping is known to the two communicating VT-service users.

Given the view that the display object is accessible to both users, the operations on the display object conceptually appear to take effect instantaneously. The fact, however, remains that the users are located in two different open systems. They, therefore, use the VT-service to update each other's copy of the display object. Thus, updates to the two copies of the display object, and to the control objects, do not take place instantaneously. This gives an opportunity to users to control the delivery of updates to the copy at the remote end. These delivery controls are discussed as part of VT-services in Section 13.4.

13.3.3 Control Objects

Control objects enable a user to convey control information to its peer user. A control object is conceptually a simple data structure, of the type integer, character string, boolean vector, symbolic, or transparent. The size of the data structure is relatively small. For instance, the size of the character string or of the boolean vector can be at most 16. Access to a control object may be controlled, in which case the user with the corresponding write access token, WAVAR, WACI, or WACA, may update its value.

The only operation that may be performed on a control object is that of updating its contents. The contents are updated as a whole.

With each control object there is an associated *trigger* mechanism, which may or may not be selected. If the trigger for a given control object is selected, then, whenever the user process updates the contents of the control object,

1. the corresponding display object is updated with all previously requested updates, and,

2. in case of S-mode of communication, an update to the control object results in the access control token, WAVAR, being transferred to the peer user.

An example of a control object is given in Table 13.6. This control object may be used to control *echoing* of characters, either locally or by the remote host. Obviously, echo control is meaningful only in the context of A-mode of communication. If its access control is WACA, then it is for the Association-*accepting* application process to decide, by suitably writing into it, whether echoing is to be performed locally or by the peer process. If the value stored in the *Echo* control object is *true,* then the terminal process displays updates to the display object on the terminal. Otherwise, inputs from the terminal process are echoed locally.

**TABLE 13.6 Definition of a
Control Object: An Example**

Control object parameter	Value
Name	Echo
Type-identifier	VT-ECHO
Access control	WACA
Priority	normal
Trigger	selected
Category	Boolean
Size	1

Any number of named control objects may be defined by the users. More generally, the semantics to be associated with the value stored in a control object is jointly determined by the users. Further, there is a default control object associated with each device object.

13.3.4 Device Objects

Device objects provide a mechanism for specifying the characteristics of real devices. Or, device objects are simply a user specification of how information stored in display and control objects is mapped onto real devices. Each device object is associated with one display object, one or more control objects, and one real device.

Consider, for instance, the device object given in Table 13.7. It is a specification of a device to be used as a default device in A-mode, unless a different device object is defined. The real device to be used as a display terminal must have a buffer capacity of at least one in each dimension, thereby implying that there are no constraints on the size of the display terminal associated with the display object, DA. The default control object is the only associated control object. It is initially as-

TABLE 13.7 Definition of a Device Object: An Example

Device object parameter	Value
Name	Device 1
Default-CO- initial-value	true
Min. x-array-length	1
Min. y-array-length	1
Display object	DA
Termination:	
event-list	$<< 1, < CR >>, "null" >, << 1, < LF >>, "null" >,$ $<< 1, < FF >>, "null" >, << 1, < VT >>, "null" >$
length	80

signed a value *true,* which may be taken to mean that the contents of the display object are being mapped onto the real device.

The *termination parameters,* both *event list* and *length,* define the events or conditions which enable an update to the associated display and control objects to take place. The event list in Table 13.7 is a collection of tuples, *<event,event - id>,* where an *event* is the text insertion of a character, *<CR>, <LF>, <FF>,* or *<VT>* from the repertoire of the display object DA. In case a termination control object (of the type integer) is defined and associated with the device object, then it is updated with the *event- id.* In this case since a termination control object is not defined, the event-id is *null.* The parameter, termination length, denotes the number of element updates after which the corresponding objects must be updated, unless one of the events, discussed above, occurs first.

13.3.5 Conceptual Communication Area

We now consider the CCA. The CCA consists of five sub-structures:

1. *CDS (Conceptual Data Store)* containing one or more display objects,

2. *CSS (Control, Signalling and Status Store),* which contains any number of control objects,

3. *ACS (Access Control Store),* which records which user owns the WAVAR access token in case of S-mode operation, and WACI and WACA access tokens in case of A-mode operation,

4. one or more device objects, and

5. *DSD (Data Structure Definition),* which contains the definitions of the above display objects, control objects, and device objects.

Figure 13.4 illustrates the components of a CCA, and the correspondence between them. It also shows the paths taken by user-data and control information. The CCA is initialized at the time of connection establishment with values drawn from a profile of the virtual terminal to be used over the connection.

13.3.6 VT Environment and VTE Profiles

The transfer of user data and control information, or equivalently manipulation of CCA objects, takes place within a *Virtual Terminal Environment (VTE).* A VTE is defined by a logically consistent set of *VTE parameter* values. The VTE parameters together completely describe:

1. the mode of communication, and the related write-access control tokens, and

2. the display, control, and device objects, together with the semantics associated with each object.

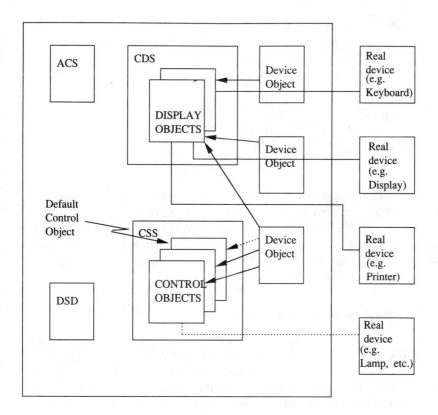

Figure 13.4 Components of the CCA and their relationship.

At any time, one and only one VT environment exists. It is initially negotiated between the users at the time of association establishment. Once established, it may be modified or totally replaced by another environment. The ability on the part of the users to modify or replace the VTE depends upon the availability of corresponding VT-service elements.

At the time of VTE negotiation, one may specify the value of each VTE parameter, and thereby, determine the complete VTE to be established. Alternatively, the negotiation is based upon a logically consistent set of VTE parameters that are pre-specified as part of a named and *registered VTE-profile*. In order to permit certain flexibility, one or more VTE parameters may be left unspecified. VTE parameters that are not assigned values are called VTE-profile *arguments*. Values of these argu-

TABLE 13.8   The Default A-mode VTE Profile

Objects	Names (with description)
Display objects	DA (see Table 13.5)
	DB (see Table 13.5, but
	with Access control = WACI)
Control objects	E (see Table 13.6)
Device objects	Device 1 (see Table 13.7)
	Device 2 (see Table 13.7, but
	with Display object = DB)

ments must be negotiated before the desired profile can be established as a *full-VTE*. Otherwise, the VTE continues to be a *draft-VTE*.

Two default VTE-profiles have been defined in [ISO 9040], one for each S-mode and A-mode of communication. Table 13.8 summarizes the default A-mode profile. Additional VTE-profiles may be defined by user groups or organizations and registered.[7]

13.4   Virtual Terminal Services

The Basic Class of Virtual Terminal Service offers a range of services to enable users to establish an association and to then exchange user data and control information through the Conceptual Communication Area. Such exchange is subject to write access control. More specifically, the following capabilities may be available (see also Table 13.9):

1. the means to establish an association between peer VT-service users. Such an association is called *VT-association*. As part of association establishment procedure, they negotiate and establish an initial VT environment including:
   (a) the mode of communication,
   (b) initial assignment of the WAVAR token, in case of S-mode of communication, and
   (c) the VTE-profile and its arguments.
   The use of optional services over the association in the form of functional units is also negotiated, provided these are available;
2. the means to transfer user data and control information. Such information, logically, updates the display and control objects in the CCA. Of course, all information is conveyed transparently by the VT-service provider using Presentation services. It thereby ensures that the semantics of all information is preserved;

---

[7]A number of profiles have been developed, or are being developed by user organizations (see [NIST 88] and [NIST 89], for instance).

TABLE 13.9   Virtual Terminal Service: Functional Units and Its Primitives

Functional unit	Facility	Service primitives	Type of service
Kernel	Establishment	VT-ASSOCIATE	confirmed
	Termination	VT-RELEASE	confirmed
		VT-U-ABORT	un-confirmed
		VT-P-ABORT	provider-initiated
	Delivery Control	VT-DELIVER	un-confirmed
		VT-ACK-RECEIPT	un-confirmed
	Access control	VT-GIVE-TOKENS	un-confirmed
		VT-REQUEST-TOKENS	un-confirmed
	Data Transfer	VT-DATA	un-confirmed
Switch Profile Negotiation	Switch Profile	VT-SWITCH-PROFILE	confirmed
Multiple Interaction Negotiation	Multiple Interaction Negotiation	VT-START-NEG	confirmed
		VT-END-NEG	confirmed
		VT-INVITE-NEG	un-confirmed
		VT-OFFER-NEG	un-confirmed
		VT-ACCEPT-NEG	un-confirmed
		VT-REJECT-NEG	un-confirmed
Negotiated Release	Termination	VT-RELEASE	confirmed
Urgent data	Data Transfer	VT-DATA	un-confirmed
Break	Interrupt	VT-BREAK	confirmed

3. the means to control the delivery of user data and control information;
4. to obtain and provide acknowledgments to user data;
5. the means to request or give the access control token WAVAR, in the case of S-mode of communication;
6. the means to re-negotiate the VT environment; and
7. the means to terminate the association in an organized manner, or abruptly by aborting the association.

13.4.1   Association Phases

Figure 13.5 summarizes the major states, or phases, of a VT-Association. Initially, the association is *idle*. Subsequently, it may move to *Data transfer* state directly, or through the *Negotiation quiescent* state in case some of the VTE parameters are not completely negotiated. In Data transfer state, or in the Negotiation quiescent state, if it becomes necessary to re-negotiate the VTE, a transition to the *Negotiation active* state is made. In Negotiation active state users negotiate a new VTE using the procedure, *Multiple Interaction Negotiation*. The procedure allows users to update values of VTE parameters by making offers or

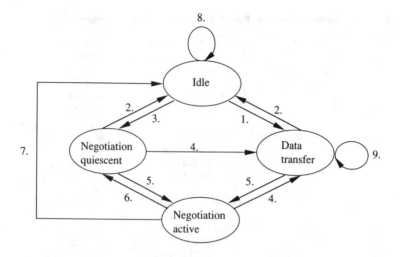

1. Successful establishment of Association
2. Release or Abort of Association
3. Successful establishment of Association, but with VTE partially established
4. Successful establishment of VTE
5. Start of VTE negotiation
6. Partially established VTE
7. Association Abort
8. Unsuccessful establishment of Association
9. Successful switching of VTE-profile

Figure 13.5 The phases of a VT-Association.

counter offers, and to accept or reject offers. Alternatively, while continuing to remain within the Data transfer state, users may simply switch to a different VTE-profile, without going through the above elaborate negotiation procedure. Of course, the association may be aborted from any state. But, it may be released only if the association is in Data transfer or Negotiation quiescent states.

Constraints regarding service primitives that may be issued when the association is in a given state, are summarized in Table 13.10. There are additional constraints on initiating VT-services. In S-mode, a confirmed service (except *VT-BREAK*) and the unconfirmed service, *VT-DELIVER*, may be initiated by a VT-service user only if it owns the write access token, WAVAR. Further, no service may be initiated by a VT-user if it has initiated a confirmed service for which the corresponding confirm primitive is outstanding. Similarly, if a VT-user has received an indication primitive, it must issue a response primitive, if applicable, before initiating another service.

TABLE 13.10   Services Available to Users in Each Phase of VT-Association

Service	Idle	Data Transfer	Negotiation Active	Negotiation Quiescent
VT-ASSOCIATE	yes	-	-	-
VT-RELEASE	-	yes	-	yes
VT-U-ABORT	-	yes	yes	yes
VT-P-ABORT	-	yes	yes	yes
VT-DELIVER	-	yes	-	-
VT-ACK-RECEIPT	-	yes	-	-
VT-GIVE-TOKENS	-	yes	yes	yes
VT-REQUEST-TOKENS	-	yes	yes	yes
VT-DATA	-	yes	-	-
VT-SWITCH-PROFILE	-	yes	-	yes
VT-START-NEG	-	yes	-	yes
VT-END-NEG	-	-	yes	-
VT-INVITE-NEG	-	-	yes	-
VT-OFFER-NEG	-	-	yes	-
VT-ACCEPT-NEG	-	-	yes	-
VT-REJECT-NEG	-	-	yes	-
VT-BREAK	-	yes	-	-

13.4.2 Functional Units

Many of the above Basic Class VT-services are optional. These services have been grouped into a number of *functional units,* thereby providing corresponding capabilities to users. Thus, services within a functional unit are all supported or not supported at all. Similarly, use of optional services is negotiated in the form of functional units rather than as individual service elements. The available functional units are listed in Table 13.9 together with the services that constitute each functional unit. A brief description of the functional units is given below.

1. An association may be released by any user using *VT-RELEASE* primitives. However, the user responding to the VT-RELEASE indication has no option except to release the Association. *Negotiated release,* on the other hand, enables a VT-user to reject the release of the association. The corresponding functional unit is optionally made available by the VT-service provider and its use must be specifically negotiated as part of association establishment.

2. The *Urgent data* functional unit provides to a user the capability to convey small amounts of user data to its peer VT-user on an urgent basis, and possibly overtaking data transfers which may have been requested earlier. This capability may be used to interrupt the peer user without disrupting prior data exchanges.

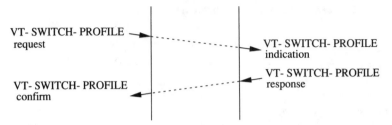

Figure 13.6   Illustration of switching of VTE-profile.

3. The *Break* functional unit also provides the users with a means to interrupt a peer VT-user. The effect of invoking the corresponding primitive, VT-BREAK, is very different. The service provider may discard all previous undelivered data exchanges between the users. Data transfer may subsequently begin only after the protocol machines of the service provider have synchronized themselves to an earlier state.

4. The functional units, *Switch-Profile* and *Multiple Interaction Negotiation,* provide users with the capability to establish a new VTE-profile. These are discussed in the next sub-section.

13.4.3   Re-Negotiation of VTE-Profile

The *switch-profile* capability enables VT-users to switch to a new VTE-profile using a single confirmed service, *VT-SWITCH-PROFILE.* The interaction takes the form of a proposal made by a VT-user, which is then either accepted or rejected. The proposal names a VTE-profile and, where required, its argument values. The VTE-profile arguments are those that do not have a pre-assigned value as part of the VTE-profile definition. The profile itself is not negotiated, but the offered argument values are negotiated between the users and the service provider. Figure 13.6 illustrates the procedure to switch to a new VTE-profile. The VT-SWITCH-PROFILE primitives include the name and arguments of the profile, and the outcome of the procedure, together with the reason in case of failure.

Multiple interaction Negotiation permits users to define and re-negotiate a new VTE-profile and its parameters. As its name implies, the procedure requires multiple interactions between the users and the service provider. The primitives, *VT-START-NEG, VT-END-NEG, VT-INVITE-NEG, VT-OFFER-NEG, VT-ACCEPT-NEG,* and *VT-REJECT-NEG,* may be used to arrive at a definition of a new VTE-profile. These primitives may only be invoked in a particular sequence. The possible sequences are given in Figure 13.7. An example sequence is illustrated in Figure 13.8. Further, there are additional constraints on who may issue

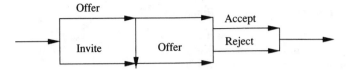

Figure 13.7 Permissible sequences under multiple interaction negotiation.

these primitives. The constraints are different for the two modes of communication, S-mode and A-mode. In S-mode, the user with the WAVAR access right may issue the primitives. In A-mode the initiator of the multiple interaction negotiation procedure may issue the first VT-INVITE-NEG or VT-OFFER-NEG primitives and is also the one that ends the negotiation with a VT-END-NEG request primitive.

13.4.4 Association Establishment

As part of association establishment, a number of parameters, including the VTE are negotiated. Table 13.11 lists the parameters that may be negotiated. If a parameter is not negotiated, the corresponding default value is assumed.

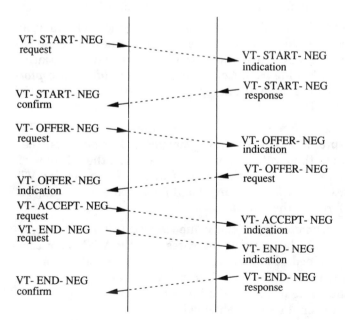

Figure 13.8 Illustration of multiple interaction negotiation.

TABLE 13.11 Parameters of VT-ASSOCIATE Primitives

Parameters	Present in which primitives
Calling Application Entity title	request, indication
Called Application Entity title	request, indication
Responding Application Entity title	response, confirm
VT-Class	request, indication
Functional units	all
Mode	request, indication
WAVAR owner	all
VTE-profile name	request, indication
VTE-profile argument offered list	request, indication
VTE-profile argument values list	response, confirm
Result	response, confirm
Failure reason (user rejected)	response, confirm
Failure reason (provider rejected)	confirm

1. The *Application entity titles* are those of the communicating entities, and are processed in accordance with the procedure for association establishment (see Section 9.2).

2. The *VT-Class* specifies the class of VT-service, which in this case, is *BASIC*.

3. The optional parameter, *Functional Units,* permits users to negotiate the use of available functional units (see Table 13.9).

4. The parameter, *Mode,* allows users to select the mode of communication. If the selected mode is S-mode, then users negotiate the initial owner of the WAVAR access token. The association-initiating user specifies its value as *initiator-side, acceptor-side,* or *acceptor-chooses.* In the latter case, the accepting user determines the initial owner of WAVAR access token.

5. *VTE-profile-name* forms the basis for negotiating the initial VTE. If the VTE-profile has one or more unspecified arguments, then users negotiate their values. For each parameter, the initiator offers a value, list of values, or a range of values. The accepting VT-user supplies a value for each argument for which a list or range of values is offered by the initiator.

6. The *Result* parameter takes the value *success, failure,* or *success-with-warning.* The latter value indicates that the VTE is not completely determined. In that case, the resulting state of the VT-Association is Negotiation quiescent. Subsequently, users must negotiate the value of the remaining VTE-profile arguments, before Data transfer state is established.

7. The reason for failure to establish the association is given in the *Failure reason* parameter.

13.4.5 Data Transfer

Data may be exchanged between VT-users using *VT-DATA* primitives. Each data transfer causes an update to a display object and/or control objects.[8] VT-DATA primitives contain two parameters:

1. *VT-object-update,* which is a sequence of updates to display and control objects. Each item identifies the object and the specific update operation, together with user data; and

2. the optional parameter, *echo-now,* used only in A-mode. It indicates to the peer user whether it is alright for it to echo the updates onto its terminal soon after processing this update.

The echo-now parameter is used by the remote VT-user to control echoing by the VT-user local to the input/display terminal. It has relevance only when remote echo has been enabled.

13.4.6 Delivery Control

Users may control delivery of updates to the display objects, or equivalently to the peer user. Four different forms of delivery control are available. These affect issuing of VT-DATA indication primitives corresponding to updates to display and control objects. The specific form of delivery control to be used is defined as part of the current VT environment.

1. *Implicit delivery,* where outstanding VT-DATA indication primitives, if any, are issued before processing or completing some other service. All pending VT-DATA indication primitives are issued by the service provider before issuing the corresponding indication or confirm primitive, VT-RELEASE, VT-SWITCH-PROFILE or VT-START-NEG, for instance. In S-mode, a similar implicit delivery takes place before the control token WAVAR is re-assigned to the peer user.

2. *No-delivery control* implies that except for implicit delivery, there are no delivery controls available to the users. Of course, users may still use a control object with its trigger mechanism selected to effect instantaneous delivery of user data.

3. *Simple delivery control* may be exercised by users to ensure that all updates to the display objects and control objects are delivered

---

[8]The primitive VT-DATA is also used to transfer both *normal* and *urgent* data. *Priority* of data transfers is determined by the priority associated with each control object. The priority of a display object is normal, whereas the priority of a control object may be normal, high or urgent. If data contained in VT-DATA primitives is to update a control object with urgent priority, then it is delivered as soon as possible, in spite of delivery control and flow control.

immediately. They do so using VT-DELIVER primitives. A VT-DE-LIVER indication primitive when issued by the service provider also has the effect of indicating an end to the sequence of data updates. A user may also request in a VT-DELIVER request primitive that an acknowledgement be provided by the peer user. The receiving VT-user's acknowledgement is contained in a *VT-ACK-RECEIPT* primitive (see Figure 13.9(a)).

4. *Quarantine delivery control,* if negotiated, provides the user with simple delivery control with the added qualification that the service provider may not deliver any VT-DATA before being specifically requested to do so. The service provider may deliver, in fact, the *net-effect* of all changes to the display and control objects (see Figure 13.9(b)).

Net-effecting may be used to reduce the amount of data exchanged, and to enable a terminal user to make corrections, if any, before the input is presented to an application.

13.4.7 Access Control

In A-mode of Virtual Terminal operation, there are no controls on who may issue a service primitive. In other words, each VT-user owns the required write access token, WACI or WACA. These are not re-assigned. But, in S-mode, the write access token, WAVAR, is owned by at most one VT-user at any time. The ownership of WAVAR token is established soon after the VT-Association is established or after a VT-BREAK service is completed successfully. The token may be re-assigned using *VT-GIVE-TOKENS* primitives. *VT-REQUEST-TO-KENS* primitives may be used to request the peer VT-user to give the tokens. Alternatively, the ownership of WAVAR token is automatically transferred to the peer user whenever a VT-user updates a control object with its trigger enabled.

13.5 Virtual Terminal Protocol

The Basic Class Virtual Terminal service is implemented using a protocol which operates between two protocol machines in the Application layer. The machines are also called *Virtual Terminal Protocol Machines (VTPMs)*. While from the VT-service point of view, the virtual terminal is modelled as a shared Conceptual Communication Area, or CCA, each VT protocol machine includes a local realization of the CCA (see Figure 13.10). Thus, whenever a user invokes a service primitive, the corresponding VTPM not only updates the local copy of the CCA, but also communicates the updates to its peer VTPM to enable the latter to update its copy of the CCA.

Additionally, each VTPM maintains a copy of the CCA contents, as existing at the time of the establishment of the current VTE. This copy

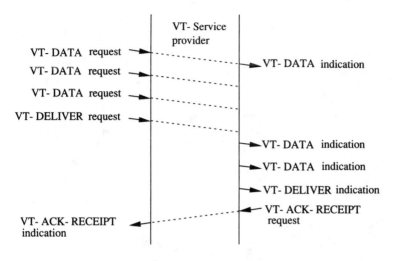

(a) Simple delivery control.

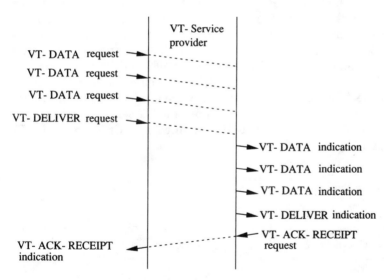

(b) Quarantine delivery control.

Figure 13.9 Illustration of two forms of delivery control.

of the CCA, also known as *reset-context,* is used to synchronize the protocol machines soon after a break operation is initiated by a user. The reset-context is changed whenever a new VTE is established.

The structure of an Application entity which uses Virtual Terminal capability is shown in Figure 13.11. The user element is either the ter-

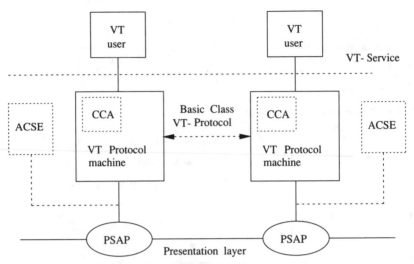

Figure 13.10 A model of the Virtual Terminal Protocol.

minal user or the application it accesses. It includes the mapping from the CCA onto the real devices. The *Virtual Terminal Service Element* (*VTSE*) is the protocol machine responsible for providing the VT-service. In Figure 13.11 we also show that a VTSE service element uses the Association control service element (ACSE) and Presentation services to implement the VT-protocol.[9] The specific services that it requires of the ACSE and Presentation service are listed in Table 13.12.

The abstract syntax required for supporting VT-services includes the syntax of protocol-data-units (PDUs) defined by ACSE protocol, VT-protocol, and by the application itself.

---

[9]See Chapters 8 and 9.

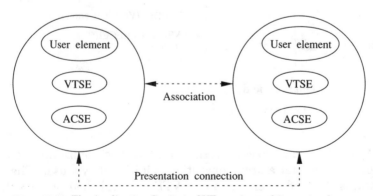

Figure 13.11 The Application Context of VT-service and its protocol.

TABLE 13.12 ACSE and Presentation Services Required by the VT-Protocol

Functional unit	ACSE services	Presentation services
Kernel	A-ASSOCIATE A-RELEASE A-ABORT A-P-ABORT	P-DATA P-TYPED-DATA P-TOKEN-GIVE P-TOKEN-PLEASE
Switch Profile Negotiation		P-SYNC-MAJOR
Multiple Interaction Negotiation		P-SYNC-MAJOR
Negotiated Release		
Urgent data		P-EXPEDITED-DATA
Break		P-RESYNCHRONIZE

13.5.1 VT-Protocol Subsets

Three subsets of Basic Class VT-protocol have been defined (see [ISO 9041]) with a view to support optional functional units. These subsets are *VT-A, VT-B,* and *VT-C.* The procedures included in each of them are summarized in Table 13.13, and are discussed in the next sub-section. Depending upon the functional units requested by the VT-users, the protocol machines select the subset which meets user requirements.

13.5.2 VT-Protocol Procedures

The VT-protocol defines the procedures to be followed regarding Association establishment, termination, abort, data transfer, delivery control, dialogue control, and re-negotiation of VT environment. Dialogue control is applicable only in S-mode of communication. We discuss

TABLE 13.13 Subsets of the VT-Protocol

Protocol subset	Protocol procedures
VT-A	association establishment association termination data transfer delivery control dialogue management error handling
VT-B	those of VT-A, above profile switch negotiation
VT-C	those of VT-B, above multiple interaction negotiation

some of the procedures.

1. Association establishment,
2. Association release,
3. transfer of data with normal, high or urgent priority, and
4. re-negotiation of VT environment, including the use of major synchronization points.

In doing so we also make references to procedures for:

1. control of write access tokens, and the use of supporting *data, major,* and *release tokens* relating to the Session layer,
2. delivery control, and
3. the break procedure and consequent re-synchronization.

13.5.3 Association Establishment

The procedure for establishing a VT-Association is illustrated in Figure 13.12(a). The protocol-data-units, *ASQ* and *ASR* (for association request and response), convey the semantics of *VT-ASSOCIATE* primitives. One of the parameters of the PDUs, *result,* as indicated earlier, may take the value *success, failure,* or *success-with-warning.* The two sequences given in Figures 13.12(b) and (c) illustrate failure to establish the association due to rejection by the responding VTPM or by the responding VT-user, respectively. In the case where the Association is established successfully, the *reset-context* is established using the initial contents of the control and display objects. Otherwise, if the result is success-with-warning, the reset-context is stored only after the full-VTE is established in Negotiation quiescent state.

The PDUs, ASQ and ASR, are conveyed in A-ASSOCIATE primitives. Once the association is established, the collection of Presentation services (and by implication the Session services) available for use by the VTPMs is determined (see also Table 13.12).

With the establishment of the association, the availability of Session layer tokens is also determined. These are summarized in Table 13.14. Note that data token is available only in S-mode of VT operation. The major and release tokens are required only if re-negotiation of VTE and negotiated release are agreed to. The ownership of the write access WAVAR token is equivalent to owning all available Session layer tokens. In A-mode operation, the available major and release tokens are always transferred together between the two VTPMs.

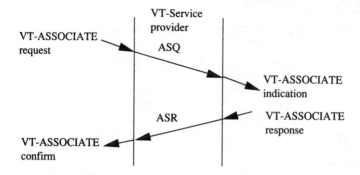

(a) Successful establishment.

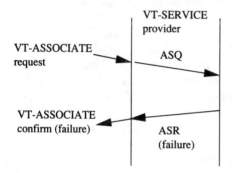

(b) Rejection by the responding VTPM.

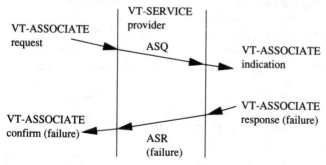

(c) Rejection by the responding VT-user.

Figure 13.12 Establishment of a VT-Association.

TABLE 13.14   Available Session Layer Tokens in Different Modes of VT- Service

VT Functional Unit	S-mode	A-mode
Kernel	data	-
Switch profile neg.	major	major
Multiple interaction neg.	major	major
Negotiated release	release	release
Urgent data	-	-
Break	-	-

13.5.4   Association Release

A VT-Association is terminated by an abort procedure either by the service provider or by a VT-user. Such a termination possibly results in loss of data. Alternatively, its release may be orderly and non-destructive. The release may even be negotiated provided the corresponding service is available. The latter two possibilities are illustrated in Figure 13.13(a) and (b). There we have also shown that all undelivered data is delivered before release actually takes place. The figures assume that, in case of S-mode, the VTPM initiating the release owns the release token and that the corresponding PDU, RLQ (for Release request) does not collide with any other PDU.

In A-mode, the release operation may be initiated by either user. However, the actual release starts only after the release token has been re-assigned to the initiating-VTPM. The VTPMs use the related PDUs, RTQ and GTQ (for Request Token and Give Token request) to request or give the token. This is illustrated in Figure 13.13(c).

If the RLQ PDU collides with another PDU, then the release procedure may fail. In Figure 13.13 (d) the RLQ PDU is shown to collide with the PDU, DLQ (for Deliver request), containing a request for acknowledgement. The responding VTPM ignores the RLQ PDU, whereas the initiating VTPM considers the release operation to have failed as soon as it detects collision. (For details on other possible release sequences, see [ISO 9041].)

The PDUs RLQ and RLR are conveyed by A-RELEASE primitives of the ACSE service elements, while the PDUs used to obtain tokens, RTQ and GTQ, are conveyed in P-TOKEN-PLEASE and P-TOKEN-GIVE primitives.

13.5.5   Data Transfer

The procedure for data transfer is illustrated in Figure 13.14(a) through (c). Clearly, only some of the possible sequences are considered. Figure 13.14 (a) illustrates transfer of data with normal priority in S-mode. It assumes that simple delivery control is in effect, and that an acknowledgement is sought by the initiating VT-user. In Figure 13.14(b), data is

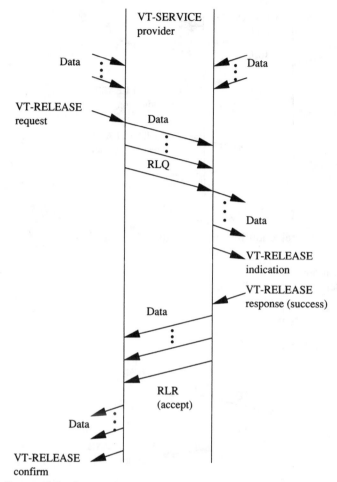

(a) Successful release when the initiator holds the token.

Figure 13.13   Release of a VT-Association.

being written to a control object with its trigger selected. Note how the write access WAVAR token, together with all available Session layer tokens, are transferred automatically to the peer VTPM.

In Figure 13.14(c) transfer of data with different priority is illustrated. Three distinct PDUS, *NDQ, HDQ,* and *UDQ* are used to transfer data with normal, high, or urgent priority, respectively. Note how the sequence of data transfers may not be preserved. This is made possible since the PDUS, NDQ HDQ and UDQ, are conveyed in different Presentation primitives, viz. P-DATA, P-TYPED-DATA and P-EXPE-DITED-DATA.

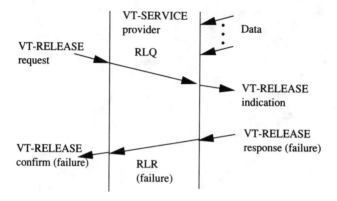

(b) Release rejection by the responding VT-user.

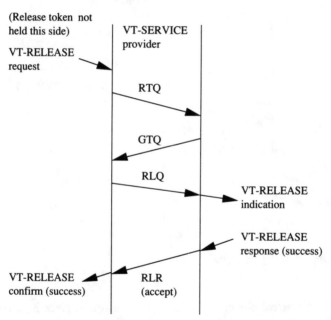

(c) Successful release when the initiator does not hold the token.

Figure 13.13 (*Continued*)

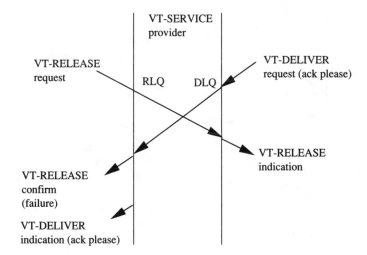

(d) Collision of release with request for data acknowledgement.

Figure 13.13 (*Continued*)

13.5.6   Re-Negotiation of VTE

The VT environment may be re-negotiated using VT-SWITCH-PRO-FILE or Multiple Interaction Negotiation procedure. Figure 13.15 illustrates the procedure to switch to a new VTE profile in A-mode of operation. First, all user data awaiting transfer must be forwarded before switching can take place. Further, if the initiating VTPM does not own the supporting major token, then it must obtain it. The PDUs, *SPQ* and *SPR* (for Switch Profile request and response), carry the semantics of VT-SWITCH-PROFILE primitives. These PDUs are mapped onto the supporting P-SYNC-MAJOR primitives.

With the switching of VTE profile, the VTPMs re-establish the reset-context. This context is used to re-initialize the Association in case a user initiates a *break* procedure, illustrated in Figure 13.16. The corresponding PDUs, *BKQ* and *BKR,* are mapped onto P-RESYNCHRO-NIZE primitives using the *restart* option (see Chapter 7 as well). In S-mode, the WAVAR token is re-assigned as determined by the VT-users. In A-mode, however, the supporting Session layer tokens are assigned to the initiating VTPM.

13.5.7   VT-Protocol-Data-Units

Table 13.15 summarizes the correspondence between VT-service primitives and protocol data units exchanged between VTPMs. As discussed

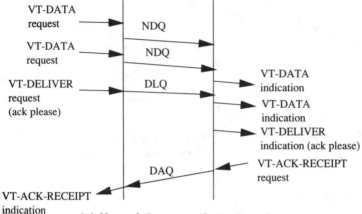

(a) Normal data transfer in S-mode.

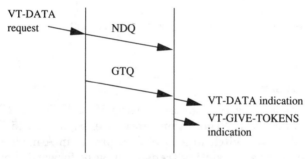

(b) Update of control object with trigger selected.

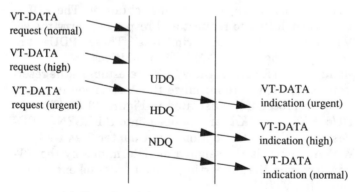

(c) Transfer of data with different priority.

Figure 13.14 Data transfer procedures.

above, a VTPM may exchange a number of related PDUs before exchanging PDUs corresponding to the service initiated by users.

The structure and contents of the protocol-data-units defined by the VT-protocol is formally defined using the ASN.1 notation in [ISO 9041].

The PDUs of the VT-protocol are transferred using ACSE and Presentation services (see also Table 13.12). In particular, Table 13.16 summarizes the manner in which the VT-protocol uses the lower layer services to transfer its PDUs.

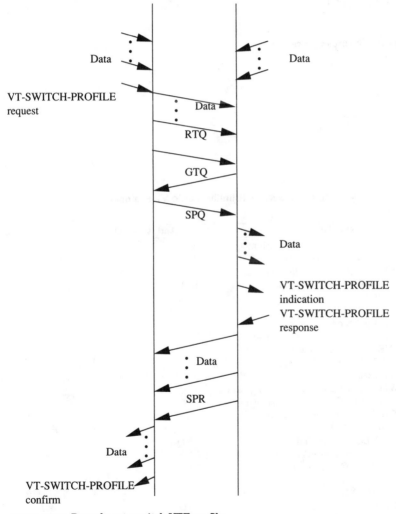

Figure 13.15 Procedure to switch VTE profile.

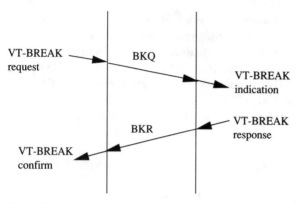

Figure 13.16 The break procedure.

TABLE 13.15 **Mapping of VT-Service Primitives onto VT-Protocol-Data-Units**

VT-service primitive	Related VT-PDUs
VT-ASSOCIATE request, indication	ASQ
VT-ASSOCIATE response, confirm	ASR
VT-RELEASE request, indication	RLQ
VT-RELEASE response, confirm	RLR
VT-U-ABORT request, indication	AUQ
VT-P-ABORT indication	APQ
VT-DELIVER request, indication	DLQ
VT-ACK-RECEIPT request, indication	DAQ
VT-GIVE-TOKENS request, indication	GTQ
VT-REQUEST-TOKENS request, indication	RTQ
VT-DATA request, indication	NDQ, HDQ, UDQ
VT-SWITCH-PROFILE request, indication	SPQ
VT-SWITCH-PROFILE response, confirm	SPR
VT-START-NEG request, indication	SNQ
VT-START-NEG response, confirm	SNR
VT-END-NEG request, indication	ENQ
VT-END-NEG response, confirm	ENR
VT-INVITE-NEG request, indication	NIQ
VT-OFFER-NEG request, indication	NOQ
VT-ACCEPT-NEG request, indication	NAQ
VT-REJECT-NEG request, indication	NJQ
VT-BREAK request, indication	BKQ
VT-BREAK response, confirm	BKR

13.6   Summary

With availability of a variety of computing resources on a computer network, it is possible to access these resources from different locations using terminals. As it turns out, a large number of terminal types are in use today. The purpose of virtual terminal protocols is to provide a uniform mechanism by which any terminal can communicate with any host or application, without causing a significant burden on either. The approach discussed in this chapter is to define a Virtual Terminal with a generic set of capabilities. Each application provides an interface to the Virtual Terminal, while a physical terminal interacts with an application by looking like the Virtual Terminal to the application.

Another approach supported by the virtual terminal protocols is a parametric one, where related parameters of terminals supported by the application are defined by the application itself or by the terminal user.

The Virtual Terminal protocol defines the procedures to be followed in using Virtual Terminal services. Both, Virtual Terminal services and protocols have been discussed in this chapter.

TABLE 13.16   Use of Lower Services to Transfer VT PDUs

VT PDU	Supporting service primitive
ASQ	A-ASSOCIATE request, indication
ASR	A-ASSOCIATE response, confirm
RLQ	A-RELEASE request, indication
RLR	A-RELEASE response, confirm
AUQ	A-ABORT request, indication
APQ	A-P-ABORT indication
DLQ	P-DATA request, indication
DAQ	P-TYPED-DATA request, indication
GTQ	P-TOKEN-GIVE request, indication
RTQ	P-TOKEN-PLEASE request, indication
NDQ	P-DATA request, indication
HDQ	P-TYPED-DATA
UDQ	P-EXPEDITED-DATA request, indication
SPQ	P-SYNC-MAJOR request, indication
SPR	P-SYNC-MAJOR response, confirm
SNQ	P-SYNC-MAJOR request, indication
SNR	P-SYNC-MAJOR response, confirm
ENQ	P-SYNC-MAJOR request, indication
ENR	P-SYNC-MAJOR response, confirm
NIQ	P-DATA request, indication
NOQ	P-DATA request, indication
NAQ	P-DATA request, indication
NJQ	P-DATA request, indication
BKQ	P-RESYNCHRONIZE request, indication
BKR	P-RESYNCHRONIZE response, confirm

14

Other
Applications and
Related Issues

Once OSI based networks become accessible to many people and organizations it is natural for a variety of new applications to develop. Remote execution of programs and their manipulation is supported using Job Transfer and Manipulation services. Exchange of documents between organizations that use different document preparation systems is feasible using the standard Office Document Architecture and Interchange Format. Remote access to data bases and distributed transaction processing are other applications that may be supported in an OSI environment. These applications, together with management and security issues, are discussed in this chapter.

14.1 Job Transfer and Manipulation

14.1.1 Introduction

The term *job* has traditionally been used to denote a request for processing to be carried out in batch mode by a central system. Such jobs are submitted at the local site, or through a remote job entry terminal, as a deck of cards or a tape containing JCL commands, program(s), and data. The processed output is made available to the user in the form of printed reports or on tapes. In an OSI environment, where a number of open systems are interconnected, a user may initiate a job from any open system, and have it processed at one or more connected open systems using files located at other systems. The output may be directed to peripherals or to files located at other systems.

The purpose of *Job Transfer and Manipulation (JTM)* facility is to provide a set of communication-related services which can be used to support processing of jobs in an OSI environment (see [ISO 8831] and [ISO 8832]). The JTM protocol covers movement of not only job-related input/output data and programs, but also data concerning monitoring and manipulation of related activities.

14.1.2 JTM Architecture

A major building block of the JTM is a *work specification* which is a conceptual data structure used to specify the work to be done. It contains fields which may be used (among others):

1. to identify the open systems that are to perform portions of the work,

2. to specify the type of work to be performed by the target open systems,

3. to define the nature of reports to be made available, and

4. to specify the locations to which reports are to be sent.

The work specification is created by the JTM service provider from parameters supplied by the initiating user in a *J-INITIATE* request primitive. Thereafter, the JTM service provider takes full responsibility to ensure that the job is processed by the target systems. A key feature of the JTM protocol is that this responsibility for progressing the activity is passed over to other open systems, as work progresses.

As part of the JTM protocol, *transfer elements,*[1] each containing a part of the work specification, are exchanged between concerned open systems. In doing so, an open system takes responsibility for the part of the work specification contained in the transfer element. When a transfer element is received, the concerned JTM service user may provide a document, accept a document for printing or display, or process one or more documents and dispose of the resulting documents in a specified manner. From the viewpoint of the JTM service, a *document* is a collection of data which forms a unit of interaction between the JTM service provider and the users. It also forms the basis for creating a work specification.

The JTM facility provides for transfer of documents to a system for processing, together with necessary instructions on how the resulting documents should be handled or disposed of. The specific processing to be carried out by a system is of no consequence to the JTM service provider and its protocol.

---

[1]These are one or more protocol-data-units that together convey a part of the work specification.

The term *OSI job* is used to refer to the total work on all open systems arising directly or indirectly from an *initial* work specification. An OSI job may, in the process of being executed, spawn a number of *OSI subjobs,* which in turn may also spawn other OSI subjobs.

The JTM *architecture* defines the notion of an *agency.* An agency is an abstraction of an open system viewed only from the point of providing or using JTM services. The role of each agency, however, is assigned relative to each job. An *initiation agency* causes a work specification to be created. Every other system participating in processing the corresponding work specification takes on the role of a *source agency, execution agency* or a *sink agency.*

1. A source agency can provide a named document for inclusion in a work specification. The document provided is either locally stored, or is obtained from another system using a file transfer protocol, FTAM for example.

2. A sink agency can receive a document and dispose of it by either printing it or simply filing it. Such a document may have resulted from processing a part of the work specification.

3. An execution agency is any part of an open system which acts as a sink for documents first and then, after processing, acts as a source for related documents.

The JTM service primitives most often used are *J-INITIATE, J-GIVE* and *J-DISPOSE.* A work specification is created by the JTM service provider from parameters of a J-INITIATE request primitive. A source agency is accessed by the JTM service provider through the J-GIVE indication primitive, while a sink agency is provided with a document for disposal using the J-DISPOSE indication service primitive. An execution agency is accessed using a J-DISPOSE indication followed by J-GIVE indication primitives.

In the normal mode of operation, all necessary documents are collected from source agencies and made available to an execution agency. After processing is complete, the documents produced by an execution agency are transferred to another sink or execution agency. Processing of an OSI job, as characterized by its work specification, is thus carried out through an arbitrary sequence of J-GIVE and J-DISPOSE primitives. The processing of an OSI job is illustrated in Figure 14.1.

14.1.3 Related Issues

Issuing of JTM service primitives and transfer of corresponding transfer elements takes place as one or more atomic actions (see Section 9.5) resulting in partial or complete protection against application and communication failure. The JTM service standard defines a number of lev-

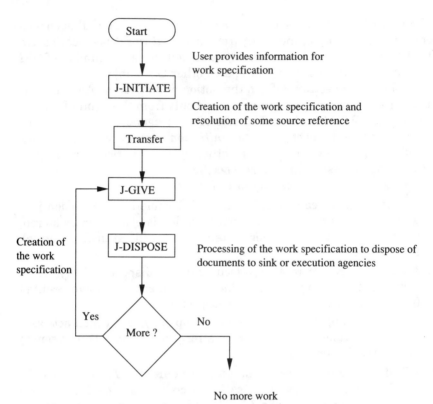

Figure 14.1 The processing of a work specification in JTM.

els of commitment. The highest level is termed *Completion,* where the entire OSI job is treated as an atomic action. If commitment takes place, then it implies that all related work has been completed and secured. Otherwise, the entire processing is rolled back. This is also referred to as *on-line processing.*

The lowest level of commitment is *Provider-Acceptance.* Here, commitment of the atomic action simply results in securing the work specification created by the service provider. There is no guarantee that other open systems have been accessed. This level of commitment is also called *off-line processing.*

The JTM facility has a provision whereby a user may monitor the progress of an OSI job submitted earlier. Upon request from the user at submission time, the JTM service provider can create reports and deliver them to one or more OSI job *monitors.* The initiating user may enquire about the progress of the job from these monitors. Alternatively, it may identify itself to be the monitor to which all reports are sent.

Once a job has been submitted for processing, the initiating user may at a later time manipulate the work specification in a limited manner. These operations include terminating the job prematurely, or modifying one or more parameters in the work specification. For more details see [ISO 8831] and [ISO 8832].

14.2 Office Document Architecture

14.2.1 Introduction

A common use of communication facilities by an organization is to exchange information. Frequently, the information originates in the form of a document, for example letter, invoice, form, or a report. The *Office Document Architecture (ODA)* recognizes such a need, and therefore, provides a framework in which information in the form of documents can be exchanged between open systems (see [ISO 8613-1] as well as other parts). During its exchange, the ODA preserves information about editing and formatting of the document, and its presentation, as envisaged by the originator of the document. Further, it permits documents to contain text, images, graphics and sound (with future extensions for spreadsheet, etc.).

Editing pertains to creation of a document and to changes in its structure or contents. Formatting determines the layout of the document, or the appearance of its contents on a paper or video screen. Presentation is the process by which a document is rendered on paper or screen. A given document may or may not be in a form which can be further processed by way of editing or formatting. Therefore, a document is classified as one of the following types:

1. *processable form,* if the document can be edited or re-formatted,
2. *formatted form,* if it is in a form ready for presentation, as originally intended, or
3. *formatted-processable form,* if it can be presented or edited and re-formatted before presentation.

Structuring of a document is a key concept in ODA. A document is divided and further subdivided into smaller parts called *objects*. An object which is not subdivided further is called a *basic object*. Thus, a structured document can be treated as a tree, where each node represents an object. The subdivision may be on the basis of whether the document is *logically* or *physically* structured. The logical structure is created based on the meaning of the information in the document, while the physical structure is based on its layout. Note that these two structures provide alternative but complementary views of the same document.

For instance, a document may contain a title, an abstract, one or more sections (each containing a section title followed by one or more paragraphs), and a list of references. The physical structure of the same document may be that it consists of a title page, followed by one or more article pages. Each section, and the list of references, begins on a new page. Further, each page consists of a header (containing a section title and page number), and one or more blocks of text or graphic images.

A document may consist of text, images, graphics, etc. The basic elements that form the contents of such documents are characters, picture elements (*pels*) and graphics elements (lines, arcs, etc.), respectively.

14.2.2 ODIF

The ODA defines a framework for developing applications that process and exchange office documents. The significant contribution of ODA is the definition of a standard *Office Document Interchange Format* (*ODIF*). This defines the format of the data stream used to interchange the structure and contents of office documents that are logically and/or physically structured in accordance with ODA.

As an example, consider two organizations A and B. Organizations A uses WordPerfect[2] for preparing and printing documents while organization B has standardized the use of T_EX. When organization A sends a document to organization B, the document is prepared using WordPerfect following all its conventions. Before sending it to organization B, the document interchange application program changes the document into its ODIF format. The ODIF version of the document is transported across the network and delivered to the application processor of organization B. The receiving application processor converts the document from the ODIF structure to the T_EX structure so that organization B can treat this document in the same way it treats any other document. A similar operation takes place when organization B sends a document to organization A.

Office documents, that are structured in accordance with ODA/ODIF, may be transported using a message handling system (X.400 based system, for example) or using a file transfer service, FTAM for example.

As part of ODA, detailed content architectures for character, raster graphics, and geometric graphics contents have also been defined. Similarly, a framework for defining document profiles has also been provided along with a few applications.

Clearly, the interchange of office documents is one of the major ap-

---

[2]WordPerfect is a trademark of WordPerfect Corp.

plications of ODA/ODIF. The importance of ODA, in this regard, is likely to increase.[3]

14.3   Remote Database Access

14.3.1   Introduction

It is common for organizations to maintain large databases and to use them extensively to support their computational requirements. With availability of OSI based networks, it is feasible to support applications that require access to databases located on one or more hosts. These databases may have different structures, management, or complexity.

The purpose of *Remote Database Access (RDA)* is to support development of applications that require access to a variety of databases (see [ISO 9579]). The access mechanism is largely independent of the data base being accessed. RDA services and its supporting protocol have been defined so that retrieval or update operations, specified by the remote database, can be invoked by a client application. These services are defined as abstract remote operations which are mapped by corresponding RDA Application service elements onto ACSE or ROSE services. CCR services, when available, may be used to ensure atomicity of access operations (see also Chapter 9).

14.3.2   RDA Services

The RDA service permits an application program in an open system to access a database in another open system. A client/server model is, therefore, used to model the asymmetric relationship between the two users of RDA service. A database implementation acts as a server, while an application program accessing the database takes on the role of a client. From the viewpoint of the RDA service, both application programs are treated as users. The client/server relationship between users is established at the time an Application association is established between corresponding Application entities. Only a client may use RDA services to invoke operations on the database server. The structure of this interaction is shown in Figure 14.2.

As mentioned earlier, RDA services are defined as abstract remote operations. *RDA-BIND* and *RDA-UNBIND* operations may be used to establish or release an Application association. These operations are mapped onto relevant ACSE services by supporting RDA Application

---

[3]One of the applications that may develop in the near future relates to electronic publishing of journals, newspapers, magazines and perhaps books. Such documents could be printed or displayed by users, or processed by an application program.

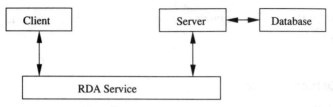

Figure 14.2 The RDA Service.

service elements. Further, if the remote database is highly structured, then it may be necessary for a client to open (and identify) a particular database resource before an access operation can be invoked. The RDA operation *r*-INVOKE may be used to identify a *statement* (together with its arguments) and to request its execution by the remote database server. Such a statement is part of the *database language*. The correspondence between the statement and its identifier is stored in the database server. Alternatively, a user may request execution of a statement by supplying the statement itself as part of an *r-EXE-CUTE* operation. There is also a provision for a user to describe a statement, using an *r-DEFINE* operation, and later request its execution by simply identifying it.

14.3.3 Related Issues

The RDA service allows a sequence of abstract operations to be considered as an atomic action, thereby ensuring that the operations are performed without interference from database operations initiated by other clients. Further, the operations either complete successfully (committed) or they terminate with no change in the remote database (rolled back). The sequence of operations, thus viewed, is called a *transaction* (see also Section 14.4, below). The facility to manage transactions is made possible by making CCR services directly available to RDA service users.

The database server, on its part, may process transactions concurrently on behalf of other clients as well. In that case it becomes the responsibility of the server to guarantee *serializability*. That is, the processing is such that it yields the same result as obtained from processing them in a particular sequence. To ensure this, the server has to put in place concurrency controls that permit users to select between exclusive access, concurrent read access, or concurrent update access.

Above, we have discussed RDA services briefly. These services, also referred to as *generic* RDA services, may be *specialized* for use with specific database servers and client processes. Among other things, a specialization of the generic RDA facility requires definition of the available data resources, the structure of data objects, and the permissible operations. For more details see [ISO 9579].

14.4 Transaction Processing

14.4.1 Introduction

A *transaction* is a unit of work with the properties of atomicity, consistency, isolation, and durability. *Atomicity* implies that the unit of work is either performed completely, or not done at all. *Consistency* implies that a successful transaction transforms the data from one consistent state to another. *Isolation* implies that partial results of a transaction are not accessible. For concurrent transactions the implication of isolation is serialization. *Durability* implies that the effects of a completed transaction are not altered by any subsequent failure.

When a transaction requires access to resources located in two or more open systems, it is called a *distributed transaction.* In such cases a transaction is composed of two or more components, each of which is a transaction, itself. This allows a transaction to be modelled in the form of a tree[4] as illustrated in Figure 14.3.

The purpose of distributed *Transaction Processing (TP)* service elements is to support communication between Application programs that are jointly responsible for processing a distributed transaction. It supports, among other things, distribution of transaction for processing, maintenance of dialogue between communicating user programs, atomicity of transactions, and error recovery (see also [ISO 10026-1]).

---

[4]As with atomic actions (see Section 9.5).

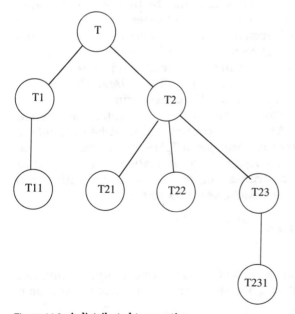

Figure 14.3 A distributed transaction.

14.4.2 TP Architecture

Each node in a transaction processing tree represents processing of a component of the transaction. The processing is carried out by a TP service user entity (*TPSU*). A branch in the transaction processing tree, therefore, models a dialogue between two TPSUs, one of which initiates processing of the transaction, while the other processes it. In this respect, a distributed transaction is processed by a number of TPSUs. The TPSUs are themselves organized (logically) in the form of a tree identical to the transaction tree. Physically, two or more TPSUs may be located in the same host, but they represent different invocations of the TPSU. The TPSU corresponding to the root is the one responsible for successful completion of the entire transaction. The TPSU corresponding to the root of a sub-tree is responsible for processing the transaction modeled by the sub-tree.

Before a distributed transaction is processed, the TPSU responsible for processing it establishes a *dialogue* with every TPSU that is responsible for processing its sub-transactions. The dialogue establishes the *superior-subordinate* relationship between the TPSUs and the context required for processing the transaction. At any time, a dialogue has a one-to-one correspondence with the supporting Application association. However, an association may support a number of consecutive dialogues, or a dialogue may span a number of Application associations in case of communication failure.

The responsibility to ensure atomicity, consistency, isolation and durability of the processed transaction may be that of the concerned TPSUs or of the TP service provider. In the former case, the concerned TPSUs communicate with each other to determine whether the transaction can be committed or is required to be rolled back. The TP service provider simply acts as a courier. In the latter case, it processes related service primitives, for instance, it issues a *TP-COMMIT-COMPLETE* indication in response to a *TP-COMMIT* request primitive.

The distributed TP protocol requires that Application service elements corresponding to Association control and CCR be available as part of the Association context. Further, a TP service element is so designed as to handle multiple Application associations, an essential requirement if a node in the transaction tree is associated with two or more branches. For further details, see [ISO 10026-1].

14.5   Network Management

14.5.1   Introduction

An OSI environment may consist of a large number of interconnected heterogeneous open systems. A systematic and continued operation of such an environment requires that availability and access to its resources be controlled, coordinated and monitored. It is the purpose of network management functions to facilitate resource management. Since systems may have local resources which are not part of the OSI environment, the management of local resources is beyond the scope of network management functions.

From the viewpoint of management, the OSI environment is viewed as consisting of a collection of *managed objects*. A managed object is any resource in the OSI environment, access to which is supervised, controlled and accounted for. OSI management is concerned with tools and services needed to control and supervise interconnection activities and managed objects. These services provide capabilities for gathering data, exercising control and developing reports on the status of managed objects.

14.5.2   Management Functions

The OSI management architecture covers the following functions:

1. *Fault Management:* These facilities enable detection, isolation and correction of abnormal operations due to faults. Faults are recognized as error events in the system. As part of fault management the system has to maintain error logs, accept and act upon error notifications, trace faults, carry out diagnostic tests, and correct faults.

2. *Accounting Management:* These facilities permit attribution of resource utilization to users so that appropriate charges can be levied on the users. The charging structure should permit timely reporting of charges as well as setting of accounting limits.

3. *Configuration and Name Management:* These facilities assist managed objects in their continuous operation by providing control over, and providing data to, the managed objects. These facilities set system parameters, initialize or close down managed objects, collect routine data, change system configuration in response to specific events, and associate names with sets of managed objects.

4. *Performance Management:* These facilities evaluate the behavior of managed objects and the effectiveness of communication activities. In the process statistical data may be gathered and analyzed, and logs of system histories maintained.

5. *Security Management:* These facilities address those aspects of OSI management which are concerned with security. Security related functions are essential to operate OSI management facilities correctly and to protect managed objects (see Section 14.6, as well).

OSI management functions collect and maintain necessary data in the form of *management information*. The *Management Information*

Base is a conceptual composite of management information within an open system. OSI management is organized in three parts, *systems management, (N)-layer management,* and *(N)-layer operation.* System management provides mechanisms for monitoring, control and coordination of all managed objects in any one or several layers. Communication support for systems management is accomplished using protocols implemented by the Application layer *Systems Management Application-entity (SMAE).*

Management of objects within a layer is carried out by (N)-layer management. (N)-layer management entities interact with each other to control and coordinate the proper operation of the (N)-layer communication functions. On the other hand, (N)-layer operation manages a single instance of communication.

Management of resources is effected through a set of management processes all of which may not be located in one local system. These processes receive information from people and software as well as remote systems, and exercise control directly over the managed objects within the same open system and through protocol exchanges with managed objects in other open systems.

14.6   Security

14.6.1   Introduction

The purpose of OSI is to facilitate the flow of information among Application processes running in a collection of open systems. In many situations it becomes essential that controls on the flow of information be imposed so as to permit proper use of the information. It is recognized that facilities for providing secure communication have to be built in as a part of system design, and that it cannot be added strictly as Application layer functions. The general structure for secure communication is defined as *Security Architecture* in [ISO 7498-2]. The OSI Security Architecture requires that security services and mechanisms be built into each of the seven layers in the OSI architecture.

In order to make a system secure it is necessary that the end system, as well as its users, follow appropriate security procedures. The security architecture of OSI is concerned with securing only the visible aspects of communication between peer entities.

14.6.2   Security Services

A set of basic security services have been defined which may be invoked from appropriate layers within the OSI structure and used in conjunction with non-OSI services. Security mechanisms have been defined that may be used to implement security services. The following security services have been defined:

1. *Authentication:* Authentication of peer entities and the source of data may be achieved using these services.
2. *Access Control:* Unauthorized use of resources accessible within the OSI environment may be prevented using these services.
3. *Data Integrity:* Unauthorized modification, deletion, insertion or replay of data may be prevented using these services.
4. *Non-repudiation:* These services are used to provide the recipient of data with a proof of the origin of data, or to provide a sender with a proof of delivery of data.

14.6.3 Security Mechanisms

A number of security mechanisms are available to provide the above security services. Some of the mechanisms already identified are:

1. *Encipherment:* This may be used to maintain confidentiality of data or traffic flow. Secret key encipherment, public key encipherment as well as irreversible encipherment algorithms may be used. When using an encipherment mechanism, a key management mechanism has also to be used.
2. *Digital Signature:* These mechanisms provide for signing of a data unit by the sender using information which remains private to the user. Verification of the signature can be done using publicly available information.
3. *Access Control Mechanisms:* These mechanisms ensure enforcement of access rights of entities. The identity of entities is authenticated using other mechanisms. Access control mechanisms not only prevent unauthorized access, but may also report such attempts to appropriate authorities.
4. *Data Integrity Mechanisms:* These mechanisms provide for integrity of single data units as well as a stream of data. These mechanisms are in two parts, one of which is implemented at the sender's end, while the other at the receiver's end.
5. *Authentication Exchange Mechanisms:* Mechanisms such as passwords and cryptographic techniques, may be used for authentication exchange. If peer entity authentication fails, any attempts to establish a connection may be aborted and reported to security management center.
6. *Traffic Padding Mechanisms:* These mechanisms are aimed at protection against any inferred information from traffic analysis.

7. *Notarization Mechanisms:* An assurance of the properties of data communication such as integrity, origin, time and destination may be provided by a third party. Such a party is a trusted entity, also called *notary.*

14.6.4 Pervasive Security Mechanisms

Several security mechanisms, not specific to any particular service, may be required as part of security management. Some of these mechanisms are presented below.

1. *Trusted Functionality:* These mechanisms are used to extend the scope or effectiveness of other security mechanisms. Clearly, to maintain security, functions which have access to security mechanisms must be trustworthy themselves. It is recognized that such procedures are costly and difficult to implement.

2. *Security Labels:* Various resources and data items may be assigned security labels which indicate the sensitivity level, for example. Such labels have to be identifiable so that they can be checked easily by enforcement mechanisms.

3. *Event Detection:* Detection of apparent violation of security, and other such events, plays a major role in any security system. Security-related *Event Handling Management* may be used to define events of interest and the actions required for each.

4. *Security Audit Trail:* These mechanisms provide an audit trail for all events related to security. All security-related information is recorded as a part of the audit trail. The analysis and report generation is a management function.

5. *Security Recovery:* These mechanisms deal with requests from other mechanisms, such as event handling, to initiate recovery actions.

14.6.5 Relation between Services, Mechanisms and Layers

The allocation of security services to layers has been carried out using a number of principles. An attempt has been made to minimize the number of alternate ways of implementations. It is considered acceptable to build a secure system by providing security services in more than one layer. Of course, one must avoid duplication of services and must ensure that the functionality of each layer can be independently developed. Additional security functions should permit implementation as a self-contained module. Based on these principles, the basic

TABLE 14.1   Security Services in OSI Layers

Service	Layer						
	1	2	3	4	5	6	7
Peer Entity Authentication	N	N	Y	Y	N	N	Y
Data Origin Authentication	N	N	Y	Y	N	N	Y
Access Control Service	N	N	Y	Y	N	N	Y
Connection Confidentiality	Y	Y	Y	Y	N	Y	Y
Connection-less Confidentiality	N	Y	Y	Y	N	Y	Y
Selective Field Confidentiality	N	N	N	N	N	Y	Y
Traffic Flow Confidentiality	Y	N	Y	N	N	N	Y
Connection Integrity	N	N	Y	Y	N	N	Y
Connection-less Integrity	N	N	Y	Y	N	N	Y
Non-repudiation	N	N	N	N	N	N	Y

structure for provision of protection services, operation of a protected connection, and protected connection-less data transfer has been defined. The basic services and their placement in the OSI layers is summarized in Table 14.1.

14.6.6   Security Management

Security management in OSI is concerned with the management of security services and mechanisms. In a distributed open system many security policies may be imposed by the system administration. All entities which are subject to a single security policy are included within a single *security domain* and administered by a single authority.

Security management requires collection as well as distribution of security related information. Examples of such information include distribution of cryptographic keys and reporting of events. Conceptually, all security related information in open systems is organized in a *Security Management Information Base*. This information is distributed to appropriate entities for enforcement of the security policy.

Three categories of security management have been defined. *System security management* is concerned with management of security aspects of the overall OSI environment. *Security services management* deals with the management of specific services. *Security mechanism management* manages the security mechanisms. These functions involve specific activities such as event handling, audit, recovery, key distribution, etc.

Security aspects in OSI are continually evolving with development of new applications that require additional security features. For instance, message handling systems and directory services rely heavily upon secure communication (see Chapters 10 and 11). They also demonstrate the wide variety of security features that need to be implemented to make corresponding services secure. Standards in this area are likely to evolve further as new techniques become available not just in communication-related security, but in computing systems in general.

15

Implementing OSI Protocols

In earlier chapters we have seen that the OSI architecture encompasses a large variety of applications. To support each application, the OSI standards define an Application service element, together with the services that it offers and the protocol that it uses to accomplish the task. Similarly, each layer is specified in terms of services that the layer offers and the protocol that it uses. Several issues still remain to be resolved before OSI based products and networks can be put in place. These are discussed in this chapter.

15.1 Conformance Testing

The first issue we discuss relates to testing a protocol implementation which claims conformity to one or more OSI standards, and its interworking with implementations by other vendors.

15.1.1 Introduction

The objectives of developing standards would be achieved only if different OSI implementations are able to communicate with each other effectively. Before communication between two implementations is attempted, it is necessary to test *a-priori* whether each implementation complies with the requirements of the relevant ISO, CCITT or IEEE standards. Because if they all do, then there is greater chance that communication between them would take place. Such testing is called *conformance testing* (for details see [CCITT X.290]). It is important to note that conformance testing is concerned with the *external behavior* of an implementation, but only to the extent of communication with similar systems. Further, it is an assessment of the *capabilities* that have been implemented.

Conformance testing does not include an assessment of the performance nor robustness of the implementation. Further, it does not pass a judgement on the manner in which the abstract service primitives have been realized, or the mechanism used to pass primitive parameters. It does, however, ensure that the syntax and semantics of all its interactions are consistent with those specified in the relevant protocol standard documents.

15.1.2 Static and Dynamic Tests

The observed behavior and the capabilities of an implementation are compared against the conformance requirements laid down in the protocol standard. These fall mainly into two categories, *static* and *dynamic* requirements. Static conformance requirements define the minimum capabilities that must be supported by an implementation which claims conformance. These requirements are specified in terms of functional units, service subsets, protocol classes and/or the range of parameters. Other capabilities may be optionally provided. The options allow an implementor to select the capabilities that he believes are required by users. Static conformance requirements also make reference to capabilities of the underlying layers that an implementation requires.

Dynamic conformance requirements are concerned with observable behavior of the implementation. It is specified as a set of admissible sequences of protocol-data-unit exchanges between communicating systems. No doubt, all protocol-data-units must conform to the specified syntax.

Before testing is actually undertaken, it is necessary that the implementor provide a statement of the capabilities and options which have been implemented, as well as a statement on the capabilities expected of the underlying layer(s). Such a statement ensures that both, static and dynamic, conformance tests are carried out against the relevant requirements only. Further, if an implementation of a stack of protocols is under test, then the implementation of each protocol layer must be tested for conformance to the relevant standard.

Since the number and combinations of events and their timing is infinite, static and dynamic testing are necessarily limited in scope. Therefore, there is a need to develop a standard suite of tests for carrying out conformance tests. As a consequence, conformance testing enables an implementor (and a user) to gain greater confidence that the system will effectively communicate with other systems that also conform to the same standards. Conformance tests have been developed and standardized for a number of protocols (see [CCITT X.403], for instance).

15.1.3   Interoperability Tests

Recall that an OSI standard includes a number of optional capabilities. Whether or not an optional capability is implemented, an implementation can claim conformance to the standard, and pass all relevant tests. However, two implementations that conform to the same standard may still not be able to communicate with each other effectively, unless they implement the same subset of optional capabilities. On the basis of furnished statements about the implementations, it is possible to determine *a-priori* whether two conforming systems will interwork with each other or not. However, they may not interwork because of factors that are not covered by conformance testing. These factors include:

1. differences in protocol versions,
2. known deficiencies and ambiguities in the protocol standard itself,
3. selection of options not accounted for under conformance testing,
4. existence of timers with substantially differing values,
5. incompatibility at other levels of the protocol stack, or even
6. performance related parameters.

Therefore, additional testing, known as *interoperability testing*, is required to determine whether or not the system is capable of effectively interworking with other similar implementations. If a system passes such tests, then there is a reasonable chance that the system will interwork with similar systems on the network.

15.2   Functional Standards

In this section we discuss an approach used to resolve incompatibility between implementations resulting from different choices of optional capabilities. Such an approach is based on a subset of optional capabilities agreed between a large community of users and manufacturers.

15.2.1   Profiles

Recall that optional capabilities that are built into OSI standards are necessary to permit users to select the required functionality of a given layer, or an application, to meet their specific requirements. The OSI standards are, therefore, also referred to as *Base Standards*. On one hand such a flexibility is desirable from the point of view of the users. But, as noted above, it makes interworking between systems difficult, since users are likely to opt for different capabilities. It is, therefore, necessary that a group of users agree on a consistent set of services and supporting protocols for use within the community. Such a consistent set of services and protocols is called a *profile*.

A profile consists of a specification of several aspects of the protocol, including:

1. the set of OSI services and protocols, together with a reference to the base standards,
2. optional features of the above services and protocols which must be implemented,
3. the use of underlying layers,
4. use of optional parameters of service primitives and protocol-data-units,
5. the manner in which two different versions of the same protocol can be made to interwork, and
6. values of various timers, or the range of their values.

A profile *may* also address issues relating to naming, addressing, layer management and security.

Several user groups and agencies are currently developing profiles for implementation of a complete stack of OSI protocols. In fact, the attempt is to reach wider agreement between several user groups, industry and government agencies. These efforts are expected to result in standardized profiles, also called *functional standards*. A functional standard additionally specifies further tests to be conducted to determine whether an implementation conforms to the functional standard. Functional standards are being developed by a number of organizations, including:[1]

1. *NIST Workshop on Implementation of OSI,* activities of which are coordinated by the *National Institute of Standards and Technology (NIST),* U. S. A. Its proceedings are published as *Working Implementation Agreements for OSI Protocols,* which ultimately result in *Stable Implementor's Agreements* (see [NIST 88] and [NIST 89]).

2. *European Workshop on Open Systems (EWOS)* organized by the *Joint European Standards Institution,* Brussels. The resulting functional standards are known as *European Pre-standards* (or *ENV).* For example, see [ENV 41201] for EWOS's functional standard on Message Handling Systems.

3. *Asia-Oceania Workshop for Open Systems,* the secretariat of which is located at *Interoperability Technology Association for Information Processing (INTAP),* Tokyo. The current activity centers around developing functional standards for use by member organizations. These are also being submitted for standardization by ISO's *Joint Technical Committee, JTC 1.* (See also *Implementation*

---

[1]Similar activities are also being undertaken by individual countries including Australia, Canada, China, India, and South Korea.

Specifications published as annex to *Japanese Industrial Standards* [INTAP S001].)

The above Workshops are actively supported by way of contributions by individuals, and user and vendor organizations. These include *Corporation for Open Systems (COS)* in U. S. A., *MAP/TOP*[2] users' forum in U. S. A. and Europe, *Promoting Conference for OSI (POSI)* in Japan, and *Standards Promotion and Applications Group (SPAG)* in Europe.

15.2.2 International Standardized Profile

The efforts described above result in a number of profiles or functional standards. While these profiles have been agreed to by user, vendor and/or government organizations in different parts of the world, *harmonization* of profiles themselves is necessary if global connectivity between users and systems is to be ensured. Thus, the next step in the evolution of OSI standards is the development of *International Standardized Profile* or *ISP* by ISO's JTC 1. As mentioned above, the committee relies upon contributions from different workshops and other organizations to carry out the exercise.

15.2.3 GOSIPs

Since federal governments form a major user of computer and communication products, a number of government agencies are also active in developing profiles. These profiles, also known as *Government OSI Profile* or *GOSIP,* are used not only to guide the development of networks in the respective countries, but also to determine procurement specifications. A government may make it obligatory for all its agencies or ministries to acquire and operate only those systems that comply with the corresponding GOSIP. Therefore, a GOSIP goes far beyond a functional standard.

A GOSIP, aside from making specific references to base and functional standards, lays down the procurement policies in respect of OSI based products. Further, it addresses the following issues:

1. naming and addressing,

2. management and security,

3. registration procedures for various user-defined objects,

---

[2]For *Manufacturing Automation Protocol/Technical and Office Protocol.* See also [Jones 88].

4. performance requirements,

5. migration, or transition, to OSI based protocols and applications, and

6. additional conformance and interoperability testing.

Several governments have initiated work in the area. Prominent among these are US GOSIP and UK GOSIP. We shall briefly discuss the US profile.

15.2.4 U.S. Government Profile

One of the largest users of communications technology is the U.S. government. Computers are used extensively by nearly every agency of the government. Over the years, most agencies have developed advanced network systems. In order to promote interoperability between end systems and between networks, the U.S. government is developing its own GOSIP (see [FIPS 146] and [Boland 88]). It is *the* standard reference to be used by all federal agencies when planning and acquiring computer communication systems or services.

US GOSIP is based on agreements reached at NIST Workshop for Implementors of OSI and on *MAP/TOP* protocols.

The general structure of the GOSIP architecture is shown in Figure 15.1. The basic concept is to use a single method to perform routing and reliable data transfer. The Transport layer protocols selected by US GOSIP are Transport Protocol Class 4 and Class 0, which requires a connection-less network service. These two protocols form the basis for ensuring interoperability. Users may select the lower layer protocols from among a set of available ones. In Figure 15.1 the lower layer protocols included are CSMA/CD over Bus [IEEE 802.3], Token Bus [IEEE 802.4], Token Ring [IEEE 802.5], and CCITT's Recommendation X.25. Other possibilities including ISDN and FDDI are to be included in the later versions of GOSIP.

The current application layer protocols included in GOSIP version 1 are File Transfer, Access and Management, and Message Handling Systems. Virtual Terminal Protocols are to be added to version 2. Other applications will be added as and when corresponding protocols mature and stable agreements become available. An application may use a selected set of Application Control Service Elements, Presentation and Session services. Further, layers 5, 6 and 7 are treated as an integral package for each specific application. An example of such packaging for FTAM is shown in Figure 15.2.

In order to support interoperability a uniform naming and addressing structure is necessary. NIST has been named as the *Address Registration Authority* for civilian applications. This provides central control over the use of addressing structure by various agencies.

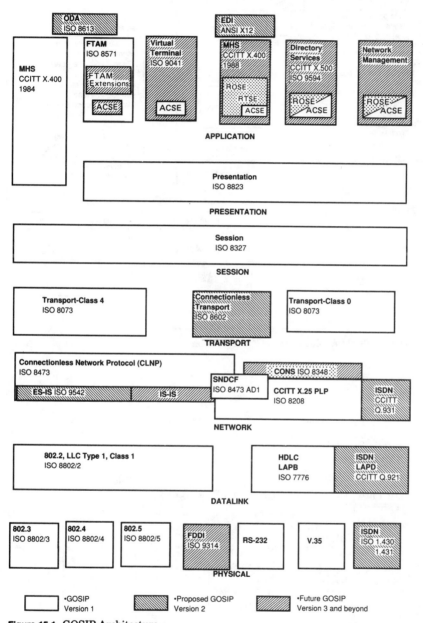

Figure 15.1 GOSIP Architecture.

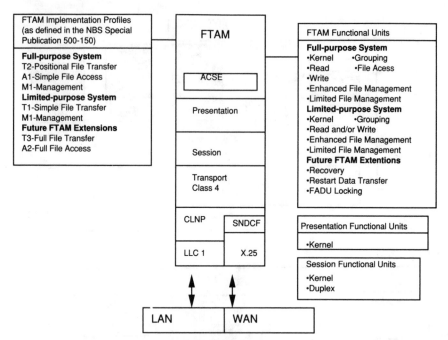

Figure 15.2 FTAM Applications in GOSIP version 1.

TABLE 15.1 GOSIP Milestones

1988	1989	1990	1991	1992
GOSIP 1.0	GOSIP 2.0	GOSIP 3.0	GOSIP 4.0	GOSIP 5.0
FTAM, X.400	VTP (Telnet), ODA	X.500, VTP(page, scroll, form), X.400(1988), FTAM Ext.	Transaction Processing, RDA, EDI	
802.x, HDLC/ LAPB, CLNP, X.25, TP0, TP4	ISDN, CONS, ES-IS, CLTP	FDDI, 100Mb Ring, TP2		
Session, Pre-sentation, ACSE				
Security				
	Network Management			

The first GOSIP standard, called GOSIP 1.0, was issued in 1988, and the second, GOSIP 2.0, in 1989. It is anticipated that GOSIP 3.0, 4.0 and 5.0 will be issued during the following three years. The structure of current milestones for GOSIP is shown in Table 15.1.

15.3   Transition to OSI Networks

Several organizations developed networks much before the formulation and adoption of OSI standards. These are primarily based on TCP/IP, SNA, uucp, and DECNET. The *Internet,* however, is the major binding force among many of the existing networks. Organizations using these networks have made significant investments in equipment and software. They support a large user population already trained in the use of services provided by the current networks.

With adoption of OSI as the standard by many organizations, transition from current network protocols to OSI based network protocols becomes a major issue. There are four aspects to the problem:

1. conversion of current implementations, both hardware and software, to support OSI protocols,
2. management and security of OSI based networks,
3. retraining of users, and
4. interworking with other OSI and non-OSI based networks,

A major investment is necessary to convert pre-OSI based equipment and software to OSI based implementation, and to retrain users in the use of current as well as new applications and services. While network management and security issues are being addressed by a number of agencies, managing the change itself is a challenging task. Such a change must be brought about without unduly disrupting critical services.

One approach is to put gateways between existing networks and emerging OSI based machines and networks. Gateways could be Transport layer gateways or even Application layer gateways. For instance, the public-domain implementation of OSI protocols, *ISO Development Environment*[3] (*ISODE*), provides a capability whereby OSI protocols can be made to run over a TCP/IP based Transport network. Such an implementation can be made to interwork with OSI based Transport services. Alternatively, one may develop an Application layer gateway which allows interworking between X.400 based MHS and other electronic mail systems (SMTP or uucp, for in-

---

[3]ISODE software is available from Northrop Research and Technology Center.

stance). Further, user interfaces for current applications need not be drastically different, thereby, minimizing the cost of user retraining.

15.4 Related Issues

Several implementations of OSI based protocols are becoming available to users. It is likely that, in the near future, OSI capabilities will be integrated with the rest of system software and marketed as such, as with TCP/IP under UNIX BSD 4.3. Performance of OSI implementations is likely to be a major concern, particularly for users experienced in the use of TCP/IP based services. Not enough effort seems to have gone into the study of performance related issues in OSI implementations. This is perhaps an opportunity for implementors to optimize their designs with a view to improve performance.[4]

If the rate of growth of networking in the last decade is any indication, networking in the 1990's will play an even more significant role. With internetworking of systems and networks at a global level becoming feasible, new applications in areas as yet unanticipated are likely to come up. The standards developed so far, and those that are being formulated, provide an excellent base for the development of many new applications.

Recent development in communications technology are aimed at providing very high speed links over long distances. As use and availability of such links becomes wide spread, protocols no longer need to be concerned with optimal utilization of bandwidth. This requires taking a fresh look at existing protocols and their design. *Lean protocols,* while resulting in larger protocol overheads, are likely to reduce the processing load on end systems as well as intermediate open systems.

---

[4]From a researcher's point of view, ISODE may provide a good test-bed for conducting measurement and performance studies.

OSI Standards Documents

In the main text, we have concentrated on aspects of OSI services and protocols that we believe are the foundation of the seven layer OSI architecture. There are several other related standards which necessarily could not be covered in the text. These cover, for instance, protocols for other application layer services, issues concerning network security or management, procedures for conformance testing. Below, we list standards documents (mainly ISO) that may be used for further study of related issues or an implementation of corresponding procedures. The documents referred to have either been accepted as standards, or are under active consideration.[1]

OSI Reference Model

ISO CD 7498-1   Basic Reference Model, to be published [second edition of ISO 9478 incorporating Addendum 1].

ISO 7498-2   Security Architecture, 1988.

ISO 7498-1/Add. 1   Addendum 1: Connection-less Data Transmission [will be superseded by ISO 7498-1 second edition].

ISO 7498-3   Naming and Addressing, 1989.

ISO 7498-4   Management Framework, 1989

ISO TR 8509 (CCITT X.210)   OSI Service Conventions, 1987.

ISO DTR 10730   Tutorial on Naming and Addressing, in preparation.

ISO DIS 10731   Conventions for the Definition of OSI Services, in preparation.

---

[1]Citations refer to documents already listed in the Bibliography.

Conformance Testing

ISO 9646-1 OSI Conformance Testing Methodology and Framework, Part 1: General Concepts, in preparation.

ISO 9646-1/PDAM1 Amendment 1: Protocol Profile Testing and Methodology, in preparation.

ISO 9646-1/PDAM2 Amendment 2: Multi-party Testing, in preparation.

ISO 9646-2 Part 2: Abstract Test Suite Specification, to be published.

ISO 9646-2/PDAM1 Amendment 1: Protocol Profile Testing and Methodology, in preparation.

ISO 9646-2/PDAM2 Amendment 2: Multi-party Testing, in preparation.

ISO 9646-3 Part 3: Tree and Tabular Combined Notation, in preparation.

ISO 9646-3/PDAM1 Amendment 1: TTCN Extensions, in preparation.

ISO 9646-4 Part 4: Test Realization, 1991.

ISO 9646-4/PDAM1 Amendment 1: Protocol Profile Testing and Methodology, in preparation.

ISO 9646-4/PDAM2 Amendment 2: Multi-party Testing, in preparation.

ISO 9646-5 Part 5: Requirements on Test Laboratories and Their Clients for the Conformance Assessment Process, in preparation.

ISO 9646-5/PDAM1 Amendment 1: Protocol Profile Testing and Methodology, in preparation.

ISO 9646-5/PDAM2 Amendment 2: Multi-party Testing, in preparation.

ISO CD 9646-6 Part 6: Test Laboratory Operations, in preparation.

ISO CD 9646-7 Part 7: Implementation Conformance Specification, in preparation.

Abstract Syntax Notation

ISO 8824 (CCITT X208) Specification of Abstract Syntax Notation 1 (ASN.1), 1990 [includes Addendum a, ASN.1 Extensions].

ISO 8824/PDAM2 Amendment 2, in preparation.

ISO CD 8824-2 Part 2: Information Object Specification, in preparation.

ISO CD 8824-3 Part 3: Constraint Specification, in preparation.

ISO CD 8824-4 Part 4: Parameterization of ASN.1 Specifications, in preparation.

ISO 8825 (CCITT X.209) Specification of Basic Encoding Rules for Abstract Syntax Notation 1 (ASN.1), 1990 [includes Addendum 1, ASN.1 Extensions].

ISO 8825/PDAM2 Amendment 2, in preparation.

ISO CD 8825-2 Part 2: Packed Encoding Rules, in preparation.

ISO CD 8825-3   Part 3: Distinguished Encoding Rules, in preparation.

Security

ISO 9796   Security Techniques—Digital Signature Scheme Giving Message Recovery, 1991.

ISO 9798-1   Security Techniques—Entity Authentication Mechanisms, Part 1: General Model, 1991.

ISO CD 9798-2   Security Techniques—Entity Authentication Mechanisms, Part 2: Entity Authentication using Symmetric Techniques.

ISO CD 9798-3   Security Techniques—Entity Authentication Mechanisms, Part 3: Entity Authentication using Public Key Algorithms.

ISO 9979   Data Cryptographic Techniques—Procedures for the Registration of Cryptographic Algorithms, 1991

ISO CD 10181-1   Security Frameworks, Part 1: Overview, in preparation.

ISO DIS 10181-2   Part 2: Authentication, in preparation.

ISO CD 10181-3   Part 3: Access Control, in preparation.

ISO CD 10181-4   Part 4: Non-repudiation, in preparation.

ISO CD 10181-5   Part 5: Confidentiality, in preparation.

ISO CD 10181-6   Part 6: Integrity, in preparation.

ISO CD 10181-7   Part 7: Security Audit, in preparation.

ISO CD 10745   Upper Layers Security Model, in preparation.

CCITT X.800   Security Architecture for OSI for CCITT Applications, in preparation.

Multi-layer Standards (Profiles)

ISO TR 10000-1   Framework and Taxonomy of International Standardized Profiles, Part 1: Framework, 1990

ISO TR 10000-2   Part 2: Taxonomy of Profiles, 1990.

ISO ISP 10607-1   International Standardized Profile AFTnn—File Transfer, Access, and Management, Part 1: Specification of ACSE, Presentation, and Session protocols for the use of FTAM, 1990.

ISO ISP 10607-2   Part 2: Definition of Document Types, Constraint Sets, and Syntaxes, 1990.

ISO ISP 10607-2/Am. 1   Amendment 1: Additional Definitions, 1991.

ISO ISP 10607-3   Part 3: AFT11—Simple File Transfer Service (unstructured), 1990.

ISO ISP 10607-4   Part 4: AFT12—Positional File Transfer Service (flat), 1991.

ISO ISP 10607-5 Part 5: AFT22—Positional File Access Service (flat), 1991.

ISO ISP 10607-6 Part 6: AFT3—File Management Service, 1991.

ISO PDISP 10608-1 International Standardized Profile TA—Connection-mode Transport Service over Connection-less Network Service, Part 1: General Overview and Subnetwork-independent Requirements, in preparation.

ISO PDISP 10608-2 Part 2: TA51 Profile Including Subnetwork-dependent Requirements for CSMA/CD LANs, in preparation.

ISO PDISP 10608-5 Part 5: TA1111/TA1121 Profiles Including Subnetwork-dependent Requirements for X.25 Packet Switched Data Networks Using Switched Virtual Circuits, in preparation.

ISO DISP 10609-1 International Standardized Profiles TB, TC, TD, and TE—Connection-mode Transport Service over Connection-mode Network Service, Part 1: Subnetwork-type Independent Requirements for Group TB, in preparation.

ISO DISP 10609-2 Part 2: Subnetwork-type Independent Requirements for Group TC, in preparation.

ISO DISP 10609-3 Part 3: Subnetwork-type Independent Requirements for Group TD, in preparation.

ISO DISP 10609-4 Part 4: Subnetwork-type Independent Requirements for Group TE, in preparation.

ISO DISP 10609-5 Part 5: Definition of Profile TB 1111/TB 1121, in preparation.

ISO DISP 10609-6 Part 6: Definition of Profile TC 1111/TC 1121, in preparation.

ISO DISP 10609-7 Part 7: Definition of Profile TD 1111/TD 1121, in preparation.

ISO DISP 10609-8 Part 8: Definition of Profile TE 1111/TE 1121, in preparation.

ISO DISP 10609-9 Part 9: Subnetwork-type Dependent Requirements for Network Layer, Data Link Layer, and Physical Layer Concerning Permanent Access to a Packet Switched Data Network Using Virtual Call, in preparation.

ISO DISP 10610-1 International Standardized Profile FOD 26—Office Document Format—Simple Document Structure—Character Content Only, Part 1: Document Application Profile, in preparation.

ISO DISP 11181-1 International Standardized Profile FOD26—Office Document Format—Enhanced Document Structure—Character, Raster Graphics, and Geometric Graphics Content Architectures, Part 1: Document Application Profile, in preparation.

ISO DISP 11182-1 International Standardized Profile FOD36—Office Document Format Extended Document Structure, Part 1: Document Application Profile, in preparation.

ISO DISP 11183-1 International Standardized Profiles AOMnn—Management Communication Protocols, Part 1: Specification of ACSE, Presentation, and Session Protocols for Use by ROSE and CMISE, in preparation.

ISO DISP 11183-2 International Standardized Profiles AOMnn—Management Communication Protocols, Part 2: AOM12, Enhanced Management Communications, in preparation.

ISO DISP 11183-3 International Standardized Profiles AOMnn—Management Communication Protocols, Part 3: AOM11, Basic Management Communications, in preparation.

Application Layer Standards

ISO 9545 (CCITT X.207) Application Layer Structure, 1989.

ISO 9545/DAM1 Amendment 1: Extended Application Layer Structures, in preparation.

Association Control (ACSE)

ISO 8649 (CCITT X.217) Service Definition for the Association Control Service Element, 1988.

ISO 8649/Am. 1 Amendment 1: Peer-entity Authentication during Association Establishment, 1990.

ISO 8649/Am. 2 Amendment 2: Connection-less ACSE Service, 1991.

ISO 8650 (CCITT X.227) Protocol Specification for the Association Control Service Element, 1988.

ISO 8650/Am. 1 Amendment 1: Peer-entity Authentication during Association Establishment, 1990.

ISO DIS 8650-2 Part 2: PICS Proforma, in preparation.

ISO 10035 Connection-less ACSE Protocol Specification, 1991.

ISO 10169-1 Conformance Test Suite for the ACSE Protocol, Part 1: Test Suite Structure and Test Purposes, 1991.

Reliable Transfer (RTS)

ISO 9066-1 (CCITT X.218) Reliable Transfer, Part 1: Model and Service Definition, 1989.

ISO 9066-2 (CCITT X.228) Part 2: Protocol Specification, 1989.

Remote Operations (ROS)

ISO 9072-1 (CCITT X.219) Remote Operations, Part 1: Model, Notation, and Service Definition, 1989.

ISO 9072-2 (CCITT X.229) Part 2: Protocol Specification, 1989.

Commitment, Concurrency, and Recovery (CCR)

ISO 9804 (CCITT X.861) Service Definition for the Commitment, Concurrency, and Recovery Service Element, 1990.

ISO 9804/PDAM1 Amendment 1: Service Enhancements, in preparation.

ISO 9804/DAM2 Amendment 2: Support for Session Mapping Changes, in preparation.

ISO 9805 (CCITT X.871) Protocol Specification for the Commitment, Concurrency, and Recovery Service Element, 1990.

ISO 9805/PDAM1 Amendment 1: Service Enhancements, in preparation.

ISO 9805/DAM2 Amendment 2: Support for Session Mapping Changes, in preparation.

ISO CD 9805-2 Part 2: PICS Proforma, in preparation.

Remote Procedure Call (RPC)

ISO CD 11578-1 Remote Procedure Call Specification, Part 1: Model, in preparation.

ISO CD 11578-2 Part 2: Service Definition, in preparation.

ISO CD 11578-3 Part 3: Protocol Specification, in preparation.

ISO CD 11578-4 Part 4: Interface Definition Notation, in preparation.

ISO CD 11578-5 Part 5: PICS Proforma, in preparation.

The Directory

ISO DIS 9594-1 (CCITT X.500) The Directory, Part 1: Overview of Concepts, Models, and Services, 1990.

ISO 9594-1/PDAM1 Amendment 1: Replication, Schema, and Access Control, in preparation.

ISO DIS 9594-2 (CCITT X.501) Part 2: Information Framework, 1990.

ISO 9594-2/PDAM1 Amendment 1: Access Control, in preparation.

ISO 9594-2/PDAM2 Amendment 2: Schema Extensions, in preparation.

ISO 9594-2/PDAM3 Amendment 3: Replication, in preparation.

ISO DIS 9594-3 (CCITT X.511) Part 3: Access and System Services Definition, 1990

ISO 9594-3/PDAM1 Amendment 1: Access Control, in preparation.

ISO 9594-3/PDAM2 Amendment 2: Replication, Schema, and Enhanced Search, in preparation.

ISO DIS 9594-4 (CCITT X.518) Part 4: Procedures for Distributed Operation, 1990.

ISO 9594-4/PDAM1 Amendment 1: Access Control, in preparation.

ISO 9594-4/PDAM2 Amendment 2: Replication, Schema, and Enhanced Search, in preparation.

ISO DIS 9594-5 (CCITT X.519) Part 5: Access and System Protocols Specification, 1990.

ISO 9594-5/PDAM1 Amendment 1: Replication, in preparation.

ISO DIS 9594-6 (CCITT X.520) Part 6: Selected Attribute Types, 1990.

ISO 9594-6/PDAM1 Amendment 1: Schema Extensions, in preparation.

ISO DIS 9594-7 (CCITT X.521) Part 7: Selected Object Classes 1990.

ISO 9594-7/PDAM1 Amendment 1: Schema Extensions, in preparation.

ISO Dis 9594-8 (CCITT X.509) Part 8: Authentication Framework, 1990.

ISO 9594-8/PDAM1 Amendment 1: Access Control, in preparation.

ISO DIS 9594-9 Part 9: Replication and Knowledge Management, in preparation.

Message Handling System (MHS)

ISO DIS 10021-1 (CCITT X.400) Message Oriented Text Interchange System (MOTIS) [Message Handling], Part 1: System and Service Overview, 1990.

ISO DIS 10021-2 (CCITT X.402) Part 2: Overall Architecture, 1990.

CCITT X.403 Message Handling: Conformance Testing, to be published.

ISO DIS 10021-3 (CCITT X.407) Part 3: Abstract Service Definition Conventions, 1990.

CCITT X.408 Message Handling: Encoded Information Type Conversion Rules, to be published.

ISO DIS 10021-4 (CCITT X.411) Part 4: Message Transfer System—Abstract Service Definition and Procedures, 1990.

ISO DIS 10021-5 (CCITT X.413) Part 5: Message Store—Abstract Service Definition, in preparation.

ISO DIS 10021-6 (CCITT X.419) Part 6: Protocol Specifications, 1990

ISO DIS 10021-7 (CCITT X.420) Part 7: Interpersonal Messaging System, 1990.

ISO CD 10021-11 Part 11 MTS Routing, in preparation.

CCITT X.435 MHS Application for EDI Messaging, in preparation.

File Transfer, Access, and Management (FTAM)

ISO 8571-1 File Transfer, Access, and Management (FTAM), Part 1: General Introduction, 1988.

ISO 8571-1/Am. 1   Amendment 1: Filestore Management, to be published.

ISO 8571-1/DAM2   Amendment 2: Overlapped Access, in preparation.

ISO 8571-1/PDAM3   Amendment 3: Service Enhancement, in preparation.

ISO 8571-2   Part 2: The Virtual Filestore Definition, 1988.

ISO 8571-2/Am. 1   Amendment 1: Filestore Management, to be published.

ISO 8571-2/DAM2   Amendment 2: Overlapped Access, in preparation.

ISO 8571-2/PDAM3   Amendment 3: Service Enhancement, in preparation.

ISO 8571-3   Part 3: The File Service Definition, 1988.

ISO 8571-3/Am. 1   Amendment 1: Filestore Management, to be published.

ISO 8571-3/DAM2   Amendment 2: Overlapped Access, in preparation.

ISO 8571-3/PDAM3   Amendment 3: Service Enhancement, in preparation.

ISO 8571-4   Part 4: The File Protocol Specification, 1988.

ISO 8571-4/Am. 1   Amendment 1: Filestore Management, to be published.

ISO 8571-4/DAM2   Amendment 2: Overlapped Access, in preparation.

ISO 8571-4/PDAM3   Amendment 3: Service Enhancement, in preparation.

ISO 8571-5   Part 5: PICS Proforma, 1990.

ISO 8571-5/PDAM1   Amendment 1: Filestore Management and Overlapped Access, in preparation.

ISO DIS 10170   Conformance Test Suite for the FTAM Protocol, Part 1: Test Suite Structure and Test Purposes, in preparation.

Virtual Terminal (VT)

ISO 9040   Virtual Terminal Service—Basic Class, 1990 [includes Addendum 1, Extended Facility Set], in preparation.

ISO 9040/Am. 2   Amendment 2: Additional Functional Units, to be published.

ISO 9041   Virtual Terminal Protocol—Basic Class, 1990 [includes Addendum 1, Extended Facility Set], in preparation.

ISO 9041/Am. 2   Amendment 2: Additional Functional Units, to be published.

ISO DIS 9041-2   Part 2: PICS Proforma, in preparation.

ISO DIS 10184-1   Terminal Management, Part 1: Model, in preparation.

ISO CD 10184-2   Part 2: Service Definition, in preparation.

ISO CD 10184-3   Part 3: Protocol Specification, in preparation.

ISO DIS 10739-1   Conformance Test Suite for Virtual Terminal, Part 1: Test Suite Structure and Test Purposes, in preparation.

Management

ISO 9595 (CCITT X.710) Common Management Information Service (CMIS) Definition, 1990

ISO 9595/DAM1 Amendment 1: Cancel/Get, in preparation.

ISO 9595/DAM2 Amendment 2: Add, Remove, and SetToDefault, in preparation.

ISO 9595/PDAM3 Amendment 3: Support for Allomorphism, in preparation.

ISO 9595/DAM4 Amendment 4: Access Control, in preparation.

ISO 9596 (CCITT X.711) Common Management Information Protocol (CMIP) Specification, second edition, 1991.

ISO 9596/DAM1 Amendment 1: Cancel/Get, in preparation.

ISO 9596/DAM2 Amendment 2: Add, Remove, and SetToDefault, in preparation.

ISO 9596/PDAM3 Amendment 3: Support for Allomorphism, in preparation.

ISO DIS 9596-2 Part 2: PICS Proforma, in preparation.

ISO 10040 (CCITT X.701) Systems Management Overview, to be published.

ISO DIS 10164-1 (CCITT X.730) Systems Management, Part 1: Object Management Function, in preparation.

ISO DIS 10164-2 (CCITT X. 731) Part 2: State Management Function, in preparation.

ISO DIS 10164-3 (CCITT X.732) Part 3: Attributes for Representing Relationships, in preparation.

ISO DIS 10164-4 (CCITT X.733) Part 4: Alarm Reporting Function, in preparation.

ISO DIS 10164-5 (CCITT X.734) Part 5: Event Report Management Function, in preparation.

ISO DIS 10164-6 (CCITT X.735) Part 6: Log Control Function, in preparation.

ISO DIS 10164-7 (CCITT X.736) Part 7: Security Alarm Reporting Function, in preparation.

ISO DIS 10164-8 (CCITT X.740) Part 8: Security Audit Trail Function, in preparation.

ISO CD 10164-9 (CCITT X.741) Part 9: Objects and Attributes for Access Control, in preparation.

ISO CD 10164-10 (CCITT X.742) Part 10: Accounting Meter Function, in preparation.

ISO CD 10164 (CCITT X.739) Part 11: Workload Monitoring Function, in preparation.

ISO CD 10164-12 (CCITT X.745) Part 12: Test Management Function, in preparation.

ISO CD 10164-13 (CCITT X.738) Part 13: Measurement Summarization Function, in preparation.

ISO CD 10164-sm (CCITT X.744) Part sm: Software Management Function, in preparation.

ISO CD 10164-tc (CCITT X.737) Part tc: Confidence and Diagnostic Test Classes, in preparation.

ISO CD 10164-ti (CCITT X.743) Part ti: Time Management Function, in preparation.

ISO DIS 10165-1 (CCITT X.720) Structure of Management Information, Part 1: Management Information Model, in preparation.

ISO DIS 10165-2 (CCITT X.721) Part 2: Definition of Management Information (replaces original parts 2 and 3), in preparation.

ISO DIS 10165-4 (CCITT X.722) Part 4: Guidelines for the Definition of Managed Objects, in preparation.

ISO CD 10165-5 Part 5: Generic Management Information, in preparation.

ISO CD 10165-6 Part 6: Requirements and Guidelines for Management Information Conformance Statement Proformas, in preparation.

Job Transfer and Manipulation (JTM)

ISO 8831 JTM Concepts and Services, 1989.

ISO 8832 Specification of the Basic Class Protocol for JTM, 1989.

ISO 8832/DAM1 Amendment 1: Full Class Protocol for Job Transfer and Manipulation, in preparation.

Office Document Architecture (ODA)

CCITT T.400 Document Transfer, Access, and Manipulation (DTAM)— General Introduction, in preparation.

ISO 8613-1 (CCITT T.411) Text and Office Systems—Office Document Architecture and Interchange Format, Part 1: Introduction and General Principles, 1989.

ISO 8613-1/DAM1 Amendment 1: Document Application Profile Proforma and Notation, in preparation.

ISO 8613-1/DAM2 Amendment 2: Conformance Testing Methodology, in preparation.

ISO 8613-2 (CCITT T.412) Part 2: Document Structures, 1989.

ISO 8613-4 (CCITT T.414) Part 4: Document Profile, 1989.

ISO 8613-4/PDAM1 Amendment 1: Additive Extensions for Filing and Retrieval Attributes, in preparation.

ISO 8613-4/PDAM2   Amendment 2: Document Application Profile Proforma and Notation, in preparation.

ISO 8613-5 (CCITT T.415)   Part 5: Document Interchange Format, 1989.

ISO 8613-6 (CCITT T.416)   Part 6: Character Content Architectures, 1989.

ISO 8613-7 (CCITT T.417)   Part 7: Raster Graphics Content Architectures, 1989.

ISO 8613-7/DAM1   Amendment 1: Tiled Raster Graphics Content Architectures, in preparation.

ISO 8613-8 (CCITT T.418)   Part 8: Geometric Graphics Content Architectures, 1989.

ISO CD 8613-9   Part 9: Audio Content Architectures, in preparation.

ISO CD 8613-10   Part 10: Formal Specifications, in preparation.

ISO 8613-10/DAM1   Amendment 1: Formal Specifications of the Document Profile, 1991

ISO 8613-10/DAM2   Amendment 2: Formal Specifications of the Raster Graphics Content Architectures, in preparation.

ISO 8613-10/DAM3   Amendment 3: Annex C: Formal Specification of the Character Content Architectures, in preparation.

ISO CD 10033   Text and Office Systems—Office Document Interchange, Flexible Disks, in preparation.

ISO DIS 10175-1   Text and Office Systems—Document Printing Application, Part 1: Abstract Service Definition and Procedures, in preparation.

ISO DIS 10175-2   Text and Office Systems—Document Printing Application, Part 2: Protocol Specification, in preparation.

CCITT T.419   Document Transfer, Access, and Manipulation (DTAM)—Composite Graphics Content Architectures, in preparation.

CCITT T.431   Document Transfer, Access, and Manipulation (DTAM)—Introduction and General Principles, in preparation.

CCITT T.432   Document Transfer, Access, and Manipulation (DTAM)—Service Definition, in preparation.

CCITT T.433   Document Transfer, Access, and Manipulation (DTAM)—Protocol Specification, in preparation.

CCITT T.441   Document Transfer, Access, and Manipulation (DTAM)—Operational Structure, in preparation.

Remote Database Access (RDA)

ISO DIS 9579-1   Remote Database Access, Part 1: General Model, Services, and Protocol, in preparation.

ISO DIS 9579-2   Part 2: SQL Specialization, in preparation.

Transaction Processing (TP)

ISO DIS 10026-1 Distributed Transaction Processing, Part 1: Model, in preparation.

ISO DIS 10026-2 Part 2: Service Definition, in preparation.

ISO DIS 10026-3 Part 3: Transaction Processing Protocol Specification, in preparation.

ISO CD 10026 Part 4: PICS Proforma, in preparation.

ISO DIs 10026-5 Part 5: Application Context Proforma, in preparation.

ISO CD 10026-6 Part 6: Unstructured Data Transfer, in preparation.

CCITT X.850 Distributed Transaction Processing Model for OSI and CCITT Applications, in preparation.

CCITT X.860 Distributed Transaction Processing Service Definition for OSI and CCITT Applications

CCITT X.870 Distributed Transaction Processing Protocol for OSI for CCITT Applications, in preparation.

Electronic Data Interchange (EDI)

ISO 9735 EDIFACT Syntax Rules, 1988.

Presentation Layer Standards

ISO 8822 (CCITT X.216) Connection Oriented Presentation Service Definition, 1988.

ISO 8822/Am. 1 Amendment 1: Connectionless-mode Presentation Service, 1991.

ISO 8822/PDAM2 Amendment 2: Support of Session Symmetric Synchronization Service, in preparation.

ISO 8822/PDAM3 Amendment 3: Unlimited User Data, in preparation.

ISO 8822/PDAM4 Amendment 4: Procedures for Registration of Abstract Syntaxes, in preparation.

ISO 8822/DAM5 Amendment 5: Incorporation of Additional Synchronization Functionality, in preparation.

ISO 8823 (CCITT X.226) Connection Oriented Presentation Protocol Specification, 1988.

ISO 8823/PDAM2 Amendment 2: Support of Session Symmetric Synchronization Service, in preparation.

ISO 8823/PDAM3 Amendment 3: Unlimited User Data, in preparation.

ISO 8823/PDAM4 Amendment 4: Procedures for Registration of Transfer Syntaxes, in preparation.

ISO 8823/DAM5 Amendment 5: Incorporation of Additional Synchronization Functionality, in preparation.

ISO DIS 8823-2 Part 2: PICS Proforma, in preparation.

ISO 9576-1 Connectionless Presentation Protocol Specification, 1991.

ISO DIS 9576-2 Part 2: PICS Proforma, in preparation.

ISO DIS 10729-1 Conformance Test Suite for the Presentation Layer, Part 1: Test Suite Structure and Test Purposes for the Presentation Protocol, in preparation.

ISO CD 10729-2 Part 2: Test Suite for ASN.1 Encodings, in preparation.

ISO CD 10729-3 Part 3: Embedded Abstract Test Suite for CO Presentation Protocol, in preparation.

Session Layer Standards

ISO 8326 (CCITT X.215) Basic Connection Oriented Session Service Definition, 1987.

ISO 8326/Add. 1 Addendum 1: Session Symmetric Synchronization, to be published.

ISO 8326/Add. 2 Addendum 2: Incorporation of Unlimited User Data, to be published.

ISO 8326/Am. 3 Amendment 3: Connectionless Session Service, to be published.

ISO 8326/DAM4 Amendment 4: Incorporation of Additional Synchronization Functionality, in preparation.

ISO 8327 (CCITT X.225) Basic Connection Oriented Session Protocol Specification, 1987.

ISO 8327/Add. 1 Addendum 1: Session Symmetric Synchronization, to be published.

ISO 8327/Add. 2 Addendum 2: Incorporation of Unlimited User Data, to be published.

ISO 8327/DAM3 Amendment 3: Incorporation of Additional Synchronization Functionality, in preparation.

ISO CD 8327-2 Part 2: PICS Proforma, in preparation.

ISO 9548 Connectionless Session Protocol, 1989.

ISO CD 9548-2 Part 2: PICS Proforma, in preparation.

ISO TR 9571 LOTOS Description of the Session Service, 1989.

ISO TR 9572 LOTOS Description of the Session Protocol, 1989.

ISO 10168-1 Conformance Test Suite for the Session Protocol, Part 1: Test Suite Structure and Test Purposes, to be published.

ISO CD 10168-2 Part 2: Generic Test Suite, in preparation.

ISO CD 10168-3 Part 3: Abstract Test Suite for CS Method, in preparation.

ISO DIS 10168-4 Part 4: Test Management Protocol Specification, in preparation.

Transport Layer Standards

ISO 8072 (CCITT X.214) Transport Service Definition, 1986.

ISO 8072/Add. 1 Addendum 1: Connectionless-mode Transmission, 1986.

ISO 8073 (CCITT X.224) Connection Oriented Transport Protocol Specification, 1988 [consolidated text under preparation].

ISO 8073/Add. 1 Addendum 1: Network Connection Management Subprotocol (NCMS), 1988.

ISO 8073/Add. 2 Addendum 2: Class 4 Operation over Connectionless Network Service, 1989.

ISO 8073/Am. 3 Amendment 3: Protocol Implementation Conformance Statement Proforma, to be published.

ISO 8073/DAM4 Amendment 4: Transport Protocol Enhancements, in preparation.

ISO 8602 Protocol for Providing the Connectionless-mode Transport Service, 1987.

ISO DTR 10023 LOTOS Description of ISO 8072, in preparation.

ISO DTR 10024 LOTOS Description of ISO 8073, in preparation.

ISO DIS 11570 Transport Protocol Identification Mechanism, in preparation.

ISO DIS 10025-1 Transport Protocol Conformance Testing, Part 1: General Principles

ISO CD 10025-2 Part 2: Test Suite Structure and Test Purposes

ISO DIS 10025-3 Part 3: Transport Test Management Protocol Specification, in preparation.

ISO DIS 10737-1 Elements of Management Information Related to OSI Transport Layer Standards, Part 1: Transport Protocol Management Specification, in preparation.

ISO DIS 10736 Transport Layer Security Protocol, in preparation.

ISO 10736/PDAM1 Amendment 1: Security Association Establishment, in preparation.

Network Layer Standards

ISO 8348 (CCITT X.213) Network Service Definition, 1987 [consolidated text for second edition under preparation].

ISO 8348/Add. 1   Addendum 1: Connectionless-mode Transmission, 1987.

ISO 8348/Add. 2   Addendum 2: Network Layer Addressing, 1988.

ISO 8348/Add. 3   Addendum 3: Additional Features of the Network Service, 1988.

ISO 8348/DAM4   Amendment 4: Removal of the Preferred Decimal Encoding of the NSAP Address, in preparation.

ISO 8348/PDAM5   Amendment 5: Allocation of a New AFI Value and IDI Format for the NSAP Address, in preparation.

ISO 8648   Internal Organization of the Network Layer, 1988.

ISO 8880-1   Protocol Combinations to Provide and Support the OSI Network Service, Part 1: General Principles, 1990.

ISO 8880-2   Part 2: Provision and Support of the Connection-mode Network Service, 1990.

ISO 8880-2/DAM1   Amendment 1: Addition of the ISDN Environment, in preparation.

ISO 8880-2/DAM2   Amendment 2: Addition of the PSTN and CSDN Environments, in preparation.

ISO 8880-3   Part 3: Provision and Support of the Connectionless Network Service, 1990.

ISO TR 9577   Protocol Identification in the Network Layer, 1990.

ISO TR 10172   Network/Transport Protocol Interworking Specification, 1991.

dpANS X3.216   Structure of the Domain-Specific Part (DSP) of the OSI Network Service Access Point (NSAP) Address [ANSI public review period ended 92-02-15].

ISO 8473   Protocol for Providing the Connectionless-mode Network Service (Internetwork Protocol), 1988.

ISO 8473/Add. 3   Addendum 3: Provision of the Underlying Service Assumed by ISO 8473 over Subnetworks which Provide the OSI Data Link Service, 1989.

ISO 8473/PDAM4   Amendment 4: PICS Proforma, in preparation.

ISO 8473/PDAM5   Amendment 5: Provision of the Underlying Service for Operation over ISDN Circuit-switched B-channels, in preparation.

ISO 8208   X.25 Packet Layer Protocol for Data Terminal Equipment, second edition, 1990.

ISO 8208/Am. 1   Amendment 1: Alternative Logical Channel Identifier As-0signment, 1991.

ISO 8208/Am. 3   Amendment 3: Static Conformance Requirements, 1991.

ISO 8878 (CCITT X.223)   Use of X.25 to Provide the Connection-oriented Network Service, 1987.

ISO 8878/Add. 1   Addendum 1: Priority, 1990.

ISO 8878/Add. 2   Addendum 2: Use of an X.25 PVC to Provide the OSI CONS, 1990.

ISO 8878/Am. 3   Amendment 3: Conformance, 1991.

ISO DIS 8878-2   Part 2: PICS Proforma, in preparation.

ISO 8881   Use of the X.25 Packet Level Protocol in Local Area Networks, 1989.

ISO 8882-1   X.25 DTE Conformance Testing, Part 1: General Principles, to be published.

ISO 8882-3   Part 3: Packet Level Conformance Suite, 1991.

ISO 8882-3/PDAM1   Amendment 1: Use of Data Link Service Primitives, in preparation.

ISO TR 10029   Operation of an X.25 Interworking Unit, 1989.

ISO 10177   Intermediate System Support of the OSI CONS using ISO 8208 in Accordance with ISO 10028, to be published.

ISO DIS 10588   Use of X.25 PLP in Conjunction with X.21/X.21 bis to Provide the OSI CONS, in preparation.

ISO DIS 10732 (CCITT X.614)   Use of X.25 PLP to Provide the OSI CONS Over the Telephone Network, in preparation.

ISO 9542   End System to Intermediate System Routing Information Exchange Protocol for Use in Conjunction with the Protocol for the Provision of the Connectionless-mode Network Service, 1988.

ISO 9542/PDAM1   Amendment 1: Dynamic Discovery of OSI NSAP Addresses by End Systems, in preparation.

ISO TR 9575   OSI Routing Framework, 1990.

ISO DIS 10028   Definition of the Relaying Functions of a Network Layer Intermediate System, in preparation.

ISO 10028/DAM1   Amendment 1: Connectionless Relaying Functions, in preparation.

ISO 10030   End System to Intermediate System Routing Information Exchange Protocol for Use in Conjunction with ISO 8878, 1990.

ISO 10030/PDAM1   Amendment 1: Dynamic Discovery of OSI NSAP Addresses by End Systems, in preparation.

ISO 10030/PDAM3   Amendment 3: Intermediate System Interactions with a SNARE, in preparation.

ISO DIS 10030-2   Part 2: PICS Proforma, in preparation.

ISO 10589   Intermediate System to Intermediate System Routing Information Exchange Protocol for Use in Conjunction with ISO 8473, to be published.

ISO CD 10747   Protocol for Exchange of Inter-Domain Routing Information among Intermediate Systems to Support Forwarding of ISO 8473 PDUs, in preparation.

ISO DIS 10733   Specification of the Elements of Management Information Related to OSI Network Layer Standards, in preparation.

ISO CD 11577   Network Layer Security, in preparation.

Data Link Layer Standards

ISO DIS 8886 (CCITT X.212)   Data Link Service Definition, 1988 [revision under preparation].

ISO CD 11575   Protocol Mappings for the OSI Data Link Service, in preparation.

ISO 3309   High-level Data Link Control (HDLC)—Frame Structure, fourth edition, 1991.

ISO 3309/Add. 1   Addendum 1: Start/Stop Transmission, to be published.

ISO 3309/Am. 2   Amendment 2: Extended Transparency Options for Start/Stop Transmission, 1992.

ISO 3309/DAM3   Amendment 3: Seven-bit Transparency Option for Start-Stop Transmission, in preparation.

ISO 4335   HDLC Consolidation of Elements of Procedures, fourth edition, 1991.

ISO 4335/Add. 1   Addendum 1 (no title; contains UI and SREJ extensions), 1987.

ISO 4335/Add. 2   Addendum 2: Enhancement of the XID Function Utility, in preparation.

ISO 4335/Add. 3   Addendum 3: Start/Stop Transmission, to be published.

ISO 4335/Am. 4   Amendment 4: Multi-Selective Reject Option, 1991.

ISO 7478   Multi-link Procedures, third edition, 1984.

ISO 7776   HDLC—Description of the X.25 LAPB-compatible DTE Data Link Procedures, 1986.

ISO 7776/DAM1   Amendment 1: PICS Proforma, in preparation.

ISO 7809   HDLC—Consolidation of Classes of Procedures, second edition, 1991.

ISO 7809/Add. 1   Addendum 1, 1987.

ISO 7809/Add. 2   Addendum 2: Description of Optional Functions, 1987.

ISO 7809/Ad. 3   Addendum 3: Start/Stop Transmission, to be published.

ISO 7809/DAM5   Amendment 5: Connectionless Class of Procedures, in preparation.

ISO 7809/Am. 6   Amendment 6: Extended Transparency Options for Start/Stop Transmission, in preparation.

ISO 7809/Am. 7   Amendment 7: Multi-Selective Reject Option, 1991.

ISO 7809/DAM9   Amendment 9: Seven-bit Transparency Option for Start/Stop Transmission, in preparation.

ISO 8471   HDLC Balanced Classes of Procedures—Data Link Layer Address Resolution/Negotiation in Switched Environments, 1987.

ISO 8885   HDLC-General Purpose XID Frame Information Field Content and Format, second edition, 1991.

ISO 8885/Add. 1   Addendum 1: Additional Operational Parameters for the Parameter Negotiation Data Link Layer Subfield and Definition of a Multilink Parameter Negotiation Data Link Layer Subfield, 1989.

ISO 8885/Add. 2   Addendum 2: Start/Stop Transmission, to be published.

ISO 8885/DAM3   Amendment 3: Definition of a Private Parameter Negotiation Data Link Layer Subfield, in preparation.

ISO 8885/Am. 4   Amendment 4: Extended Transparency Options for Start/Stop Transmission, in preparation.

ISO 8885/Am. 5   Amendment 5: Multi-Selective Reject Option, 1991.

ISO 8885/PDAM6   Amendment 6: Seven-bit Transparency Option for Start/Stop Transmission, in preparation.

ISO 8885/PDAM7   Amendment 7: Frame Check Sequence Negotiation Using the Parameter Negotiation Subfield, in preparation.

ISO TR 10171   List of Standard Data Link Layer Protocols that Utilize HDLC Classes of Procedures, to be published.

ISO 10171/PDAM1   Amendment 1: Registration of XID Format Identifiers and Private Parameter Set Identifiers, in preparation.

Local Area Networks (LANs)

ISO 8802-1   Local Area Networks, Part 1: Introduction, to be published.

ISO DIS 8802-1E   Local Area Networks, Part 1: Introduction, Section E: System Load Protocol, in preparation.

ISO 8802-2   Part 2: Logical Link Control, 1990.

ISO 8802-2/DAM1   Amendment 1: Flow Control Techniques for Bridged Local Area Networks, in preparation.

ISO 8802-2/DAM2   Amendment 2: Acknowledged connectionless-mode service, Type 3 operation, in preparation.

ISO 8802-2/PDAM3   Amendment 3: PICS Proforma, in preparation.

ISO 8802-2/DAM4   Amendment 4: Editorial Changes and Technical Corrections, in preparation.

ISO 8802-2/PDAM5 Amendment 5: Bridged LAN Source Routing Operation by End Systems, in preparation [was PDTR 10734].

ISO 8802-3 Part 3: Carrier Sense Multiple Access with Collision Detection-Access Method and Physical Layer Specifications, second edition, 1990.

ISO 8802-3/DAM1 Amendment 1: Medium Attachment Unit and Baseband Medium Specifications for Type 10BASE2, in preparation.

ISO 8802-3/DAM2 Amendment 2: Repeater Set and Repeater Unit Specification for use with 10BASE5 and 10BASE2 Networks, in preparation.

ISO 8802-3/DAM3 Amendment 3: Broadband Medium Attachment Unit and Broadband Medium Specifications, Type 10BROAD36, in preparation.

ISO 8802-3/DAM4 Amendment 4: Physical Medium, Medium Attachment, and Baseband Medium Specifications, Type 1BASE5 (StarLAN), in preparation.

ISO 8802-3/DAM5 Amendment 5: Medium Attachment Unit and Baseband Medium Attachment Specification for a Vendor Independent Fiber Optic Inter-repeater Link, in preparation.

ISO 8802-3/DAM6 Amendment 6: Summary of IEEE 802.3 First Maintenance, in preparation.

ISO 8802-3/DAM7 Amendment 7: LAN Layer Management, in preparation.

ISO 8802-3/DAM9 Amendment 9: Physical Medium, Medium Attachment, and Baseband Medium Specifications, Type 10baseT, in preparation.

ISO 8802-4 Part 4: Token-passing Bus Access Method and Physical Layer Specification, 1990.

ISO DIS 8802-5 Part 5: Token Ring Access Method and Physical Layer Specification, in preparation.

ISO 8802-5/PDAM1 Amendment 1: 4 and 16 Mbit/s Specification, in preparation.

ISO 8802-5/PDAM2 Amendment 2: MAC Sublayer Enhancement, in preparation.

ISO 8802-5/PDAM3 Amendment 3: Management Entity Specification, in preparation.

ISO 8802-5/DAM4 Amendment 4: Source Routing MAC Bridge, in preparation.

ISO 8802-5/DAM5 Amendment 5: PICS Proforma, in preparation.

ISO CD 8802-51 Part 51: MAC Sublayer Conformance Test Purposes, in preparation.

ISO CD 8802-6 Part 6: Distributed Queue Dual Bus (DQDB) Access Method and Physical Layer Specification, in preparation.

ISO 8802-7 Part 7: Slotted Ring Access Method and Physical Layer Specification, to be published.

ISO DIS 10038 MAC Bridging, in preparation.

ISO 10038/PDAM1   Amendment 1: Specification of Management Information for CMIP, in preparation.

ISO 10038/DAM2   Amendment 2: Source Routing Supplement, in preparation.

ISO 10039   MAC Service Definition, 1991.

ISO TR 10178   The Structure and Coding of Logical Link Control Addresses in Local Area Networks, to be published.

ISO DTR 10735   Standard Group MAC Addresses, in preparation.

ISO DIS 8882-2   X.25 DTE Conformance Testing, Part 2: Data Link Layer Test Suite, in preparation.

ISO DTR 10174   Logical Link Control (Type 2 Operation) Test Purposes, in preparation.

ISO CD 10742   Elements of Management Information Related to OSI Data Link Layer Standards, in preparation.

Physical Layer Standards

ISO 10022 (CCITT X.211)   Physical Service Definition, 1990.

ISO TR 7477   Arrangements for DTE to DTE Physical Connection Using V.24 and X.24 Interchange Circuits, 1985.

ISO 7480   Start-Stop Transmission Signal Quality at DTE-DCE Interfaces, 1991.

ISO 8480   DTE-DCE Interface Backup Control Operation Using the 25 Pin Connector, 1987.

ISO 8481   DTE to DTE Physical Connection Using X.24 Interchange Circuits with DTE-provided Timing, 1986.

ISO 8482   Twisted Pair Multipoint Interconnections, 1987.

ISO 9067   Automatic Fault Isolation Procedures Using Test Loops, 1987.

ISO 9543   Synchronous Transmission Signal Quality at DTE-DCE Interfaces, 1989.

ISO 9549   Galvanic Isolation of Balanced Interchange Circuits, 1990.

Abbreviations

Here is a complete list of abbreviations used in this book.

ACS	Access Control Store
ACSE	Association-Control Service Element
AE	Application Entity
AFI	Authority and Format Identifier
ANSI	American Standards Institution
AP	Application Process
APDU	Application Protocol Data Unit
ASE	Application Service Element
ASN	Abstract Syntax Notation
AU	Access Unit
AVA	Attribute Value Assertions
BAS	Basic Activity Subset
BCS	Basic Combined Subset
BSS	Basic Synchronized Subset
CASE	Common Application Service Element
CCA	Conceptual Communication Area
CCITT	Comiteé Consultatif International de Télégraphique et Téléphonique
CCR	Commitment, Concurrency and Recovery
CDS	Conceptual Data Store
CEP	Connection-endpoint
CLNP	Connection-less Network Protocol
conf	confirm
CONS	Connection-oriented Network Service
COS	Corporation for Open Systems
CRC	Cyclic Redundancy Checksum

CSS	Control, Signalling and Status
DCE	Data Circuit-terminating Equipment
DCS	Defined Context Set
DECNET	Digital Equipment Equipment's Network Architecture
DIB	Directory Information Base
DIS	Draft International Standard
DIT	Directory Information Tree
DL	Distribution List
DLC	Data Link Connection
DLCEP	Data Link Connection End-point
DLPDU	Data Link Protocol Data Unit
DLS	Data Link Service
DLSAP	Data Link Service Access Point
DLSDU	Data Link Service Data Unit
DMD	Directory Management Domain
DP	Draft Proposal
DSA	Directory Service Agent
DSD	Data Structure Definition
DSP	Domain Specific Part
DTE	Data Terminal Equipment
DU	Data Unit
DUA	Directory User Agent
EIA	Electronics Industry Association
ENV	European Pre-standards
EWOS	European Workshop on Open Systems
FADU	File Access Data Unit
FTAM	File Transfer, Access and Management
GOSIP	Government OSI Profile
HDLC	High Level Data Link Control
IADCS	Inter-activity Defined Context Set
IDI	Initial Domain Identifier
IEEE	Institution of Electrical and Electronic Engineers
ind	indication
INTAP	Interoperability Technology Association for Information Processing
IPM	Interpersonal Message
IPMS	Interpersonal Messaging System
IPN	Interpersonal Notification

IS	International Standard
ISO	International Standards Organization
ISODE	ISO Development Environment
ISP	International Standardized Profile
ITU	International Telecommunications Union
IWU	Interworking Unit
JTC	Joint Technical Committee
JTM	Job Transfer and Manipulation
LAN	Local Area Network
LCN	Logical Channel Number
LI	Length Indicator
LLC	Logical Link Control
MAN	Metropolitan Area Network
MAP	Manufacturing Automation Protocol
MD	Management Domain
MHS	Message Handling System
MS	Message Store
MTA	Message Transfer Agent
MTS	Message Transfer System
NC	Network Connection
NCEP	Network Connection End-point
NIST	National Institute of Standards and Technology
NPAI	Network Protocol Control Information
NPDU	Network Protocol Data Unit
NS	Network Service
NSAP	Network Service Access Points
NSDU	Network Service Data Unit
O/R	Originator/Recipient
ODA	Office Document Architecture
ODIF	Office Document Interchange Format
OSI	Open Systems Interconnection
PAD	Packet Assembler/Dissembler
PCEP	Presentation Connection End-point
PCI	Protocol Control Information
PDU	Protocol Data Unit
pels	picture elements
PhC	Physical Layer Connection
PhCEP	Physical Connection End-Point

PhL	Physical Layer
PhPDU	Physical Layer Protocol Data Unit
PhS	Physical Layer Service
PhSAP	Physical Layer Service Access Point
PhSDU	Physical Layer Service Data Unit
PLP	Packet Level Protocol
PM	Protocol Machine
POSI	Promoting Conference for OSI
PPDU	Presentation Protocol Data Unit
PS	Presentation Service
PSAP	Presentation Service Access Point
PSDU	Presentation Service Data Unit
PTT	Post Telegraph and Telecommunication
QOS	Quality of Service
RDA	Remote Database Access
RDN	Relative Distinguished Names
req	request
resp	response
RESYNC	Resynchronization
RM	Reference Model
ROSE	Remote Operations Service Element
rsp	response
RTSE	Reliable Transfer Service Element
SAP	Service Access Point
SASE	Specific Application Service Element
SC	Session Connection
SCEP	Session Connection End-point
SDU	Service Data Unit
SMAE	Systems Management Application Entity
SMTP	Simple Mail Transfer Protocol
SNA	Systems Network Architecture
SNAcP	Subnetwork Access Protocol
SNDCP	Subnetwork Dependent Convergence Protocol
SNICP	Subnetwork Independent Convergence Protocol
SNPA	Subnetwork Point of Attachment
SPAG	Standards Promotion and Applications Group
SPDU	Session Protocol Data Unit

SS	Session Service
SSAP	Session Service Access Point
SSDU	Session Service Data Unit
SYNC	Synchronization
T	Transport
TC	Transport Connection (or Technical Committee)
TCEP	Transport Connection End-point
TCP/IP	Transmission Control Protocol/Internet Protocol
TOP	Technical and Office Protocol
TP	Transport protocol (or Transaction Processing)
TPDU	Transport Protocol Data Unit
TPSU	Transaction Processing Service User
TS	Transport Service
TSAP	Transport Service Access Point
TSDU	Transport Service Data Unit
UA	User Agent
uucp	UNIX-to-UNIX communication protocol
VT	Virtual Terminal
VTE	Virtual Terminal Environment
VTP	Virtual Terminal Protocol
VTPM	Virtual Terminal Protocol Machines
VTSE	Virtual Terminal Service Element
WACA	Write Access Connection Acceptor
WACI	Write Access Connection Initiator
WAN	Wide Area Network
WAVAR	Write Access Variable
WG	Working Group

Bibliography

[Berns 87]   Bernstein, P. A., Hadzilacos, V., Goodman, N., Concurrency Control and Recovery in Database Systems, Addison Wesley, Reading, MA, 1987.

[Black 89]   Black, U., Data Networks: Concepts, Theory and Practice, Prentice-Hall, Englewood Cliffs, NJ, 1989.

[Boland 88]   Boland, T., Government Open Systems Interconnection Profile, Users Guide, NCSL, NIST, Gaithersburg, MD, 1988.

[CCITT X.3]   CCITT, PAD facility in a public data network, CCITT Recommendation X.3, 1988.

[CCITT X.21]   CCITT, Interface between DTE and DCE for synchronous operation on PDNs, CCITT Recommendation X.21, 1988.

[CCITT X.25]   CCITT, Interface between DTE and DCE terminals operating in packet mode, CCITT Recommendation X.25, 1988.

[CCITT X.28]   CCITT, DTE/DCE interface for start-stop mode DTE accessing PAD facility, CCITT Recommendation X.28, 1988.

[CCITT X.29]   CCITT, Procedures for exchange of control information and user data, CCITT Recommendation X.29, 1988.

[CCITT X.75]   CCITT, Packet-switching signalling system between public networks, CCITT Recommendation X.75, 1988.

[CCITT X.121]   CCITT, International numbering plan for public data networks, CCITT Recommendation X.121, 1988.

[CCITT X.200]   CCITT, Reference model of open systems interconnection CCITT application, CCITT Recommendation X.200, 1988.

[CCITT X.208]   CCITT, Specification of Abstract Syntax Notation One, CCITT Recommendation X.208, 1988.

[CCITT X.209]   CCITT, Specification of basic encoding rules for Abstract Syntax Notation One, CCITT Recommendation X.209, 1988.

[CCITT X.210]   CCITT, Open systems interconnection layer service definition conventions, CCITT Recommendation X.210, 1988.

[CCITT X.211]   CCITT, Physical service definition of OSI for CCITT applications, CCITT Recommendation X.211, 1988.

[CCITT X.212]   CCITT, Data link service definition for OSI for CCITT applications, CCITT Recommendation X.212, 1988.

[CCITT X.213]   CCITT, Network service definition for OSI for CCITT applications, CCITT Recommendation X.213, 1988.

[CCITT X.214]   CCITT, Transport service definition for OSI for CCITT applications, CCITT Recommendation X.214, 1988.

[CCITT X.215]   CCITT, Session service definition for OSI for CCITT applications, CCITT Recommendation X.215, 1988.

[CCITT X.216]   CCITT, Presentation service definition for OSI for CCITT applications, CCITT Recommendation X.216, 1988.

[CCITT X.217]   CCITT, Association control service definition for OSI for CCITT applications, CCITT Recommendation X.217, 1988.

[CCITT X.218]   CCITT, Reliable Transfer: model and service definition, CCITT Recommendation X.218, 1988.

[CCITT X.219]   CCITT, Remote Operations: Model, notation and service definition, CCITT Recommendation X.219, 1988.

[CCITT X.220]   CCITT, Use of X.200 series protocols in CCITT applications, CCITT Recommendation X.220, 1988.

[CCITT X.223]   CCITT, Use of X.25 to provide OSI connection-mode network service, CCITT Recommendation X.223, 1988.

[CCITT X.224]   CCITT, Transport protocol specification for OSI for CCITT applications, CCITT Recommendation X.224, 1988.

[CCITT X.225]   CCITT, Session protocol specification for OSI for CCITT applications, CCITT Recommendation X.225, 1988.

[CCITT X.226]   CCITT, Presentation protocol specification for OSI for CCITT applications, CCITT Recommendation X.226, 1988.

[CCITT X.227]   CCITT, Association control protocol specification for OSI for CCITT applications, CCITT Recommendation X.227, 1988.

[CCITT X.228]   CCITT, Reliable transfer: protocol specification, CCITT Recommendation X.228, 1988.

[CCITT X.229]   CCITT, Remote operations: protocol specification, CCITT Recommendation X.229, 1988.

[CCITT X.290]   CCITT, OSI Conformance Testing Methodology and Framework for CCITT Applications. CCITT (Draft) Recommendation X.290, 1988.

[CCITT X.400a]	CCITT, MHS - System and service overview, CCITT Recommendation X.400, 1988.
[CCITT X.400b]	CCITT, MHS - System and service overview, CCITT Recommendation X.400, Red Book, 1984.
[CCITT X.402]	CCITT, MHS - Overall architecture, CCITT Recommendation X.402, 1988.
[CCITT X.403]	CCITT, MHS - Conformance testing, CCITT Recommendation X.403, 1988.
[CCITT X.407]	CCITT, MHS - Abstract service definition conventions, CCITT Recommendation X.407,1988.
[CCITT X.408]	CCITT, MHS - Encoded information type conversion rules, CCITT Recommendation X.408, 1988.
[CCITT X.410]	CCITT, Message Handling Systems: Remote Operations and Reliable Transfer Service, CCITT Recommendation X.410, Red Book, 1984.
[CCITT X.411]	CCITT, MHS - Message transfer system: Abstract service definition, CCITT Recommendation X.411, 1988.
[CCITT X.413]	CCITT, Message store: Abstract service definition, CCITT Recommendation X.413, 1988.
[CCITT X.419]	CCITT, MHS - Protocol specifications, CCITT Recommendation X.419, 1988.
[CCITT X.420]	CCITT, MHS - Interpersonal messaging system, CCITT Recommendation X.420, 1988.
[CCITT X.500]	CCITT, The Directory - Overview of concepts, models and services, CCITT Recommendation X.500, 1988.
[CCITT X.501]	CCITT, The Directory - Models, CCITT Recommendation X.501, 1988.
[CCITT X.509]	CCITT, The Directory - authentication framework, CCITT Recommendation X.509, 1988.
[CCITT X.511]	CCITT, The Directory - Abstract service definition, CCITT Recommendation X.511, 1988.
[CCITT X.518]	CCITT, The Directory - Procedures for distributed operation, CCITT Recommendation X.518, 1988.
[CCITT X.519]	CCITT, The Directory - Protocol specifications, CCITT Recommendation X.519, 1988.
[CCITT X.520]	CCITT, The Directory - Selected attribute types, CCITT Recommendation X.520, 1988.
[CCITT X.521]	CCITT, The Directory - Selected object classes, CCITT Recommendation X.521, 1988.
[Comer 88]	Comer, D., Internetworking with TCP/IP: Principles, Protocols and Architectures, Prentice Hall, Englewood Cliffs, NJ, 1988.
[Deasi 86]	Deasington, R. J., X.25 Explained Protocols for Packet

Switching Networks (Second Ed.), Ellis Horwood Ltd., Chichester, England, 1986.

[ENV 41201]   Joint European Standards Institution, Private Message Handling Systems: User Agent and Message Transfer Agent, ENV 41201, CEN/CENELEC, rue Brederode 2, B-1000, Brussels, 1987.

[FIPS 146]   US Department of Commerce, Government Open Systems Interconnection Profile (GOSIP), FIPS Pub 146, August 1988.

[Halsa 88]   Halsall, F., Data Communication, Computer Networks, and OSI, Addison Wesley, Wokingham, England, 1988.

[Horow 87]   Horowitz, E., Sahni, S., Fundamentals of Data Structures in Pascal (second ed.), Computer Sc. Press, Rockville, MD, 1987.

[IBM 75]   IBM, IBM System Network Architecture- General Information, IBM System Development Div., Department E01, PO Box 12195, Research Triangle Park, NC, 1975.

[IEEE 802.2]   IEEE, Logical Link Control, ANSI/IEEE Standard 802.2, IEEE, New York, NY, 1985.

[IEEE 802.3]   IEEE, Carrier Sense Multiple Access with Collision Detection (CSMA/CD) Access Method and Physical Layer Specification, ANSI/IEEE Standard 802.3, IEEE, New York, NY, 1985.

[IEEE 802.4]   IEEE, Token Passing Bus Access Method and Physical Layer Specification, ANSI/IEEE Standard 802.4, IEEE, New York, NY, 1985.

[IEEE 802.5]   IEEE, Token Ring Access Method and Physical Layer Specification, ANSI/IEEE Standard 802.5, IEEE, New York, NY, 1985.

[INTAP S001]   Interoperability Technology Association for Information Processing (INTAP), Overview for Implementation Specification, S001, INTAP, 1989.

[ISO 646]   International Standards Organization, ISO 7-Bit Coded Character Set for Information Interchange, ISO 646, 1983.

[ISO 2022]   International Standards Organization, ISO 7-bit and 8-bit Coded Character Set for Information Exchange; Code Extension, ISO 2022.

[ISO 7498]   International Standards Organization, OSI - Basic Reference Model, ISO 7498, 1984.

[ISO 7498-1]   International Standards Organization, OSI - Basic Reference Model - Addendum 1: Connectionless- Mode Transmission, ISO 7498 AD 1, 1987.

[ISO 7498-2]   International Standards Organization, OSI - Basic Reference Model, Addendum 2: Security Architecture, DIS 7498 AD 2, 1987.

[ISO 7498-3]   International Standards Organization, OSI - Basic Ref-
                      erence Model - Addendum 3: Naming and Addressing,
                      DIS 7498 AD 3, 1987.

[ISO 7498-4]   International Standards Organization, OSI - Basic Ref-
                      erence Model - Addendum 4: Management Framework,
                      DIS 7498 AD 4, 1988.

[ISO 7776]   International Standards Organization, High-level Data
                      Link Control Procedures - Description of the X.25 LAPB-
                      Compatible DTE Data Link Procedures, ISO 7776, 1986.

[ISO 8072]   International Standards Organization, OSI - Transport
                      Service Definition, ISO 8072, 1986.

[ISO 8072 AD 1]   International Standards Organization, OSI - Transport
                      Service Definition - Addendum 1: Connectionless-mode
                      Transmission, ISO 8072 AD 1, 1986.

[ISO 8073]   International Standards Organization, OSI - Connection
                      Oriented Transport Protocol Specification, ISO 8073,
                      1986.

[ISO 8073 DAD 1]   International Standards Organization, OSI - Connection
                      Oriented Transport Protocol Specification - Addendum 1:
                      Network Connection Management Subprotocol, ISO
                      8073 DAD 1, 1985.

[ISO 8073 DAD 2]   International Standards Organization, OSI - Connection
                      Oriented Transport Protocol Specification - Addendum 2:
                      Class Four Operation Over Connectionless Network Ser-
                      vice, ISO 8073 DAD 2, 1987.

[ISO 8208]   International Standards Organization, X.25 Packet
                      Level Protocol for Data Terminal Equipment, ISO 8208,
                      1987.

[ISO 8208 DAD 1]   International Standards Organization, X.25 Packet
                      Level Protocol for Data Terminal Equipment - Adden-
                      dum 1: Alternative Logical Channel Number Allocation,
                      ISO 8208 DAD 1, 1986.

[ISO 8208 DAD 2]   International Standards Organization, X.25 Packet
                      Level Protocol for Data Terminal Equipment - Adden-
                      dum 2: Extensions for Private and Switched Use, ISO
                      8208 PDAD 2, 1986.

[ISO 8326]   International Standards Organization, OSI - Basic
                      Connection Oriented Session Service Definition, ISO
                      8326, 1987.

[ISO 8327]   International Standards Organization, OSI - Basic
                      Connection Oriented Session Protocol Specification, ISO
                      8327, 1987.

[ISO 8348]   International Standards Organization, Network Service
                      Definition, ISO 8348, 1987.

[ISO 8348 AD 1]   International Standards Organization, Network Service

Definition - Addendum 1: Connectionless Mode Transmission, ISO 8348 AD 1, 1987.

[ISO 8348 DAD 2]   International Standards Organization, Network Service Definition - Addendum 2: Network Layer Addressing, ISO 8348 DAD 2, 1987.

[ISO 8473]   International Standards Organization, Protocol for Providing the Connectionless-Mode Network Service, DIS 8473, 1987.

[ISO 8509]   International Standards Organization, OSI - Service Conventions, ISO TR 8509, 1987.

[ISO 8571/1]   International Standards Organization, OSI - File Transfer, Access and Management, Part 1: General Introduction, DIS 8571/1, 1986.

[ISO 8571/2]   International Standards Organization, OSI - File Transfer, Access and Management, Part 2: The Virtual Filestore Definition, DIS 8571/2, 1986.

[ISO 8571/3]   International Standards Organization, OSI - File Transfer, Access and Management, Part 3: File Service Definition, DIS 8571/3, 1986.

[ISO 8571/4]   International Standards Organization, OSI - File Transfer, Access and Management, Part 4: The File Protocol Specification, DIS 8571/4, 1986.

[ISO 8602]   International Standards Organization, OSI - Protocol for Providing the Connectionless-Mode Transport Service, ISO 8602, 1987.

[ISO 8613-1]   International Standards Organization, OSI - Office Document Architecture and Interchange Format, Part 1: Introduction and General Principles, DIS 8613-1, 1988.

[ISO 8648]   International Standards Organization, OSI - Internal Organization of the Network Layer, ISO 8648, 1988.

[ISO 8649]   International Standards Organization, OSI - Service Definition for Association Control Service Element, DIS 8649, 1988.

[ISO 8650]   International Standards Organization, OSI - Protocol Specification for Association Control Service Element, DIS 8650, 1988.

[ISO 8802-2]   International Standards Organization, Local Area Networks, Part 2: Logical Link Control, DIS 8802-2.2, 1987.

[ISO 8802-3]   International Standards Organization, Local Area Networks, Part 3: Carrier Sense Multiple Access with Collision Detection - Access Method and Physical Layer Specifications, DIS 88023, 1987.

[ISO 8802-4]   International Standards Organization, Local Area Networks, Part 4: Token-Passing Bus Access Method and Physical Layer Specifications, DIS 8802-4, 1987.

[ISO 8802-5]   International Standards Organization, Local Area Net-
                 works, Part 5: Token Ring Access Method and Physical
                 Layer Specification, DIS 8802-5, 1987.

[ISO 8822]   International Standards Organization, OSI - Connection
                 Oriented Presentation Service Definition, DIS 8822,
                 1988.

[ISO 8823]   International Standards Organization, OSI - Connection
                 Oriented Presentation Protocol Specification, DIS 8823,
                 1988.

[ISO 8824]   International Standards Organization, OSI - Specifica-
                 tion of Abstract Syntax Notation One (ASN.1), ISO 8824,
                 1987.

[ISO 8825]   International Standards Organization, OSI - Specifica-
                 tion of Basic Encoding Rules for Abstract Syntax Nota-
                 tion One (ASN.1), ISO 8825, 1987.

[ISO 8831]   International Standards Organization, OSI - Job Trans-
                 fer and Manipulation Concepts and Services, DIS 8831,
                 1987.

[ISO 8832]   International Standards Organization, OSI - Specifica-
                 tion of the Basic Class Protocol for Job Transfer and
                 Manipulation, DIS 8832, 1987.

[ISO 8878]   International Standards Organization, Data Communi-
                 cations - Use of X.25 to Provide the OSI Connection-
                 Mode Network Service, ISO 8878, 1987.

[ISO 8880-1]   International Standards Organization, Protocol Combi-
                 nation to Provide and Support the OSI Network Service,
                 Part 1: General Principles, DIS 8880-1, 1987.

[ISO 8880-2]   International Standards Organization, Protocol Combi-
                 nations to Provide and Support the OSI Network Ser-
                 vice, Part 2: Provision and Support of the Con-
                 nection-Mode Network Service, DIS 8880-2, 1987.

[ISO 8880-3]   International Standards Organization, Protocol Combi-
                 nations to Provide and Support the OSI Network Ser-
                 vice, Part 3: Provision and Support of the Connec-
                 tionless-Mode Network Service, DIS 8880-3, 1987.

[ISO 8881.3]   International Standards Organization, Data Commun-
                 ications - Use of the X.25 Packet Level Protocol in Local
                 Area Networks, DIS 8881.3, 1987.

[ISO 8886.2]   International Standards Organization, Data Commun-
                 ication Data Link Service Definition for Open Systems
                 Interconnection, DIS 8886.2, 1987.

[ISO 9040]   International Standards Organization, OSI - Virtual
                 Terminal Service - Basic Class, DIS 9040, August 1988.

[ISO 9041]   International Standards Organization, OSI - Virtual Ter-
                 minal Protocol - Basic Class, DIS 9041.2, December 1987.

[ISO 9066-1]   International Standards Organization, OSI - Reliable Transfer, Part 1: Model and Service Definition, DIS 9066-1, 1988.

[ISO 9066-2]   International Standards Organization, OSI - Reliable Transfer, Part 2: Protocol Specification, DIS 9066-2, 1988.

[ISO 9068]   International Standards Organization, Provision of the Connectionless Network Service Using ISO 8208, DP 9068, 1986.

[ISO 9072-1]   International Standards Organization, OSI - Remote Operations, Part 1: Model, Notation and Service Definition, DIS 9072-1, 1988.

[ISO 9072-2]   International Standards Organization, OSI - Remote Operations, Part 2: Protocol Specification, DIS 9072-2, 1988.

[ISO 9542]   International Standards Organization, Data Communications - End System to Intermediate System Routing Exchange Protocol for Use in Conjunction with the Protocol for Providing the Connectionless-Mode Network Service, DIS 9542, 1988.

[ISO 9545]   International Standards Organization, OSI - Application Layer Structure (ALS), DP 9545, 1987.

[ISO 9579]   International Standards Organization, Remote Database Access, DP 9579, 1988.

[ISO 9594-1]   International Standards Organization, OSI - The Directory, Part 1: Overview of Concepts, Models and Services, DP 9594-1, 1987.

[ISO 9594-2]   International Standards Organization, OSI - The Directory, Part 2: Information Framework, DP 9594-2, 1987.

[ISO 9594-3]   International Standards Organization, OSI - The Directory, Part 3: Access and System Services Definition, DP 9594-3, 1987.

[ISO 9594-4]   International Standards Organization, OSI - The Directory, Part 4: Procedures for Distributed Operation, DP 9594-4, 1987.

[ISO 9594-5]   International Standards Organization, OSI - The Directory, Part 5: Access and System Protocols Specification, DP 95945, 1987.

[ISO 9594-6]   International Standards Organization, OSI - The Directory, Part 6: Selected Attribute Types, DP 9594-6, 1987.

[ISO 9594-7]   International Standards Organization, OSI - The Directory, Part 7: Selected Object Classes, DP 9594-7, 1987.

[ISO 9594-8]   International Standards Organization, OSI - The Directory, Part 8: Authentication Framework, DP 9594-8, 1987.

[ISO 9595-1]   International Standards Organization, OSI - Management Information Service Definition, Part 1: Overview, DP 9595-1, 1987.

[ISO 9595-2]   International Standards Organization, OSI - Management Information Service Definition, Part 2: Common Management Information Service Definition, DP 9595-2, 1987.

[ISO 9596/1]   International Standards Organization, OSI - Management Information Protocol Specification, Part 1: Overview, DP 9596/1, 1986.

[ISO 9596/2]   International Standards Organization, OSI - Management Information Protocol Specification, Part 2: Com-mon Management Information Protocol, DP 9596/2, 1987.

[ISO 9646-1]   International Standards Organization, OSI Conformance Testing Methodology and Framework, Part 1: General Concepts, DP 9646-1, 1988.

[ISO 9646-2]   International Standards Organization, OSI Conformance Testing Methodology and Framework, Part 2: Abstract Test Suite Specification, DP 9646-2, 1988.

[ISO 9804]   International Standards Organization, OSI - Service Definition for the Commitment, Concurrency and Recovery Service Element, DIS 9804, 1988.

[ISO 9805]   International Standards Organization, OSI - Protocol Specification for the Commitment, Concurrency and Recovery Service Element, DIS 9805, 1988.

[ISO 10021/1]   International Standards Organization, Text Communication MOTIS: Systems and Service Overview, ISO 10021/1, 1988.

[ISO 10021/2]   International Standards Organization, Text Communication MOTIS: Overall Architecture, ISO 10021/2, 1988.

[ISO 10021/3]   International Standards Organization, Text Communication - MOTIS: Abstract Service Definition Conventions, ISO 10021/3, 1988.

[ISO 10021/4]   International Standards Organization, Text Communication MOTIS: Message Transfer System: Abstract Service Definition and Procedures, ISO 10021/4, 1988.

[ISO 10021/5]   International Standards Organization, Text Communication - MOTIS: Message Store: Abstract Service Definition, ISO 10021/5, 1988.

[ISO 10021/6]   International Standards Organization, Text Communication MOTIS: Protocol Specifications, ISO 10021/6, 1988.

[ISO 10021/7]   International Standards Organization, Text Communication MOTIS: Inter-personal Messaging System, ISO 10021/7, 1988.

[ISO 10022]   International Standards Organization, OSI Physical Service Definition, DP 10022, 1988.

[ISO 10026-1]   International Standards Organization, OSI - Distributed Transaction Processing, Part 1: Model, DP 10026-1, 1988.

[Jones 88]   Jones, W.C., MAP/TOP Networking, McGraw-Hill Book Co., New York, NY, 1988.

[Knigh 88]   Knightson, K. G., Knowles, T., Larmouth, J., Standards for Open Systems Interconnection, McGraw Hill, New York, NY, 1988.

[McNam 82]   McNamnara, J. E., Technical Aspects of Data Communication (second ed.), Digital Equipment Corp., Bedford, MA, 1982.

[NIST 88]   NIST, Stable Implementation Agreements for Open Systems Interconnections Protocols, Vol. 2, Ed. 1, NIST Pub. 500-162, Dec 1988.

[NIST 89]   NIST, Working Implementation Agreements for Open Systems Interconnections Protocols, NISTIR 89-4082, March 1989.

[OReilly 89]   O'Reilly, Tim, and Todino, G, Managing uucp and Usenet, O'Reilly and Associates, Newton, MA, 1989.

[Rives 78]   Rivest, R.L., Shamir, A., and Adleman, L., A Method for Obtaining Digital Signatures and Public-Key Cryptosystems, Comm. of ACM, Vol. 21, No. 2, 1978, pp 120-126.

[SC6 N4731]   International Standards Organization, End System to Intermediate System Routing Exchange Protocol for Use in Conjunction with ISO 8208 (X.25/PLP), SC6 N4731, 1987.

[Schwa 87]   Schwartz, M., Telecommunication Networks: Protocol, Modeling and Analysis, Addison Wesley, Reading, MA, 1987.

[Stall 87a]   Stallings, W., Local Networks (second ed.), Macmillan Publishing Co., New York, N. Y., 1987.

[Stall 87b]   Stallings, W., Handbook of Computer Communications Standards, Vol. 1: The Open Systems Interconnection (OSI), Model and OSI-Related Standards, Macmillan, New York, NY, 1987.

[Stall 87c]   Stallings, W., Handbook of Computer Communications Standards, Vol. 2: Local Network Standards, Macmillan, New York, NY, 1987.

[Stall 87d]   Stallings, W., Handbook of Computer Communications Standards, Vol. 3: Department of Defense (DOD) Protocol Standards, Macmillan, New York, NY, 1987.

[Stall 88]   Stallings, W., Data and Computer Communication (second ed.), Macmillan Publishing Co., New York, NY, 1988.

[Tanen 88] Tanenbaum, A. S., Computer Networks (second ed.), Prentice Hall, Englewood Cliffs, NJ, 1988.

Index

ABOUT THE AUTHORS

BIJENDRA N. JAIN is a professor of computer science at the Indian Insitute of Technology.

ASHOK K. AGRAWALA is a fellow of the IEEE, a professor of computer science at the University of Maryland, and a coauthor of *Real-Time Systems Design*.